D0861323

ASPA Classics

Conceived of and sponsored by the American Society for Public Administration (ASPA), the ASPA Classics Series publishes volumes on topics that have been, and continue to be, central to the contemporary development of the field. The ASPA Classics are intended for classroom use, library adoptions, and general reference. Drawing from the *Public Administration Review* (*PAR*) and other ASPA–related journals, each volume in the series is edited by a scholar who is charged with presenting a thorough and balanced perspective on an enduring issue.

Each volume is devoted to a topic of continuing and crosscutting concern to the administration of virtually all public-sector programs. Public servants carry out their responsibilities in a complex, multidimensional environment, and each collection will address a necessary dimension of their performance. ASPA Classics volumes bring together the dialogue on a particular topic over several decades and in a range of journals.

The volume editors are to be commended for volunteering to take on such substantial projects and for bringing together unique collections of articles that might not otherwise be readily available to scholars and students.

ASPA Classics

Administrative Leadership in the Public Sector
Montgomery Van Wart and Lisa A. Dicke, eds.

Public Personnel Administration and Labor Relations
Norma M. Riccucci, ed.

Public Administration and Law
Julia Beckett and Heidi O. Koenig, eds.

Local Government Management
Current Issues and Best Practices
Douglas J. Watson and Wendy L. Hassett, eds.

Administrative Leadership in the Public Sector

An ASPA Classics Volume

Edited by

Montgomery Van Wart and Lisa A. Dicke

Routledge
Taylor & Francis Group

LONDON AND NEW YORK

First published 2008 by M.E. Sharpe

Published 2015 by Routledge
2 Park Square, Milton Park, Abingdon, Oxon OX14 4RN
711 Third Avenue, New York, NY, 10017, USA

Routledge is an imprint of the Taylor & Francis Group, an informa business

Library of Congress Cataloging-in-Publication Data

Administrative leadership in the public sector / edited by Montgomery Van
Wart and Lisa A. Dicke.
   p. cm. — (ASPA classics)
Includes bibliographical references and index.
   ISBN 978-0-7656-1348-6 (cloth : alk. paper)—ISBN 978-0-7656-1349-2 (pbk. : alk. paper)
   1. Public administration—United States. 2. Leadership—United States. 3. Civil service—
United States—Personnel management. 4. Employees—Training of—United States.
I. Van Wart, Montgomery, 1951– II. Dicke, Lisa A., 1960–

JK421.A545 2007
352.23´6—dc22   2007002134

ISBN 13: 9780765613493 (pbk)
ISBN 13: 9780765613486 (hbk)

CONTENTS

TABLES AND FIGURES

Tables

Figures

PREFACE

This ASPA classic volume is designed to fill a much-needed gap in the public administration leadership literature. Although a substantial body of work on leadership exists, it is scattered and only loosely connected. Indeed, leadership theory and research have suffered significantly from the fragmentation of the field. For the first time, in this volume, the authors bring together significant contributions to the public-sector leadership literature in a coherent fashion. It is hoped that this compilation will provide students and scholars with a resource that allows them to view conceptual, historical, and intellectual relationships more easily.

The value of the volume for scholars and libraries, then, is that these materials fill a large gap in the administrative leadership monograph literature. Although such a literature does exist (see Van Wart's assessment of the field in part 1), it is largely specialized or narrowly focused. The drawing together of the various theoretical strands (which occurred in the mainstream literature in the 1990s) is only now beginning to occur in the public-sector arena. The literature assembled here, along with the comprehensive overviews of the subareas, should help this cause. Indeed, it is hoped that scholars may see the gaps in the literature more clearly with this compilation.

The value to instructors teaching various public administration classes should also be substantial. Classes in administrative leadership have been almost entirely dependent on the private-sector literature. Management classes have had to resort to broad theoretical treatments or hypothetical case studies instead of materials discussing the concrete elements of leader-manager effectiveness. Organization theory and behavior courses can be enhanced through a more comprehensive treatment of the subject of administrative leadership. Edited volumes are not generally intended as primary texts, but the substantial introductions provide an ample overview to the field and the sequential nature of the materials provides excellent structure for the instructor who chooses to use it as such for a course or a portion of it. The text will find more use at the graduate level but should be quite accessible to upper-division college students as well.

Although it really goes without saying, it is useful to remind ourselves that "oldies" are invaluable in so many ways. First, if we do not know where we have been and what our history is, we are, as the saying predicts, doomed to repeat it. How often we declare new insights only to discover later that they have been long known and documented if only we were aware! Second, "oldies" are generally "goodies" because of the felicity of phrase, the clarity of concept, and the vibrancy that they exhibited. Some of the most sparkling pieces in the collection, as well as some of the most insightful, are fifty years old. That is to say, classics have achieved their status because they have stood the test of time, and still have valuable lessons (and historical perspective) to share.

The editors would also like to thank those who have assisted in this project. Marc Holzer, the series editor, deserves enormous credit as the person who conceived of the series and encouraged us specifically to take on the project despite busy schedules and the challenges involved with compiling quality edited texts. We appreciate the efforts of Evelyn Nobles, Jodi Gonzalez, and Stacey Pollard in facilitating the completion of this project. We would also like to thank Paul Suino for proofing everything once, and sometimes twice, as well as for his general patience. We also want to thank Floyd Rosenkranz for his support and consideration.

Administrative Leadership in the Public Sector

PART 1

INTRODUCTION

Leadership studies are important for many reasons. First, leadership is a topic of great interest to practitioners, academics, and the lay public. The topic applies to nearly every aspect of human endeavor when groups of individuals are working together.

Second, the quality of leadership makes a difference. Even in the case of a first-level supervisor in a highly rule-bound work setting where differences are marginalized, employee turnover is frequently directly related to the quality of leadership. Further, leaders are called upon to make decisions that affect the quality of life for thousands of people and sometimes involve life-and-death decisions.

Third, the study of leadership is important because it is complex (Bass 1990). Although everyone assumes an intuitive working knowledge of the topic, it is beyond most people's ability to do more than make a few vague assertions about the nature of leadership, who ideal leaders are, how you cultivate leaders, and so on. Part of the complexity arises from the fact that leadership is inevitably nested among so many related fields—politics, organizations and systems, management, motivation, learning, and ethics to mention only a few. Another aspect is the complexity of the phenomenon itself, with its substantial subjective component. That is, since leadership is entirely a social construct, it can be defined in an almost infinite number of ways, depending on the value preferences of the commentator.

Some Important Distinctions

Some preliminary distinctions are important for those new to the field of leadership. One important distinction is that types of leadership vary substantially. This book will focus primarily on organizational leaders but there are many other fundamentally different types of leadership. One of the first types of leaders we customarily think about are political leaders. There are also leaders of social networks and even of intellectual movements. Different types of leaders do have some extremely broad similarities. However, the differences in various types of leaders are as important as the unifying elements. For example, two of the more fundamental conceptions of leaders are that they lead followers and motivate them. Yet consider the differences among the types of followers—voters, paid employees, volunteers, and ideological and intellectual consumers. The manner in which a politician motivates a self-interested constituent is different from the way a boss motivates a new hire, a religious leader inspires a zealot, or an intellectual stimulates an unknown reader-follower. Here, the dissimilarities can be more critical than the similarities. Even within the organizational leader setting, the differences among private- and public-sector leaders are not insignificant (R. Terry 1993; L. Terry 1995). There are vast differences between a corporate profit-making environment in which loyalty to shareholders is key and a nonprofit agency within a democratic political system in which accountability to the public at large is essential (Goodsell 1994).

A second important distinction has to do with the difference between descriptive/analytic research and prescriptive analysis. Descriptive research attempts to clarify facts and analytic research attempts to identify relationships. For example, what is decisiveness and how does it relate (if at all) to leadership? Prescriptive research, on the other hand, seeks to provide guidelines for effective action. For example, if decisiveness and leader effectiveness are shown to be highly related to situational characteristics, then leaders should learn to identify when those factors are present (e.g., during crises, in situations with extreme time constraints, when a leader has a good command of the facts, when followers' self-interests are likely to cloud logic, etc.).

A related variant of this distinction is the difference between the study of leadership to expand basic knowledge and the study of leadership for applied purposes. This is a classic bifurcation of purposes, which at its extreme results in very different types of writings and analysis, although it results in useful overlap as well.

Basic research on leadership is interested in identifying underlying principles of leadership and verifying them in a scientifically rigorous manner. It is concerned with conceptualization, methodological validity and reliability, lack of bias, and generalizability. At a minimum this perspective seeks accurate descriptive accounts of narrowly circumscribed processes; at a mid-level it seeks to explain processes; at its most rigorous it seeks to reliably predict outcomes.

Applied research is more apt to study leadership in its natural settings. Therefore, applied research generally studies leadership as a complex process and takes advantage of natural comparative examples, but it rarely has anything approaching more scientifically rigorous controlled settings. Applied researchers will more often report on findings after analyzing a specific case, or after analyzing the leadership survey instruments of many managers. Greater emphasis is placed on the proper way to be an effective leader and on prescription (advice).

Ideally, basic scientific research provides the detailed conceptualizations and broader theories that are then tested in multiple, different, applied settings. These applied settings should transfer knowledge to practitioners in useful ways. At its worst, basic scientific studies can be trivial, rarified, and/or unnecessarily obscure; applied research can be overly simplistic, overly generalized, and theoretically naïve.

A third useful distinction is the level of focus of various theories: organization, group, dyadic (two people), or intra-level characteristics. These distinctions provide a useful variety in the readings but also make comparisons more difficult. For example, nearly all the articles in parts 2 and 3 are at the organization level, looking at such issues as agency structure, quality systems, systems priorities and assessments, and accountability. A focus on the relationship between the leader and individual follower (dyadic) also occurs frequently in research on behaviors and leadership exemplars. For example, Daley and Naff consider a variety of behavioral differences with an eye to gender: do men and women behave differently toward their subordinates, and is this good, bad, or indifferent in terms of effectiveness? Looking more closely at the internal cognitive workings of leadership, Marshall Dimock (in part 4) focuses on the deeply personal and imaginative aspects of administrators in "Creativity." This is a common focus for many articles on leadership traits and skills.

Organization of the Book

After the introductory section, the book is organized to emphasize the normal causal chain of events that generally affect individual leaders. In the first phase, a leader assesses the environment in which s/he will act (part 2), sets goals (part 3), utilizes and improves personal traits (part 4), and adjusts her/his style to suit the situations and personality of the leader (part 5). In the next phase, the leader acts using an assortment of techniques in a variety of functional domains (part 6). Finally, the leader evaluates the success and failures that s/he has had in the organizational setting (part 7). Preceding and concurrent with these phases, leaders are engaged in development (part 8). Finally, it is useful to consider concrete examples of administrative leaders as they range from exemplars to autocrats (part 9).

The introduction offers an overview of leadership as a field of study. It provides a background on the leadership literature and the perennial debates, the strengths and weaknesses of that literature, and the differences between the mainstream organizational literature and the public-sector subset, which sometimes seems to function as a distant cousin. It also provides a contrast between the research perspectives of the leadership literature and the broader public governance model.

Contrary to some overly simplistic notions of leadership that prescribe identical actions regardless of the situation, leaders must engage in preliminary assessment to act effectively. Leaders must be able to assess the dynamics occurring in the organization, the external environment, and the constraints that they face in carrying out routine functions and nonroutine changes. How well do followers understand their roles, do they have all the skills necessary, and are they motivated to work hard? Are organizational processes supportive of productivity, teamwork, and morale? Is the organization creative and innovative enough to stay abreast of contemporary organizational practice? Does the organization have an eye to the opportunities and threats occurring outside its boundaries, and is it able to adapt quickly and flexibly? In addition, leaders must know their constraints: by law, by position, by resources, and by their own leadership limitations. They must know how to push these bounds back (with the exception of the law in the public sector), when necessary over time, in order to meet the challenges leaders face.

In conducting this ongoing assessment, leaders must be able to set goals and priorities for themselves and for their organizations. They must make decisions about where to focus their attention and their time in daily activities. To what degree are leaders going to focus on technical and operational issues, on the motivation and development of people, and/or on the alignment and success of the organization at large? While these different foci are ultimately self-supporting, leaders' time and resources are always limited, and choices must be made about the relative importance of each. Further, leaders must decide the degree to which operations and organizational structures, culture, and so on should be maintained, refined, or changed. Even when a change orientation is appropriate, leaders must decide whether an incremental or a radical change strategy is more appropriate.

Leaders come to various situations in varying stages of readiness. Leader characteristics are a large part of that readiness. Although no absolute set of characteristics is necessary in all leadership situations, certain traits and skills tend to be significantly more important than others. Traits are those characteristics that are primarily inherent and become a part of one's personality (e.g., self-confidence, energy, the need for achievement, etc.), while skills are characteristics that are primarily learned (e.g., communication, analytic, and influence skills). This is not to say that traits cannot be enhanced, especially through training and/or indoctrination; nor is it to say that some people do not have a natural gift with some skills. For example, self-confidence tends to be an innate personality characteristic; nonetheless, with training and experience an individual can become far more self-confident. Likewise, while communication skills take practice and study to master, some people clearly have greater native abilities in oral and writing skills.

Leaders also bring a leadership "style" to situations. A style can be thought of as the dominant pattern of leader behavior in a position or situation. Rather than referring to all aspects of leadership, *style* most commonly refers to the pattern of follower inclusion in decisions, although it can also refer to the communication patterns, individual versus group/team patterns of leadership, and use of influence tactics. People have a preferred mode of leadership. Good leaders generally have alternate modes so that they are not dependent on a single style and can adjust to a variety of situational needs. Like leader characteristics, styles are antecedent to leadership in that they are prior aspects of the leaders' repertoire and to some degree are an explicit method of accomplishing specific goals. Yet styles, like leader characteristics, are expressed through the concrete actions that leaders take in doing their jobs.

Leaders act. These actions or behaviors can be thought of as occurring in three domains. First, leaders have tasks to accomplish. Their organization, division, or unit has work that it must produce, no matter whether it is a concrete product or a relatively nebulous service. Second, leaders have followers and it is the followers who actually accomplish the mission of the organization. Thus, good leaders never lose sight of the fact that they accomplish their goals through and, as importantly, with others. Finally, leaders are expected to know more than how to design and coordinate work processes; they are expected to know how the product of these efforts will integrate and compare with other organizations and external entities. If production and people constitute the mission of leadership, then organizational alignment and adaptability constitute the vision of leadership. Today more than ever, good leaders must not only be competent in their professional skills, they must also be able to articulate a vision that is compelling to a wide variety of constituencies.

From time to time leaders must be able to evaluate (and be evaluated on) how they have done. This is an ongoing and complex activity. It requires balancing numerous competing interests. It also requires adjusting plans and priorities as new operational problems occur, problems are resolved, and, less frequently but very critically, new opportunities and threats materialize. It requires continual examination of one's own performance as well as the performance of the organization.

Developing leaders is also no easy task. The type of leadership training that is required depends in part upon the level of leader being trained: lower-level supervision, mid-level management, or executive. It also depends on the type of function being performed, such as staff or line. It even depends on the type of organization and inherent characteristics of the business: auditing or corrections versus economic development or public relations. To what degree do certain leaders need more technical, interpersonal, or basic management skills training, or preparation on abstract executive competencies such as change management or visioning? Even when it has been decided what is to be taught, there are questions about the best methods for doing so, such as technical briefings, mentoring, or case studies in executive seminars.

The final section of the book takes a brief look at some examples of administrative leaders. As discussed earlier, much can be learned by looking at examples of those who are successful or not successful in fulfilling the leadership function. Such cases are particularly useful in thinking about the larger roles that administrators do or should play in a democratic system. In particular, to what degree should nonelected leaders shape public policy, and just what is policy and what are simply large implementation issues?

Review of the Selections in Part 1

James Fesler's 1960 editorial on administrative leadership "Leadership and Its Context" provides an inspirational call for more attention to the subject. What is remarkable about this single-page editorial is that it surveys so much history and asks just about every major question in the leadership literature. What are the ideal qualities of the good administrator? Who is the great leader? What is the difference between private and public leaders? What are and should be the roles of education, wealth, experience, and specialized training? How do the situational requirements of leadership vary, and how do you put together teams of leaders who build off one another's differences? The editorial was written in a period before the training for the State Department was routinized (although it was being discussed), and prior to the creation of the Federal Executive Institute in 1968. His pithy comment bears repeating: "History, administrative experience, and behavioral science research all testify that when leadership is defined without reference to destination or to the particular waters to be navigated, we may be led around in circles or, indeed, simply drift."

Montgomery Van Wart's "Public-Sector Leadership Theory: An Assessment" (2003) serves several functions for the collection. His assessment of the literature provides an overview of the history of leadership research in both the mainstream and the narrower public-sector veins. He begins with a review of the various historical phases—the great man school of the nineteenth century, the trait approach of the first half of the twentieth century, the basic situational (transactional) approaches from the 1950s through the 1980s, the ethical-normative perspectives beginning in the 1970s, the transformational approaches also beginning in the late 1970s, and finally more integrative approaches beginning in the 1980s. Paralleling this review is a discussion about the administrative (public-sector) literature. It has focused on different issues and, generally speaking, has not been as robust (with the exception of the ethical leadership). Nonetheless, the literature is extensive, if sometimes oblique in comparison to the mainstream literature. He also reviews the perennial debates about the proper focus, the degree to which leadership makes a difference, the development of leaders, and the proper style for leaders. These debates have echoes in this book with reference to goal setting (part 3), evaluation (part 7), leader training (part 8), and leader style (part 5). Finally, he asserts that "a more sophisticated model able to accommodate entirely different missions and environments" is lacking and calls for more empirically based studies.

One example of a more sophisticated model, but based on empirical observation, is provided by Matthew Fairholm in "Different Perspectives on the Practice of Leadership." He differentiates five separate approaches to leadership: scientific management, excellence management, values leadership, trust-cultural leadership, and whole-soul leadership. He integrates these with approaches to followers and tools and behaviors. Thus scientific management leadership tends to use incentivization, control, and direction as the primary follower approaches and monitoring, organizing, and planning as its tools.

The final piece in this section is a portion of a book review, "Leaders and Leadership" (1980), by John Corson. Corson served as the president of the American Society for Public Administration in 1948–49, and was a prolific writer and commentator about administrative leadership. The excerpts used here incorporate the perspectives of two major authors on the subject, James MacGregor Burns and John Gardner. Burns discusses transformational leadership types as intellectual, reform, revolutionary, and heroic and transactional leadership types as opinion, group, party, and executive. Burns's work incorporates a far broader perspective on the subject of administrative leadership than is common even today.

Gardner's taxonomy comes from a paper he delivered before the White House Fellows Alumni Association, but that was later subsumed in his own major work on leadership. He discusses four macro-level types of leaders with a different but complementary approach to Burns's transactional-transformational analysis. For Gardner there are the clarifiers and definers, the implementers, the mobilizers, and the integrators. Thus, some leaders are good at identifying problems, others are good at bringing together the resources to fix them, still others excel at devising concrete solutions once the public has agreed that something must be done, and finally, some leaders are good at integrating the "big picture" and balancing competing interests.

References

Bass, Bernard M. 1990. *Bass and Stogdill's Handbook of Leadership*. New York: Free Press.

Goodsell, Charles T. 1994. *The Case for Bureaucracy: A Public Administration Polemic*. Chatham, NJ: Chatham House.

Terry, Larry D. 1995. *Leadership of Public Bureaucracies: The Administrator as Conservator*. Thousand Oaks, CA: Sage.

Terry, Robert W. 1993. *Authentic Leadership: Courage in Action*. San Francisco: Jossey-Bass.

CHAPTER 1

LEADERSHIP AND ITS CONTEXT

JAMES W. FESLER

Who is the good administrator? Who is the great leader? Who is the best public servant? We persist in asking theses questions, just as Confucius, Plato, and philosophers ever since have asked, "Who is the good ruler?"

It seems strange that so many should attempt to answer these questions by a single generalizing sentence or a master list of ideal characteristics. Administrative practice offers such a variety of answers that we could plausibly assume that the problem's complexity had been perceived.

Macaulay and Trevelyan hit on a formula for choosing administrative leaders that stressed academic excellence at two major universities and subordinated or ignored specialized knowledge of the concerns of government. American military tradition long banked on the selection of leaders from a group of youths nominated by members of Congress, screened by admission examinations, and educated at a special school emphasizing engineering subjects. The American civil service system relied for decades on voluntary applications from those who habitually scan bulletin boards in post offices, qualify by training and experience to fit into narrowly carved niches near the base of the administrative pyramid, and subsequently prove adept at finding notches by which to scale the pyramid. Later the civil service system regarded long service in specialized staff and auxiliary functions as the appropriate mediating experience between a liberal education and the emergence of major program administrators. For a number of leadership positions, "deserving" political partisans have been recruited or, in another era, executives of large business corporations have been borrowed short-term. The nation's representation abroad, even in a single time period, has been composed of three diverse groups: careerists initially chosen for their college education, poise, and linguistic ability; persons drawn from other careers who are motivated to aid less developed peoples even without the security of a structured career system; and private citizens willing to subsidize both their parties' campaigns and their embassies' operations. And recently, as if completing the circle, proposals have been made for a Foreign Service Academy to be filled with high school graduates nominated by members of Congress and ranked by examinations.

Though such variety of practice demonstrates the complexity of men's perceptions of the leadership problem, it gives no assurance that the choices made reflect accurately

From *Public Administration Review,* vol. 20, no. 2 (1960): 122. Copyright © 1960 by American Society for Public Administration. Reprinted with permission.

the differing requirements of the tasks to be performed. For this purpose our original questions need recasting so that they specify: good administrator of what? great leader of whom? in pursuit of what goals? in what government? at what stage of a nation's or organization's life? in what economic and social conditions? against what challenges at home and abroad? in association with what other leaders?

Consider, for example, what a variety of types of persons may be needed in a single group of leaders. A Bradley and a Patton, a Truman and an Acheson, a Teller and an Oppenheimer may play distinctive, often complementary, and sometimes fruitfully conflicting roles. So, too, leaders of quite different casts of mind and temperament in succession to each other can weave history's web the more tightly—one may be energetic, innovate, and upset the traditional orthodoxies; his successor may preside over the legitimatizing, consolidating, and stabilizing of the new social organization. The patterns of chief and deputy-chief, of constitutional monarch and prime minister, of chairman of the board and president of the corporation, of naval ship's captain and executive officer suggest the variety in our attempts to fix the mold that shapes the function of leadership.

History, administrative experience, and behavioral science research all testify that when leadership is defined without reference to destination or to the particular waters to be navigated, we may be led around in circles or, indeed, simply drift.

CHAPTER 2

PUBLIC-SECTOR LEADERSHIP THEORY

An Assessment

MONTGOMERY VAN WART

In 1995, Larry Terry noted the neglect of administrative or "bureaucratic leadership" in the public-sector literature. This article assesses the state of the administrative leadership literature. It examines the following questions:

- Is the study of administrative (that is, bureaucratic) leadership important?
- What are the reasons for the neglect of administrative leadership, including the difficulties associated with this type of research?
- Has the administrative leadership literature made significant strides since Terry's observation in 1995? If not, why?
- What are the specific strengths and weaknesses of the literature, whatever its overall robustness? In particular, how does it compare with the mainstream (that is, largely private-sector-focused) literature?
- What areas are ripe for research?

To address these questions, a relatively exhaustive review of public-sector leadership was conducted, as well as a thorough review of the major schools in the mainstream literature. Because of the many weaknesses in the literature (in scope, in numerous gaps, and in theory building), it is hoped this article can make a major contribution in defining the terrain of this complex and difficult area so that more rapid and coherent progress can be made.

The Importance and Challenges of Leadership Research

The Importance of Leadership

To most people, the importance of leadership is self-evident no matter what the setting. In organizations, effective leadership provides higher-quality and more efficient goods and services; it provides a sense of cohesiveness, personal development, and higher levels

From *Public Administration Review,* vol. 63, no. 2 (March/April 2003): 214–28. Copyright © 2003 by American Society for Public Administration. Reprinted with permission.

of satisfaction among those conducting the work; and it provides an overarching sense of direction and vision, an alignment with the environment, a healthy mechanism for innovation and creativity, and a resource for invigorating the organizational culture. This is no small order, especially in contemporary times.

Leadership is difficult in all eras, to be sure, but it seems that today's leaders face additional challenges. While the shared-power environment created in the second half of the twentieth century enhanced many aspects of democracy, "it also makes leadership more difficult" (Henton, Melville, and Walesh 1997, 14). The public has greater access to view leaders today—especially public-sector leaders—through the media focus, the Internet, and greater levels of public awareness. Yet the public shows less tolerance for leaders' mistakes, foibles, and structural challenges as its skepticism has grown (Yankelovich 1991). Further, there is evidence that as competition in the organizational universe has intensified in the new global economy, even among public-sector organizations, the range of skills necessary for leaders has grown (Bass 1985).

Reasons for Neglect and Difficulties in Administrative Leadership Research

If we accept—as most people do—that leadership is important and that leaders have a tough job in the best of times, it stands to reason that leadership research would be both prolific and valuable. Although the first part of this statement is documented in the mainstream literature—more than 7,500 empirical and quasi-empirical references were cited in the major handbook for the literature in 1990 (Bass 1990)—the latter is disputed among leadership experts. The most prominent researcher of his day, Ralph Stogdill urged his colleagues to largely abandon forty years of work as utterly inconclusive in 1948 (which, as a whole, they did). In his landmark 1978 study on leadership thirty years later, James MacGregor Burns acidly stated, "Leadership is one of the most observed and least understood phenomena on earth" (1). Another particularly eminent scholar—Warren Bennis—came to the same conclusion in the mid-1980s: "Never have so many labored so long to say so little," and "leadership is the most studied and least understood topic of any in the social sciences" (Bennis and Nanus 1985, 4, 20). Although I will argue the situation improved dramatically in the mainstream in the 1990s, it is easier to understand the incredibly slow progress of leadership research, for all the attention, when one examines the challenges leadership research faces in generalizing beyond relatively small subsets.

One set of difficulties has to do with what Brunner calls "contextual complexity" (1997, 219). While there are significant similarities among leaders that are generally agreed upon (for instance, they have followers and affect the direction of the group), from a research perspective, the differences among leaders are far greater and more challenging. For example, the leader of paid employees and the leader of volunteers have very different jobs. Issues of contextual complexity apply to mission, organizational and environmental culture, structure, types of problems, types of opportunities, levels of discretion (Baliga and Hunt 1988, 130), and a host of other critically important areas. These types of issues led one of the earliest commentators on public-sector administrative leadership to conclude that "the differences in individuals who find themselves in executive positions and the variations in the life cycles of organizations produce practically limitless permutations and combinations" (Stone 1945, 210). As if these contextual, complex challenges were not enough, however, a researcher has other problems that inhibit generalizations in social science research when highly complex human phenomena are studied. An additional confounding factor in our list is the issue of proper definition, which is ultimately a normative problem. Because science cannot solve normative issues (Dahl 1947), this problem is central to the ability to build a body of work that is coherent as research and applied use. The final technical problem is the effect of observation and the observer. Even the "hardest" of the sciences has rediscovered this problem (Kiel 1994), yet it is a particularly pesky dilemma in amorphous areas such as leadership. One version of the predicament, simply stated, is that observed phenomena change through the act of observation. A second version of the problem is that because the observer determines the conceptual framework of the issue, the methods to be used, and the context to be studied, the results are affected far more by the investigators' biases than might be supposed.

For all of these challenges and all of the seemingly nonadditive (but certainly not nonproductive) leadership research done until the 1980s, efforts at more sophisticated, multifaceted approaches for comprehensive models have made a substantial improvement (Chemers 1997, 170; Hunt 1996). However, administrative leadership research (literature that is most interested in leadership in public-sector bureaucratic settings) has experienced neither the volume nor the integration of the mainstream. Why? Building on the ideas of Doig and Hargrove (1987), Terry (1995, 2–3) speculates on some reasons beyond the technical issues raised above, which certainly have not slowed down mainstream interest in leadership research. He offers three types of reasons.

First, there may be some belief that administrative leadership does not (or should not) exist to an appreciable degree because of a belief in a highly instrumental approach to leadership in the public sector. This is a legacy of both scientific management, with its technocratic focus, and beliefs in a strong model of overhead democracy (Redford 1969). The stronger these beliefs, the less likely administrative leadership would receive attention. Second, bureaucracies may be guided by powerful forces that are largely beyond the control of administrative leaders, making their contributions relatively insignificant. Both arguments tend to delimit the role and contribution of public administration. Finally, there may be a problem with attention being diverted from leadership research by related topics. Given the relatively small size of the pool of researchers compared to the number of possible topics in the field, this is a significant possibility. Researchers who are more empirically inclined may find bureaucratic routines (frontline and mid-level management) more accessible. Many of those interested in executive leadership may find political leadership more attractive, with its dramatic and accessible policy debates and discussions, rather than administrative leadership, with its more subtle and nuanced decision-making routines. Finally, those interested in the philosophical nature of leadership may be pulled into the normative debates about the amount of and manner in which discretion should be exercised by administrative leaders, rather than the changing and unchanging characteristics of administrative leadership. Although it is not conclusive, my assessment of the causal weights will be offered in the conclusion.

Figure 2.1

A Generic Practitioner Model of Organizational Leadership

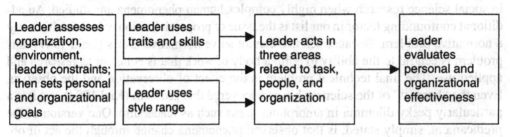

Operationally, "administrative leadership" in this article refers to leadership from the frontline supervisor (or even lead worker) to the nonpolitical head of the organization. The focus is not on elected legislative leaders and only on elected executives and their political designees, such as agency secretaries and directors, commissioners, or legislatively approved directors, to the degree that they include nonpolicy functions as a significant component of their responsibilities. There are many instances in which the line is hard to draw. The article first will review the mainstream leadership research as well as the administrative (public-sector) research. Next, the perennial debates (and research questions) of mainstream leadership theory will be compared to administrative leadership theory. This will culminate in a discussion of the state-of-the-art in administrative leadership research and a conclusion suggesting areas that may be productively mined in the future by scholars and pursued by practitioners.

Background on Leadership Research

Dominant Themes in the Mainstream Leadership Literature

It is certainly impossible to pigeonhole all of the mainstream leadership literature[1] into tight eras with sharp demarcations; however, it is possible to capture the dominant themes and interests for a heuristic overview. For those interested in a detailed history and more complex analysis, an excellent, exhaustive review can be found in *Bass and Stogdill's Handbook of Leadership* (Bass 1990). However, Figure 2.1 provides a simple, contemporary, practitioner-oriented model as a mental framework for the development of the leadership literature. Such practitioner models emphasize leader assessment, leader characteristics, and leader styles, all of which affect actual leader behaviors. As leaders evaluate their own and their organizations' effectiveness, they begin the cycle again. Scientific models tend to de-emphasize the leader-assessment phase (as difficult to observe) and emphasize intervening organizational variables that affect leader success.

The nineteenth century was dominated by the notion of the "great man" thesis. Particular great men (women invariably were overlooked despite great personages in history such as Joan of Arc, Elizabeth I, or Clara Barton) somehow move history forward because of their exceptional characteristics as leaders. The stronger version of this theory holds that history is a handmaiden to men; great men actually change the shape and direction of history. Philosophers such as Friedrich Nietzsche and William James firmly asserted that history would be different if a great man suddenly were incapacitated. Thomas Carlyle's 1841 essay on heroes and hero worship is an early popular version of this, as is Galton's 1869 study of hereditary genius (cited in Bass 1990). Such theories generally have an explicit class bias. A milder version of the theory is that as history proceeds on its irrevocable course, a few men will move history forward substantially and dramatically because of their greatness, especially in moments of crisis or great social need. Although these lines of thinking have more sophisticated echoes in the later trait and situational leadership periods, "hero worship" is certainly alive and well in popular culture and in biographies and autobiographies. Its core belief is that there are only a few, very rare, individuals in any society at any time with the unique characteristics to shape or express history. Although this thesis may serve sufficiently for case studies (essentially biographies), it is effectively irrefutable and therefore unusable as a scientific theory.

The scientific mood of the early twentieth century fostered the development of a more focused search for the basis of leaders. What traits and characteristics do leaders seem to share? Researchers developed personality tests and compared the results against those perceived to be leaders. By the 1940s, researchers had amassed very long lists of traits from numerous psychologically oriented studies (Bird 1940; Jenkins 1947). This tactic had two problems: First, the lists became longer and longer as research continued. Second—and more importantly—the traits and characteristics identified were not powerful predictors across situations. For example, leaders must be decisive, but they also must be flexible and inclusive. Without situational specificity, the endless list of traits offers little prescriptive assistance and descriptively becomes little more than a laundry list. In 1948, Ralph Stogdill published a devastating critique of pure trait theory, and it fell into disfavor as being too one-dimensional to account for the complexity of leadership (Stogdill 1948).

The next major thrust was to look at the situational contexts that affect leaders in order to find meaningful patterns for theory building and useful advice. One early example was the work that came out of the Ohio State Leadership Studies (Hempill 1950; Hempill and Coons 1957), which started by testing 1,800 statements related to leadership behavior. By continually distilling the behaviors, researchers arrived at two underlying factors: consideration and initiation of structure. Consideration describes a variety of behaviors related to the development, inclusion, and the good feelings of subordinates. Initiating structure describes a variety of behaviors related to defining roles, control mechanisms, task focus, and work coordination, both inside and outside the unit. Coupled with the humanist or human relations revolution that was occurring in the 1950s and 1960s, these (and similar studies) spawned a series of useful—if often simplistic and largely bimodal—theories (Arygris 1957; Likert 1959; McGregor 1960; Maslow 1965; Fiedler 1967; Fiedler, Chemers, and Mahar 1976; Blake and Mouton 1964, 1965; Hersey and Blanchard 1969, 1972).

These early implicit and explicit situational theories were certainly useful, for several reasons. First, they were useful as an antidote to the excessively hierarchical, authoritarian styles that had developed in the first half of the twentieth century with the rise and dominance of large organizations in both the private and public sectors. Second, they were useful as teaching tools for incipient and practicing managers, who appreciated the elegant constructs even though they were descriptively simplistic. As a class, however, these theories generally failed to meet scientific standards because they tried to explain too much with too few variables. Among the major theories, only Vroom's normative decision model broke out of this pattern because it self-consciously focused on a single dimension of leadership style—the role of participation—and identified seven problem attributes and two classes of cases (group and individual) (Vroom and Yetton 1973; Vroom and Jago 1988). Although the situational perspective still forms the basis of most leadership theories today, it has done so either in a strictly managerial context (that is, a narrow level of analysis) on a factor-by-factor basis, or it has been subsumed by more comprehensive approaches to leadership at the macro level.

While ethical dimensions were mentioned occasionally in the mainstream literature, the coverage was invariably peripheral because it avoided normative issues. The first major text devoted to ethical issues was Robert Greenleaf's book, *Servant Leadership* (1977), but it did not receive mainstream attention. In contrast, James Macgregor Burns' book on leadership burst on the scene in 1978 and had unusually heavy ethical overtones.[2] However, it was not the ethical dimension that catapulted it to prominence, but its transformational theme. Both Greenleaf (a former business executive) and Burns (a political scientist) were outside the normal academic circles in leadership, which primarily came from business and psychology. A number of contemporary mainstream leadership theorists, both popular and academic, continue in this tradition to one degree or another, such as DePree (1989), Rost (1990), Block (1993), Gardner (1989), Bennis, Parikh, and Lessem (1994, in contrast with Bennis' other work), and Zand (1997), among others. This theme was covered earlier and more frequently (at least in terms of ethical uses of discretion) in the public-sector literature, but that was not part of the mainstream literature and will be discussed separately.

Until 1978, the focus of the mainstream literature was leadership at lower levels, which was amenable to small group and experimental methods and simplified variable models, while executive leadership (and its external demands) and the more amorphous abilities to induce dramatic change were largely ignored.[3] Burns' book on leadership dramatically changed that interest by introducing the notion that transactional leadership was what was largely being studied, and that the other highly important arena—transformational leadership—was largely being ignored.[4] This hit an especially responsive cord in the nonexperimental camp, which had already been explicitly stating that, nationally, there was a surfeit of managers (who use a "transactional" mode) and a terrible deficit of leaders (who use a "transformational" mode) (Zaleznik 1977). Overall, this school agreed that leaders have a special responsibility for understanding a changing environment, that they facilitate more dramatic changes, and that they can energize followers far beyond what traditional exchange theory would suggest. Overstating for clarity, three subschools emerged that emphasized different aspects of these "larger-than-life" leaders.[5] The transformational school emphasized vision and overarching organizational change (Burns 1978; Bass 1985; Bennis and Nanus 1985; Tichy and Devanna 1986). The charismatic school focused on the influence processes of individuals and the specific behaviors used to arouse inspiration and higher levels of action in followers (House 1977; Conger and Kanungo 1998; Meindl 1990). Less articulated in terms of leadership theory was an entrepreneurial school that urged leaders to make practical process and cultural changes that would dramatically improve quality or productivity; it shared a change emphasis with the transformational school and an internal focus with the charismatic school (Peters and Austin 1985; Hammer and Champy 1993; Champy 1995).

The infusion of the transformational leadership school(s) led to both a reinvigoration of academic and nonacademic studies of leadership and a good deal of confusion initially. Was the transactional leadership that the situationalists had studied so assiduously really just mundane management? Or was the new transformational leadership just an extension of basic skills that its adherents were poorly equipped to explain with more conventional scientific methodologies? Even before the 1980s, some work had been done to create holistic models that tried to explain more aspects of leadership (Yukl 1971; Winter 1979). Yet it was not until the 1980s that work began in earnest and that conventional models routinely incorporated transactional and transformational elements.

Bass' work is a good example in this regard. Even his original work on transformational leadership (1985) has strong transactional elements (transformational leaders being those who not only master transactional skills, but capitalize on transformational skills as well),[6] which were strengthened in later work (Bass and Avolio 1990; Bass 1996). In the authoritative *Bass and Stogdill's Handbook of Leadership*, Bass asserted that the field "has broken out of its normal confinement to the study of [small group and supervisory] behaviors" to more studies on executives, more inclusion of perspectives from political science, and more cross-fertilization among schools of thought (Bass 1990, xi). Not surprisingly, fresh efforts to find integrative models were common in the 1990s (Hunt 1996; Chemers 1997; Yukl 1998) (see Table 2.1 for a summary of the eras of mainstream leadership theory and research). To be sure, this cursory review does not do justice to the wealth of perspectives on specific leadership topics, but space and purpose preclude a more in-depth treatment.[7]

The Public-Sector Literature on Leadership Theory and Research

Although the literature on leadership with a public-sector focus is a fraction of that in the private sector, it is has been substantial albeit relatively unfocused. One way to begin a brief review is to look at the track record of *PAR*. In doing an informal content analysis of the journal since its inception—using a rather loose definition of leadership that includes the broader management topics, most executive topics, much of the explicit discretion literature, and that part of the organizational change literature that has a strong leadership component—the author found 110 articles relating to the topic in 61 years. However, using a stricter criterion—that leadership was an explicit focus of the article—only about twenty-five articles qualified, or about four per decade on average.

Table 2.1

Eras of Mainstream Leadership Theory and Research

Era	Major time frame	Major characteristics/example of proponents
Great man	Pre–1900; continues to be popular in biographies	• Emphasis on emergence of a great figure such as a Napoleon, George Washington, or Martin Luther, who has substantial effect on society. • Era influenced by notions of rational social change by uniquely talented and insightful individuals.
Trait	1900–48; current resurgence of recognition of importance of natural talents	• Emphasis on the individual traits (physical, personal, motivational, aptitudes) and skills (communication and ability to influence) that leaders bring to all leadership tasks. • Era influenced by scientific methodologies in general (especially industrial measurement) and scientific management in particular (for instance, the definition of roles and assignment of competencies to those roles).
Contingency	1948–80s; continues as the basis of most rigorous models but with vastly expanded situational repertoire	• Emphasis on the situational variables leaders must deal with, especially performance and follower variables. Shift from traits and skills to behaviors (for example, energy levels and communication skills to role clarification and staff motivation). Dominated by bimodal models in its heyday. • Era influenced by the rise of human relations theory, behavioral science (in areas such as motivation theory), and the use of small group experimental designs in psychology.
Transformational	1978–present	• Emphasis on leaders who create change in deep structure, major processes, or overall culture. Leader mechanisms may be compelling vision, brilliant technical insight, and/or charismatic quality. • Era influenced by the loss of American dominance in business, finance, and science, and the need to re-energize various industries which had slipped in complacency.
Servant	1977–present	• Emphasis on the ethical responsibilities to followers, stakeholders, and society. Business theories tend to emphasize service to followers; political theorists emphasize citizens; public administration analysts tend emphasize legal compliance and/or citizens. • Era influenced by social sensitivities raised in the 1960s and 1970s.
Multifaceted	1990s–present	• Emphasis on integrating the major schools, especially the transactional schools (trait and behavior issues largely representing management interests) and transformational schools (visionary, entrepreneurial, and charismatic). • Era affected by a highly competitive global economy and the need to provide a more sophisticated and holistic approach to leadership.

In the 1940s, articles by Finer (1940) and Leys (1943) defined the administrative discretion debate—how much discretion should public administrators have, and under what conditions—that was taken up so vigorously again in the 1990s. Donald Stone wrote "Notes on the Government Executive: His Role and His Method" in 1945, which is as good an equivalent to Follett's "The Essentials of Leadership" ([1933] 1996) or Barnard's *Functions of the Executive* ([1938] 1987) as ever appeared in the journal.

The trickle of high-quality pieces continued in which Lawton (1954) followed in Stone's footsteps, and Dimock (1958) provided a well-grounded assessment of leadership development. The first piece based exclusively on empirical evidence was by Golembiewski (1959), in which he brought together the literature on small groups in public-sector settings.

Guyot (1962) presented the only empirical study in the 1960s to study variation in the motivation of public and private leaders. Fisher (1962) complained that federal managers do not have management training, and James Fesler (1960) provided a superb editorial comment on the importance of studying leadership and its many contexts. Other topics addressed were influence and social power (Altshular 1965; Lundstedt 1965).

No important articles appeared in the 1970s, which mirrors the low profile of leadership publication in the popular literature. Yet the lacuna is made up by the resurgence of interest in leadership topics in the 1980s. Dilulio (1989) reasserted the importance of both leadership and the management component. Probably the three best articles on the training and development of leaders were written during this time (Likert 1981; Flanders and Utterback 1985; Faerman, Quinn, and Thompson 1987). Stone (1981) and Dimock (1986) wrote essays on the importance and nurturing of innovation and creativity in organizations by leaders. Empirical pieces also appeared on followership (Gilbert and Hyde 1988) and leader action planning (Young and Norris 1988).

Because leadership is so highly related to reform, and because of the volume and debate over the proper type of reforms to make that occurred throughout the decade, leadership is at least indirectly discussed in nearly every issue after 1992. This is particularly true for the debate about administrative discretion, which largely pitted an "entrepreneurial" camp against a "stewardship" camp. Although they cannot do justice to the full range of topics in these two idealized perspectives, good examples are provided in Bellone and Goerl's "Reconciling Public Entrepreneurship and Democracy" (1992) and Terry's "Administrative Leadership, Neo-Managerialism, and the Public Management Movement" (1998). Some of the best and most focused empirically based studies in *PAR* appeared in the 1990s (Hennessey 1998; Moon 1999; Considine and Lewis 1999; Borins 2000).

Generalizing about the leadership literature in *PAR* as one barometer of the field, the following observations can be made: First, until the last decade, leadership was largely considered an executive phenomenon, and thus when small group and lower-level leadership was the focus of the mainstream leadership literature in the 1960s and 1970s, leadership topics were lightly covered. Second, there were only a handful of empirical pieces on leadership in the first fifty years of the journal. Finally, in terms of the "thoughtful essay" tradition, many of the best examples occur in book reviews, with Donald Stone, John Corson, and Paul Appleby being frequent contributors. Though important, *PAR* is but one source—what other contributions were being made to a distinctively public-sector leadership literature?

In the first half of the century during the trait period, public-sector sites were frequently examined, although no distinctive perspective emerged (Jenkins 1947). The first in an important genre of executive studies was done by Macmahon and Millett (1939), in this case regarding federal administrators. The tradition of biographies and autobiographies of important administrative leaders was also established (Pinchot 1947). In the 1950s, a series of good leadership studies in the administrative realm was produced, most notably by Bernstein (1958). However, Selznick's classic, *Leadership in Administration* (1957), is probably the single best overall treatment of the subject in terms of timelessness. In the 1960s, Corson (with Shale) wrote his second book on senior administrative leaders (1966), and Graubard and Holton edited a series of essays on political and administrative leadership (1962). Downs' (1967) well-known book on bureaucracy is notable for its popular, if negative, typology of leaders. Again, the 1970s produced little of special note, with the exception of the administrative role in iron-triangle politics (Heclo 1977) and several good studies of military and quasi-military leadership (Winter 1979; Jermier and Berkes 1979).

With the introduction of the transformational and charismatic literatures in the 1980s, the resurgence of more general interest in leadership was mirrored in the administrative leadership literature. The administrative leader as entrepreneur was introduced by Eugene Lewis (1980) and expanded upon by Doig and Hargrove (1987). Kaufman provided a definitive executive study (1981); Cleveland (1985) and Gardner (1989) provided masterfully well-rounded essays in the Selznick tradition. The more specialized studies on public-sector leadership continued to be primarily for the military (Van Fleet and Yukl 1986; Taylor and Rosenback 1984).

The volume of materials produced in the 1990s requires more selectivity for the present purpose. Many public-sector leadership books have elements that are applicable for administrative leaders but really focus on local and national policy makers (such as councils, mayors, state legislators, etc.) and civic leaders (Chrislip and Larson 1994; Heifetz 1994; Svara 1994; Henton, Melville, and Walesh 1997; Luke 1998). Some emphasize specific elements of leadership such as planning (Bryson and Crosby 1992), complexity (Kiel 1994), problem focus (R. Terry 1993), public-service values (Rost 1990; Fairholm 1991; Riccucci 1995), and frontline leaders (Vinzant and Crothers 1998). Larry Terry (1995) provided a full-length argument supporting leadership as stewardship (which he calls conservatorship). Much of the more narrowly focused leadership literature continued to be for the military (Hunt, Dodge, and Wong 1999). The *International Journal of Public Administration* sponsored a symposium about transformational leadership, edited by the distinguished leadership expert Bernard Bass in 1996. In 2001, Rusaw provided the first book designed as an overarching textbook with a review of the literature. Previously, broad treatments had been available only in chapter formats in most of the standard generic textbooks in the field.

No review of the literature would be complete without some mention of leadership education and training—that is, the application of scholarly work and the genesis of applied research from training settings. Although some of the larger public administration programs with greater resources have substantial offerings in organizational leadership, few of the moderate and smaller programs nationally have the faculty resources to do so. Nonetheless, leadership books and articles are sprinkled throughout management classes in educational curricula, even if in an auxiliary capacity. There are numerous leadership training programs for leaders at all levels of government and at various levels in organizations. Many use leadership-feedback instruments (often called 360-degree instruments) that provide anonymous feedback from subordinates, superiors, and sometimes colleagues. For example, the Center for Creative Leadership uses the proprietary assessment tool "Benchmarks" as the basis of one of its programs. Some rely heavily on case studies, such as the State and Local Executive Program at Harvard's Kennedy School. Many are eclectic or holistic, such as the Federal Executive Institute. Nearly all major federal agencies have their own leadership programs, and the military and public safety areas are particularly keen on leadership training. Many fine state and local programs are located at universities, such as the University of Virginia (Center for Public Service), University of Texas–Austin (Governor's Center), and Arizona State University (Advanced Public Executive Program). A number of the scholars who publish in this area are affiliated with such programs. Finally, it should be noted that the Office of Personnel Management has done a good deal of applied research (OPM 1997, 1999), which it shares with its partners in state governments.

Why do the literatures vary today? The mainstream was pushed into more integrative leadership models in the 1980s by the "new economy," which was triggered by the economic shocks of the 1970s. Substantially higher levels of productivity and customer focus required a much more encompassing model or set of models than the largely transactional approaches had achieved. Reformation efforts in the public sector lagged by nearly a decade (despite the fanfare of 1992–94). Integrative models tailored to public-sector settings simply may be following traditional delayed development, but they also may have been stymied by the enormous normative debates that typified the field in the 1990s.

Perennial Debates in Mainstream Leadership Theory

Another way to review the leadership literature is to examine the major debates that have shaped both leadership paradigms and research agendas. For simplicity, only four of the broadest are discussed here:

- The "proper" focus?
- Does it make a difference?
- Are leaders born or made?
- The best style?

What Should Leaders Focus On: Technical Performance, Development of People, or Organizational Alignment?

We expect leaders to "get things done," to maintain good systems, to provide the resources and training for production, to maintain efficiency and effectiveness through various controls, to make sure that technical problems are handled correctly, and to coordinate functional operations. These and other more technical aspects of production are one level of leadership focus. This focus is implicit in much of the management literature from scientific management, classical management (for example, POSDCORB), the productivity literature, and the contemporary measurement and benchmark literature. It is particularly relevant for leadership in the lower levels of the organization closest to production.

Another perspective is that leaders do not do the work: They depend on followers to actually do the work. Therefore, followers' training, motivation, maturation and continued development, and overall satisfaction are critical to production and organizational effectiveness. Indeed, some of the foremost researchers on the stumbling blocks for leaders state, "many studies of managerial performance have found that the most critical skill for beginning managers, and one most often lacking, is interpersonal competence, or the ability to deal with 'people problems'" (McCall, Lombardo, and Morrison 1988, 19). This strain of thought blossomed during the humanist era, beginning with Maslow in the 1940s and peaking during the 1960s with writers like Argyris, McGregor, and Likert and the situationalists in the 1970s. In the situational leadership research, it was the other half of the task-people dualism. It is still very popular today, especially in the team leadership literature (Katzenbach and Smith 1993), the excellence literature such as Tom Peters (1994), and the charismatic elements of the transformational leadership literature.

The emergence of the transformational leadership paradigm in the 1980s brought the idea that "the essential function of leadership is to produce adaptive or useful change" (Kotter 1990). This notion was, in reality, resurrected from the great man theories in political science and Weberian charismatic theory in sociology. Similarly, Edgar Schein asserted that *"the only thing of real importance that leaders do is to create and manage culture"* (1985, 2, emphasis in original).

Certainly not a major theme in the mainstream, if not altogether absent, was the notion that leadership is a service to the people, end consumers, society, and the public interest (rather than followers). It is common for biographies of religious and social leaders to advance this most strongly, but exemplars in public service do so nearly as strongly (Cooper and Wright 1992; Riccucci 1995). This notion does not displace technical performance, follower development, or organizational alignment, but it often largely ignores these dimensions as "givens." Although relatively uncommon in the mainstream, it has been a prominent element of the scholarly discussion in the public administration literature.

Lastly—and logically—leadership can be seen as a composite of several or all of these notions. Such a composite perspective has both logical and emotional appeal. Leaders typically are called upon to do and be all of these things—perform, develop followers, align their organizations, and foster the common good. Yet it also sidesteps the problem to some degree. Most leaders must make difficult choices about what to focus on and what they should glean from the act of leadership. What is the appropriate balance, and who determines it? Such normative questions loom large when reckoning the merits of the checkered histories of administrative leaders such as Robert Moses (Caro 1974), J. Edgar Hoover (Powers 1987), and more recently, Robert Citron. For an array of possible definitions related to administrative leadership, see Table 2.2.

Table 2.2

Possible Definition of Leadership in an Administrative Context

Leadership can focus strictly on the ends (getting things done), the means by which things get done (the followers), or aligning the organization with external needs and opportunities (which can result in substantive change). A definition of leadership can also emphasize the spirit with which leadership is conducted: In the public sector, this is invariably a public service commitment. Of course, definitions are a blend of several of these elements but with different emphases. One's definition tends to vary based on normative preferences and one's concrete situation and experience.

1. **Administrative leadership is the process of providing the results required by authorized processes in an efficient, effective, and legal manner.** (This narrower definition might apply well to a frontline supervisor and would tend to be preferred by those endorsing strict political accountability.)

2. **Administrative leadership is the process of developing/supporting followers who provide the results.** (Since all leaders have followers, and since it is the followers who actually perform the work and provide its quality, it is better to focus on them than the direct service/product. This is a common view in service industries with mottos such as Our Employees Are Our Number 1 Priority.)

3. **Administrative leadership is the process of aligning the organization with its environment, especially the necessary macro-level changes necessary, and realigning the culture as appropriate.** (This definition tends to fit executive leadership better and emphasizes the "big picture." Many public sector analysts are concerned about the application of this definition because of a breakdown in democratic accountability.)

4. **The key element to administrative leadership is its service focus.** (Although leadership functions and foci may vary, administrative leaders need to be responsive, open, aware of competing interests, dedicated to the common good, etc., so that they create a sense of public trust for their stewardship roles.)

5. **Leadership is a composite of providing technical performance, internal direction to followers, external organizational directions—all with a public service orientation.** (This definition implicitly recognizes the complex and demanding challenge for leaders; however, it eschews the tough decision about defining the proper emphasis or focus that leaders may need to—and operationally do—make.)

To What Degree Does Leadership Make a Difference?

Burns (1978, 265) tells the cynical story of a Frenchman sitting in a cafe who hears a disturbance, runs to the window, and cries: "There goes the mob. I am their leader. I must follow them!" Such a story suggests that, at a minimum, we place too great an emphasis on the effect that leaders have. At its loftiest level—do leaders make a difference?—the question is essentially philosophical because of its inability to provide meaningful control groups and define what leadership means, other than in operational terms. No matter whether it is the great man or transformational theorists comparing Hitlers to Chamberlains, or situational theorists working with small groups comparing the results of finite solution problems, the answer is generally yes. Nonetheless, it is important to remember that leaders do not act in a vacuum—they are a part of the flow of history and set in a culture filled with crises, opportunities, and even dumb luck. In practical terms, however, the question of whether leaders make any difference gets translated into the questions of how much difference and when?

In its various permutations, the question of how much difference leaders make takes up the largest part of the literature, especially when the question relates to the effect of specific behaviors, traits, and skills or their clusters. At a global level, the transformational and great man devotees generally assert that great leaders can make a great difference. Some of the best practical writers, however, caution that leaders' effects are only modest because of the great constraints and the inertia they face (Barnard [1938] 1987; Gardner 1989). The stories about Truman pitying the incoming Eisenhower because his orders would not be followed as in the Army, and Kennedy ordering the missiles out of Turkey only to find out during the Cuban missile crisis that they were still there, reflect this perspective. It is likely that this wisdom is directed at the excessive reliance on formal authority and insulated rationalistic thinking that some inexperienced or weaker leaders exhibit.

Another particularly important dimension of the effect of leadership relates to the levels at which leadership occurs. At the extreme, some theorists emphasize leadership that is almost exclusively equivalent to grand change (Zaleznik 1977) and minimize and even denigrate the notion that leadership occurs throughout the organization. To the contrary, the small group research of the 1950s through the 1970s seemed to suggest that leadership is fundamentally similar at any level. A few, especially the customer service and excellence literatures, emphasize the importance of frontline supervisors (Peters 1994; Buckingham and Coffman 1999). More comprehensive models of the current leadership literature tend to emphasize the idea that different types of leadership are required at different levels, especially because of the increasing levels of discretion allowed as one climbs higher in the organization (Hunt 1996). Different styles simply require different types of skills (Katz 1955).

Are Leaders Born or Made?[8]

An implicit assumption of the great man theory is that leaders (invariably the heads of state and major businesses such as banks and mercantile houses) are essentially born, probably allowing for some significant early training as well. That is, you either have the "stuff" of leadership or you do not, and most do not. Of course, in an age when leadership generally required either membership in the privileged classes (that is, the "right stuff" included education, wealth, connections, and senior appointments) or, in rare instances, extraordinary brilliance in a time of crisis (such as a Napoleon),[9] this has more than a little truth to it. In a more democratic era, such factors have less force, especially because leadership is conceived so much more broadly in terms of position.

Today, the question is generally framed as one of degree rather than as a strict dichotomy. To what degree can leaders be "made," and how? The developmental portion actually has two major components according to most researchers and thoughtful practitioners. While part of leadership is the result of formal training, it actually may be the smaller component. Experience is likely the more important teacher. In the extreme, this position states that leadership cannot be taught, but it can be learned.

More formal training is not without its virtues, too, providing technical skills and credibility, management knowledge, external awareness, coaching, and encouragement for reflection. Leaders must have (or in some instances acquire) the basic technical knowledge of the organization, often more for credibility than the executive function itself; formal training can assist greatly here. Management is a different profession altogether from doing line work; again, training can greatly facilitate the learning process, especially for new managers. Thus, while the black-and-white debate about leaders being made or born is largely considered sophomoric, the more sophisticated debate about the relative importance of innate abilities, experience (unplanned or rotational), and formal training is alive and well.

What Is the Best Style to Use?

Although leadership style is really just an aggregation of traits, skills, and behaviors, it has been an extremely popular topic of research and debate in its own right. One of the most significant issues has been definitional: What is leadership style? Although leadership style can be thought of as the cumulative effect of all traits, skills, and behaviors, it generally describes what is perceived as the key—or at least a prominent—aspect of the universal set of leadership characteristics. Examples include follower participation, such as Zand (1997, 143), who discusses command, consign, consult, and concur styles; change styles, such as risk averse or risk accepting; and personality styles, such as those based on the Myers-Briggs Type Indicator. Other leadership style definitions involve communication, individual versus group approaches to leadership, value orientations—especially involving integrity, and power-and-influence typologies.

A slightly different approach to style looks at it related to function. Much of the situational literature addresses style in this light. Leaders have to get work done ("initiate structure") and work through people ("consideration"). How they are perceived to balance these factors can be defined operationally as their style. A somewhat different, but very useful, insight into functional style preference has to do with the type of situation the leader prefers or excels in: a maintenance situation, a project or task force situation, a line versus function situation, a startup, or turning a business around (McCall, Lombardo, and Morrison 1988).

Another important set of issues regarding style has to do with whether and to what degree style can be changed in adults.[10] Not many have taken the hard line that changing style is nearly impossible. Fiedler (1967; Fiedler, Chemers, and Mahar 1976) is probably most prominent in this regard, largely advising that it is better to figure out the situation first and find the appropriate leader second. Yet, even assuming that change in style is possible, most serious researchers warn against excessive expectations of dramatic change, although radical style change anecdotes pepper the popular literature. If style can be changed, then the important issue that emerges is how (which largely becomes an applied training issue)? Hersey and Blanchard (1969, 1972) have been the most popular in this regard, teaching people to compare their style preference (defined by worker participation in decision making) with the style needs of various situations. In addition to style need (situational demands), style preference, and style range (a leader's repertoire of different styles) is the issue of style quality. Just because one practices a style extensively does not mean that one is proficient in its use.

Although these debates have strong echoes in the public-sector literature, the differences in the debate structures are as important as the similarities.

Debates and Discussions in Administrative Leadership Theory

Of the four major questions, only the first (focus) is discussed as robustly in the public-sector literature as it is in the mainstream; indeed, from a normative philosophical basis, the administrative leadership literature probably argues this issue even more thoroughly. However, the question of proper focus is translated into the discretion debate, which has taken numerous forms affecting the proper role of administrative leaders. For the sake of simplicity, the first era (1883–1940s) can be conceptualized as a time when the dichotomy between the political world of policy decisions and the world of technical and neutral implementation was the overarching ideal. It was argued that good administrative leaders made many technical decisions but referred policy decisions to their political superiors. The role of discretion was largely ignored or downplayed. The second era (1940–80s) was a less idealistic model that recognized that the interplay of the political and administrative worlds is far more intertwined than a simple dichotomy would explain. The dominant model during this period was administrative responsibility, that is, the appropriate and modest use of significant discretion. The recent era (since the 1990s), driven by a worldwide government reform agenda, has interjected entrepreneurial uses of discretion for public administrators. The debate about what to reform in government (the size, the cost, the processes, the structures, the accountability mechanisms, etc.) and how to reform it has stirred huge controversies in the scholarly community. To the degree that it is embraced, the newest model encourages creative and robust uses of discretion and diffuses authority among more stakeholders and control mechanisms.

The discretion debate has shaped the proper focus debate primarily in terms of a management orientation (transactional) versus a change orientation (transformational). If leaders should not exercise significant discretion or be too activist, then they should not play a substantial change role but should focus more on management issues. In a contrary position, many in the New Public Management school echo the mainstream school of the 1980s in asserting that public administrators are uniquely qualified to play a large role, which otherwise would leave a critical leadership vacuum. Another element in the proper focus discussion that is robust in the public-sector literature adds—or sometimes substitutes altogether—the inclusion of customers/clients/citizens and the public good generally. Although the different schools disagree rather caustically about the way to frame these notions and the proper terms to use, there tends to be rather impressive agreement that external constituencies and the common good are a fundamental focus of public-sector administrators that is not to be taken for granted.

The debate about the importance of leadership is much more muted and underdeveloped. Although some argue from the perspective of democratic theory that administrative

leaders should not be important from a strictly political perspective, most public administration scholars and almost all practitioners simply assume or assert the importance of
public administrators. Unfortunately, there is a tendency to treat all situations in which
leadership is important as a single monolith, rather than exploring the ramifications of
different types of leadership in different contexts with varying missions, organizational
structures, accountability mechanisms, environmental constraints, and so on. This means
that the technology of leadership is much less articulated on the public-sector side than
the private-sector side. Attempts at scholarly syntheses that reflect sophisticated multi-
functional, multilevel, and multisituational models that were in evidence in the mainstream by the 1990s are largely lacking in either monographs or the journal literature in
the public sector.

Part of the weakness of the literature resides in its nonintegrated character, with the
ironic exception of many surprisingly good chapter overviews on leadership in general
public administration and public management textbooks. The serious debate about the
best style to use is cut into many parts and is rarely as explicitly or holistically discussed
as in the mainstream leadership literature. Fragments of this literature are found in
management topics such as total quality management, motivation, and routine problem
solving in places such as *Public Productivity and Management Review*, and part of the
literature is found in executive topics such as strategic planning and organizational change
and development in journals such as *Public Administration Quarterly*. The ethics-values
literature, for all of its normative robustness, generally offers few concrete recommendations on this score beyond general admonitions to be responsive, trustworthy, honest,
courageous, and prudent.

The final debate, about whether leaders are born or made, is also not particularly well
developed from a theoretical perspective. In the 1960s, the situational models presented
relatively elementary task-people matrices. Both task and people skills could be taught,
and a more humanistic approach that was less reliant on directive styles was generally
encouraged. This was generally adopted in the public-sector literature. In the 1980s, when
the mainstream field was searching for a more comprehensive and complex model, some
good examples of sophisticated training models did emerge on the public-sector side
(Flanders and Utterback 1985; Faerman, Quinn, and Thompson 1987) but this part of the
literature was largely dormant in the 1990s. The "born" side of the argument recognizes
the importance of recruitment and selection of exceptional individuals. Such discussions
have been relatively common in a human resources context, especially in reports recommending ways to strengthen the public sector (for instance, the Volcker Commission in
1990 and the Winter Commission in 1993), but have not been integrated into an explicit
leadership discussion.

Conclusion

The mainstream leadership literature, which is a multidisciplinary field dominated by
business administration and psychology, has been huge. Although the field has been active for a century, partial and simplistic approaches to this complex phenomenon did not

really contribute much to the overall understanding of leadership until the 1980s, when transformational approaches were (re)introduced. That is, many of the elements of leadership—select traits, skills, or behaviors—were better understood, but a more sophisticated model that could accommodate entirely different missions and environments was lacking. A major effort in the 1990s was to provide syntheses that are sophisticated enough for researchers and elegant enough for practitioners. Although some have contributed or used public-sector examples in the mainstream literature, they have not been integrated into a distinctive public-sector leadership literature focusing on the significant constraints and unique environment of administrative leaders. The administrative leadership literature is substantial if very broadly defined, especially in the last decade. However, the broader, tangential literature about administrative leadership is dispersed in topics such as reform, ethics, and management, and an explicit focus on the detailed dynamics of leadership is largely lacking.

Although it is hard to determine the exact reasons for neglect in this area, it is possible to assess the broad reasons. The technical difficulties of leadership research, especially the empirical elements, have not deterred those in the mainstream. Yet given the subtle nature of decision making by administrators in a system of democratically elected leaders with multiple branches of government, this seems to have been a significant detraction for public-sector researchers. This has been compounded by a noticeable lack of administrative leadership theory development that has not been in the service of organizational, ethical, policy, or political studies. Beliefs that activist administrative leadership styles are not appropriate, or insignificant given the other powerful players, seem to have produced self-selection before the decision to research the area. That is, those with these beliefs have already largely gone into political science and policy areas rather than public administration and public management. If this has been a significant problem in the past, it seems the call for organizational excellence, reform, entrepreneurialism, and robust stewardship over the last twenty years has compensated for this tendency. The final problem—the diversion of attention—seems to be a major problem when examining much of the leadership-related materials. Most of the best empiricism, coupled with disciplined theory building and testing, is at the management level. The most problematic diversion (in terms of extending understanding of administrative leadership), albeit a healthy discussion in its own right, has been the normative debate about administrative discretion in which schools use extreme cases to make arguments rather than more balanced assessments and recommendations of realistic trends.

The strength of the administrative leadership literature, such as it is, has been its hearty normative discussions about the proper role of administrators in a democratic system. Entrepreneurial behavior cannot be blithely endorsed when public administrators are entrusted with the authority of the state. Yet the increased size, cost, and regulatory intervention of the state means that new modes must also be considered—no matter whether they are explicitly entrepreneurial or more robust stewardship roles—as enormous pressures for reform escalate.

As a literature, the weaknesses are more pronounced than the strengths. The normative debate about the right amount and use of more activist leadership approaches for administrative leaders has long since stopped producing useful insights in terms of leadership studies. All schools of thought have tended to treat transformational elements of leadership either too simplistically or too universally. After all, the leadership of a frontline supervisor and a chief executive officer, or the leadership of an auditor as opposed to a state lottery executive, are likely to be remarkably different. Good leadership theory, if it is at the macro level, must accommodate these substantial differences. The field has had remarkably few empirical studies that are not largely descriptive and has overly emphasized leadership as an executive function. Finally, contemporary syntheses of public-sector leadership models that define the actual relationships of the numerous leadership competencies in various environmental contexts are simply absent. Indeed, no matter where you look in or for this subfield, the needs are great and the research opportunities are manifold.

These needs can be crystallized into a dual leadership agenda. First, there is a striking need for a comprehensive leadership model that integrates transactional and transformational elements. While simplistic models such as Figure 2.1 are good for heuristic purposes, such a comprehensive model must be far more articulate to have the requisite explanatory power for the variety of situations and factors inherent in the vast world of public-sector leadership.[11] Second, such comprehensive models must be subjected to empirical research to test the strength of relationships under various conditions and over time. This is particularly important in an age when change skills, vision articulation, and innovation are in greater demand. With well-articulated models, this is not as difficult as it might seem. Such models should undergird leadership survey feedback programs (360-degree instruments used in leadership training), which in turn provide excellent (and large) databases. Another way to examine such models is through the types of surveys commissioned by the International City/County Management Association. Yet another way is to do a series of in-depth interviews with key organizational leaders. The key is to discipline ourselves to create models that are powerful enough to handle the complex leadership phenomenon and then to harness them in our research. Not only will it produce better science, it will be extremely useful in sharing our insights with the practitioner community.

Notes

1. By "mainstream," I refer to literature that self-consciously labels itself as a part of the leadership literature and addresses itself to broad audiences. I exclude literatures that are meant for the consumption of a single discipline with specialized interests and terms. Thus, although many of the studies of public-sector administration are found in the mainstream, many of the issues and materials are not. Needless to say, as with all distinctions regarding large bodies of work, such differentiations are meant more for general insight and convenience than as rigorous taxonomies.

2. For example, Burns states that "moral leadership emerges from and always returns to, the fundamental wants and needs of followers" (4), and later he adds that "transforming leadership ultimately becomes moral in that it raises the level of human conduct and ethical aspiration of both the leader and the led, and thus it has a transforming effect on both" (20).

3. Of course, Weber ([1922] 1963) introduced the notion of charismatic leadership quite clearly, and it had been used by those influenced by sociology and political science such as Willner (1968), Dow (1969) and Downton (1973). Even Freud made it clear that leadership involved more than simple exchange processes implicit in most situational theories.

4. Although part of this avoidance may have been the result of a pro-experimental or positivist perspective, part of it may have been an eschewal of the great man school (which clearly has transformational trappings), which was disdained as antiscientific.

5. Because the overlap is so extensive for the subschools, these distinctions are more for analytical insight than articulation of groups that would necessarily self-identify with these monikers.

6. For example, he notes, "We find that leaders will exhibit a variety of patterns of transformational and transactional leadership. Most leaders do both but in different amounts" (1985, 22).

7. Examples of these topics include the types of leaders, leadership styles, the types and effects of followers, the relevance of societal and organizational cultures on leadership, and the operation of power, or mid- and micro-level theory such as leader role theory, group development theory, path-goal theory, leader-member exchange theory, and attribution theory, among many others.

8. This is a variation of the nature-nurture debate found in some form in most of the social sciences.

9. The time-of-crisis motif is prominent in the change literature (Kanter, Stein, and Jick 1992) as well as the leadership literature. Transformationalists reminded us there are exceptional leadership opportunities, which may or may not be filled, when there is a dramatic crisis, a leadership turnover, or at select stages of the organizational life cycle (especially the birth-to-growth and the maturity-to-decline phases).

10. This debate is related to the made-born argument, but with a critical difference. While the made-born argument is about whether a leader can master any style, the style debate focuses on whether a leader can learn styles other than their native or preferred style.

11. For example, I am completing a book that uses an overarching framework somewhat more articulated than Figure 2.1 and that incorporates sixty-two sub-elements.

References

Altshular, Alan. 1965. "Rationality and Influence in Public Service." *Public Administration Review* 25(3): 226–33.

Argyris, Chris. 1957. *Personality and Organization.* New York: Harper.

Baliga, B. Rajaram, and James G. Hunt. 1988. "An Organizational Life Cycle Approach to Leadership." In *Emerging Leadership Vistas,* edited by James G. Hunt, B. Rajaram Baliga, H. Peter Dachler, and Chester A. Schriesheim, 129–49. Lexington, MA: Lexington Books.

Barnard, Chester I. [1938] 1987. "The Functions of the Executive." In *Classics of Public Administration,* edited by Jay M. Shafritz and Albert C. Hyde, 96–101. Chicago: Dorsey Press.

Bass, Bernard M. 1985. *Leadership and Performance Beyond Expectations.* New York: Free Press.

———. 1990. *Bass and Stogdill's Handbook of Leadership.* New York: Free Press.

———. 1996. *A New Paradigm of Leadership: An Inquiry into Transformational Leadership.* Alexandria, VA: U.S. Army Research Institute for the Behavioral and Social Sciences.

Bass, Bernard M., and Bruce J. Avolio. 1990. "The Implications of Transactional and Transformational Leadership for Individual, Team, and Organizational Development." In *Research in Organizational Change and Development,* edited by William Pasmore and Richard W. Woodman, vol. 4, 231–72. Greenwich, CT: JAI Press.

Bellone, Carl J., and George F. Goerl. 1992. "Reconciling Public Entrepreneurship and Democracy." *Public Administration Review* 52(12): 130–34.

Bennis, Warren, and Burt Nanus. 1985. *Leaders: Strategies for Taking Charge.* New York: Harper and Row.

Bennis, Warren, Jagdish Parikh, and Ronnie Lessem. 1994. *Beyond Leadership: Balancing Economics, Ethics and Ecology.* Oxford, UK: Basil Publishing.

Bernstein, Marver H. 1958. *The Job of the Federal Executive.* Washington, DC: Brookings Institution.

Bird, Charles. 1940. *Social Psychology.* New York: Appleton Century.

Blake, Robert R., and Jane S. Mouton. 1964. *The Managerial Grid.* Houston: Gulf.

———. 1965. "A 9, 9 Approach for Increasing Organizational Productivity." In *Personal and Or-*

ganizational Change through Group Methods, edited by Edgar H. Schein and Warren G. Bennis, 169–83. New York: Wiley.

Block, Peter. 1993. *Stewardship: Choosing Service over Self Interest.* San Francisco: Berrett-Koehler.

Borins, Sandford. 2000. "Loose Cannons and Rule Breakers? . . . Some Evidence about Innovative Public Managers." *Public Administration Review* 60(6): 498–507.

Brunner, Ronald D. 1997. "Teaching the Policy Sciences: Reflections on a Graduate Seminar." *Policy Sciences* 39(2): 217–31.

Bryson, John M., and Barbara C. Crosby. 1992. *Leadership for the Common Good: Tackling Problems in a Shared-Power World.* San Francisco: Jossey-Bass.

Buckingham, Marcus, and Curt Coffman. 1999. *First, Break All the Rules: What the World's Greatest Managers Do Differently.* New York: Simon and Schuster.

Burns, James MacGregor. 1978. *Leadership.* New York: Harper and Row.

Caro, Robert A. 1974. *The Power Broker: Robert Moses and the Fall of New York.* New York: Vintage Books.

Champy, James. 1995. *Reengineering Management: The Mandate for New Leadership.* New York: HarperBusiness.

Chemers, Martin M. 1997. *An Integrative Theory of Leadership.* Mahwah, NJ: Lawrence Erlbaum Associates.

Chrislip, David D., and Carl E. Larson. 1994. *Collaborative Leadership: How Citizens and Civic Leaders Can Make a Difference.* San Francisco: Jossey-Bass.

Cleveland, Harlan. 1985. *The Knowledge Executive: Leadership in an Information Society.* New York: E.P. Dutton.

Conger, Jay A., and Rabindra N. Kanungo. 1998. *Charismatic Leadership in Organizations.* Thousand Oaks, CA: Sage Publications.

Considine, Mark, and Jenny M. Lewis. 1999. "Governance at Ground Level: The Frontline Bureaucrat in the Age of Markets and Networks." *Public Administration Review* 59(6): 467–80.

Cooper, Terry L., and N. Dale Wright, eds. 1992. *Exemplary Public Administrators: Character and Leadership in Government.* San Francisco: Jossey-Bass.

Corson, John J., and Paul R. Shale. 1966. *Men Near the Top: Filling Key Posts in the Federal Service.* Baltimore: Johns Hopkins University Press.

Dahl, Robert A. 1947. "The Science of Public Administration: Three Problems." *Public Administration Review* 7(1): 1–11.

DePree, Max. 1989. *Leadership Is an Art.* New York: Doubleday.

Dilulio, John J., Jr. 1989. "Recovering the Public Management Variable: Lessons from Schools, Prisons, and Armies." *Public Administration Review* 49(2): 127–33.

Dimock, Marshall E. 1958. "Executive Development after Ten Years." *Public Administration Review* 18(2): 91–97.

———. 1986. "Creativity." *Public Administration Review* 46(1): 3–7.

Doig, Jameson W., and Erwin C. Hargrove. 1987. *Leadership and Innovation: A Biographical Perspective on Entrepreneurs in Government.* Baltimore: Johns Hopkins University Press.

Dow, Thomas. 1969. "The Theory of Charisma." *Sociological Quarterly* 10(3): 306–18.

Downs, Anthony. 1967. *Inside Bureaucracy.* Boston: Little, Brown.

Downton, James V. 1973. *Rebel Leadership: Commitment and Charisma in the Revolutionary Process.* New York: Free Press.

Faerman, Sue R., Robert E. Quinn, and Michael P. Thompson. 1987. "Bridging Management Practice and Theory: New York State's Public Service Training Program." *Public Administration Review* 47(4): 310–19.

Fairholm, Gilbert. 1991. *Values Leadership: Toward a New Philosophy of Leadership.* New York: Praeger.

Fesler, James W. 1960. "Leadership and Its Context." *Public Administration Review* 20(2): 122.

Fiedler, Fred E. 1967. *A Theory of Leadership Effectiveness.* New York: McGraw-Hill.

Fiedler, Fred E., Martin M. Chemers, and L. Mahar. 1976. *Improving Leadership Effectiveness: The Leader Match Concept.* New York: Wiley.

Finer, Herman. 1940. "Administrative Responsibility in Democratic Government." *Public Administration Review* 1(4): 335–50.

Fisher, John. 1962. "Do Federal Managers Manage?" *Public Administration Review* 22(2): 59–64.

Flanders, Lorretta R., and Dennis Utterback. 1985. "The Management Excellence Inventory: A Tool for Management Development." *Public Administration Review* 45(3): 403–10.

Follett, Mary Parker. [1933] 1996. *Mary Parker Follett: Prophet of Management.* Boston: Harvard Business School Press.

Gardner, John. W. 1989. *On Leadership.* New York: Free Press.

Gilbert, G. Ronald, and Albert Hyde. 1988. "Followership and the Federal Worker." *Public Administration Review* 48(6): 962–68.

Golembiewski, Robert T. 1959. "The Small Group and Public Administration." *Public Administration Review* 19(3): 149–56.

Graubard, Stephen R., and Gerald Holton, eds. 1962. *Excellence and Leadership in a Democracy.* New York: Columbia University Press.

Greenleaf, Robert K. 1977. *Servant Leadership: A Journey into the Nature of Legitimate Power and Greatness.* New York: Paulist Press.

Guyot, James F. 1962. "Government Bureaucrats Are Different." *Public Administration Review* 22(4): 195–202.

Hammer, Michael, and James Champy. 1993. *Reengineering the Corporation: A Manifesto for Business Revolution.* New York: HarperCollins.

Heclo, Hugh. 1977. *A Government of Strangers: Executive Politics in Washington.* Washington, DC: Brookings Institution.

Heifetz, Ronald A. 1994. *Leadership without Easy Answers.* Cambridge, MA: Belknap Press.

Hempill, John K. 1950. *Leader Behavior Description.* Columbus, OH: Ohio State University, Personnel Research Board.

Hempill, John K., and Alvin E. Coons. 1957. "Development of the Leader Behavior Questionnaire." In *Leader Behavior: Its Description and Measurement,* edited by Ralph M. Stogdill and Alvin E. Coons, 6–38. Columbus, OH: Ohio State University, Bureau of Business Research.

Hennessey, J. Thomas. 1998. "Reinventing Government: Does Leadership Make the Difference?" *Public Administration Review* 58(6): 522–32.

Henton, Douglas, John Melville, and Kimberly Walesh. 1997. *Grassroots Leaders for a New Economy: How Civic Entrepreneurs Are Building Prosperous Communities.* San Francisco: Jossey-Bass.

Hersey, Paul, and Kenneth H. Blanchard. 1969. "Life Cycle Theory of Leadership." *Training and Development Journal* 23(1): 263–64.

———. 1972. "The Management of Change." *Training and Development Journal* 26(2): 20–24.

House, Robert J. 1977. "A 1976 Theory of Charismatic Leadership." In *Leadership: The Cutting Edge,* edited by James G. Hunt and Lars L. Larson, 189–207. Carbondale, IL: Southern Illinois Press.

Hunt, James G. 1996. *Leadership: A New Synthesis.* Newbury Park, CA: Sage Publications.

Hunt, James G., George E. Dodge, and Leonard Wong, eds. 1999. *Out-of-the-Box Leadership: Transforming the Twenty-first Century Army and Other Top-Performing Organizations.* Stamford, CT: JAI Press.

Jenkins, William O. 1947. "A Review of Leadership Studies with Particular Reference to Military Problems." *Psychological Bulletin* 44(1): 54–79.

Jermier, John M., and L.J. Berkes. 1979. "Leader Behavior in a Police Command Bureaucracy: A Closer Look at the Quasi-Military Model." *Administrative Science Quarterly* 24(1): 123.

Kanter, Rosabeth Moss, Barry A. Stein, and Todd D. Jick. 1992. *The Challenges of Organizational Change: How Companies Experience It and Leaders Guide It.* New York: Free Press.

Katz, Robert L. 1955. "Skills of an Effective Administrator." *Harvard Business Review* 33(1): 33–42.

Katzenbach, Jon R., and Douglas K. Smith. 1993. *The Wisdom of Teams: Creating the High Performance Organization.* Boston: Harvard Business School Press.

Kaufman, Herbert. 1981. *The Administrative Behavior of Federal Bureau Chiefs.* Washington, DC: Brookings Institution.

Kiel, L. Douglas. 1994. *Managing Chaos and Complexity in Government.* San Francisco: Jossey-Bass.

Kotter, John P. 1990. *A Force for Change: How Leadership Differs from Management.* New York: Free Press.

Lawton, Frederick J. 1954. "The Role of the Administrator in the Federal Government." *Public Administration Review* 14(2): 112–18.

Lewis, Eugene. 1980. *Public Entrepreneurship: Toward a Theory of Bureaucratic Political Power.* Bloomington, IN: Indiana University Press.

Leys, Wayne A.R. 1943. "Ethics and Administrative Discretion." *Public Administration Review* 3(1): 10–23.

Likert, Rensis. 1959. "Motivational Approach to Management Development." *Harvard Business Review* 37(4): 75–82.

———. 1981. "System 4: A Resource for Improving Public Administration." *Public Administration Review* 41(6): 674–78.

Luke, Jeffrey S. 1998. *Catalytic Leadership: Strategies for an Interconnected World.* San Francisco: Jossey-Bass.

Lundstedt, Sven. 1965. "Administrative Leadership and Use of Social Power." *Public Administration Review* 25(2): 156–60.

Macmahon, Arthur W., and John D. Millett. 1939. *Federal Administrators: A Biographical Approach to the Problem of Departmental Management.* New York: Columbia University Press.

Maslow, Abraham. 1965. *Eupsychian Management.* Homewood, IL: Dorsey.

McCall, Morgan W., Michael M. Lombardo, and Ann M. Morrison. 1988. *The Lessons of Experience: How Successful Executives Develop on the Job.* New York: Lexington Books.

McGregor, Douglas. 1960. *The Human Side of Enterprise.* New York: McGraw-Hill.

Meindl, John R. 1990. "On Leadership: An Alternative to the Conventional Wisdom." In *Research in Organizational Behavior,* edited by B.M. Staw and L.L. Cummings, vol. 12, 159–203. Greenwich, CT: JAI Press.

Moon, Myung Jae. 1999. "The Pursuit of Managerial Entrepreneurship: Does Organization Matter?" *Public Administration Review* 59(1): 31–43.

National Commission on the Public Service (Volcker Commission). 1990. *Leadership for America.* Lexington, MA: Lexington Books.

National Commission on the State and Local Public Service (Winter Commission). 1992. *Hard Truths/Tough Choices: An Agenda for State and Local Reform.* Albany, NY: Nelson A. Rockefeller Institute of Government.

Office of Personnel Management (OPM). 1997. *MOSAIC: Occupational Study of Federal Executives, Managers, and Supervisors.* Washington, DC: Office of Personnel Management.

———. 1999. *High-Performing Leaders: A Competency Model.* Washington, DC: Office of Personnel Management.

Peters, Thomas, and Nancy Austin. 1985. *A Passion for Excellence: The Leadership Difference.* New York: Random House.

Peters, Tom. 1994. *The Pursuit of WOW! Every Person's Guide to Topsy-Turvy Times.* New York: Vintage Books.

Pinchot, Gifford. 1947. *Breaking New Ground.* New York: Harcourt, Brace.

Powers, Richard G. 1987. *Secrecy and Power: The Life of J. Edgar Hoover.* New York: Free Press.

Redford, Emmette. 1969. *Democracy in the Administrative State.* New York: Oxford University Press.

Riccucci, Norma M. 1995. *Unsung Heroes: Federal Execucrats Making a Difference.* Washington, DC: Georgetown University Press.

Rost, Joseph C. 1990. *Leadership for the Twenty-first Century.* Westport, CT: Praeger.

Rusaw, A. Carol. 2001. *Leading Public Organizations: An Integrative Approach.* Orlando, FL: Harcourt.

Schein, Edgar H. 1985. *Organizational Culture and Leadership: A Dynamic View.* San Francisco: Jossey-Bass.

Selznick, Philip. 1957. *Leadership in Administration.* New York: Row, Peterson, and Company.

Stogdill, Ralph M. 1948. "Personal Factors Associated with Leadership: A Survey of the Literature." *Journal of Psychology* 25(1): 35–71.

Stone, Donald C. 1945. "Notes on the Government Executive: His Role and His Methods." *Public Administration Review* 5(3): 210–25.

———. 1981. "Innovative Organizations Require Innovative Managers." *Public Administration Review* 41(5): 507–13.

Svara, James H., ed. 1994. *Facilitative Leadership in Local Government: Lessons from Successful Mayors and Chairpersons.* San Francisco: Jossey-Bass.

Taylor, Robert L., and William E. Rosenback, eds. 1984. *Military Leadership: In Pursuit of Excellence.* Boulder, CO: Westview Press.

Terry, Larry D. 1995. *Leadership of Public Bureaucracies: The Administrator as Conservator.* Thousand Oaks, CA: Sage Publications.

———. 1998. "Administrative Leadership, Neo-Managerialism, and the Public Management Movement." *Public Administration Review* 58(3): 194–200.

Terry, Robert. 1993. *Authentic Leadership: Courage in Action.* San Francisco: Jossey-Bass.

Tichy, Noel M., and Mary Anne Devanna. 1986. *The Transformational Leader.* New York: John Wiley and Sons.

Van Fleet, David D., and Gary Yukl. 1986. *Military Leadership: An Organizational Perspective.* Greenwich, CT: JAI Press.

Vinzant, Janet C., and Lane Crothers. 1998. *Street-Level Leadership: Discretion and Legitimacy in Front-Line Public Service.* Washington, DC: Georgetown University Press.

Vroom, Victor H., and Arthur G. Jago. 1988. *The New Leadership: Managing Participation in Organizations.* Englewood Cliffs, NJ: Prentice Hall.

Vroom, Victor H., and Phillip W. Yetton. 1973. *Leadership and Decision-Making.* Pittsburgh, PA: University of Pittsburgh Press.

Weber, Max. [1922] 1963. *The Sociology of Religion.* Beacon, NY: Beacon Press.

Winner, Ann Ruth. 1968. *Charismatic Political Leadership: A Theory.* Princeton, NJ: Princeton University, Center for International Studies.

Winter, David G. 1979. *Navy Leadership and Management Competencies: Convergence among Tests, Interviews and Performance Ratings.* Boston: McBer.

Yankelovich, Daniel. 1991. *Coming to Public Judgment: Making Democracy Work in a Complex World.* Syracuse, NY: Syracuse University Press.

Young, Frank, and John Norris. 1988. "Leadership Challenge and Action Planning: A Case Study." *Public Administration Review* 48(1): 564–70.

Yukl, Gary. 1971. *Leadership in Organizations.* Englewood Cliffs, NJ: Prentice Hall.

———. 1998. *Leadership in Organizations.* 4th ed. Englewood Cliffs, NJ: Prentice Hall.

Zaleznik, Arthur. 1977. "Managers and Leaders: Are They Different?" *Harvard Business Review* 55(5): 67–78.

Zand, Dale E. 1997. *The Leadership Triad: Knowledge, Trust, and Power.* New York: Oxford University Press.

CHAPTER 3

DIFFERENT PERSPECTIVES ON
THE PRACTICE OF LEADERSHIP

MATTHEW R. FAIRHOLM

Public administrators not only need practical and intellectual permission to exercise leadership, they need practical and intellectual understanding of what leadership actually is. Training public managers in the skills and techniques of leadership and management has become a major part of public human resource efforts (Day 2000; Sims 2002; Rainey and Kellough 2000; Ink 2000; Pynes 2003). Articles and essays have surfaced in the literature about the need for and legitimacy of public managers exerting leadership in their work, complementing the traditional functions of organizational management and policy and program implementation. Books have emerged to lend more specificity to the topic of leadership in the public sector. Still, in the face of technicism, strict policy implementation, and a fear of administrative discretion, it has often been a significant struggle to discuss the philosophy of leadership in public administration.

This article offers empirical insight, both descriptive and prescriptive, about what leadership actually looks like as practiced by public managers, and it supports a growing focus on leadership in the literature (Behn 1998; Terry 1995; Van Wart 2003). The research findings influence public administration and the individual public administrator by first growing our basic understanding of leadership, refining our perceived public administration roles consistent with that understanding, and finally, reshaping the professional training of public administrators. These new ideas about how public managers view and practice leadership legitimize the notion that leadership is inherent in and a crucial part of public administration, and it offers public managers the chance to improve or enhance those legitimate leadership activities. The hope is that the current trend of building leadership and management capacity among practitioners will be undertaken with a more proper focus and with renewed theoretical and practical vigor.

Background: The Leadership Apology in Public Administration

Public administration traditionally is the study and work of management in public organizations. It is also the study and work of leadership in those organizations. Public administration emerged with a bias toward management science—the expert, the decision maker—but

From *Public Administration Review,* vol. 64, no. 5 (September/October 2004): 577–90. Copyright © 2004 by American Society for Public Administration. Reprinted with permission.

management science has not sufficiently served public administration (McSwite 1997). Bennis (1993) suggests that managers focus on doing their work right (that is, correctly), while leadership is concerned with selecting the right things—programs, policies, values, goals, etc.—to work on. In today's environment, it makes more sense for us to describe public administration as the practice and theory that grapples with doing the right things right in the service of society. In short, public administration is the work of management and leadership. In contemporary literature, the concepts of management and leadership are constantly being defined, compared, and differentiated.[1] A simple way to see the distinction is that if you can count it, you can control it, you can program it, and therefore, you can manage it. If you cannot count it, you have to do leadership. While some still may not see a distinction, the leadership literature today by and large accepts the differences. Notions of leadership, for instance, grounded the government reinvention efforts so prevalent in the 1990s (Ingraham, Sanders, and Thompson 1998). For example, Sanders (1998) argues that leadership is essential in the working and transformation of government. He suggests the key ingredients of leadership in government reinvention include "single-minded purpose and a strategic perspective with a proclivity for risk . . . participation and persistence" (55).

Behn (1998) says that leadership is required in the world of public administration to resolve its inherent imperfections. He suggests that no matter what we call the work of public managers, managing the systems and procedures are only part of the job. Initiative, motivation, inspiration—the things of leadership—also play a critical role in making government and government organizations work. Behn offers that the question is not whether they should lead, but rather what kind of leadership should public administrators be practicing. For him it is "active, intelligent, enterprising leadership . . . that takes astute initiatives designed to help the agency not only achieve its purposes today but also to create new capacity to achieve its objectives tomorrow" (224). Terry's (1995) view of leadership serves as a backdrop to much of Behn's discussion. While Behn focuses on the traits and behaviors of public managers, Terry emphasizes a normative, values-laden approach to leadership, dismissing the heroic leadership constructs in favor of the leader as conservator of institutional and organizational values and goals. The idea of public managers infusing values into an organization is not a new one, even if it is often ignored. Selznick (1983) states that the point of leadership is to "infuse the organization with values." And Denhardt (1981) says the theory and practice of public administration are integral to the development of the state and its allocation of values in society. It follows, therefore, that public administration must encompass far more than technical concerns (Hart 1984). Fairholm (1991) focuses a discussion of values leadership in the work of public administration, presenting a model of leadership that is consistent with the fundamental constitutional values that guide and shape the work of public managers. Luminaries in the field, such as Follett (1918), Barnard (1938), and Waldo (1980), have also discussed leadership issues in terms of values and relationships. This focus has been renewed in the leadership literature discussing emotional intelligence, or the ability to understand people and act wisely in human relations (Goleman 1995). Nevertheless, for most, leadership is only one of many supporting elements of public administration's success or efficacy, not a major factor in public administration theory and practice.

In fact, some public administration theorists avoid the topic of leadership altogether. James MacGregor Burns (1978) offers a reason. In modern times, he writes, leadership research and theory have been misfounded in social and political thought. Burns emphatically argues that an encompassing leadership theory has suffered both from an ill-advised intellectual trip "down a blind alley," leading only to misguided ideas of authority, and from the inadequacy of empirical data (23). Researchers have denigrated the idea of leadership, he contends, because they misunderstand the evolving nature of authority derived from changing social structures, and because they have missed opportunities to tie in research procedures and focuses from intellectual interests such as psychology, sociology, history, and political science, not just scientific management, Weberian bureaucracy, and the like. Following Burns's argument, perhaps public administrators are still afraid of the concepts of raw power, authority, and domination, with which a misguided history of leadership theory has endowed us with. Specifically, many in public administration suffer from a preoccupation with traditional arguments surrounding the potential evils of authority. This preoccupation revolves around typical public administration issues and concerns that are described in ways contrary to the focus on leadership found in recent literature. These concerns can be summarized by what might be termed the "three Ds": (1) dichotomy arguments that say leadership looks too much like politics and therefore should be eschewed; (2) discretion arguments that simply define leadership as a maverick and undesirable version of administrative discretion; and (3) domination/authority arguments that suggest leadership is merely another form of domination and authority and, therefore, is inherently dangerous because it tends to create societal units that are dominated by the whims of unchecked (that is, unelected), morally hegemonic "men of reason" (McSwite 1997).

Despite these objections (indeed, perhaps because of them), studying what leadership actually is and how it is applied makes sense in the world of public administration. As Burns once optimistically declared, "At last we can hope to close the intellectual gap between the fecund canons of authority and a new and general theory of leadership" (1978, 26). Certainly, studying leadership in public administration offers an opportunity to jump the practical hurdles that history and intellectual narrowness have presented. Such endeavors can begin to close an intellectual and practical gap and help complete the field.

Beginning to Fill the Public Administration Leadership Gap

For public administration, the leadership gap has really only existed in the academic realm. Practitioners have been "doing leadership" and dealing with authority and influence all along, but without a good model for what they are doing. While some writers in the field have focused on leadership, overall, public administration scholars have done little to help understand what leadership in public organizations is. Van Wart (2003) suggests it is still an area worthy of more thought and especially more research. His review of public administration articles suggests that leadership itself has not been in the mainstream of public administration literature and that a dearth of empirical research on leadership is evident.

Many public administration academics are, at best, ignoring leadership issues and, at worst, rejecting the concept. Practitioners, on the other hand, are trying to gain sufficient training or grounding in leadership to deal with the relationship-based issues they face daily. Because of this practitioner focus, a few universities have started programs explicitly linking leadership and the public sector environment. Increasingly, government agencies are devoting time and financial resources to leadership and management-development programs.[2] Many state governments have committed to offering the nationally recognized certified public manager training to their employees. And most federal agencies have leadership-development programs for senior executives, middle managers, and new recruits with significant leadership potential.

You Know It When You See It

Even with all of this focus on leadership development, public administration as a field has not devoted sufficient scholarly attention to the topic. People often lump all executive functions or behavior into the word "leadership." They disregard the unique leadership techniques that have prompted contemporary leadership scholars to differentiate leadership and management. Thus, they may say that virtually everything done in organizations is leadership—which also means that nothing is. One reason for this lack of attention is that understanding leadership is hard. In part, this is true because of the many extant management and leadership theories, approaches, and definitions. To some extent, though, these definitions of leadership simply reflect the theory that each individual researcher has about the leadership phenomenon. One authority on leadership suggests, "Leadership is like beauty. You know it when you see it." As Stogdill (1974, 7) suggests, "there are as many definitions of leadership as there are persons who have attempted to define the concept." Understanding leadership, then, may entail understanding people's conceptions or mind-sets about the phenomenon and framing these perspectives in a useful model. Studying practitioner views on leadership, therefore, is an appropriate and valuable start to understanding what leadership looks like in public administration to public administrators.

This article deals with the author's study focusing on what leadership looks like to public managers. This research develops empirical evidence that different perspectives on leadership exist that shape the behavior of individual practitioners in ways specific to their mind sets. This is a "personal conceptions" or "perspectival" approach to leadership study. This perspectival approach reveals the different ways that individual public managers see their leadership activities every day—how they conceive of leadership from their perspective. Therefore, it provides a richer, more meaningful understanding of the concept of leadership and facilitates a more complete analysis of the leadership phenomenon. It also suggests it is likely that practitioner leaders can grow in their understanding of leadership. Importantly, this research better informs the work of public administrators by emphasizing both the leadership and the management responsibilities that are evident as practitioners ply their craft.

Leader and Leadership

Two main approaches to studying leadership emerge. The most popular is a focus on the leader, suggesting that leadership is best understood by studying specific individuals in specific situations (Bennis 1984; Kouzes and Posner 1990; Carson 1987; Sanders 1998). Proponents of this method focus on the qualities, behaviors, and situational responses of those who claim to be or are given the title of leader. In this first approach, leadership is what leaders are or do, and therefore the meaning of leadership derives from the work of the leader: Leaders define leadership.

The second approach recognizes that studying individual leaders may not get you to a general understanding of leadership (DePree 1992; Wheatley 1999; Heifetz 1994; Burns 1978; Greenleaf 1977). This approach rejects the idea that leadership is a summation of the qualities, behaviors, or situational responses of individuals in a position of author-ity at the head of organizations. Proponents of this approach accept that leadership is something larger than the leader—that leadership encompasses all there is that defines who a leader may be. Hence, the meaning of "leader" (or who may be labeled a leader) depends on the leadership techniques displayed, not the position held. This second ap-proach differs from the leadercentric approach mainly by asking the question, "what is leadership?" instead of "who is a leader?" This second, more philosophical approach guides this research exploring how public managers view leadership.

Applying the Perspectival Approach to Understanding Leadership

Paradigmatic, perspectival, or worldview conceptions of how we look at the world are not new in literature. Barker (1992) uses the term "paradigm" to suggest a system or pattern of integrating thoughts, actions, and practices. Graves (1970) describes different states of being, each of which determines actions, relationships, and measures of success. Although the states of being are somewhat hierarchically arranged, Graves's research shows that a person need not necessarily grow to higher levels or states of being. Harman (1998), in reviewing the history of science and knowledge, suggests there are three fundamental ways (perspectives) of seeing and knowing the world and the phenomena of social interaction. Other authors see culture as shaping the way we view things in our everyday experiences (Quinn and McGrath 1985; Schein 1996; Herzberg 1984; Hofstede 1993).

McWhinney (1984) explains the importance of looking at paradigmatic perspectives in studying leadership. He argues the different ways people experience reality result in distinctly different attitudes toward change, and understanding these different concepts contributes to new understanding about resistance to change and modes of leadership. Morgan (1998) also suggests that the way we see organizations influences how we operate within them and even shapes the types of activities that make sense within them.

The Theory of Leadership Perspectives

The research draws on the perspectives outlined by Gil Fairholm (1998). He suggests that people view leadership in at least five different ways. These perspectives not only shape how one internalizes observation and externalizes belief sets, they also determine how one measures success in oneself and others. Thus, Fairholm says, "defining leadership is an intensely personal activity limited by our personal paradigms or our mental state of being, our unique mind set" (xv). Our leadership perspective defines what we mean when we say "leadership" and shapes how we view successful leadership in ourselves and others. He explains that while the leadership perspective that someone holds may not be the objective reality about leadership, people holding that view behave as if it is. Individuals immediately draw on their own conceptions to internalize conversations about leadership. They define leadership for themselves and use their perspective as the basis for judging whether others are exercising leadership. Frustration, confusion, and even conflict may arise because individuals may simply have multiple, competing, even conflicting conceptions of what leadership is.

Fairholm posits five distinct leadership mind-sets that emerge from experience and literature from the past 100 years or so. The first is *leadership as (scientific) management*. This perspective equates leadership with the type of management that draws on the scientific management movement of the early part of the twentieth century, which still has relevance for many even today. In this perspective, much emphasis is placed on managers understanding the one best way to promote and maintain productivity among the employee ranks. Gulick's (1937) famous mnemonic, POSDCORB (plan, organize, staff, direct, coordinate, report and budget), had great influence on the work of public administrators by legitimizing and routinizing the administration of government and fits squarely in this perspective.

The second perspective, *leadership as excellence management*, suggests that leadership is management but focuses on what has been called the "excellence movement." Popularized in the 1980s by Peters and Waterman (1982), Deming (1986), and Juran (1989), this perspective focuses on systematic quality improvements with a focus on the people involved in the processes, the processes themselves, and the quality of products that are produced.

The third perspective is *leadership as a values-displacement activity*. This perspective defines leadership as a relationship between leader and follower that allows for typical management objectives to be achieved primarily through shared values, not merely direction and control. Leadership success depends more on values and shared vision than on organizational authority. Although the values-leadership perspective differentiates leadership and management, it still focuses much on the role of the leader in the relationship. The fourth perspective, *leadership in a trust culture*, shifts the focus toward the ambient culture where interaction between the leader and the led is based on trust founded on shared values, recognizing the follower as having a key role in the leadership relationship. This mind-set emphasizes teams, culture, and mutual trust between leader and follower, which are the methods leaders use to institutionalize their values.

The last perspective is *whole-soul (spiritual) leadership*. This perspective builds on the ideas of displacing values and maintaining a culture of trust, as it focuses attention on the whole-soul nature of both the individual leader and each follower. This perspective assumes that people have only one spirit, which manifests itself in both our professional and personal lives, and that the activity of leadership engages individuals at this core level. "Spirit" is defined in terms of the basis of comfort, strength, happiness; the essence of self; the source of personal meaning and values; a personal belief system or inner certainty; and an emotional level of being. Equating spiritual leadership with the relatively new idea of emotional intelligence may seem natural. Emotional intelligence is indeed related to social intelligence and wise human relations. It involves the ability to monitor one's own emotions, to discriminate among them, and to use the information to guide one's thinking and actions (Salovey and Mayer 1990). Emotional intelligence is a useful concept (perhaps for all of the perspectives, but especially from values leadership on), but it involves only a part of what spiritual leaders might use in their larger-scoped task of capturing the spirit (the soul, the heart, or the character) of followers at the emotional, but also at the value, intellectual, and technical levels. Whole-soul (spiritual) leadership integrates the components of work and personal life into a comprehensive system that fosters continuous growth, improvement, self-awareness, and self leadership in such a way that leaders see others as whole persons with a variety of emotions, skills, knowledge, and abilities that go beyond the narrow confines of job needs. Spiritual leadership is essentially the linking of our interior world of moral reflection with our outer world of work and social relationships.

The theory suggests these five perspectives are distinct but related hierarchically, leading to a more accurate and comprehensive conception of leadership. This hierarchy suggests that succeeding perspectives encompass and transcend lower-order perspectives, and that individuals must move through simpler perspectives before being able to comprehend and engage in leadership activities characterized by more complex perspectives. To gain a full picture of leadership, the theory suggests, we should take into account how a "holarchy" of leadership perspectives offers a compilation of leadership elements that produces a more comprehensive view of the leadership phenomenon (Koestler 1970). Within this compilation of leadership elements, some transcend others to such a degree as to make the less encompassing elements look less like true leadership. As we move up the model, the distinctive elements of leadership as differentiated from management become more refined.

The Leadership Perspectives Model

The *leadership perspectives model* explains leadership in terms of these encompassing perspectives (Figure 3.1). The model shows five concentric triangles, the smallest of which is scientific management and the largest of which is whole-soul leadership. Thus, in two dimensions, we are able to see how one perspective can encompass and transcend another perspective. For example, values leadership encompasses the ideas of scientific management and excellence management, but transcends them in ways that help us to see distinct activities and approaches that create a line between management theories of the past and leadership ideas in contemporary literature.

The leadership perspectives model operationalizes significant elements of Fairholm's initial theory, illustrating how these constructs, along with operational categories and key leadership elements, relate. The specific leadership elements are ones that are found in contemporary leadership literature. Overall, the model points the way not only to understand the phenomenon of leadership better, but also to teach leadership and develop individuals in their leadership activities.

Figure 3.1

Leadership Perspectives Model (LPM)

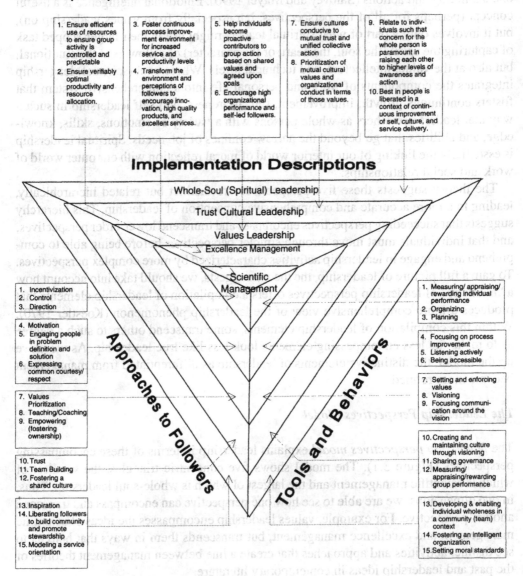

1. Ensure efficient use of resources to ensure group activity is controlled and predictable
2. Ensure verifiably optimal productivity and resource allocation.

3. Foster continuous process improvement environment for increased service and productivity levels
4. Transform the environment and perceptions of followers to encourage innovation, high quality products, and excellent services.

5. Help individuals become proactive contributors to group action based on shared values and agreed upon goals
6. Encourage high organizational performance and self-led followers.

7. Ensure cultures conducive to mutual trust and unified collective action
8. Prioritization of mutual cultural values and organizational conduct in terms of those values.

9. Relate to individuals such that concern for the whole person is paramount in raising each other to higher levels of awareness and action
10. Best in people is liberated in a context of continuous improvement of self, culture, and service delivery.

Implementation Descriptions

Whole-Soul (Spiritual) Leadership

Trust Cultural Leadership

Values Leadership

Excellence Management

Scientific Management

Approaches to Followers

1. Incentivization
2. Control
3. Direction

4. Motivation
5. Engaging people in problem definition and solution
6. Expressing common courtesy/respect

7. Values Prioritization
8. Teaching/Coaching
9. Empowering (fostering ownership)

10. Trust
11. Team Building
12. Fostering a shared culture

13. Inspiration
14. Liberating followers to build community and promote stewardship
15. Modeling a service orientation

Tools and Behaviors

1. Measuring/appraising/rewarding individual performance
2. Organizing
3. Planning

4. Focusing on process improvement
5. Listening actively
6. Being accessible

7. Setting and enforcing values
8. Visioning
9. Focusing communication around the vision

10. Creating and maintaining culture through visioning
11. Sharing governance
12. Measuring/appraising/rewarding group performance

13. Developing & enabling individual wholeness in a community (team) context
14. Fostering an intelligent organization
15. Setting moral standards

Key Research Findings

This researcher performed a content analysis on 103 essays written by middle managers in the District of Columbia government describing their conception of leadership. Data were also collected from thirty-one interviews of public managers (balanced in terms of government function, personnel grade level, gender, and ethnicity) in three metropolitan

Washington-area jurisdictions—Arlington County, Virginia; Washington, DC; and Prince George's County, Maryland—as a supplement and verification of the essays' analysis. The content analysis and interview data reveal the following general findings about the leadership of public managers in terms of the five leadership perspectives.

Five Leadership Perspectives. The content analysis revealed four distinct, "pure" leadership perspectives and one transitional perspective (that is, excellence management). The scientific management, values leadership, trust culture leadership, and whole-soul leadership perspectives were evident as distinct mind-sets held by practicing public executives. Fifteen of 103 essays (14.6 percent) reflected completely distinct leadership perspectives. All perspectives were evident in mixed or combination forms. The scientific management perspective was identified as the perspective of choice most often, receiving the most hits at 24 percent, while the excellence management perspective received the least at 15 percent. Each hit measures the existence of at least one description or reference to a leadership element in the leadership perspectives model. The evidence for each leadership perspective is reinforced by the analysis of both the essays and the interviews.

Excellence management garnered the least concrete support. It is the only perspective that did not have a pure form found in the essays—that is, no one was identified as solely in this perspective—and almost one-third of the essays had no hits relevant to this perspective. However, the interview data show it to be the most frequently described perspective. This finding suggests that excellence management may be more appropriately labeled a transition or bridge perspective from scientific management to values leadership. This perspective may reflect people's tendency to mix the vocabularies of management and leadership as they try to express what it is they actually do. People hear the newer terms of leadership, but they may not yet be able to shake off the traditions of management theory and the vocabulary of the industrial revolution. The result is a description of leadership that mixes the efficiency and productivity mantra of scientific management with the relationship, teamwork, values, and empowerment vocabulary of recent leadership literature, such as that found in the values-based leadership and emotional intelligence literature.

Hierarchical Leadership Perspectives. The five perspectives of leadership tend toward a hierarchy. The public managers described perspectives that related in loosely hierarchical ways—perspectives that encompass and transcend other perspectives. In this sense, the scientific management perspective is of a lower order in the leadership perspective hierarchy. All of the other perspectives encompass and transcend it. Whole-soul leadership is of a higher order, transcending the other four. The interview data verify essay data and confirm the five perspectives relate in a hierarchical manner. Through trial and error, by increasing their awareness of leadership activities, or by increasing their levels of responsibility in the organization, individuals may progress from lower-order perspectives to higher-order perspectives. This suggests that some people may extend their understanding and practice of leadership over time. This could happen if a career is maintained at the same organizational level or if it spans multiple levels.

Data illustrate that adopting a new perspective transcends the previous one. For instance, the tools and behaviors of a lower-order perspective may be the building blocks for the tools and behaviors of succeeding perspectives, but they are not adopted unchanged from one perspective to another. As one moves up the hierarchy of leadership perspectives, the tools, behaviors, and approaches one uses are encompassed and transcended and can, at certain levels, be totally sublimated by other tools and behaviors so as to be obsolete or even antithetical to the work of a leader in higher-order perspectives.

Distinctiveness Through the Operational Categories. The perspectives can be distinguished by understanding how someone describes the implementation (or doing) of leadership, the tools and behaviors used, and the approaches to followers taken in the leadership relationship. The content analysis of all 103 essays suggests that specific leadership elements within the "approaches to followers" category distinguish a person's leadership perspectives (such as giving orders, motivating, team building, inspiring). However, the tools and behaviors that individuals describe in "doing leadership" are more helpful in differentiating leadership perspectives than either of the other two. Table 3.1 summarizes the number of times a leadership element within the operational categories of the leadership perspectives was distinctly described in the essays. A total of 1,343 distinct references to the leadership elements that define the categories outlined in the leadership perspectives model were found in the 103 essays. The interview data reinforce the fact that the operational categories in the model are useful in distinguishing leadership perspectives.

Seeing More the Higher Up You Are. The higher in the organizational hierarchy public managers are, and the more time in service they have, the more likely they are to subscribe to higher-order perspectives. Perhaps this is a commonsensical notion, but rarely, if ever before, born out by research (though by no way is it to say that by virtue of promotion individuals necessarily adopt more encompassing views of the leadership responsibilities). Comments from interview subjects validate this idea. One mid-level manager within the whole-soul leadership perspective stated bluntly that "my views have changed over a number of years." Another response from a senior executive within the trust culture leadership perspective indicated, "If you were to ask me five years ago I would have a different answer, I'd have different thoughts." As this individual began to understand different aspects of the job, especially aspects dealing with values and relationships, new ideas and technologies began to emerge and were viewed as successful. These statements, typical of many this researcher received, lend evidence that people can and do move from one perspective to another and that the movement is toward higher-order perspectives—perspectives that are more encompassing and transcendent than previous conceptions. There may even be a point at which they realize what they thought they were doing in terms of leadership actually turned out to be more managerial in nature. A realization of how leadership differs from management causes them to focus their leadership effort differently. One public administrator confided that "in this current job, I jumped right into management (there was a lot wrong in that area) and I was frustrated that I hadn't taken the time to do the leadership. Now I am starting from scratch all over focusing on the 'leadership piece' because the office still did not function well."

Table 3.1

Summary of Hits Within Each Perspective by Leadership Elements and Operational Categories

Leadership perspective	Operational categories	Leadership elements	Number of hits	Percent for element	Percent for category
Scientific management	Implementation description	Ensure efficient use of resources to ensure group activity is controlled and predictable	39	11	
		Ensure verifiably optimal productivity and resource allocation	24	7	18
	Tools and behavior	Measuring/appraising/rewarding individual performance	57	17	
		Organizing (to include such things as budgeting, staffing)	54	16	
		Planning (to include such things as coordination and reporting)	64	19	51
	Approaches to followers	Incentivization	15	4	
		Control	15	4	
		Direction	74	22	30
Total			342	100	
Excellence management	Implementation description	Foster continuous process improvement environment for increased service and productivity levels	18	10	
		Transform the environment and perceptions of followers to encourage innovation, high quality products, and excellent services.	38	21	31
	Tools and behavior	Focusing on process improvement	25	14	
		Listening actively	6	3	
		Being accessible (to include such things as managing by walking around, open door policies)	9	5	22
	Approaches to followers	Motivation	59	32	
		Engaging people in problem definition and solution	15	8	
		Expressing common courtesy/respect	13	7	48
Total			183	100	
Values leadership	Implementation description	Help individuals become proactive contributors to group action based on shared values and agreed upon goals	59	17	28
	Tools and behavior	Encourage high organizational performance and self-led followers	35	10	
		Setting and enforcing values	19	6	
		Visioning	81	24	

(continued)

Table 3.1 (continued)

Leadership perspective	Operational categories	Leadership elements	Number of hits	Percent for element	Percent for category
		Focusing communication around the vision	44	13	42
	Approaches to followers	Values prioritization	15	4	
		Teaching/coaching	61	18	
		Empowering (fostering ownership)	26	8	30
Total			340	100	
Trust cultural leadership	Implementation description	Ensure cultures conducive to mutual trust and unified collective action	16	7	
		Prioritization of mutual cultural values and organizational conduct in terms of those values	15	6	13
	Tools and behavior	Creating and maintaining culture through visioning	28	12	
		Sharing governance	23	10	
		Measuring/appraising/rewarding group performance	37	16	37
	Approaches to followers	Trust	24	10	
		Team building	77	32	
		Fostering a shared culture	18	8	50
Total			238	100	
Whole soul leadership	Implementation description	Relate to individuals such that concern for the whole person is paramount in raising each other to higher levels of awareness and action	28	12	
		Best in people is liberated in a context of continuous improvement of self, culture, and service delivery	19	8	20
	Tools and behavior	Developing and enabling individual wholeness in a community (team) context	20	8	
		Fostering an intelligent organization	36	15	
		Setting moral standards	55	23	46
	Approaches to followers	Inspiration	51	21	
		Liberating followers to build community and promote stewardship	14	6	
		Modeling a service orientation	17	7	34
Total			240	100	

Gender and Racial Congruence. All five perspectives were evident in male and female public managers at the same relative frequencies. However, females tended slightly more toward the excellence management perspective, while males tended slightly more toward the scientific management perspective. All five perspectives were evident in African American and white public managers at the same relative frequencies. These facts suggest the leadership perspectives model applies regardless of the gender or race of the person engaging in leadership.

Functional Incongruence. The data reveal the functional area of government in which public managers operate may influence leadership perspectives. Public managers in the public safety and justice function tend toward the first three perspectives in the hierarchy: scientific management, excellence management, and values leadership. Public managers in the government support, direction, and finance function revealed all but the trust culture leadership perspective. Public managers in human services and education, economic regulations, and public works reflected all five leadership perspectives, although they tended toward the lower-order perspectives.

Discussion: Implications for Public Administration

The leadership perspectives model posited in this study emerges as a valid way to test both the descriptive and prescriptive potential of the perspectival research approach and helps to frame a more comprehensive view of leadership. It is descriptive in the sense that it defines and explores how one may view leadership and positions that perspective into an overarching leadership model. To some, leadership is scientific management, but that perspective may not be as encompassing (as complete a description of the phenomenon) as another perspective. The section of the model from values leadership to whole-soul leadership describes leadership in a more refined manner (and more in line with contemporary literature on leadership, such as emotional intelligence), with whole-soul leadership perhaps being the better overall description of what transcendent leadership looks like. The model is prescriptive in the sense that it explains which activities, tools, approaches, and philosophies are required to be effective or successful within each perspective.

This research suggests that in order to fully understand what leadership is, we have to take into account that some of what we call leadership is often encompassed and transcended by other, more enlightening conceptions. The more enlightened we become in terms of transcending leadership elements, the more able we are to see leadership as distinct from what contemporary literature would distinguish as management. Burns (1978) refused to use the term "management." Instead, he used the term "transactional leadership" to distinguish lower-order organizational technologies from the ideas of higher-order leadership, which he termed "transforming leadership." This model adds new light (and support) for why Burns may have chosen to use leadership to describe his more managerial descriptions of organizational activities, in that some do view management as leadership. However, we are able to understand through this model that some perspectives of what we do are not leadership at all, but rather management—perhaps good management, but management only. In other words, everything we call leadership may not actually conform to the distinctive technologies of leadership.

This leadership perspectives model allows public administrators to more easily recognize their day-to-day leadership (and management) efforts and to see those efforts in broader, more encompassing ways. The research and findings based on the model can influence public administration and the individual public administrator by (1) growing their understanding of leadership, (2) helping to refine public administrators' roles and recognize that their measures of success in these roles will reflect activities consistent with their leadership perspective, and (3) reshaping the professional training of public administrators.

Growing One's Understanding of Leadership

This research suggests that one's understanding of leadership depends on the perspective that one brings to the question. The perspectival approach to leadership assumes it is possible to expand and grow one's understanding of leadership, even to the point of realizing what one thought was leadership may more accurately be called management or, as Burns put it, transactional leadership. It does not assume one must necessarily move from one perspective to another, but it does suggest that movement can and does occur. Interview subjects reflected a sincere and reflective approach to leadership, which they felt comfortably fit their views of how they interact with other people and how other people interact with them. These were not expressions of leadership styles (that is, calculated activities to achieve some specific goal or achieve a particular agenda depending on the situation or follower maturity). Rather, the perspective a person holds defines (1) the truth to them about leadership, (2) the leader's job, (3) how one analyzes the organization, (4) how one measures success in the leadership activity, and (5) how they view followership. The leadership perspective is the umbrella under which different leadership styles may be pursued or expressed (Hersey and Blanchard 1979). Leadership perspectives, therefore, are not leadership styles to be changed willy-nilly. Rather, leadership perspectives are paradigms and worldviews (leadership philosophies) that need not necessarily change over a lifetime, but may be grown and changed through concerted training efforts, life experiences, and learning opportunities.

One interviewee in the public library system suggested the things she did and believed as a first-line manager were totally different from the things she does and believes now as a senior executive. She said that what got her to her current position was no longer effective where she currently sits in the organization. As she progressed through different levels of the organization, she also progressed through different perspectives of what leadership meant to her and how she practiced it as a public administrator.

Redefining and Refining the Roles of Public Administrators

Just as leadership can be viewed in multiple ways, so can the roles of the public administrator. This research reinforces the idea that the perspective of leadership that public administrators accept (implicitly or explicitly) determines their actions and how they measure the relative success or failure of those actions. Therefore, the leadership perspectives within which public administrators operate most likely influences the roles they choose to play.

Public administrators who sit squarely in the scientific management perspective accept that the traditional public administration principles of efficiency and effectiveness and the activities summarized by POSDCORB fully explain the purposes and processes of their work. To them, technical managerial skill and scientific, reasoned precision must be the purview of public administration without the pressures of political activity, which "rightly" belong to politicians. Public administrators holding to the excellence management perspective add an emphasis on process improvement and stakeholder involvement to discover and resolve potential problems in efficient and effective processes. These first two perspectives, scientific management and excellence management, focus on the administrative side of the classic public administration dichotomy. Together, they ground the traditional measures of success for public administrators, which the leadership perspectives model suggests may actually be based on transactional management ideas—not leadership at all.

However, as we have seen, there are those who claim more for the profession of public administration than the technical and predictable. Many say that the politics-administration dichotomy is no longer relevant, if it ever was. These public administration leaders bring a values perspective to the work they do and recognize their potentially influential place in society (Marini 1971; Waldo 1971; Frederickson 1997). Some focus on the societal impact they can make. Others focus on the organizational impact they can make. Others find meaning in creating great public administrators one by one, either by teaching, mentoring, or going about their public-sector jobs in inspiring ways. These views of public administration may fit more comfortably with the philosophies of higher-order leadership perspectives.

No wonder, then, there are still disagreements within the field as to its proper role and stance in society: There are public administrators who honestly measure success and implement leadership from dramatically different leadership mind-sets. They use different tools and engage in behaviors and approaches toward others very differently. These perspectives also guide how they view the work of other public administrators, always gauging the success or failure or the appropriateness of another's work based on how they conceive of leadership in public administration. Not only does this sometimes cause confusion and frustration within public organizations, where public servants are doing the day-to-day work of government, but it also adds to the confusion and frustration in debates about the field itself. Perhaps these debates might better focus on the perspectives of leadership among public administrators that dictate their values, goals, and behavior more so than the academically defined roles that public administrators are said to play. The perspectival approach to leadership, therefore, may encompass a way to analyze the field of public administration itself.

Some public administrators who hold to lower-order leadership perspectives may never see a reason to progress through different perspectives. The research findings in this study conclude, however, that there are perspectives of leadership that encompass and transcend lower-order perspectives, that growth and progression is evident in the ways people conceive of leadership, and that moving to higher-order perspectives increases a public administrator's capacity to cope with increasingly complex issues, organizations, and relationships. Hence, there are ways of conceiving of leadership in public administration that transcend and encompass more limiting perspectives. This translates to public administrators who seem more organizationally sophisticated and emotionally intelligent, as well as more attuned to the personal or individual issues of their jobs. They deal more with people, public issues, and policies (both within the organizations and outside it) and are able to facilitate more success in an increasingly complex world.

The perspectival approach to leadership also points to a clearer way to understand the different measures of public administration success. The hierarchical nature of the leadership perspectives model suggests the role of public administrators encompasses the technical implementer and skilled mediator roles, but transcends them as well. It suggests that public administrators may rightly play a more facilitative, policy-making, and collaborative role—roles that are more in line with higher-order leadership perspectives—and those roles may be more appropriate (if not necessarily more effective) roles in general.

Shaping Professional Training, MPA Curricula Designs, and the "Oughts" of Public Administration

Understanding leadership perspectives as they are applied to the work of public administration can be used not only to refine (and redefine) the field, but also to provide a foundation for training new public administrators. As important as the technical and traditional management skills of public administration are, there is also a need to focus on the recently recognized skills and perspectives of leadership such as relationship building, inspiration, culture creation, values change, creativity, and flexibility. If such a focus is neglected in the training and work of public administration, the field may never get past the continual debates about its legitimacy, usefulness, and place in government and society.

In today's organizational climate, where technology and information are expanding rapidly, along with the knowledge base and professional and personal requirements of the workforce, higher-order leadership perspectives and the public administration roles associated with them may indeed be more effective. Public administrators are often in a better position to suggest new programs and new directions for government. Higher-order mind-sets assume, or at least allow for, this function as a part of doing leadership in public administration. The leadership perspectives model helps to redefine the field to focus on public service as an opportunity to engage in leadership within public organizations. It supports our continual efforts to teach others to seek the highest ideals of public service, and thereby to leave to citizens a legacy of trust, integrity, and responsibility, as well as high-quality service delivery and accountability. This implies there are approaches to public administration that should be adopted over others (such as community building, value shaping, visioning, and stewardship). It implies there are approaches to public administration that are more encompassing and transcendent than others.

The research describes what leadership looks like in the work of public administration, emphasizing that the work within public organizations influences the work of public organizations. Public administrators can, therefore, better understand their work as leaders inside the organization—not just middle managers, but middle leaders as well (G. Fairholm 2001; M. Fairholm 2002). Remember the one public manager who "jumped right into management," but then realized he had to start "from scratch all over focusing on the 'leadership piece' because the office still did not function well." Well-functioning offices are key to well-delivered services and good government.

Another public administrator explained that "leaders need to be modeling behavior, what you want from people you must model. If you want to have a certain type of communication from others you must communicate that way. If you want people to develop people, you must develop people. You must model the work ethic; do what is required to help. I believe in having respect for the position one holds, but I also believe in equality. You need to work to build a community." This perspective outlines a kind of organizational work that influences how both the internal and external mission of the organization is carried out.

The leadership perspectives model clarifies leadership as distinct from discretion or mere uses or abuses of authority. The different perspectives of leadership make the work of public administration look and feel different depending on the different mind-sets public managers hold from which they view their craft. These perspectives prescribe how public administration ought to be. Indeed, the "oughts" of public administration are shaped by the perspective of leadership that one holds. What the leadership perspectives model also offers, however, is that not all perspectives are equal in application. Some perspectives are more encompassing and transcendent than others—that is, some are more operationally useful today than others. Recognizing this potential measure of our work should influence how this work is taught and how individuals are trained.

Current (and past) master of public administration programs still teach mostly management skills and techniques. Often programs add the word "strategic" to the planning function to give it a top-box orientation, but it is still focused on institutional planning and numbers, not values. A course on managerial leadership is emblematic of this approach, and it is not sufficiently comprehensive. MPA curricula and professional development programs would benefit from discussing the descriptions of leadership perspectives and the type of public administration consistent with those descriptions. They should train specific skills, competencies, and technologies that the different perspectives demand, including emotional intelligence or other higher-order concepts about values, relationships, and dealing with stakeholders at the emotional level. MPA programs should include leadership specialties as a core competency with courses to reinforce it.

The leadership perspectives model itself offers fundamental skills and approaches that can be used as a framework to shape a training and development program or even as part of an MPA curriculum. For example, a five-day leadership training program might use the perspectives to outline each day's activities. Each day would include a section on implementing leadership from that perspective, coupled with skills-development activities for the leadership elements within the "tools and behavior" and "approaches to followers" categories. Each day might then end with the implications for public administration from that perspective. Table 3.2 outlines such a training design. These curricula and programs should recognize some of the more normative issues about these perspectives and devote

Table 3.2

Generic Leadership Training Program for Public Administrators

General daily format	Day 1: Leadership as scientific management	Day 2: Leadership as excellence management	Day 3: Values leadership	Day 4: Trust cultural leadership	Day 5: Whole-soul leadership
Introduction	Implementation description—What leadership looks like	Implementation description—What leadership looks like	Implementation description—What leadership looks like	Implementation description—What leadership looks like	Implementation description—What leadership looks like
Skills development	• Measuring/appraising/ rewarding individual performance • Organizing (to include such things as budgeting, staffing) • Planning (to include such things as coordination and reporting)	• Focusing on process improvement • Listening actively • Being accessible (to include such things as managing by walking around, open door policies)	• Setting and enforcing values • Visioning • Focusing communication around the vision	• Creating and maintaining culture through visioning • Sharing governance • Measuring/appraising/rewarding group performance	• Developing and enabling individual wholeness in a community (team) context • Fostering an intelligent organization • Setting moral standards
Follower relationship concepts	• Incentivization • Control • Direction	• Motivation • Engaging people in problem definition and solution • Expressing common courtesy/respect	• Values Prioritization • Teaching/coaching • Empowering (fostering ownership)	• Trust • Team-building • Fostering a shared culture	• Inspiration • Liberating followers to build community and promote stewardship • Modeling a service orientation
Conclusion	Public administration practice—Each day discuss what this leadership perspective tells me about my work.				

attention to answering the questions about how public administration should be thought about and practiced in encompassing and transcendent ways.

Conclusion

As public administration begins to include discussions of leadership more explicitly in its work and training, the field will not only better understand its legitimate role in society, it will also produce men and women who are competently and confidently prepared to do the work of public leaders. The task of public administration today—both intellectually and operationally—is to better understand these perspectives and ensure the field is adopting the most appropriate and encompassing approaches to and measures of our work in the societies we live in, the organizations we work in, and the individual lives we influence. Overall, the perspectival approach to understanding leadership is a credible and valid way to better understand how people can operate in this complex yet intensely personal world within which public administration finds itself staunchly entrenched.

Notes

1. This debate centers on some general ideas. Management embodies the more reasoned, scientific, position-based approach to organizational engagement, such as setting and maintaining organizational structure, dealing with complexity, solving organizational problems, making transactions between leader and those being led, and ensuring control and prediction. Leadership embodies the more relationship-based, values-laden, developmental aspect of the work we do in organizations, such as changing organizational contexts, transforming leaders and those being led, setting and aligning organizational vision with group action, and ensuring individuals a voice so that they can grow into productive, pro-active, and self-led followers (Burns 1978; Kolter 1990; Taylor 1915; Urwick 1944; Zaleznik 1977; Ackerman 1985; Rosener 1990).

2. Examples of these universities and programs include the Farber Center for Civic Leadership at the University of South Dakota, the Center for Excellence in Municipal Management at The George Washington University, the Management Institute at the University of Richmond, and several programs at Harvard, Stanford, and the University of Chicago. Washington, DC, has also devoted considerable resources to building and sustaining a public-private partnership with the academic, business, and philanthropic communities to focus on developing management and leadership capabilities in its mid- and senior-level management tier, though budget cuts now threaten the endeavor (CEMM 1996). See also Wimberley and Rubens (2002) for more on leadership development programs through partnerships.

References

Ackerman, Leonard. 1985. "Leadership vs. Managership." *Leadership and Organization Development Journal* 6(2): 17–19.

Barker, Joel. 1992. *Future Edge: Discovering the New Paradigms of Success*. New York: W. Morrow.

Barnard, Chester. 1938. *The Functions of the Executive*. Cambridge, MA: Harvard University Press.

Behn, Robert. 1998. "What Right Do Public Managers Have to Lead?" *Public Administration Review* 58(3): 209–25.

Bennis, Warren. 1984. "Where Have All the Leaders Gone?" In *Contemporary Issues in Leadership*, 2nd ed., edited by William E. Rosenbach and Robert L. Taylor, 5–23. Boulder, CO: Westview Press.

————. 1993. *An Invented Life: Reflections on Leadership and Change.* Reading, MA: Addison-Wesley.

Burns, James MacGregor. 1978. *Leadership.* New York: Harper and Row.

Carson, Clayborne. 1987. "Martin Luther King, Jr.: Charismatic Leadership in a Mass Struggle." *Journal of American History* 74(2): 448–54.

Center for Excellence in Municipal Management (CEMM). 1996. *The Academy for Excellence in Municipal Management.* Washington, DC: George Washington University.

Day, David. 2000. "Leadership Development: A Review in Context." *Leadership Quarterly* 11(4): 581–611.

Deming, W. Edwards. 1986. *Out of the Crisis.* Cambridge, MA: Massachusetts Institute of Technology, Center for Advanced Engineering Study.

Denhardt, Robert. 1981. "Toward a Critical Theory of Public Organization." *Public Administration Review* 41(6): 628–36.

DePree, Max. 1992. *Leadership Jazz.* New York: Dell.

Fairholm, Gilbert. 1991. *Values Leadership: Toward a New Philosophy of Leadership.* New York: Praeger.

————. 1998. *Perspectives on Leadership: From the Science of Management to Its Spiritual Heart.* Westport, CT: Quorum Books.

————. 2001. *Mastering Inner Leadership.* Westport, CT: Quorum Books.

Fairholm, Matthew. 2002. "Leading from the Middle: The Power and Influence of Middle Leaders." *Public Manager* 30(4): 17–22.

Follett, Mary Parker. 1918. *The New State: Group Organization—The Solution of Popular Government.* Edited by Benjamin R. Barber and Jane Mansbridge. University Park: Pennsylvania University Press, 1998.

Frederickson, H. George. 1997. *The Spirit of Public Administration.* San Francisco: Jossey-Bass.

Goleman, Daniel. 1995. *Emotional Intelligence.* New York: Bantam Books.

Graves, Clare. 1970. "Levels of Existence: An Open Systems Theory of Values." *Journal of Humanistic Psychology* 10(2): 131–54.

Greenleaf, Robert. 1977. *Servant Leadership: A Journey into the Nature of Legitimate Power and Greatness.* New York: Paulist Press.

Gulick, Luther. 1937. "Notes on the Theory of Organization." In *Papers on the Science of Administration,* edited by Luther Gulick and Lyndall Urwick, 3–13. New York: Institute of Public Administration.

Harman, Willis. 1998. *Global Mind Change: The Promise of the 21st Century.* 2nd ed. San Francisco: Berrett-Koehler.

Hart, David. 1984. "The Virtuous Citizen, the Honorable Bureaucrat, and 'Public' Administration." *Public Administration Review* 44 (Special Issue): 111–20.

Heifetz, Ronald. 1994. *Leadership without Easy Answers.* Cambridge, MA: Belknap Press.

Hersey, Paul, and Kenneth Blanchard. 1979. "Life Cycle Theory of Leadership." *Training and Development Journal* 3(6): 94–100.

Herzberg, Frederick. 1984. "Mystery Systems Shape Loyalties." *Industry Week,* November 12, 101–4.

Hofstede, Geert. 1993. "Cultural Constraints in Management Theories." *Academy of Management Executive* 7(2): 81–94.

Ingraham, Patricia, Ronald Sanders, and James Thompson, eds. 1998. *Transforming Government: Lessons from the Reinvention Laboratories.* San Francisco: Jossey-Bass.

Ink, Dwight. 2000. "What Was Behind the 1978 Civil Service Reform?" In *The Future of Merit,* edited by James Pffifner and Douglas Brook, 39–56. Washington, DC: Woodrow Wilson Center Press.

Juran, J. 1989. *Juran on Leadership for Quality: An Executive Handbook.* New York: Free Press.

Koestler, Arthur. 1970. "Beyond Atomism and Holism—The Concept of Holon." In *Beyond Reductionism: New Perspective in the Life Sciences,* edited by Arthur Koestler and J.R. Smythies, 192–232. New York: Macmillan.

Kotler, John. 1990. "What Leaders Really Do." *Harvard Business Review* 68(3): 103–11.

Kouzes, James, and Barry Posner. 1990. *The Leadership Challenge: How to Get Extraordinary Things Done in Organizations*. San Francisco: Jossey-Bass.

Marini, Frank. 1971. *Toward a New Public Administration: The Minnowbrook Perspective*. Scranton, PA: Chandler Publishing.

McSwite, O.C. 1997. *Legitimacy in Public Administration: A Discourse Analysis*. Thousand Oaks, CA: Sage Publications.

McWhinney, Will. 1984. "Alternative Realities: Their Impact on Change and Leadership." *Journal of Humanistic Psychology* 24(4): 7–38.

Morgan, Gareth. 1998. *Images of Organization: The Executive Edition*. San Francisco: Berrett-Koehler.

Peters, Tom, and R. Waterman. 1982. *In Search of Excellence: Lessons from America's Best-Run Companies*. New York: Warner Books.

Pynes, Joan. 2003. "Strategic Human Resource Management." In *Public Personnel Administration: Problems and Prospects*, edited by Steven W. Hays and Richard Kearney, 93–105. Upper Saddle River, NJ: Prentice Hall.

Quinn, Robert, and Michael McGrath. 1985. "The Transformation of Organizational Cultures: A Competing Values Perspective." In *Organizational Culture*, edited by Peter Frost, Larry Moore, Meryl Louis, Craig Lundberg, and Joanne Martin, 315–34. Beverly Hills: Sage Publications.

Rainey, Hal, and Edward Kellough. 2000. "Civil Service Reform and Incentives in the Public Service." In *The Future of Merit*, edited by James Pfiffner and Douglas Brook, 127–45. Washington, DC: Woodrow Wilson Center Press.

Rosener, Judy. 1990. "Ways Women Lead." *Harvard Business Review* 68(6): 119–25.

Salovey, P., and J. Mayer. 1990. *Emotional Intelligence: Imagination, Cognition, and Personality*. New York: Harper.

Sanders, Ronald. 1998. "Heroes of the Revolution: Characteristics and Strategies of Reinvention Leaders." In *Transforming Government: Lessons from the Reinvention Laboratories*, edited by Patricia Ingraham, Ronald Sanders, and James Thompson, 29–57. San Francisco: Jossey-Bass.

Schein, Edgar. 1996. *Organizational Culture and Leadership*. 2nd ed. San Francisco: Jossey-Bass.

Selznick, Phillip. 1983. *Leadership in Administration: A Sociological Interpretation*. Los Angeles: University of California Press.

Sims, Ronald. 2002. "Understanding Training in the Public Sector." In *Public Personnel Management: Current Concerns, Future Challenges*, edited by Carolyn Ban and Norma Riccucci, 194–209. New York: Longman.

Stogdill, Ralph. 1974. *Handbook of Leadership: A Survey of Theory and Research*. New York: Free Press.

Taylor, Frederick. 1915. *The Principles of Scientific Management*. New York: Harper and Row.

Terry, Larry D. 1995. *Leadership of Public Bureaucracies: The Administrator as Conservator*. Thousand Oaks, CA: Sage Publications.

Urwick, Lyndall. 1944. *The Elements of Administration*. New York: Harper and Brothers.

Van Wart, Montgomery. 2003. "Public-Sector Leadership Theory: An Assessment." *Public Administration Review* 63(2): 214–28.

Waldo, Dwight, ed. 1971. *Public Administration in a Time of Turbulence*. Scranton, PA: Chandler.

———. 1980. *The Enterprise of Public Administration: A Summary View*. Novato, CA: Chandler and Sharp.

Wheatley, Margaret. 1999. *Leadership and the New Science: Learning about Organization from an Orderly Universe*. San Francisco: Berrett-Koehler.

Wimberley, Terry, and Arthur Rubens. 2002. "Management Support Organizations and University Partnership in Nonprofit Education, Training and Consultation." *Social Science Journal* 39(1): 129–36.

Zaleznik, Abraham. 1977. "Managers and Leaders: Are They Different?" *Harvard Business Review* 55(3): 67–78.

CHAPTER 4

LEADERS AND LEADERSHIP

JOHN J. CORSON

Confucius, Plato, and Plutarch wrote about leadership. They explored where leaders came from, how they were developed and how they led followers without being wholly led by followers. Since their times we have seen a host of leaders come and go. Scores of authors have explored the nature of leadership. Why now reexplore the role and talents of leaders? What remains to be said?

There are four answers to these questions and four reasons that warrant such a book as claims our attention in this review. "Leadership is" in the opinion of the author, "one of the most observed and least understood phenomena on earth."[1] Second the nature of leadership required differs with time and context; the Ayatollah Khomeni could not have brought about the modernization that made of a poor, backward nation in the 1950s, the modern Iran of the late 1970s. Third, "One of the most universal cravings of our times" is ". . . a hunger for compelling and creative leadership."[2] Remember the prevailing view as to the inadequacy of both candidates for the presidency in 1980.

Narrowing the focus to our own country, the fourth reason for such writings is an urgent and immediate need. Ronald Reagan has called for "a rebirth of the American tradition of leadership at every level of government and in private life as well."[3] That call cannot be dismissed as campaign oratory at a time when our industrial growth rate is down, our population growth rate is down, our technological growth rate is down, we are rivaled, if not outdone, in terms of productivity by the Japanese and the Germans, and we are outmatched militarily by the Russians. We are increasingly dependent for raw materials, as well as oil, on nations that once looked up to us and now delight in making this country dance to their music. Some economists predict a future of no growth. A president's commission (the McGill Commission) strives to develop a "National Agenda for the Eighties" while scores of separate pressure groups—trade associations, labor unions, racial groups, feminists, environmentalists, and others—fight unyieldingly for their objectives with little regard for a "national interest." Yes, we need leaders—leaders for each sector and at every institution—if this country is to maintain its preeminence and our social and economic standards. . . .

Excerpted from *Public Administration Review*, vol. 40, no. 6 (November/December 1980): 630–34. Copyright © 1980 by American Society for Public Administration. Reprinted with permission.

The Nature of Leadership

James MacGregor Burns' *Leadership* is a book that will be drawn from library shelves during the 2000s. It is encyclopedic. It reflects a vast breadth of reading. It is interdisciplinary. As an historian Burns examines the records of leaders from Napoleon to Margaret Thatcher. As a psychologist, he studies the relationship between leaders and followers. As a sociologist, he explores the forces—family, school, conflict, and others—which develop leaders. As a political scientist, and that is his trade, he explores the social (a labor union, the press) and political (a party or a legislature) institutions that identify, develop, push forward or destroy leaders.

He describes various kinds of leadership—intellectual (Voltaire, Hobbes, Locke, Madison, and Keynes), reform (Charles Grey in Britain, Tsar Alexander II in Russia, and Franklin Roosevelt in the United States), revolutionary (Lenin, Mao Tze Tung, and Fidel Castro), heroic (Ataturk in Turkey, Nkrumah in Ghana, and again Mao in China). These types of leadership he brands as "transformational," i.e., "leadership that raises both the leader and his followers to higher levels of motivation and morality."

Then Burns turns to "transactional leadership" in which the leader leads by the exchange of values with followers—his acts for their votes or his views for their subscriptions. Within this category, he pictures "opinion leadership" (a Martin Luther King, a Franklin Roosevelt, or now a Katherine Graham and earlier a Henry Luce, or a Walter Reuther or even the shop foreman), "group leadership" that is the leadership of enterprises, of a bureaucracy or of the League of Women Votes, "party leadership" (a Ronald Reagan, a Lyndon Johnson, Bob Taft, or Robert Byrd) and "executive leadership" (Charles de Gaulle or Robert McNamara).

In summary, Burns leaves us with (1) a definition of leadership, (2) the identification of numerous qualities and skills demonstrated by leaders, and (3) a four-part statement of how a leader exerts influence. Most important is this definition: "Leadership is the reciprocal process of mobilizing, by persons with certain motives and values, various economic, political, and other resources, in a context of competition and conflict, in order to realize goals independently or mutually held by both leaders and followers."[4] . . .

Organizational Leadership

. . . The foregoing book describes well what is expected of public servants—legislative or executive—if they would be leaders rather than mere doers. But in the university, in a state or city government, a federal bureau or in any other public agency, it is not *a* leader that is needed. There has to be effective leadership at many levels and in each part of the organization.

For these numerous leaders, John W. Gardner[5] has defined the tasks well. He contends that the leadership of an organization involves four tasks, no two of which need to be performed by any one leader. There is need, first, for "clarifiers" and "definers," i.e., legislators or executives who help their constituents or their subordinates identify what needs be done, what changes need be made, and what priorities should prevail. The individuals who measure up to this task demonstrate (1) imagination and initiative, (2) the moral courage to urge what may be unpopular change, (3) the capacity to articulate their ideas in simple, truthful terms, and (4) the ability to persuade.

Second, there is need for "implementers" or "problem solvers." Such individuals can conceptualize and design the organizational system and sub-systems—budgeting, planning, personnel, purchasing, grant making, etc.—needed to convert ideas into functioning programs and policies. These individuals possess a high order of intelligence. They possess a command of techniques and program content. Above all they must have a sensitive understanding of human response to the interrelationships they would establish.[6]

Third, there is need for "mobilizers." Cyert writes of "the art of stimulating human resources." Burns writes of "transformational leadership that raises the group to higher levels of motivation and morality." Woodrow Wilson called for leaders who could "lift" people out of their everyday selves. The men and women that can "mobilize" the human beings who make up constituencies as well as staffs (in the long run not just after a new organization is created or a new program established), are articulate, convincing and persuasive. More important, they manifest commitment, a deep belief in the rightness of what they are doing and asking others to do.

Fourth, there is need for individuals who can see beyond the ends of their noses; for "integrators" who recognize the needs of the whole society or the whole organization, not alone the division they head. Such individuals recognize that our society and our organization are terribly splintered into narrow, selfish groups constantly warring with each other. They are capable of weaving the minds and efforts of interacting constituencies (e.g., management and labor, industrialists and environmentalists) or interacting agencies (the departments of Defense and State, or federal and state agencies) together.

These four types—the "clarifies" or "definers," the "implementers" or "problem solvers," "the mobilizers" and the "integrators"—make up, I submit, the leaders needed in the public service.[7] They are needed to pump fresh ideas and new life into (1) the pressure groups that aid or thwart social change, (2) the legislatures that stand at the threshhold of advance, and (3) the agency staffs that must be helped to accept new directions and new processes.

Notes

1. Burns, *Leadership*, p. 1.

2. Burns, ibid., p. 2.

3. Mr. Reagan's speech accepting the Republican nomination for president, *Washington Post*, p. A10, July 18, 1980.

4. Burns, ibid., p. 425.

. . .

[5]. In unpublished papers: one presenting remarks before the White House Fellows Alumni Association, Washington, DC, Thursday, May 5, 1978, and a second entitled, "Responsibility Networks," dated August 5, 1980, not yet used or printed.

[6]. J. Douglas Brown contends that ". . . in human organization the leader's sensitive understanding of human nature is more vital to his performance than a vast accumulation of knowledge or skills concerning science, technology, statistics or abstract reasoning." *The Human Nature of Organizations*, AMACOM, 1973, p. 20.

[7]. The ideas summarized here are effectively supplemented by Philip Selznick, in his classic volume, *Leadership in Administration*, Row, Peterson and Company, 1957, particularly Chapter 5, pp. 134–54.

PART 2

THE PRELIMINARY ASSESSMENTS
THAT LEADERS NEED TO MAKE

Logically, leader assessment of the organization comes first. This is clearest with new leaders, who often conduct appraisals of work systems by reviewing data banks and interviewing people throughout the organization. Assessment, like all leadership activities, is a cyclical process and leaders are generally working in all phases of the cycle on a regular basis. Good leaders have the analytic ability to review large amounts of data and sift out important trends—especially those that need to be acted upon. Adapting a framework from Yukl (2002), eight major leadership functions that can be factored into organizational assessments are reviewed below.

Task skills. Do subordinates have the education and training to do the job? Do they have experience doing it? Are their abilities well matched to their current jobs? Problems can occur in this area when recruitment is faulty, people are hired with weak training and experience, a formal training system is meager or nonexistent, and the informal on-the-job system does not correct worker errors. Examples include situations in which new recruits are so poorly prepared when accepting their jobs that new-worker training programs are overwhelmed, or supervisors are inundated with their own tasks and are unable to properly review the work of subordinates.

Role clarity. Even if workers are skilled and experienced in their current jobs, do they know what they are supposed to do and with whom? Does the unit have areas where too many people seem to be responsible for some things but other important work needs are unattended? This is generally less of a problem in highly automated or formalized systems that are well organized. When such "mechanized" systems must be retooled to accommodate new technologies or mandates, however, problems can arise. Further, because so much front-line production work in government today is contracted out, much of what is left is complex work requiring extensive amounts of coordination. Role clarity is also a problem when formal rewards are not well matched to important role responsibilities.

Innovation and creativity. Does the unit or organization handle routine problems well and flexibly, does it generally "see most problems coming," and then does it actually look for entirely new ways of better accomplishing the work? These are related, but different, worker skills. Many problems may be relatively routine and handled as regular work if workers have the experience, training, and empowerment to do so. Nonroutine problems may simply be unusual exceptions, requiring one-time solutions, or may be an early predictor of new problem trends. An entirely different level of creativity is required when the work process is examined for revision or replacement because of a new technology or mandate. Leaders are often prime actors or facilitators in exercising innovation and creativity; however, research shows that high-performing organizations diffuse this function throughout the organization, rather than allowing it to be an exclusively executive or senior management prerogative.

Resources and support services. It is rare for leaders to have all the resources they would like. Resources include the manpower to accomplish the work, pay and benefits for employees, tools and equipment, and the work environment such as office space. Some leaders in chief executive officer positions are nearly wholly focused on resource expansion while most line supervisors can do little to change their bureaucratic allocation. Resource expansion (or protection) is an important leader function but one that is highly time- and energy-consuming. Support services are also a kind of resource that, when missing, detract from an organization or unit's ability to function at peak capacity. Support services include line departments such as personnel, information technology support, and specialized services such as transportation or repair units.

Subordinate effort. How hard do subordinates perceive they work? How hard do they seem to work relative to standards using comparative output measures? The difference of just a 10 percent additional routine productivity in a unit of ten people is a full-time equivalent position. Subordinate effort may play an even more important function in problem solving, special project accomplishment, and professional growth. Providing motivation through direct actions and indirect system support is an enormous part of a leader's generally perceived role.

Cohesiveness and cooperation. This is a significant portion of what is often referred to as organizational climate. Are there interpersonal fights? Are team members wary of one another? Do groups distrust one another? Finally, is there a shared sense of purpose, mission, and pride in work? Severe cases of conflict management may require leaders to impose strict directives until interpersonal interventions can be affected. As difficult, but more subtle, is the task of building a sense of common purpose that binds individuals and groups together for high performance.

Organization of work and performance strategies. When work is relatively routine and repetitive, policies and procedures about how work is to flow through the organization can be established. Bureaucratic organizations must be on guard against excessive formalization ("red tape"), which may provide review but may also introduce inefficiency, rigidity, and worker anomie. As work becomes more complex and involves professional judgment, worker discretion escalates and optimal coordination becomes a never-ending goal for leaders.

Another aspect of the organization of work has to do with performance strategies. How do workers and units know how well they are doing? How do senior managers and policy makers know how well the organization is doing in broad outputs and outcomes? Measuring work performance is fundamental for all leaders, but is often difficult in the public sector because of multiple goals, vague outputs, and complex services.

External coordination and adaptability. Organizations and units do not work in a vacuum; the work processes must connect well with external users and stakeholders. This is an important leader responsibility, no matter whether it is a supervisor interacting with other units or a chief executive officer interacting with special interest groups and legislators. To what degree are external consumers and funders pleased with the agency? Leaders also have the special responsibility to scan the external environment to see what types of opportunities and threats exist to which the organization (or unit) may need to adapt so that change can be anticipated and crisis averted.

Not only do leaders need to assess the organization and their environment, but prior to any goal setting the leader must also assess their constraints (Stewart 1982). Constraints, especially in the public sector, are often what make a leader's job exceedingly difficult. One constraint is the legal-contractual nature of public-sector organizations. Generally specified in law are the mission, procurement policies, personnel policies, and substantive policies related to the agency's focus such as the environment, education, and so on. Another constraint for the leader is the scope of authority for a particular position. All positions, no matter how senior, have limitations, but it is axiomatic that those positions closest to line work have the least scope of authority. Another important constraint for leaders is the availability of resources. Since funding for most agencies is generated through appropriations processes rather than through a market mechanism, many resources that a leader needs to produce work, such as the number of people to do the work, the amount they will be paid, and the conditions under which they will work, are legislatively constrained. Resource redeployment strategies, common for private-sector leaders (such as a layoff in one area to pay for the acquisition of strategic product in another), are generally less plausible for public-sector leaders. The final constraint is a leader's own abilities. A technically trained leader may be constrained when considering a "cultural" revolution in an agency, and an externally recruited leader may be constrained when considering a series of important technical process changes with which they are not personally familiar. Since there are a number of strategies for dealing with this, a weakness in leadership abilities is not as rigid as most constraints, but unrecognized and unacknowledged may be the iceberg that ultimately sinks a major effort (McCall 1998).

Review of the Selections in Part 2

The first selection is by Paul Appleby, the author of *Big Government* (1946) and *Policy and Administration* (1949). Appleby provides the basis of an assessment of structural relations in large agencies in an executive system. How is the appointed administrative leader going to organize the department? What are the relationships between the elected and appointed executives, among appointed executives, between the appointed executive and her/his management team, among staff and line managers, and so on? Appleby provides a particularly lucid discussion about different types of staff and their roles: the chief of staff and personal staff (senior aides and career aides), and the technical staff (what Mintzburg would refer to as the analysts in the technostructure). His observations have become almost axiomatic, such as when he points out that almost inevitably department heads "are more competitive than cooperative" and "no staff organization should be permitted to get into an operating position where it is competitive with an operating agency." Structural issues are key to both the selection of senior-level administrators and the potential for reorganization. These types of issues may even precede more detailed organizational analyses.

The selection by Garrity, "Total Quality Management: An Opportunity for High Performance in Federal Organizations" (1993), uses a systems perspective that is one of the strengths of the TQM literature. A systems approach emphasizes the big picture of management, and when it was initially introduced in the 1980s in the private sector and the 1990s in the public sector, it reminded managers about a number of aspects necessary for long-term effectiveness and productivity. Certainly little in TQM was genuinely new and it heavily adopted insights from the academic systems theory literature as well as the organizational development literature. Nonetheless, it packaged old ideas very well and the times were right for its messages. Among the key reminders were: the importance of clients' (customers') perceptions, the value of striving for high quality as opposed to mediocrity, the importance of change for dynamic organizations, the complexity of change processes and the need for expertise in change, and the underutilization of team structures (as well as the liabilities of the overuse of hierarchical structures). Garrity's list of twelve principles includes all of these aspects and more. His list and the list provided in this introduction provide excellent comparative examples of assessment frameworks. The excerpt also includes a passage about a high-performing organization being like a jazz ensemble. Even though the analysis of the pieces is useful for improvement and to ensure that the "basics" are in place, in the final analysis, a really good organization allows the unique and creative harmonies to emerge rather than expecting to plan everything in advance.

The final selection, by Hale and Franklin (1997), "Reevaluating Methods of Establishing Priorities for Governmental Services," reviews the nuts and bolts of different policy assessment strategies. The strategies are called the incremental, conceptual, performance, and reevaluation frameworks. The incremental framework is the traditional one in most governmental settings because it assumes a marginal change and is politically most expedient except in extraordinary circumstances. The conceptual framework reexamines fundamental principles—societal, governmental, and humane—to ensure that government is playing the proper role. Traditionally, the authors argue, however, the discussions occurring in the conceptual framework are centered on political elites and neglect robust citizen input. It also does not allow for rigorous comparative analysis of scarce resources among programs. The performance framework uses "organization and clarification of accomplishment criteria to advance decision making." The authors provide an excellent example of how the performance framework can be used to prioritize funding needs. The final or reevaluation framework is an amalgam of all three of the preceding ones. It takes into account political realities at the outset such as the budgetary environment (expanding or austere), incorporates a review of governmental purposes to ensure both technical compliance and alignment with shifting public values, and uses concrete performance data to assess implementation quality. Its main liability is that, like any sophisticated and elaborate approach, it takes well-trained staff to carry it out. Also, a more limited and targeted approach (such as those provided in the first three frameworks) may be more appropriate in a variety of circumstances.

References

McCall, M.W. Jr. 1998. *High Flyers: Developing the Next Generation of Leaders*. Boston: Harvard Business School Press.
Stewart, R. 1982. *Choices for the Manager: A Guide to Understanding Managerial Work*. Englewood Cliffs, NJ: Prentice Hall.
Yukl, G. 2002. *Leadership in Organizations*, 5th ed. Upper Saddle River, NJ: Prentice Hall.

CHAPTER 5

ORGANIZING AROUND THE HEAD OF A LARGE FEDERAL DEPARTMENT

PAUL H. APPLEBY

I

Professor Carl Brent Swisher in his recent book, *The Growth of Constitutional Power in the United States,* makes the point too often forgotten that the primary purpose of written constitutions, including our own, is to grant adequate power to govern. Checks on the power to govern, important as they are felt to be, follow—they do not precede. In a very similar way, consideration of administrative organization begins with the arrangements essential to authority and responsibility. Delegation, decentralization, and all of the techniques making for a diffusion of influence and for zealous and reciprocal collaboration enormously enrich administration—but they are secondary. True and effective decentralization can only follow effective centralization.

In this paper I wish to discuss organization around the head of a great governmental department in the primary terms of his needs as an important factor in the process of governmental integration. These needs, like the primary purpose of a constitution, are too often forgotten. Any citizen—of whatever degree of acquaintance with government—is aware of *his* needs to influence the course of government and to modify the impact of government on him. Any government employee of whatever rank is aware of the need for the wind of authority to be tempered to his sensitive individuality. In a democracy these awarenesses work constantly for the betterment of certain important aspects of our organized society. But few are so constantly alert to the competing but complementary need for adequate organization. And too often even those functionally assigned to the business of supporting the essential centralized authority go through their labors in an unthinking manner—throwing away necessary controls with one hand and holding tenaciously to unfruitful routines with the other.

In one sense, consideration of the administrative aspect of government begins, of course, with the people for whom the government exists. In another sense, its consideration begins with the means by which government in administration may do effectively that which it is required to do. In this sense, consideration of public administration in the national government begins with the fact that the executive government must be *manage-*

From *Public Administration Review,* vol. 6, no. 3 (1946): 205–12. Copyright © 1946 by American Society for Public Administration. Reprinted with permission.

able by the President who is held responsible for the executive government. There would be little national profit from assigning responsibility to the President if we were to equip him insufficiently with authority and with other means by which he may act responsibly. Ultimate controllability by the President is the keystone of the arch—if we are to have an arch: coordinated, integrated government within the bounds covered by the executive process; responsible executive action responsive as a whole to the whole people and not merely responsive in its parts to special-interest groups.

The phrase "ultimate controllability" requires elucidation. I am speaking, of course, about executive controllability as a necessary preliminary to congressional and popular controllability. Even with respect to programs of acknowledged political content any President can exercise usually only a general control. He must delegate much of his responsibility for control. He must rely generally upon the principal executive to whom he has delegated responsibility until that executive is felt to be unsatisfactory; when the unsatisfactory executive is replaced, similar general reliance must be placed on the new appointee. Yet when the delegated responsibility can be clearly concentrated in one person and the power to replace is unhampered, this power is the basis for essential presidential control. There are areas where administrative control can be relatively lax; these are areas where programs have become uncontroversial and operations stable. Presidential power in practice, with respect to such areas, will be more remote—at any moment more in reserve, more of an ultimate power, less of a present and direct power—than in the case of new or newly controversial programs.

There are some other areas in which presidential powers may need to be somewhat restricted in law—forcing the President to exercise a more general, more reserved, more "ultimate" power of control, a less quick and direct control. It is my belief that such areas are much smaller than they commonly are believed to be and that legal restrictions on the President's control should be less drastic than they frequently are. The areas in question include those of "administrative law"—the regulatory process involving "quasi-judicial" functions. These particular areas are actually to be distinguished somewhat from areas of other types of action programs, but I believe that even with respect to them the tendency has been to restrict presidential powers too much. "Ultimate controllability" here takes on a very important meaning. But both here and in still other areas where there is less justification, the tendency has been to deprive the President and his responsible executives of even an ultimately real control. These are areas where the cry is to "take administration out of politics." In such instances the unconscious effort is actually to take administration out of democracy. Laws in some of these instances would force administration for a long time to continue in accordance with the ideas of the pressure group sponsoring the original enactment. In other specific cases the effort is to throw policy control away from the people and into the hands of a specific group of experts—lawyers, scientists, military men, etc. With or without bases in laws, sub-administrators do seek and do develop administrative autonomy. This tendency is dangerously effective principally as it is supported by practices that permit particular private interests or groups of private interests largely to dominate the bureaus or programs concerned. The proper influence and ultimate control of the whole people are violated by such autonomous administration. Coordination and integration are difficult, intricate, and important means by which all programs of the government are brought under the influence and control of the nation at large. Don Price has stated it this way: "The real issue of representation and responsibility is not between the chief executive and legislature, but between the chief executive and the legislature on the one hand, and on the other hand, the departments, bureaus and legislative committees that seek to go their own ways."[1] The subject of organizing around the head of a department must be approached first of all in terms of the relationship of a department head to the central business of securing representative and responsible government—making democracy effective. Bureau autonomy is a denial of democracy. Departmental autonomy is an even more thoroughgoing denial.

II

In this paper, then, we begin our consideration of the situation of a department head by thinking of him in the executive level next below the President. It is a familiar picture of Cabinet members, but I wonder how much we—or they—reflect upon the picture. The Cabinet member who consciously and systematically organizes his department to positively and imaginatively to contribute to the presidential function of governmental integration is yet to appear on the scene. The usual performance is so markedly in another direction as to lead one of the profoundest observers of our government to declare seriously that Cabinet members are characteristically "the President's worst enemies."

Certainly among themselves and individually in relationship with the President it is true that Cabinet members are more competitive than cooperative. They are champions of special and competing private interests, of groups functionally specialized. They are competitors with respect to appropriations, authority, and prestige. Seeking to simplify and make manageable *their* jobs, they resent and resist efforts directed toward governmental integration. Quietly even carrying their differences with the President to congressional committees, they may at any time block his proposals. (If an example is required, consider the history of reorganization efforts.) Congressional committee structure reflects special interests in much the same way as do the executive departments. On the Hill as in the Executive Branch, the need is to translate special policy into better general policy; cross-lots dealing of bureau and department with congressional committees tends to prevent this translation. Department heads, then, throw into the presidential lap a very great many more differences than they prevent from landing there. Probably this would be true in the best of circumstances, but no one can doubt that the government would profit from a greater effort by and under department heads to work imaginatively toward a better fulfillment of presidential, government-wide needs.

I am not speaking about any particular Cabinet, of course, and I intend no extravagant laboring of the point. I wish simply to indicate that proper organization around a department head needs to be pointed upward to the President and outward to the rest of the government—not merely downward for the sake of the secretary's own essential controls. Indeed, the downward flow of authority assumes a new significance if adequate integration of a department is seen as preliminary to adequate integration of the government. Often the worst sins of competition between departments are committed without the participation or knowledge of department heads. So far as department heads are concerned, these are sins of omission; commission is within the bureaus.

The problems of integration in terms both of policy and of administration are more staggering today than ever before because of the enormously increased complexity of our society. The intertwining of interests on the part of various governmental departments is akin to the increased intertwining of, let us say, physics and chemistry. But the most vivid and urgent development is the way in which so many domestic policies now impinge upon and require reconciliation with international relations. In the future, domestic policy simply cannot be permitted to develop without the check of international considerations, and foreign policy cannot be permitted to develop in a vacuum unrelated to the thousand and one relevant domestic policies. Here is the most compelling new requirement for integration of manifold matters. It cannot be achieved by a President individually, or by heads of departments singly or together, or by the State Department alone. It requires intricate, institutional coordination and wholly new methods of governmental organization. The trenches of isolationist sentiment are no longer out in the country. They are held in Washington by officials who *believe* internationally but who *act* less than nationally—departmentally or bureau-mentally. How to overcome this isolationism is the supreme problem in public administration today. This is so because the translation of many segmented, special interest policies into sound national policy and the translation of national policy into effective international policy is the supreme public policy problem today. Organization and administration are means by which we produce policy as well as the means by which we carry it out.

Departments of the future, then, must be better and especially organized for interdepartmental functioning and for better projection of policy and administration into presidential, whole-public-interest terms. This can be done at the departmental level, I feel confident, by an administrative program having generally this form: staff organisms around department heads whose sole reason for being rests in the functions of projecting policy and administration into governmental and international terms; behind these, staff agencies adequate to develop bureau policy and administration into departmental terms and into forms sufficiently controllable by the secretary to be capable of the still higher projection.

Coordination and adequate centralization, then, are words reflective of the administrative aspect of the primary function of government: the provision of means by which 140,000,000 people reach common action, the parts related to the whole, the whole related to the parts. The responsibility is by no means wholly within departments. We are very inadequately organized as a *government*. Aside from the lack of adequate governmental institutions, we have many specific lacks. We tend, for example, to have departmental or bureau career services and not much of a governmental career service. But if it is true at the presidential level, as I have suggested it to be, that the Chief Executive cannot effectively administer the government simply through department heads, it is equally true that no department head can administer his department adequately simply through his bureau chiefs. One reason why department heads take positions hostile to presidential needs and policy is in the fact that they defend or are governed by bureaus they themselves do not control. To a degree they are merely "fronts" for bureaus.

It would require another paper to discuss as it merits the tendency to autonomy in organizational segments of which the bureau is a chief example. And it would require still another paper to suggest the more specific and detailed ways by which loose federations of bureaus might be knit into actual departments. Here it is impossible to do more than to present some general thoughts by way of orientation. But it is necessary to recognize that it is much easier to unify a division than it is to unify a bureau, very much easier to unify a bureau than it is to unify a department, and very, very much easier to unify a department than it is to unify the Executive Branch. Most of the persons engaged in public administration are at levels or in segments where this problem is insufficiently revealed. They need better to understand it if for no other reason than to be able more equably to adjust to it. I am indicating belief in need for greater departmental unification; if it is achieved it will be at the cost of considerable emotional strain on the part of those who have been working in relatively autonomous isolation.

On the other hand, it should be recognized that the choice is not between this stress and an absence of stress; it is between stresses. The stress that results from governmental confusion produces frustration in citizens generally, including government personnel, and it has a special, additional impact on workers within government.

The secretary who does not have essential control of his department does have many real powers the exercise of which can work havoc within the organization. Adjustments to succeeding secretaries in ways not warranted by policy change or by mere personality differences are perhaps as destructive of individual and organizational performance and morale as any other single phenomenon. After adequate unification, therefore, I am inclined to rank administrative continuity through institutional means as only second in importance. Perhaps it is only the obverse side of the same coin.

Most heads of departments come—and probably will continue to come—to their posts without some of the most desirable qualifications. We have no system by which young men of political promise are given experience and trial in administration. By the time members of Congress come to Cabinet posts, they are likely to be set in a nonadministrative pattern of individual performance. Business executives usually have come to dominate particular organizational situations rather than having developed a flexible general administrative ability that might enable them to adjust to the wholly strange political environment. Bankers and farmers, insofar as they are qualified for specific Cabinet posts, are qualified in technical familiarity with some aspect of the subject matter rather than as political leaders and administrators. Editors, lawyers, and educators tend to have more general policy understanding but are primarily individualists without actual administrative understanding.

Even in a particular case where a department head may prove to be a competent administrator, it is difficult for him to bequeath anything of administrative value to a successor. He tends to build a structure of his own way of working, and its very novelty and history invite early abandonment of it.

In a broad way, then, the problem seems to turn upon setting up a permanent basic structure for departmental administration so firmly that it cannot readily be disregarded or dispensed with, yet elastic enough to provide for the injection of a few personally selected aides to help insure policy shift and to permit change in keeping with changes in administrative needs. A large part of the machinery for departmental management and policy integration must exist ready-made, so placed as not readily to be ignored, and not exclusively dependent on the favor of the incoming secretary. If they are to be at the same time a responsive and useful tool, the organic arrangements must be nicely made by custom and the weight of administrative arrangements, and not by law.

If it is true, as I have asserted, that no secretary can administer a department wholly through bureau chiefs, I think it is also true that no secretary can administer his department wholly through career aides. He needs a few aides—two or three or four or five—who as distinctly personal selections extend his reach. Such aides usually are amateurs and usually they act in a semidetached manner that invites disorder and whimsy. It has seemed to me important that their yeasty interest in policy innovation should be associated quickly and directly with organic staff entities. Assuming responsibility for continuing administrative functions and the organs concerned with those functions, the new aides could be expected to draw more quickly upon the wisdom of experience and at the same time to have at their command the most effective controls and tools for effecting change. A definite provision for new persons to be given responsibility for career staffs should make room for both dynamics and continuity.

I am inclined to believe that heads of staff units under these personal appointees should have a special recognized status on a special register of key government administrative personnel with eligibility for transfer under general controls exercised by the Executive Office of the President and a special board. All of the necessary arrangements can and should be made under existing laws; a rigid, special corps must be avoided. Properly safeguarded, the maintenance and development of such a register should effect a considerable improvement in public administration; it should result in building more and better administrators, and they, because of government-wide status and opportunity, should contribute to greater administrative unification.

III

We come, then, to specific consideration of the form and utilization of *departmental* staffs. It should begin with thought about the nature of the policy and action to be served and developed. It therefore also has to do with qualifications needed for high staff personnel.

Speaking with an English friend recently I remarked casually, "Perhaps you will be surprised to hear me say it, but I believe that the thing in shortest supply in Washington is *political* sense." He said in reply that he agreed with me, but that he would say it differently: "The thing in shortest supply in Washington is ability to *think*—to think in whole terms encompassing all of the elements of the scene, all of the relationships, including especially the human and social factors; people in Washington are equipped to think and do think in too highly specialized ways." I could agree with no statement more completely than with this one of my English friend.

We very much want breadth in the levels around the secretary and in all levels of staff serving the secretary. The primary staff purpose is to help translate the specialized thinking, specialized policy, and specialized administration of departmental segments and individuals into *public* policy and *public* administration.

There is a great tendency on the part of budget people to see all policy as budgetary policy or fiscal policy, all administration at budgetary control. There is a similar tendency for attorneys to see all policy as legal policy. There is a similar tendency for personnel officers to see all administration as administration of personnel. There is a tendency for economists to see all policy as economic policy. There is a tendency for politicians to see all policy as partisan policy or to see it in other narrowly political terms. All of these things are simply some of the aspects of public policy. Of all the terms used, the term political is the broadest and the one most difficult for the more narrowly specialized to accept. Really sound and effective political policy comes very close to describing really sound and effective public policy. In general understanding, however, the phrase has some connotations that drag its meaning to a lower level of abstraction. For purposes of this paper, then, let me minimize the truly, properly, and necessarily political nature of both policy and administration by saying again that the staff function is to help translate narrower, more specialized thinking and action into terms that will enable the secretary in his sphere and auxiliary to the presidential function to develop and maintain truly public policy and truly public administration.

If this is the staff function, it follows that no staff member especially responsible for a specialized segment of the staff function should have dominance over the total staff function. This is to say that the budget officer, the director of administrative planning, the director of personnel, the solicitor, the economic adviser, the head of any economic policy group, and the head of any planning group—important as they all are—should be excluded from any position analogous to chief-of-staff. Although a political staff function should be broader than any of the others, I believe that in practice any specialized political aide, as one responsible for congressional, national committee, state, and local government contacts, also should be excluded from the post of staff leader.

Actually, I believe that the staff leader should be merely that—a chairman whose only preeminence is in his responsibility for staff cross reference and synthesis.

It follows, of course, that no staff leader should have a monopoly on the function of staff representation to the secretary.

The preliminary purpose of the staff is to synthesize its product and the product of the bureaus. Without explicit *authority* to do so, it does it within the limits fixed by an absence of authority. Beyond these limits, the staff purpose is to serve the authority of the secretary by providing him with perspective in terms of his interests, functions, and responsibilities. Reporting and recommending from their several vantage points—all at the secretarial level—they equip him with various views and judgments from which—in connection with the reports and recommendations from bureau heads, and in the light of his dealings with the President, the Congress, and the public—he is enabled to arrive at the best judgment of which he is capable. Where there is sharp controversy, one view would provide him with nothing more helpful than a picture of head-on collision. A three-dimensional view is a minimum for internal perspective.

There is at least one other important aspect to the limitation of the chairman of the secretary's staff. Chester I. Barnard, in *The Functions of the Executive,* indicates that all of the executives reporting to a single executive should be as nearly as possible equal to each other, and that all of them together are roughly equal to their superior officer. It may be that in some respects all of the second-level executives are greater than the superior executive; they might, for example, by common action easily ruin their chief. But in another respect the superior executive ought to be equal to a little more than the sum of the next-level-executive parts. The staff, at least, certainly should not usurp the whole role of the principal executive, but since their function is based on his function there is always some tendency toward usurpation. Staff plus bureau chiefs should equal a little less than the secretary, and staff minus bureau chiefs should, of course, equal a good deal less. The two military departments of our government have had a great part in developing the staff idea, but in recent years they have appeared to me to have violated many basic principles of organization and administration. Neither of these departments has balanced departmental organization, and in both, staff and operations have been so combined as to minimize secretarial functions. This latter situation constitutes a victory of the technician, the specialist, over the generalist, and results, I believe, in less truly public policy. The staff should not usurp the role of the operating chiefs. The staff and the secretary together should definitely be superior to, greater than, and different from, the sum of the operating chiefs. The chairman of the staff should be less than the whole staff, and, of course, less than the secretary.

A few other thoughts I would suggest dogmatically as desirable rules: the staff should have a collegial character in which the principal discipline would be in the enforcement of cross reference. The principal responsibility of the staff chairman should be this enforcement of cross reference and as much synthesis as could be derived from it. No staff aide should have a function or field coextensive with that of a single bureau; preferably the function and field of each principal staff aide should be department wide as a contribution to the process of translating material into secretarial terms. No staff organization should be permitted to get into an operating position where it is competitive with an operating agency. The regular staff function should not involve the review of bureau judgment in the same terms, but review and anticipation in terms above the field of special bureau competence.

To go further than this into the detailed arrangements for staff functions would go much beyond the purpose of this particular paper. Here begin knotty problems so involved with particular program situations, so in need of flexibility with which to meet changing conditions, that they would require very detailed analysis.

The kinds of activities by means of which a secretary does his job are surprisingly few: he sees people—individual citizens, representatives of organized groups, members of Congress, other national officials, state and local officials, party leaders, his own executives; he signs letters, orders, documents; he issues statements, makes speeches, testifies before congressional committees, sees the press; he reads newspapers, gets news and opinion reports, reads memoranda, reports, and recommendations. The staff organization needs to take account of all these things, for here is where confusion or integration takes place. These things involve the whole of departmental policy and administration in secretarial terms. They suggest staff organization giving attention to these things: personnel selection and utilization; budgetary and financial management; interdepartmental and Executive Office relationships; international relationships; congressional and party relationships; general public relationships and information; coordination of the department's procedures in terms of law; coordination in terms of operating programs; administrative organization and practice; program development and planning; review of public papers; interviews and conferences. The management of these things *in their interrelationships* and *in terms of the secretary's responsibilities* is the business of departmental—as distinguished from bureau—personnel.

Note

1. In a chapter entitled "Democratic Administration," in a volume, *Elements of Public Administration,* edited by Fritz Morstein Marx and soon to be published by Prentice Hall.

CHAPTER 6

TOTAL QUALITY MANAGEMENT

An Opportunity for High Performance in Federal Organizations

RUDOLPH B. GARRITY

Introduction

This article presents an argument for the new federal government Total Quality Management (TQM) initiative by showing that TQM principles and practices should be foundational considerations when refocusing national attention on the challenges of the 1990s and beyond. Nothing less than a major American culture enhancement is required to sustain and improve the standard of living desired by most Americans. TQM reinforces the positive philosophies, values, behaviors, and norms organizational development academicians and practitioners have long known to be significant in attaining high levels of employee satisfaction and organizational performance. We now have an organizational language called TQM that integrates what we know can work. We need to learn the talk, and then, walk that talk.

Foundational TQM Principles and Practices

A number of directives and guidelines are in place that require the federal government to begin quality and productivity management initiatives. A review of just a single set of these, with focus on the Department of Defense, include:

1. Executive Order 12637, Productivity Improvement Program for the Federal Government, April 1988, states: "There is hereby established a government-wide program to improve the quality, timeliness, and efficiency of services provided by the Federal Government."
2. OMB Circular No. A-132, Federal Productivity and Quality Improvement in Services Delivery, April 1989, states: "The objectives are to make continuous, incremental improvements and implement quality and productivity management practices in executive departments and agencies."
3. DoD Directive (Draft), Total Quality Management, June 1989, states: "TQM is the vehicle to drive out waste and maximize the effectiveness of overall DoD performance.

From *Public Administration Quarterly,* vol. 16 (Winter 1993): 430–59. Copyright © 1993 by Southern Public Administration Education Foundation, Inc. Reprinted with permission.

This includes improving efficiency and effectiveness, innovation, productivity quality of worklife, and providing products and services that satisfy or exceed customer requirements at a cost that represents best value."

The comments that inevitably are made include: "Isn't this just another one of those management and productivity programs that have previously failed to make a significant impact?" and "Government is different than industry. What they do won't work here" and "You'd have to change the culture around here if you want to see any improvement." The responses to these concerns are, respectively, No, Yes and No, and Yes.

This article will show that the TQM motto of "Doing the right thing, right the first time on time, all the time; always striving for improvement, and always satisfying the customer" is right for our time and is doable. Individuals, private and public sector organizations, and the nation are well served by learning the TQM language and modifying our cultural philosophies, values, behavior, and norms to include the demonstration of TQM principles and practices. What distinguishes TQM from other improvement programs that have been tried with limited success over the years is an unflagging dedication to the following:

1. focus on customer, product and service satisfaction;
2. recognizing quality as a presence of value rather than the absence of defects;
3. top management participation, direction, and support;
4. employee involvement and responsibility;
5. effective and renewed communication;
6. cross-functional orientation and teamwork;
7. analysis of management systems and procedures using standards, measures, and fundamental statistical techniques;
8. a long-term commitment to continuous process improvement;
9. rewards and recognition for performance;
10. workforce training—awareness, management, skills;
11. achieving organizational discipline for practicing the new behaviors every day, forever; and
12. developing a supporting organizational culture.

Emphasis in TQM is on behavior rather than attitude, participation rather than observation, measurement rather than guessing, integration rather than separation, multiple approaches rather than one right way, rewarding rather than punishing, motivation rather than apathy, growing rather than stagnating, doing rather than saying, and win/winning rather than win/losing. As we will see in the text that follows, there is something for everyone here—the individual, the organization, the nation.

What Do We Want from the Private Sector?

The extraordinary events of the 1980s have launched society explosively into the 1990s. For those attuned to current events it may appear that challenges and opportunities are arriving so fast that any attempt to order personal, organizational or national priorities rationally is at best difficult and may even be hopeless. Political, social, economic, technical, and ecological issues abound in both the private and public sectors in such an integrated and layered manner that any attempt to bound a problem to arrive at potential solutions is certain to raise other issues and the concern of other players in the arena.

Fortunately, there are a few studied, experienced, and insightful persons in a wide variety of disciplines and endeavors who observe the trends that flow out of the complexities and interdependencies that most of us struggle to deal with on a daily basis. Through their guidance we may all benefit by finding the course of action necessary for our personal, organizational, and national fulfillment. The perspectives of some of the more notable individuals are herein offered to address the question: What do we want from the private sector?

Naisbitt (1984) directs our attention to ten trends that portend significant change in the what, where, and how of our organizational lives. His research indicates that the United States is headed away from a hierarchical, centralized, industrial, short-term, representative, national structure to one driven by networks, decentralization, information production, long-term thinking, participative management, and international business concerns. The economic resurgence of Japan, demise of the Soviet Union, potential of a reunified Germany, solidification of the European Economic Community, and a worsening U.S. trade deficit should raise great concern in the U.S. regarding our ability to maintain sufficient international credibility and influence to assure U.S. economic growth.

In his well-regarded book, *The Zero-Sum Solution*, Thurow (1985) tells us that America's effortless economic superiority is being matched by other countries' economic achievements which could possibly cause the U.S. to compete only on the basis of lower wages. By inference, it is probably accurate to conclude that lower private sector sales and wages mean less tax revenue for government services at the same time that more services are being demanded. In time, most Americans could end up with a smaller piece of a shrinking national economic pie.

Thurow makes the point that, wherever good ideas originate, such ideas may be used in America. He also observes that no nation can expect to maintain international significance if it fails to maintain its industrial production capability. An information production economy cannot succeed if that is all it offers the rest of the world.

Two major figures arose during the 1980s to sound the alarm concerning the diminishing quality of American products, our loss of world markets, and the inevitable decline of our standard of living. In *Out of Crisis,* Deming (1989) suggests that a transfer of wasted man and machine hours to better products and services occurs when quality improvement becomes a firm's major concern. The results are better products at lower prices and an increase in available jobs. Deming's "14 Points" are regarded by some as the way "out of the crisis."

Juran and Gryna (1988) contribute immensely to this discussion by adding their learning from years of informational experience. The text, *Juran's Quality Control Handbook,* is considered by some to be the most important American work on quality management. Juran's understanding of the relationships among quality and productivity, organizational management, and international business is indicated when he observes that Japanese successes were made possible because of a consistent and supporting social, cultural, and economic environment. Western failures to gain similar benefits from such practices occur when the prerequisites for success do not exist; that is, the personal systems and work climate to encourage, enable, and reward workers for contributing their energies and ideas have not been established by the organization.

Juran (1988, 10) continues to say: "The recent experiences of American and Japanese companies suggest that workers cannot and will not contribute fully if the company operates in a manner that is inconsistent with workers' abilities, needs, values, and expectations which have been conditioned by the larger society." As for the education level of workers, Juran says: "Workers are better educated than their predecessors, both technically and in financial aspects of the business. They want the democratic freedoms, rights, and responsibilities they exercise in private life extended to the workplace" (Ibid., 17).

Regarding the contributions of social science to improved organizational performance, Juran (1988, 10, 20) explains: "It is not easy to translate the behavioral scientist's concepts, principles and research findings into action . . . Internal psychological events e.g., motives, attitudes, needs . . . need to be transformed into concrete actions a manager can use. Organizational effectiveness . . . is dependent on three related categories of systems: technical processing systems, social/cultural systems, and process management systems." Juran's list of lessons learned covers the same general topics as Deming's 14 Points and includes an emphasis on customer focus, top management leadership, worker participation and training, and on quality planning, control, and improvement.

Now then, what do we want from the private sector? We want American industry to be effective in producing and marketing the products and services desired by consumers the world over. We want it to provide those products and services at world-class quality levels and at competitive prices so that American employment grows and our standard of living increases. To do this, however, requires revolutionary thinking and behavior on the part of managers and workers. Improved quality and productivity in our private sector organizations can no longer be just goals; they must be achievements.

Bennis and Nanus, in *Leaders: The Strategy for Taking Charge,* tell us that leaders are needed who have vision and judgment as well as managers who focus on mastering routines. In other words, we need greater effectiveness and efficiency from our private organizations. They suggest a focus on attaining (1) attention through vision, (2) meaning through communication, (3) trust through positioning, and (4) the deployment of self. The concept of Transformative Leadership is developed in which "leadership is the power to translate intention into reality . . . [E]ffective leadership can move organizations from current to future states, create visions of potential opportunities for organizations, instill within employees commitment to change and instill new cultures and strategies in organizations that mobilize and focus energy and resources" (Ibid., 17–18).

Throughout the above commentary, the concepts of visionary leadership, cultural change, employee involvement, improved quality and productivity, customer focus, and enhanced communication were mentioned with regularity. These are fundamental principles and practices needed by America's private sector to survive the competition that is growing. Quality management programs hold out the promise that we can do better together—if we want to succeed together. Reich (1985, 48) cautions us: "There is no way that a rigid, hierarchical, standardized production system can compete for long with a flexible system that enjoys the complete support of all its people. For the U.S., however, the shift has been slow and painful . . . the transition requires a basic restructuring of business, labor and government."

What Do We Want from the Public Sector?

Quite often we hear comments that "business and government must cooperate" and "government should learn from business." While this is often true, we must recognize that public sector organizations have different customer expectations, leadership strategies, and organizational cultures. These and many other factors require attention when determining the level of similarity between public and private sector organizations. For example, public sector customer demand is influenced by a wider variety of factors and services are often legislated without popular demand.

In the public sector, bottom line performance criteria are harder to define and even harder on which to collect performance data. This makes leadership effectiveness more difficult to measure. Should the public sector manager focus on representativeness and accountability or on effectiveness and efficiency? And what about organizational culture? While the private employee may be able to see the relationships among competition, company image, productivity, sales levels, profits, performance levels, personal advancement, and pay levels, the public sector employee may be more concerned with political trends, key personnel moves, personal contacts, and resource allocations. His vision of what he does, why he does it, and the way work should be done may differ to some degree.

Having said the above, however, it is important to note that work accomplished within the technical core of public organizations is very likely to focus on effectiveness and efficiency even though political turmoil is being experienced at higher levels. Constituent needs, legislative activity, political maneuvers are the stuff of appointed senior executives and most career personnel are willing to leave these activities in their hands.

We do realize that, for the public organization to fulfill its mission, it needs to balance pressure for representativeness and accountability with pressures for effectiveness and efficiency. This means that top and middle managers are required to strike an agreement on priorities and procedures that enable each to their respective objectives.

Bower (1983) does a commendable job of defining the similarities and differences between public and private sector organizations. He offers the following observations concerning similarities: (1) Organizations do not work unless members are willing to contribute effort. Authority is grounded in the reasons that a member has chosen to work. There is an implicit contract. (2) The only way to measure whether an organization is effective is relative to the common purpose around which it is organized. An opportunity to succeed along with sufficient resources must be linked to the purpose. (3) An effective organization is one that meets enough of the purposes common to the group of members so that they are willing to contribute their contributions.

To this point, the conclusion that may be drawn is that a federal organization, like its private sector counterpart, has objectives to accomplish, needs knowledgeable, skilled, and motivated employees to do so, and can be led more effectively by capable administrators who understand both the external environment and internal organizational culture. Contemporary issues that currently vie for attention include (1) how to balance the needs of the client and the constituent of the organization, (2) how to improve the image and ethics of federal managers and organizations, and (3) how to improve management in these organizations. Each of these is addressed below.

Viteritti (1990, 425) explains: "The term 'client' comes to us from the sociological literature on organizations and refers to customers or service recipients." On the other hand, "The term 'constituent' is derived from the political literature . . . to whom an official is accountable." The distinction is meaningful in that evaluation of organizational performance requires the determination of the criteria with which to measure customer satisfaction.

He concludes that, contrary to much of the literature that suggests that responsiveness to client needs is enhanced through organizational focus on constituent influence (open system), equitable distributions are more likely to be achieved in the client interest when the needs are addressed directly in terms of more objective bureaucratic criteria. The implication for improving organizational performance, therefore, is to understand the needs of the client, establish criteria of performance, and follow and improve established procedures. TQM includes this strategy for improving the effectiveness and efficiency of organization processes.

On the subject of image and ethics, it is obvious that the ethical behavior of public officials and the image of the federal organization are inextricably related. The public is quick to recognize incidents in which an individual's behavior seems to betray the public trust. Mitchell and Scott (1987) indicate that the public administrator's legitimacy is usually thought to be based on expertise, entrepreneurship and/or stewardship. He finds no empirical evidence that the expertise or entrepreneurial ability of the administrators that have been studied are any greater than that of individuals in society. When it comes to stewardship, he claims that public representatives and administrators have failed in significant numbers so as to damage the public perception of government. He believes that action is needed to convince the public that its trust is not misplaced.

Wildavsky (1988, 753) claims that the civil servants are unable to do much themselves "because the situation is the effect, not the cause." He makes the point that it is important for the situation to be turned around because civil servants "must appear to represent society or risk undermining the state as legitimate."

Another contributor on this theme is Denhardt and Jennings (1989, 77) who state that the Reagan administration violated a previous norm which stated, "The traditional ethic of public service, [is] based on the idea of [the] existence of a public interest that exceeds private interest." Instead, what was seen to be operating was the idea that "as long as one operates within the bounds of law, the use of public office for private gain is perfectly reasonable." An opposite point of view, however, is contributed by McCarthy (1988, 3) who states: "The reality is that the burden of changing the poor image of the government falls to federal employees. It is their words and deeds that must make the difference."

Beaumont (1989) suggests a greater emphasis on education in ethics and recommends a list of essential values that all public servants should adhere to for ethical problem solving. Included are the "pursuit of excellence" and "accountability." Cleary (1989) contributes the point that the American Society for Public Administration has added two more criteria, "personal responsibility" and "professional responsibility" to assure the highest standard of personal integrity.

The last subject for consideration on "What do we want from the public sector?" concerns actions to improve federal management. Garrity (1988) reports that in June 1988 a Leading the Federal Workforce Survey indicated that a cross section of federal managers wanted the next President to focus on (1) improving leadership, (2) developing a quality workforce, and (3) improving the federal image among other topics.

Shortly before his election, George Bush (1988, 7) penned his thoughts on the subject of the Federal Service and stated that "improving the quality, morale, and performance of the public service will be a high priority." He continued, "Many of the past failures of government have occurred—not because federal employees lack talent and energy—but because byzantine rules and procedures imprison talents and sap morale." Finally, he emphasized the need to make public service more effective, efficient, productive, and more satisfying as a place to work.

The final reference in this section comes from the Volker Commission Summary (1989, 62). The original report called for emphasis on leadership, talent, and performance along with a renewed sense of commitment. Recognition was given to a requirement to "set higher goals for government performance productivity and to provide more effective training and executive development." The report also called on civil servants to commit to efficiency, responsiveness, and integrity.

Once again, as in the previous section, the themes of improved leadership, employee involvement and commitment, improved communication, emphasis on quality and productivity, customer focus, and improved skill training and problem solving continue to be salient concerns. What has been established so far is that both the private and public sectors are ready for a comprehensive initiative that has the potential to change the way we think about our organizational responsibilities and opportunities. How we lead, follow, and participate in the life of our organizations is important for our personal success and that of our organizations. Nothing less than a major cultural effort will suffice. In the public sector, we must achieve greater accountability, effectiveness, and efficiency—and the public must see it in us.

Success Stories in Both Sectors

In their much-acclaimed *A Passion for Excellence,* Peters and Austin (1985) relate the success stories of dozens of American companies and organizations. Not all their strategies were the same, but the common elements that emerge include: (1) a focus on the needs of the customer; (2) top management leadership and commitment to improvement; (3) a highly motivated, innovative workforce; (4) a commitment to attain the highest level of product and service quality; (5) attention to the processes used to produce the product or service; and (6) a recognition that people are the most important link in the process.

Similarly, Nora (1985) speaks to the integration of quality, productivity, and quality of worklife for the global challenge. Examples like General Motors Corp. Livonia Engine Plant are given to demonstrate what can be accomplished when management and employees commit to improved performance, personal rewards, and organization results. In this case, improved measurement techniques were applied with the result of increased quality, increased production, decreased per unit cost, and increased employee suggestions and pride. Success stories abound in other areas also. Hamlin (1985) provides numerous detailed examples of product and service organization improvements including efforts to measure successfully work formerly thought to be unmeasurable.

In the federal government, Burstein (1988, 133) notes, "What is clear from an analysis of the improvement methods that agencies employed is that no single best solution predominates." Much publicity has been given to the former Secretary of Commerce Malcolm Baldridge's effort to "run government like a business." Bulow (1988–89) reflects that Baldridge was committed to make Commerce the best managed department in the government. Following the belief that "we can't manage what we can't control," Commerce streamlined administrative practices, made major structural overhauls, and established a Management by Objectives (MBO) system to achieve the kind of accountability that is common in the business world.

Collamore (1989) claims that MBO at Commerce resulted in better planning, performance measurement, decision making, communications, management commitment, and reduced crisis management. A lesson learned was that no new system of improvement can work unless it is used and supported over the long run. Collamore (1989, 40) states: "It took patience, persistence, flexibility, special effort, and sustained top management to turn 'yet another fad' into a management philosophy for the entire institution." He cites Drucker, the father of MBO, with saying that the business enterprise needs a principle of management that will give full scope to individual strength and responsibility, as well as common direction to vision and effort, to establish team work and to harmonize the goals of the individual with the commonweal. Management by Objectives and self-control make the commonweal the aim of every manager and are seen as a philosophy of management.

The above statement is particularly impactful. Drucker skillfully integrates the individual, team work, business interests, and the public interest (commonweal) for the benefit of all concerned. Could there be synergy among individual, business, and government goals, performance, and rewards? There just might be if common cultural elements could be synchronized. Perhaps TQM could be the language and behavior that stimulate this integration.

The last item for consideration in this section is the establishment and award of the Malcolm Baldridge National Quality Award. Haavind and Whiting (1989, 34) explain that the purpose of the award is "to boost quality at all levels so that Americans can take pride in the quality of U.S. goods and services, and that the global market can see the United States as a source of the finest goods and services." The criteria for the award indicate the type of management that is desired in American organizations. Focus is on (1) leadership, (2) information and analysis, (3) strategic quality planning, (4) human resource utilization, (5) quality assurance of products and services, (6) quality results, and (7) customer satisfaction. Among others, Motorola and Xerox have been recipients of the award in the last two years.

Across the United States, private and public sector organizations are stepping up to the challenge of improving quality and productivity. Florida Power and Light received a 1989 Deming Award for Quality—the first U.S. firm to do so. Numerous other success stories can also be told, including Ford, Harley-Davidson, 3M, Alameda Naval Aviation Depot, Ochoco National Forest, Phoenix Arizona Municipal Services, New York City Department of Juvenile Justice, and the National Theater for the Handicapped. Where there are people who care for quality, improvements are possible.

As we will see in the following sections, TQM is integral to, and a logical outcome from, lessons of experience and intellectual study in individual, group, culture, and organization development.

TQM and Individual Development

Consideration is given in this section to the contributions of four authors: C.G. Jung, B.F. Skinner, Michael S. Gazzaniga, and Stephen R. Covey. Each, in turn, offers a prospective on human needs, behavior, and development that may be explored for relationship to TQM.

Jung (1968) offers the concept that each person makes use of ectophysic (sensation, thinking, feeling, and intuition) functions for gathering information and making decisions. He notes that a fully functioning person uses all these capabilities but not all in equal measure or with equal skill. We might extrapolate from this concept that a person who has ample opportunity to develop greater competence in the use of these functions will develop improved self-awareness and gain more esteem in social situations.

TQM principles and practices provide opportunity for employees to participate, learn, and grow both individually and from one another. Problem solving and data collection and analysis can only work well when one's ectophysic functions operate in an orderly manner and under control of the individual. TQM process action teams (PATs) provide opportunity for employees to gather data and make decisions together. They can learn personally from this process and the organization will also benefit.

Jung shows concern about the ill-effects of individual isolation (a breeding ground for neurosis) and emphasizes the importance of learning to achieve a sense of balance wherein the "whole" is recognized from the "parts" and the superior and inferior functions are working in balance. Essentially, TQM training in team participation and in statistical techniques, along with encouragement to be innovative, is geared toward helping the employee function well and to do so with others. The importance of an active imagination is also contributed by Jung and applies here in that the individual learns to use his functions appropriately under conditions of support and low stress. By keeping the individual "in control of self," greater participation, patience, and thinking may result.

Skinner (1971) contributes the idea that the change agent needs to control and engineer the new environment intentionally when planning to elicit a change in a person's behavior.

This is useful because TQM requires a change in individual employee behavior and in the organizational culture to support other changes and changes in others. Skinner says that greater use of positive reinforcers are indicated to assure that new behaviors become part of the enhanced culture.

Providing greater employee freedom and self-direction is seen as an important goal in TQM with the expectation that empowered employees will be more willing to solve problems and improve organizational efficiency. While Skinner would not likely agree that this will necessarily follow, he would agree that establishing an environment to encourage changed behavior and then rewarding the behavior is the way to make change occur. He would also caution that too many controlling and reinforcing activities would likely be dysfunctional or cause apathy because there would be little opportunity for employees to value themselves as self-managing individuals. TQM supports the self-managing team concept, thereby remaining consistent with these concerns.

If one accepts the behavior-interpretation-belief relationship suggested by Gazzaniga (1985), TQM should be implemented more on the basis that individuals should be held accountable for learning and participating in the practices and methods than on the basis of their first changing their attitude and belief systems. It is worth noting here that Juran has made this point regularly in his lectures—first, ensure that employees participate and see the benefits of improved operating methods and then they will change their attitudes more willingly.

Gazzaniga also suggests that stimulating both the left and right sides of the brain with appropriate stimuli may be constructive in helping the individual create a new consciousness. This concept is intriguing when one considers the difficulty normally encountered in making change in the organizational culture.

Finally, in *The 7 Habits of Highly Effective People,* Covey (1989) reveals the results of his study into the wide variety of personal improvement literature. His findings help us put a personal development emphasis on this section and provides an opportunity to suggest that TQM is right for the individual too, not just for the organization.

Covey points out that, after one considers the "character ethic" advice of the 1800s and early 1900s and the "personality ethics" advice over the last fifty years, there emerges a clear pattern of fundamental principles and practices. When used regularly, Covey says, these principles and practices become habits for personal success. The habits are: (1) be proactive, (2) begin with the end in mind, (3) put first things first, (4) think win/win, (5) seek first to understand then to be understood, (6) synergize, and (7) continue to improve. Putting this in a TQM perspective, we could say that individuals should learn to be active in the pursuit of their goals and priorities. They should first understand themselves, then seek to understand and work effectively with others. They should also look to build on one another's strengths for personal effectiveness and seek to improve their individual performance continuously.

A reflection on the TQM principles and practices shows similar guidance for an organization attempting to improve the quality of its products and services and its level of productivity. Perhaps it is reasonable to suggest that TQM as a language for communicating commitment among employees, and as a group problem-solving method to improve performance, is a vehicle for integrating individual and organizational objectives for the benefit of all concerned.

TQM and Group Development

When individuals come together in groups to accomplish an objective, their interaction and its effect on their ability to complete the task successfully become areas of academic study and organizational concern. This section addresses a number of group dynamic issues from the perspective of process action teams (PATs) which are central to the TQM problem-solving method. In PATS, the participants learn to (1) become a team, (2) play appropriate group roles, (3) do group problem solving and decision making, (4) deal with intergroup conflict, and (5) build trusting relationships.

Groups are often involved in problem-solving and decision-making efforts. PATs are specially constructed for these purposes. Lippitt in "Improving Decision-Making with Groups" (Bradford 1978, 83) states: "Group decision making is possible. The use of the consensus method over voting or unanimity is realistic, but it is not easy. Careful attention to the decision making process, mature group membership, and democratic leadership combine to contribute maximally to those situations where groups can meet most effectively their obligation in problem solving." TQM emphasizes consensus decision making and is consistent with Lippitt's observations and cautionary note.

Because of the multi-disciplined team approach to problem solving advocated by TQM, it is possible that PATs may be working on overlapping problems and this may cause intergroup problems. Schein in "Group and Intergroup Relationships" (Ott 1989, 216) suggests: "The over-all problem, then, is how to establish high-productive, collaborative intergroup relations."

To avoid intergroup competition, he suggests (1) give greater emphasis to "total organizational effectiveness" and give credit for total, rather than individual effectiveness, (2) create frequent intergroup communications and give rewards based in part on help given, (3) rotate members between the groups to gain mutual understanding, and (4) attempt to avoid win/lose situations between groups.

Once again, TQM applies in that emphasis is on effective group work with maximum communications and the recognition of group, rather than individual contributions.

TQM requires a high level of trust among top, middle, and lower levels of management as well as trust that employees will give their best for the organization in response to empowering efforts by management. Also, there needs to be trust among group members that other members will respect and protect their interests and points of view. Zand in "Trust and Managerial Problem Solving" (Bradford 1978, 196) "conceptualizes trust as a behavior that conveys appropriate information, permits mutuality of influence, encourages self-control, and avoids abuse of the vulnerability of others." It would not be an exaggeration to say that no organization can realize the benefits of TQM without establishing a high degree of trust among large numbers of its members.

The TQM principles and practices are wholly consistent with the recommendations of noted authors on group development. In fact, TQM advocates group problem solving using consensus decision-making as the best approach for gathering information and getting organizational buy-in to recommended solutions. There should be little doubt that TQM is not only consistent with expert opinion on effective group dynamics; it in fact derives from it.

Organizational Culture and Performance

A reminder to the reader seems appropriate at this point. The theme throughout is that TQM is a legitimate and valuable strategy for improving federal organizations. We have considered what Americans appear to want from their private and public sector organizations, reviewed a number of success stories where an emphasis on quality and productivity were the basis for improved performance, learned from the experts the essential factors in understanding personal development and group dynamics, and have seen that most, if not all, of the TQM principles and practices have evolved from or are in direct support of the fundamental issues in each of these areas.

Emphasis now turns from what might be termed "the objective requirements" of individuals, groups, and the citizenry to the "cultural processes" in terms of beliefs, behaviors, and norms we have created for ourselves. This section suggests that "organizational culture" is a pervasive phenomenon that includes much of what was discussed above. As such, an understanding of organizational culture, TQM's relationship to this culture, and the impact of culture on the organization's performance are central to the argument for TQM implementation in federal organizations.

To begin with, culture is not easily defined. Some knowledgeable contributors have suggested the following.

Schein (1985, 4) says: "Organization culture is a pattern of basic assumptions—invented, discovered, or developed by a given group as it learns to cope with its problems of eternal adaptation and internal integration—that has worked well enough to be considered valid and, therefore, to be taught to new members as the correct way to perceive, think, and feel in relation to these problems."

Deal and Kennedy (1988, 4) state: "Culture, as Webster's New Collegiate Dictionary defines it, is the integrated pattern of human behavior that includes the thought, speech, action, artifacts and depends on man's capacity for learning and transmitting knowledge to succeeding generations. The elements of culture include the business environment, values, heroes, rites and rituals, and the cultural network."

Kilmann et al. (1985, 5) contributes that culture is "the shared philosophies, ideologies, values, assumptions, beliefs, expectations, attitudes, and norms that knit a community together. These psychological qualities reveal a group's agreement, implicit or explicit, on how to approach decisions and problems: the way things are done around here." He also observes that culture has impact to the degree that it (1) provides direction, (2) has strength, and (3) is pervasive. Direction refers to the course culture is causing the organization to follow; strength refers to the level of pressure the culture exerts on its members; and pervasiveness is the degree to which the culture is shared.

What is clear from the above definitions is that culture is a social reality created iteratively over time as members of a group or organization set a course of action, face problems and opportunities, learn from their experiences, communicate that learning to others in the group, and reinforce the beliefs and behaviors that result. Questions to be asked next, then, are: "If we agree that culture(s) can be seen operating in groups and organizations, to what use can this knowledge be put?" "Can we use that knowledge to advance a desired goal or organizational change?"

Poupart and Hobbes (1989) speak of productivity being linked closely to culture and of both depending on the organization's major strategic thrust. They think that most managers would prefer a strong or widely shared culture to a weak one—one that stresses customer satisfaction and product innovation. Here we see the potential of TQM to strengthen the culture, make it entrepreneurial, and use it for organizational improvement.

What follows builds on the theme that infusing an organization's culture with a large dose of TQM principles and practices can lead to improved product and service quality and productivity. This theme is consistent with the quality and productivity success stories referenced earlier and is thought to be a useful strategy in refocusing private and public sector organizations toward the needs of the citizenry.

Shafritz and Ott (1987) suggest that there is a high correlation between a strong culture and organization goal attainment, and that there are a number of organizational culture issues upon which there is a wide consensus. These include: (1) organization cultures exist; (2) each organization culture is relatively unique; (3) organizational culture provides organizational members a way of understanding and making sense of events and symbols; and (4) organization culture is a powerful lever for guiding organization behaviors. It functions as an organizational control mechanism approving or prohibiting patterns of behavior. The last point here is particularly insightful—maybe the TQM principles and practices can be made part of the lever that guides organization behavior.

The question that comes to mind is: "If it makes sense to enhance an organization (improve its performance) by changing its culture, how can this be done?" Deal (1988, 158) says: "When we speak of organizational or cultural change we mean real changes in the behavior of people throughout the organization . . . new role models . . . telling different stories . . . asking different questions . . . different work rituals. This takes a long time to achieve. To get people in a culture even to begin to change, management has to capture 5 to 10 percent of their time for a year." One may wonder who should do this and if it is worth the effort.

The answer from Schein (1985) is that it is possible that the only thing of real importance that leaders do is to create and manage culture and that the unique talent of leaders is to work with culture. TQM supports this perspective in that it articulates the essential need for top management participation, direction, and support. Top management must "walk the talk" for any organizational change to occur, notwithstanding the intellectual correctness of any set of principles and practices.

If an organization's leaders desire a culture change based on TQM and wish to demonstrate the new thinking and order of things, they should consider the desirability of (1) creating organizational meaning, (2) establishing the zone of acceptable decision making, and (3) establishing appropriate administrative rituals. Mahler (1988) observes that, in complex organizations, stories are told about the organization's founding, the exploits of its members, their successes, and the obstacles they overcame along the way. He points out that these stories help define the organization and its mission, often by portraying it in heroic and noble terms to members. The importance here is that successful TQM–related accomplishments offer examples of "doing it" the organization way.

Roe (1989) raises the issue of a "zone of acceptance" in organization decision making that has applicability in building a TQM–based culture. He suggests that each organization member has a zone of acceptance; that is, a set of organizational orders and instructions which he rarely challenges. The TQM issue is one of establishing an organization-wide framework of thinking that assures that individuals anywhere in the organization include fundamental TQM principles and practices in their zone of acceptance. For TQM to become part of the "way of doing business around here" requires extensive effort on the part of all key personnel to talk, demonstrate, and reward the decision making thought processes and outcomes desired.

Another useful perspective in understanding the potential for changing culture is that offered by Goodsell (1989, 161–62) regarding "Administration as Ritual." He states: "Although the organization-culture movement has of late greatly expanded the discussion of symbols, myths, and rites in administrative organizations, no one has attempted to conceptualize public administration systematically in ritualistic terms." He continues: "Ritual is a culturally constructed system of patterned and ordered sequences of words and acts. When performed socially (rather than individually), it has the effect of endowing certain interpretations of reality with a legitimacy that is recognized by the social group. Ritual, by dramatic means, both declares and demonstrates—through display and enactment—certain propositions to be unquestionably true." Finally, he argues that "rituals both carry forward past traditions and shape current culture. In doing so, they may consist of explicitly staged performances . . . Collective ritual has six formal properties: repetition, role playing, stylization, order, staging, and social meaning."

Goodsell notes: "Administrative rituals are played out before two general categories of audience, the one inside the organization and the other outside." This is a very important point in that a government organization, as addressed in a previous section, needs to balance its effort toward improved effectiveness and efficiency with its responsibility for representativeness and accountability. Also noted earlier, image and stewardship are important factors to the citizenry and are largely the way the citizens judge the value of a government organization.

Goodsell refers to the internal audience as the "Back Region" and those outside the organization as being in the "Front Region." The contribution of the language and practice of TQM appears to be the potential for linking the Back and Front Regions into a larger operational framework that reduces current polarized thinking around the issue of efficiency versus accountability. TQM, when practiced, also creates the appearance of better stewardship and enhances the government image.

From the above discussion, one can begin to see the importance of thinking of TQM as a cultural phenomenon. In the United States the effort to evolve an organization, private or public, to a higher level of product or service delivery is an attempt at refocusing employee common values and behavior. To the degree that the principles and practices of TQM become part of the core beliefs and operating style of an organization, a shared sense of the "corporate whole" is ingrained into each person. This, in turn, strengthens the ability of the organization to maintain its focus and achieve coherence in its day-to-day processes.

It is important to note that the specific TQM principles and practices are not "the culture" but are more accurately described as integrated activities carried out within the culture. The unique way in which these activities are accomplished (the how to do it) is the real indicator of the underlying culture of the organization. It might properly be said that no organization may actually achieve its TQM potential unless it enhances its culture in a way that persuades a large majority of its personnel to believe in, and continually practice, the desired organizational behaviors.

The culture, as a metaphor, encourages a reinterpretation of traditional management concepts and processes. Greater emphasis is placed on leadership as the management of meaning. Organization leaders create organizational reality through their establishment of a system of shared meanings. The philosophies, values, behavior, policies, and procedures created express the unique attitude and style of the organization and are said to reflect its culture.

It appears obvious that the implementation of TQM in an organization requires an enhancement of that organization's culture. Morgan (1986) cautions the ambitious change agent that culture is not so mechanistic as it might seem to the casual observer. In actuality, it is quite diffused and more of a holographic experience for those who are a part of it. He states that managers can influence the evolution of culture by being aware of the symbolic consequences of their actions and by attempting to foster desired values, but they cannot control culture. The implication for those preparing to implement a TQM initiative is to recognize that the proposed TQM principles and practices will be learned and used by employees within the content of the social realities already established. At best this is an incremental approach to management improvement. However, what are the alternatives?

Finally, Siehl and Martin (1987) offer the thought that an essential task of the leader is the creation and maintenance of a system of shared values. First, leaders can use role modeling to communicate core values effectively. Second, they can establish formal training programs as a powerful means of reinforcing the value system and generating employee commitment. The lesson here is that TQM can, and should be, incorporated into an organization's culture. To do so, however, requires the commitment of leaders throughout the organization who should demonstrate their new behaviors, establish the appropriate administrative structures, and devise cultural interventions. Considering the potential leverage of cultural change, many organizations should plan their strategy and implement it with vigor.

TQM and Federal Organization Development

The argument that TQM principles and practices provide a language of commitment to improved organizational performance has been advanced. The author has considered the need for improved product and service quality and organizational productivity in both the private and public sectors, and has identified some success stories in which TQM–like approaches were utilized. We have seen that TQM is a logical outgrowth of individual development and group development theory. Finally, the author has reflected on the relationship between organization culture and organization performance with the belief that, if the TQM principles and practices can become integrated in the culture, then improved organizational performance is a reasonable expectation.

This section draws on many of the concepts and expectations developed above and additional contemporary literature in an attempt to project how life will be in tomorrow's federal organization with the aid of TQM. The assumption is that the organization has applied a long-term change strategy to achieve a recognizable modification of the organization's culture, and that improved performance in the form of better product and service quality and greater productivity has been demonstrated. This conceptualization of the future federal organization is facilitated by the perspectives and recommendations that follow. Drucker (1988) speaks of the "Coming of the New Organization" in which business will be knowledge-based and composed of specialists who direct and discipline their own performance. Because of this, he says that the number of managers and management levels can be reduced. He postulates that the organization will go beyond the matrix and that it will require greater self-discipline and even greater emphasis on individual responsibility for relationships and for communications. The connection to TQM may be seen in the emphasis on skill development, self-disciplined and self-managed teams, and the importance of effective communications.

Kanter (1983) speaks to the type of leaders who will hopefully emerge who see an opportunity to redirect the organization and take it. These "change masters" are diverse people in diverse circumstances who share an integrative mode of operating which produces innovation. They work across boundaries, reach beyond the limits of their jobs, and are good builders and users of teams. TQM applies in that it encourages cross-functional orientation and problem solving using process action teams (PATs).

Kitsopoulos (1989, 217) adds a concern for creativity to Kanter's concept by stating that "we observe a globalization of markets, an intensification of competition on an international level, and highly differentiated needs and quality demands by customers" and "that the creativity of the individual as well as the team must be consciously fostered in order to ensure continuous innovation . . . Obstacles to communication and the creative development of all workers must be eliminated." While he is referring to the private sector, one can see that challenges in the public sector may cause similar concern. TQM focuses on the need for continuous process improvement and for individuals and teams to become involved in, and responsible for, finding new ways to accomplish the organization's mission.

Manz (1987) stresses the need to develop "self-managing teams." The use of self-managing groups involves a shift of focus from individual methods of performing work to group methods. Further, he offers that employees become members of a self-managing group and tend to define their work roles in terms of their values as contributors to the group's primary task rather than in relation to one specific job.

As for his research on group performance, he notes productivity gains significantly greater than 20 percent when compared to other plants using traditional management methods. From a TQM perspective, process action teams are trained in problem solving and team development skills. When they attain cohesion in group process, their output should be significant for improved organizational performance.

McBriarty (1988, 10) addresses the status of public personnel administration in the content of declining resources and increasing challenges and suggests that "the public sector professional is likely to share a general disenchantment with the legalistic imper- sonality of big bureaucracy and to reject the idea that hierarchy is the 'one best way' to organize cooperative human effort." Further, he says that they prefer "greater opportunity for participation and control of their own activities . . . explanations of the 'why' of those activities . . . and believe that organizations should adapt to the peculiarities and human needs of the membership."

The value of TQM is that it provides a forum for self-expression, recognition, and contribution separate from the hierarchy for the time the individual participates in the process action team. The PAT is a place for individuals to grow in problem-solving skills, group relationships, and managerial skills. It may even be termed an experiential training ground for learning and managerial development.

Schon's (1983) *The Reflective Practitioner* concept has applicability if one considers the uncertainty pervading the striving organization. While technocratic, rational decision- making has its place when problems can be reasonably bound, he says that much manage- ment is accomplished among uncertainty and ambiguity. He proposes that managers (and other professionals) think while they work, do not know where they are going beforehand, but when they start to work act intelligently. He calls this behavior "reflection-in-action" and suggests that it is a central "art" which makes situations of uncertainty, instability, uniqueness, and value conflict manageable.

Once again, TQM applies in that top managers and other professionals need to appreci- ate the iterative process of setting objectives, taking action, learning from results, making incremental corrections in course, and then doing it over again. The critical element is the recognition that, even while this process is occurring, the following guidance must be provided to others in the organization: (1) a vision of the future; (2) priorities to be worked; (3) parameters within which to work; (4) articulation of customer needs; and (5) the quality of product or service desired.

Senge (1986, 134–35) contributes the idea that it is important to recognize the different competencies that distinguish the leader from the manager in complex organizations. He restates Bennis (1985) to identify four distinct competencies for successful leadership: management of attention, management of meaning, management of trust, and manage- ment of self. Senge believes: "Effective leaders in the more democratic organizations of the future will not only encourage and inspire people to trust themselves, take risks, and innovate. They will also create a learning environment in which the lessons of experience can be distilled and transmitted far more efficiently than in the traditional authoritarian organization."

His comment of greatest interest and potential is on the importance of the leader being able to recognize leverage points. "Leverage points are the relatively small number of policy changes that can radiate desirable influence throughout a system." A TQM policy can be a leverage point for the organization's top leadership to launch the organization into its future. Assuming that TQM principles and practices are integral to developing individuals and organizations thereby contributing to America's renewal and economic resurgence, why not coax our leaders to learn the talk and to walk the talk.

Any discussion of the future that only views the organization through the eyes of the manager is bound to be limited because it only considers "downward action orientation" without sufficient appreciation for the attitudes and behaviors that are likely to result or attention to those that are desired. Gilbert and Hyde (1988) report that there are eight empirically derived dimensions of followership that, when in sufficient presence, will contribute impressively to organizational performance. These are: (1) partnership with the supervisor; (2) commitment to the job; (3) technical competence; (4) sense of humor; (5) dependability; (6) positive working relationships; (7) tendency to speak up; and (8) proper comportment.

They say: "Supervisors need to expect excellence in followership from their subordinates. The system needs to measure it, provide feedback to subordinates about it, and reward it where it occurs. These study findings suggest that followership is a 'crucial element' in job performance and productivity . . ." (Ibid., 967).

The question arises: "What does TQM contribute here?" The answer is that TQM implementation requires organizational-wide education and training in problem-solving skills, group dynamics, employee development, and manager coaching. It is a "full court press" strategy to penetrate and become systematized within the organizational culture. Attempts at mutual growth and development, improving trust and communications, and focusing on common goals are believed to be a win/win strategy with a chance to succeed. Make no mistake, however, this is hard work and requires significant resources over a long time period.

The picture presented in this section is one of a federal organization with a renewed concern for developing top leaders with vision for the future, managers with employee empowerment skills, and employees at all levels with commitment to being skillful followers. Should this occur, it portends a new era in government-private sector relations. The government may have learned to change its image from that of a "referee" among private entities battling for influence and reward to that of a "coach" assisting all players to become as worthwhile and productive as they can be for the public good.

In terms of U.S. economic issues, Hampden-Turner (1988, 45) suggests that "the coached economy is likely to be more effective in terms of both economic growth and humanitarian goals than the . . . free markets refereed by government." Also: "Enterprises learn to organize themselves for work of ever-increasing quality, sophistication, and efficiency. Governments can facilitate learning by acting as catalysts."

The Jazz Ensemble: A New Metaphor

Morgan (1986, 335, 336) explains: "The images and metaphors through which we read organizational situations help us describe the way organizations are, and offer clear ideas and options as to how they could be." Also: "There is a close relationship between the way we think and the way we act, and . . . many organizational problems are embedded in our thinking." Finally he argues: "People who learn to read situations from different (theoretical) points of view have an advantage over those committed to a fixed position. For they are better able to recognize the limitations of a given perspective. They can see how situations and problems can be framed and reframed in different ways, allowing new kinds of solutions to emerge."

This section concerns how we think about the future federal organization after considering the prescriptions for change advanced earlier in this article. A new lens or metaphor is suggested to stimulate leaders to emerge and create the organizations we both need and want as we race (tumble?) into the future.

The metaphor suggested is the performance of a jazz ensemble. The elements of the ensemble include the musicians (professional, skilled, empowered, adaptable, innovative), the conductor (participant-leader, coach, focus provider, integrator, source of inspiration), the music (theme, guideline, discipline), the instruments (tools, methods, characteristics), the stage setting (mood, comfort, support structure), and the audience (customer, judge, reward-giver). During the performance, the conductor selects the song to be played to meet the interests of the audience and participates himself by orchestrating the outcome.

The ensemble adheres to the theme (core values) of the selection but each player maintains an independence of technique and expression (decentralization) as he learns from and builds on the contributions of other players. The quality of the performance of a particular song evolves as it is played again and again by the group—although it is never played exactly the same way twice (situational effects). Group members value the outcomes from their combined effort along with the respective contributions of individual players. The sense of accomplishment is high when rewarded with audience applause.

The creation of the new metaphor derives from an integration of the organizational behavior contributions of Peter Vaill, David Brown, and Michael Gazzaniga. According to Vaill (1989, 21), "The organizational world of permanent white water has evolved requirements for the leader-manager for higher quality thought and action than ever before. It is not merely the action capacity of the traditional can-do problem solver. And it is not merely the intellectual capacity of the traditional inhabitant of the ivory tower. It is a genuine mix . . . (of) truly wise leaders." From this it appears that the leader operates as a proactive conductor-participant, using a mix of knowledge and technique appropriate to the situation and the environment.

Vaill (1989, 170) also contributes: "Members of high-performing systems typically find working with their bosses thrilling. Such people's understanding of what needs to be done is astonishing (focus), their availability and willingness to stay on something until it is done is refreshing (time), and through it all they are memorable people to be around (feeling)." This statement captures the spirit and excitement of high performance whether it be in a musical ensemble or in an organization.

Brown (1989) stresses the importance of looking at the organization as a "concert in action" with emphasis on integration of activities and on team building with the manager's (conductor's) role in it. From a systems perspective, he states that those with managerial responsibilities are finding that organizational objectives can best be achieved by an approach which involves a greater sharing of their duties and responsibilities in the system. It takes team play to produce systems that can and will do what is asked of them in an efficient, economical, and lasting way.

The implication here is that organizational outcomes, like the outcome from a symphony orchestra, result from individuals and groups working as teams within the larger system of activity to achieve a quality (harmonious) outcome. The jazz ensemble metaphor is thought to be more representative of tomorrow's organization than the symphony orchestra due to the flexible and innovative style of management and work processes that will be employed.

Finally, with the theory of the "social brain," Gazzaniga (1985) provides a physiological contribution to the jazz ensemble metaphor. He postulates that (1) the human brain is organized in a modular manner with relatively independent units that function in parallel and (2) that this parallel processing results in iterative behavior-interpretation-belief activity which defines the person and, by extension, the group and the organization. It is well known that the accomplished person in any specialty, particularly in the arts, senses the gestalt of a situation and acts with intuitive and motor skill correctness without giving much attention to the specifics of that situation. This is certainly true for the musician. Perhaps it will also be true of the leaders and their "associates" in tomorrow's dynamic federal organization.

Summary

It has been argued that Total Quality Management is the language of those committed to individual, organizational, and national excellence and that TQM should be implemented in federal organizations. This was done by looking at what is needed from our private and public sector organizations, considering expert opinion on individual and organizational development, exploring ways to enhance organizational culture and performance, and conceptualizing the federal organization of the future. If this work is at all convincing let's do it. Better yet, let us do it anyway and become motivated by the results.

References

Beaumont, Enid (1989). "The Ethical Public Manager." *The Bureaucrat* (Spring):14–19.

Bennis, Warren and Burt Nanus (1985). *Leaders: The Strategies of Taking Charge.* New York: Harper & Row.

Bower, Joseph L. (1983). *The Two Faces of Management.* Boston: Houghton Mifflin.

Bradford, Leland P. (ed.) (1978). *Group Development.* San Francisco: University Associates.

Brown, David S. (1989). "Management's New Goal: Concert Building." *The Bureaucrat* (Summer):27–30.

Bulow, Kay (1988–89). "Running Government Like a Business." *The Bureaucrat* (Winter):12–13.

Burstein, Carolyn and Kathleen Sedlak (1988). "The Federal Productivity Improvement Effort: Current Status and Future Agenda." *National Productivity Review* (Spring):122–133.

Bush, George H.W. (1988–89). "On the Federal Service." *The Bureaucrat* (Winter):7.

Cleary, Robert E. (1989). "Making MBO Work in the Public Sector." *The Bureaucrat* (Fall):37–40.

Covey, Stephen R (1989). *The 7 Habits of Highly Effective People.* New York: Simon and Schuster.

Deal, Terrence E. and Allen A. Kennedy (1982). *Corporate Cultures: The Rights and Rituals of Corporate Life.* New York: Addison-Wesley.

Deming, W. Edwards (1986). *Out of Crisis.* Cambridge: MIT Center for Engineering Study.

Denhardt, Robert B. and Edward T. Jennings, Jr. (1989). "Image and Integrity in the Public Service." *Public Administration Review* (January–February):74–77.

Drucker, Peter F. (1988). "The Coming of the New Organization." *Harvard Business Review* (January–February):45–53.

Garrity, Rudy (1988). "Leading the Federal Workforce." *The Bureaucrat* (Fall):22.

Gazzaniga, Michael S. (1985). *The Social Brain.* New York: Basic Books.

Gilbert, G. Ronald and Albert C. Hyde (1988). "Followership and the Federal Worker." *Public Administration Review* (November–December):963–967.

Goodsell, Charles T. (1989). "Administration as Ritual." *Public Administration Review* (March–April):161–166.

Haavind, Robert and Rick Whiting (1989). "Baldridge Quality Award: Industry's Version of Oscar." *Electronic Business* (Oct. 16):34–45.

Hamlin, Jerry L. (ed.) (1985). *Success Stories in Productivity Development.* Atlanta: Industrial Engineering & Management Press.

Hampden-Turner, Charles (1968). "Three Images of the Government: The Referee, The Coach, The Abolitionist." *New Management* (Fall):43–49.

Jung, C.G. (1968). *Analytic Psychology: Its Theory and Practice.* New York: Vintage Books.

Juran, J.M. and Frank M. Gryna (1988). *Juran's Quality Control Handbook.* New York: McGraw-Hill.

Kanter, Rosabeth Moss (1983). *The Change Masters.* New York: Simon and Schuster.

Kilmann, Ralph J., Mary J. Saxton, Roy Serpa, and Associates (1985). *Gaining Control of the Corporate Culture.* San Francisco: Jossey-Bass.

Kitzopoulos, S.C. (1989). "Creativity and Innovation in the High-Technology Era." In Howard S. Didsbury, Jr. (ed.), *The Future: Opportunity Not Destiny.* Bethesda, MD: World Future Society.

Mahler, Julianne (1988). "The Quest for Organizational Meaning." *Administration & Society* (November):344–368.

Manz, Charles C. and H.P. Sims, Jr. (1987). "Leading Workers to Lead Themselves: The External Leadership of Self-Managing Work Teams." *Administrative Science Quarterly* 32:106–128.

McBriarty, Mark A. (1988). "Toward the Year 2000: Are We Ready?" *The Bureaucrat* (Summer):8–12.

McCarthy, Thomas G. (1988–89). "Changing the Public's Perception." *The Bureaucrat* (Winter):3–4.

Mitchell, Terence R. and William G. Scott (1997). "Leadership Failures, the Distrusting Public, and Prospects of the Administrative State." *Public Administration Review* (November–December):445–451.

Morgan, Gareth (1986). *Images of Organization.* Beverly Hills: Sage.

Naisbitt, John (1984). *Megatrends.* New York: Warner Books.

Nora, John, C. Raymond Rogers, and Robert J. Stramy (1986). *Transforming the Work Place.* Princeton: Princeton Research Press.

Ott, J. Steven (1989). *Classic Readings in Organization Behavior.* Belmont, CA: Brooks/Cole.

Peters, Tom and Nancy Austin (1985). *A Passion for Excellence.* New York: Warner Books.

Poupart, Robert and Brian Hobbes (1983). "Changing the Corporate Culture to Ensure Success: A Practical Guide." *National Productive Review* (Summer):223–238.

Reich, Robert B. (1983). "The Next American Frontier." *Atlantic Monthly* (March):48.

Roe, Emery M. (1989). "The Zone of Acceptance in Organization Theory: An Explanation of the Challenger Incident." *Administration & Society* (August):234–261.

Schein, Edgar H. (1985). *Organization Culture and Leadership.* San Francisco: Jossey-Bass.

Schon, Donald A. (1983). *The Reflective Practitioner.* New York: Basic Books.

Senge, Peter M. (1986). "Systems Principles for Leadership." In John D. Adams (ed.), *Transforming Leadership: From Vision to Results.* Alexandria, VA: Miles River Press.

Shafritz, Jay M. and J. Steven Ott (1987). *Classics of Organization Theory.* Chicago: Dorsey Press.

Siehl, C. and J. Martin (1982). "Learning Organization Culture." Unpublished manuscript, Stanford University.

Skinner, B.F. (1971). *Beyond Freedom and Dignity.* New York: Bantam Books.

"The Volker Commission Report" (1989). *Public Administration Review* (Summer):60–62.

Thurow, Lester C. (1985). *The Zero-Sum Solution.* New York: Simon and Schuster.

Vaill, Peter B. (1989). *Managing as a Performing Art.* San Francisco: Jossey-Bass.

Viteritti, Joseph P. (1990). "Public Organization Environments: Constituents, Clients, and Urban Governance." *Administration & Society* (February):425–447.

Wildavsky, Aaron (1988). "Ubiquitous Anomie: Public Service in an Era of Ideological Dissensus." *Public Administration Review* (July–August):753–755.

CHAPTER 7

REEVALUATING METHODS OF ESTABLISHING PRIORITIES FOR GOVERNMENTAL SERVICES

MARY M. HALE AND AIMEE L. FRANKLIN

Evolving welfare reform at the national level has put pressures on local governments to bear the burden of adjustment. Community-level policy makers and leaders must initiate efforts to protect the governmental safety net, ensure access, reform financing structures, and engineer new service delivery models. Local governments will continue to face resource limitations; therefore, careful financial management requires decision-making procedures that support consistent, fair, and rational determination of resource allocation priorities. This article presents fresh methods for local governments to use in setting priorities for funding governmental services.

The first section discusses historically and currently popular methods for prioritizing funding for government programs. The second section introduces a new framework for determining which programs will receive funding and the level of funding to be dedicated to each program. The reevaluation framework capitalizes on the strengths of previous approaches to decision making and offers specific criteria and strategic guidelines useful in prioritizing government services.

Research regarding the strategies that local governments use at both the county and city levels shows that new processes can guide priority setting in a wide range of service areas. The presentation of these contrasting and emergent approaches aims to assist decision makers in analyzing competing priorities for limited funds and modifying processes for ranking key result areas and service categories.

Historical and Current Prioritization Methods

Determining priorities in local government often requires deciding what matters most in terms of consequences for the collective residents of the community. Basic considerations in prioritizing include obligations, responsibilities, value growth, and personal reasons. Critical to all of the methods reviewed in this article are the initial answers to the following questions:

From *Public Productivity & Management Review*, vol. 20, no. 4 (June 1997): 384–96. Copyright © 1997 by Sage Publications, Inc. Reprinted with permission of M.E. Sharpe, Inc.

- What is the government mandated to provide?
- What is local government's responsibility?
- What conditions are most desirable?
- What image does the community wish to promote?
- What is the influence of the decision maker's prior background with the issue or desire to make a good impression on the community?

Several methods are available to help decision makers determine programmatic priorities that are in line with constrained funding levels. Three frameworks and methods are outlined to provide a basis for analyzing an emergent method that has tremendous potential to correct deficiencies in other approaches. The respective frameworks are based on incrementalism, conceptualization, and performance. These frameworks and related criteria are offered to provoke critical thinking, not to supply detailed points or answers that will, without doubt, arise.

The Incremental Framework

Much has been written about the budgetary decision makers' historical reliance on incremental approaches to resource allocation. Using this approach, resource decisions are made on the marginal amount of change from year to year, and entrenched interests are thus not challenged regarding their fair share of the budgetary pie (Wildavsky 1988). As Caiden (1992) has observed, historically, this type of resource allocation worked best because the emphasis on year-to-year marginal adjustments used the recent past as a good guide to the immediate future. The essence of this approach was that it reaffirmed funding decisions by labeling them part of the base budget and, in effect, removed previous funding levels from consideration in budgetary discussion. One outcome of this approach was that discussions were then limited to making decisions on the increment (or decrement) of change from previous funding levels.

The fundamental attraction of this approach is that it emphasizes stability and routinized decision-making processes in an attempt to minimize uncertainty (Axelrod 1995). In addition, it accommodates the politicalness of the prioritization process by allowing for a series of trade-offs in funding decisions without explicitly considering previous decisions made on programs and policies. From a policy perspective, the drawback of this approach is that it is minimally responsive to changes in the environment. As a result, it encourages "meat-ax" budgeting techniques such as across-the-board reductions (Mikesell 1995).

The Conceptual Framework

A conceptual framework focuses policy discussion on the proper role of government by asking questions about the underlying purpose for service provision. For example, are government programs designed to reinforce the self-sufficiency of citizens, or should local government limit its responsibilities to providing a safety net and only those services that provide for basic human needs?

Criteria used in conjunction with this framework are consistent with the conventional legal responsibilities and political philosophy of the United States. The criteria state that local governments should prioritize according to three major guidelines (Grace 1995):

- First, adequately meet mandated responsibilities, then offer optional programs providing important services for large numbers of people or helping government meet its legal responsibilities.
- Second, give special consideration to programs with capacity for long-term benefits and a ripple effect; to programs that help maintain and stimulate a humane, compassionate community; and to programs showing promise of becoming independent of governmental funding.
- Third, support programs for persons without physical, mental, or emotional capacity to work only when other governmental resources are not adequate.

The conceptual framework considers three points of view: the societal view, the structural/government view, and the humane perspective. Examination of each of these different perspectives can be used to guide public decision making (Grace 1995). A brief description of each is presented next.[1]

The Societal View. The societal view is most concerned with the productivity of all adult members of society so that the basic needs of individuals for food, shelter, and clothing are met. When making prioritization decisions using this view, the emphasis is on helping citizens achieve self-sufficiency through the provision of services that emphasize education and training in anticipation of long-term benefits such as a reduction in future public expenditures (Grace 1995). Examples of government functions in this area include helping disabled persons and elderly individuals remain or become self-sufficient; increasing the productivity of adults by supporting programs that encourage volunteerism, especially among the elderly; providing support to programs that train adults to become better parents so that their children are more likely to become responsible, productive members of society instead of participants in antisocial behavior; and sponsoring children's programs that address physical health, mental health, socialization, and education and training.[2]

The Structural/Governmental View. Communities of people have historically united "to create facilities and services . . . impossible for individuals to provide for themselves" (Grace 1995, 3). Programs that meet the basic needs of the community—such as public safety, housing, education, and water and sanitation services—are commonly acknowledged as primary responsibilities of the community acting together through its government. The formation of nonprofit agencies is a means of providing other services basic to the needs of the community while partially relieving government of its responsibility. The government has no legal responsibility for helping to sustain these nonprofit services. When the choice to do so is made, the community's decision makers must be convinced both of the need and effectiveness for such services. The interest of the community is served, through private donations and public taxes, when *needed* service provision is sustained, when service delivery is *effective,* and when service provision is more *cost-effective* than when offered through government agencies.

The Humane Perspective. The humane perspective stands in sharp contrast to the other two approaches in the conceptual framework. This perspective "involves basic societal values about governmental actions and funding support for meeting the needs of groups within the society, based on *compassion and empathy* for those in need" (Grace 1995, 4, italics added). This type of compassionate response is usually couched in terms of humane values and the desirability of responding in acute crisis situations. Examples of programs that traditionally receive funding priority under this view of the conceptual framework are those that provide for basic human needs such as food, shelter, clothing, or health care.[3] The action of many local governments to meet such needs is often undertaken because such response is seen as a compassionate, moral responsibility rather than as a legal duty.

The fundamental benefit of the conceptual framework is that it forces an examination of the proper role of government in providing the range of services desired by a community. It also promotes democratic action in the consideration of community-wide values. However, the conceptual framework is limited in its ability to fulfill the promise of democratic decision making because it is not conducive to citizen participation; instead, the discussion tends to be limited to the political elite who have the greatest voice in the community and its decision-making processes. In addition, the lack of ability or willingness of political elites to articulate and consider program and service trade-offs, which is enhanced by current institutional structures (Peterson, Rabe, and Wong 1986), makes it difficult to engage in a meaningful, deliberative process that carefully assesses the underlying purpose for government service provision.

The Performance Framework

Performance frameworks use organization and clarification of accomplishment criteria to advance decision making. This type of approach gives primary emphasis to the systematic measurement of outcomes as they reflect desired results, rather than a traditional focus on inputs and processes as a means to prioritize funding choices (the Government Performance and Results Act of 1993 and the Arizona Governor's Office of Strategic Planning and Budgeting [1995] are examples at the federal and state level, respectively). A performance framework clarifies and simplifies prioritization and decision making by providing a method of identifying and analyzing multiple variables (e.g., goals, programs, values) and promoting a common basis for decision making. Five ideas support the performance framework. The first idea is that most people make decisions based on personal and professional background, experiences, and preferences for abstract concepts (deLeon 1995). The second idea is that the overall goal is to minimize the negative impact and maximize the positive benefit of decisions. The third point is that the choice of measurements can reflect process and/or product. The fourth is that indicators should be specific and measurable. The fifth assumption is that it is important to maximize analytic skill and minimize the potential for political manipulation.

Table 7.1

Design Principles for Effective Performance Measurement Systems

Formulating a clear, coherent mission, strategy, and objectives;
Developing an explicit measurement strategy;
Involving key users in the design and development phase;
Rationalizing the programmatic structure to ground measurement;
Developing multiple sets of measures for multiple users, as necessary;
Considering program and systems clients throughout the process;
Providing sufficient detail for a clear picture of performance;
Periodically reviewing and revising the measurement system;
Accounting for complexities; and
Avoiding excessive aggregation of information.

Source: Adapted from Kravchuk, R.S., and Schack, R.W. (1996), p. 357.

Requirements for appropriate performance measurement of government services are threefold. First, decision makers (i.e., administrators, analysts, funders) must understand the real nature of these delivery systems; for example, the services provided are clearly defined, reliable, and of high quality. Second, they must be willing to agree on strategic objectives (outcomes), provide incentives to influence each organization's behavior to be objective- and performance-based, and evaluate each program on the degree to which it achieves the outcomes. Third, performance measurement data must be properly collected, analyzed, and clearly presented. All these requirements must be met if the performance framework is to inform decision makers.[4] In using this framework, it is critical that relationships between government and the private sector are adequately and effectively managed and that local government monitor performance.[5]

Kravchuk and Schack (1996) offer a set of design principles for effective performance measurement (see Table 7.1). Using these principles, a fairly simple ranking process has been developed to assist in the prioritization process. Unlike other decision-making aids that rely on complicated quantitative analysis, the strategy suggested here is based on creation of a utility scale to establish a matrix of preferences and orderings and to evaluate alternatives. The result is a prioritization ordering of alternatives useful for making funding decisions.

The process involves seven steps:

1. Identify decision alternatives (e.g., organizations or services being considered for funding).
2. Build consensus on attributes for evaluation (e.g., organization mission, program objectives, operation areas).
3. Identify explicit factors for evaluating attributes (e.g., value criteria, performance measures).
4. Establish a utility scale (e.g., a 1–3, 1.0, or 1–5 point scale).

Table 7.2

The Performance Framework Matrix for Prioritizing Funding to Organizations

| | Organizations | | | | | |
	A	B	C	D	E	Total
General climate for services						
Service need	.03	.01	.02	.03	.01	1.0
Service importance to community	.02	.02	.02	.02	.02	1.0
Duplication	.00	.00	.04	.04	.02	1.0
Service quality	.02	.02	.02	.02	.02	1.0
Target population	.04	.01	.02	.03	.00	1.0
Reputation						
Administrative capacity	.02	.02	.02	.02	.01	1.0
Fiscal accountability	.02	.03	.02	.01	.03	1.0
Programmatic accountability	.02	.02	.03	.02	.01	1.0
Staff quality	.02	.02	.01	.02	.03	1.0
Clientele support	.02	.02	.01	.02	.03	1.0
Use of performance-based budgeting	.02	.02	.02	.01	.03	1.0
Maintain prior funding level	Yes	No	Yes	Yes	Yes	
Utility totals	.23	.19	.23	.24	.21	

5. Determine relative weights for each attribute and factor (e.g., .00 to .09). If the utility scale used is 1.0, a number is placed in each cell and the total of all numbers across each row should equal 1.0.

6. Calculate total utility for each decision alternative.

7. Prioritize according to descending order of decision alternatives' totals.

The effectiveness index may rely either on weighting specific program measure indicators according to presumed relative importance or on calculating total scores of factor values among various decision alternatives. Both procedures have inherent difficulties related to subjectivity, the potential multiplicity of alternatives, and uneven dimensions of program performance. However, the latter method is advantaged in its simplicity and potential for defusing conflict.

When performing the analysis, program objectives and criteria are cross-referenced with organizations. The criteria are related to ideas of organizational capability and competency. Organizations being considered for funding are listed horizontally, and criteria are listed vertically (see Table 7.2).

The example provided in Table 7.2 assumes that funding decisions should be prioritized according to four attributes and a determination concerning whether each organization is willing to keep next year's request at the current fiscal year's funding level.[6] The attributes are as follows:

1. the general climate or market for an organization's services (i.e., the demonstrated need for services, importance of services to the community, the target population(s) being served, and the existence or duplication of services by other providers);

2. the professional reputation of the organization (related to the organization's ad-

ministrative capacity, fiscal and programmatic accountability for service delivery, and staff quality);

3. clientele support; and

4. use of performance-based budgeting (including percentage of administrative costs, unit costs of major services provided, and realistic agency goals).

As can be seen in Table 7.2, the utility totals for each organization being considered range from .19 to .24. Based on this example, the end result is that the sum total value of services provided by a group of agencies depends on three factors: (1) the value of the services provided by each member agency, (2) the impact of other agencies' values on each agency, and (3) the perceived percentage contribution of each agency's value to the total. Given current funding constraints, one obvious choice is that funding will be distributed to agencies that keep requests for funding at prior-year levels and that have the highest utility total. Therefore, in Table 7.2, funding prioritizations would be arranged as follows: organizations D, A, C, E, and none to B.

The strength of the performance framework approach lies in its versatility. It can be constructed with simplicity or complexity, and it can be used with individuals and in groups.[7] Examining fewer rather than a larger number of decision alternatives at any one time is preferable. In the case of a large number of programs to consider, it would make sense to construct multiple matrices and put like agencies on the same matrix. In addition, the performance framework strives to identify desired results to be used as the benchmark for judging the achievements of government programs. The primary drawback of this approach is that it is difficult to quantify the outcomes or results of government programs, which has often led to an emphasis on input and workload measures in traditional decision-making processes. Part of the historical reason for why this weakness has been difficult to overcome is the lack of resources—both trained staff to evaluate and modify existing performance measures and automated performance monitoring systems (Affholter 1994). The lack of automated systems has also contributed to the fact that there are few uniform measurement metrics (as demonstrated by the multiple definitions of participants in workforce development programs) and data collection techniques (Wholey 1989).

A drawback of this approach is the tendency to rely on quantitative analysis as the sole decision-making tool. It is but one part of rational decision making. Other important components that should be considered in tandem with the performance matrix are expert knowledge, shared communication, and direct experience with organizational management and program development (Kravchuk and Schack 1996). Of course, undue confidence should not be placed in rational decision-making techniques. Any approach to prioritization must be able to adapt to the vagaries of the political process embedded in governmental decision making (Chelimsky 1995).

Emergent Approaches for Prioritizing Services

The previous section described different methods that have been used for establishing priorities in governmental service provision. In this section, an emergent framework—the reevaluation framework—is introduced. This framework examines the fit between service needs and funding choices and goal accomplishment. It is a preferred approach because it capitalizes on the benefits of other approaches. For example, it merges the emphasis on the political process described in incremental budgetary theories with the economic principles of utility maximization present in the conceptual framework and the results orientation of decision making under the performance framework. After an introduction to the reevaluation framework and the two approaches within its structure, this section concludes with an examination of the relative strengths and weaknesses of each of the approaches presented.

The Reevaluation Framework

A reevaluation framework uses new or alternative methods to alter or realign whole systems. When successfully employed, this approach can be used to skillfully mesh service needs and funding choices. Although much remains unknown regarding how federal policy change affects outcomes in communities, we do know that changing funding relationships and patterns inevitably involves changing value(s). Future methods and processes that examine the fit between service needs and funding choices are also likely to lead to a different way of thinking about what is important and how to accomplish desired goals.

Funding choice decisions are fundamentally related to what we value. All government services are value areas and, as such, changing funding in these areas creates changes in values. That is, an increase in funding is likely to lead to an increase in value for the organization and the community. In addition, an increase or decrease in funding for one organization (or set of organizations) affects other organizations. It also affects the overall budget or value of the funder(s). Therefore, two important questions to be asked are, "How does a change in dollars (or value) in any one organization affect other organizations providing like or related services?" and "How does a change in dollars (or value) in one service area affect the total dollars (or value) of the city government (or the community)?"

How local governments respond to federal budget cuts; how providers respond to proposed reductions; and how changes affect service access, price, and competition are key concerns. Decision makers ultimately choose among three basic alternatives related to funding choices. They can (1) maintain funding to the existing set of agencies, (2) increase funding to these or other agencies, or (3) reduce funding to the existing set of agencies. The first two options are obviously desirable but may not be feasible. Should this be true and the third option is indicated, it is possible to reduce spending on government services without cutting the delivery of these services. Chernick and Reschovsky (1995) offer various strategies to reduce spending without cutting service delivery. One common element of these strategies is that they each seek to improve the administrative structure of the program through evaluation and budgetary techniques.

Within the reevaluation framework are two different approaches that could assist in the establishment of priorities among competing programs: value assessment and service integration. A description of each is provided next.

The Value Assessment Approach. The value assessment approach is concerned with how a funding change (increase or decrease) to one or more agencies (within a set of agencies) is thought to likely alter the value (or benefit) of services that agency can provide. In addition, this approach is concerned with how funding changes to individual agencies are likely to affect the total perceived value provided to the community by all agencies. This strategy recognizes the difficulty in quantifying the relationship between budgets and outcomes, particularly when the outcomes, their indicators, and valid measurements of those indicators are not quantifiable. It also recognizes that, even though outcomes may be quantifiable, the relationship between those measures and their value to the community is also difficult to establish. The term *value* is, in the balance, a human perception rather than a measurement, and determining the relative value of the outcomes for different agencies is the result of education, experience, personal needs, and perceptions of the community as a whole.

The existence of two facts underlies this approach. First, for a given budget level for a fiscal year and in the absence of executive office guidance to the contrary, an agency will spend nearly 100 percent of its budget. By spending roughly 100 percent of its allocated budget, an agency delivers 100 percent of the services it can and, thus, provides 100 percent of the value it can (within budget constraints).[8] Second, within a limited percent budget range, there is a linear relationship between dollars provided and services delivered; that is, the value per dollar (value/dollar) for each agency. Simply put, with more money, an agency can provide more services and create more value. Conversely, an agency with less money can provide fewer services and create less value (Bock, personal communication, July 1996).

Determining the change in value resulting from various budget allocation scenarios is not a simple mathematical process.[9] Even so, it is possible to determine the value of services provided by individual agencies as well as the total value of services delivered among all agencies, the impact of funding changes on the values of a set of agencies, and the relative contribution of each agency's value to the overall service delivery system in the community.

Using value assessment criteria to evaluate the impact of funding changes on the services and value of various agencies within a community can lead to better understanding of the interconnections and interdependencies of the service delivery system among funders, agencies, and elected officials. The method recommended to facilitate this type of deliberation would prioritize according to evaluated participation in a three-step process.

- First, a coordinated coming together of service providers, elected officials, and program clientele is used to analyze the current system (in terms of overlaps, communications, referrals, case management, etc.) and to identify service gaps and capacities.
- Second, a set of focus groups or electronic meetings are held to conduct a perceived impact evaluation related to potential changes (increases or reductions) in funding within the community.
- Third, ongoing commitments of affected agencies are made to form resource collaboratives. Such collaboratives would be expected to have affiliation agreements aimed at sharing resources and using outcome-based evaluations.

Should this approach be desirable to local government, attention, over time, would have to be paid to four areas. First, an effective information and data system to enhance collaboration and integration would need to be in place. Second, service providers would have to develop new ways of working with clients and each other. Third, a method for resolving conflicts among agencies would need to be ensured. Finally, funding mechanisms appropriate for resource collaboratives would have to be developed. Despite such development effort, the strength of this approach lies in its potential to bring providers together in a community over the long term.

The Service Integration Approach. Service integration is a process for developing an integrated framework within which ongoing programs can be incorporated and improved to make services better available within existing commitments and resources (Yessian 1995). Recent changes in federal rules and regulations better allow service integration efforts that improve management and delivery of services. In recent years, service integration has gained the interest of decision makers in both the federal government and private foundations.

Service integration models can bring needed order to a fragmented system and can ensure that efforts to improve the community fit together and support resources already in place (Morgan 1995). Effective integration can result in reexamination of core processes, colocation of services (i.e., concentrating a number of services in one place, such as one-stop centers), redesigned funding or management procedures, and job reassignments (Moss 1994). Types of service integration range from small-scale efforts to improve referrals and points of access (e.g., through information/resource and referral centers) to larger scale efforts of organizational realignment and consolidation.

Guidelines for integrating services emphasize the importance of community-based collaboratives and long-term fundamental change (Morgan 1995, 1971; Yessian 1995). General guidance from each of these authors emphasizes the need for linkages between programs that have the target group in mind and are flexible enough to change based on ongoing performance review. In addition, a centralized leadership structure is necessary to pursue sufficient funding and regulatory flexibility while remaining accountable for results in line with those identified in the system's strategic plan. These broad guidelines can be coupled with other approaches to conduct value assessment or to achieve effective service integration. The keys to using the evaluation approach successfully are to develop collaborative actions requiring the involvement of key actors, the media, and public input into the planning process; implementing a monitoring and data-collection mechanism; and establishing a method for resolving conflicts.

Both approaches within the reevaluation framework share similarities in terms of reducing duplication, understanding linkages, encouraging collaboration, establishing accountability through performance-based evaluation and funding, and looking at the service system from an eagle-eye[10] vantage point. A primary advantage of this method for establishing priorities is that it encourages a comprehensive and systematic view of both a policy issue and the network of services and providers surrounding the policy issue. An important component of this framework is the consensus-building process necessary to

Table 7.3

Comparative Review of Different Frameworks

Framework	Benefits	Problems
Incremental	Accommodates the politicalness of the prioritization process	No periodic review of entire policy networks; minimally responsive to changes in the environment
Conceptual	Forces an examination of the proper role of environment and consideration of community-wide values	Not conducive to wide-ranging participation, particularly that of citizens
Performance	Identifies desired results and allows for utility ranking of multiples alternatives/ organizations	Difficult to develop uniform, objective quantifications; minimizes the role of the political process
Reevaluation	Establishes priorities based on a comprehensive and systematic view of the policy issue by multiple stakeholders	Lack of dedicated resources for staff trained in needs assessment and outcome evaluation techniques

identify the results desired. In conclusion, the benefits of reevaluation are twofold: This approach encourages collaboration of a wide range of stakeholders, making the process more democratic; it also has the ability to accommodate the politicalness of governmental decision-making processes by linking policy objectives to funding decisions.

Table 7.3 summarizes the major benefits and problems evident in each of the four approaches to establishing the priorities that have been discussed in this article. After reviewing this table, it can be concluded that the reevaluation framework offers a fresh approach to the task of analyzing competing needs for government services when faced with constrained resources. This approach offers the potential to minimize problems evident in other approaches, such as the difficulty of involving multiple participants in a discussion of policy trade-offs or the overwhelming complexity of comparing measures of results across dissimilar governmental services. And, as described previously in this article, the reevaluation framework uses public input in combination with strategic planning and funding mechanisms to strengthen prioritization decisions in a more cooperative, policy-focused process.

Conclusion and Recommendation

In considering the status of governmental programs in the next two to three years, one thing is evident: Funding is likely to be fragile (Grace 1995). In responding to shifting funding demands, local government faces two interrelated problems. The first problem is attracting alternative funding sources when most citizens are politically unwilling or economically unable to bear the burden of more taxes. The second problem is that previously used methods of establishing funding priorities will not promote decision making on the basis of adherence of deliberate discussions to determine policy priorities.

Decisions regarding future funding and prioritization choices should be made through self-conscious analysis and reflection, considering the likely consequences of different actions. To heighten commitment to services in any functional area of government, it is important to increase collaborative community vehicles to sell investment in these areas and to base funding decisions on sound information and analysis. Three specific recommendations are appropriate.

- First, each organization that provides services should be encouraged to reconsider its mission, eliminate duplication, and coordinate where possible with other organizations of like purpose to retain an appropriate local network of services.
- Second, a public input and strategic planning effort should be undertaken to build and strengthen local resource collaboratives. Such collaboratives are integral to long-term community development and necessary to gain and retain stable and adequate funding for needed services.
- Third, local government should establish a small-group partnership initiative composed of "opinion leaders" and representatives of the community. The primary advantage of this grouping is that it can ensure a minimum winning coalition in decision-making processes. This community council of business and community "partners" should have a cataloguing mechanism through which to create and update current profiles of service needs in their service delivery area and be critically involved in making judgments regarding service delivery development. Building a broad consensus regarding long-range goals and objectives, with a focus on high-value community development and quality outcomes, will create the movement necessary to sustain support for a continuing prioritization, will maximize the potential of positively changing policy, and will minimize the negative impact throughout the community.

The task for deliberation about priorities is twofold: (1) making the local government's self-interest clear by carefully documenting the fiscal linkages among long-term economic development, resource development, funding and service outcomes; and (2) having careful consideration of alternatives to reprioritize services. In the end, choosing a proper framework for programmatic selection decisions and budget allocations is best seen as the beginning rather than the end of a collaborative effort to strengthen the choices regarding the selection of services local governments will provide.

Authors' Note

We gratefully acknowledge Fred Bock and Scott Combs for their comments and assistance in the preparation of this article. The localities that supplied information regarding their strategies in dealing with the elimination of significant federal funds for welfare and health reform are Hillsborough County, Florida; three communities (Calhoun, Muskegon, and St. Clair counties) in Michigan; and two cities (Phoenix and Tempe) in Arizona.

Notes

1. Economic and political aspects are embedded in each of these perspectives.
2. "While some of the programs discussed above can be sustained by volunteers and donations,

many will seek governmental support because of the basic importance of the program functions to the community" (Grace 1995, 3).

3. "The poor frequently elicit a humane response to their need, but in this case people are more cautious about the 'circumstances beyond their control'—often wanting some proof that the persons involved have lost jobs due to economic displacement or lack of educational and technical skills needed in the current marketplace" (Grace 1995, 5).

4. See Kravchuk and Schack, 1996, for a discussion of the challenges and design principles involved in performance measurement.

5. Efforts to reduce the local government workforce risk undermining its performance measure ability. To assure capability in this area, strategic planning should be used to drive cuts and guarantee that cuts fall in the right places.

6. Alternately, funding decisions could be simply based on which organizations meet basic needs and provide essential services, reflect direct benefits to local residents, or indicate precisely how city funds are to be used; all others experience a reduction or are not considered for funding in the next few years.

7. It is often useful for all stakeholders and/or decision makers to initially meet as a group to agree on the items to be cross-referenced and the value weight range to be used. The aggregation of completed matrices is then used to produce a group-based priorities list. The advantages of this course are that it helps limit influences of social pressure and power politics and can enlarge the scope of participation (e.g., to community organizations or advocacy groups).

8. This discussion is simplified to assist in ease of understanding; for example, the argument does not consider the indirect costs for administrative and overhead or service functions that may be assessed to the program. In addition, when considering the "linear relationship" between dollars provided and services delivered, attention must be given to the limits of service provision within existing infrastructures and attempts must be made to calculate the threshold of economies of scale when additional units of services are identified.

9. In theory, it is desirable to have an absolute scale of value, with a quantifiable relationship between the budget of an agency delivering services and the value of the outcomes (but not necessarily the outcomes themselves).

10. See Morgan, 1995, for elaboration on the advantages offered by the eagle-eye (versus organization-centric) approach.

References

Affholter, D.P. (1994). "Outcome Monitoring." In J.S. Wholey, H.P. Hatry, and K.E. Newcomer (eds.), *Handbook of Practical Program Evaluation* (pp. 96–118). San Francisco: Jossey-Bass.

Arizona Governor's Office of Strategic Planning and Budgeting (1995). *Managing for Results: Strategic Planning and Performance Measurement Handbook.* Phoenix, AZ: Author.

Axelrod, D. (1995). *Budgeting for Modern Government* (2nd ed.). New York: St. Martin's Press.

Caiden, N. (1992). "Public Budgeting amidst Uncertainty and Instability." In J.M. Shafritz, and A.C. Hyde (eds.), *Classics of Public Administration* (pp. 485–496). Pacific Grove, CA: Brooks/Cole.

Chelimsky, E. (1995). "The Political Environment of Evaluation and What It Means for the Development of the Field." *Evaluation Practice,* 16, 215–225.

Chernick, H., and Reschovsky, A. (1995). *Urban Fiscal Problems: Coordinating Actions Among Governments.* The LaFollette Policy Report, 7(1), 8–13.

deLeon, L. (1995). "Policy Analysis and Policy-making: Never the Twain Shall Meet?" *Public Administration Quarterly,* 19(1), 104–125.

Government Performance and Results Act of 1993, Pub. L.N0.103–62, 107 Stat. 286 (1993).

Grace, J.M. (1995). *Philosophy of Public Philanthropy: A Conceptual Framework* (Report prepared for the Tempe community council). Tempe, AZ: Cultural and Human Service Agency Funding.

Kravchuk, R.S., and Schack, R.W. (1996). "Designing Effective Performance-measurement Systems under the Government Performance and Results Act of 1993." *Public Administration Review,* 56, 348–358.

Mikesell, J.L. (1995). *Fiscal Administration: Analysis and Applications for the Public Sector* (4th ed.). Orlando, FL: Harcourt Brace.

Morgan, G.C. (1971). *Evaluation of the 4-C Concept.* Washington, DC: Day Care and Child Development Council of America.

Morgan, G.C. (1995). "Collaborative Models of Service Integration." *Child Welfare,* 74, 1329–1342.

Moss, M. (1994). "From Reengineering to Service Integration." *Nursing Management,* 25(8), SE-80E.

Peterson, P.E., Rabe, G.B., and Wong, K.K. (1986). *When Federalism Works.* Washington, DC: Brookings Institution.

Wholey, J.S. (1989). "Introduction: How Evaluation Can Improve Agency and Program Performance." In J.S. Wholey, K.E. Newcomer, and Associates (eds.), *Improving Government Performance* (pp. 1–12). San Francisco: Jossey-Bass.

Wildavsky, A. (1988). *The New Politics of the Budgetary Process.* Glenview, IL: Scott, Foresman.

Yessian, M.R. (1995). "Learning from Experience: Integrating Human Services." *Public Welfare,* 53(3), 34–39.

PART 3

WHAT ARE THE PROPER GOALS AND PRIORITIES OF ADMINISTRATIVE LEADERS?

Setting goals and establishing priorities logically follows the assessment function (which was discussed in part 2). After surveying organizational strengths and weaknesses, and reviewing the constraints that they must work within, administrative leaders must decide what they want to accomplish and prioritize those goals. However, as with the assessment function, administrative leaders will quickly discover that setting goals and establishing priorities is far more complex than initially meets the eye. If goals and priorities are hastily established based upon superficial data collection and consideration, the most important function that leaders perform—decision making—has been frittered away. In addition, prioritizing goals can be quite controversial.

In many ways all decision-making processes, from trivial choices to the most important selection of goals, are in a psychological "black box." It is impossible to know exactly how the mind processes the multitude of facts and values that underlie the simplest of decisions. Nonetheless, it is easy to point to coherent decision-making processes that substantially increase the likelihood of good decisions. Three key factors are commonly identified in good goal selection. First, it is difficult to set good goals if a proper organizational assessment has not occurred. For the veteran leader this may occur through experience, but for the new or the ongoing leader facing a rapidly shifting environment, it may mean a formal process and an allocation of significant personal and/or organizational resources. Second, good goal setting requires an appraisal of alternative goals and strategies and a comparison of their relative strengths and weaknesses. Organizational goals are too important not to test assumptions with rigor. Third, and related to the first two factors, is the allocation of the necessary time and energy to create goals that are lucid, coherent, and compelling. Among the most important motivational forces in the organization are goals that are so clear that they need little or no explanation. Coherence is obtained by ensuring that goals are not inconsistent with one another, or too numerous. Goals that are compelling are emotionally satisfying to employees because they point out the fundamental significance of the work. Because the public sector is frequently assigned problematic areas (e.g., child welfare) and required to enforce conflicting values (e.g., economy, efficiency, due process, and compassion) simultaneously, it is generally an even more difficult process than in the private sector.

Making this process more difficult still is the uncertain role of *administrative* leaders (Heifetz 1994). In what ways and how involved should non-elected leaders be in the goal-setting process? Since the earliest days of the republic this debate has been enjoined in different guises. Alexander Hamilton fought with the anti-Federalists about the power and size of the executive branch. At the turn of the twentieth century, Progressives championed the idea of substantial, if technical, decision making being made by professionals (with the guidance of authoritative laws and rules) who were immune from political "interference and corruption." The Finer-Friedrich debate of the early 1940s recrystallized the discussion of administrative discretion in an era when the role of government was expanding at all levels. In the 1990s the academic literature revisited the debate about the propriety of "entrepreneurial" behavior by administrative leaders in the public sector, a taste of which is excerpted here (see, for example, Piotrowski and Rosenbloom 2002; deLeon and Denhardt 2000).

Because of the complexity of the topic and the different perspectives of various writers, five types of questions are identified below. Authors not only emphasize different questions in their analyses, but in some cases provide profoundly different answers. Those questions are:

- What is a goal?
- Who is the decision maker?
- Where do the decision makers' cues come from?
- What should the administrative leaders' level of focus be? and
- How much responsibility for incremental change, process innovation, and system transformation should the administrative leader have?

What Is a Goal?

A goal is something that a person or group wants to achieve. Goals for individuals can range from something as simple as items on a dayplanner list to lifelong aspirations. Goals for organizations can range from overarching purposes embedded in authorizing legislation that affect millions of people and cost billions of dollars to complete, to small projects that affect a handful of people and cost little more than an investment of time. Goals can be as clear-cut as following the directions of a cooking recipe or as complex as incorporating the ambiguity of maintaining peace among structurally competitive constituents. This range of response, however, begs for a more sophisticated response to the question than that provided by the dictionary.

From strategic planning we derive useful taxonomic hierarchies such as goals, objectives, strategies, plans, and measures. At the broadest level, the goal is the overarching purpose to be achieved. Objectives break the goal down into its constituent parts, or subgoals. Strategies are the general means by which an objective is implemented. Plans include the details of operationalization. Measures keep track of progress toward goals at various levels. A city transportation division's goal may be to enhance city transportation. The objectives may be to provide a system of transportation that is efficient, safe, economical, and environmentally appropriate. The strategies may be incorporated into the missions of the various departments: streets, public transportation, and airports. The streets department has plans for new roads, road maintenance, road signs, and so on. Although this type of planning hierarchy is ubiquitous and helps to answer the question at one level, for administrative leaders it raises several very challenging questions. Are overarching goals strictly policy decisions that administrative leaders should eschew being involved in formulating and making? What is the exact cut-off between higher-level decision plans that are of a policy nature and those of a lower level that are clearly technical and administrative?

Highly related to the issue of goal specificity is the size of the system involved. It is much easier to divide policy and administrative functions with the elected county official who personally supervises a small office and reports directly to a board of supervisors, than it is to do so in a multibillion dollar agency such as the Department of Defense. Clearly general increases or decreases in appropriations are policy issues. Clearly review of promotions is an administrative matter. But to what degree is missile selection a technical matter and does it become a political matter if manufacturing locations are considered? To what degree should the military have a say in base closings? How involved should Congress be in designating the rules for the wearing of religious paraphernalia and how involved should the president become regarding gender and racial discrimination scandals? How active should the military be in proposing preemptive strikes, undeclared wars, and state-building initiatives? In war, at what point do tactical decisions in the field take precedence over the more general orders issued through the authorized hierarchy?

Finally, there is the issue of the type of goal or the goal context. Some goals are highly concrete and specific due to the nature of the goal environment. For example, the goals to be achieved in building administrative offices, the establishment of authorized personnel levels (the single largest operational expense in government), and the regulations of large programs are generally relatively well defined. The goal-setting process can be systematically surveyed in advance and relatively few major surprises should occur. However, some goals are by their nature vague, poorly understood, or consistently in dispute so that the policy arm of government finds it neither politically expedient nor efficient to specify them in concrete terms. Such is the case, for example, with environmental protection, in which standards shift; natural resource management, in which constituent conflicts are inherent; and economic development, in which fiscal nimbleness is crucial.

In the four articles in this section, the authors take a variety of positions regarding goal definition. One author posits that all decisions reflect goals and have policy ramifications. Some point to the complexity of defining goals and the difficulty of making clear policy-administration distinctions. Another identifies conditions that require a healthy dose of administrative discretion, and considers the liabilities of an activist approach.

Who Is the Decision Maker?

A second important preliminary question has to do with the identification of the decision maker. Some of the authors do not stipulate the decision makers clearly. Thus, their discussions are curiously abstract and overgeneralized. Distinctions between legislative and executive branch elected officials are not minor, however. Appointed officials range from those selected largely on ideological grounds to those who have moved up from merit systems. Merit employees range from bureau chiefs to frontline supervisors. The types of responsibilities vary enormously among these various types of leaders, as do the requirements for their effectiveness (Jacques 1989; Hunt 1996).

Only when one has a clear sense of these two questions—the nature of the goal and who the decision maker is—can one really interpret the position on the next three, sometimes controversial, issues.

Where Do the Decision Makers' Cues Come From?

In the public sector, cues for decision makers in making decisions, no matter whether they are elected, appointed, or merit, can come from a variety of sources. Particularly important sources are the laws and ordinances enacted, and the regulations and rules flowing from them. No matter whether they are of high quality or not, laws and their ilk have the benefits of being the result of an authorized process, open to public input and review, and generally providing a level of consistency in the administrative mechanisms charged with implementation. Laws and rules also have numerous failings. They may lead to planning rigidity and fallible implementation. They can lead to challenges of interpretation requiring judicial intervention. Of course sometimes laws are purposely vague in their directions, thereby delegating great authority down the administrative hierarchy.

Another source of cues is the voters, whose macro-level preferences are a vital element of the democratic mix. Such cues come from voting results after listening to different platforms, referenda, and indirectly through the people's voice, the media. Certainly this is an authoritative source and is often rightly interpreted as a "mandate." Nonetheless, cues from voters suffer from a variety of drawbacks. First, voting is a blunt instrument. Voters have neither the expertise, the time, nor the interest to be directly managing government through electoral mechanisms. Further, like all groups, even voters have biases, such as in the corrections area, in which voters want extremely high service volumes but where, if left on their own, voters would not fund that service at constitutionally required levels. Finally, the same applies to the people's elected representatives, who are generally walled off from all but policy-level hiring decisions and from most procurement decisions for fear of nepotism, fraud, and cronyism.

A sub-element of voters is constituent or special-interest groups. Special-interest groups do represent the public interest in a variety of ways. They represent the interests of those who are either directly affected or care strongly enough to be involved. The actions of competing special-interest groups serve to ensure that the level of debate is thorough and robust. When there is no counterbalancing side, however, the weaknesses of special interests bleed through. Among these are extreme self-interest with the concomitant lack of concern for the common good, the ability to form iron triangles with select politicians and bureaus, and the strong tendency to resist system-wide solutions as they fight for special treatment.

A last source of cues in the public sector is the market itself. Market incentives have been gaining favor in public-sector environments in the last twenty years: vouchers, contracting out, and outright privatization are some of the more common variants. Markets are strong at maintaining dynamic systems through a balanced mix of micro- and macro-level incentives. Nonetheless, the market often does a poor job of providing cues in many areas for which the public sector is responsible, such as messy, nearly intractable social problems. The market, if not carefully supervised, is prone to distortion and even outright corruption.

All four of these sources of cues are essentially external to leaders, but leaders themselves can be considered a final source of cues about what decisions to make. Leaders have legitimacy in this regard when they have two key characteristics, expertise and virtue. We want decision makers to be knowledgeable and we want to be able to trust that the decisions they reach are in the public interest. Reliance on virtue means that leaders can use their professionalism, enhance their involvement, and increase customization. The problems with relying excessively on virtue are also well known. Excessive power (i.e., excessive discretion) all too frequently leads to self-dealing, distortions, policy and administrative fragmentation, and inconsistency.

The selection of authors in part 3 promotes different mixes and emphases regarding the goals and priorities of administrative leaders. One author is loath to acknowledge any sources except those coming from law and voters. Another argues that constituent input must be substantial. Other authors focus on market cues in public-sector settings.

What Should Administrative Leaders Focus On?

To effectively allocate their time, leaders must prioritize what is most important to them and "size-up" their situations. Does the leader want to spend the bulk of her/his time on technical issues such as monitoring, operations planning, informing, or problem solving? This is called a results focus in the current popular literature, and a production orientation, task orientation, or initiating structure in the academic literature. Leaders can also choose to emphasize the support and development of those who actually do the work—followers. In organizational settings this requires training, motivating, listening and coaching, team building, and so on. In the academic literature this is called consideration, relationship behavior, or a people orientation. A third aspect of leaders' jobs has to do with organizational responsibility: scanning the environment, networking, articulating and renewing the vision of the organization, transforming the culture, and so on. Of course, leaders invariably perform all of these functions and in the ideal they should perform them all—and equally well. However, given the scarce time and energy that leaders have, the relative focus that they choose can be extremely important. In fact, there is a good deal of evidence to support the notion that as the organization matures the changes are significant enough so that often different types of leaders are needed. This question is pursued more fully and directly in parts 6, 7, and 8.

None of the authors directly addresses this question at length, but indirectly their relative positions are implied. The first author clearly emphasizes the technical role for administrative leaders, even at the executive level. All the other authors acknowledge that leaders have to address all of these roles. The last author discusses what environmental situations would tend to require different foci in a financial context.

How Much Responsibility for Change Should Administrative Leaders Have?

Although many commentators place the change function as among the most crucial and distinctive leadership responsibilities, the question is very much complicated in the public sector. Ideological positions vary with regard to the proper role of the different decision makers in the system. A constitutional purist might argue that only duly elected officials, and their appointed representatives, should make any substantial decisions with regard to public resources or authority. One of the authors in part 3 does take this position.

All the other authors take a more pragmatic approach to the question because administrative realities make such a posture unrealistic in the extreme. The messy nature of administrative realities, the nature of the work itself, the need for change based on the environment, and the structure of implementation mandates are all reasons that lead these authors to ascribe a more discretionary role to the administrative decision maker.

Review of the Selections in Part 3

The Herman Finer piece, "Administrative Responsibility in Democratic Government" (1940), is a classic assertion by a political scientist of the primacy of the electoral function over the administrative function. It is a nearly perfect expression of the politics-administration dichotomy in vogue in the Progressive era. Although still popular as an ideological position and as an ideal to strive for in some circles, it is largely invalidated as an accurate description of administrative realities.

Carl J. Bellone and George F. Goerl, in "Reconciling Entrepreneurship and Democracy" (1992), tackle the value issues related to entrepreneurial administrative behavior. They begin by discussing the evolving nature of the state, and the need for flexibility. Next, and very importantly, they discuss the tensions between the democratic values of accountability, citizen participation, transparency, and concern for long-term good, and the entrepreneurial values of autonomy, vision, secrecy, and risk taking. While acknowledging the liabilities of entrepreneurial values in administrative settings, they argue that these values should not be dismissed out of hand given their potential benefits and the availability of a variety of accountability mechanisms. Although not reprinted here, even their moderate position regarding entrepreneurial values has been much disputed in the literature.

The last two selections emphasize more concrete examples. In James M. Banovetz's "City Managers: Will They Reject Policy Leadership?" (1994), the focus is on city managers, who are appointed by city councils to be administrative leaders. Like Bellone and Goerl, Banovetz emphasizes the historical shift in expectations not only of city managers, but of their elected masters as well. That is, city councils in larger cities increasingly have full-time staff, spend greater time doing the job, and are elected on a narrow rather than a broad platform. Using survey data, Banovetz notes that the acknowledged policy function for city managers grew in the last half of the twentieth century until, in 1989, 56 percent "reported that the policy role was the most important for success in their jobs," up from 22 percent twenty-four years earlier. However, he concludes that this may be the high-water mark of the policy function, with future city managers serving in less-visible and less-active policy roles. His table on the evolution of perceptions about government and governmental leadership is particularly useful in the context of thinking about public-sector goal setting.

The last article, by Kevin P. Kearns, "Accountability and Entrepreneurial Public Management" (1995), looks at goal setting in the financial context. He uses the fascinating case study of the financial debacle in the Orange County Treasurer's Office as the means to tease out different types of systems needs and organizational responses. Robert Citron, the Orange County treasurer, provides the perfect example of the liabilities of entrepreneurial values gone amuck. To analyze the different types of situations that can be encountered in the public sector, Kearns sets up a four-cell matrix. One axis is determined by the need for explicit versus implicit accountability. Explicit accountability means that defined rules or standards can be used, whereas implicit accountability means that more discretion and professional judgment is called for. A second axis identifies reactive versus proactive responses. Sometimes the administrative system can afford to take corrective actions after the fact and at other times it is incumbent upon administrators to determine future directions or take action to prevent future problems. The resultant accountability cells are, from the most technical and specific to the least so: compliance accountability, negotiated accountability, advocacy accountability, and entrepreneurial accountability. They argue that no model is inherently superior; rather, it depends upon the nature of the work, the environment, and the conscious values of those designing the system.

References

deLeon, Linda, and Robert Denhardt. 2000. "The Political Theory of Reinvention." *Public Administration Review* 60 (2): 89–97.
Heifetz, Ronald A. 1994. *Leadership Without Easy Answers*. Cambridge, MA: Belknap Press.
Hunt, James G. 1996. *Leadership: A New Synthesis*. Newbury Park, CA: Sage.
Jacques, Elliott. 1989. *Requisite Organization*. Arlington, VA: Cason Hall.
Piotrowski, Suzanne J., and David H. Rosenbloom. 2002. "Nonmission-Based Values in Results-Oriented Public Management: The Case of Freedom of Information." *Public Administration Review* 62 (6): 643–57.

CHAPTER 8

ADMINISTRATIVE RESPONSIBILITY IN DEMOCRATIC GOVERNMENT

HERMAN FINER

Administrative responsibility is not less important to democratic government than administrative efficiency; it is even a contributor to efficiency in the long run. Indeed, it is tempting to argue that the first requisite is responsibility, and if that is properly instituted efficiency will follow. Elaboration of this point should be unnecessary in the era and under the stress of the events which now make up our days.

To the subject of administrative responsibility, Professor Carl J. Friedrich has made several interesting and sagacious contributions,[1] and he deserves our gratitude for having reintroduced its discussion among primary problems. Yet these contributions have by no means said the last word on the subject. Indeed, he has put forward a number of propositions which must arouse earnest dissent. In answer to an earlier contribution of his I said,

> It is most important clearly to distinguish a "sense of duty" or a "sense of responsibility" from the fact of responsibility, that is, effective answerability. I am anxious to emphasize once again that the notion of *subjective* responsibility (in my definition of it), whether as intellectual integrity or general loyalty to the spirit and purpose of one's function, is of very great importance in maintaining the level of efficiency. It is stimulating and sustaining, like the will to believe. But we must first of all be perfectly clear about its nature in order that we may not burke the question of whether or not such responsibility is sufficient to keep a civil service wholesome and zealous, and how far, in its own nature, it is likely to break down so that political responsibility must be introduced as the adamant monitor of the public services. For the first commandment is, Subservience.[2]

My chief difference with Professor Friedrich was and is my insistence upon distinguishing responsibility as an arrangement of correction and punishment even up to dismissal both of politicians and officials, while he believed and believes in reliance upon responsibility as a sense of responsibility, largely unsanctioned, except by deference or loyalty to professional standards. I still maintain my belief while in a more recent article[3] Professor Friedrich still maintains his, so far as I am able to follow his argument. I propose therefore to treat the subject in two divisions, first, a more extended version of my own beliefs and, second, a critical examination of his article.

Excerpted from *Public Administration Review*, vol. 1, no. 4 (1941): 335–50. Copyright © 1941 by American Society for Public Administration. Reprinted with permission.

I

Most of the things I have to say are extremely elementary, but since it has been possible for a writer of eminence to discount their significance I may be forgiven for reaffirming them. The modern state is concerned with a vast sphere of services of a mixed nature. They are repressive, controlling, remedial, and go as far as the actual conduct of industrial, commercial, and agricultural operations. The state, which used to be negative—that is to say which was concerned to abolish its own earlier interventions and reduce such controls as ancient and medieval polity had caused it to undertake—has for some decades now abandoned laissez faire and can be called ministrant. Its work ranges over practically every sector of modern individual and social interest, from sheer police work, in the sense of apprehending and punishing assaults on person, peace, and property, to the actual ownership and management of utilities. I need not dwell on this point further, nor upon the range and detailed intensity of the state's operation, nor the large percentage of men and women among the gainfully occupied population it employs in the strategic positions in society. The weight and immensity and domination of this behemoth, for our good as well as for our control, are well known to all of us. But academic persons are less subject to the power of the colossus than the worker, the economic entrepreneur, the sick and the needy of all kinds. The academic person is therefore likely to regard the weight of the administrator's hand as not needing to be stayed or directed by the public custodian.

Are the servants of the public to decide their own course, or is their course of action to be decided by a body outside themselves? My answer is that the servants of the public are not to decide their own course; they are to be responsible to the elected representatives of the public, and these are to determine the course of action of the public servants to the most minute degree that is technically feasible. Both of these propositions are important: the main proposition of responsibility, as well as the limitation and auxiliary institutions implied in the phrase, "that is technically feasible." This kind of responsibility is what democracy means; and though there may be other devices which provide "good" government, I cannot yield on the cardinal issue of democratic government. In the ensuing discussion I have in mind that there is the dual problem of securing the responsibility of officials, (1) through the courts and disciplinary controls within the hierarchy of the administrative departments, and also (2) through the authority exercised over officials by responsible ministers based on sanctions exercised by the representative assembly. In one way or another this dual control obtains in all the democratic countries, though naturally its purposes and procedures vary from country to country.

What are we to mean by responsibility? There are two definitions. First, responsibility may mean that X is accountable for Y *to* Z. Second, responsibility may mean an inward personal sense of moral obligation. In the first definition the essence is the externality of the agency or persons to whom an account is to be rendered, and it can mean very little without that agency having authority over X, determining the lines of X's obligation and the terms of its continuance or revocation. The second definition puts the emphasis on the conscience of the agent, and it follows from the definition that if he commits an error it is an error by his own conscience, and that the punishment of the agent will be merely the twinges thereof. The one implies public execution; the other hara-kiri. While reliance on an official's conscience may be reliance on an official's accomplice, in democratic administration all parties, official, public, and Parliament, will breathe more freely if a censor is in the offing. . . .

Democratic systems are chiefly embodiments of the first mentioned notion of responsibility, and dictatorial systems chiefly of the second. . . .

Democratic governments, in attempting to secure the responsibility of politicians and officeholders to the people, have founded themselves broadly upon the recognition of three doctrines. First, the mastership of the public, in the sense that politicians and employees are working not for the good of the public in the sense of what the public *needs* but of the *wants* of the public as expressed by the public. Second, recognition that this mastership needs institutions, and particularly the centrality of an elected organ for its expression and the exertion of authority. More important than these two is the third notion, namely, that the function of the public and of its elected institutions is not merely the exhibition of its mastership by informing governments and officials of what it wants, but the authority and power to exercise an effect upon the course of which the latter are to pursue, the power to exact obedience to orders. . . .

Democratic government proceeded upon the lines mentioned because the political and administrative history of all ages, the benevolent as well as the tyrannical, the theological as well as the secular, has demonstrated without the shadow of a doubt that sooner or later there is an abuse of power when external punitive controls are lacking. This abuse of power has shown itself roughly in three ways. Governments and officials have been guilty of nonfeasance,[4] that is to say, they have not done what law or custom required them to do owing to laziness, ignorance, or want of care for their charges, or corrupt influence. Again there may be malfeasance, where a duty is carried out, but is carried out with waste and damage because of ignorance, negligence, and technical incompetence. Third, there is what may be called overfeasance, where a duty is undertaken beyond what law and custom oblige or empower; overfeasance may result from dictatorial temper, the vanity and ambition of the jack in office, or genuine, sincere, public-spirited zeal. As a matter of fact, the doctrine of the separation of powers as developed by Montesquieu was as much concerned with the aberrations of public-spirited zeal on the part of the executive as with the other classes of the abuse of power. Indeed, his phrase deserves to be put into the center of every modern discussion of administrative responsibility, *virtue itself hath need of limits.* We in public administration must beware of the too good man as well as the too bad; each in his own way may give the public what it does not want. If we wish the public to want things that are better in our estimation, there is a stronger case for teaching the public than for the imposition of our zealotry. A system which gives the "good" man freedom of action in the expectation of benefiting from all the "good" he has in him, must sooner or later (since no man is without faults) cause his faults to be loaded on to the public also.

As a consequence of bitter experience and sad reflection, democratic governments have gradually devised the responsible executive and an elected assembly which enacts the responsibility. Within the system, there has been a particular concentration on the subservience of the officials to the legislature, ultimately through ministers and cabinet in a cabinet system, and through the chief executive where the separation of powers is the essential form of the organization of authority. Where officials have been or are spoils- men, the need for holding them to subservience is particularly acute, since the spoilsman has not even a professional preparation to act as a support and guide and guarantee of capacity. With career men, the capacity may be present. What is needed, however, is not technical capacity per se, but technical capacity in the service of the public welfare as defined by the public and its authorized representatives.

Legislatures and public have realized that officials are monopolist no less than the grand men of business who have arrogated to themselves the exclusive control of the manufacture or sale of a commodity and therewith the domination, without appeal by the victim, of an entire sector of national life. The philosophy and experience of the Sherman Antitrust Act have significant applications to administrative procedures in public administration. The official participates in the monopoly of a service to society so outstanding that it has been taken over from a potential private monopolist by the government. This monopoly is exercisable through a sovereign agency armed with all the force of society and subject to no appeal outside the institutions which the government itself creates. This is to be subject to a potentially grievous servitude. . . .

To overcome the potential evils flowing from public monopoly, democratic governments have set up various controls. It is these controls, and especially their modern deficiencies, which seem to have worried Professor Friedrich into a position where he practically throws the baby out with the bath. He feels that there is need of some elasticity in the power of the official, some discretion, some space for the "inner check," and he sees also that existent controls (either intentionally or by the accident of their own institutional deficiencies) do actually leave some latitude to the official. He argues therefore that heavy and, indeed, primary reliance in the making of public policy and its execution should be placed on *moral* responsibility, and he pooh-poohs the efficacy of and need for political responsibil- ity. He gives the impression of stepping over the dead body of political responsibility to grasp the promissory incandescence of the moral variety.

Let us review the chief controls exercised over politicians and officials in democratic government, and their deficiencies and the remedy of these deficiencies. In traversing their inadequacies I am dealing with those loopholes for administrative discretion or the poli- cymaking power of officials which have given Professor Friedrich so much concern. First, the legislative definition of the duties and powers of officials may not be precise because the legislators were not very clear about what they wanted. It is doubtful, for example, whether the planning clauses in the T.V.A. statute represented any clarity of purpose in the legislative mind. Legislative draftsmanship may be slipshod. Or the statute may be simply misunderstood, thus offering latitude to officials. If all the items of administrative determination arising out of the elbowroom allowed by these causes were gathered together they would no doubt be considerable. Since this latitude exists, it calls for one or both of the available remedies: the continuing control of the representative and judicial agencies over the official and an omnipresent sense of duty *to the public* on the part of the official. But the remedy is not, as Professor Friedrich suggests, the institution of specific legislative policies which may please the heart of the technical expert or the technocrat. I again insist upon subservience, for I still am of the belief with Rousseau that the people can be unwise but cannot be wrong. The devices for securing the continuing responsiveness of the official are, of course, the law courts, the procedure of criticism, question, debate, and fact-finding, and parliamentary control of the purse within the assembly, and, in the United States, the election of executive or administrative officials and their recall.

It has been suggested by Professor Laski that to overcome judicial bias in the interpretation of social legislation a preamble might be set at the head of every statute so that the intention of it should be rendered less mistakable.[5] Such a device might serve the purpose of making the official amenable to the legislature, except that I have grave doubts whether the legislature can express its intention any better in a preamble than it does in the particulars of the whole statute.

Next, the enormous congestion of modern legislative assemblies and the heritage of antiquated procedure mean that a sufficiently frequent review of legislation and its administrative outcrops cannot be secured to remedy, or to punish, or to act by power of anticipation on the official mind. But these are not insuperable problems and there is no need for us, seeing contemporary deficiencies, to jettison political responsibility prematurely.

Third, there may be a want of understanding by members of Parliament and congressmen of technical issues involved in the law and the administration, and this shortcoming has meant a leaning upon the supply of these things available in public employees. But the growth of advisory bodies, formal and informal, in the major governments of our own time has tremendously limited the need to rely wholly upon official initiative. Attention to the further development of advisory bodies is the line of progress here, not surely the handing over of our fate to officials who, by the way, are themselves only too grateful for instruction by such bodies.[6]

It is true, further, that the exercise of the power of control by the legislature, such for example as Congress' detailed attention to and itemization of financial appropriations, may destroy movement, flexibility, and the like, on the part of the administration. This point is stressed by Professor Friedrich; queerly enough, he does not deduce from this criticism that a more rational parliamentary procedure is required, but that there is need of more administrative discretion. He even goes to the inexplicable extreme of proposing that some action is better than none, whatever the action is!

In short, these various drawbacks of political control can be remedied. They can be highly improved, and it is therefore unnecessary to proceed along the line definitely approved by Professor Friedrich of more administrative policy making. As a democrat, I should incline to the belief that the remedying of these drawbacks is precisely our task for the future. The legitimate conclusion from the analysis of the relationship between Parliament and administration is not that the administration should be given its head, but on the contrary that legislative bodies should be improved. Conceding the growing power of officials we may discover the remedy in the improvement of the quality of political parties and elections, if our minds are ready to explore.

Even then I am willing to admit an external agency could not attend to every administrative particular without introducing an element of coercion and fear into administration which might damage originality, joy in work, the capacity for creative suggestion, and day-by-day flexibility. No external agency could do this; and none that we know would want to. But because some latitude must be given—both owing to the technical impossibility of complete political coverage, and the wise recognition that the permitted latitude can be used for technically good policy which though not immediately acclaimed or wanted may become so in a short while upon demonstration to the public—there is no need to overstress the auxiliaries to political control. Such auxiliaries as approved by Professor Friedrich are: referenda by government departments, public relations offices, consultation of academic colleagues in order to temper "partisan extravagance," "education and promotional functions," the administrative scrutiny of a congressman's mail. These are harmless enough.

But when Professor Friedrich advocates the official's responsibility to "the fellowship of science," the discard of official anonymity, the entry of the official into the political arena as an advocate of policy and teacher of fact versus "partisan extravagance," the result to be feared is the enhancement of official conceit and what has come to be known as "the new despotism." . . .

II

In the article in *Public Policy*, . . . Professor Friedrich takes a position radically different from my own as hitherto stated, though most of the facts to which both of us refer are common ground. Before turning to a detailed criticism of his thesis, it is useful to state his position in general. He argues (1) that the responsibility of the official that is of any moment to us today is not political responsibility but moral responsibility; (2) that the quality of administration and policy making depends almost entirely (and justifiably so) upon the official's sense of responsibility to the standards of his profession, a sense of duty to the public that is entirely inward, and an adherence to the technological basis of his particular job or the branch of the service in which he works; (3) that the public and the political assemblies do not understand the issues of policy well enough to give him socially beneficial commands in terms of a policy; (4) that, in fact, legislatures and the public have been obliged to allow or positively to organize more and more latitude for official policy making; (5) that there are satisfactory substitutes for the direction of officials and information as to the state of public opinion through the electorate and the legislature in the form of administratively conducted referenda, public relations contacts, etc.; and, therefore, (6) that political responsibility, i.e., the responsibility of the administrative officials to the legislature and the public, is and should only be considered as a minor term in the mechanism of democratic government, so much so, indeed, that officials may rightly state and urge policies in public to counteract those advocated by the members of the elected legislatures.

Let us commence the critical discussion with a passage of Professor Friedrich's on Goodnow's *Politics and Administration*. In 1900 Professor F. J. Goodnow's work, one of the pioneer incursions into a fairly untilled field, made the following distinction between politics and administration. "There are then, in all governmental systems, two primary or ultimate functions of government, viz. the expression of the will of the state and the execution of that will. There are also in all states separate organs, each of which is mainly busied with the discharge of one of these functions." Professor Friedrich imputes to Goodnow "an almost absolute distinction" in this functional difference. As a matter of fact, Goodnow uses the term *"mainly* busied with the discharge of one of these functions," and deserves credit for the broad distinction.

The distinction in the present writer's mind is this. By the "political" phase of government we mean all that part which is concerned with eliciting the will and winning the authority of the people. The process is carried on differently in democratic and dictatorial states. The elements of coercion and persuasion differ in magnitude and kind, and the place of the electorate, parties, parliaments, and ministers differs. This process ends with a law; with the approval (by positive ratification or by lapse of time for rejection) of administrative rules based on the original statute; and with control of the application of the law. The distinctive mark of this political part of the governmental process is that its agencies are practically unfettered in their authority over the making of policy and its execution. Where a written constitution and judicial review are absent, these political agencies are bounded only by the hopes and fears arising out of the electoral process. What of the administrative side? Administration begins where the legislature says it shall begin. It begins where the administrator begins, and the legislature decides that. Administration may include the making of rules and policy, which *looks* like legislation or politics. But its essence is that the administrator, elected or appointed (and most usually in modern states the latter), cannot himself determine the range or object of that policy. He has authority, but it is a conditioned, derived authority.

Thus, in the governmental process in general, there are agencies which are concerned with making and executing policy, and there is a descending narrowing latitude of discretion in the making of policy. The latitude is greatest where electorate meets legislature; it then tapers down through a descending line of the administrative hierarchy until the discretion left to the messenger and the charwoman and the minor manipulative grades is almost nil. There have been polities where there was an almost complete fusion of these functions, e.g., at some stages of Athenian democracy. But modern states are obliged at some point convenient to each in a different degree to distinguish them, with the first as authority and master over the second.

Professor Friedrich calls this distinction of Goodnow's (shared by all other authorities I can recall) "misleading," a "fetish," a "stereotype," in the minds of theorists and practitioners alike. Are we then to be permitted to offer worship only to fallacies? He produces the queerest explanation for this alleged "absolute antithesis" of Goodnow's. It is this:

> That it is built upon the metaphysical, if not abstruse, idea of a will of the state. This neo-hegelian (and Fascist) notion is purely speculative. Even if the concept "state" is retained—and I personally see no good ground for it—the idea that this state has a will immediately entangles one in all the difficulties of assuming a group personality or something akin to it.[7] (6)

This explanation is surely very fanciful. Later on, Professor Friedrich is constrained to admit: "Politics and administration play a continuous role in both formation and execution [of policy], though there is probably more politics in the formation of policy, more administration in the execution of it." "More" is a delicious understatement. But the understatement is not intended; it is part of a thesis that the amount of policy made by modern officials is of very great magnitude, in terms of proposing and later executing with latitude of interpretation. But this is only a play on the words "making" and "policy." What important "policy" does any federal official "make"? Has any federal official more authority than to propose? Certainly we expect those who are paid by the public to think and propound solutions to do their job well. But this is nothing new. By misusing the word "make" to suggest instituting and carrying into the law of the land, and only by this torsion of meaning, can Professor Friedrich's thesis at all come into court—that administrative responsibility to the legislature, the real policy-forming body of the nation, is in modern conditions impossible or unnecessary.

Professor Friedrich then reiterates an earlier statement of his: "Nor has the political responsibility based upon the election of legislatures and chief executives succeeded in permeating a highly technical, differentiated government service any more than the religious responsibility of well-intentioned kings." He then says, "An offended commentator from the British Isles [who appears to be the present writer] exclaimed that if I imagined that to be true of England I was 'simply wrong.'" Yes! That the power of the House of Commons is permeating the British civil service, right down to its local offices, and making it responsive to the House as the master delegate of the electorate, is most effective, is true, is demonstrably true, and ought not be denied. Nor can it be compared in delicateness or constancy with the "religious responsibility of well-intentioned kings," which appears to be an enthusiasm of Professor Friedrich's, for he undertakes to defend it by history, though he does not do so. Does it hold good of the Tudors, Stuarts, and Hanoverians? If so, why has British history been one long resolute struggle for the supremacy of Parliament and the reduction of the monarch to a dignified cipher? . . .

Professor Friedrich argues that "even under the best arrangements a considerable margin of irresponsible conduct of administrative activities is inevitable." He is sanguine enough to continue (4): "Too often it is taken for granted that as long as we can keep the government from doing wrong we have made it responsible. What is more important is to ensure effective action of any sort." Of any sort! This surely is exactly the doctrine to stimulate a swelling of the official head. Though I am not inclined to argue by *reductio ad absurdum*, such a phrase, if taken seriously, must encourage public employees to undertake actions which would very soon arouse the cry of Bureaucracy! and New Despotism! Friedrich himself tones down his own objurgation shortly afterward, but does not discard it.

. . . In the effort not to let reconsideration correct his first misconception of "responsibility," Professor Friedrich finds himself compelled to adopt quite an undemocratic view of government, and to throw scorn upon the popular will. I do not think for a moment that he really is antidemocratic, but his line of argument presses him to enunciate views which might lead to this suspicion. The error in his conception leads to an error in the consequence; and the error in the consequence is precisely what officials (not constrained by principle and institutions to the dictates of political responsibility) would begin to use as an argument to justify their irresponsibility: conceit of themselves and scorn of the popular will. Thus (12),

> The pious formulas about the will of the people are all very well, but when it comes to these issues of social maladjustment the popular will has little content, except the desire to see such maladjustments removed. A solution which fails in this regard, or which causes new and perhaps great maladjustments, is bad; we have a right to call such a policy irresponsible if it can be shown that it was adopted without proper regard to the existing sum of human knowledge concerning the technical issues involved; we also have a right to call it irresponsible if it can be shown that it was adopted without proper regard for existing preferences in the community, and more particularly its prevailing majority.

The answer to this argument is this. It is demonstrable that the will of the people *has* content, not only about what it desires, but how maladjustments can be remedied, and some of its ideas are quite wise. The popular will may not be learned, but nevertheless the public's own experience teaches it something, the press of all kinds teaches it more, and political parties and the more instructed members of the community play quite a part. "The people" consists of many kinds of minds and degrees of talent, not of undifferentiated ignorance and empty-mindedness. Legislative assemblies created by election, in which political parties play a vital part, also exist; and they are not so dumb. Their sagacity is not to be ignored or derided. Second, a policy which is based upon an incomplete or faulty grasp of technical knowledge is *not* an irresponsible policy, for to use the word "irresponsible" here is to pervert it by substituting it for the words "incomplete" or "faulty" or "unwise." It is surely wisest to say that the full grasp of knowledge is to be used by the official within the terms of the obligation and policy established for him by the legislature or his departmental superior; otherwise it looks as though an independent position were being claimed for the official. Nor is it wise to make responsibility to "the community" an addendum to a "proper regard to the existing sum of human knowledge, etc., etc." And, by the way, the state seems to have cropped up again in the word community!

"Consequently," continues Professor Friedrich, "the responsible administrator is one who is responsible to these two dominant factors: technical knowledge and popular sentiment. Any policy which violates either standard, or which fails to crystallize in spite of their urgent imperatives, renders the official responsible for it liable to the charge of irresponsible conduct." But just as surely there is no responsibility unless there is an obligation to someone else; no one is interested in a question of responsibility as a relationship between a man and a science, but as it involves a problem of duty and the problem of duty is an interpersonal, not a personal, matter. Responsibility in the sense of an interpersonal, externally sanctioned duty is, then, the dominant consideration for public administration; and it includes and does not merely stand by the side of responsibility to the standards of one's craft in the dubious position of a Cinderella. If the community does not command, there is no call for the technical knowledge whatever; and, however magnificent the grasp of technical knowledge and the desire to use it, it must be declared irresponsible whenever it becomes operative except under a direct or implied obligation. Many a burglar has been positively hated for his technical skill.

There is another consequence of his thesis which Professor Friedrich would not like, I feel certain, if he had developed its implications. He declares: "Administrative officials seeking to apply scientific 'standards' have to account for their action in terms of a some-what rationalized and previously established set of hypotheses. Any deviation from these hypotheses will be subjected to thorough scrutiny by their colleagues in what is known as the 'fellowship of science.'" What is the force of the phrase "have to account for their action?" Exactly to whom? By what compulsion? Does this phrase mean only that there is left to the official the vague, tenuous reaching out of his qualms in view of the known or possible public opinions of the men with whom he studied or those who are the present leaders of the profession? Suppose he despises their grasp of knowledge and scorns their judgment—is he therefore irresponsible? Suppose that they are conservative, while he is one of a minority of progressive practitioners? When is he responsible and when irresponsible? When he follows the ancients or marches with, perhaps even leads, the pioneers? . . .

I do not deny all value to such guild organization; I affirm and applaud some of these organizations. Yet, appraised from the very angle of the theory which I am here opposing, they must be seen as broken reeds in a long-run view of governmental devices to keep men in the van of social progress, technically defined, and still less to satisfy progress as the populace, the consumer, asks for it. Professor J.M. Gaus, who is quoted in support of the claim that responsibility is professional, is by no means so zealous in the service of the notion as Professor Friedrich who quotes him, for he says: "The responsibility of the civil servant to the standards of his profession, *in so far as those standards make for the public interest,* may be given official recognition." I have italicized the proviso, and it is essential, I am sure, to Professor Gaus's view. Who would define the public interest—who could define it? Only the public, I believe, or its deputies.

* * *

I come now to the last matter in which I care to take issue with Professor Friedrich, the relationship between administrative responsibility and the doctrine of official anonymity. Professor Friedrich believes:

> It must seriously be doubted whether technical responsibility, which, as we have shown, is coming to play an ever more important role in our time, can be effectively secured with-out granting responsible officials considerable leeway and making it possible for them to submit their views to outside criticism. The issue is a very complex one. Opinions vary widely. People try to escape facing these difficulties by drawing facile distinctions, such as that officials might discuss facts but not policy. It might cogently be objected that facts and policies cannot be separated. (22)

The rejoinder to this statement in the first place is that it is possible in some cases at any rate to distinguish facts and policy quite clearly. For example, the government or the representative assembly in seeking a policy to deal with rural water supplies might properly expect to receive from an official a description of the existing situation, in terms of the total water resources of the country, the supplies and the sources of supply in various rural vicinities, what those supplies cost per thousand gallons, whether the nearest supplies beyond the jurisdiction of each unit need pumping stations or whether the water will come down by being piped, what are the costs of pumping and distribution in various other areas, and so on. What the assembly shall do about it, once these facts are before it, is a matter of policy. A wise civil servant, careful to preserve his own usefulness and that of his colleagues, and not reckless in the face of the always imminent cry of bureaucracy and despotism, would not urge a policy upon it. Still less would he use public advocacy to spur on his political chief or connive with reformist groups having a purposeful policy. He would rather confine himself to frank private demonstration of the alternatives and their advantages and disadvantages, to his political chief, or where the political system requires, to the committee of the assembly at their request.

That, however, is not all. If Professor Friedrich really believes that the severance of fact and policy is impossible, then a fortiori the civil servant should preserve his anonymity, on pain of bringing himself and his colleagues into partisan contempt. And Professor Friedrich does really seem to contemplate a war of all against all. He seems to approve of the fact that six reporters proceeded to a federal department whose head had ruled that his subordinates were not to give interviews and violated the chief's rule by getting six different stories. Is this the way to promote official responsibility to the chief? To the technical standards? To the "fellowship of science"? Does Professor Friedrich approve of this piece of press impudence? Has he ever investigated what such impudence cost the T.V.A. in prestige, morale, and administrative efficiency in the old days? Nor can I view with equanimity the grave consequences of such proposals as this: "In matters of vital importance the general public is entitled to the views of its permanent servants. Such views may often provide a salutary check on partisan extravagances. Such views should be available not only to the executive but to the legislature and the public as well" (23).

This doctrine surely is to set up the official against the political parties, to make the official the instrument of conflict between the "general public" (which I thought had already been thrown out of court earlier in Friedrich's article) and the legislature. He would set the official, I suppose, against the chief executive also, for he has been elected by the general public, and may utter as many "partisan extravagances" as he pleases in the course of a four-year term. It is not clear whether Professor Friedrich thinks that the civil servant shall pursue moral responsibility as far as a crown of thorns, whether once he has embroiled parties and public and legislature he must resign. As matters are, he would certainly be kicked out by the legislature or chief executive, and it would serve him right. For democracy is ill served by and justifiably abhors those who, appointed to be its servants, assume the status and demeanor of masters.

III

The foregoing critical analysis of Professor Friedrich's view on administrative responsibility as stated in *Public Policy* shows, I think, its untenability both in its main drift and in most of its particular secondary though related aspects. The analysis reveals the following propositions as cogent and justifiable, in contradiction to Professor Friedrich's contentions.

Never was the political responsibility of officials so momentous a necessity as in our own era. Moral responsibility is likely to operate in direct proportion to the strictness and efficiency of political responsibility, and to fall away into all sorts of perversions when the latter is weakly enforced. While professional standards, duty to the public, and pursuit of technological efficiency are factors in sound administrative operation, they are but ingredients, and not continuously motivating factors, of sound policy, and they require public and political control and direction.

The public and the political assemblies are adequately sagacious to direct policy—they know not only where the shoe pinches, but have a shrewd idea as to the last and leather of their footwear: and where they lack technical knowledge their officials are appointed to offer it to them for their guidance, and not to secure official domination; and within these limits the practice of giving administrative latitude to officials is unsound.

Contemporary devices to secure closer cooperation of officials with public and legislatures are properly auxiliaries to and not substitutes for political control of public officials through exertion of the sovereign authority of the public. Thus, political responsibility is the major concern of those who work for healthy relationships between the officials and the public, and moral responsibility, although a valuable conception and institutional form, is minor and subsidiary.

Notes

1. "Responsible Government Service under the American Constitution," in Friedrich and others, *Problems of the American Public Service* (McGraw-Hill, 1935).

2. 51 *Political Science Quarterly* 582 (1936).

3. "Public Policy and the Nature of Administrative Responsibility," in *Public Policy, 1940* (Harvard, 1940), pp. 3–24.

4. I use the terms nonfeasance and malfeasance in a common sense, not a legal sense—they are convenient.

5. Committee on Ministers' Powers, *Report, 1932, Addendum.*

6. Cf. R.V. Vernon and N. Mansergh, *Advisory Bodies* (Allen and Unwin, 1941).

7. Page references are to *Public Policy, 1940.*

CHAPTER 9

RECONCILING PUBLIC
ENTREPRENEURSHIP AND DEMOCRACY

CARL J. BELLONE AND GEORGE FREDERICK GOERL

The 1980s have been labeled the "age of the entrepreneur." Several commentators have given the Reagan administration credit for promoting the virtues of private enterprise, "leaner" governments, and entrepreneurial budgets (those that lower tax burdens). The rise of the public-sector entrepreneur is found in the advent of tax limitation movements, declining federal grants to state and local governments, growing fiscal crises faced by governments at all levels of the federal system. Public administrators as entrepreneurs and agents of entrepreneurial states seek to find new sources of revenue, besides the more traditional taxes, to increase tax bases through economic development projects and to augment the number of private-sector entrepreneurs within their boundaries. Current attention paid to public-private partnerships as solutions to the fiscal and social problems of government symbolizes the importance currently attached to both private and public entrepreneurship.

However, the characteristic behavior of public entrepreneurs (as well as traditional public administrators), must be evaluated in terms of administrative responsibility if their actions are to be compatible with democratic values. Administrative responsibility can be viewed as simply following policies and directions of hierarchical superiors. Because this approach can lead to the Eichmann phenomenon, some authors have argued that administrative responsibility must include certain democratic values when administrators are carrying out administrative directives. Other authors have even described responsibility as requiring the administrator to become an active agent of democratic education and reform. John Burke urges administrators to correct any departures from democratic principles by politicians, to feel an obligation to democratic government as a whole, and to act effectively to achieve policy ends (Burke 1986, 42, 45, 50–54). Terry Cooper argues that public administrators, as "citizen-administrators," should be political educators for a citizenry that needs more information in order to play important political and citizenship roles (Cooper 1984). In these two cases, theorists of administrative responsibility assume that the public administrator has a responsibility for furthering democratic values in the political process, in policy implementation, and for developing better opportunities for citizenship.

From *Public Administration Review*, vol. 52, no. 2 (March/April 1992): 130–34. Copyright © 1992 by American Society for Public Administration. Reprinted with permission.

As entrepreneurs, public administrators have taken on the added responsibility of finding new and additional sources of revenue; but they have, at the same time, a vested political self-interest. The legitimacy of public entrepreneurs would seem to rest on their exercising administrative responsibility in the democratic manner described above so as to make public entrepreneurship compatible with democratic values and institutional roles. Four important characteristics of public entrepreneurs—autonomy, a personal vision of the future, secrecy, and risk-taking—need to be reconciled with the fundamental democratic values of accountability, citizen participation, open policymaking processes, and concern for the long-term public good (stewardship).

Entrepreneurial Autonomy Versus Democratic Accountability

First, a conflict exists between the autonomy/discretion desired by entrepreneurs and democratic accountability. With an increase in the complexity of revenue problems facing many governments, public administrators ask for greater discretion to carry out their entrepreneurial revenue searches (Lewis 1980; Goerl and Bellone 1983). Revenue crises have made public policy goals relatively less important in comparison to economic goals or revenue acquisition. In the name of revenue generation, programs and projects are set in motion that threaten to change drastically the character of a community and the authority relationships between professional public administrators and the citizenry. For example, user fees, redevelopment agencies, off-budget enterprises, investment revenues, tax-increment financing, and development fees can be seen as measures to avoid voter approval and, thereby, increase the autonomy of public officials and public administrators. Together with privatization, they contribute to the autonomy and discretion of public entrepreneurs while often making public accountability more difficult.

Because the public sector's bottom line is hard to measure, public accountability is most often attempted by measuring inputs or regulating administrative processes. Thus, through the budget process and administrative rules and regulation, legislative bodies have long sought to circumscribe the actions of public agencies in the belief that budgets and regulations ensure accountability (Gruber 1987). A characteristic of public entrepreneurs, however, is their attempt to increase their influence over budget processes in order to be free from excessive rules and regulations. Public entrepreneurs ask for autonomy from line-item budget controls in order to be more effective and efficient. They want discretion to spend "their money" (public entrepreneurs are encouraged to see themselves as owners) for measures that they deem important and on items they, not others, choose. This means that, if public entrepreneurs are to be held accountable, measures of accountability must shift from an input or process focus to one based on an outcome analysis. Analysis of outcomes as a means to measure administrative accountability can be traced to the 1960s with program budgeting and evaluation.

A current example of outcome accountability for public entrepreneurs can be found in Fairfield, California, where the city council spends little time going over the city manager's budget or in holding budget hearings. Fairfield's budget is determined on a formula basis that includes cost of living, population growth, and available revenue indicies. Each department gets a predetermined percentage of the overall budget. Near the end of the year, however, each department head must come before the council and explain how the allocated money was spent to achieve the agreed-upon goals of the department. It should be noted, however, that because the goals of departments can be hard to measure, the open-line of credit given department heads may not always result in effective public accountability.

Public Entrepreneurial Vision Versus Citizen Participation

A second conflict for a public entrepreneur who desires democratic legitimacy is between entrepreneurial vision and democracy's need for citizen input. Terence Mitchell and William G. Scott have suggested that entrepreneurs may be no more prescient and knowledgeable than the rest of us (Mitchell and Scott 1987, 447–48). Democratic politics and administration both demand that citizens be able to contribute views on issues of importance to them. However, if entrepreneurs are to be innovators, it means that they need to come with visions or ideas that are, by definition, uncommon. The Reagan administration's Iran-Contra arms entrepreneurial scheme, implemented by Oliver North and others, and the vision of the former mayor of Oakland, California, and others to reacquire the Oakland Raiders by guaranteeing ticket sales, are examples of private visions which, by most standards, were not compatible with the tenets of democratic participation and approval.

The Los Angeles Olympic Organizing Committee's decision to have the 1984 Olympics privately financed and the decision of the City of Santa Clara, California, to buy a $100 million amusement park in order to save it from closing, although not widely held visions, gained acceptance by the public and public officials through open discussion. In the latter case, the citizenry of Santa Clara got to vote on the proposal.

Only by testing entrepreneurial vision through a meaningful public-participation process can public administrators and others ensure that public entrepreneurship is compatible with the values of democratic participation.

Entrepreneurial Secrecy Versus Democratic Openness

A third conflict is between the entrepreneur's need for secrecy and the democratic value of conducting the public's business in the open. Openness is defined as disclosure of information in policymaking stages that permits the public to be informed participants in the policymaking process. The Iran-Contra arms deal is a good example of an entrepreneurial activity requiring secrecy to be successful. Given the competitive nature of local governmental finance and land development, public-private entrepreneurial partnerships frequently require secrecy if they are to be successful. In the interest of the private developer, land-use decisions are often kept as secret as possible and, in the process, compromise the public's right to know.

Because many entrepreneurial deals are done in the face of competition from other cities, as in the case of auto malls in California and elsewhere, the pressure to help subsidize the private entrepreneur can yield large outputs of public money (Bellis 1987). The wisdom of these, or, in the case of Oakland's fight to get "their" Raiders back, can produce major budgetary outlays, which may not prove to be very productive when open to public scrutiny and measured in term of the overall public interest.

Entrepreneurial Risk Taking Versus Democratic Stewardship

Fourth, entrepreneurial risk taking may conflict with the obligation to be a steward of the public good. Democratic stewardship is concerned with the prudent use of the public trust to achieve both long- and short-term goals compatible with a concept of the public interest. When directed by legislative or executive mandate, public administrators engage in risk-taking behavior (such as economic development projects) that are subject to changing business cycles. The administrator may face professional and ethical dilemmas if he or she believes that the risk taking demanded is unwise. When engaging in nonmandated risk taking, the responsibilities of the public administrator become even more a stewardship issue. High-risk investment schemes that have gone wrong and resulted in economic losses, failed arbitrage efforts in investing federal grant funds, and short-term borrowing to pay operating costs, as in the case of New York City's fiscal crises of the seventies, are all examples of entrepreneurial risk taking that ignored the prudent concern for the long-term public good (Shefter 1985).

Entrepreneurial risk taking may be more congruent with democratic stewardship if it is preceded by public information, discussion, and formal acceptance by those who will have to bear the risks should they fail. Indianapolis found a professional football team to fill its stadium, but other cities have had a difficult time finding private developers to make their public entrepreneurial ventures profitable.

Toward a More "Public" Public Entrepreneurship: The Case for a Civic-Regarding Entrepreneurship

The range of administrative and democratic responsibilities of public entrepreneurs helps describe the tension between such entrepreneurship and a democratic polity. Public administrators who seek to be entrepreneurial have added to their responsibilities by trying to generate new sources of revenue for financing public services and providing more services that pay for themselves. Given current fiscal crises, they have needed to be adept economic and political entrepreneurs. Although Mitchell and Scott (1987) raise questions as to how entrepreneurial public entrepreneurs or any entrepreneurs actually are, there is also the important question of how "public" are public entrepreneurs. The answer to this is to be found in the earlier discussion of administrative responsibility. Public entrepreneurs need to take their political authority seriously and follow the principles of democratic theory in policy design and implementation as Burke and Cooper stated. We propose that, following Cooper's line of reasoning, they also need to be concerned with a more active approach to administrative responsibility which includes helping to facilitate increased citizen education and involvement. We call this a civic-regarding entrepreneurship.

Certainly, not all public administrators are concerned with citizenship and public participation, although many observers argue that they should be (e.g., Frederickson 1982). However, given the areas of conflict between public entrepreneurship and democracy listed above, it is important for a truly "public" entrepreneurship to be civic regarding.

To borrow from Benjamin Barber's distinction between thin and strong theories of democracy (strong theories being participatory), we maintain that only a thin theory of public entrepreneurship presently applies (Barber 1985). The thin theory, in accord with liberal democratic theory, is of a public entrepreneurship that effectively and responsively generates public revenue in order to provide public services. To do this, public entrepreneurs must have the autonomy and discretion to demonstrate their economic and political talents in the public interest. The citizenry's role is one of evaluation and trust in the entrepreneur's success and responsiveness. However, the evaluation and trust asked of the citizenry is problematic because public service delivery quality is difficult to measure, and entrepreneurs can often fail. Consequently, a citizen's continued passivity may only be a sign of political alienation.

A strong theory of public entrepreneurship (a civic-regarding entrepreneurship), following Barber's distinction, should be participatory or one where the citizenry have greater opportunities to participate in the design and delivery of their public goods and services. As a result of the more-services-less-revenue paradox handed the public administrator by the voter, citizens can be held accountable, in part, for current deficiencies in public services and financial resources. These deficiencies have lead to the growth of a public entrepreneurship characterized by increased efforts by administrators to be free of voter and taxpayer control. It is the citizen's distrust of "big" government and the services that it provides that has led administrative theorists to call for greater citizen participation and an improved citizenship as a way of helping to regain the trust of the voter or citizen. Greater cooperation between administrator and citizen is the desired goal.

A civic-regarding entrepreneurship emphasizing public participation offers a remedy for over-zealous pursuits of self-interests. It offers a program of action that could make public entrepreneurship and democracy more compatible. Through developing citizens' opportunities to participate, the quality of citizenship could be raised to a level where citizens themselves become more responsible agents of efforts to provide more public goods and services within the parameters of acceptable tax burdens.

At the highest level of political aspiration, a civic-regarding entrepreneurship can be seen to be attempts, to use George Frederickson's words, to "recover civism," which embraces among other things, political community, self-aware citizens, and more adaptable and responsive government (Frederickson 1982). Expanding on Frederickson's call for our discipline to rediscover its own citizenship responsibilities, administrative theorists have stressed that public administrators should be held responsible for helping further "civic literacy" (Mathews 1984, 124), civility (as in forbearance [Hart 1984, 1161]), and "civic capital." "Civic capital" can be defined as: "problem solving knowledge possessed by citizens, attitudes that guide civic action, and civic capacity for governance" (McGregor 1984, 128). The goals of such efforts would be, to cite Charles Levine's (1984, 180) list, the raising of citizen trust in government, the citizen's sense of efficacy, and, hopefully, a shared conception of the common good.

A strong theory of public entrepreneurship requires a strong theory of citizenship. Better citizen participation, along with new sources of public revenue and better public policies and services, are high standards for public administrators to try to reach. These lofty aspirations, however, are abstract without clearer identification of the type of citizenship role one is talking about and specifications as to how opportunities for citizenship and a citizen's public education can be enhanced.

At a minimum, a civic-regarding entrepreneurship is no different from all other endeavors to increase citizen participation. However, as Dwight Waldo reminds us, not all citizen participation is of a public or collective character (Waldo 1984); it can simply be expressions of self-interest, interest group liberalism, or special pleading. In addition, it can be more manipulative than facilitative and more symbolic than effective. It may also be more divisive than facilitative or benevolent. Lastly, it may require more concern for social-equity considerations than are found in liberal democracy (Bellah et al. 1985; Frederickson and Hart 1985).

There are different degrees or levels of political participation (Milbrath 1965, 5–38). In the case of administrative democracy, the same may be said. At a minimum, citizens can only take part in public service delivery systems if they receive public services. Not all do. Thus, considerable doubts exist as to fairness in such distributions of services. Equal access to high-quality public services should be a basic citizenship right that should not be jeopardized. However, fiscal limits threaten the provision of public goods and services. Thus, the entrepreneurial talents of public administrators are crucial to a civic-regarding entrepreneurship.

However, public administrators, as civic-regarding entrepreneurs, can go much further. They can increase the ability of citizens to complain about the quality of their public services and help to facilitate correcting efforts (Sharp 1986). In similar fashion, New York City and other local governments that create uniform-service districts that enable a citizen to use a single site for reaching the appropriate service providers are also increasing the opportunities for greater involvement in ensuring service systems that are responsive (Mudd 1984).

When it comes to providing the rationale for spending public funds, a civic-regarding entrepreneurship would entail creating citizen budget committees to help set priorities before any formal budget approval is made by the executive and legislative branches. Portland, Oregon; Dayton, Ohio; and, in some respects, New York City all try to get citizens more involved earlier in the budgetary process.

Because public entrepreneurship often is manifested in the form of economic development projects, any effort at a civic-oriented entrepreneurship needs to increase the ability of citizens to see, comprehend, criticize, amend, and jointly design the projects so that their neighborhood or community is not disrupted or victimized by the development efforts of others. Where neighborhoods are well defined, neighborhood associations, citizen advisory boards, etc., may be in order if citizens are to defend and enhance their own community (White 1983; Marcuse 1990). Although criticized for possibly raising the Not In My Back Yard problem, overall social equity concerns are better served by mutually agreeable zoning and development than when the citizenry and neighborhoods have no say.

Elevating citizen choice, as in the case of voucher systems, may still be the best way for enhancing citizen participation. Budget and land-use decisions are among the most important for all stakeholders. Being urged to become more responsible for one's public choices, with public sector staff providing needed information, may make citizen input far more informative for city staff and elected officials.

The use of citizen volunteers to help provide and produce public services has been suggested as another way of increasing opportunities for citizen participation. Volunteerism has increased in many fiscally troubled cities and counties out of self-defense. Neighborhood safety patrols and arson-prevention volunteers are cases in point. In upper-class suburbs, a highly educated citizenry often demands a high level of participation for themselves in the design and delivery of their public services. Such citizen volunteerism is a show of civic obligation and duty. It is a way of stretching scarce resources to enable citizens to provide more and better services than they would otherwise have received. It may also be a way of increasing the citizenship rights and especially the citizenship obligations of many people who would otherwise remain outside the service delivery systems of governments.

From an historical perspective, it has been entrepreneurial volunteers who have first provided most public services from the postal service, to the police, down to present-day neighborhood mediation services (Ellis and Noyes 1978). Volunteers, when aided by government offices of volunteerism, have been crucial to a delivery of many services, especially new and more innovative social services that facilitate compassion, benevolence, and the equal distribution of public goods.

Conclusion

De Tocqueville and John Stuart Mill saw the jury as a key to a citizen's public education. Today, there are more vehicles for increasing the opportunities for a citizen's participation and civic education (Barber 1985, 261–311). Not all citizens may want to participate, and they should not be forced to do so under the tenets of liberal democratic theory (Meyers 1990). However, as Morris Janowitz and Gerald Suttles have argued, there may not be enough opportunities for those who want to participate (Janowitz and Suttles 1978). A civic-regarding entrepreneurship is about finding those opportunities. For those who find the opportunity to do so, a more deeply felt obligation to be better citizens may develop and perhaps a willingness to give more of themselves for the provision of needed public services. The willingness to pay is one important sign that civic-oriented entrepreneurship is present. A civic-regarding entrepreneurship is a reminder of our roles as both agents (participants) and members (with political obligations) to the polity (Tussman 1960).

References

Barber, Benjamin. 1985. *Strong Democracy*. Berkeley: University of California Press.
Bellah, Robert, et al. 1985. *Habits of the Heart*. Berkeley: University of California Press.
Bellis, David. 1987. "Inner-City Competition over Auto-Mall Development (or, How to Win Friends by Stealing Auto Dealers from Your Neighbors)." *Western Governmental Researcher,* vol. III (September), pp. 15–29.

Burke, John. 1986. *Bureaucratic Responsibility.* Baltimore: Johns Hopkins University Press.

Cooper, Terry. 1984. "Public Administration in an Age of Scarcity: A Citizenship Role for Public Administration." In Jack Rabin and James S. Bowman, eds., *Politics and Administration.* New York: Marcel Dekker, pp. 306–9.

Ellis, Susan J. and Katherine Noyes. 1978. *By the People.* Philadelphia: Energize Press.

Frederickson, H. George. 1982. "The Recovery of Civism in Public Administration." *Public Administration Review,* vol. 42 (November/December), pp. 501–8.

Frederickson, H. George and David K. Hart. 1985. "The Public Service and the Patriotism of Benevolence," *Public Administration Review,* vol. 45 (September/October), pp. 547–54.

Goerl, George F. and Carl J. Bellone. 1983. "The Democratic Polity's Search for the Knowledgeable Public Administrator: An Argumentative Essay." *International Journal of Public Administration,* vol. 5(3), pp. 217–66.

Gruber, Judith. 1987. *Controlling Bureaucracies.* Berkeley: University of California Press.

Hart, David K. 1984. "The Virtuous Citizen, the Honorable Bureaucrat and 'Public' Administration." *Public Administration Review,* vol. 44 (special issue), pp. 111–20.

Janowitz, Morris and Gerald Sutties. 1978. "The Social Ecology of Citizenship." In Rosemary Saari and Yesheskel Hansenfield, eds., *The Management of Social Services.* New York: Columbia University Press.

Levine, Charles. 1984. "Citizenship and Service Delivery: The Promise of Coproduction." *Public Administration Review,* vol. 44 (special issue), pp. 178–87.

Lewis, Eugene. 1980. *Public Entrepreneurship: Toward a Theory of Bureaucratic Power.* Bloomington, IN: Indiana University Press.

Marcuse, Peter. 1990. "New York City's Community Boards: Neighborhood Policy as Results." In Naomi Carmon, ed., *Neighborhood Policy and Programmes.* New York: St. Martin's Press, pp. 145–63.

Mathews, David. 1984. "The Public in Practice and Theory." *Public Administration Review,* vol. 44 (special issue), pp. 120–25.

McGregor, Eugene B. 1984. "The Great Paradox of Democratic Citizenship and Public Personnel Administration." *Public Administration Review,* vol. 44 (special issue), pp. 126–32.

Meyers, Diana. 1990. "Democratic Theory and the Democratic Agent." In John Chapman and Alan Westheimer, eds., *Majorities and Minorities.* New York: New York University Press, pp. 126–50.

Milbrath, Lester. 1965. *Political Participation.* Chicago: Rand McNally.

Mitchell, Terence and William G. Scott. 1987. "Leadership Failures, the Distrusting Public and Prospects of the Administrative State." *Public Administration Review,* vol. 47 (November/December), pp. 445–52.

Mudd, John. 1984. *Neighborhood Services.* New Haven: Yale University Press.

Sharp, Elaine B. 1986. *Citizen Demand-Making in the Urban Context.* University, AL: University of Alabama Press.

Shefter, Martin. 1985. *Political Crises/Fiscal Crises.* New York: Basic Books.

Tussman, Joseph. 1960. *Obligation and the Body Politic.* New York: Oxford University Press.

Waldo, Dwight. 1984. "Response." *Public Administration Review,* vol. 44 (special issue), pp. 107–9.

White, Louise G. 1983. "A Hundred Flowers Blossoming, Citizen Advisory Boards and Local Administrators." *Journal of Urban Affairs,* vol. 5 (Summer), pp. 221–30.

CHAPTER 10

CITY MANAGERS

Will They Reject Policy Leadership?

JAMES M. BANOVETZ

Ever since Karl Bosworth opined that "The City Manager Is a Politician" (Bosworth 1958), many local government administrators and scholars have embraced that job description, suggested that Woodrow Wilson's politics-administration dichotomy was invalid, and predicted a growing political-policy role for city and county managers in the future (Frederickson 1989; Stillman 1974; Loveridge 1971; Sherwood 1976; Newland 1979; Graves 1982; Mikulecky 1980; Gaebler 1983). Even the best contemporary discussions of the city management profession[1] have reiterated this evolutionary process: Ammons and Newell (1989) recently noted that the "politics-administration dichotomy . . . continues to erode in practice . . . in the constant quest for the leadership necessary to solve the problems of the nation's cities" (170), and Svara (1990) predicted that "a continuing shift toward the policy and political roles (for city managers) is likely since younger and professionally trained managers are likely to devote more time to them and less to the management role" (181).

City managers, too, report that such a shift is occurring. Ammons and Newell (1989) found that, in 1988, 56 percent of city managers in their study reported that the policy role was the most important for success in their jobs, whereas Wright in 1965 found only 22 percent of the city managers giving such a response (Ammons and Newell 1989).

Despite such evidence, however, there is now reason to speculate that this trend might not continue, but rather that the city manager's role in the early twenty-first century might be more like the role of managers in the mid-twentieth century than of managers in recent decades. City managers of the future may find that their job, like their job tenure, is more similar to that of baseball managers than to political leaders, and that the resulting insecurity, as well as job demands, will cause them to focus on managerial rather than policy responsibilities.

To be sure, the city manager's job has changed during the course of the twentieth century, and the typical manager's job description has included a growing list of policy responsibilities. Keller (1989) argues that city managers must be "chief executives of

From *Public Productivity & Management Review,* vol. 17, no. 4 (Summer 1994): 313–24. Copyright © 1994 by Jossey-Bass. Reprinted with permission of M.E. Sharpe, Inc.

appropriate interorganizational network economies and polities"; Newland (1979) has charged the manager to be a futurist; Mikulecky (1980) has labeled the manager a diplomat in intergovernmental relations; and Toffler (1980) has called the manager a broker of interests. Gaebler (1983) has used the term *entrepreneur* to describe the manager's role, and the International City/County Management Association (ICMA) itself has suggested that the title *city manager* might give way to the label *city coordinator* (Rutter 1980). The ICMA prediction may have been right, but for the wrong reasons: city managers may be city coordinators, but managerial coordination will take precedence over policy coordination.

Trend Conflict

The difference between these two perspectives is rooted in different interpretations of trends. Scholars and practitioners who predict a growing policy role for city managers do so on the basis of a linear extension of the manager's evolving role. Although frequently used, this methodology is based on the perilous assumption that the environment is stable. It presumes that the circumstances in which city managers operate—the forms of government, political attitudes and values, political behaviors, citizen expectations, socioeconomic trends, organizational milieus, and work patterns—will remain relatively constant or change in a parallel linear manner.

The notion that the city manager's role will revert to a stronger managerial focus, with a lessening of its policy focus, is predicated on evidence that the managerial environment will not stay stable; indeed, it is not stable now. The assumption of linearity in policy roles assumes a constancy in relationships between managers and their bosses—elected mayors, city council members, county board presidents, and county board members—that simply does nor exist. The political behaviors of such elected officials are themselves undergoing changes that are more dialectic than linear in nature.

City managers are fond of saying that their term of office "extends until the next council meeting." The accuracy of this assertion necessarily (and intentionally, given the precepts of democratic theory; see Mosher 1982) makes the manager's role a function of the behavior and expectations of elected council members. The "behavior and expectations" are evolving in a dialectic fashion, and the same behavior and expectations may force managerial roles to deviate from the linear pattern sketched by scholars and practitioners.

Dialectic Evolution of Council Behavior

The behavior of elected local government officials, and thus the role development of city management, has been profoundly affected by four distinct sets of public attitudes toward government, each of which was rooted in its own period of twentieth-century history. These attitudes, summarized in Table 10.1, have run the gamut from revulsion toward government to reliance upon government as a paternalistic guarantor of personal and economic well-being.

Table 10.1

Public Attitudes Toward Government

Era	Public perception	Exemplifying factors
Early twentieth century	Government is corrupt	Spoils system Machine politics "Shame of the Cities"
1915–35	Government should be limited	Dillon's Rule Substantive due process Reform legislation
1935–65	Government is paternalist	New Deal Great Society War on poverty Civil rights
1965–present	Government is excessive	Antiwar (Vietnam) demonstrations Taxpayers' revolt Reaganism

Attitudes toward government in the early twentieth century were products of the corruption of the late nineteenth century. (For a discussion of this early history and its impact on the council-manager plan of local government, see Judd 1979.) Partisan machine politics and its accompanying corruption led voters, and especially the emerging middle class, to distrust government and restrain it through legal controls. These controls were written into restrictive state laws and further embellished by narrow construction in the interpretation of governmental powers. At the local level, popular hostility toward government led to the formation of suburban governments, where the new middle class could separate itself from the big-city machines and enjoy control over neighborhood governments. In this environment, the council-manager plan was sold to local voters on the basis of (1) its structural parallels with contemporary business models, and specifically the business corporation,[2] which gave the plan validity in terms of the middle-class values of economy and efficiency; and (2) the dichotomy between politics and administration, noting that the council-manager plan guaranteed administrative expertise divorced from political considerations.

Attitudes toward government changed markedly with the onslaught of the depression and the postwar economic expansion. The New Deal spawned the expectation that government had a responsibility to provide economic well-being for all, including responsibility to provide educational opportunity, economic security, housing, health care, transportation, recreation, and civil rights (Frisch and Stevens 1971, 13–21). The attitudes stemming from these changed popular expectations also affected cities, which found themselves responsible for an ever-increasing range of human services; city managers found themselves supervising a growing list of programs and responding to a widening spectrum of citizen demands (Banovetz 1971, 18). The popularity of the council-manager plan expanded rapidly during this and the following era as popular suspicion of government was replaced with popular demands for more government. The people's mood had swung from popular distrust of government to popular enthusiasm for it, from dialectical thesis to antithesis. The turbulent decade of the 1960s brought the dialectical synthesis. Popular support for government programs and services did not lessen, but the people revolted against the "excesses" of government. Reacting to the turbulence associated with U.S. involvement in the Vietnam War, government-ordered desegregation plans, increasingly burdensome taxes, and the expanding scope of government regulatory activity, people viewed the role of government in society as too pervasive.

In short, public attitudes toward government are now a synthesis of high expectations for personal benefits and strong convictions that the scale and cost of government activity must be substantially reduced.

Linear Evolution of the Managerial Role

In his description of the "rise" of the city manager profession, Stillman (1974) described several eras in the profession's history, eras that relate in interesting ways to changing public expectations of government. He divided the profession's evolution into four periods. The first, 1914–24, was the period when the profession established its identity, culminating in the approval of its first code of ethics in 1924, which described the profession's role in strictly administrative terms. In the second period, 1924–38, the profession reflected the values of the scientific management philosophy; it culminated with the amendment of the code of ethics in 1938 to establish clearly the politics-administration dichotomy and to suggest a role, but a strictly limited role, for the manager as an adviser to the council.

Whereas the first two periods reflected public interest in a limited government, the second two periods reflected the changing public mood toward government. The third period, 1938–52, was described by Stillman as a period during which the profession went through an identity crisis as it sought to reconcile its precepts to "the New Political Realism." It culminated in 1952 revisions to the code of ethics that defined the manager as "a community leader (who) submits policy proposals to the council and provides the council with facts and advice on matters of policy." The fourth era began in 1952 and was marked by 1969 code amendments that continued to delineate a political role for the manager.

Stillman's analysis should be updated to take account of the ICMA's 1980 pronouncement on the profession's future, which suggested a much more proactive and forceful role for the profession in addressing the problems of local governments during the remaining decades of the century and beyond (Rutter 1980).

These trends are set forth and embellished in Table 10.2. The city manager's executive functions and the change in informal descriptive titles significantly parallel the job's changing and expanding responsibilities. Although city managers have been loath to acknowledge this operational job title change in public, many do so in private conversation.

Unfortunately, the extent to which the linear progression in managerial role (see Table 10.2) has already occurred may be sufficiently extreme to provoke a counterreaction in the opposite direction, a dialectic antithesis. Such a reaction is made more likely by the changes occurring in the behavior of the managers' bosses, local elected officials.

Table 10.2

Evolution of the City Management Profession

Era	The manager's job focus	Descriptive job title
1914–24	Administrative technician Eliminate corruption Establish scientific management methods	City administrative officer
1924–38	Administrative technician Organization director Policy leader	City administrator
1938–52	Organization leader Policy adviser	Chief administrative officer
1952–80	Organization leader Policy adviser and initiator Intergovernmental manager Program initiator Decision-making catalyst	Executive officer
1980–present	Coordinator of administrative operations Policy initiator and coordinator Decision-making catalyst Community development leader Policy and program evaluation	Chief executive officer

Changes in Elected Official Behavior

However, no matter how clearly managers see or want a more active policymaking role for themselves, that role will not emerge unless it is compatible with the political expectations of the public and their elected representatives. The city management profession, with its history of resignations and terminations, has learned that lesson only too well.

Predicting the public's future expectations for government bears some similarity to predicting school enrollments. Enrollments can be predicted into the near future with some degree of certainty because children are born some years before they enroll in school. Similarly, public expectations of government can be predicted in advance with some (albeit less) certainty because those expectations are based on attitudes and values that are formed in advance. People acquire their political attitudes and values during youth and young adulthood, arguably between the ages of fifteen and twenty-five. The attitudes and values learned during those ages become the basis for political expectations and behaviors that shape public policy when those persons reach the ages when they are most likely to be politically active and hold public office, the ages between thirty-five and sixty. Thus attitudes and values formed at an early period of life become operative in government at a later period of life.

Viewed from this perspective, the political role expansion of the city manager from 1952 to the present, and particularly between 1960 and 1985, can be attributed to the elected city officials who developed their political attitudes and values when government was viewed as paternalistic, a source of support and service. People with such political attitudes welcomed city managers who could help government deliver more of the services being desired. This reaction was in marked contrast, however, to the much slower growth of city management in the period 1914–52, when city councils were populated by people who were in favor of limited government, people who had been raised to view government with suspicion. Such persons were much less willing to trust the management of their local affairs to an "outsider."

This dialectic swing in popular attitudes toward government has occurred again. As Table 10.1 suggests, a new generation has emerged in American public life, a generation that grew up viewing government with hostility and mistrust. Just as past generational changes affected the city management profession and city manager roles, so, too, will the hostility and mistrust of the generation now being elected to public office.

The post–1960s generation experienced yet another change that will affect, and is affecting, evolutionary trends. It is a generation with a new and stronger sense of political efficacy and commitment. Political activities associated with the antiwar movement and civil rights demonstrations gave participants a sense of personal, individual empowerment to bring about government change. It opened new avenues for popular participation in government and encouraged markedly increased levels of political activism by people from all walks of life and at all levels of government. This generation is empowered by its youthful experiences to take a more personal and active role in government at all levels.

This sense of empowerment, of the ability of the individual to make a personal mark upon government, will not diminish with age. Braungart and Braungart (1991), in a life-history study of former activist leaders, suggest that "a political generation takes a lifetime to end. Although the collective-activist phase of their youth ceased more than two decades ago, the spirit of the 1960s political generation endures. Whether these men and women who led SDS and YAF in the 1960s viewed their earlier experiences as 'life transforming' or a 'learning experience,' they continue in their middle-age years to try to implement their youthful values—in high public office as well as in 'little niches'" (297).

Sociological studies of generational impacts confirm that sociopolitical orientations tend to endure over the life span (Alwin and Krosnick 1991; Braungart and Braungart 1991; Krosnick 1991); historical evidence also documents the cyclical nature of political change in the American polity and the ability to base predictions for the future on such changes (Smith 1990). Changes in the political attitudes and behaviors of the American electorate are coming, and their coming will significantly affect the role of the city manager in council-manager government.

Some of these changes have already come, and they are presenting problems for council-manager government. The makeup of city councils has changed: the membership of such bodies is more diverse, and the behavior of the members is different. Many more council members are being elected from districts: more and more city managers are finding that they must shift to accommodate ward-based politics, which brings new, and many more, stresses.

The role of the mayor in council-manager government has also been changing. As early as 1979 city managers were discussing the impact of the "strong mayor/manager" form of government at their annual meeting. More recently, the *Municipal Yearbook* (1988) has noted a convergence of the council-manager plan and the mayor-council plan, noting "excellent prospects for the further interchange of aspects of structure and function" (9). Svara (1990, 181) has also noted this convergence and the likelihood that it will bring increased conflict in council-manager cities.

Ehrenhalt (1991) has identified still another pattern of change that will have an impact on city managers and their roles, and that, in fact, may have a decisive impact on managerial involvement in policy processes. Ehrenhalt has found that elected office holders have changed in nature. They have changed from persons elected to office with the support of parties or groups in the community to persons who gain election as a result of personal incentive and effort. They have changed from persons whose primary occupation was in the private sector and who held public office as a community service to persons whose primary time and energy commitment is to public office and only secondarily to other professional activity. They have changed to increasingly include those who have been willing to make a major investment of time and talent to gain and exercise political influence. Such people typically want more than to serve the community; they want to make a significant difference.

Ehrenhalt describes the new style of office holder in the following terms:

> Seeking and holding office take up more of a politician's time than they did a generation ago. It is much harder now to combine politics and a career in private life. . . .

People in local government—city council members, county commissioners, and their equivalents—nearly all have some discretion in how much time they devote to their work. . . . Local politicians can hold down private jobs and most of them do. But a variation on Gresham's law has come to operate in local politics: full-timers drive part-timers out of circulation. The city councilman who spends his days building political coalitions, meeting with constituents, and cultivating financial support sets a standard of political sophistication that colleagues pretty much have to meet if they are going to stay effective or even stay in office. Once a city council attracts its first full-time member, it is on the way to becoming a de facto full-time institution, even if it does not think of itself as one.

What matters . . . is ambition. Political careers are open to ambition now in a way that has not been true in America in most of this century. . . . The real barriers are the burdens that a political career has come to impose on people who pursue it—the burdens of time, physical effort, and financial sacrifice. Politics is a profession now, not just in Congress, but in many state legislatures and in countless local governments, where a casual part-time commitment used to suffice. . . .

Every individual is a faction unto himself.

> Such a public office holder is not a linear extension of political predecessors but the antithesis of elected local officials of a generation ago. Yet this new breed of office holder is becoming increasingly familiar to city managers; it is a kind of office holder to whom city managers must adapt if they wish to survive as policy leaders.

City Manager Adaptations

Some city managers are adapting to, and will survive in, this new political environment. Particularly well suited will be those in cities sufficiently well staffed to employ professionals as department heads and management assistants and in middle-management positions; those who enjoy the policy game; and particularly those sufficiently fortunate to avoid too many of Ehrenhalt's new breed of politicians on their councils. But many others will have difficulty: they will not have sufficient staff support; they will have difficulty adapting to the multiple, and often conflicting, demands of the political activists on the council; and they will hesitate to risk their job in an uncertain employment market.

Newell, Glass, and Ammons (1989) have already uncovered evidence of change in city manager policy activity that, although it does not involve less attention to policy, does suggest a difference in approach: "As the political environment of council-manager cities has changed, city managers have apparently relinquished the mantle of community leadership to elected officials while not only spending more time on but regarding as more important the policy role, which encompasses policy development and council relations."

Managers of the future will increasingly face the dilemma of the baseball manager. With no control of the people above them in the organizational hierarchy, with limited choice and control over those whom they must manage, and with publicly visible responsibility for organizational success, they will find themselves the easy target of those, on the council and in the community, who have reason to find fault with organizational performance. Just as the unhappy owners of losing baseball teams find it easiest to fire the manager, so too will dissatisfied city council members find that "firing the manager" offers a quick, convenient way to give constituents the impression that they are taking charge of events and moving to make improvements.

In such a milieu, many—perhaps most—city managers will "hunker down" in their jobs, focus their energies on delivering services and resolving citizen complaints, and avoid, whenever possible, entanglement with the personalities on the council. Such managers may still list "involvement in policy" as their primary activity, but it will be a kind of involvement that is much different from that of their predecessors in the 1970s and 1980s. It will not be a proactive involvement that seeks to identify policy needs, detail policy alternatives, and encourage optimization in decision making. Instead, it will be a reactive involvement, addressing issues that arise from other sources, waiting for council direction before charting alternatives, and willingly accepting "satisficing" solutions.

Managers are, after all, only human. Faced with increasing political uncertainty and the possibility of imminent job loss, they will sacrifice rationality for incrementalism in decision making; work diligently more to avoid mistakes than to achieve success; perfect standard routines rather than assume the risks of innovation; and seek anonymity rather than leadership. In short, they will become government bureaucrats. In the process, they will have lost their distinctive place in the field of public management, their ability to be "unique in the degree to which they can rather openly assert their special quality and status in the exercise of leadership" (Sherwood 1976, 586).

Implications for Professional Development

The city management profession, in short, may find that its role in local government ceases to advance in a linear fashion, building on past achievements. Instead, it may begin to experience dialectic change similar to the pattern characteristic of society's political values and leadership. If it does, the manager of the future will represent a synthesis of the administrative officer of the pre–1938 era and the policy activist/leader of the present era. Such a managerial role will be very different from what will occur if Svara's vision of "a continuing shift toward the policy and political roles" is realized.

In either event, managers of the future will need more sophisticated and developed "political skills" if they are to survive and succeed. Whether they are "hunkered down" trying to avoid dismissal by politically ambitious council members or aggressively, perhaps even politically, providing policy leadership, they will have to take a page from the book of the nineteenth-century government reformers who learned that structural reform, by itself, does not resolve the problems of local government. Rather, reformers found that "the missing ingredient was a need for wider human understanding and concern. . . . All the reasoning in the world that the reformers' policies of efficiency and economy would benefit the masses would not, did not, and could not compensate for a lack of contact, caring, and empathy. These were all qualities that these same masses met and recognized in probably the majority of the precinct and ward leaders of the political machine" (Griffith 1938).

These qualities continue even now to be projected by successful political leaders. Unless city managers of the future can project these same qualities, they are not likely to survive the future milieu projected either by Svara or this article. If they are to play aggressive policy and political roles, then they must project the qualities of successful public leaders; if they are to survive as government bureaucrats in a position not unlike that of baseball managers, then they must portray the caring and empathy needed to give each of their individual council members a sense of personal fulfillment and political success.

To prepare for such roles, managers must match their technical competence with human relations skills. The field of administration has long recognized the need for such skills in working with subordinates. The literature, from Mary Parker Follett to contemporary OD (Organization Development) theorists, is replete with admonitions regarding the human factor in management. What is now needed is the development of OD-type skills, competencies, and methodologies for dealing with organizational superiors—with the council members, other political leaders, members of local advisory boards and commissions, neighborhood organization leaders, and the proverbial taxpayers who make demands on city hall.

These OD skills will be different from those employed in the technology of making the organization work. Although people are always people, relationships are not always the same. The people above the manager in the organization may be just as human as those below, but their relationships are vastly different.

Managerial relationships with elected officials are changing as the behavior—the objectives, involvement, and expectations—of elected officials changes. New OD-type competencies and insights must be developed so that city managers can adjust to, capitalize on, or simply survive in whatever changing role is now emerging for their profession.

Notes

1. County managers, professional twins of city managers, have come into their own as local government administrators in recent years, but for simplicity's sake this article will use the more widely accepted generic term *city managers* to refer to city and county management professionals.

2. Judd (1979, 104–9) describes the theme used by proponents of council-manager government to sell the plan to Dallas voters in 1930: "Why not run Dallas itself on a business schedule by business methods under business management? . . . The city manager plan is after all only a business management plan. . . . The city manager is the executive of a corporation under a board of directors. Dallas is the corporation. It is as simple as that. Vote for it." The voters did.

References

Alwin, D., and Krosnick, J. "Aging, Cohorts. and the Stability of Sociopolitical Orientations over the Life Span." *American Journal of Sociology*, 1991, 97 (1), 169–95.

Ammons, D., and Newell, C. *City Executives*. Albany: State University of New York Press, 1989.

Banovetz, J. *Managing the Modern City*. Washington, DC: International City Management Association, 1971.

Bosworth, K. "The City Manager Is a Politician." *Public Administration Review*, 1958, 18, 216.

Braungart, M., and Braungart, R. "The Effects of the 1960s Political Generation on Former Left- and Right-Wing Youth Activist Leaders." *Social Problems*, 1991, 38 (3), 297.

Ehrenhalt, A. *The United States of Ambition*. New York: Times Books, 1991.

Fisher, F. The New Entrepreneurs." *Public Management*, 1981, 63 (6), 2.

Frederickson, H. *Ideal and Practice in Council-Manager Government*. Washington, DC: International City Management Association, 1989.

Frisch, M., and Stevens, R. *American Political Thought*. New York: Charles Scribner's Sons, 1971.

Gaebler, T. "The Entrepreneurial Manager." *Public Management*, 1983, 65 (1), 14.

Graves, C. "Guidelines for the Black Urban Administrator." *Public Management*, 1982, 64 (6), 15.

Griffith, E. *A History of American City Government: The Conspicuous Failure*, 1870–1900. New York: Praeger, 1938.

Judd, Dennis R. *The Politics of American Cities: Private Power and Public Policy*. Boston: Little, Brown, 1979.

Keller, L. "City Managers and Federalism." In H. Frederickson (ed.), *Ideal and Practice in Council-Manager Government*. Washington, D.C.: International City Management Association, 1989.

Krosnick, J. "The Stability of Political Preferences: Comparisons of Symbolic and Nonsymbolic Attitudes." *American Journal of Political Science*, 1991, 35 (2), 547–76.

Loveridge, R. *City Managers in Legislative Politics*. New York: Bobbs-Merrill, 1971.

Mikulecky, T. "Intergovernmental Relations Strategies for the Local Manager." *Public Administration Review*, 1980, 40 (4), 379.

Moser, F.C. *Democracy and the Public Service*. 2nd ed. New York: Oxford University Press, 1982.

Municipal Yearbook 1988. Washington, D.C.: International City Management Association, 1988.

Newell, C., Glass. J., and Ammons, D. "City Manager Roles in a Changing Political Environment." In H. Frederickson (ed.), *Ideal and Practice in Council-Manager Government*. Washington, DC: International City Management Association, 1989.

Newland, C. "Future Images: Urban Diversity and Democracy." In *Municipal Yearbook 1979.* Washington, DC: International City Management Association, 1979.

Renner, T. "Appointed Local Government Managers: Stability and Change." In *Municipal Yearbook 1990.* Washington, DC: International City Management Association, 1990.

Rutter, L., for the ICMA Committee on Future Horizons of the Profession. *The Essential Community: Local Government in the Year 2000.* Washington, DC: International City Management Association, 1980.

Sherwood, F. "The American Public Executive in the Third Century." *Public Administration Review*, 1976, 36 (5), 586.

Smith, T. "Liberal and Conservative Trends in the United States Since World War II." *Public Opinion Quarterly*, 1990, 54, 479–507.

Stillman, R., II. *The Rise of the City Manager.* Albuquerque: University of New Mexico Press, 1974.

Svara, J. *Official Leadership in the City.* New York: Oxford University Press, 1990.

Toffler, A. "New Worlds of Service." *Public Management*, 1980, 62 (1), 8.

CHAPTER 11

ACCOUNTABILITY AND ENTREPRENEURIAL PUBLIC MANAGEMENT

The Case of the Orange County Investment Fund

KEVIN P. KEARNS

On December 6, 1994, the financial world was rocked by news that Orange County, California, had declared bankruptcy. Its vast $20 billion investment pool, representing over 180 county and municipal agencies, had experienced $1.7 billion in unrealized losses due to the fund's heavy reliance on investments that fell in value as interest rates rose in 1994. Nervous creditors who had made loans to the fund to finance its aggressive investment strategies liquidated $11 billion in collateral on the loans. Then, with its leverage hopelessly constricted, the county fund filed for protection under Chapter 9 of the U.S. Bankruptcy Code, much like the way private firms seek protection under Chapter 11 of the Code. It was the largest municipal bankruptcy in the history of the federal code.

The news was especially shocking because the manager of the Orange County fund, county treasurer Robert Citron, had built a reputation as a successful public sector entrepreneur. Under Citron's direction, the Orange County fund had been hailed as an example of how an aggressive investment strategy could help diversify local government revenues, thereby reducing reliance on property taxes and other traditional revenue sources. Orange County's investment portfolio included a class of derivative securities, which fluctuated inversely with interest rates. The fund also used short-term leverage borrowing to purchase certain securities as well as reverse repurchase arrangements in which securities in the portfolio were used as collateral on the short-term loans. This approach has been embraced by several other California communities as well as by government agencies in several other states.[1]

The potential gains from such a strategy can be enormous, but the risks are proportional to the gains. For several years, Citron played the financial markets masterfully and his approach may have helped the Orange County jurisdictions hold their own when property values and tax revenues fell in recent years.[2] But Citron's strategy was based on one key assumption: that interest rates would continue to fall as they did in 1992 and 1993. His investment strategy backfired when rates began to climb.

From *Public Budgeting & Finance*, vol. 15, no. 3 (Fall 1995): 3–21. Copyright © 1995 by Blackwell Publishers. Reprinted with permission.

The Orange County investors lost millions, Robert Citron lost his job, and the citizens lost confidence in their government. Ripple effects within the financial world and among state and local governments will likely be felt for a very long time.

It is *not* the intent of this article to analyze the fine details of the Orange County case in terms of the specific investment securities chosen by Robert Citron and his advisors or the decision processes they used to make these investments. Nor does the article discuss the specifics of the regulatory environment in which Citron and his financial advisors operated. The details of the Orange County debacle will unfold in the months (and perhaps years) ahead as investors, creditors, regulators, and the courts put together the pieces of the puzzle.

Instead, this article examines the broad facts and general context of the case from a conceptual and theoretical perspective of public sector accountability. Specifically, this article presents a conceptual framework that illuminates four different types of accountability environments facing public managers today. The framework is a heuristic tool that may be helpful in retrospective analysis of cases like the Orange County bankruptcy and many other accountability controversies in the public sector. The framework can also be used in a prospective way by public officials to help them diagnose their accountability environment and develop targeted strategies to enhance their role as stewards of the public trust.

The "Reinvention" of Public Sector Accountability

In some important respects, the Orange County case is a story of how prevailing standards of accountability, and the management systems that support those standards, can shift in response to the economic, political, and intellectual environment.[3]

In the field of public financial management, the prevailing standard of accountability historically has been rooted in stewardship of the public trust. Financial managers in the public sector generally are not risk-takers and certainly there are very few incentives—financial or political—to gamble with the investment of public funds. Consequently, the priorities of public financial managers traditionally have been: first, to protect the investment's principal, generally through relatively safe instruments such as government securities and certificates of deposit; second, to maintain liquidity, guaranteeing that cash is readily available to meet expenditure obligations; and, third, to derive a reasonable yield or return on investments within the limits imposed by the first two principles. Naturally, this conservative approach does not produce dramatic returns on investment, but in most cases it does ensure the safety and liquidity of public funds. Many states, in fact, have laws restricting public investments to conservative and relatively liquid instruments.

In Orange County and other California communities, the shift in the accountability environment began in 1978 when voters there approved Proposition 13, essentially capping property tax revenues on which local governments had come to rely as a predictable and steadily growing source of revenue. Public officials in California, and in several other "tax revolt" states, responded to this challenge with determination and, in some cases, with remarkable success by finding creative and entrepreneurial ways to diversify government revenues and by improving the efficiency and effectiveness of government services.

It was in this political and economic environment that California removed some of the legal and regulatory constraints on financial managers like Robert Citron, freeing them to be more entrepreneurial with public investments. In fact, Citron helped draft the California law that allowed county treasurers, with permission of their boards of supervisors, to use reverse repurchase agreements in which investment securities serve as collateral on loans for the purchase of additional securities.[4] Proposition 13 was designed to limit the discretionary authority of public officials to raise tax rates, and it certainly succeeded in doing that. Ironically, the environment created in part by Proposition 13 had the opposite effect in the domain of investment management by shifting the standard of accountability away from compliance with strict legal and regulatory constraints and toward greater reliance on professional discretion and entrepreneurship. Within this environment, an emerging generation of public sector entrepreneurs are attempting to manage government organizations "like a business" with aggressive strategies to diversify revenues, privatize operations, tailor services to customer needs, and generally enhance government responsiveness and flexibility.

This free-market, entrepreneurial paradigm of public management was given intellectual credibility with the publication of *Reinventing Government*.[5] The philosophy espoused by David Osborne and Ted Gaebler sent shock waves through bureaucratic and political circles. Their book was the first public administration text to become a best-seller, and their philosophy was given political legitimacy when it was endorsed by candidate Bill Clinton during the 1992 presidential campaign. More than just esoteric theory, *Reinventing Government* provided the blueprint for Vice President Al Gore's National Performance Review, which recommended actions, currently being implemented, to improve the effectiveness and efficiency of the federal government.[6] The post–Proposition 13 environment in California provided much of the inspiration for Osborne and Gaebler. Many of the case histories and illustrations used in their book are drawn from the experiences of local governments in California.

Briefly, Osborne and Gaebler believe that government organizations must be liberated from the strangle-hold of regulations, bureaucratic procedures, line-item budgets, and risk-averse organizational cultures if they are to be more entrepreneurial and customer-focused. They argue persuasively, and with many examples, that bureaucracy is the ultimate obstacle to improving government responsiveness and performance. Among their many recommendations are that management systems in government should be less rule-driven and more mission-focused. Public officials, they argue, should be given more discretion and authority to develop strategies to earn money rather than simply spend money. Essentially, they say that governments can and should adapt business management principles to the public sector context in order to more effectively meet the needs of citizens, taxpayers, and future generations.

Intellectually, these are very attractive and exciting themes. In practice, however, they require fundamental shifts in the accountability environment of government agencies at the federal, state, and local levels.[7] The bureaucratic structures and red tape, which Osborne and Gaebler denounce, do indeed inhibit the flexibility and entrepreneurship of government agencies. But the bureaucracy, with all of its well-documented shortcomings, is still the primary instrument of public sector accountability, and its ultimate purpose is to prevent abuse of power and to limit the autonomy and discretion of public officials. Historically, for better or worse, we have relied on these bureaucratic mechanisms—rules, regulations, operating procedures, chains of command, checks and balances—to constrain administrative discretion and to ensure proper stewardship of the public trust.[8] Eliminating this red tape, and the larger bureaucratic framework that produces it, will require the development of new instruments of accountability to replace the old.

Osborne and Gaebler claim that their management philosophy does not supplant the notion of accountability, but rather redefines it by freeing public officials to manage more strategically in response to rapidly changing conditions and emerging public needs. In effect, the Osborne and Gaebler philosophy calls for higher standards of accountability based on professionalism, expertise, delegation, and empowerment of citizens to play a larger and more meaningful role in public affairs.

Let there be no misunderstanding here. This article is not suggesting that the Orange County fiasco can be laid at the feet of Osborne and Gaebler or of anyone who follows their philosophy. But the Orange County case does present a classic example of the risks associated with any "reinvented" notion of accountability that is based on an entrepreneurial model of public management. A more constructive approach, employed in this article, is to try to learn something from the Orange County case by studying it within an expanded framework of accountability. This framework, unlike the narrow and confining bureaucratic framework, is capable of surfacing some plausible public management strategies that are both responsive to changing needs and accountable to the overriding notion of serving the public interest.

Some Definitions of Accountability

The notion of accountability is perhaps *the* core philosophical concept in public management. Still, there remains considerable debate on its meaning. In its most narrow interpretation, accountability involves answering "to a higher authority—legal or organizational—for one's action in society at large or within one's organization."[9] This narrow definition of accountability draws a very clear distinction between two fundamental questions: (1) To *whom* is the organization (or individual worker) *accountable*? and (2) for *what* is the organization (or individual worker) *responsible*?

Strictly speaking, only the first question pertains to "accountability" per se. It deals primarily with mechanisms of supervision, oversight, and reporting to a higher authority in a formal chain of command. Formally, the second question has more to do with concepts like professional *responsibility* and *obligation*, which are distinct and are often treated as such in the scholarly literature.[10]

Others have eschewed the bureaucratic bias implied in these traditional definitions of accountability. A performance-based (versus compliance-based) notion of accountability says that it involves some standard with which to "hold individuals and organizations responsible for performance measured as objectively as possible."[11] Naturally, performance includes the exercise of professional judgement. Therefore, Rosen argues that accountability involves, among other things, the exercise of "lawful and sensible administrative discretion" and efforts to "enhance citizen confidence in . . . administrative institutions."[12] Then, of course, there is the on-going debate, beginning with the seminal exchange between Carl Friedrich[13] and Herman Finer,[14] on how to monitor professional discretion—whether accountability is best enforced by outside oversight or internal management controls. Finally, a strategic perspective on accountability is put forth by Romzek and Dubnick, who say that "accountability involves the means by which public agencies and their workers manage the diverse expectations generated within and outside the organization."[15]

These broader perspectives on accountability introduce an element of strategic management whereby public officials attempt to anticipate shifting public expectations, interpret changing standards of accountability, and position their agencies for proactive as well as reactive responses. In the process, public managers are transformed from a role of passive compliance into one of active participation in framing the accountability standards by which they are judged.[16]

This article embraces the broader concept of accountability—one that is more messy than precise operational definitions but probably more consistent with the "popular" usage of the term. In this view, accountability includes much more than just the formal processes and channels for reporting to a higher authority. Rather, the term "accountability" generally is used to refer to a wide spectrum of public expectations and performance standards that are used to judge the performance, responsiveness, and even "morality" of government organizations. These expectations often include implicit performance criteria that are far more subjective and ill-structured than are formal mandates or explicit rules. And, in this broader conception of accountability, the range of people and institutions to whom government officials must "account" includes not only higher authorities in the institutional chain of command but also the general public, the news media, peer agencies, donors, and many other stakeholders.

As a member of the scholarly community, I have some misgivings about blurring formal distinctions between terms and concepts that have been so carefully defined and articulated by my colleagues. But, as a pragmatist, I sense that the broader conception of accountability is a fact of life in terms of how this topic is discussed in the real world of professional practice. Thus, with apologies to the purists, I will use the term "accountability" throughout this article to refer to the broader notions described above.

A Conceptual Framework for Analyzing Accountability

Elsewhere, I have proposed a conceptual framework for identifying four different types of accountability and some important management issues associated with each.[17] The framework assumes that any system of accountability contains at least two dimensions: (1) a set of accountability standards—explicit or implicit—generated by the organization's strategic environment; and (2) a response—reactive or proactive—from inside the organization.

Even novice public officials quickly learn that they are accountable to at least two types of performance standards. First, they are accountable for explicit performance standards

Figure 11.1   **Four Types of Accountability**

		Accountability Standards	
		Explicit	**Implicit**
Internal Response System	Tactical (Reactive)	(1) Compliance Accountability	(2) Negotiated Accountability
	Strategic (Proactive)	(4) Anticipatory (Advocacy) Accountability	(3) Discretionary (Entrepreneurial) Accountability

Source: Adapted from Kevin P. Kearns, "The Strategic Management of Accountability in Nonprofit Organizations: An Analytic Framework," *Public Administration Review* 54 (March/April 1994): 188.

that are often codified in law, administrative regulations, or contractual obligations. These accountability standards represent the bureaucratic and regulatory environment that public officials confront on a daily basis. Second, they are accountable for *implicit* standards that involve generally accepted notions of appropriate administrative action, professional discretion, and organizational performance. These implicit standards are defined not so much by laws and regulations as by societal values, beliefs, professional norms, and assumptions. Any public official who has confronted the wrath of a citizen ("So *this* is how you are spending my hard-earned money!") is familiar with these implicit and subjective standards of accountability.

The second dimension of the framework assumes that public managers have several options with which to respond to accountability standards. First, they may respond with *tactical* (reactive) approaches when accountability standards are presented to them either in the form of explicit requirements or of implicit expectations. The tactical approach is essentially a stimulus-response, driven by intense pressure from the accountability environment to take some action. Second, they may take *strategic* (proactive) actions to anticipate new or emerging accountability standards and to position their organization within a dynamic accountability environment. The strategic approach requires foresight and a willingness to take corrective action before the organization is forced or pressured to do so.

Superimposing these two dimensions yields a matrix with four cells as illustrated in Figure 11.1.

Let us examine each cell of the matrix in greater detail and with illustrations from the Orange County case. Keep in mind that these four cells are conceptual representations of important segments of the accountability environment. In the real world, the boundaries between the cells may not be as clear and precise as those represented here. But this tool provides a point of departure for additional in-depth analysis and, perhaps, adaptation by decisionmakers to the unique context of their organization.

Compliance Accountability (Cell #1)

The upper left quadrant of the matrix denotes the most familiar, and most narrowly interpreted, form of accountability—*compliance* by a government organization with an explicit and publicly stated standard of performance or operational procedure. The accountability standards in this cell are often codified and enforced by an outside oversight organization and, therefore, carry the force of law. Alternatively, the standards might be embedded in the bureaucratic procedures, chains of command, hierarchies of authority, and checks and balances *within* the organization. While these internal bureaucratic mechanisms do not always carry the force of law, they are very explicit and vigorously enforced as part of the organization's management control system.

Whether the accountability standards are enforced externally or internally, compliance is viewed as essentially *reactive* in nature. That is, the organization (or the individual worker) awaits the formulation of precise and clearly articulated standards and then tries to follow the rules, subject to oversight and periodic audits, or evaluations. This type of accountability environment requires a clear hierarchy of authority that is recognized as legitimate by all actors. Also, compliance involves a relatively heavy reliance on the traditional notion of *bureaucracy* that, especially in government, has been a principal instrument for ensuring that the public trust is not abused.

While compliance is always reactive, it is rarely a *passive*, or knee-jerk, response. Indeed, truly effective compliance requires active participation from the people and organizations that are subject to these explicit standards of accountability. For example, they must design administrative and operational procedures in accordance with the laws and regulations. They must train employees and volunteers to work within those parameters. They must anticipate problems and barriers to overcome during implementation. They must allocate (and perhaps reallocate) sufficient resources to the effort. And, of course, they must monitor their own behavior and compile appropriate information in order to demonstrate (literally "account" for) their compliance. Still, all of these actions are essentially in response to the *stimulus* provided by the law, the regulation, or the bureaucratic standard of accountability that is imposed upon them.

This cell of the framework is used by many states and localities to regulate the investment practices of government jurisdictions, and it is the cell in which Orange County operated prior to the liberalization of California's public investment regulations. Also, it is the cell used by the Securities and Exchange Commission (SEC) to regulate the activities of financial advisors and brokers.

Negotiated Accountability (Cell #2)

The cell in the upper right corner of Figure 11.1 addresses several different accountability contexts. First, government organizations are often held accountable to emerging performance standards that are implicit—that is, standards that arise from shifting societal values and beliefs or from emerging political values and priorities that have not yet been codified in law, administrative regulations, or bureaucratic controls. In such cases, the accountability standards are only loosely defined (or completely undefined) and, therefore, open to debate.

A second circumstance in this cell, and one that also is quite familiar to public administrators, is the need to be accountable or performance standards that are, in fact, codified, but where the laws and regulations (or other contractual arrangements) are vaguely worded and, therefore, subject to interpretation and "translation" by public administrators charged with their implementation.

In both cases, the accountability standards are implicit and imprecise, leading to conflicting standards of performance and relatively high levels of uncertainty among all stakeholders. Even with their ambiguity, however, these accountability standards (or their advocates) are often powerful enough to capture the organization's immediate attention, providing a catalyst for tactical actions and relatively rapid response. Often this response involves some form of negotiation between the organization and its environment. The purpose of the negotiation is to clarify the ambiguous circumstances and to reach agreement on commonly understood standards of accountability.

Thus, this cell of the framework is labeled *negotiated accountability*. In some cases, the negotiations may take place with a particularly powerful (or interested) constituency—individuals or groups who have an unusually high stake in the outcome—such as citizen groups, advocacy organizations, and other coalitions of stakeholders. In other cases, the negotiations may involve a regulating body that enforces a vaguely worded law, regulation, or contract.

The concept of negotiated accountability could apply to several aspects and phases of the Orange County case. First, at the front-end (before the bankruptcy), there is the prospect that everyone associated with the Orange County investment pool—investors, creditors, the County Board of Supervisors, the SEC, and even citizens—would, in retrospect, have wanted to negotiate and reach agreement on: (1) a specified set of objectives for the investment pool, expressed in terms of acceptable levels of risk in relation to potential returns on investment; (2) a portfolio of investment instruments that would best meet the fund's objectives; and (3) how best to manage the portfolio to ensure internal oversight and accountability. Immediately following the crisis, there was speculation that some investors may not have been fully informed regarding the management of the portfolio and, in particular, the use of a single broker for the fund.[18] Also, there is the curious aspect that school districts in Orange County were mandated to participate in the fund, thereby removing any opportunity for them to negotiate.

Second, at the back-end (in the wake of the bankruptcy), there is the very real prospect that some form of negotiated accountability will be required to clarify the obligations of Orange County and the rights of investors under Chapter 9 of the U.S. Bankruptcy Code.[19] Some people believe that Chapter 9 inappropriately relieves the jurisdiction of its legitimate accountability to its creditors since, in theory, the governments involved still have at their disposal certain options to generate more revenue.[20] According to some legal experts, there is even a possibility that Merrill Lynch & Co., the sole broker for the Orange County investment pool, may be liable for some of the fund's losses, just as a bartender is liable for the consequences of serving an obviously intoxicated patron.[21] The legal concept of fiduciary responsibility can be murky and, of course, Merrill Lynch denies any liability. Still, ten years ago the firm negotiated a modest settlement arising from losses incurred by San Jose, California, which employed an investment strategy very similar to that of the Orange County fund. Other securities firms paid a total of $26 million in judgments and penalties arising from the San Jose crisis. Not surprisingly, Merrill Lynch's stock (which itself is a noteworthy instrument of "negotiated accountability") fell 3.4 percent following news of the Orange County bankruptcy.[22]

The concept of negotiated accountability is a very important domain of public management, but it has received relatively little attention in the literature. What are the implicit standards of accountability by which the organization is judged? Are there external stakeholders who are particularly interested in the enforcement of these standards? Are any of these accountability standards negotiable? Would it be in the organization's best interest to negotiate now or later? On what philosophical or legal grounds should the organization negotiate?

These questions may highlight several types of *threats* for the organization. As described above, this cell of the matrix often involves disagreements among stakeholders regarding accountability standards and measures, leading to *conflict* between the organization and its environment. Conflict, in turn, generally involves *risk* and uncertainty because the outcome of the dispute and its long-term effects cannot be fully controlled or easily predicted. Also, low-level conflicts can quickly and unpredictably *escalate* to major controversies, especially when one party or the other perceives that escalation will enhance their power and control of the situation.

However, decisionmakers may perceive several types of opportunities in this cell of the accountability environment. *Timing* is one factor that can offer opportunities. Zartman and Berman say that negotiations may be especially timely when some type of significant change has taken place in the environment that alters the relative power of stakeholders or their respective perceptions of the situation.[23] Negotiations may provide the opportunity to *clarify expectations* and performance standards, thereby reducing uncertainty and risk. In the process, there may be opportunities to *build trust* among participants, especially when negotiations take place in good faith and with mutual disclosure of information.

Discretionary (Entrepreneurial) Accountability (Cell #3)

The cell in the bottom right corner of Figure 11.1 portrays the context in which accountability standards and expectations are implicit. But, unlike the previous cell, these standards are not yet powerful enough to demand an immediate tactical response, such as negotiations with the external environment. In fact, in this cell there may be no identifiable parties with whom to negotiate. Instead, there is tremendous latitude for the exercise of professional judgement and discretionary authority by government officials on behalf of their constituents. This cell recognizes knowledge and expertise as the primary instruments of accountability rather than laws, bureaucratic hierarchies, or negotiated agreements on performance standards. As John Burke says, "Professional responsibility is grounded in the public's high regard for and recognition of knowledge and expertise, and it reflects the great value placed on specialization and professional skill in modern bureaucracies."[24]

This cell is labeled *discretionary (entrepreneurial) accountability* because there is very little meaningful oversight other than the self-defined and self-enforced norms and standards of professional practice. In the absence of meaningful threats or sanctions from the external environment, public officials must take personal and professional responsibility for anticipating and interpreting emerging standards of acceptable professional behavior and organizational performance, weighing long-term risks as well as short-term benefits. Consequently, there can be enormous pressures on public managers in this cell of the matrix. North Carolina's state treasurer, Harlan Boyles, said that, prior to the Orange County incident, he was under intense political pressure from local governments in his state to liberalize investment regulations and restrictions so that they too could begin reaping the high investment dividends enjoyed by communities in California, Texas, Ohio, and elsewhere. Boyles said that he received more than a dozen calls a month from brokers around the country hoping to sway his views. "It's a constant pressure. They'll call and say, 'Let us show you what we did in California.' Thankfully, our General Assembly has never been inclined to liberalize the investment laws."[25]

There is also pressure from peer organizations in this cell of the accountability matrix. David Bronner, director of Alabama's pension fund, said, "I remember a group outing two years ago with the Orange County people. They were very boastful about how well they were doing and how antiquated I was." Bonner also noted that, until recently, he had unilateral discretionary authority to make investments in whatever instruments he deemed appropriate, regardless of their risk.[26]

This is the cell in which Robert Citron was operating when he was managing the Orange County investment pool. In California's deregulated, post–Proposition 13 environment, Citron was given substantial discretionary authority. In his defense, Citron responded by achieving steady gains in the portfolio's value. Clearly, however, there are enormous risks, as well as potential benefits, associated with the notion of discretionary (entrepreneurial) accountability.

Significantly, this is the cell of the matrix that Osborne and Gaebler suggest be enhanced by, in effect, giving government officials more discretionary authority to respond to public needs as they arise. The dilemma, only partially addressed by Osborne and Gaebler, is how to reconcile an entrepreneurial spirit, which requires swift unilateral responses to emerging opportunities, with the fundamental principles of representative bureaucracy, which require time-consuming efforts to build consensus on long-term as well as short-term goals. Indeed, this is the dilemma that has drawn some of the sharpest critiques of the entrepreneurial paradigm in the literature. Bellone and Goerl foretold the Orange County debacle:

> When engaged in *non-mandated risk taking*, the responsibilities of the public administrator become even more a stewardship issue. High-risk investment schemes that have gone wrong and resulted in economic losses, failed arbitrage efforts in investing federal grant funds, and short-term borrowing to pay operating costs . . . are all examples of entrepreneurial risk-taking that ignored the prudent concern for the long-term public good. (emphasis added)[27]

However, the authors go on to suggest that the notions of entrepreneurship and democracy can be reconciled by providing more opportunities for meaningful citizen participation in the affairs of government. They state that a "strong theory of entrepreneurship requires a strong theory of citizenship."[28] This argument is also made by Osborne and Gaebler. But this optimistic view of citizen participation is not shared by everyone. For example, Terry responds that entrepreneurship requires dangerous concentrations of power and a commitment to fundamental change in the traditional notion of political authority and representative bureaucracy on which the profession of public administration is based. He concludes that "we should abandon the misconceived quest to reconcile public entrepreneurship with democracy," and that Bellone and Goerl's notion of civic-regarding entrepreneurship "seems to be a wolf in sheep's clothing."[29]

Coincidentally, there is evidence in the Orange County case that seems to confirm suspicions about the limited ability of citizens to provide a meaningful check on entrepreneurship, especially in a specialized domain like public investment strategies. Robert Citron was reelected to the treasurer's office in June 1994, only six months before the financial crisis. His opponent in the race was John Moorlach, a certified public accountant who based his campaign on Citron's risky investments and the vulnerability of the Orange County investment fund to fluctuating interest rates. Moorlach captured barely one-third of the vote and failed to generate any meaningful or lasting public dialogue on the Orange County investment strategy. Evidently, the voters were either: (1) unconcerned about Citron's management of the investment pool; (2) incapable of making informed judgements because of the complexity of the issues; or (3) distracted by another political issue, Proposition 187 (limiting the rights of illegal immigrants), which had more emotional appeal than did the intellectually challenging notions of reverse repurchase agreements, derivatives, and fluctuating interest rates. Even after the bankruptcy, citizen reactions seemed mixed. A local radio station sponsored "an hour of rage" after the financial crisis, allowing callers to vent their anger. The station received very few angry calls.

While most of us readily embrace the democratic notions of citizen participation and consultation, it is highly unlikely that "typical" citizens would be able to engage in informed and reasoned discourse on this issue. Still, this cell raises important strategic issues for public managers. What opportunities (if any) exist for citizen input on a given entrepreneurial venture? Can such opportunities be created or enhanced? In the absence of citizen input, is the organization prepared to defend its actions in terms of the public interest and in both long-term and short-term perspectives? To what extent are the organizational cultures and professional norms of public agencies compatible with this entrepreneurial paradigm? Are public administrators and elected officials professionally competent to play the entrepreneurial game?

There are many threats in this cell that can be attributed directly to the freedom that public and nonprofit organizations enjoy under these conditions. A major threat in this cell involves increased *exposure to risk*. When discretionary initiatives in this cell fail, the organization cannot hide behind the skirts of a formal regulatory framework by saying, "Well, yes, things did go dreadfully wrong, but we were only following the directives from above!" In effect, this segment of the accountability environment sometimes gives public officials enough rope to hang themselves.

Another type of threat in this cell relates to the culture of the organization. Within an unregulated environment, the organization can become inebriated with the seemingly endless possibilities to enhance or diversify revenues, to reallocate resources, to revise programs and procedures, to reach out to new clients, and so on. In the process, the organization can gradually "drift" from its traditional values and comparative advantages. Also, it can lose sight of its ultimate accountability to the public, even drifting from its legal mandate.

A related type of threat concerns the *core competencies* of the organization. Some government professionals are accustomed to working in a free-market competitive environment, but many are not. They are more comfortable (and more competent) in an environment structured by guidelines, rules, regulations, and other explicit parameters of accountability.

However, the relatively unregulated environment in Cell #3 provides the organization with opportunities for greater *flexibility* and *responsiveness* to changing needs. A related opportunity involves the prospect of seeking *input* and meaningful *participation* from clients, donors, and other stakeholders in designing accountability measures that are relevant to their needs and their perceptions of the public interest. This approach holds the prospect of building support and trust for the organization as well as generating creative ideas that would otherwise not be explored. Another type of opportunity involves the prospect of exercising *leadership* by serving as a *benchmark* of excellence for comparable organizations.

Finally, this environment provides organizations with the opportunity to invest in the *professional development* of staff and elected officials. As described above, this segment of the accountability environment requires new skills to fulfill professional obligations and responsibilities. It requires people who are self-starters and proactive in their efforts to serve the public trust. It requires creativity and innovation. It requires vision and leadership. But most of all, it requires competence.

Anticipatory (Advocacy) Accountability (Cell #4)

Finally, the bottom left cell of the matrix portrays situations in which government agencies face the prospect of explicit accountability standards imposed from the outside. The strategic choices are: (1) to position themselves for compliance with these standards; or (2) to actively participate in developing the new standards. For example, a legislative body or regulatory agency may be considering steps to tighten (or loosen) regulatory controls. In this cell, the decisionmakers seek to anticipate the formulation of these standards in order to position the organization for eventual compliance. Members of the organization may even attempt to play an advocacy role in shaping and defining the standards that they believe will eventually be imposed.

The notion of anticipatory (advocacy) accountability requires that public officials try to stay "ahead of the curve" by being prepared for likely changes in their accountability environment. It also places responsibility on public administrators to educate elected officials and other policy actors on emerging public needs and the risks and benefits associated with contemplated political actions. Thus, the notion of anticipatory accountability is consistent with the concept of "administrative advocacy,"[30] wherein public managers are not only responsible for implementing policy initiatives dictated from above, but also for advocating legislative or administrative initiatives to serve the public interest. This responsibility implies additional burdens of accountability. Summarizing Paul Appleby's normative model of administrative morality, Stephen Baily says, "Politics and hierarchy induce the public servant to search imaginatively for a *public-will-to-be*. In this search, the public servant is often a leader in the creation of a new public will, so he is in part accountable to what he in part creates."[31]

Most likely, in the wake of the Orange County problem, there will be renewed calls for a stricter regulatory environment governing investment of public funds. Naturally, state and local agencies will be well advised to closely monitor these developments as they unfold and, if appropriate, attempt to influence the outcome of these legislative debates.

Significantly, the Orange County case also illustrates the pitfalls of accountability from the standpoint of administrative advocacy. In 1979, Robert Citron, acting as head of the state association of county treasurers, was a prime architect and vocal promoter of legal and regulatory changes, which allowed the use of reverse repurchase arrangements with oversight and approval by local elected officials.[32] As such, Citron and other advocates bore responsibility (at the time they advocated the change) to: (1) relate it to a pressing need in the public interest; (2) build in meaningful oversight mechanisms to monitor impacts and to prevent abuse; and (3) educate legislators and, by extension, the general public regarding risks as well as benefits. Having successfully advocated the new legislation, they bore responsibility to follow the spirit as well as the letter of the law, as suggested by the notion of compliance accountability discussed above.

There are several threats that are unique to this segment of the accountability environment. First, there are *political risks* associated with any form of advocacy. The organization's direct involvement in the formal policy-making process can galvanize widespread debate and controversy, potentially focusing unwanted attention and scrutiny on the organization itself. Also, there is the risk of *alienating powerful constituencies* and jeopardizing the organization's traditional base of support. Finally, there are potential *legal threats*, especially for organizations that have strict limits on their political activity. For these organizations, it is wise to seek professional legal counsel before engaging in any political activity.

However, there are opportunities as well as threats in this accountability environment. There is the opportunity to build *networks* and *coalitions* of other stakeholders who share similar interests and objectives. These coalitions can have beneficial effects long after the political issue has been resolved. Also, there is the opportunity to exercise *leadership* and to focus *favorable attention* on the organization if its motives are widely perceived to advance the public interest. As in Cell #2 (negotiation), there are opportunities to *educate* relevant stakeholders and to *preempt* events that might lead to the imposition of inappropriate standards.

Discussion

The matrix presented in Figure 11.1 illustrates four types of accountability that can be used to highlight, retrospectively, certain aspects of the Orange County situation. Also, embedded within each cell of the matrix are management issues and plausible strategies that public administrators might use to their advantage and, ultimately, to the public's advantage, as they apply strategic management approaches while fulfilling their obligations as stewards of the public trust.

Compliance Accountability

Public organizations—even those operating under an entrepreneurial paradigm—must occasionally conduct a compliance audit. At the most elementary level, this audit should attempt to document the organization's legal obligations as follows:

- a complete listing of oversight agencies to which the organization is generally accountable or that have jurisdiction over selected portions of the organization's mandate and mission;
- a compilation and analysis of the legal or regulatory standards of accountability to which the organization is bound by its mandate, charter, authorizing legislation, and contractual arrangements with other organizations;
- assessments of how well the organization has performed in meeting these standards;
- assessments of compliance with the "spirit" and the "letter" of the law; and
- demonstrated efforts to provide full disclosure of the organization's performance in both the "spirit" and the "letter" of the law.

These approaches, of course, address the most narrowly interpreted aspects of accountability—answering to a higher authority regarding performance and compliance with explicit mandates; they are also among the most important questions decisionmakers will ask when conducting an accountability audit.

Negotiated Accountability

Most of the literature on negotiation approaches the topic from an adversarial perspective—that any form of negotiation is, in effect, a zero sum game wherein the interests of one or more players are advanced at the expense of others. But when attempting to enhance accountability in public management, the adversarial approach to negotiation is unacceptable. Instead, the objective of negotiated accountability is to clarify and define the "public interest" and to reach agreement on what mechanisms and strategies best serve those interests. A cursory list of objectives would include:

- to clarify the multiple and, perhaps, conflicting interpretations of the "public interest" and "accountability" to those interests within the context of specific programmatic activities or proposals;
- to clarify which (if any) accountability issues in a specific programmatic domain are "negotiable" and to distinguish them from those that are "nonnegotiable;"

- to clarify the respective objectives and interests of various policy stakeholders and to separate these objectives and interests from specific proposals or programs to achieve them;
- to clarify and agree on reasonable standards of compliance or performance to which an organization or an individual should be held accountable;
- to reach agreement on reasonable measures, behaviors, processes, or outcomes with which to assess organizational or personal accountability;
- to reach agreement on whether there are uncontrollable factors and contingencies that may affect the accountability relationship in order to ensure, in advance, that actors are not held responsible for events beyond their control;
- to reach agreement on what resources and investments are needed to maintain given levels of accountability and the marginal costs and benefits of incrementally greater (or lesser) degrees of control; and ultimately,
- to build trust among the participants in the negotiation process.

Toward these objectives, the philosophy of "principled bargaining," advanced by Fisher and Ury,[33] seems appropriate. Naturally, considering the high financial and political stakes involved, it is very likely that any negotiations emerging from the Orange County case will be more "adversarial" than "principled."

Discretionary (Entrepreneurial) Accountability

Managers at all levels of government are feeling the same types of pressures, to a greater or lesser degree, as those experienced by Robert Citron. Taxpayers are quick to demand higher levels and improved quality of government services, but they are not inclined to provide additional resources. Moreover, the fiscal pressures on state and local governments are likely to increase with the new Republican leadership in Washington. These fiscal and political pressures, combined with the seemingly endless stream of "antibureaucracy" proposals—in the media, the scholarly literature, the popular literature, and in government—ensure that public managers will continue to use discretionary judgement and entrepreneurial approaches.

But there must be a democratic process—rooted in the political authority of elected officials—through which to decide when professional autonomy and discretion are warranted and when they are not, especially when ". . . professional practice is likely to conflict with the desires and interests of the public or its representatives."[34]

What principles should guide public managers to maintain accountability in a relatively unregulated environment?

- above all, discretionary actions or entrepreneurial ventures must be consistent with the legal mandate and formal authority of the organization;
- such actions or ventures should be mission-focused, guided by an explicit and publicly slated set of goals, operating philosophies, and measures of success;
- all participants must take professional responsibility to obtain full information on the risks as well as the potential benefits;

- discretionary programs, especially entrepreneurial ventures, should have an internal (preferably formal) system of checks and balances to avoid concentrations of power and authority in the hands of one or of several people;
- less formally, participants should foster an organizational culture or "climate" wherein dissenting opinions among participants and stakeholders are not only tolerated but also encouraged and facilitated;
- discretionary initiatives, especially entrepreneurial ventures, should be informed by a formal process of scenario construction wherein the participants examine probabilities of various chains of events (however improbable) and consequences of those events, leading to "best case, worst case, and most likely case" scenarios;
- in the absence of meaningful citizen input, participants in discretionary ventures should engage in a "rehearsal of defenses"[35] by asking, "how and to whom would we defend our actions if called upon to do so?";
- in the absence of citizen input, there should be a mechanism for periodic disclosure of how well the initiative has performed in meeting its objectives;
- discretionary initiatives, especially entrepreneurial ventures, must have a contingency plan that allows the organization to withdraw or otherwise adjust its commitment if the public interest becomes threatened by unforeseen or uncontrollable events; and
- discretionary investments should be overseen by a review body, with prohibitions against single-bet, winner-take-all investment strategies.

Certainly, Robert Citron and his advisors made certain assumptions that interest rates would continue to drop. What we do not know is whether there were mechanisms or processes built into the management systems (or even the organizational culture) that allowed and facilitated the expression of counter-assumptions and alternative strategies for consideration.

The professional obligation to be fully informed and knowledgeable in any entrepreneurial venture was expressed by Charles Cox, finance director of Farmers Branch, Texas, when he said, "If I don't understand it, and I don't know how it works, I'm not going to invest in it."[36] A recent survey of members of the Government Finance Officers Association (GFOA) found that only 4 percent were knowledgeable about derivative securities, 20 percent said that they had limited knowledge, and 76 percent said that they had some or no knowledge.[37]

Anticipatory Accountability

Levine, Peters, and Thompson state that "accountability tends to serve democracy best when administrators anticipate the legitimate preferences of elected officials and adjust their behavior accordingly."[38] Certainly, there is no crystal ball issued to public managers when they take their office. Still, several principles should guide their efforts to remain accountable to the public trust when operating in this type of accountability environment:

- develop and nurture organizational routines for continuously scanning changes in the accountability environment;
- use multiple methods to stay in touch with citizens, elected officials, and peers in order to continuously monitor emerging needs; and
- work with legislators in a bi-partisan or nonpartisan way to craft legislative proposals that are responsive to the public interest.

These steps will help ensure that public managers stay on top of emerging issues and position themselves and their organizations accordingly.

Summary

This article has examined the cursory facts of the Orange County bankruptcy within a conceptual framework that recognizes four perspectives on accountability. Also, the article presents a set of management strategies to enhance public sector accountability within a shifting environment.

It would be the height of arrogance to suggest that these methods could have prevented an incident like the Orange County debacle. But they do provide a heuristic device that can be used by practitioners and scholars to assess the multiple dimensions of accountability and the management systems appropriate to each.

Acknowledgment

The author gratefully acknowledges the constructive comments of the anonymous reviewers as well as his colleague, Professor Iris Young, at the Graduate School of Public and International Affairs, University of Pittsburgh.

Notes

1. Leslie Wayne, "The Search for Municipal Cowboys." *New York Times*, December 8, 1994, p. cl.

2. Seth Mydans, "Shock and Confusion in Offices and Streets." *New York Times*, December 8, 1994, p. C16.

3. See also, Barbara Romzek and Melvin J. Dubnick, "Accountability in the Public Sector: Lessons from the Challenger Tragedy." *Public Administration Review* 47 (May/June 1987): 227–38.

4. Sallie Hofmeister, "A Strategy's Creator Also Drafted the Law." *New York Times*, December 8, 1994, p. c16.

5. David Osborne and Ted Gaebler. *Reinventing Government* (Reading: Addison-Wesley, 1992).

6. Vice President Al Gore. *Creating a Government That Works Better and Costs Less: Report of the National Performance Review* (Washington, DC: U.S. Government Printing Office, 1993).

7. See Larry D. Terry, "Why We Should Abandon the Misconceived Quest to Reconcile Public Entrepreneurship with Democracy." *Public Administration Review* 53 (July/August 1993): 393–95; see also, Ronald C. Moe, "The 'Reinventing Government' Exercise: Misinterpreting the Problem, Misjudging the Consequences." *Public Administration Review* 54 (March/April 1994): 111–22.

8. Charles T. Goodsell. *The Case for Bureaucracy: A Public Administration Polemic*, 3rd ed. (Chatham, NJ: Chatham House, 1985).

9. Jay M. Shafritz. *The HarperCollins Dictionary of American Government and Politics* (New York: HarperCollins, 1992), 4.

10. Terry L. Cooper. *The Responsible Administrator* (San Francisco: Jossey-Bass, 1990), 59–62.

11. Samuel Paul. "Strengthening Public Sector Accountability: A Conceptual Framework" (Washington, DC: World Bank Discussion Paper #136, 1991), 2.

12. Bernard Rosen. *Holding Government Bureaucracies Accountable*, 2nd. ed. (New York: Preager, 1989), 4.

13. Carl J. Friedrich, "Public Policy and the Nature of Administrative Responsibility," in *Public Policy*, 1940, ed. Carl J. Friedrich (Cambridge: Harvard University Press, 1940).

14. Herman Finer, "Administrative Responsibility in Democratic Government," *Public Administration Review* 1 (Summer 1941): 335–50.

15. Romzek and Dubnick, "Accountability in the Public Sector," 228.

16. For a full discussion of both the positive and negative aspects of professional discretion in setting accountability standards, see John Burke, *Bureaucratic Responsibility* (Baltimore: Johns Hopkins University Press, 1986).

17. Kevin P. Kearns, "The Strategic Management of Accountability in Nonprofit Organizations: An Analytical Framework," *Public Administration Review* 54 (March/April 1994): 185–92.

18. G. Bruce Knecht, "Merrill Lynch's Role as Broker to Fund May Expose It to Liability, Lawyers Say," *Wall Street Journal*, December 8, 1994, p. A9.

19. Tom Herman and Wade Lambert, "Filing Spotlights Murky Corner of Finance," *Wall Street Journal*, December 8, 1994, p. A9; see also, Harrison Golden, "How Orange County Can Dig Out of Its Hole," *Wall Street Journal*, December 14, 1995, p. A12.

20. John E. Petersen, "It's Better Not to Belly-Up," *Governing* (February 1995): 56.

21. Knecht, "Merrill Lynch's Role," A9.

22. Ibid., A9.

23. I. William Zartman and Maureen R. Berman. *The Practical Negotiator* (New Haven: Yale University Press, 1982), 47–54.

24. Burke, *Bureaucratic Responsibility*, 25.

25. *Wall Street Journal*, "Public Finance Chiefs Are Often Very Boring: That's the Good News," December 8, 1994, p. C1.

26. Ibid., C1.

27. Carl J. Bellone and George Frederick Goerl, "Reconciling Public Entrepreneurship and Democracy." *Public Administration Review* 52 (March/April 1992): 132.

28. Ibid., 133.

29. Terry, "Why We Should Abandon the Misconceived Quest," 394–95.

30. Shafritz, *The Dictionary of American Government*, 10.

31. Stephen K. Baily, "Ethics and the Public Service" in *Public Administration: Concepts and Cases*, ed. Richard J. Stillman (Boston: Houghton Mifflin, 1984), 480.

32. Hofmeister, "A Strategy's Creator," C16.

33. Roger Fisher, William Ury, and Bruce Patton. *Getting to Yes: Negotiating Agreement Without Giving In*, 2nd ed. (New York: Penguin, 1991).

34. Burke, *Bureaucratic Responsibility*, 148.

35. Terry Copper. *The Responsible Administrator* (San Francisco: Jossey-Bass, 1990), 23.

36. *Wall Street Journal*, "Public Finance Chiefs," 1.

37. Ibid., 1.

38. Charles H. Levine, B. Guy Peters, and Frank J. Thompson. *Public Administration: Challenges, Choices, Consequences* (Glenview: Scott, Foresman/Little Brown, 1990), 190.

PART 4

WHAT ARE THE BEST TRAITS AND SKILLS FOR LEADERS IN THE PUBLIC SERVICE?

For the first fifty years of the twentieth century the field of leadership research studied traits and skills of leaders in order to determine which were most important. Then Ralph Stogdill (1948) and others concluded that a "pure" theory of traits and skills was insufficient to explain leadership. Leadership varies too much by individual differences and situations to build the *primary* structure of a theory of leadership around the possession of a select series of traits and skills. Yet that is not to say that these variables are not important or that the possession of certain traits and skills does not lead to the emergence of leadership more frequently than does their absence. We now turn to a review of those more significant personal, motivational, and value traits and skills.

Personal traits are among the most powerfully correlated with leadership. Some of the most commonly cited include self-confidence, decisiveness, resilience, flexibility, energy, willingness to assume responsibility, and emotional maturity. Yet despite their general importance, no traits are absolute. Further, they may peak in the moderate range or be highly linked with at least one other mitigating characteristic. Thus, *self-confidence* leads others to want to follow (even if the leader has a poor idea) but excessive self-confidence can turn into egotism, stubbornness, or aloofness. *Decisiveness* is key because decisions have to be made so that work can proceed; yet numerous situations call for deliberation and slower participative processes such as those with poorly structured problems, leader ignorance, and problems with longer time horizons (Vroom and Jago 1988). *Resilience* (or persistence) is an important trait of leaders because long-term, higher-range goals may mean hard work, occasional failures to overcome, and temporary discomfort. Yet excessive resilience may lead to insensitivity of follower needs and an unwillingness to acknowledge unproductive strategies. Resilience is normally softened with *flexibility*. Flexible leaders understand that situations evolve, resources may need adaptation, and original plans may be improved with learning. Yet an excessively flexible leader may be perceived as weak, indeterminate, or too willing to compromise. Because of the demands of leadership it is hard to have too much *energy*. Nonetheless, energy focused on excessively narrow work goals can lead to pathological consequences such as obsessiveness, poor quality of personal life, and even ill health. *Willingness to assume responsibility* is an important factor that many people lack because they have different life goals or simply prefer to avoid positions of high visibility.[1] Finally, *emotional maturity* is simply having a balanced ego regarding self and others (e.g., a realistic sense of self-worth), as well as an absence of emotional or personal issues that drain energy from the work setting.

Just as leaders tend to have certain personal traits, they are likely to have certain motivational traits (McClelland 1985). Perhaps the most important is the *need to achieve.*[2]

Organizations have work to produce and have changes to make; effective leaders help them produce and change. Thus leaders who are driven by a need for achievement tend to project this through the accomplishments of their organization. An achievement orientation tends to result in higher and harder goals with more determination to reach them. Excesses of an achievement orientation can lead to frustration when progress is slow or bitterness over a lack of personal advancement that may have more to do with bad luck than a lack of ability and drive. Leaders also have a slightly greater tendency to seek power, which is certainly a requisite for most leaders and can lead to the productive study of influence, but which can also become self-serving or dysfunctional if unchecked.

Effective leaders also tend to share certain value traits; these traits have a special cast in the public sector. Nearly every study of followers' top preferences of leaders puts the *honesty/integrity/fairness* cluster before competence. Possession of this trait tends to result in follower trust, even when the leader must judge and make tough decisions. Because of the stewardship role of public administrators, honesty and fairness have a nearly hallowed stature that, when absent, quickly tarnishes leaders' reputations (Fairholm 1991; Terry 1995; Riccucci 1995). Another value trait is the *drive for excellence*, which is related to achievement but has more of an aesthetic quality. Value traits that tend to be significantly more desirable in the public sector than in the business sector include a *public service motivation* and *cultural sensitivity*.

Some additional traits associated with leadership are intelligence (which can be bolstered by education and training and can be captured in analytic skills), verbal fluency (as a charismatic trait rather than as a skill; see below), and creativity (see continual learning below). Important though they may be, they are largely captured in other concepts for purposes of this brief review. Many people would like to think that physical traits do not bear on leadership, or at least should not. Research has shown that many physical traits, such as height, attire, gender, and attractiveness, have generally positive but weak correlations (Bass 1990, 80–81). A more significant feature, however, is comportment. An effective leader's physical presence tends to give others a sense of confidence and well-being.

Although the distinction between traits and skills is a useful heuristic tool, which we will employ here, in reality it is impossible to sharply demarcate traits (innate and very early-imprinted characteristics) and skills (acquired characteristics most susceptible to improvement with learning, especially in adulthood). We will discuss six skill clusters: technical, communication, social, influence/negotiation, analytic, and the skill of continual learning.

All leaders need *technical skills,* but the amount and type of those skills tends to shift according to the level of the position in an organization (Katz 1955). Technical skills include the content or generic knowledge of the subject, but also the knowledge of the processes actually used in the organizational setting. Technical credibility—expertise— can also be an important source of power (French and Raven 1959). An example of the complex relationship of technical skill is illustrated by McCall, Lombardo, and Morrison (1988), who studied the patterns that lead executives to become derailed in their careers. They found that one prevalent pattern was for technically sophisticated front-line supervisors to become too reliant on narrow technical expertise, which at higher levels led to insensitivity and arrogance.

Another large domain of skills commonly needed by managers and leaders is the area of communication, including the use of verbal, oral, and nonverbal media. *Communication skills* include relaying and sometimes "selling" information (technical information), ideas (concepts), and ideals (norms and values) as well as collecting information, sentiments, and ideas from others. Thus, it is often true that leaders are strong in some areas, weak in others, and need to develop different types of communication skills if they are to be effective across the levels and areas of their organization. For example, explicitly relaying technical information is an important skill for a supervisor with many new employees, whereas it would be significantly less so for a chief executive officer. Another important dimension of communication quality is linguistic form and subtlety. A good leader will use a linguistic format that will encourage the appropriate exchange of information and have the finesse to encourage maximum effort without being perceived as being domineering or manipulative. For example, a time-sensitive crisis may need a short "crisis mode" prelude preceding a command; or a directive might be placed in a request format, allowing the recipient some implementation latitude.

A large related area has to do with *social skills*. Different aspects of social skills include friendliness or sociability, expressiveness, and sensitivity (social perceptiveness). People who enjoy others (commonly called extroverts) have an edge in social skills but introverts can also learn to be highly adept socially and to enjoy social interaction. People who can be expressive in appropriate and tactful ways about feelings as well as about shared goals tend to be more successful as leaders. Finally, social skills require a sensitivity to the specific abilities and needs of others, and appropriate responses.

A moment's reflection about power in administrative settings (*influence and negotiation skills*) provides an easy dichotomy: power stems partially from the organizational role position and partially from the occupant of the position. In extreme cases, some people wield power entirely through formal position (generally without much popularity) and, though less common, some people wield considerable power without any position. In their classic analysis of social power, French and Raven (1959) further specify types of social power. Position power includes legitimate power that is authorized through the position, coercive power is the power to punish people who do not comply, and reward power is the power to provide benefits to those who do. Personal power stems from expert power, which is the power of knowledge, and referent power, which is the power of being liked and/or trusted. Weber (1946) pointed out long ago that public bureaucracies are structurally inclined to emphasize legitimate power through finely detailed authorizing processes and expert power because of the preference to hire and promote based on merit. He also pointed out that referent power (charisma) is generally required from leaders bent on great changes, although it is substantially less critical in mature organizations. From contemporary practice we know that coercive and reward power are relatively difficult to exercise in the public sector, at least in comparison to the private sector, and we will simply assert for our current purposes that referent power is significantly underutilized. Generalizing for simplicity, leaders are best advised to use positional power sparingly and strategically, and to try to rely most heavily on their personal power (Barnard 1938).

Analytic skills concern the ability to remember, make distinctions, and deal with complexity. They include memory, discrimination, cognitive complexity, and a tolerance for ambiguity. Memory is useful for both technical data and social interaction. Discrimination has to do with the ability to make distinctions and identify critical trends and useful data from the welter of information bombarding leaders. Cognitive complexity means that a leader can work at different levels simultaneously, and balance different types of situation, domains of responsibility, and timelines. A tolerance for ambiguity is necessary so that leaders do not exercise decisiveness prematurely and can allow situations (or their understanding) to mature to the point that action is necessary (or will be effective).

Although *continual learning* has become a more popular concept in the last decade and has been democratized to cover most of the workforce, it has long been recognized as an important executive/leadership skill (Argyris and Schön 1974). At a minimum, leaders are required to handle daily problems, and more often than not, they are working on a number of major decisions. Such activities generally require large amounts of new data that must be related to unique situations. Old solutions must be adapted, or entirely new ones must be devised. Although some aspects of continual learning have an innate quality resulting from traits such as flexibility and drive for excellence, it seems to be a largely learned mind-set that is affected by training and organizational culture. Mentors are particularly helpful in showing how to work through one problem at a time.

Comparing Skill and Trait Taxonomies

One of the greatest challenges for both the general reader as well as the researcher is to adopt a taxonomy of leadership traits and skills. That entails both (1) establishing a set of terms (a nomenclature) with definitions and (2) ensuring that the conceptual map is relatively comprehensive (i.e., that there are no large gaps) *and* elegant (i.e., not excessively long for practitioners or too conceptually overlapping for researchers). For example, should the need for achievement, the drive for results, and ambition be considered separate concepts or a single concept? If they are considered overlapping enough to be a single concept, which term should be the trait label, and which should define sub-elements? Because there are so many candidates for important leadership traits and skills (even excluding a huge behavioral list), if a single taxonomic list is *not* adopted (at least as a point of reference), one is likely to get lost in a blizzard of synonymous terms and overlapping concepts.

The editors of this volume have proposed a list of ten traits and six skill clusters above. Both longer and shorter lists are available; see for example the American Management Association and researcher John Sussman (in Stone 1981). Table P4.1 is a rough equivalence of the terms from those lists. (See also the list provided by Daley and Naff in part 6, items 13–21 labeled effectiveness characteristics).

It is important to note that few of the readings cover all, or even most, of the leader characteristics in these lists. Rather most of them focus on a few of the traits and/or skills in depth.

Table P4.1

A Comparison of Trait and Skill Taxonomies

Van Wart and Dicke	AMA	Sussman
(16 concepts)	(17 concepts)	(11 concepts)
Traits		
Self-confidence	Perceived objectivity	Aggressiveness (a)
Decisiveness	Proactivity	Aggressiveness (b)
Resilience	Adaptability	Concern for results (a)
Energy	Stamina	
Need for achievement	Concern with impact	Ambition
	Efficiency orientation	Concern for results (b)
Responsibility	Development of others	Desire for responsibility
Flexibility	Spontaneity	Social adaptability
Service motivation and customer orientation	Positive regard	Concern for people
Personal integrity	Self-control	Integrity
Emotional maturity	Accurate self-assessment	Loyalty
		Appearance
		Exceptional intelligence
Skills		
Technical skills		
Communication skills	Self-presentation	
Social skills	Management of groups	
Influence and negotiation	Use of unilateral impact	
Analytic skills	Conceptualization	
	Logical thought	
	Diagnostic use of concepts	
Continual learning ability		Creativity

Notes: Sussman's list was intended solely as a trait list. Because of the broadness of Sussman's terms, some were used twice, as designated by (a) and (b). Although some of these terms are close equivalents (e.g., resilience and stamina), many of these terms are only rough equivalents (e.g., self-confidence and aggressiveness).

Review of the Selections in Part 4

The first article, "Government Bureaucrats *Are* Different" (1962), is by James F. Guyot. His piece was one of the first empirical studies to look at the similarities and differences between private- and public-sector managers. Two questions arise: Are the two sectors different in significant ways, and, Are those that carry out the functions in these two sectors different? It is the second question that he addresses particularly well and that is so pertinent to the examination of traits and skills. Because part of his research provides a sociological perspective on the background of government bureaucrats, his piece was placed first. He also presents data regarding the traits/skills of the need for achievement, the need for affiliation, the need for power, energy, willingness to accept responsibility, and service motivation, among others. Specifically he finds that business bureaucrats have a higher level of affiliation, while the indicator for achievement was higher on the public-sector side. Although these findings have been disputed, he does an excellent job of placing them in historical context.

The second selection is "A Technique to Capitalize on Human Intelligence in Organizations: Brain Skill Management" (1996) by Weston Agor. He discusses the classic left-right brain functions, people's natural preferences, and the placement and training of employees based on these preferences. For example, he notes that lower-level managers have more programmed decisions to make (decisions with few ambiguous or unspecified factors), requiring left-brain skills, while top-level managers make more non-programmed decisions, using a right-brain capacity. He also examines the strengths and weaknesses of analytical types versus intuitive types. Although he is careful not to suggest that certain jobs *must* be filled by certain personality types (which would lead to unhealthy stereo-typing), he does argue for the need to be cognizant of inherent job demands, manager characteristics, and subsequent training needs based on a coherent analysis. Organizations need all types of managers and they become high-performing, he asserts, when they consciously select intuitive types for idea generation, analytic types to critically evaluate the ideas, and integrative types to refine implementation plans.

Marshall Dimock's (1986) "Creativity" asserts the primacy of creativity for government using Toynbee's long-term argument: "civilizations survive only when they have creative minorities that are adequately motivated toward worthy goals," in which public administration inevitably must play a vital role. He not only acknowledges the innate and learned aspects of creativity, but argues that the supportiveness of the environment is the most important factor. Dimock dissects the nature of creativity using five schools of thought. *Intuitionism* emphasizes the innate aspects of creativity based on psychological "hard-wiring" and preferences that have been dominated by the left-right brain research. *Synthesizing* is the type of creativity that brings concrete disparate ideas together, such as in a master plan. *Imagination* is the ability to see how things that do not have a concrete reality might be, such as the establishment of an entirely new program. *Levels-of-attention* is a school of thought that emphasizes the ability to translate or superimpose one reality on another in order to come up with new perceptions or insights such as those that might occur by benchmarking with an organization in a different industry. He points out that although these four theories of creativity emphasize harmony, the fifth points out that creativity can occur because of *conflict and discord,* properly channeled, such as the working agreements that must be reached when administrators preside over contending special interests. Finally, he points out that these theories are not mutually exclusive and may operate in different contexts. Therefore, administrators should be sensitive to the different types of creativity and find ways to encourage and harness them all.

The last two selections are from practitioners describing their experiences in the field. In "Successful Leadership in Local Government Programs: Hillsborough County's Productivity Initiatives" (1991), Helen Levine identifies five attributes for successful entrepreneurial leadership in local government. The first is an intellectual savvy to see opportunities and be able to instinctively assess their timeliness. Another is having the courage to take risks when the time is right. A third characteristic is having credibility within the organization for honesty and technical competence. A fourth trait is a sense of humor and the emotional maturity to be resilient and flexible in the turbulent environment that typifies the dynamic organization. The final trait is the drive to achieve results, despite obstacles and setbacks.

The final article is by Donald Stone, who is very much writing as a practitioner—"Notes on the Governmental Executive: His Role and His Methods" (1945). His is a global assessment addressing the skills needed for governmental leadership in large agencies, while implying the traits needed (resilience, flexibility, energy, emotional maturity, etc.). (It also discusses a number of structural elements, similar to the piece by Lawton.) He emphasizes the need for honing social and influence-negotiation skills, rather than relying on position power, which must be used in an "economical fashion." Relatedly, he stresses communication skills to create a team and to excite admiration, similar to the views of the transformationalists. He takes a sophisticated position regarding the role of technical skills depending on level of authority, the need for credibility, and the requirement to provide genuine technical guidance and first-hand analysis of technical suggestions. Finally, regarding the nature versus nurture argument about the source of leadership, he seems to think that many people have what it takes and can be coached to be much better, but that if "he doesn't have it, no amount of boning up on what experience has taught us will help him much."

Notes

1. This is often seen in the professions in which it is common to return to front-line work after a stint in a leadership position.

2. In addition to achievement, McClelland was also highly interested in the need for power and the need for affiliation.

References

Argyris, Chris, and Donald A. Schön. 1974. *Theory in Practice.* San Francisco: Jossey-Bass.

Barnard, Chester. 1938. *The Functions of the Executive.* Cambridge, MA: Harvard University Press.

Bass, Bernard M. 1990. *Bass & Stogdill's Handbook of Leadership.* New York: Free Press.

Fairholm, Gilbert. 1991. *Values Leadership: Toward a New Philosophy of Leadership.* New York: Praeger.

French, J., and B.H. Raven. 1959. "The Bases of Social Power." In D. Cartwright (ed.), *Studies of Social Power.* Ann Arbor, MI: Institute for Social Research, 150–67.

Katz, Robert. 1955. "The Skills of an Effective Administrator." *Harvard Business Review* (January–February): 33–42.

McCall, Morgan W. Jr., Michael M. Lombardo, and Ann M. Morrison. 1988. *The Lessons of Experience: How Successful Executives Develop on the Job.* New York: Lexington Books.

McClelland, D.C. 1985. *Human Motivation.* Glenview, IL: Scott, Foresman.

Riccucci, Norma T. 1995. *Unsung Heroes: Federal Execucrats Making a Difference.* Washington, DC: Georgetown University Press.

Stone, Donald C. 1981. "Innovative Organizations Require Innovative Managers." *Public Administration Review* 41 (5): 507–13.

Terry, Larry D. 1995. *Leadership of Public Bureaucracies: The Administrator as Conservator.* Thousand Oaks, CA: Sage.

Vroom, Victor H., and Arthur G. Jago. 1988. *The New Leadership: Managing Participating in Organizations.* Upper Saddle River, NJ: Prentice Hall.

Weber, Max. 1946. *From Max Weber: Essays in Sociology,* H.H. Gerth and C. Wright Mills (eds.). New York: Oxford University Press.

CHAPTER 12

GOVERNMENT BUREAUCRATS *ARE* DIFFERENT

JAMES F. GUYOT

At the sound of the word "bureaucrat" the man in the street will probably imagine some time-serving Post Office clerk or a power-hungry New Dealer. At the same time a sociologist will conjure up the "ideal type" of an official occupying a defined position within a large-scale, rational organization (be it church, army, trade union, or telephone company), where he plays out his role according to prescribed rules and becomes more like those rules day by day. Perhaps it is a fault of our language that one word carries two such different meanings, yet there is a common referent. Both layman and academic would agree that a GS-9 Qualifications Rating Examiner in the U.S. Civil Service Commission is a "bureaucrat." But which is the more appropriate characterization? How might we distinguish government bureaucrats from their opposite numbers in the business world? Or are they both running the same race under different colors?

The Togetherness of Person and Position

Underneath a characterization of bureaucrats in terms of what kinds of positions they hold in what kinds of organizations lies the assumption that there exists a particularly appropriate relationship between an individual and his occupational position. Speculation on the nature of this relationship has led to the flowering of a number of interesting social theories such as Max Weber's delineation of the role of the "Protestant Ethic" in the development of capitalist institutions, the influence of class on consciousness in Marxian sociology, and Robert K. Merton's often quoted essay on "Bureaucratic Structure and Personality," which concludes that:

> ... the bureaucratic structure exerts a constant pressure upon the official to be "methodical, prudent, disciplined." If the bureaucracy is to operate successfully, it must maintain a high degree of reliability of behavior. ... Discipline can be effective only if the ideal patterns are buttressed by strong sentiments.[1]

Here the question arises, to what extent do occupational situations shape personality or to what extent do personality needs influence the selection and continuation in an oc-

---

From *Public Administration Review*, vol. 22, no. 4 (1962): 195–202. Copyright © 1962 by American Society for Public Administration. Reprinted with permission.

cupation? Sociologists and psychologists tend to give different weights to occupational role and personality factors. Others give up the game and label the interaction of organizational and individual forces the "fusion process." Another set of theoretical questions has to do with the latitude of personal behavior that "fits" into what may be defined as a particular role. The present state of role theory is too unstable to provide much guidance here. Nevertheless, there is general agreement that some sort of a relationship does exist between personalities and occupational roles. From this it follows that significant differences or similarities in the character of bureaucratic roles in government agencies and large business organizations, should appear also in the personality characteristics of people playing comparable roles in these two structures.

Who Goes with Whom?

What motives propel a bureaucrat along his career in the federal government, and how are they different from those of his counterpart in a large business organization? What tells us more about the structure of a man's motives: knowing whether he works in a public or a private bureaucracy or knowing whether he is an engineer, an accountant, or a public relations man? Speaking concretely, does the personality of a production engineer in the Air Materiel Command run along lines somewhat similar to a budget assistant in the Office of Naval Research, or is it closer to the personality of a managing foreman at General Motors?

To answer this question and probe the reality behind the public and the sociological images of bureaucrats personality tests were given to comparable samples of 247 middle managers coming from several government departments and a range of large private firms.[2] To aid the comparison, these parallel samples are cross-cut into five types of occupational roles similar to those used in the *Dictionary of Occupational Titles* and other research on occupations. The three motives measured by these tests—motivation for *Achievement,* for *Affiliation,* and for *Power*—are particularly relevant to the characteristics of these two images. *Achievement* motivation resembles loosely the "Protestant ethic," a desire to accomplish something as an end in itself, a concern with standards of performance. *Affiliation* motivation, on the other hand, as a concern with acceptance or rejection by others comes close to the "social ethic" which Whyte finds motivating the organization man. *Power* motivation is simply the desire to dominate or influence others and, as a crucial variable in any governmental system, its importance grows with the increasing effectiveness of the machinery of government.[3]

A Split Decision

Table 12.1 shows the average motive scores for matching the samples of governmental and business bureaucrats. Checking the position of our hypothetical production engineer in the Air Materiel Command, it can be seen that in *Achievement* and *Affiliation* motivation he resembles his fellow government employees and is not much like his opposite number on the business side. In *Power* motivation, however, he seems closer to his business counterpart.

Table 12.1

Achievement, Affiliation, and Power Motivation Scores by Sector and by Role for a Sample of Business and Federal Government Middle Managers

Occupational roles	Cell govt.	Size bus.	Achievement			Affiliation			Power		
			Govt.	Bus.	Av. for role	Govt.	Bus.	Av. for role	Govt.	Bus.	Av. for role
Sales and public contact	8	21	6.00	7.467	6.738	14.71	18.79	16.75	19.42	16.72	18.07
General management	33	30	8.758	5.233	6.995	17.90	20.02	18.96	15.41	14.33	14.87
Budget and personnel	53	15	6.019	5.333	5.676	16.94	17.49	17.22	14.92	15.15	15.03
Science and research engineering	23	8	7.783	3.875	5.872	15.73	16.61	16.17	16.97	18.60	17.79
Production engineering	30	26	7.00	5.385	6.193	15.91	22.74	19.33	15.18	15.18	15.18
Average for each sector			7.112	5.460		16.24	19.13		16.38	16.00	

A statistical analysis of variance in the average motive scores finds these relationships true for the sample at large. *Achievement* motivation distinguishes significantly between government and business bureaucrats as a whole but not between different occupational roles encompassing both government and business middle managers. The same is true for *Affiliation* motivation, except that some of the variation can be attributed to a combination of role and sector factors. But, with *Power* motivation occupational roles are clearly distinguished while differences between business and government are not. In the first two motives there are fundamental differences between bureaucrats who work for the government and those who work for private business.[4] Do these findings mean that the sociological image of bureaucracy is a mirage? Not at all. There are significant similarities along the lines of occupation in *Power* motivation and occupational roles bear some relation to differences in *Affiliation* motivation. Although occupational roles do not distinguish motivations across the board, some other organizational characteristic or combination of characteristics such as size of organization, degree of centralization, etc. might do so. Do these findings mean that the popular image is a true copy? We must look at the nature of the differences in motivation between government and business bureaucrats to answer this question.

Distinguishing Between Bureaucrats

Overall differences in motivation between government and business bureaucrats appear in Figure 12.1. Here the government bureaucrats show a higher level of *Achievement* motivation while the businessmen are higher in *Affiliation* motivation. This is quite the opposite from what an examination of American folklore would lead one to expect. Furthermore, the expected distinction in *Power* motivation is too small to be significant. How can we explain research

Figure 12.1 **Relative Levels of Achievement, Affiliation, and Power Motivation in Comparable Samples of Government and Business Bureaucrats**

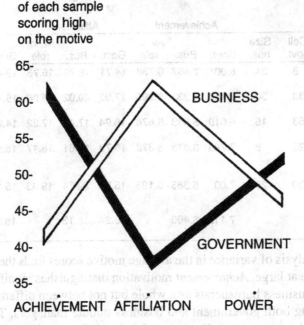

Note: In comparing samples of 147 government and 100 business bureaucrats, the differences in achievement and affiliation motivation are statistically significant ($X2 = 8.70$, $P < .02$ and $X2 = 5.47$, $P < .04$, respectively) while the difference in Power motivation is not. ($X2 = 0.448$, $P > .50$).

results which fly in the face of widely if not altogether reasonably held beliefs, and what significance does this have for the role of the government bureaucracy in the United States?

First of all, let us keep in mind the time and space dimensions of the samples from which these results were drawn. These are men who held middle management rank in large-scale government and business organizations during the late 1950s and who probably selected their particular bureaucratic career sometime before or shortly after World War II. The spread of the government sample does not include such stereotyped departments as State and the Post Office but covers rather heavily the area of the defense agencies. Neither does the business sample cover all kinds of businesses but only those firms large enough and "progressive" enough to ship young men off for a year or so to high priced executive development programs. Taking account of these limitations four generalizations can be suggested to explain these results.

1. The merit system has made at least some of the impact it was intended to make on the character of the civil service.
2. "Bureaucratic" recruitment to management positions draws more from the lower socio-economic groups than do the usual processes of business succession.

3. The money motive and the Protestant Ethic are not the same thing.
4. The civil service is no special preserve for the quest for power.

The Protestant Ethic, the Social Ethic, and the Merit System

Perhaps the most general formal distinction in character between public and private bureaucracies lies in that bundle of personnel practices known as the "merit system." In theory, regularized and objective criteria rather than caprice and personal favor govern the selection, retention, and promotion of civil service employees while careers in the business world are shaped by a complex of factors among which favoritism and nepotism may play a significant role. If there really exists such a difference in the character of these two bureaucracies, then a prima facie case could be made for finding a higher level of *Achievement* motivation in one and a higher level of *Affiliation* motivation in the other just as they appear in Figure 12.1.[5]

Another factor contributing to a heavy concern for the affections of others on the part of rising junior executives would be the relatively longer apprenticeship to the "human relations approach" which business organizations, especially the progressive ones, have enjoyed.

In the *Organization Man* Whyte describes how he believes the Social Ethics or reliance on the group, as both the mode of action and the source of values, is displacing the Protestant Ethic as a guide for those on the way up in business and other large organizations. Here is a psychological complement to the bureaucratization of society described by the sociologists. Of course the sweep of any social trend varies from place to place. The evidence of the study in motivations reported here suggests that one element of this trend, belongingness as an aspect of personnel administration, is in fact more advanced in the private than in the public sector. At the same time, another element of this trend toward bureaucracy, the requirement of specific or professional qualifications for office, which has advanced further in the government sector, probably offers a better environment for the Protestant Ethic. The balance struck by the elements of this trend at a particular point in time is shown in Figure 12.1. What are the chances that in the future more rationalized personnel methods in business and more judicialized personnel procedures in government will push the balance toward another direction?

Bureaucratic Recruitment and Social Mobility

The rational model of bureaucracy also suggests that individuals of modest social origins have more opportunity to advance to the top ranks in organizations where selection and promotion are based on training and achievement than where family connections, ethnic origins, personal wealth, and other considerations help determine who will fill the room at the top. This democratizing aspect of bureaucratic recruitment should be particularly prominent in government during periods of rapid expansion such as the New Deal and war years. While the children of the managerial elite have both the incentive and the opportunity to follow the career paths of their fathers, children of professional families

182

Figure 12.2 A Comparison of the Social Origins of Top Executives and Middle Managers in Business and Government

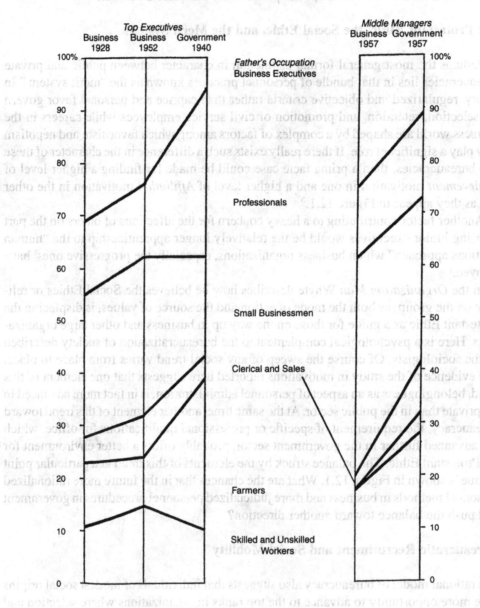

Sources: The percentages for business executives in 1928 and government executives in 1940 are both derived from Reinhard Bennis, *Higher Civil Servants in American Society: A Study of the Social Origins, the Careers, and the Power-Position of Higher Federal Administrators* (University of Colorado, 1949), pp. 22, 26, 27. The percentages for business executives in 1952 are derived from W. Lloyd Warner and James C. Abeggien, *Big Business Leaders in America* (Harper, 1955), p. 25.

may be oriented more toward government careers by the conflict between major business values and the values associated with professional life—responsibility and service to the community, economic status as a by-product rather than the immediate goal.

It is not the intention here to discuss how closely government administration approximates the rational model of bureaucracy or what the value orientations of professional children really are. Rather, it is intended to show that research, as illustrated in Figure 12.2, bears out two conditions which follow as consequences of those two hypotheses. These conditions are, (1) a greater proportion of the government than of the business elite coming from lower socio-economic backgrounds, and (2) of those from high status backgrounds, a greater proportion of the government elite come from professional families.

In 1928 Professors Taussig and Joslyn of Harvard surveyed a large sample of American business leaders and discovered that the great majority of them were sons of business and professional families. Warner and Abegglen repeated the survey in 1952, pointing out that social mobility is still a vital force in American life, since the percentage of business leaders whose fathers held lower status occupations had increased even though these occupations represented a smaller segment of the occupational structure in their fathers' generation than in the generation of the fathers of 1928's business leaders. If the third column of Figure 12.2, the higher civil servant studied by Bendix in 1940, is compared with both the earlier and later generations of business leaders, it is evident that government is in the vanguard of this democratizing trend. Forty-three per cent of 1940s top level government bureaucrats came from clerical, farming, or working-class families. As late as 1952 only 32 percent of top level business bureaucrats were recruited from these strata. On the high status end of the scale the overwhelming majority of government men came from professional rather than managerial families while the reverse is true of both business groups.

These social differentials in recruitment to the top levels of government and business are paralleled in my samples of the middle management level. As columns four and five of Figure 12.2 show, twice as many government as business middle managers come from the three lower strata and twice as many business as government middle managers come from the families of major executives. Where does *Achievement* motivation fit into this picture? Common sense suggests that men who have climbed a greater distance up the social ladder probably did so with a lot of motivation to achieve. In fact, a study of this motive in a national sample found it higher in the upwardly mobile than in others of the same social class background.[6] Thus, the finding here that government middle managers are highly motivated to achieve may be in part a measure of the personal equipment that enabled many of them to climb up to their current status level in contrast to the larger proportion of business middle managers whose career movement was more lateral than upward.

When two independent studies show that civil servants and their business counterparts are recruited from overlapping yet significantly different social backgrounds, we can seriously raise several questions. Does the "neutral" civil servant carry an automatic leftward bias along with him from his relatively humble origins? How might social class differences in personnel hinder communication and magnify policy conflicts between government and business organizations in, for instance, the regulatory field? What weight does this lend to recent suggestions for the exchange of executives between the two sectors?

The Profit Motive and the Motivation to Achieve

Frequently the fundamental difference in character between business and government organizations is defined as the operation of the "profit motive" in one and its absence in the other. From this it follows that high *Achievement* motivation should be more characteristic of business than government. But, what role does the profit motive play in large-scale business organizations these days, and how congenial is the pursuit of money with the *Achievement* motive as defined in this research?

The middle manager in mid-century seems a far cry from the rational economic man or the lonely free enterpriser of an earlier era. It would be difficult to define what meaning "profits" carries with any but the very top level employees of many of today's large-scale, complex, business organizations. Probably, the closest approximation to "profits" as an operative incentive would be a sense of identification with the organization and its successes, which successes may be measured in terms of growth in size, developing and maintaining a reputation for craftsmanship and service, or technical leadership within its field, as well as a high rate of profits. Similarly, a government employee may measure the success of his particular agency in both concrete and more abstract ways—the launching of an earth satellite, the fair distribution of welfare benefits, or a high rate of returns in the collection of income tax.

But, assume that businessmen are fundamentally more concerned with making money for themselves and perhaps others, for they do bring in greater incomes than do government servants. This concern in itself is not enough to qualify them as devotees of the Protestant Ethic or the *Achievement* motive. Speaking of the Protestant Ethic, Weber points out that "the ideal type of capitalistic entrepreneur . . . gets nothing out of his wealth for himself, except the irrational sense of having done his job well."[7] Experimental studies with the *Achievement* motive indicate that money is an effective stimulus for people high in the motive only when it is perceived as a measure of success. In fact a survey of the occupational values of college students distinguished the pursuit of money quite strongly from those values logically associated with the *Achievement* motive—creativity, originality, and the opportunity to use special abilities and aptitudes. Furthermore, the study found that "money and security, which have traditionally been considered polar opposites as occupational values, are, on the contrary psychologically close together."[8]

The profit motive in its mid-century form may not have been a great attraction for men with a lot of *Achievement* motivation. On the other hand, the challenge of the New Deal, coming at a time when many of today's middle managers were shaping their career images, may well have provided an incentive for such men to join the government service. If this was the pattern of the past, what can we say about the appeals of the government service in the 1950s and what will it be in the 1960s? Is the prospect as dark as it was painted in Edward H. Litchfield's, "Apostasy of a Merit Man," at the Public Personnel

Association's International Conference in 1960?[9] Does the enthusiastic response of the college generation to the Peace Corps mean that at least in certain areas government service offers the main challenge?

The Benevolent Leviathan

The popular image of the character of government employees mentioned at the beginning of this article is made up of two opposing elements: (1) laziness and incompetence, and (2) malevolence and an attempt to control the lives of the citizens. If this article has shown that the first of these elements is not as characteristic as commonly thought, does that increase the threat posed by the second?

Certainly the "First Problem of Politics" in the democracies today is how to maintain effective citizen control over the growing apparatus of government. Not only the size and scope of government activity but improvements in social technology as well have brought about a concentration of power in the government bureaucracy which some fear may be able to pursue an autonomous course armed with its special information, expertise, and indispensability. From time to time *Horrible Examples* of this possibility are drawn from the operations of the Department of Defense. Frequently solutions to this problem are sought in institutional controls working within the bureaucracy or through Congress and the courts.

On the psychological side the problem seems more ominous. Elaborating on the folk wisdom that "power is of an encroaching nature," Michels forged inevitably into his "iron law of oligarchy" when he demonstrated how in the German social revolutionary parties holding a position of power induces the official to displace the general goals of the organization in favor of his own power interests. Pessimists claim that the opportunity to tyrannize over their fellow men attracts the worst sort of people to public office in a welfare state. To what extent does the availability of the means to power draw out the motive for power, or how much hope is there that self-restraint may supplement the institutional checks placed on the autonomy of the bureaucrat?[10]

The research results reported in Figure 12.1 suggest that the opportunity to exercise power in a government bureau is no more enticing than it is in an executive suite in a business organization. Looking at those particular occupations which exercise power on the clientele of the organizations we find that income tax collectors are lower than the average in *Power* motivation while salesmen are the highest of any group. Perhaps the existing institutional controls have placed such curbs on individual autonomy that the civil service is not an unusually attractive field for those absorbed in the pursuit of power. Here, a comparison with the motivations of men in the elective branch of the government could be interesting.

Image and Reality

In the age of the Welfare State and Competitive Coexistence special demands are placed on government. How well these demands are met depends in part on the image government

Table 12.2

Age and Education of the Samples of Business and Federal Government Middle Managers

		Government	Business
Age	Range	29–46	27–42
	Average	37.8	35.3
Education	Attended college	92.5%	94.0%
	Advanced degree	16.0%	9.0%
Total in sample		147	100

servants hold of themselves and the image of them held by those who deal extensively with them—congressmen; the business and academic communities; students, who are potential recruits to the government service; and citizens, who must ultimately sanction the behavior of government servants.

Empirical test of the popular and an academic image of the civil servant seems to show both images to be erroneous. The government bureaucrat of this study emerges as more energetic, less dependent, and no more power-hungry than his opposite number on the business side.

A Note on Methodology

Middle managers were selected for this study because, as C. Wright Mills suggests, "It is in the middle brackets of managers that bureaucratic procedures and styles are most in evidence," and it seemed worthwhile to compare two kinds of bureaucracy. At higher levels of the government the bureaucrat's special relation to Congress might reduce this comparability. Since the term "middle management" carries a variety of meanings, samples of businessmen were decided upon who had been selected for middle management development programs and government members of similar programs who ranged between grades GS-12 and GS-15. The two samples that resulted are well matched in age and education as shown in Table 12.2.

The next question is, how representative are the samples? The fact that these people were chosen by their organizations for executive development programs indicates at least that they are not misfits and, perhaps, that they are the ideal type of business and government bureaucrats. To the extent that these samples represent such a vanguard they may be quite unlike the average government or business middle manager. The "vanguard" aspect of the government sample is supported also by the heavy weighting given the currently significant Department of Defense (80.3 percent of the sample yet only 50 percent of total civilian government employment). To reflect some of the diversity of government the Treasury Department (8.8 percent of the sample) was included as one of the traditional agencies, the Department of H.E.W. (7.5 percent) as one of the welfare agencies, and some men from research and intelligence agencies (3.4 percent) who happened to be attending the business training programs. While the diversity of business organizations would be even more difficult to represent in detail, the business sample moves in that direction by drawing from a variety of industrial and consumer goods industries and utilities throughout the nation.

To the extent that the size of a sample controls its breadth of representativeness, these samples of 100 business and 147 government middle managers are about as representative as samples of higher level bureaucrats such as Reinhold Bendix's 192 higher civil servants and W.E. Henry's over one hundred business executives. In this respect they may be less representative than the more than eight thousand big business leaders who answered Warner and Abegglen's questionnaire or the 400-member sample to be interviewed with T.A.T.'s in the Warner-Van Riper-Martin study of federal executives.

In time perspective the samples represent middle managers of the middle and late 1950s. Two groups of the business sample were tested by Professor McClelland of Harvard in the spring of 1957. Mr. David Berlew of the Social Relations Department at Harvard tested another group in the summer of 1958. The government sample was tested in the late fall of 1957 through the assistance of Mr. Chester A. Evans of the Department of the Navy, Mr. Joseph G. Colmen of the Department of the Air Force, Mrs. Elizabeth Mulholland of the Social Security Administration, and Mr. E.N. Montague of the Internal Revenue School. While the assistance of these persons is fully acknowledged the analysis and interpretation of the results are the author's responsibility.

Notes

1. R.K. Merton et al. (eds.), *Reader in Bureaucracy* (Free Press, 1952), p. 365.

2. The characteristics of these samples are discussed in the note on page 186 at the end of this chapter.

3. For discussion of the origins, measurement, and social significance of these motives see David C. McClelland, et al. *The Achievement Motive,* (Appleton-Century-Crofts, 1953), John W. Atkinson (ed.), *Motives in Fantasy, Action, and Society,* (D. Van Nostrand, 1958), and particularly McClelland's forthcoming book, *The Achieving Society.*

4. In *Achievement* motivation sector differences are significant with $P < .05$ in *Affiliation* motivation both sector and a combination of sector and role factors were significant with $P < .01$, while in *Power* motivation role factors are significant with $P < .05$.

5. Evidence of such a difference in the weight of personal advantage is hard to come by although there is general agreement that government has traditionally led business in the use of objective selection techniques. Paul P. Van Riper, *History of the United States Civil Service* (Row, Peterson, 1958), pp. 279–82. Sharper evidence in this direction comes from analysis of subsamples within the groups tested. One of the business groups shows a slight but not statistically significant relation between success in the organization (salary divided by age) and high affiliation motivation while John Hill has found in a selected government subsample a significant and *inverse* relation between success (GS grade dived by age) and high affiliation motivation. See Chapter 7 of the forthcoming book by David C. McClelland, *The Achieving Society.*

6. See H. Crockett's forthcoming dissertation at the University of Michigan, "Achievement Motivation and Social Mobility."

7. Max Weber, *The Protestant Ethic and the Spirit of Capitalism,* Talcott Parsons (trans.) (Charles Scribner's, 1958), p. 71.

8. Morris Rosenberg et al., *Occupations and Values* (Free Press, 1957), pp. 5, 14.

9. *Public Personnel Review* 85–89 (March–April 1961).

10. See Michels' *Political Parties* (Free Press, 1949).

CHAPTER 13

A TECHNIQUE TO CAPITALIZE ON HUMAN INTELLIGENCE IN ORGANIZATIONS

Brain Skill Management

WESTON H. AGOR

> Brains are what business runs on. We need more people out there
> showing how to use them better.
> *Larry Prusak, Ernst & Young*

> If new organizational designs can tap these creative (brain's right hemisphere)
> possibilities, they will provide further means of extending and transforming
> organizational capacities for rational action.
> *Gareth Morgan, Images of Organization*

We have learned more about how the human brain functions in the last quarter century than we have in all of man's previous history of research on this topic. Coupled with what we also learned in the same time period about organizational decision making, we are now poised to make major breakthroughs in how to assess, organize, and develop this human capital asset in ways never dreamed of before.

This article summarizes what we now know about productivity using human brain skills in organizational decision making, and it will describe how a process called Brain Skill Management (BSM) has been used to cultivate and mine these skills to enhance managerial/organizational decision making in a wide variety of applied settings. The paper concludes with an agenda for action which is likely to produce even more productive techniques for cultivating this human capital asset.

What We Know About Human Brain Skills

We have learned a great deal over the last quarter century concerning the pattern of human brain skills, and this knowledge has major practical implications for decision making—both at a personal level and at the level of organizational operations (Gardner 1991; Benfari 1991).

From *Review of Public Personnel Administration,* vol. 16, no. 3 (Summer 1996): 14–22. Copyright © 1996 by Sage Publications, Inc. Reprinted with permission.

First of all, we know the brain is an information processing system that may well record and store data and experiences in a holographic (complex contextual) pattern (Pribram 1971). The brain also has a capacity to specialize into so-called "left brain" and "right brain" functions (Sperry 1968). More significant still, we know that humans differ systematically by sex, by ethnic background, and by management level in terms of the brain skills we tend to prefer and with which we typically demonstrate capabilities (Agor 1984). This variability is reflected at the organizational level in such ways as the specific occupation we prefer and perform well at, and the style of decision making we prefer and exhibit (Agor 1986). Further, there is growing evidence to suggest that brain skill abilities and preferences may be in part genetically imprinted, passed on from generation to generation within given gene pools (Neubauer and Neubauer 1990).

Previous research has suggested that managers and organizations can never be perfectly rational because as humans we have limited information processing abilities; these limitations give rise to "bounded rationality" (Simon 1947). However, more recent findings suggest that the brain has holistic, analogical, intuitive, and creative capacities that may well enable us to break free from this more limited view of human capacities (Mintzberg 1994; 1989). At an organizational level, this means we have a capacity to break out of unproductive processes such as "groupthink," to question the relevance of existing operating norms, and to generate new and more productive paradigms for decision making (Robbins and DeCenzo 1995). Technically, this critical and creative potential is known as the brain skill of double-loop learning (Morgan 1986).

Practical Implications for Decision Making

What we have learned from the above research has tremendous practical implications for decision making in organizations.

First, it is likely that we can enhance productivity and job satisfaction by proactively employing brain skill assessments to help structure such important organizational activities as job recruitment and placement. Second, it is likely that we can enhance how organizations and teams within them double-loop learn by using brain skill assessments to guide and develop new and more productive decision making processes than we presently use. Finally, it is also likely that we will have high potential payout from investing personal and organizational time in developing further our knowledge about how the brain functions and cataloging more completely than we know now the brain skills that may in fact exist. Learning how such skills might be channeled for applied use would represent a valuable contribution to organizational performance.

Why should we be optimistic in this regard? A large body of research findings suggests that there is a high probability of such projections being realistic. The literature in organizational behavior indicates that workplace decisions can be classified usefully as programmed (well structured, familiar, routine, easily defined problems) and nonprogrammed (new problems where information is ill-structured, information is ambiguous or incomplete (Nelson and Quick 1994). Extensive research in related fields has indicated that "left brain" dominant managers are more comfortable and skilled at programmed decision making situations while "right brain" dominant managers prefer unprogrammed decision making organizational environments (Agor 1986). We have also found linkages between management levels and brain skill preferences and abilities. For example, field research demonstrates rather conclusively that top management positions are characterized by frequent nonprogrammed decisions while lower level management positions generally entail a preponderance of programmed decision making (Schermerhorn 1993). Survey sample studies indicate that top managers tend to be more "right brain" dominant than lower level managers, and that this brain skill is one key resource for reaching this level of management. We also know that brain skill dominance systematically differs by sex and by occupational specialty (Agor 1989a).

In addition, research is available to indicate still further that managers vary considerably by brain skills with respect to their ability to deal with certainty, periodic uncertainty, and risk in decision making. "Left brain" dominant managers tend to prefer highly structured, predictable, and routine situations and tend to recruit other managers with similar preferences. This in turn often leads to the creation of a "groupthink" atmosphere and a dearth of entrepreneurship or inclination to be innovative from within an organization. In contrast, "right brain" dominant managers tend to prefer crisis decision making settings, considerable uncertainty, and tend to be skilled at generating new creative ways of doing things (Robbins 1994).

We also know from recent brain skills research that it is quite possible to enhance substantially the functioning of groups within organizations by structuring how organizational groups are formed and how they are sequenced in the decision making process. For example, we know that "right brain" managers are most skilled at generating new and different ways of solving a problem, but they also have a tendency to be careless with detail and unreliable with respect to follow through. Some of their ideas are not very practical to implement, and their enthusiasm often passes from one subject to another in a short period of time. On the other hand, "left brain" dominant managers are skilled at detail, enjoy the implementation process, and can provide excellent critical evaluation of other managers' ideas, although they are not as skilled in generating innovative ideas themselves. When placed on the same team to work on a pending problem, "left" and "right" brain dominant managers tend to fight with each other about the style of the most appropriate decision-making process to adopt, often leading to unproductive results for the organization (Benfari 1991). A more productive alternative suggested by recent research is to form decision-making groups guided first-and-foremost by brain skills rather than by job title, occupational specialty, or years of experience in the organization (Agor 1991). Further, it appears to be more productive to sequence the brain skills found consistent with the stage in the decision-making process or problem at hand (Agor 1993).

Finally, it should be noted that research and applied case studies of brain skill use demonstrate that a number of important aspects of human intelligence can be enhanced and developed through training programs of various types (Gardner 1993). One major finding is that the simple process of paying attention to selected brain skills and devoting time to their cultivation and development will not only enhance the potential for using a particular skill, but also facilitate its applied use in organizational decision making (Henry and Walker 1991).

Figure 13.1 **Pattern of Brain Skills and Decision Making in Organizations**

Management level	Lower-level managers	Middle-level managers	Top-level managers
Type of problem	Programmed	Mixed	Nonprogrammed
Brain skills required	Left	Mixed	Right
Style	Analytical vertical thinker	Mixed	Intuitive lateral thinker
Task preference	• Routine • Precision • Detail • Repetitive • Implementation	Mixed	• Non-routine • Broad issues • Relationships • Constant new assignments and problems • Idea generation

Brain Skill Management: The Process

The central implication to be drawn from the body of research cited above is that there is a strong probability that brain skill data can be used proactively by human resource management professionals and public sector managers to capitalize more productively on the ability and potential of human intelligence than we presently are doing (Stewart 1994). Further, it is likely that developing and using brain skill information to help guide such organizational processes as human capital recruitment, training, and placement could well have the additional payoff of enhancing the personal job satisfaction of employees (Bruhn and Chesney 1994).

The complete process by which brain skills can be assessed, developed, and used to guide personal and organizational decision making is called Brain Skill Management (BSM).[1] A BSM program consists of three major components: (1) diagnostic testing; (2) custom placement; and (3) training in brain skill development (Agor 1989b).

Diagnostic testing should be used at the very beginning of a problem solving or decision-making process (see Figure 13.1). Such testing can be used to increase productivity in a variety of ways. For example, testing can be used to assemble management teams that are more likely to work together effectively. Testing can also be used to locate personnel who are most skilled at developing new and more innovative ways of delivering services in your organization. At the same time, testing can be employed to find those persons who have the greatest ability to evaluate critically the proposed ideas of others in detail, and the talent to guide a program at the implementation and evaluation stage of the decision-making process.

Organizations of all types rarely make use of such diagnostic testing and the information it can provide when designing and implementing programs. All they usually know about their employees is their formal job title, responsibilities, and record of experience; they

Figure 13.2   **Management Capabilities and Limitations by Brain Skills**

Brain skills	Analytical	Intuitive
Capabilities	• Works well with detail, precision	• Sees relationships, new levels emerging
	• Good at critical evaluation	• Good creative problem solver
	• Careful in implementation	• Can generate new ideas, options
	• Comfortable with repetition, routine	• Comfortable with crisis, rapid change, unknowns
Limitations	• Inflexible	• Careless with detail and follow through
	• Tends to be too critical	• Tends to take on more projects than can be handled
	• Has difficulty seeing new ways of doing things	• Finds it hard to say no

Figure 13.3   **How to Use Management Brain Skills in the Decision-Making Process**

Action	Step 1	Step 2	Step 3
	Select/assign intuitive managers first	Select/assign analytical managers second	Integrate managers for action third
Task	Generate new solutions to problem	Critically evaluate list of proposed solutions	Reach agreement on best solutions for implementation
Capabilities	Sees possibilities Ingenious Can deal with complexities	Sees facts Can analyze, organize, and find flaws	Can identify new solutions that can also be practically implemented

seldom know or have a very sophisticated assessment of the brain skills their employees possess or how they might be used. As our knowledge of the brain expands, new assessment instruments are being devised for practical use that have a high level of reliability and validity (Agor 1992a).

Custom placement based on brain skill assessments can enhance the design and implementation of decision-making processes at both a personal and an organizational level in several ways. Broadly speaking, employees tend to divide into two types—intuitive persons and analytical persons (see Figure 13.2). Those persons who score as being highly intuitive are the most innovative in their problem solving and tend to be creative in their thinking about organizational activities. They would be best grouped at the beginning of the problem-solving process, being assigned such tasks as creating new or more productive ways of providing existing services. When grouped together, these employees tend to use thinking styles that other "like types" find comfortable to work with (see Figure 13.3).

Once a list of potential problem solving solutions has been identified and developed by the intuitive group, analytical type employees would be best grouped and assigned the task of evaluating this proposed project list. This is the case because analytical type managers are most skilled at detailed analysis and evaluation. They are more capable of identifying missing links in a proposed plan of action and in managing a program plan's implementation once agreed upon by all participants.

Once a detailed list of problem solving proposals has been prepared and evaluated, step three is to bring the intuitive and analytical groups back together to discuss and refine a final plan of action. At this stage, custom placement based on testing can again be useful. For example, selecting a leader who is skilled at facilitating effective interaction between the different styles that exist between the two groups is critical. A skilled facilitator can help make each member feel ownership in the final product, which of course enhances the probability of successful implementation.

The third component in BSM is training in brain skill development. Despite the fact that we have learned a good deal about how the brain functions in recent years, organizations in the main have been slow to use and develop what we have learned for problem solving or decision making. A number of tools and techniques now exist which can be taught to enhance supervisory and executive learning about their brain skills for productive decision making. For example, such techniques as mind-mapping and modified Delphi can be used to free up the creative side of the brain so that it can be used for practical applications to think up new and different ways of solving a particular problem or issue at hand (Wycoff 1991). They can also be used to help break habitual ways of thinking (e.g., groupthink, vertical thinking) so that other possible solutions and relationships can be conceptualized—or help insure the accurate perception of an emerging trend that might bear on a particular problem or issue (Parikh 1991).

Using a BSM program to develop and guide a decision-making process requires transformational change concerning how an organization will make decisions in the future. If one hopes to maximize productivity, it must become a learning organization (Senge 1990). To make this transformation from programmed to creative operations requires the adoption of an organizational management model that is relatively open and flexible. A highly hierarchical authority structure will probably no longer be as functional as it once was (if ever). A commitment must be made to asking for and accepting answers from everyone in the organization—not just from department heads or other formal organizational leaders. Since leadership is situational, years of experience with the organization will probably be less valued than they were in the past. Risk taking and exploring totally new ways of accomplishing objectives will be not only entertained, but rather encouraged and rewarded (Agor 1992b).

Employing a BSM program to develop and guide an organization's decision-making process means you will have to be committed on a day-to-day basis to creating an atmosphere in which innovation is encouraged. It means being willing to organize groups and meetings in a somewhat less traditional manner, and it means dropping old management practices when they do not serve any productive purpose. It may be necessary, for example, to "structure" some meetings so that the agenda is not formally outlined in great detail. Instead, the meeting's common general purpose can be stated in one sentence, allowing group members to decide more informally how to actually deal with the problem. Another useful technique is to segment meetings into creative open times to complement structured times. During these open periods, evaluation of proposed ideas is held in abeyance until this "brain storming" meeting segment has been completed (Kroeger and Thuesen 1992).

Brain Skill Management: Findings from Field Testing

Over the last fifteen years numerous BSM program workshops have been conducted to enhance the decision-making capabilities of existing personnel within a wide variety of public and private sector organizations. Among the public sector sample set of case studies, organizations at every level of government are represented (Agor 1989c, 1988a, 1988b, 1985a, 1985b). An analysis of structured exit interview questionnaires from participants reveals that: implementing a BSM program to help solve real problems these organizations faced resulted in the following products and processes that did not exist before the program was implemented:

- the quantity and quality of proposed problem solutions in each case was enhanced (as measured by range and depth);
- the process by which this product was developed took less time than had been required in the past and was achieved with less unproductive conflict;
- participants left the process measurably more committed to implementing the chosen course of action than had been previously experienced in similar problem-solving situations;
- brain skills were identified (both at an individual and group level) for lateral use across department lines on other future organizational problems. These brain skills were not identified prior to this exercise;
- brain skill networks were identified and facilitated throughout participating organizations across traditional department lines and outside traditional job title classifications. These networks had not existed prior to this exercise;
- brain skill support groups emerged which had not previously existed with pledges to assist each other in the future (both formally and informally) to enhance skill development for applied use;
- participants indicated that they left the BSM process with a greater appreciation and understanding of not only their own brain skills but also those of their "opposites."

Implications for the Future

Public sector organizations are faced with growing pressure to be more productive. This often means real term dollar (after discounting for inflation) cutbacks in existing program support. Frequently, organizational constraints unique to public sector organizations (e.g., civil service systems, affirmative action requirements, categorical grant programs) demand that productivity must be achieved with existing personnel. Implementing a BSM program holds high potential for locating, tapping, and developing the human intelligence capital that we have only just begun to understand and channel for the betterment of all.

Note

1. The assessment instrument designed for use in a brain skill management program is available by contacting Dr. Agor at UTEP, P.O. Box 614, El Paso, TX 79968-0547.

References

Agor W.H. 1993. "Use Intuitive Intelligence to Increase Productivity." *H.R. Focus* 9: 9.

———. 1992a. *The Role of Intuition in Decision Making.* El Paso, TX: Global Intuition Network.

———. 1992b. *Intuition in Decision Making.* El Paso, TX: Global Intuition Network.

———. 1991. "How Intuition Can Be Used to Enhance Creativity in Organizations." *Journal of Creative Behavior* 25: 11–19.

———. (ed.). 1989a. *Intuition in Organizations: Leading and Managing Productively.* Newbury Park, CA.

———. 1989b. "Using a Brain-Skill Management Program to Increase Productivity in the Public Sector," pp. 521–23 in *Prentice Hall Law and Business: Public Personnel Administration Policies and Practices for Personnel.*

———. 1989c. "Intrapreneurship and Productivity." *The Bureaucrat* 18: 41–44.

———. 1988a. "Nurturing Executive Intrapreneurship with a Brain-Skill Management Program." *Business Horizons* 31: 12–15.

———. 1988b. "Finding and Developing Intuitive Managers." *Training and Development Journal* 42: 68–70.

———. 1986. *The Logic of Intuitive Decision Making: A Research Based Approach for Top Management.* Westport, CT: Greenwood.

———. 1985a. "Intuition as a Brain Skill in Management." *Public Personnel Management* 14: 15–24.

———. 1985b. "Managing Brain Skills to Increase Productivity." *Public Administration Review* 45: 864–868.

———. 1984. *Intuitive Management: Integrating Left and Right Brain Management Skills.* Englewood Cliffs, NJ: Prentice Hall.

Benfari, R. 1991. *Understanding Your Management Style.* Lexington, MA: D.C. Heath.

Bruhn, J.G. and A.P. Chesney. 1994. "Diagnosing the Health of Organizations." *Health Care Supervisor* 13: 21–33.

Gardner, H. 1993. *Multiple Intelligences: The Theory in Practice.* New York: Basic Books.

Henry, J. and D. Walker. 1991. *Managing Innovation.* Newbury Park, CA: Sage Publications.

Kroeger, O. and J.M. Thuesen. 1992. *Type Talk at Work.* New York: Delacorte Press.

Mintzberg, H. 1994. *The Rise and Fall of Strategic Planning.* New York: Free Press.

Mintzberg, H. 1989. *Mintzberg on Management.* New York: MacMillan.

Morgan, G. 1986. *Images of Organization.* Newbury Park, CA: Sage.

Nelson, D.L. and J.C. Quick. 1994. *Organizational Behavior.* St. Paul, MN: West Publishing.

Neubauer, P.B. and A. Neubauer. 1990. *Nature's Thumbprint: The New Genetics of Personality.* Reading, MA: Addison-Wesley.

Parikh, J. 1991. *Managing Yourself.* Cambridge, MA: Basil Blackwell.

Pribram, K. 1971. *Languages of the Brain.* Englewood Cliffs, NJ: Prentice Hall.

Robbins, S.P. 1994. *Management.* Englewood Cliffs, NJ: Prentice Hall.

Robbins, S.P. and D.A. DeCenzo. 1995. *Fundamentals of Management.* Englewood Cliffs, NJ: Prentice Hall.

Schermerhorn, Jr., J.R. 1993. *Management for Productivity*. New York: John Wiley & Sons.

Senge, P.M. 1990. *The Fifth Discipline: The Art or Practice of the Learning Organization*. New York: Doubleday.

Simon, H.A. 1947. *Administrative Behavior*. New York: MacMillan.

Sperry, R.W. 1968. "Hemisphere Deconnection and Unity in Conscious Awareness." *American Psychologist* 23: 723–33.

Stewart, T.A. 1994. "Intellectual Capital: Your Company's Most Valuable Asset." *Fortune Magazine* 10: 68–73.

Wycoff, J. 1991. *Mindmapping: Your Personal Guide to Exploring Creativity and Problem Solving*. New York: Berkeley Books.

CHAPTER 14

CREATIVITY

MARSHALL DIMOCK

Creativity is originality. But it is more than that. It is bringing something into the world that is relatively new and possibly revolutionary in its wide circle of effects. Like atomic fission. Or understanding the circulation of blood in the human system.

Creativity goes on all the time. Innovation is sometimes the result of accident, as the discovery of penicillin is said to have been. Discovery may be the accomplishment of the little-educated as well as the savant, of the poor as well as the rich. While creativity occurs in every nation, some innovate a great deal more than others and some nations hardly at all. This may be explained by nations' mores, social systems, and organization and management.

Creativity is not always fully accepted, or it may even be discouraged and punished by sanctions of various kinds. In some countries it is forbidden to draw the human form, for instance, because it is an insult to a jealous god. Or it may be taken as a matter of faith that anything manmade, no matter how charming, must have an imperfection of some kind. To do otherwise would tend to rival the deity, and only the founder of the universe is capable of perfection.

I mention these social influences and controls because many people—perhaps most— believe that creativity is so inborn, or at any rate internalized, that it is like a song in the heart that comes out in a person's voice. In other words, it is temperament, an uncontrollable inner urge of some kind, something mysterious that cannot be fully explained. It borders on genius. Members of both sexes learn to play musical instruments, dance or draw—or even perform original mathematical solutions—at a tender age. Creativity is something less than this, but in most people's minds it bears a strong family resemblance.

Now which of these two views is correct? Is creativity inborn or is it produced socially? This question is so important that it should not be answered offhandedly, or on the basis of personal preference, possible prejudice, or human conceit.

Throughout history, most near geniuses do seem to have had this inner urge. Something called a passion, the madness of the gods. Or merely a deft touch.

But, equally, the encouragement and training of the mind, either by self or outside teaching, does seem to produce innovation of a high order. And certainly there can be no question that social environment is a universal factor. The prosperity or decline of na-

From *Public Administration Review,* vol. 46, no. 1 (January/February 1986): 3–7. Copyright © 1986 by American Society for Public Administration. Reprinted with permission.

tions seems to depend more upon creativity than upon any other factor. If this were not the case, resource-rich nations would invariably be the most opulent; the innovative, but resource-poor ones only second class. But how about Japan? Or Britain, a small island, at her peak? Or even Rome or Constantinople which, at the height of the empire, spread over most of the then known world? Their resources were quite limited. China, of course, is another story, because she always had enormous resources. But India? This subcontinent is by no means puny in scale or in resources.

Yes, the social factor is important. And some, if they could, would like to reduce all knowledge of creativity to environmental factors. Like turning on or off a spigot. But this is so extreme as to be absurd.

One thing remains certain. Those who have the most control in setting the congenial or hostile atmosphere for creativity—such as government officials—are primarily responsible for determining whether potential creativity is encouraged or otherwise. This explanation may also account for the constant tension existing between rigid bureaucracy and its antithesis, freedom of self-expression.

Granting that both inner and outer influences contribute to creativity, the question remains whether all creativity is a reflection—a mere mirroring—of individual effort or whether social organizations, per se, have the innate capacity to produce creative results. This clearly is one of the key issues of communism versus capitalism and mammoth organizations versus ones of smaller size.

Three questions are present here. Do large organizations inherently discourage originality and breakthroughs? Alternatively, is it true that, the smaller the organization (with adequate resources), the greater is the likelihood of innovation? And third, if all organizations (including those that are near monopolies) were small enough to allow individual self-expression, could this system be relied upon to produce more efficiency and social satisfaction than any other? If this were true, communism might work toward such a goal and advanced capitalist countries might reconsider their drift toward socialistic monopoly.

Of course it is possible to bypass all the questions I have been raising and junk the term creativity completely. In fact it can be done relatively easily. One simply holds that some individuals, skills, and accomplishments are "exceptional," and let it go at that. However, this will not help us in our desire to understand and put to use a knowledge about creativity. When you consider what is at stake, such a cop-out seems inadvisable.

And what is at stake? Well, to begin with, if more people believed in using their inner resources, more individuals might try. This might not be a very "scientific" statement, but it makes for good political economy. Secondly, a lot of people might achieve satisfactions—some bordering on peak experiences—out of expressing their creative urges. In such cases these same people might previously have lacked the self-confidence to try. Thirdly, if there were more creative individuals, the nation would probably be more contented. Of course individuality also creates problems, and temperament even more stormy ones, but most people would probably assume such a risk in preference to the alternative of increasing automation and knee-jerk responses.

The potential social accomplishments are equally inviting. In highly developed industrial systems more money is being made from innovating new products, methods, and appeals than from any other single factor. Again, Japan is a good example. If she lacks something potentially enriching, she simply goes out to do it better than anyone else.

This line of thought also supports Toynbee's conclusion that civilizations survive only when they have creative minorities that are adequately motivated toward worthy goals. But this is only true when creativity takes the long view and not the narrow.

A third accomplishment, if government and its administration could be made more creative, would be a development away from public cynicism, distrust, and defeatism and toward approval. Lastly, if society were innovative enough and free enough, an endless sequence of cause-and-effect consequences might result. A larger number of creative individuals might be produced, and if their thirsts and passions were strong and deep enough, this in itself might almost guarantee social stability and satisfaction, which is the stuff from which real culture is made.

This is not merely Utopianism; to me it seems like quite sensible logic.

What Is Creativity?

Directly or indirectly, and over a long period of time, a great deal has been written about creativity. But no one theory is presently completely accepted.

One reason for this is that different fields of knowledge require different factors in combination. The difference between painting and dance compared with mathematics and Einstein's theory, for example. Or the deftness with which a surgeon uses a scalpel or sews up an incision. Or the ability to do embroidery or etchings. Or the ability to tell stories and paint word images. But even in these illustrations common skills are present. Scientists such as Einstein say that imagination is more important in higher mathematics than mere logic. And embroiderers have skills similar to good surgeons.

A second factor is that some commentators stress one factor and others stress different ones in their evaluations of relative importance. This is not so unusual for it occurs in any kind of analysis.

Still another explanation is that creativity, being individual and highly personal, requires much self-analysis when assessing the relative significance of the factors that make up creativity.

But what *are* the main approaches?

One of the oldest and most widely supported is intuitionism. "Don't ask me how I do it, I just know." This is what a "born" carpenter often says, and he may have little or no formal education. We say he has manual dexterity. He has more than this. He has a mental picture of how things are put together and work, and hence he knows intuitively what to do and in what order to do them. Others try just as hard but never seem to succeed. These are the left-handed ones, like myself.

Intuitionism is a highly respectable approach to creativity. Some of the best scientists give this as the principal explanation of creativity. W.I.B. Beveridge, for example, in *The Art of Scientific Investigation* (1950), divides all scientist innovators into two groups,

A and B, the As being the ones who know that something is true before completing the proof and the Bs being the ones who excel in facts and in patient building of mounds of data which they continually test. The As are like predators—they devour the facts, but only as a means of whetting their appetites for confirmation of what they sense is true in the first place.

Of course, some of the best painters of modern times, notably the impressionists, or writers such as the existentialists, often testify that intuitionism and creativity are the same thing.

A second school of thought, equally valid and growing rapidly in importance, even in scientific circles, is the synthesis school. Chester Barnard belonged to this school. The creative person is the one who is most skilled at including all factors, and especially the psychological ones, and coming forth with a conclusion that is better than others because it stands the test of time. It is analogous to a group of officials going into a huddle and coming up with a solution that turns out to be the best possible one. The difference is that in the first illustration it is the brain of one individual that does the synthesizing.

Brain research in this area is clearly a main frontier of science today. Take, for example, Marilyn Ferguson's book, *The Aquarian Conspiracy* (1980). All kinds of questions arise from this area of research. How do the right and left lobes of the brain work together? Is it true that left-handed persons are more creative than right-handed ones? Is parapsychology the "coming" field because it holds the key to extrasensory perception? Is brain research the key to "consciousness" (social solidarity, compassion) which widely read authors, such as the author of *The Greening of America* (1970), consider to be the key to human well-being?

Of course, once consciousness is mentioned other accompanying concepts such as imagination, sensitivity, acuteness, and empathy immediately come to mind, so synthesis is obviously a Thesaurus term with many connotations (but what key word is not?).

The third major emphasis finds the solution to creativity in imagination. Its devotees probably outnumber any other point of view that might be mentioned. It is particularly favored by literary people. "What are you writing?" someone asks. "I don't know, the idea hasn't matured yet." Often they seem to suggest that they personally do not come up with ideas. The ideas come out of the blue. There is an element of magic or mystery in writings that have stood the test of time. Like Alice, most people from time to time take imaginary trips. They fantasize, then return to the real world refreshed and relaxed.

But is the process all that mysterious? Or is it merely the subconscious at work? Does the writer get an idea and gradually build around it until he has an overwhelming compulsion to reduce his brainchild to paper? The clinical psychologists may think one thing, the seasoned novelists another. Many of the latter are on record as saying that imagination is something over which they have no active control. It is like writing a novel. You decide on characters and situations and the plot "takes off." The author is more the vehicle, not the guide.

Another major theory about the origin of creativity is that made notable by Arthur Koestler in his large and influential book, *The Act of Creation* (1964). Koestler immediately drew respect because he was not only a successful literary figure but a much admired psychologist. Koestler's might be called the levels-of-attention approach to creativity. Koestler agreed with Beveridge that there are two kinds of people (simplified for analytical purposes), namely the imaginative and the precise. The former typically have a more outgoing personality and more social skills than the paragons of factual analysis, who tend to be introspective and not nearly so expressive. The essence of creativity, thought Koestler, is the ability to operate on more than one plane. The dull and the drudge operate only on one. This is habitual and repetitive. Hence if the pattern is deeply ingrained this person cannot easily break with tradition, take chances, and create something original. Beveridge's "A" type person, on the other hand, finds that this shifting of gears comes easily. It is most likely to occur during periods of relaxation and repose following periods of intense work and application. But in addition to this fluctuation from intensity to relaxation, which most students of creativity acknowledge, Koestler argued that because of both native and acquired traits the highly creative individuals are able "to turn it on" almost at will. They shift from one plane to another. The higher plane requires more synthesis. It coordinates experience and imagination. Such a person has images (mind images) of what is possible or even ideal. It closely resembles a mystical experience. Some writers and painters—perhaps most—encounter it almost every day. They are so "elevated" and carried away that they lose track of time, experience a kind of ecstasy, have to be called to meals.

The more adept a person is at rising from lower, applied areas, to higher, intellectual and imaginative planes, the more creative such a fortunate individual is likely to become. But it must be done naturally, not artificially, because if the latter, the artificiality will show in the person's product.

A fifth approach to creativity seems at odds with these four, which have all emphasized integration and harmony. The one we are about to consider is Freudian, assuming that creativity arises out of conflict and the clash of opposites. It is analogous to the theory found in some social science writing that everything worthwhile arises out of crisis situations. This theory is essentially a dualistic philosophy, whereas those we have been considering show strong marks of monistic thinking. Perhaps the best example of this approach is Rollo May's book, *The Courage to Create* (1976).

The theory is that both good and evil are found in all creation, one dominating at one time and the other at another. There are certain deep drives, such as sex, or power, or anger, and when one is frustrated a transference or sublimation occurs which the public judges creative. John Steinbeck's writings are often cited as a prime example of this kind of creative output.

For a number of reasons, this type of plot is thought to have wide public appeal. Often there is violence. At least things are not dull. People see themselves in the passions and plots that unfold. People cry, get aroused emotionally. Such writing is an antidote to excessive pietism. And when one writes with passion, as Steinbeck did most of the time, one cannot help admiring his prose even though one may not sympathize with his cavalier attitude toward sacred symbols. When people speak of "realism," this kind of plot and portrayal of human nature is often what they mean.

Reconciliation

So there are five main approaches to the question of what causes creativity. These are intuition, synthesis, imagination, levels of attention, and conflict.

Personally I see no difficulty in accepting substantial parts of all these theories. There are relatively few people like John Steinbeck, for example, because most creative people are doubtless more tranquil. They may have as much emotion, but they express it differently.

As for the other factors: intuition, synthesis, imagination, and levels of attention, they have a good deal of congruence. It has already been remarked, for example, that imagination clearly involves an innate disposition to project, coordinate, integrate, and reproduce on command images which often have a certain novelty. This type of personality has a quality akin to what David McClelland calls "the achievement motive." Some individuals have, from birth, a drive to achieve. Others have a parallel ability to imagine and give it form.

Similarly, I doubt if from the standpoint of psychological research, any one method is all-sufficient to explain the very real existence of creativity. Study of the brain and of the crossover between the two lobes? To be sure. But that certainly is not the whole of the matter. The entire body and personality are all connected with the brain; everything about a person is connected with an endless web of social influences. So what is personal and discrete cannot wholly be divorced from that which is influenced by environmental impacts. The only thing that can be said for sure is that it takes a bold or crazy person to adventure, and sometimes the two seem to be related. Even then, the person has to be strong, or desperate, or he would never take big risks. And it is risks that break new ground.

One additional point is a widely held view today that people really have not "lived" unless they are constantly involved in inner and outer turmoil of some kind. This view is by no means confined to devout Freudians, whose father symbol is the psychiatrist. And as has been said, they regard their outlook as "realism."

Where they go wrong, however, is in assuming that only inner struggle, or outer crisis, represents the hard work syndrome. What they overlook is that the integrated, tranquil person—often a poet—has to work just as hard. But since he is more integrated, it does not show on the surface as much.

One reason this distinction seems so important to me is that in the United States at the present time, and in some other countries as well, it is increasingly intimated in the press and elsewhere that the only time people really integrate is when they are slipping or in disarray. People *do* often innovate at such times. More often, they turn to violence or war. As William James, John Dewey, Albert Schweitzer, Rene Dubos, and a number of others have insisted, therefore, the responsible citizen is constantly seeking "moral equivalents." And often they have to work just as hard, or harder, than those who are regarded as more unruly.

From Person to Institution

Perhaps now we are ready to consider the question raised at the outset, whether institutions, independently of outstanding individuals, have the innate capacity to be productively creative.

But why should we expect any organization to be independent of human personalities? Is not the human factor the most important one in any calculus and the reason for its existence?

Having studied the relation of bureaucracy to enterprise all of my adult life, I have no doubt that institutions appear to have personality, vitality and self-perpetuating qualities. There is also no doubt that these institutions quickly disappear when whatever produced these energies in the first place also disappears.

Toynbee believed in the possibility of energizing whole societies and thus increasing their survival prospects to the point of speaking of their personalities, radiating capabilities, atmosphere and tone. In other words, he hypothesized that institutions can, over a period of time, acquire human characteristics. Others more closely identified with the management field refer to such things as atmosphere and spirit. A chief of staff in the Pentagon recently remarked, for example, that our military have everything except the requisite spirit and then added that it is spirit that wins battles and wars. And was not it Haldane, the great British administrative theorist, who said that the best way to evaluate an organization is to sense its atmosphere when you walk in the door? Some types of public relations are cosmetic and artificial, but others are genuine and more revealing than anything else.

Much has been written about what the factors are that produce an organizational atmosphere that is productive, satisfying, and durable at the same time. But in the next few years, if I judge correctly, we shall have to redouble our energies along this line.

The relevant question just now is, what may be the correlation betwixt creativity and administrative vitality?

In an article called "Bureaucracy Self-Examined" which appeared in the *Public Administration Review* in 1944, I argued that bureaucracy can be fully understood only when one examines carefully every component of administration. If you accept this premise, then you ask questions such as "What kind of organization is best designed to make participants and the program, as well, creative?" Then you ask the same thing about control, personnel systems, public relations, goal setting, planning, policy, and all the rest. Nothing is excepted. No higher law than creativity exists because creativity is the essence of humanness, both for the supplier and for the beneficiary.

If there are enough creative people and if they are given sufficient freedom and encouragement, their number will multiply. And if the number becomes large enough and the spirit widely pervasive, the public will be drawn to the program's attractiveness and surrounding aura, like butterflies are attracted to a flower's nectar or little girls to miles of narcissus on a Swiss hillside.

Juxtaposition of Factors

I believe this poesy is not too outrageous if one next considers how naturally the five theories of creativity we have been examining correlate with the maxims of public administration that are widely subscribed to in the United States today.

Beginning with the last of the five, crisis, we cannot escape the realization that threats to survival are what shake people up the most. These threats take many forms: physical destruction, surrender, violence, obliteration of value and belief systems, threats to ways of life considered worth struggling to maintain. Or endangering Social Security checks, equality of opportunity, and the chance to rise. All these and many more are threats of loss which cause us to do certain things: question our goals and our methods. Discover what our friends and competitors may be doing better. Deciding whether we are too habit-ridden, unimaginative, and indolent. Or possibly too greedy and smug.

Once we innovate we are performing the creative act. And if we should become skilled and inspired enough to raise the standards in any field (from art to agriculture) then we are providing proof that all five of the creative factors can be combined programmatically.

I myself believe that the essence of public administration is problem solving. Problem solving takes place only when problems are approached creatively. When the approach is in bits or pieces, or puts technique above purpose, or is a cover-up for outworn ideas or systems, then in the long run such efforts are bound to fail. And I think there has been entirely too much of this prissy, manipulative spirit in the efforts of both Britain and the United States in dealing with their declining political economy fortunes the past several years.

As for the other four theories of creativity, they can, I think, be dealt with conveniently as a unit. This because of the congruence noted earlier.

Public administration deals with human needs and how those needs can be met with imagination, empathy and practical means—or at least somewhat allayed by these attributes. Public administration has no corpus or justification outside this dedication to needs.

Such being the case, see how the administrative mind uses creativity to achieve these goals:

Intuition is divination, through empathy and intelligence, of the appropriate means needed to achieve personal and social goals. It is defining the public interest, as a philosopher or humanist would.

Imagination is a revelation, an image, of the way things ought to be. Nothing is ever so good that it cannot be made better.

Synthesis is a deft and experienced melding of all ingredients to form a whole that is viable and progressive. It is a future, medium-range, and present all rolled into one.

Levels of attention are not hierarchical but constitute a bond of mutual trust and dependency, like a marriage or any successful partnership. It is believing two things that appear to be completely opposite. The first belief is that policy and inspiration occur at the top. The accompanying belief is that all motivation and practical accomplishment come from the bottom. The connection between the two is operating administration, which is the point on which all TLC should focus, just as in management generally everything reduces to humanness before creativity can be assured.

What this adds up to, it seems to me, is a philosophy of balance. Creativity is both an idea and a canvas, a vision of city parks and stable neighborhoods, of profit-making enterprises sharing a dedication to the common interest.

There would be less conflict if there were more poets. There would be more poets if there were doers capable of making dreams a living reality.

Reading Suggestions

Barnett, H.G. *Innovation, the Basis of Cultural Change.* New York: McGraw-Hill, 1953.

Beveridge, W.I.B. *The Art of Scientific Investigation.* London: Heinemann, 1950.

Ferguson, Marilyn. *The Aquarian Conspiracy; Personal and Social Transformation in the 1980s.* Los Angeles: T. Ptarcher, 1980.

Koestler, Arthur. *The Act of Creation: A Study of the Conscious and Unconscious Processes in Humor, Scientific Discovery and Art.* New York: Macmillan, 1964.

May, Rollo. *The Courage to Create.* New York: W. Norton, 1975. Bantam edition, 1976.

McClelland, David. *The Achievement Motive.* New York: Appleton-Century-Crofts, 1953.

Retch, Charles A. *The Greening of America.* New York: Random, 1970.

Ulam, Stanislaus M. *Adventures of a Mathematician.* New York: Charles Scribner's, 1976.

CHAPTER 15

SUCCESSFUL LEADERSHIP IN LOCAL GOVERNMENT PROGRAMS

Hillsborough County's Productivity Initiatives

HELEN D. LEVINE

Hillsborough County, containing Tampa, Florida, and approximately 825,000 people, has a comprehensive program built around four strategies that, in a very traditional local government, bring about change:

• Communicate clearly why change is necessary. We were asking employees to change everything about how they felt about work, what they did at work, to whom they reported at work. We needed a consistent change message. We needed to reinforce the importance of implementing change to get support not just from our employees but also from our board members, interest groups, and the community at large. Our approach was not radical. What was radical was the way we put the package together, combining a high-quality employee newsletter, an award-winning monthly video news program; the county administrator's annual report, with an emphasis on improvements each department made; Partners in Progress (a political group); and the Intersolve Steering Committee, which was our public and private partnership experience (although we experienced mixed success in working with the private sector on some projects).

• Provide the necessary resources to implement productivity improvements. For the first time we joined groups: Public Technology Inc., International City Management Association, Florida Innovation, National Association of Counties, and American Society for Public Administration. We told our people to go to meetings, and we paid for them to go. We created and supported two new departments: Operations Improvement and Development and Information Technology. Information Technology sets a strategic direction for information systems and telecommunications, assists departments in the development of prototype systems, and advises departments in the acquisition of hardware and software. Operations Improvement and Development is an in-house consulting group that provides work-flow analysis improvement teams, organization development, performance measures, strategic planning, and training for our line employees and management.

One of our most innovative efforts was to establish employee improvement groups. We first emphasized that we are not in the audit business or from the finance or budget office. Setting up the improvement teams showed that we actually believe in the power of employees to say, "This is my problem. I need a tool called pack-a-punch. I will be able to go through and get my pipes in sooner and not disturb Mrs. Smith's yard." The improvement teams gave employees a way of getting involved and of believing in and buying into the process.

Over one hundred projects have been addressed by employee improvement teams. Direct and indirect savings totaled well over $2 million in the first year, $6 million in the second year. The message we wanted to convey was our interest: How can you do your job better? Is your supervisor helping you? What tools do you need? This is a different and, I think, important message. Our training program has increased over 25 percent each year. This year we will offer over eighty classes.

• Build organizational structures that foster and support entrepreneurial activity. We flattened the organization to only five levels. Access to decision making and improved accountability were significant by-products of the reorganization. We have some departments in which our biggest skeptics have been convened. In particular, we have changed patterns of communication and of work.

• Rearrange incentives to reward performance. We have all heard the maxim that what gets rewarded is what gets done. But how do you reward those civil servants who are willing to take risks? In Hillsborough County, we still offered cost-of-living increases; all you had to do to get your 5 percent merit increase was to punch in. We had to change that "rhythm," the codex of how people did work, how supervisors thought about it, and what the rewards were.

To do this, we increased the number of unclassified employees, those who serve at the pleasure of the county administrator, from about 20 to 220. They are required to define quarterly objectives. The departments that are most successful are those that took this change most seriously. In each of our performance agreements, there is a section that addresses improved service delivery, which is an important message.

A performance innovation that I have never seen anywhere else is that 30 percent of my performance has to do with how I function as a manager in terms of the process. Am I good at decision making? Am I motivated? Do I have leadership skills?

We also initiated a classification study with the Civil Service Board. As a consequence, we are doing away with cost-of-living increases and reclassifying or consolidating many positions.

So what are the rewards? We started an awards program. It is a successful, well-attended annual event that recognizes team efforts and outstanding achievers. Additionally, extra-meritorious raises are available for individual employees who have excelled.

Based on my experience and discussions with others, my idea of successful productivity programs are those with the following attributes:

• the demonstrated and consistent support of the chief administrator, who establishes and communicates the vision to employees and the community;

- the formal support of elected officials;
- a designated leader of the program, who preferably reports directly to the chief administrator;
- the endorsement and support of an outside constituency who support and understand productivity improvements;
- flexibility in the improvements but inflexibility in the values surrounding the productivity program;
- broad organization from the front line to senior management;
- professionally trained staff to facilitate the programs and provide technical support to the organization;
- the ability to set the expectation for participation in productivity programs through performance agreements and the ability to recognize and reward participants.

What about the attributes of a leader in local productivity programs? There seem to be five: a critical thinker who understands the dynamics of change in the public sector setting (that is, that a narrow "window of opportunity" exists to bring about substantive changes and that pacing is critical to the success and longevity of the program); a risk taker who has and can give permission to fail in the search for innovative strategies; an individual with personal credibility in the organization and in the community and who can "walk the walk" of productivity and change; a person with a keen sense of humor and the ability to provide the perspective necessary to negotiate the permanent white water of local government; and a person who succeeds at having a positive impact on an organization, not merely receiving a gold watch for longevity.

Will the program formally exist a year from now in the face of a large projected deficit? Will my program exist? Will I have a position? I wish I knew. But will the differences that we made be in place? Will those utility people remember the rhetoric, go through the exercise, and know how to work the system? I think they will, and I think that is what our legacy is. We as bureaucrats cannot be too invested in our job titles or even our jobs, in some cases. To make the difference, you have to be willing to take a risk. I think we have done that, and I think we have made a difference.

CHAPTER 16

NOTES ON THE GOVERNMENTAL EXECUTIVE

His Role and His Methods

DONALD C. STONE

Governmental executives—what they do and do not do and what they should and should not do—have received their full measure of popular attention in recent years. They have been pulled apart and discussed pro and con. They have been demolished vocally; sometimes they have been given the stamp of approval. More often than not, however, these oral onslaughts have failed to take cognizance of the essential character of the executive job in large establishments. In the public press, and even in the textbooks, such phrases as "delegation of authority," "sharply defined responsibilities," "elimination of duplication and overlapping" are worked over repeatedly to the point of weariness. In the public administration societies it is the old stand-bys of organizing, coordinating, analyzing, budgeting, controlling, *ad infinitum,* that get the spotlight.

Discussion focused in these directions often misses the crux of the problem the executive must solve if he is to be able to guide and direct his organization so that it can carry out the program for which he is made responsible. What does the executive have to do if his leadership is to be effective? How does he meet the limitations and obstacles that are inherent in most management situations? It is with this point, the position of the executive and how it is implemented, that I am here concerned. It is not the planning, development, and execution of program that I propose to discuss, but rather the conduct of a large organization in discharging its assignment.

There is, of course, no standard prescription, no patent medicine that can be given to the executive, guaranteed to solve all his problems and leave him free of frustration and dismay. The differences in individuals who find themselves in executive positions and the variations in the life cycles of organizations produce practically limitless permutations and combinations. The pattern is never the same, and only after penetrating inquiry of the circumstances in each case would a wise man undertake to suggest what might be required to assist the executive in establishing reciprocal relationships with his organization.

A new organization set up to perform an emergency function—a War Production Board, an Office of Price Administration—puts very different demands upon its execu-

From *Public Administration Review,* vol. 5, no. 3 (1945): 210–25. Originally published in *New Horizons in Public Administration* (University of Alabama Press, 1945).

tives than an organization that has had time in which to mature its program and develop its precedents and traditions—for example, the New York State Department of Education, the U.S. Forest Service, or the Cincinnati Public Works Department. Similar contrasts run through the entire catalogue of agency characteristics. Requirements differ in an organization rendering a routinized service or engaged in a paper processing job such as the Postal Service or a dependency benefits office, from requirements in a planning or development commission. They differ within the life of an organization, between the time when it is moving in an accustomed pattern and the time when external pressures or events are forcing drastic changes—the Department of Agriculture in the early years of the century and in the 1930s. They differ between an organization in which activities are conditioned to a large extent by outside circumstances and one in which the product to be developed is relatively definitive and tangible—the U.S. State Department versus the Railroad Retirement Board.

When the variations in the personalities of executives are intermingled with the kaleidoscopic aspects of organization, the possible results become almost infinite. On the one hand, there are those who function by giving their staffs full rein and, on the other, those who believe in relying more on executive drive and push; the idea men and those whose expertness lies more in salesmanship and negotiation; the men skillful in legislative and public relationships and those whose forte is internal management; those with a great fund of administrative experience and those without. Both institutional and personality factors affect the sum total of what any organization is and both must be taken into account in estimating what is needed to make the thing work.

We have had sufficient experience in analyzing the variables, however, to have acquired some useful benchmarks. We have learned enough to know in a general way what is required if the executive is to be able to fulfill his role and what may stand in the way of success. It is in this context that I have assembled these notes in the hope that they might illuminate in some degree a few of the many facets of the problem of large-scale public management.

By large scale, I mean organizations of such size as to preclude face-to-face dealing by the executive with all of the constituent elements. Although there will be many modifications in the method of executive leadership between an organization of 500 or 1,000 employees and one of 10,000 or 20,000 employees, the variations are not crucial for the problem with which I am concerned: How results can be achieved when the activity is of such scope that it is beyond the ability of the executive to keep personally in touch with all of its aspects or to apply his personal efforts to very many of its problems.

Much of what I have to say is true of any large organization, public or private. In this discussion, however, I am directing my attention more specifically to the executive in the environment of the public service. By this I do not mean the Chief Executive: mayors, governors, the President, although many of my comments apply also to these top officials. What I am concerned with primarily is the number one man in an agency or department, or bureau or other major subdivision which presents the problem of leadership through an institutional framework.

The specialized conditions surrounding governmental programs put extraordinary demands on their directors in terms of knowing how to weave the competing and disparate elements into a unified whole and producing an organization capable of accomplishing its mission. Public pressures, the need to adjust to the views of legislative bodies, the rigidities in procedures attendant upon management according to law and executive regulation are elements present in any public service enterprise. All of these are related to that central characteristic that distinguishes executive positions in the public service from those in private management—the fact that the government executive is the guardian of the public interest and is accountable to the electorate, directly or indirectly, for what he does. This is very different from the concern for the public which the private executive has in relation to the marketability of his product and the good name of his firm.

In addition, many present-day governmental organizations directed toward mobilization of the nation's resources for war and preparation of the United States for support of international commitments have inherent complexities in program that are unique. The problems we have faced and are still facing in finding and developing sufficient executive leadership for these unprecedented enterprises are indicative of the need of further probing and further understanding of what it takes to bring the public service and the demands that are now placed upon it into balance.

The Executive's Role

This discussion of the job of being a successful governmental executive is predicated on the assumption that the product of any organization is an institutional product, not the executive's personal product. What the executive can accomplish—his impact on the organization—at any one point in time is conditioned by the state of his organization, and what he achieves is largely the product of his influence rather than his command. Therefore, in long-range terms, the job of an executive is to create an environment conducive to concerted effort in pursuit of the organization's objectives. In short-run terms, his job is to know what is going on in the organization and to be in a position to act on the issues which require his personal attention and still to retain sufficient freedom to deal with those outside his organization—superiors, legislators, public. Stated differently, the executive's job is one of maximizing his influence throughout his organization as distinguished from relying exclusively upon his formal authority and the power of command. A good many aspects of these propositions have been probed by others, notably by Mr. Chester Barnard in his numerous writings on executives and their work, and perhaps require no further comment. In many quarters, however, these concepts seem to be insufficiently understood.

Whatever may be the notions of what executives do and how they do it, the bedrock fact is that the executive must rely on his staff for the achievement of his objectives. Most issues in his organization will be settled without ever reaching him. And on those that do reach him his choice will generally be a restricted one. By the time a report or instruction has been developed, worked over, revised, reviewed, level by level, what finally remains for the executive to say in most cases is "OK." He may be inclined to make some changes, but he will soon learn that something else will demand his attention before he is through. Unless what comes to him involves an issue of great importance, he will, therefore, frequently have to accept what he considers to be an inferior product. When the issue is a crucial one for the organization's program and involves high-level judgments on the consequences of a given course of action, the executive may be called upon to choose among two or three alternative solutions, but secondary questions are likely to have to go by the boards. Consequently, unless the executive's objectives are wholeheartedly accepted by his organization, the chances that they will be achieved are problematical.

Failure on the part of the executive to seek aggressively his organization's support may leave him in a precarious position. The forces militating against an effective working together toward a common goal are many and powerful in any large organization: Unreconciled points of view, tradition and routine, inertia, the distortions that grow out of specialist interests, personal ambitions. These internal resistances singly or in combination can cancel out the executive's efforts. To be sure, some of the drives in any established organization represent forces of stability that will keep the organization running when there is no leadership and will save the new executive from many mistakes. Furthermore, the necessary adjustment of the executive to the facts of his environment can contribute to his development by increasing his understanding of how he can function in relation to what goes on around him. On the other hand, if the executive is entirely unsophisticated in the ways of institutional behavior and does not consciously and continuously take steps to offset the divisive elements in his environment, he will find himself dominated by rather than dominating his organization.

The executive is often seen as the man sitting at the top of the organization possessed of a dangerous amount of authority, hiring and firing at will, whose every suggestion or order is responded to promptly and completely. This view reflects one of the greater misconceptions about the nature of executive work. The government executive may have a large grant of legal authority, but he will find that, in actual fact, it must be used in an economical fashion. If he lacks discrimination in the use of his power, he will debase its value and perhaps find himself impotent at a moment of crucial importance. He must guard against destroying the organizational support on which he must depend in executing his program. As Paul Appleby has often remarked, the new executive in an organization may fire a few persons but not very many. Reducing the point to an absurdity, he can not issue an order, "Now and henceforth all employees shall wear red neckties," and expect to get a response. By persuasion, by indoctrination, by leadership—in other words by influence—he may, however, be able to accomplish what he cannot accomplish by fiat. This is by no means a universally understood truth. There are too many executives who fail to recognize that because the members of their organizations are creatures of reason their positions would be strengthened if they bolstered their formal authority with the support that comes from conviction.

I do not mean to suggest, however, that awareness of the importance of influence as a method of reaching institutional goals is strictly a milk and honey proposition of dubious effectiveness in moments of crisis. If the executive is skillful and knows how to establish his position, he can be the decisive element in determining the character of the organization, and he can exercise his authority with telling effect when the occasion demands it. The point is he cannot "bull his way through" any and all situations; he cannot run against the tide of organization opinion. He may buffet his way by sheer force on occasion or on specific issues, but if he does it too often he may pay for his gains by failure to carry his organization with him over the long run.

I have already commented that the executive's job has to be viewed in long-range terms as well as on a day-to-day basis. His aim will be to use his own time and talents on the activities and issues that will contribute the most to the organization's forward movement and to develop a supporting team to the point of optimum production. His success in reaching it will be, in important measure, determined by his success in developing a body of commonly shared ideas. This is a prerequisite if his staff are to have guide posts against which to judge their general direction and their specific actions and if he is to have some assurance of reliable performance. Without this kind of institutional environment, the executive will be unable to mold the organization into something more than the sum of its parts. Furthermore, cultivation of such an atmosphere is essential if the members of the organization are to have a sense of participation in an enterprise bigger than themselves and secure the satisfactions necessary to good staff work. Only then do the fragmented jobs that are the lot of most people in large organizations become a source of stimulation.

The importance of an institutional environment and of indoctrination in its meaning has long been understood by the Army and Navy, but in large part has been neglected by civilian governmental organizations. It has often been observed that indoctrination permits West Point and Annapolis trained men to function, and function well, even though the commonly accepted rudiments of good organization may be missing in a given situation. Some of the civilian organizations such as the Farm Credit Administration, the New York City Police Force, and the Tennessee Valley Authority are conspicuous for their high morale—the natural by-products of a consciously fostered environment. More often than not, however, this basic source of organization strength has been given too little attention by governmental executives in this country.

Awareness of the problem does not mean prompt solution. Almost any executive is likely to find that the contribution he can make to an organization's environment can be made only over an extended period of time. Rapid adjustments, such as customarily take place in the Army and Navy at the outbreak of war, or in a relief agency in time of distress, are the exceptions rather than the rule. The recently appointed chief of a Federal bureau with many years of tradition and precedent behind it has estimated that his job of redirection is at least a ten-year one. On occasions in the Federal Government when time considerations were crucial and other factors permitted, this problem has been solved by setting up a new agency, thus short circuiting the process of retooling a staff steeped in earlier programs and methods. This is a principal reason why some of the new war agencies were set up to do jobs which on the face of it might have been assigned to existing agencies. Normally, however, a government executive is likely to find it necessary to work with what he inherits and to develop a plan of action that can be followed without too much disruptive pulling and hauling. This may mean focusing his developmental efforts on future rather than on current activities, so that the daily work of the organization can move ahead with a minimum of uncertainty and interruption. What the executive accomplishes over the short run will depend upon the state of the institutional environment at any one time and upon the external circumstances affecting his program. His day-to-day activities and decisions may be directly in line with his long-range plans or he may be forced on occasions to accept situations or proposals that do not measure four square with his ultimate objectives. Whether the executive's job is viewed in long-range or short-range terms, however, the ways in which he can seek to maximize his influence and close the gap between present reality and the ultimate ideal of smoothly integrated activity are the same. It is on these that I shall comment briefly for the remainder of this discussion.

How He Spends His Time

The executive's concept of what his job is and the way this affects the scheduling of his time and talents will be a primary factor in the results he secures. In large part this can be encompassed under the head of "operating at his proper level." In his forthcoming book, *Big Democracy,* Paul Appleby develops the point at some length. By this he means that no head of a government department or other subdivision should do work or make decisions that should be the responsibility of officials at a lower level in the organizational hierarchy. Not only does this disrupt and confuse his subordinates but it prevents the executive from doing what is properly his job.

Dealing with people. The executive job is one of dealing with people, of judging, adjusting to, and working around personalities both inside and outside his organization. This is at the core of the business of getting people to apply their energies in harmony with each other and getting things done. I recall the case of a city manager who was extremely unpromising at the time of his appointment. He had no apparent experience or interest in such matters as working out arrangements for delegations of authority or subdivision of labor, he probably had never heard of the follow-up principle, and he was completely baffled by theoretical discussions of management. He had, however, an abiding interest in people. He attracted people, and he had an uncanny sense of whom he could trust. Anyone looking at his organization and how he functioned would say it could not work. But it did. He had a feeling for what it took to provide the cohesion and the central pull necessary for turning out services to the community.

This is in part a reflection of the fact that the executive should use a major portion of his time and talents in being the catalyst who assimilates and draws together the ideas of others, resolves lines of action, gets agreements nailed down, sees that action gets taken. He must develop and rely on his staff for the carry through on the specific elements of his program and must carefully restrain himself if tempted to dip into technical work. If he does not, he will never have time for his part of the institutional job—the never ending one of bringing about a consensus on the one hand and on the other of seeing that discussion does not protract interminably, that something decisive happens.

In doing this, he will need to take care not to go off on his own without regard for his organizational resources. If he forgets or ignores his staff in the course of operations, he runs the risk of dispensing off-the-cuff opinions which will not stand close analysis or making commitments which his organization cannot fulfill, not to mention the fact that such actions leave the staff in thin air. Unfortunately, not all governmental executives are like the one who commented to me recently that he doubted that he crossed up his staff as often as they did him. There are too many who operate as if the chief function of staff was to keep the executive from the embarrassment of explaining away their errors. This can only lead to a frittering away of strength in checking up on many small and relatively unimportant episodes.

The public arena character of the executive's responsibilities will draw upon his resources day and night, and he will find that in varying degrees, depending upon his status in the governmental scheme of things, he will not be able to live his life according to his personal choice but must govern himself in the light of the demands upon him. Nor will he be able to compensate for this by pointing at the end of the day to specific accomplishments and saying. "I did such and such." He may be able to think of a number of things that his organization did and how he tried to influence his organization and perhaps provide the capstone to some enterprise, but he can not look upon the results as his own.

It is because of these characteristics of executive life and routine that the appointment of good technicians to administrative posts is often a failure. Unless the specialist happens to possess the rare quality of administrative aptitude he cannot be remade into an executive with satisfaction either to himself or his staff. Anyone who has observed governmental operations has seen many instances of the unfortunate consequences of moving to administrative posts persons who are first and last technicians—making a physician a public health officer, a design engineer, a commissioner of public works, a social case worker, a welfare director, a program idea man in a Federal department, an assistant secretary.

Not as a technician. The need for the executive to eschew the technical and stick to the level where adjustments get made and judgments about the implications of surrounding circumstances are applied is one of the oft-repeated dictums of the public administration fraternity, but the point too frequently is oversimplified. For one thing the dividing line can never be determined with finality. The extent to which the executive concerns himself with specific issues will always be affected by such factors as the age of his organization, outside circumstances, and the extent to which he may have to compensate for failures at lower levels.

In any event, the executive must know enough of the general field not to get lost in the labyrinth. If he does not know the program at the outset, he must master quickly its major substantive elements. Otherwise he will be unable to command the loyalty and respect of his specialists and weld them together as a team. He must have sufficient understanding of the basic issues involved in his program to be able to judge whether the necessary steps have been taken to arrive at a proper conclusion. In the early days of the Federal Bureau of Old Age and Survivors Insurance, for example, the way in which individual participants were to be enumerated and their accounts identified—now numbering approximately 70 million—was one of the major technical issues. With many contending proposals advanced, members of the Social Security Board as well as the head of the

Bureau had to go into the problem sufficiently to be assured that the staff had developed the best answer.

The more background the executive develops with the passage of time, the more discriminating will be his judgments that have technical ingredients. He will learn to know when he should overrule his specialists (seldom on technical grounds) and how far he can rely on them, and he will know enough not to be cowed by them. Although the executive must be able to find his way among the technicians, his dominating concerns are more likely to be the non-technical factors affecting the resolution of a problem, particularly the general implications and potential outside acceptance of what is done. While the state highway commissioner, for example, will need to keep up with major changes in specifications or design which may become centers of controversy, he will find that his main headaches will arise out of such questions as the right of way for a road or the location of a bridge.

External affairs. This necessary concentration of the executive with what is feasible and with judging what is in the public interest should affect materially the amount of time the executive spends in becoming sensitive to and influencing the outside environment. It is the executive's job to cultivate relationships with the heads of other government agencies, with members of legislative bodies, with private institutions, and with the public so that his staff will have a favorable climate within which to function. In this way, he can increase his awareness of the ways in which programs and ideas must be carried out if they are to be accepted. The job of running interference for his organization is one that only the executive can do, and the effectiveness with which it is done will be a significant determinant of what his organization can accomplish.

His success in this part of his job will be affected in part by whether the executive confines his contacts to those that come to him or whether he consciously seeks to direct the character of these relationships. The government executive too often restricts himself to persons of his own social background or of the particular group with which his agency deals. He needs to mix with those who are against as well as for his program. If his agency's function is concerned with aids to business, he needs to understand the viewpoint of labor; if it is social welfare, he needs to mingle enough with the rugged individualists to see life from their angle. If his outside contacts are not well rounded or if he neglects them altogether, he may find that he will end up with a distorted view of the outside environment.

The executive's success in meeting these outside responsibilities will also be in part a by-product of his reaction to what his job demands of him as an individual. The broader and more generalized it is, the more important it will be for him to know what is going on not only in his general field, but in the community, in the nation, and in the world. He will need to broaden his own horizons, stretch his mind, and develop new ideas from which his whole organization can benefit. I know one Federal department head, for example, who met at regular intervals with people of ideas both inside and outside his organization, thus doing comprehensively what every executive should do at least in some degree. As a basic minimum, he should find time to keep up-to-date on the journals and books that give perspective to government enterprise, and I do not mean here administrative literature, important as that may be. If he lets himself become so preoccupied with his immediate problems that he fails to keep up with the life that is going on about him, he lets slip one of the best ways through which he can have an impact on his organization—by helping to bridge the gap between it and the world at large.

How He Saves His Time

I trust these comments on the level of activity on which the executive's energies should be focused do not give the impression that all the executive need do is have a bit of insight into what is demanded of him and proceed forthwith. It will unfortunately be an inevitable part of his lot that people and things will press for his attention far beyond his capacity to deal with them. His life will be a succession of meetings, telephone calls, documents. He cannot escape spending appreciable time handling many problems which will seem small in themselves but which may have serious implications for the status of the organization; persons who are not performing, staff troubles and worries, some aggrieved citizen, a press release. Many persons outside his organization will seek him out—citizens, legislators, newspaper men, old friends, *ad infinitum.*

Although he will need to take the greatest care not to appear inaccessible either to his staff or to those outside his organization, he must face the very practical problem of deciding whom he will see and of maintaining a balance among the competing demands for attention. If he holds himself open to deal with any problem that comes to him he will become inaccessible to his operating chiefs and he will neglect his outside responsibilities. Decisions will be delayed. He will lose perspective both on his organization and the world and will fail to provide the upward pull and unifying influence that his position requires. With a little firmness and careful planning. however, there are a number of steps he can take to conserve his time, and he can establish controls that will in reality increase rather than decrease his accessibility.

Personal staff. Judicious use of personal assistants is one of the best of these. In a large department or office, the executive may have several such assistants. Secretary of State Stettinius, in announcing new appointments in the State Department recently, designated fifteen persons to various types of assistant positions, in addition to the regular staff officers of the Department. For some of these, special areas of concern were indicated, e.g., International Organization and Security Affairs, Press Relations, Broad Management Matters; for others no special assignment was mentioned. This is probably far too many for the ordinary situation. The city manager of a city of 50,000 inhabitants, the head of a department of a medium-sized state, or a Federal division chief, for example, may find that a single administrative assistant will be sufficient.

One of the most important uses of the executive's personal staff, including his secretary, is in meeting the problem of seeing people. They can help him arrange his calendar, determine whom he should see, control the length of time he spends with visitors. They can frequently do much to satisfy those whom the executive is not able to see or arrange for their business to be disposed of by other officials. To meet the needs of subordinates they can often secure spot information or decisions from the executive. They can arrange meetings between the executive and persons both within and without the organization according to relative urgency.

The personal staff can also help identify the most pressing problems requiring the executive's attention and can pave the way for their speedy disposition by being sure that all necessary information is at hand and in order. They can sometimes pinch hit for the executive on spot jobs. They can give assistance in writing speeches and articles and can accompany him on trips when they can be useful. They can keep him up-to-date with what is going on. Sometimes one of them serves as an intimate advisor and will help select key officials and evaluate the performance of subordinates who seem to be falling down on their jobs. Obviously, each of the executive's personal assistants is not assigned to all of these tasks, as there will be specialization among them. But until his immediate office is staffed with aides who can do some or all of these things for him, he will be unnecessarily handicapped.

On the other hand, he must guard against overdoing it. A large number of personal assistants may mean that there are deadheads or blanks in the organization for whom the executive is seeking to compensate by increasing his personal staff. This can only muddy up the regular lines of communication and command and cause confusion in his organization. Personal assistants can also be a source of uncertainty if the executive fails to define their jobs so that their roles are understood by the rest of the organization.

An executive's personal assistants must not function as palace princes, accessible in varying degrees to other organization officials and pleading the cause only of favorites. They must be the same to all men, and the executive must kill any tendency to manipulate the organization or to afford an entrance through the "back door." Equally fatal is reliance on them by the executive to the point that his outlook becomes limited and warped.

Operating aides. In addition to what the personal staff can do to save the executive time and energy, there will also be need in any large organization for the kind of assistants who can share his principal operating burdens. If the executive chooses such aides judiciously he can compensate for talents which he may not have and multiply several times the impact of his leadership.

If the job of the executive requires a high level of public leadership, extensive dealing with a legislative body, a large number of outside contacts, or the devotion of much time to evolving a program or to negotiations with other executives, or if his talents do not lie in the management of an organization, a general deputy responsible in the line of command for internal administration will be needed. A permanent deputy position is likewise desirable when the executive post is one that changes with political fortunes. To be sure, it is not possible to have such a deputy in all of the situations where one could be used advantageously. In most city manager cities, for example, it is not often feasible for the manager to share his principal duties. The extent to which public attention is fixed on the centralization of responsibility in *the* city manager almost precludes the use of a double, although not other types of assistants.

Short of a general deputy, the executive may utilize a principal assistant either as an operating aide or as a chief of staff, giving him varying degrees of responsibility, or he may divide his managerial duties with one or more such assistants in a manner mutually compatible with the persons involved. The specific arrangements must be based upon the systematic analysis of tasks to be performed and of the personalities of the executive and the persons that can be secured to perform them. But even the best possible person will never fill the job as theoretically conceived.

However the matter is arranged, and it will always be difficult to work out smoothly, such assistants must think and act in terms that are appropriate to the organization at large. If they do not deal with matters that cut across the entire organization, they no longer serve as aides to the executive in his general leadership and management job but rather as operating heads of a group of specialized units. They then become preoccupied with segments of the organization and their work does little to contribute to the achievement of balance among the different parts. In the Federal Government, assistant secretaries in the departments are frequently used in this fashion—in the Interior, Commerce, Post Office, and Justice Departments among others. Generally speaking, there has been underdevelopment of the general deputy or assistant type of post I am describing here, in state and local government as well as in the Federal Government.

Time saving procedures. Apart from the help the executive can get by providing himself with staff to supplement or complement his own efforts, there is much that can be done to save his time if careful attention is given to the way in which documents, information, problems, issues are presented to him.

With a little ordinary care the amount of time the executive need spend on strictly informational material can be reduced to manageable dimensions. Summaries can be prepared for reports, lengthy memos can be briefed to one page, papers dealing with related subjects can be brought together. I am currently using a simple device in my own organization which, though small, is one in which the flow of information is enormous. My executive assistant and assistant chiefs provide me daily with a memorandum entitled "daily intelligence" in which they enumerate the things that have happened that I should know about, matters that have come up which they have arranged for others to settle, and steps they are taking to deal with affairs in which they know I have an interest. I in turn use the same device in posting the Director of the Bureau of the Budget on things he should know about. This is a very elementary but useful arrangement.

The way in which this can be done in a vast organization is illustrated by the manner in which information is packaged and presented to the Army Chief of Staff and other principal officers in the War Department. A log of selected, important messages to and from the War Department and points in all parts of the globe is the first order of business each day and takes from fifteen to forty-five minutes. This is followed by a meeting, attended by the Chief of Staff and his Deputy, the Secretary of War, and the Commanding General of the Army Air Forces, at which material on military operations throughout the world and on enemy developments and capabilities is presented and discussed. The data are organized by the Operations and Intelligence Divisions of the General Staff, and the discussion consumes from one-half to two hours. These daily informational routines are supplemented by a comprehensive system of briefing the Chief and Deputy Chief of Staff on all matters on which they must make decisions or on which they should be informed.

The Army also has an excellent system of long standing for standardizing the format and condensing the content of reports. In almost every case the essentials are reduced to a two-page memo covering statement of the problem, facts bearing on the problem, conclusions, recommendation. Explanatory discussion, if any, is put in appendices. When action is required, drafts of whatever documents may be necessary to carry out the proposals are attached. This system, referred to as "completed staff procedure," has permitted the rapid transaction of a great volume of business and has made it possible to get comprehensive studies made and implemented in short order.

Governmental executives generally could do much to simplify their lives by insisting upon the adaptation and development of this idea to meet their particular needs. More often than not, full implementation of a plan or recommendation will take a series of steps or actions. Each of these should be set up in a fashion to permit the executive to take action quickly. It is more economical of time for the executive to send documents back for change if need be than to try to make a decision on other than a specific basis. Too often executives are confronted with the statement, "Here's a problem," rather than "I propose that you do this for these reasons."

This process of simplification should not, however, be carried to the point that the executive is deprived of the opportunity of deliberation on the facts surrounding the proposal with which he is confronted. It is not always feasible nor is it necessarily desirable to reduce proposals to one recommended course of action. When there are non-technical factors entailing judgment and perspective of a level to warrant careful attention by the executive, cut-and-dried solutions will handicap rather than aid him. He should have the opportunity to consider well thought out alternative recommendations.

How He Communicates His Ideas

It will not profit the executive a great deal to be a genius in the management of his time, if he does not take steps to forge strong links between himself and the other elements in his organization. In this connection, the mobilization and indoctrination of his team of key subordinates must be near the top of any executive's agenda. When the executives sees to it that the persons in positions of responsibility have been selected and trained for the function of leadership, the way will be open for securing response to new objectives, policies, and methods. Without such a staff he will have a mob, not an organization.

If there is a free and open channel through which ideas and information can move both down and up, the influence of the executive can be felt all the way through the organization. This is not, of course, a one-way process. If the executive is skillful he will take pains to develop to the utmost the ideas and suggestions coming from his staff, both because this is the way to strengthen the net product and because only in an atmosphere where there is mutual respect are the executive's views likely to carry their maximum weight.

The kind of person the executive happens to be also has a good deal of bearing on the amount of influence he has. He is a symbol to his organization, and in the case of the higher posts, to the public as well. His attitudes and actions, both private and public, will have an effect—indirect and subtle perhaps, but nonetheless important—on the attitudes of all within his organization. If his characteristics and actions excite admiration, his staff will unconsciously be motivated to respond to his leadership and ideas. If the contrary is true, the natural reluctance of individuals to adapt themselves to the requirements of organized activity is likely to be thrice compounded.

Oral communication. In small sessions with key officials, the executive has his best opportunity for putting over his ideas. The values of such sessions can be multiplied if, when feasible, the officials primarily concerned with the resolution of an issue bring with them a principal subordinate or two, and if appropriate staff officers are included in important discussions with line officers. Any such devices that will increase the likelihood of cross-fertilization of ideas without setting undue obstacles in the way of the expeditious handling of business should be encouraged by the executive. Furthermore, to the extent that the executive makes the most of his opportunities for meeting with groups of people rather than individuals, he will be able to extend the area over which his influence is directly felt. It is not always necessary for the executive to be present in person for this result to be achieved. One of his staff officers or assistants thoroughly familiar with his point of view and attitude can often represent him.

Meetings of this character are of enormous importance as a means of facilitating the forward movement of an organization. If as issues come to the top they can be thrashed out by the principals involved, all points can be brought out on the spot and the most effective answer nailed down. This speeds the handling of important business, and through the process of dealing in unison on organization-wide matters, the principals get to know each other and how to work together. The more this understanding is developed, the more readily they will team up voluntarily when special problems confront two or more of them.

Staff meetings. General staff meetings, if well planned and confined to subjects that are of common interest and concern, can do much to aid communication. They can bring about fuller recognition by each individual of his relationship to the larger whole, and the executive can use them to bring about a common perspective and to help him in knitting the organization together. Anyone who has attended an effectively conducted meeting has observed how much more readily ideas take shape and are acted upon when an easy means of exchange is developed.

I do not wish to suggest, however, that general staff meetings are of exceptional importance. They are only one of many tools in the management kit. It is often taken for granted that every executive should get his key subordinates together—the department heads of a city or state government—as a cabinet, at frequent, regular intervals. The only useful purpose of group meetings of this character is discussion of matters of common concern. There no merit in bringing diverse officials together to consider matters that can be settled in the line of command. In a meeting of departments heads with the governor, any discussion of the welfare director's problems would put the director of public works to sleep. If the head of the agriculture department started to bring up his problems, most of the rest would be bored stiff. The reason for calling key subordinates together should be to dispose of issues requiring their collective judgment.

Written communications. Written communications are a generally understood although not too well applied method of conveying the executive's ideas from one level to another in an organization, and they can be an aid to his long-range efforts to develop his institution. In many organizations subordinates down the line are deluged with detailed instructions and regulations on every aspect of institutional life. Failure to credit staff with a certain amount of common sense and ingenuity will not generate mutual understanding and more likely than not will lead to complete indifference. In either event, the executive is not helped by the result.

On the other hand, there is only too apt to be a grievous lack of well thought out statements issued by the executive outlining specific objectives, schedules of operating requirements, and definitions of responsibilities. However good a job the executive may do in dealing with his principals and however conscientious they may be about passing on the information they get from the top, this will not cover the situation entirely. Written communications are an important supplement in getting to the entire organization the basic outlines of policies and objectives.

As important as it is that policies, and also programs and methods, be translated into clear, written communications, these should not be relied upon to get an essential thought over without the assistance that comes from personal comment on their application. Furthermore, this is the only way there can ever be assurance that staff members read or at least become aware of the written word. Written communications are useful chiefly as a point of departure and serve their primary purpose, after the actual labor of thinking them through is complete, as a basis for a discussion or series of discussions with staff of the ideas or directions contained therein. They are particularly useful for the orientation and instruction of new members of the organization.

How He Harnesses His Organization

My comments to this point have been focused on the ways in which the executive uses and extends his personality, ideas, and time. This has largely left out of account the institutional framework through which he must function. None of his personal activities, negotiations, or dealings will amount to much if his institution is not so organized that he can get a firm grip on it at crucial points and at crucial times.

Keeping up to date. Essential number one is that he must know what is going on in his organization. If he organizes for the purpose, he can keep track of the trend of affairs—weak spots and strong spots, emerging problems, bottlenecks, opportunities for progress. If he does not, he is likely to be at a loss in attempting to pursue a balanced program.

In the normal course of events he will be confronted with a vast array of paper: actions or letters requiring his signature, drafts of orders and regulations, proposed plans of work, reports of inspections or organizational studies, program appraisals, reports of progress, statistical summaries and interpretations, personnel documents, budget and fiscal analyses *ad infinitum*. With the help of his assistants in organizing and controlling these materials they can provide him with much grist for appraisal of the organization's operations.

The picture the executive gets in this fashion will be only a partial one and will lack a good deal of realism if he does not supplement these sources of information with others.

Many of the gaps the executive can fill in for himself, through conversations and dealings with his subordinates, and in some fields of governmental work, through inspections. The state conservation commissioner can see at first hand what is being done in the way of development and use of state parks and in the management of state forests. On the other hand, the head of an agency engaged in activities having little tangible or physical expression cannot rely very heavily on this device. A commissioner of internal revenue, for example, cannot learn much about the product of his organization by looking at the files of paper in process.

The executive's personal staff can help keep him posted on what is going on by passing on information that he might pick up himself if he could see more people. What I am referring to is spot news that may affect the organization and its work, information on breakdowns in the organization, on personnel maladjustments, reactions of particular persons to actions by the executive, new proposals or ideas in the making, complaints with which the executive may have to deal. They may learn of these things informally by contacts below the upper crust of the organization, or they may pick up some of it from conversations with or reports by both staff and line officers. The executive needs to differentiate between the significant and unimportant in this kind of stuff which may often be little more than rumor or gossip. He must keep a check rein on it, and not let it offset the solid help which his general staff divisions can give him directly.

Staff divisions. Perhaps the most important single tool the executive has in harnessing his organization and keeping it in focus is his general staff—the budgeting, program planning, personnel, organization and methods planning divisions. I do not include here service or auxiliary units such as statistical, procurement, and office services, as important and necessary as these may be. Neither do I include here accounting and legal services which, while providing control mechanisms for the executive, are otherwise more akin to the service units than they are to the general staff divisions. It is true, however, that because of personal competence, as well as the fact that they engage in some general staff activity, accounting and legal chiefs are often used by the executive for a variety of general staff responsibilities.

The staff divisions provide resources for the analysis and development of solutions of problems common to the whole organization. They provide a source of highest counsel and advice on matters about which the executive is uncertain or has reason to doubt the solution offered by an operating subordinate. They provide a general rather than a specialized viewpoint in review both of proposals made by the operating subdivisions and of evaluating the results of the work of such subdivisions. They can do much to help the executive bring the objectives of the organization into focus and get consistency of action. In addition, the employees of such divisions circulate around the entire outfit and provide one of the most fruitful means of gathering information and of securing understanding and acceptance of policy.

The executive needs the benefit of a group of staff advisers functioning in this fashion to help him in anticipating tasks to be done, in planning to meet contingencies that may be around the corner, in mapping out policy and program, and in working out fundamental organization and methods. Their value depends, however, on the way in which they function. They must stay in the staff role of advising, consulting, and coordinating and must avoid imposing their personal judgment on line officials on operating matters. Staff divisions can become a burden rather than a help if they diffuse the executive's line of command by dipping into operating work and if they insulate the executive from other sources of counsel. That the temptation to move outside the staff realm frequently is not resisted is reflected in the common practice of having a large number of detailed transactions referred to the budget office or personnel office for review, transactions that involve no new policy questions. Perhaps the reason staff officers often insist on this is because it is easier to review the activity of others than to do creative work or because they do not have the capacity to do staff work, or because they have never learned what real staff work is.

The staff divisions cannot fulfill their roles to the maximum if they move off on their own in separate directions. It is, therefore, essential that general staff activities be coordinated with each other. The executive or his general deputy may be able to supply this coordination. Sometimes this can be more readily achieved by placing the staff units under an executive officer or a chief of staff. The various staff elements can in this way be brought into focus by someone concerned with the management of the organization as a whole, and the total resources are more available to the executive. Furthermore, there will then be less likelihood of nonproductive competition for the attention of the executive, and the number of organizational units the executive must keep track of personally will be reduced.

But regardless of the arrangement, general staff functions must be directed by high-level officers who have a considerable amount of free access to the executive, with the executive officer performing a facilitating function and providing the environment in which the executive can most easily tap the reservoir of ideas of the individual staff officers.

Arrangement of line units. The way in which the executive arranges the subdivisions of his agency or bureau will also have a lot to do with whether he is on top of or at the mercy of his organization. There is much common knowledge of how to organize operating subdivisions, and I shall not go into the question in detail. I should like to comment particularly on the relationship between the way in which the organization is put together and the executive's opportunity to act on significant issues.

For example, a small number of operating divisions will not necessarily mean that the executive is sufficiently free of detail that he can contribute the element of overall perspective and influence. When there are so few or the establishment is so arranged that the executive is walled off from operations by many layers of supervision or the job of harmonizing and coordinating on major issues is pushed down to a subsidiary level, he may become the slave rather than the master.

Related to the question of too few operating units and the layers of supervision that this may entail, is that of the excessive independence that statutory provisions often give subordinate operating officers. When the functions of major division heads are defined by statute, the top executive is placed under a severe handicap in trying to manage what frequently become independent principalities. I recall the vivid comment of a Federal executive who complained that he had the impossible task of administering a federation of bureaus rather than a department.

In a different category are the complications that may ensue if there is too fine a break-down of activities. Not only is he unable to hold the separate units within his span of attention, which leaves them floating on their own, but those issues that do reach him may get one-sided or unbalanced consideration. Functions need to be so arranged that, to the maximum extent possible, varied points of view will be brought to bear and reconciled at points along the way. In recognition of the dangers of overspecialization, up-to-date city health departments, for example, have moved away from the system of organizing public health nursing services on the basis of specialized types of work: tuberculosis, venereal disease, infant care. Units or districts consisting of a group of nurses able to meet varied problems and situations are in large measure self-coordinating and thus reduce the burden on higher administrative positions.

There is another disadvantage in agencies or units set up with relatively narrow functions. If the agency commands the support of a specialized or single purpose type of interest or pressure group, undue influence in one direction may be exerted on the executive, and it will be more difficult for him to keep his organization in proper focus.

Almost all of these dilemmas of internal organization have been faced at one time or another in organizing the housing functions of the Federal Government. In February, 1942, the three major functions of loan insurance, mortgage banking, and public housing were brought together by Executive Order to form the National Housing Agency. In varying degrees each function has its own clientele including one or more interest groups. If any one of these functions should be reconverted to independent agency status, the executive of such a narrowly based agency would be subject to highly specialized pressures. The executive of a unified housing agency is in a far better position to balance off interest against interest and emerge with a program which reflects the national interest.

Combining the mortgage banking and housing loan insurance functions with all the other loan activities of the Government would be equally undesirable from the point of view of carrying out a housing program. Such a move would facilitate credit policy coordination by the head of the agency but would complicate the job of executives of other agencies operating in the same functional field, as well as subordinate program objectives, to fiscal considerations. The public housing chief could not, under these circumstances, easily reconcile housing credit activities with his program. The purpose of the Federal housing programs is adequate housing for all citizens. Consequently, a permanent agency encompassing all three housing functions holds greatest promise as a method of providing coordinated leadership over a comprehensive group of closely knit housing operations. This solution permits effective executive direction and control. It is for this same reason that credit agencies in the agricultural field have been placed in the Department of Agriculture, those concerned with foreign operations in the Foreign Economic Administration, and so on.

Is He a Success?

This discussion has touched on some of the things that the executive can do to harmonize and get the most out of the other elements in his organization. I have emphasized that this is the way that he builds up his influence in his organization and guides it toward its objectives. In closing, I should like to reiterate my earlier point that although the executive is not likely to succeed if he approaches his organization as something that is his own to command, he is at no disadvantage as he takes up the role of leadership.

The fact that he is the repository of formal authority in his organization is a powerful asset in the business of developing his titular position into one of genuine force and strength. Furthermore, it is up to him at any one point in time to determine the issues which he wants to have referred to him for decision. Although he may not decide much in his organization, quantitatively speaking, his choice of the decisions that he should make will determine how his organization meets its major difficulties. The point is that for the most part, he must depend upon others; therefore to the extent that the entire organization moves within a commonly accepted framework will it develop some speed and assurance in its forward movements.

My comments have been directed in large part toward some of the methods by which this team relationship can be developed. I trust that these may have proved helpful by suggesting some of the aspects of the business of managing a government enterprise beyond those generally taken for granted. All of these devices and suggestions, however, will not prove any substitute for general aptitude in the business of getting people to pull together. The real leader does not consciously rely upon any pat method of exercising leadership and influence. This is something to which he will be sensitive by his very makeup. He will feel the pulse of his organization and will understand it as a whole rather than as a lot of separate segments. He will know whether he understands it by whether it is responsive to him. If he has this sensitivity, even if he is a neophyte, he will soon learn the tricks of the trade. If he does not have it, no amount of boning up on what experience has taught us will help him much.

This can perhaps be illustrated by an analogy that is more suggestive than it is accurate. A person making his first public speech has little impression whether or not he is carrying his audience. By his one-hundredth speech he should know. If he does not, he is not a real public speaker. If he does, he will adjust his performance in many ways in order to bring the audience and himself into harmony. And so it is with the executive in relation to his organization. A good executive gets the feel of situations by the way in which those with whom he deals respond to him, and adjusts himself and his staff arrangements accordingly.

PART 5

WHAT ARE THE BEST STYLES FOR PUBLIC-SECTOR LEADERS TO USE?

Leader style refers to the dominant and defining behavioral patterns of the leader. For simplicity one can talk of a single, overall style for a leader, but in reality very few effective leaders have a single style that they use all of the time. Effective leaders vary their styles from situation to situation. Leaders may use styles consciously, but just as often they are unconscious in their use of style. Some leaders are oblivious to the fact that many of their actions belie their espoused style. Followers attribute styles to leaders from the behaviors they observe; but these observations may or may not be consistent with each other because of different observations and perceptions about the leader. Effective leaders know what styles to adopt in given situations, know what their preferred and alternate styles are, and are able to self-consciously adapt their style (Hersey and Blanchard 1969) or the situation (Fiedler, Chemers, and Mahar 1976) for maximum success. In other words, effective leaders tend to be more conscious of the style they use, have better alignment between their self-conception and the perceptions of others, and have a philosophy of leadership that assists them to act and speak coherently about what they do (Bass 1990).

Many factors impinge upon leader styles: follower characteristics, environmental contingencies, and power structures are chief among them. A leader generally should not use the same style with a group of new employees as with a group of twenty-five-year veteran employees. Nor would one use the same style with an employee about to be suspended as with an award-winning employee. In terms of environmental contingencies, the most prominent is the crisis, in which more directive modes and greater decisiveness are generally called for. Even the culture of the organization or unit will affect the style used. For example, it is common in larger organizations, where the CEO has substantial external contacts, for her/him to focus almost exclusively on those external affairs, and for the chief deputy to handle internal operations, thereby resulting in a dual leadership model substantially affecting their styles.

Just as all people have inherent personality characteristics that define their preferred and secondary personality modes, people have preferred and secondary leadership styles too. The preferred mode is the one with which a leader feels most comfortable and on which a leader will tend to rely most heavily in ambiguous situations. Secondary styles are those that the leader can employ, but generally it is a more conscious activity. The style range is the degree to which the leader can use multiple styles. Style capacity is the ability of a leader to employ a style effectively, no matter whether it is a preferred or secondary style. It is quite possible for one leader to have great capacity in one style, and rarely use any secondary styles, and for another to have a relatively comprehensive range, use all of them poorly, and be less effective overall. Of course highly effective leaders not only have competence in a wide style range, but also are able to shift styles strategically according to different situations. There is debate about how much a given leader can change his or her style (Fiedler, Chemers, and Mahar 1976) or should try to adapt him or herself to a situation. Yet even with a narrow view of adaptability, the leader is still responsible for finding the right person to handle specific situations or adapting the situations in ways amenable to his or her styles.

One of the most common style dimensions is follower inclusion in decision making, which is related to the level of leader support for followers. Starting in the 1960s, and evolving in the 1970s, this led to a series of efforts to identify an empirically supportable theory, as well as a series of practical prescriptions for leaders. Two broad approaches developed (Northouse 2001). The earlier approach suggested that there was a single ideal style—albeit broadly defined—that generally worked in all situations (a universal approach). It started with the observation from social science insights of the first half of the twentieth century that followers were an important part of the leadership process. Significantly, they had been relatively neglected in leadership theory. The human relations school asserted that an excessive task orientation was dysfunctional, and that the support and development of followers was critical for maximal effectiveness. It was not that a task orientation could be neglected, but that a people-oriented approach was also necessary. It the simplest version, this led to the authoritarian versus democratic management styles implicit in so many theories of the period. Neglect of critical management functions was generally labeled laissez-faire leadership. More sophisticated versions of this model assumed that leaders, followers, and situations evolve into an ideal management approach. In the case of the "grid leadership" described by Blake and Mouton (1964) it meant that the weakest leaders use an authoritarian style, the moderately competent leaders used both task- and people-oriented behaviors but not to maximum effect, and the strongest leaders used an ideal mix of people and task behaviors (team management, or 9–9 on their grid). Both the simpler and the more sophisticated approaches to an ideal style theory of leadership are represented in the reading selections.

The second approach to leadership emphasizes the situation (a contingency approach). Although situational models tend to espouse some of the same tenets just discussed— leaders need both task and people skills—this school of thought added two twists. First, because the situation or contingency, not an ideal, dictated the proper leadership style, it was quite possible to effectively use different styles (including an authoritarian mode) as events and context demanded. Second, these models suggest that high-performance groups can sometimes move to a level beyond full participation. That is, in some situations, groups experience a self-led mode in which full delegation occurs, and they are more driven by their own need for achievement than by the dictates of the organization through the leader.

The Hersey and Blanchard (1969) situational leadership model is the single most widely used in this perspective. It prescribes various leadership styles to use with a group or an individual in different situations, dependent on the "maturity" of the followers. Follower maturity is based on experience and willingness (cooperation and confidence). They provide a four-cell matrix of leader style based on these maturity characteristics. If an employee is unable (e.g., inexperienced) and unwilling (e.g., hesitant about how to do a job), the style to use is a "telling" mode (highly directive) and should primarily focus on the task at hand. If the employee is unable but is willing, the best style is a "selling" mode (a directive style with more interpersonal rapport). If the employee is able but not fully engaged, the best style to use is a participating mode so that the followers have greater ownership but the leader does not disengage from the situation and can focus on encouragement of correct behaviors. For fully mature followers, those who are both able and willing, the recommendation is for delegating because they need little task or interpersonal support. Because of the simplicity of the model and its face validity, it has been very popular as a training tool to help managers think about the styles they use, especially at the supervisory level. However, the model has been severely criticized by scholars for both theoretical inconsistencies and lack of empirical support. This cautions the astute user of this model to view it as a useful exploratory framework, not as a rigorous prescriptive tool.

Vroom and his colleagues have developed a very sophisticated situational approach, strictly using the idea of follower inclusion in the decision-making mix (Vroom and Yetton 1973; Vroom and Jago 1988). However, the approach most popular to researchers has been based on the work of House and is called path-goal theory (1971, 1996). The general idea is that successful leaders will clear the path for followers so that they will want to achieve jointly desired employee-organizational goals. It is based on expectancy theory, which stipulates that in order for followers to be well motivated they must first feel that they can be successful in task completion (be trained, be competent, understand the task, etc.), next feel that they will be rewarded for task completion (praise, raises, promotions, etc.), and finally value the rewards (Vroom 1964). Because different elements of follower motivation may be missing in different situations, leaders must use their style to complement each situation. Uninformed followers need direction, unsure followers need support, and high-performing followers need the rewards of greater autonomy and self-achievement. The related styles according to House are directive, supportive, participative, and achievement leadership styles.

Although situational leadership approaches are generally more sophisticated, the models have not been able to report significantly higher levels of empirical support because of their inherent complexity. Further, for basic training purposes, ideal approaches continue to be extremely popular. Two of the selections are based on situational approaches using path-goal leadership theory.

Another common conception of leadership style has to do with the orientation toward change. In fact, many debates have occurred about leaders' being primarily facilitators of change and managers as being maintainers of systems (Zalenik 1977). Putting aside the argument about whether management is a subset of leadership, leadership is a subset of management, or they are relatively autonomous activities, we can look at them as a spectrum of activities that vary both by situation and by leader preference. Typically in the leadership literature management activities are called "transactional" and change activities are called "transformational." We can further divide each category into leadership with a task focus, a people focus, or an organizational alignment focus. This typology extends the task/people dimension in the management assessments so popular in the 1960s and 1970s. A task-oriented transactional manager focuses primarily on production; a people-oriented manager focuses primarily on the employee's training and development; and an organization-oriented manager focuses primarily on aligning the unit or agency with the external environment. Thus a task-oriented line supervisor may do poorly in a middle management position requiring a lot of peer negotiation and interaction, or a middle manager promoted to an executive position may do poorly because s/he cannot let go of an exclusively operational perspective when an outward focus (e.g., public and legislative relations) is needed. In the transformational domain, leaders who change processes or technical systems radically (in the reengineering tradition) are entrepreneurial leaders. Those who inspire followers to achieve new levels of production, cooperation, and effort are charismatic leaders. Those who propose an entirely new way of organizing the enterprise or mastermind significant changes in the mission are visionary leaders. Although it is rare for a leader to be a pure type, the categories can be useful in qualifying the different emphases of different leaders. For example, Lee Iacocca was exclusively an entrepreneurial leader at Ford, championing the popular Mustang under a strong-willed company president; at Chrysler he moved away from entrepreneurial activities somewhat, and increased his charismatic and visionary style enormously as president (Iacocca 1984). One of the selections emphasizes a transformational approach to leadership.

Review of the Selections in Part 5

Carl Stover's 1958 article "Changing Patterns in the Philosophy of Management" reflects the widespread influence of the human relations school, in that ideas about management were evolving into notions about organizations being more than a "well-oiled machine." Yet management is also more than just keeping people happy. Because of the complexities of management, those in positions of authority must have a deeper understanding of what they do and why. Stover asserts (well before Mintzberg [1973] and others corroborated such findings) that in the hurly-burly of administration, it is easy to be inconsistent or unsystematic. Although having a philosophy does not guarantee good management, frequently lack of a philosophy does impede good leadership. A philosophy helps a manager systematize ideas, define what is true, determine what questions are more and less important, and prescribe values useful in making decisions. Easy examples to look at are the ideas managers have about human nature and the concomitant relationship to employee motivation; if we believe people are basically lazy, then we will rely extensively on external controls such as rules and punishments. Yet he uses philosophy in its old-fashioned sense, in which personal beliefs and scientific study are closely aligned. "Management is an intellectual understanding in which the powers of intelligent inquiry are more important than hunches." (Nonetheless, he gently decries science's tendency to eschew issues of values in its effort to be objective when it also leads to viewing management as "an enterprise without values.") He ends with a wonderful statement about the characteristics that we can look for in ideal managers: "a broad, world-encompassing view, a scientific spirit, a knowledge of the methods and tools of science, a basic understanding of the social sciences and the humanities, talents in the integration of ideas and in the solution of problems, and, above all, an idealism that will guide and stimulate them."

Sven Lundstedt's article "Administrative Leadership and Use of Social Power" (1965) is a good example of the simpler bifurcations about leadership. He begins with a traditional definition of leadership: "Leadership is the ability to influence the behavior of others in a group or organization, set goals for a group, formulate paths to the goals, and create some social norms in the group." After reviewing French and Raven's classic taxonomy of types of power, he divides leadership styles into the permissive or coercive approaches. The coercive approach assumes that people must be "controlled, directed, and threatened with punishment to make them work adequately and well." The democratic alternative is supported by the research of Maslow, McGregor, Likert, Herzberg, and others. In this perspective "responsibility is not distasteful and only becomes so in the context of unrewarding experiences." He further asserts that "extended participation in making decisions about one's own job should be the rule rather than the exception." He details the negative organizational cycle that typically occurs in an overriding authoritarian model, in which workers tend to live up to the poor expectations of leaders. However, although he makes a simplistic assertion that democratic or participative leadership is superior, he concludes that democratic leadership is vastly more complex and difficult. In other words, badly executed democratic leadership might not be an improvement over authoritarian leadership.

The next two articles are based on the path-goal situational leadership model of House and his associates. In "Leadership and Regional Councils: A Mismatch between Leadership Styles Today and Future Roles" (1993), Robert Gage looks at leadership in terms of the competencies needed by regional councils (often called councils of government). That is, he is asking, what is the best style for regional councils, and does that style change significantly over time? He finds that the dominant style of councils (in 1993), according to executive directors, was participative. Yet he asserts that the preferable pattern of leadership is directive at that historical juncture because of the need to take a stronger hand in regional planning and to make implementation a priority. Although several aspects of the study might be questioned, such as why the biases of executive directors should be the primary source of evidence and his interpretation of the implications of different leadership styles, the piece is a classic in clearly and boldly laying out its assertions (hypotheses), testing them, and interpreting the results.

Starkly contrasted with this is "Research and Interventions for Stress Reductions in a Hospital Setting" (1989) by Raynis and Cleek, which uses a hospital setting for its applied study of the best style to use in an organizational situation. They focus on several features: the high-stress environment and the professional training of staff. They immediately assert that "according to Path-Goal theory, the presence of a large number of stressors implies the need for a more participative style on the part of the supervisor, thus increasing subordinate control over the environment, and also the need to attend to subordinates' emotional needs" (supportive leadership). Their research indicated that the main stressors were uncertainty and task ambiguity stemming from the flow of work, rather than lack of training and experience by staff. Directive styles of leadership tended to parcel out bits of work such that employees could not see patterns in advance or participate in the planning. An achievement orientation frustrated employees who felt that they could not adequately affect overall results. Therefore the authors recommend that the situation lends itself to more participation and support, and less overt direction and emphasis on achievement. Again, the details of the case are not as important as the analytic process that the authors use to determine the appropriate styles.

References

Bass, Bernard M. 1990. *Bass & Stogdill's Handbook of Leadership.* New York: Free Press.

Blake, Robert R., and Jane S. Mouton. 1964. *The Managerial Grid.* Houston, TX: Gulf.

Fiedler, F.E., M.M. Chemers, and L. Mahar. 1976. *Improving Leadership Effectiveness: The Leader Match Concept.* New York: Wiley.

Hersey, Paul, and Kenneth H. Blanchard. 1969. "The Life Cycle Theory of Leadership." *Training and Development Journal* 23: 26–34.

House, Robert J. 1971. "A Path-Goal Theory of Leader Effectiveness." *Administrative Science Quarterly* 16: 321–28.

House, Robert J. 1996. "Path-Goal Theory of Leadership: Lessons, Legacy, and a Reformulated Theory." *Leadership Quarterly* 7 (3): 323–52.

Iacocca, Lee. 1984. *Iacocca: An Autobiography.* New York: Bantam.

Mintzberg, Henry. 1973. *The Nature of Managerial Work.* New York: Harper and Row.

Northouse, Peter G. 2001. *Leadership: Theory and Practice,* 2nd ed. Thousand Oaks, CA: Sage.

Vroom, Victor H. 1964. *Motivation and Work.* New York: McGraw-Hill.

Vroom, Victor H., and Arthur G. Jago. 1988. *The New Leadership: Managing Participating in Organizations.* Upper Saddle River, NJ: Prentice Hall.

Vroom, Victor H., and Paul W. Yetton. 1973. *Leadership and Decision Making.* Pittsburgh, PA: University of Pittsburgh Press.

Zalenik, Arthur. 1977. "Managers and Leaders: Are They Different?" *Harvard Business Review* 55 (5): 67–78.

CHAPTER 17

CHANGING PATTERNS IN THE PHILOSOPHY OF MANAGEMENT

CARL F. STOVER

Whether he recognizes it or not, every manager has a philosophy on which he relies in doing his job. It is rarely systematic or integrated. Typically, it is contradictory and inconsistent. If he expresses it in words, the description is likely to diverge to some degree from the philosophy he reveals in practice.

A moment's reflection should make clear why these things are true. Managers deal with complex problems in complex settings. As Herbert Simon points out, they cannot be objectively rational about their decisions because they cannot satisfy all of the conditions of rationality. They cannot know all of the facts about the situations they face. They cannot comprehend all of the implications of the alternatives before them, nor are they aware of the full range of possible alternatives. Their knowledge of the goals that should be served is limited and their ignorance of the full significance of these goals is manifold.

If the manager is to deal at all with the problems before him, he must simplify them, put them in a context he understands, relate them to some system, however imperfect, over which he has a command. He must analyze them in terms of ideas that have meaning to him and of values that he believes in and that have significance for him. To make his job manageable, then, and to make himself in some measure rational, the manager must depend on a philosophy.

What Is Philosophy?

Philosophy can mean many things. For some, it signifies a love of wisdom; for others, a body of principles, a set of values, a world view, or merely a field of study. For our purposes here, perhaps a philosophy can best be viewed as *a system of ideas* which does three things:

First, *it defines what is true*—as when communism prescribes the inevitable decay of capitalist economies or democracy asserts that men possess inalienable rights; as when Newton posited the attraction of masses or Albert Einstein asserted that $E = mc^2$. What the philosophy states to be true may not be capable of empirical proof, and sometimes

From *Public Administration Review*, vol. 18, no. 1 (1958): 21–27. Copyright © 1958 by American Society for Public Administration. Reprinted with permission.

it may be patently wrong. Nevertheless, philosophy does attempt to describe the nature of reality in abstract terms.

A second thing that philosophy does is *to determine what questions are important to ask and to rule out others.* A believer in a natural law philosophy might think it important to ask what values the moral order of the universe would impose upon him in dealing with a particular problem. A casuist would ask what precedents existed for handling a matter, whereas a utilitarian would find such a question of secondary importance.

In his *Ethics for Policy Decision,* Wayne A.R. Leys[1] makes clear the relationship between philosophy and the asking of deliberative questions. The book was prepared for managers and others who are policy makers on this premise: "If policy makers read philosophical ethics for critical questions instead of answers, they may correct some sources of bad judgment." (3) Every manager should read this book. Its first portion is devoted to an examination of the questions posed by various philosophical schools; the second applies these questions to case examples of policy-making problems in business and government. Here are some of the questions which Leys draws from different philosophical schools.

For the Stoics, he posits these questions, which reveal that every manager is indeed something of a Stoic:

1. What is not within our power?
2. What must be accepted as external conditions and what is intolerable because it destroys personal integrity?
3. To what must we be resigned in order to preserve our rationality and self-respect? (190)

The Marxians, however, would be more likely to inquire in this vein:

1. What are the fundamental changes in the mode of economic production? What economic classes are created by these changes?
2. How are all issues related to the class conflict? How do class interests determine ideology?
3. What action in the immediate situation will hasten the final showdown in the class war, regardless of the interests of the individuals immediately involved? (190–91)

Finally, we might look to the semanticists, from whom we have recently heard a great deal:

1. Is your knowledge of fact confused by emotional language?
2. Does the language that you use prejudge the issues? Can you translate your description of fact into an expression that has a less or a different emotional meaning?
3. In choosing your course of action, do you select words (as a part of your action) to which other people will respond rationally? Are you engaging in unimportant verbal quibbles? Are you expecting words to do things that words cannot do? Are

you failing to engage in verbal ceremonials that are required by other people? Should you engage in verbal trickery in dealing with irrational or preoccupied individuals and groups? (191)

The third contribution that philosophy makes is the *prescription of a set of values* useful in making decisions about right and wrong. You are all familiar with examples. The Judaeo-Christian system prescribes the Golden Rule, Aristotle the Golden Mean. In a more contemporary vein, democracy prescribes the rectitude of values related to human freedom.

As we move to an examination of management philosophy, specifically, it will be useful to keep these three aspects of philosophy in mind, for it is his philosophy which helps a manager (1) to define what is true, (2) to ask the right questions, and (3) to apply the appropriate values.

Philosophies in Practice

Different approaches to management may often be related directly to different beliefs about what is true. A stark example of this point occurred in the period following World War II, when Sears, Roebuck and Company and Montgomery Ward and Company followed divergent business policies in competing for a common market.[2] Under General Robert E. Wood, Sears expanded, on the assumption that the economy was essentially healthy and would grow in the postwar period. Sewell Avery, believing that a depression was due, held the line. As a result, Sears advanced from 57.7 percent of net sales for the two firms in 1940 to 68.6 percent in 1950, and Ward's percentage declined correspondingly. The values of the two leaders also differed. While both looked askance at the government's efforts to influence the economy, Avery's aversion was probably stronger. Possibly his failure to interpret the postwar period correctly was in some way related to his negative valuation of government economic activities. The interplay of values with perceptions of fact is not uncommon and holds many hazards for the manager.

Other revealing examples may be drawn from personnel policies and practices. Certainly, the personnel policy promulgated by an organization reflects in some measure the beliefs its leadership holds about what people are like and how they can be influenced to put out their best efforts. The sweatshop of the past was rooted in a depreciated estimate of the worth of the great mass of individuals. Today, factories and offices generally demonstrate a much different understanding.

In a similar vein, the questions asked about organization procedures reflect different views. "Are there enough controls?" is a common question in management, which when carried too far may well evidence an overemphasis on human frailty. How much better, and less frequent, is the question, "Is there sufficient individual opportunity?"

Values are implicit in all of these examples. Some personnel policies celebrate the organization, others celebrate man himself. Some view the individual as a commodity to be bartered, a machine to be exploited; others treat him with a basic humanity. What you do depends on what you believe to be right, on what your values are.

These practical examples help to demonstrate that a manager's philosophy does not exist in a vacuum. It is influenced by general social philosophies, by individual codes and temperaments, and many other factors. It is also influenced by the growing body of management literature and by the activities of professional associations. As managers are increasingly exposed to management training in schools of business or public administration, these influences are bound to grow. By the same token, the philosophical views of individual managers are reflected in their writings and other professional activities. This is a field in which practitioners, teachers, and researchers frequently exchange ideas, information, and even roles.

Thus, the literature and other professional activities in the field should provide useful clues to how management philosophy is changing or is likely to change. It is on these activities that primary reliance is placed for this analysis, but it is tempered, inevitably, with observations of the administrative milieu.

From Folklore to Science

Probably the most noticeable present trend in management philosophy is the growing belief that management can and should be a field of scientific inquiry and that the practice of management can be made more scientific. In a sense, this is the master trend, to which all others are related. For ease of reference, it might be called the movement from management folklore to management science.

The folklore of our field continues to have value. A review of some of the sprightly comments of the late Lent D. Upson, long-time director of the National Training School for Public Service and dean of the School of Public Affairs and Social Work at Wayne University, will refresh us and also our memories about what that folklore is like. In his *Letters on Public Administration*[3] he has these things to say:

> Don't ask your superior to approve of plans you are sure of. The mere asking raises the question of expediency. If it is necessary to discuss a subject with a superior, it is usually well to bring a gang with you. One of your associates will think up the right answer while you are stumbling over it—or at least will confuse the issue so thoroughly that your superior will remain in the dark. Loud talk and confusion may snatch victory out of defeat. This administrative technique is particularly good at public hearings.
>
> An alternative is always to bring in two plans—a good one and a bad one. Your boss will spend half the morning tearing your bad plan apart and then be so tired he will approve the good one without change.
>
> Your subordinates have doubtless already learned these techniques. But what to do if one of them gets out on a limb indulging in them? Yank him back if he is a good man, a mayor's appointee, or the nephew of a heavy stockholder. Otherwise, saw off the limb after about the third error—or resign yourself. . . .
>
> Occasionally ask the advice of your colleagues and subordinates on some current problem. It will flatter them and they may surprise you.

In some quarters, this approach is still popular, and I for one hope that its brighter aspects will never be fully lost. But increasingly, men are coming to believe and to demonstrate that folklore is not enough. Dating roughly from the 1920s, management has become an important object of scientific inquiry, and scientific tools have become more and more necessary in the field.[4]

Early contributors to this development were the "scientific managers"—among them, Henri Fayol, V.A. Graicunas, Luther Gulick, Lyndall Urwick, the Gilbreths.[5] The approach of this school was primarily mechanistic, involving the detailed analysis of formal and structural aspects of organization and work processes. While it is the fashion among some contemporary students to criticize this school because it laid claim to too much scientific sophistication, its contribution is of lasting value.

A related early group placed greater emphasis on the human dimension. The Hawthorne experiments are the classic example of this approach, though hardly the most sophisticated. Here one recalls Mayo, Roethlisberger, and Dickson;[6] Mary Parker Follett's dynamic administration;[7] and, more recently, Robert Merton, Sam Stouffer, Rensis Likert, Alex Bavelas, Dorwin Cartwright, and a host of others,[8] whose work carries such familiar and appealing titles as group dynamics, motivation research, participative management, and the psychology of work.

A third group influencing this trend and providing a strong foundation for it includes men like Leonard D. White[9] and John Gaus[10]—the historians and describers of management—whose principal contributions to the growth of a scientific temper have been the clear analysis of management problems, the exact recording of management data, and the stimulation of others in the field to grapple with its more important problems.

In the period since the war, the trend from folklore to science has had a major culmination, bringing with it more sophisticated methods, more powerful analytical tools, and a sounder general science of man and society. We now find not only social scientists, with their new-found sophistication, but also physicists, electrical engineers, mathematicians, biologists, and other specialists contributing to our understanding and practice of management. Operations research, the theory of games, and other specialized analytical tools are coming into play with much greater frequency.

With this prodigious development has come a better understanding of management. We now have a larger recognition of determinism in management action, reflecting our appreciation of determinism in all social activity. Events do not just happen, they are caused. Things heretofore regarded as necessary evils, ever-present problems, are now viewed as natural outgrowths of prevailing conditions and, hence, as subject to control or change.

We also realize, more fully than before, that management is an intellectual undertaking in which the powers of intelligent inquiry are more important than hunches. Greater emphasis is being given to ways of making management a rational activity, to take out of it the guesswork and put into it the laws of probability.

Management is increasingly recognized as social process, rather than simply as an exercise of authority and command, in terms of assigned responsibilities and functions. Our focus is on relationships among people, processes and currents, patterns of association and communication. It has moved away from the more formal statements of organization charts and books of procedures and the legal proscriptions of the statute books.

This broader understanding of what is true has led managers to elevate certain kinds of questions and to introduce others in their deliberations. These are the sorts of questions which reflect this change:

1. What are the underlying causes of the problem? Are they the same as those appearing on the surface?
2. What can the scholars, the scientists, and others with specialized knowledge and training contribute to solving it? What kinds of intellectual skills will be useful?
3. What is the social structure with which we are dealing? What is the informal communication pattern? How does it affect the formal relationships in the organization?
4. What are the major facets of the problem? How do they relate? What is the human dimension? What human relationships are involved?

In the realm of values, the changes brought by the growth of science in management are most difficult to grasp and describe. Viewed broadly, the increased emphasis on science has apparently led us to the incipient decline of values in management activity. It has emphasized management as a tool, to be applied to the service of any ends. In the process, the idea that the means used must be consistent with the ends sought has been dealt a serious blow.

The intrusion of prevailing scientific philosophies into management encourages the separation of fact and value, with arguments that the latter area is not subject to empirical verification by the methods of science. Values must be accepted as given. Once given, scientific techniques may be used to find ways of achieving their operationally defined elements in practice.

While the acceptance of this view may be essential to preserve the objectivity science requires, it presents two difficulties in management practice. First, it tends to discourage attention to value questions by raising doubts about whether they can be answered objectively and rationally. Second, it encourages a view of the world in which values are relegated to secondary importance. From both comes the danger that management will become an enterprise without values. Though scientific approaches may require that value questions be put aside in the course of studies and analyses of specific processes and problems, it must not be forgotten that value questions have an essential place in all management deliberations.

"From Morality to Morale"

A second trend parallels and springs from the movement from folklore to science. Borrowing a title from David Riesman's provocative book, *The Lonely Crowd*,[11] I would characterize it as the movement "from morality to morale."

At root, this is the trend to human relations, but it involves much more than that. Implicit in it is the potential recasting of the entire spirit of management activity from getting the job done to keeping the people happy.

No manager familiar with the Hawthorne experiments can doubt the importance of the human dimension in management. With them has come the twentieth century industrial recognition of that old maxim, "it pays to be nice to people." The human relations movement carries with it the realization that if people are to do their best work and contribute the most that they can, they must feel that they have a stake in the enterprise, that they are important to it, and that their worth is appreciated.

In the period between the Hawthorne experiments and today, human relations has become a major item of faith for the manager, as it is, indeed, for the whole society. The human relations proponents are many and their approach has invaded management circles with what frequently amounts to a new religion.[12]

How has this trend influenced the philosophy of management? Most important, it has taught us to recognize important elements in the human world of bureaucracy. The organization appears as a social group and work a social activity. The individual brings to his job his total personality; he is not just a single-purposed automaton. Side by side with the formal structure of the organization exists an informal social structure that is vital to the individual employees and to the life of the organization itself.

From this recognition of different elements spring new questions, of which these are indicative:

1. What is the social environment within which we operate?
2. What persons and group affiliations influence attitudes and decisions?
3. How are human needs being met within the organization?
4. How will a proposed action be received by the individuals who occupy centers of informal authority?

The value considerations resulting from this development are varied and contradictory. On the one hand, the human relations approach, when taken seriously, enthrones the democratic ideals of maximum individual development and maximum human welfare. It argues for the greatest possible release of each individual's full creative and productive powers. It preaches that each participant deserves to receive essential satisfactions from his activities.

On the other hand, there is a danger that it will debase the individual, treating him as an object to be manipulated and emphasizing the group rather than the man. Human beings become objects to be shaped with the proper psychological tools into instruments of the organization.

The value problem here must be faced directly. Unprincipled and unbridled application of human relations techniques could result in a subtle tyranny, frightening to contemplate. It could be sufficiently morally debilitating to undermine the entire field.

From Mechanistic to Dynamic Approaches

Our third important trend in management philosophy is also an aspect of the first. It is the movement from mechanistic to dynamic approaches to management.

The mechanistic character of early "scientific management" has already been mentioned. It tended to treat organizational activity like a machine process, to emphasize its static and its repetitive aspects. More recently, we find a greater acknowledgment of the constantly changing nature of organizations, their participants, and their environment. From static features, the emphasis has changed to flux and process; from repetitive features, it has turned to evolutionary development.

This change of emphasis is apparent in the work of Chester I. Barnard,[13] Herbert Simon,[14] Talcott Parsons,[15] and the less well-known Peter M. Blau, whose major book bears the revealing title, *The Dynamics of Bureaucracy*.[16] The emphasis here on movement and change leads quite naturally to problems of predicting the future under conditions of uncertainty, and thus moves us directly into the realm of game theory, probability theory, and operations research.

This trend, too, is affecting the philosophy of management. It has directed attention to the fact that an organization is a dynamic institution in a dynamic environment. It has forced us to admit that the prediction of future organization status and the analysis of problems requires the application of sophisticated methods and techniques. Under this influence, we are led to ask questions of this sort:

1. What is the real nature of the problem? What methods of experimentation and analysis can be used to determine its perimeters?
2. What other problems in this or other fields are similar to it? How were they solved? Are those solutions applicable here?
3. What are the key variables influencing our situation?
4. What kind of strategy is appropriate?

The values perpetuated here are largely those of science itself. Full knowledge, tempered and reserved judgment, and a rigorous methodology are all advanced as good, because they will encourage results that work.

There are other trends, all interrelated in some measure with those we have covered, which could be explored if there were time. The movement from individualism to group action is one; the decline of legal in favor of social considerations, another. All of these spring from and contribute to a different understanding of what is true, what questions are important, and what values should be served in management.

Conclusion

I have hoped to demonstrate that management philosophy is essential in the practice of management. Inevitably, it accompanies the act of managing, and it might be offered that the better the philosophy, the better the management. The more nearly the manager's philosophy defines what is actually true, poses the truly important questions, and prescribes the highest and most appropriate values, the better his management will be. Good management judgment requires sound philosophical views.

Our society seems to be moving rapidly to its total bureaucratization. The action of managers in both public and private enterprise is likely to have an increasing impact on the material and spiritual welfare of our people. Already, in the age of nuclear warfare and radiation fall-out, managers hold the survival of much of the human race in their grasp.

Under such conditions, we cannot be content with anything but the best. Men in management positions must be truly exceptional. They must possess qualities that will enable them to decide wisely on the proper course of action. In the light of the developments we are seeing in management, and in the range of activities for which management is responsible, these are some of the characteristics which our managers must have: a broad, world-encompassing view, a scientific spirit, a knowledge of the methods and tools of science, a basic understanding of the social sciences and the humanities, talents in the integration of ideas and in the solution of problems, and, above all, an idealism that will guide and stimulate them.[17]

This is indeed a large order. Though it may not be achieved, it must certainly be pursued. Perhaps there is no better advice to leave with those undertaking such a task than these words offered by John M. Clark, professor emeritus of economics at Columbia University:

> . . . . if we do our best and if luck does not turn too strongly against us, we may hope, not to solve our problems, but to evolve with them.

Notes

This article was originally presented as a lecture in the Air Force Advanced Management Program at George Washington University, May 7, 1957.

1. Prentice Hall, Inc., 1952.

2. Ibid., pp. 286–304.

3. Reprinted in part in Dwight Waldo (ed.). *Ideas and Issues in Public Administration: A Book of Readings* (McGraw-Hill, 1953), pp. 332–33.

4. Perhaps the best recent example of this trend is the appearance of the *Administrative Science Quarterly.* Published by the Graduate School of Business and Public Administration at Cornell University, this journal is dedicated, significantly, "to advancing basic understanding of administrative processes through empirical investigation and theoretical analysis."

5. See Luther Gulick and L. Urwick, *Papers on the Science of Administration* (Institute of Public Administration, 1937), for examples of the approach of this group.

6. See Elton Mayo, *The Human Problems of an Industrial Civilization* (Macmillan, 1933), and F. J. Roethlisberger and W.J. Dickson, *Management and the Worker* (Harvard University Press, 1946).

7. Henry C. Metcalf and L. Urwick (eds.). *Dynamic Administration: The Collected Papers of Mary Parker Follett* (Harper, 1942).

8. For examples of this work see Robert K. Merton (ed.), *Reader in Bureaucracy* (Free Press, 1952), Daniel Lerner and Harold D. Lasswell, *The Policy Sciences* (Stanford University Press, 1951), Dorwin Cartwright and Alvin Zander (eds.), *Group Dynamics: Research and Theory* (Row, Peterson, 1953), and Rensis Likert, *Developing Patterns of Management* (American Management Association, 1956).

9. For example, see Leonard D. White's trilogy on administrative history—*The Federalists* (Macmillan, 1956), *The Jeffersonians* (Macmillan, 1956), *The Jacksonians* (Macmillan Company, 1956). A fourth volume, *The Republican Era,* will be published in 1958.

10. For example, see John M. Gaus, *Reflections on Public Administration* (University of Alabama Press, 1947), and John M. Gaus and Leon Wolcott, *Public Administration and the U.S. Department of Agriculture* (Public Administration Service, 1940).

11. Yale University Press, 1950.

12. For examples of thought in the human relations field, see Robert Dubin's excellent collection of articles and cases, *Human Relations in Administration: The Sociology of Organization* (Prentice Hall, 1951). See also Thomas North Whitehead, *Leadership in a Free Society* (Harvard University Press, 1936), Harold Guetzkow, *Groups, Leadership, and Men* (Carnegie, 1951), and S.A. Stouffer et al., *The American Soldier: Combat and Its Aftermath* (Princeton University Press, 1949).

13. Chester I. Barnard, *The Functions of the Executive* (Harvard University Press, 1938).

14. Herbert A. Simon, *Administrative Behavior* (2nd ed., Macmillan, 1957). See also, by the same author, *Models of Men: Social and Rational* (John Wiley, 1957).

15. Talcott Parsons, *The Structure of Social Action* (McGraw-Hill, 1937). See also Talcott Parsons and Edward A. Shils (eds.). *Toward a General Theory of Action* (Harvard University Press, 1951).

16. University of Chicago Press, 1955.

17. For a further discussion of some of these qualities and their relationship to education for the public service, see Robert A. Walker, "The Universities and the Public Service," 39 *American Political Science Review* 926–33 (October 1945).

CHAPTER 18

ADMINISTRATIVE LEADERSHIP AND USE OF SOCIAL POWER

SVEN LUNDSTEDT

Leadership, by its very nature, involves the exercise of social power. Exerting a profound effect on personal behavior, individual and organizational productivity, adjustment to working situations, and morale in organizations, leadership should not be viewed separately from social power. Yet, the relationship between leadership and social power has been an obscure subject and the exercise of social power in leadership has not been well understood. Effective leadership in administration and optimum performance by subordinates requires such understanding. The psychological definition of these terms is fundamental to this analysis.

Leadership is the ability to influence the behavior of others in a group or organization, set goals for a group, formulate paths to the goals, and create some social norms in the group. This definition, which has consensus and technical acceptability, describes the behavior of parents, members of social groups, and work groups. Thus, leadership is the exercise of social influence, with weak leadership resulting in a loss of social influence over others.

Power has been analyzed traditionally in political, economic, and sociological units of analysis. Only recently has social power been examined as an important aspect of interpersonal behavior. Viewing social power in such terms gives a clearer view of human motivation, and knowledge of motivation is basic to an understanding of sound leadership practices.

Meaning and Bases of Social Power

Social power is a recently devised term, its focus is social influence over others. Strictly speaking, it is a psychological force which emanates from a person, and is directed toward a particular material or psychological goal which that person wants to achieve. It is social pressure exerted by others who wish to change us, or by us upon others whom we wish to change. The basic motive for using any kind of social power is a psychological, or material, reward of some kind, plus the avoidance of unpleasant experiences. In general,

From *Public Administration Review*, vol. 25, no. 2 (1965): 156–60. Copyright © by American Society for Public Administration. Reprinted with permission.

all humans relations are governed by different systems of rewards, and in part by various patterns of avoiding unpleasantness.

French and Raven[1] use five categories to describe the bases of social power. They are: *"reward power, coercive power, legitimate power, referent power,* and *expert power."*

Reward power is based on the perception that another person has the ability to give pleasurable rewards. This kind of influence is common enough. Because reward power is such a fundamental source of incentive, it has become a universal form of influence and control. Achieving rewards for certain kinds of social behavior profoundly effects the basis of social relations with others, and will usually cause one to view others positively when rewarded by them.

Coercive power is based on the perception that another person has the ability to inflict psychological, or physical, pain. This is a primitive form of influence and control, and evokes in people a different basic response from reward power. Pain inhibits behavior, produces withdrawal, and evokes aggression; it disrupts social relations and tends to change their course. Excessive frustration by the exercise of coercive power will tend to make people suspicious, mistrustful, and resistant to change.

Legitimate power is based on the perception that another person has a legitimate right to prescribe behavior, to tell one what to do in a given instance. Custom, tradition, mores, and group norms and values, are the roots of legitimate power. It is power formally sanctioned by the social system. In a sense, it can be viewed as power based on a "social contract" between members of a group, organization, or larger society. A familiar contract is social control by law, although it can be less formal as in customs, traditions, or mores. A parent's power over a child is, for example, based on more or less informal norms about child rearing passed on by tradition. A physician's power to prescribe treatment, or an elected official to govern, come directly from a formal rule, or law. The group which defines the sanctions and controls the exercise of legitimate power, also defines its practical and theoretical limits. This is one of the major sources of conflict between the individual and the group, which generates the main body of legal activity in society.

Referent power is based on one person's psychological identification with another, or group of others. Its effects can be seen dramatically in the socialization process in young children. It is often quite subtle in its influence over behavior. As a rule, it starts with norms of behavior held by another person, or group, which serve as a model. The norms are seen as having rewarding attributes and their possession is desired. The norms take hold through the psychological process of identification, and eventually their influence is felt from within the person (internalization). In other words, referent power is the influence of the value of others which become internalized as part of the conscience of the individual.

Under the influence of referent power a person will behave in a prescribed way because he wants to be like someone else, and perhaps wishes membership in a certain social group containing admired persons. The final effect of referent power is like a planted seed which, as it takes root in the personality, influences the social behavior of the individual. This is one of the most remarkable forms of social influence.

Expert power is embodied in a recognized knowledge or skill. But others usually must first recognize expert power for it to have an enduring effect. It depends to some extent, therefore, upon legitimate power although it can exist alone. One need not, for example, always have to get legitimate sanction for one's expert abilities and knowledge in order to influence others through the power of expert knowledge. Conversely, an unlicensed physician or lawyer has their expert power weakened when they are not fully accredited by law, or a jury of their peers.

The Permissive or the Coercive Leader?

These five variations in social power, when used within social relationships, invariably reflect basic differences in methods and styles of leadership. An efficient understanding of human behavior in groups and organizations depends upon knowing how control and influence over others are best exercised.

The Authoritarian View

Historically, two different philosophies about the use of social power appear in all literature dealing with enduring social relations among mankind. The authoritarian view is suspicious of social power and maintains that it should not be shared widely; the democratic view is that social power should be distributed and shared. Familiar arguments for and against the authoritarian view have been repeated by McGregor in his discussion of managerial philosophy.[2] There are certain assumptions in the authoritarian position that are again challenged, but now by present social psychological thinking.

One set of erroneous assumptions state that most people inherently dislike work, and will avoid it if they possibly can. Those who adopt this point of view assume that people must be coerced, controlled, directed, and threatened with punishment to make them work adequately and well. This assumption is made easier to accept by the authoritarian's claim that people really prefer to be directed, dislike responsibility, are lazy, and above all want security instead of psychological independence and challenge. Using a theory of motivation based on use of coercion, the authoritarians argue in a circle and thereby beg the question. Available psychological evidence does not support this view of human nature or its assumptions about intrinsic motivation which overlook the psychological needs for self expression and self fulfillment that rise above lower physiological and psychological needs.

The Democratic Alternative

Allport,[3] Murray,[4] and Maslow[5] contribute also to the theory of motivation used by McGregor to explain the desire to work. John Dewey[6] provides a modern philosophical framework for this view and it has been tested in studies reported by Likert,[7] Herzberg,[8] and others.

For most people mental and physical work is as natural as rest or relaxation. It is simply another natural human expression of a need to cope with life problems. If one approaches work with the idea that it will be more rewarding than painful, the whole character of the task changes. Positive attitudes develop only in the context of meaningful reward and it is important that *the range* of human rewards be broad enough to include many possibilities. In fact, the more the better. Salary and adequate physical surroundings are not enough of a reward. There must be psychological rewards which come from completing interesting tasks in a satisfying work setting.[9]

Given adequate opportunity for self expression and participation within an organization, people will be competent in exercising self direction and self control over their lives and will prefer to do so. External control threats of punishment, and other forms of coercive power are neither the only nor best means to increase initiative and effort. Coercive power arouses only anger, defensiveness and resistance. An individual's commitment to work hard and to perform well is dependent much more on rewards, but not any or all rewards.

According to this theory, responsibility is not distasteful and only becomes so in the context of unrewarding experiences. Laziness, avoidance of responsibility, and a preoccupation with security are not inherent, or natural, tendencies. Carried to its logical conclusion, this approach suggests that effective leadership is based on granting employees additional social power to perform their jobs, providing, however, that the goals of the organization are also kept reasonably intact. Extended participation in making decisions about one's own job should be the rule rather than the exception.

Such a distribution of social power also means that the administrator does not have to over-supervise employees. Consequently, an administrator can gain more freedom to pursue effectively his own role in the organization. *Social power is not a fixed quantity which if distributed widely results in a reduction of power available to higher administrative personnel.* Since all organizations have a division of labor which includes specialization of function, there are obvious structural restraints upon relinquishing one's *official* authority. It is a question of using that authority more effectively according to sound human relations practices. But simple distribution of influence is not enough. The distribution needs to be made with the five kinds of social power in mind, and with some understanding of their relative effects in concrete situations. One should not only regularly be given honest recognition (rewarded) by a superior for a job well done, but involved directly in important decision making in the group (given legitimate and expert power) with reference to one's own job. Under these conditions social control tends to occur by the exercise of referent power, that is, through self control based on the desire to participate independently in the activities of the organization because one identifies the organization's goals with one's own. Coercive power should be required less and less in this form of administrative leadership.

An Organizational Cycle

The goal of a frustration-free work environment is naive and Utopian. Conflicts cannot be ruled out, but they can be managed with greater effectiveness. And the conflicts which result from poor leadership can be reduced. The now classic study by Lewin, Lippitt, and

White,[10] demonstrated experimentally that when autocratic leadership results in personal frustration among group members, the over-load of frustration will turn to anger, and that anger to aggressive behavior or apathy.

Excessive use of coercive power usually precipitates a characteristic cycle of group behavior. Initial reactions to frustration often create a pattern in which the autocratic leader is forced to engage in more coercive behavior to restore a deteriorating group to its former tenuous balance. The cycle can be described as follows:

1. Because of an autocratic philosophy of human nature and leadership, the leader uses coercion to establish and enforce group norms and goals. This creates personal frustration among many group members. Temporary compliance for the sake of expediency usually occurs at first, and may continue for a time as pseudo-participation.
2. As psychological needs become increasingly frustrated, decisions about organizational or group objectives begin to be impaired. People become less cooperative. Communication deteriorates; hostility, suspicion, and distrust increase.
3. When group anger is aroused by frustration, behavior is initiated to reduce frustration and personal discomfort. Special social relationships may be formed to cope specifically with the stress and discomfort. Informal groups (cliques and factions) appear, and informal communications (rumors) increase to meet personal needs. Finally cohesiveness within the formal work group tends to disappear, and there is a loss of interest in productivity.
4. Left to run their natural course, such social relationships in a work group invariably will create increased interpersonal conflict, lowered morale, lowered productivity, increases in errors and absenteeism, and increases in grievances. Eventually, the original group may be replaced by another which may go through the same cycle of conditions within the organization. A strong relationship seems to exist between this kind of cycle and turnover.

Social relations in the autocratic group reflect an obsession with social power and its utilization, rather than regarding such power as a routine part of one's natural surroundings. Within such groups the issue of social power is exaggerated far out of proportion to its functional value. Striving for control over others, or resisting it, are often salient features in such a group. Political strategy making and in-fighting sap the energy and vitality of the organization. Like other kinds of symptoms this struggle reveals a serious underlying managerial problem which may require outside professional help for correction. New norms and values must replace those creating problems, norms that should be based on the individual's need for self expression, participation, trust, and human tolerance.

A Paradox of Authoritarianism

When coercive power becomes a "catagorical imperative" serious ethical problems about maintaining reasonable social norms can, and do, arise. In a sense, social justice is then at stake. Overcontrol can lead to impairment of judgment when individuals become too frustrated and angry to care about responsibility for individual or moral choices. When the group norms which form the basis for each individual's personal judgment of correct behavior are weakened by group and organizational conflict, individual judgment may also be weakened. In this sense, the anarchy and moral breakdown in authoritarian groups are understandable as tragedies, and comedies, of error. People may have less concern for reasonable ethical behavior in groups in which they have little, or no, personal stake, or psychological roots. After sufficient provocation and frustration, members in an autocratic group may lose interest in the group's code of behavior and break its rules indiscriminately. Social concern for others may disappear and in its place may appear the familiar reaction of "every man for himself." This last point has to take account of individual differences which are the exception to any rule.

The social psychological forces leading to the formation of the autocratic group are the basis of an interesting paradox. Because autocratic leadership makes the assumptions about human nature and motivation to which we have referred (the autocrat often believes, quite cynically, that people are basically evil), the autocratic group contains the seeds of its own destruction. The instability which such a group strives hardest to overcome by coercion, is designed into the very structure of the group from the start by use of coercion. People can hardly be expected to be motivated by constant frustration and pain without reacting rather strongly to undo the frustration. This paradox is a formidable blind spot in the autocratic point of view, because there is no mechanism within that view by which the paradox can be resolved, except by leaders in the group giving up coercion.

There are certain stereotypes, often associated with both leadership and management that contribute an unwarranted respectability to authoritarian administration. Firmness of character and clarity of thought, strangely enough, are often associated with autocratic types of leadership. Oddly, references are also made to its association with masculinity. Firmness of character is indeed a high virtue and should not be so falsely equated. This again begs the fundamental question.

Clarity of thought in decision making and strength of character are a necessary ingredient in democratic leadership because the decisions about the correct use of social power are far more complex and difficult. It is far easier to be autocratically simple minded than to make the necessary refined and complex distinctions about the use of social power within organizations and in all human affairs. Democratic leadership, in this high form, recognizes administration as part of the humanistic tradition, as well as an aspect of management science.

Notes

1. R.P. French. Jr. and B. Raven, "The Bases of Social Power." In D. Cartwright, (ed.) *Studies in Social Power* (Ann Arbor, MI: Institute for Social Research, 1959).

2. D. McGregor, *The Human Side of Enterprise* (New York: McGraw-Hill. 1960).

3. G.W. Allport. *Becoming: Basic Considerations for a Psychology of Personality* (New Haven: Yale University Press, 1955).

4. H.A. Murray, *Explorations in Personality* (New York: Oxford, 1938).

5. A.H. Maslow, *Motivation and Personality* (New York: Harper, 1954).

6. J. Dewey, *Human Nature and Conduct* (New York: Henry Holt, 1922).

7. R. Likert, *New Patterns of Management* (New York: McGraw-Hill, 1961).

8. F. Herzberg, B. Mausner, and B. Snyderman, *The Motivation to Work* (New York: Wiley, 1959).

9. W.F. Whyte, (ed.) *Money and Motivation* (New York: Harper, 1955).

10. K. Lewin. R. Lippitt, and R.K. White, "Patterns of Aggressive Behavior in Experimentally Created Social Climates" 10 *Journal of Social Psychology* 271–79 (1939).

CHAPTER 19

LEADERSHIP AND REGIONAL COUNCILS

A Mismatch Between Leadership Styles Today and Future Roles

ROBERT W. GAGE

Leadership in substate regional organizations in the United States has undergone major changes in this century. The quest for improved leadership and more effective approaches to metropolitan governance continues today. This article examines the possibility that leadership styles in regional councils today are mismatched with the future roles these entities are expected to play in the substate regional policy arena.[1] This possible incongruity has important implications for the future effectiveness of regional councils and for other organizations that work with them: local governments, citizen leagues, chambers of commerce, and various community-based organizations. All of these organizations are important stakeholders in the quest for improved leadership at the substate regional level.

This situation is especially interesting because of changes in substate regionalism that occurred in the 1980s. Today a greater number of different regional organizations play important roles in regional governance. During the 1980s, new approaches to regional problem solving emerged, encouraged by the national emphasis on public/private partnerships by the Reagan administration. Many different kinds of intercommunity partnerships emerged, initiated by leadership from the private, public, and academic sectors (Dodge 1989, 1990; Committee for Economic Development 1982; Fosler and Berger 1982). Thus, leadership today and in the future must be able to accommodate both an increased diversity of organizational actors and more involvement from the private sector.

Leadership Styles of Regional Councils

In this article, regional leadership is viewed from a situational perspective (Hersey 1984), with an emphasis on the horizontal interaction of regional councils with other actors in the regional decision-making environment. This perspective was adopted because it acknowledges the importance of interorganizational relationships and networking in maintaining an organization's leadership position in relation to its environment (Yukl 1989, 132).

Horizontal interdependence is especially important in the relationships of regional

---

From *State and Local Government Review,* vol. 25, no. 1 (Winter 1993): 9–18. Copyright © 1993 by Carl Vinson Institute of Government, University of Georgia. Reprinted with permission.

councils with their environments. External networking activities of council executive directors are critical in maintaining and expanding their influence. In such environments, policymakers and managers are likely to spend more time in horizontal interactions with actors outside their own organizations, although they must also be involved in vertical relationships. They do this to build larger, more influential networks of contacts (Yukl 1989; Kotter 1982).

Leadership in regional councils remains something of an enigma today. Regional councils frequently have been criticized for failing to take a stronger, more directive role in regional decision making. However, the history of substate regional activity in this country indicates that most councils are not accustomed to playing a directive role in regional affairs. The membership of most regional councils is voluntary and the councils traditionally have lacked authority to require member participation in programs and to require implementation of regional plans (Advisory Commission on Intergovernmental Relations [ACIR] 1966, 13).

Purpose of Study

This article examines whether current leadership styles of regional councils are mismatched with the roles the councils expect to play in the future. The premises of the research are twofold. The first is that the voluntary nature of regional council organization has caused the councils to prefer a supportive or a participative style of leadership rather than a directive style. (Styles are defined in Table 19.1.) The second premise is that the demands placed upon regional councils in this decade are likely to require a more directive leadership approach if the councils are to be effective in regional decision making.

Early criticisms of regional councils (ACIR 1973, Tables 3 and 4) imply that a more directive approach is needed. Today councils are being urged to become more proactive in identifying and solving regional problems and in helping to resolve conflict in their regions (National Association of Regional Councils [NARC] 1987, 1988).

Trends in regional council leadership will be presented in this article in a brief historical review of the development of substate regions in the United States. Current leadership styles will be reported from the results of a national survey of regional council directors. The dominant styles of leadership and their relationship to regional council roles expected in the next five years will then be analyzed.

Historical Background

In the first phase of regional council development, initiative for policy leadership came from public and private local sources. This leadership was basically participative. In the 1920s, regional planning emerged as a private foundation or civic club endeavor in New York City, Philadelphia, San Francisco, and Minneapolis–St. Paul (ACIR 1973, 54). On the public side, the first metropolitan county planning commission was established in Los Angeles, California, in 1922, and the Ohio Legislature passed the first enabling legislation for joint planning arrangements between local governments in 1923. The creation in 1945 of the Central Lane Planning Council (in the Eugene, Oregon, Metropolitan Area) opened the post–World War II era of voluntary alliance of substate regional entities (ACIR 1973, 55).

The participative style of leadership in these early efforts was effective for maintaining the voluntary basis of regional council membership. It gave local governments and civic organizations the flexibility to withdraw from the councils if serious differences arose.

A period of guided ascendancy followed the first phase of council development, beginning with the implementation of Section 701 planning grants under the Federal Housing Act of 1954. Throughout the guided ascendancy period, the federal government assumed a directive leadership role, as did many regional councils acting as agents for implementation of federal government programs and regulations. As of 1977, general purpose regional councils (metropolitan and non-metropolitan) were funded 76 percent by federal, 10 percent by state, 12 percent by local, and 2 percent by other sources (ACIR 1982, 289).

Heavy dependency upon federal funds led to a common view of regional councils as vassals of their federal sponsors. The councils established program networks to implement the dominant federal programs of the period. At the end of this period, substate regional activity was described as mature, with 671 councils covering most of the nation (McDowell 1980, 21). However, this was a pseudomaturity attained at significant cost to council independence.

In 1981, an abrupt change occurred as the Reagan administration made sweeping reductions in regional programs. Regional councils were forced to begin a third phase, a period of entrepreneurship (Gage 1988, 479–84). Pressed to fend for themselves, the councils in the 1980s had to rely much more on their own initiatives. In a survey of regional council operating funds, NARC reported that federal funding fell from 76 percent in 1978 to 45 percent in 1988 (1989, 7). With decreased federal support, regional councils became less involved with administration of national programs and with implementation of federal regulations. Consequently, regional council leadership moved away from directive leadership toward more supportive and participative styles.

Today, regional councils are at the center of new, potentially significant developments. Some observers believe that a period of resurgence for substate regional agencies has begun. For example, DeGrove indicates that involvement of regional organizations in state planning has the potential to move "regional agencies from an underfunded and generally weak position" to one with potential to "influence heavily the nature of both local and state . . . programs" (1991, 2). Stronger regional organizations "in both a planning and regulatory sense, are an emergent fact in many states, and more loom on the horizon" (DeGrove 1991, 2). Thus, the "policy window" (Kingdon 1984, 173) for regional initiatives appears to be more open now than in the past decade. In this environment, a number of questions about regional leadership become important. What forms of leadership do councils exert today? Are these forms likely to be effective or ineffective, given the roles regional councils are expected to play in the future and the challenges they will probably encounter? If the relationships of regional councils with the private sector are likely to be

Table 19.1

Leadership Styles of Regional Councils

Council leadership styles in regional decision making, in decreasing order of direct council involvement.

1. **Directive leadership role**
   Council as a director, a proactive leader, taking an aggressive role in defining issues, addressing conflict, and bargaining to reach solutions.

2. **Participative leadership role**
   Council as a participant, networking to bring people into contact with each other so that they can resolve regional conflicts, reach decisions, and pursue regional goals.

3. **Supportive leadership role**
   Council as a supporter of the regional decision-making process, providing information and planning expertise, with little direct involvement in regional conflict and decision making.

Sources: Adapted from NARC (1988) and House and Mitchell (1974).

important in the future, are the current leadership styles of regional councils appropriate for working with the private sector in regional problem solving?

Research Methodology

Data for this research were collected in the summer of 1990. Questionnaires were mailed to executive directors of the 525 regional council organizations located in 46 states and Washington, DC (Four states—Alaska, Hawaii, New Jersey, and Rhode Island—were without regional councils as of June 1990.) A total of 308 survey questionnaires were completed and returned for a response rate of 59 percent.[2]

Analysis

The analysis focuses on three leadership styles and the relationships of these styles to certain prominent regional council roles. These leadership styles—directive, participative, and supportive—are taken from the work of House and Mitchell (1974). They are defined in Table 19.1.

Executive directors were asked to indicate the emphasis their councils currently place on each leadership style, ranging from a rating of 3 (strong emphasis) to 1 (little or no emphasis).

The analysis then focuses on six regional roles and four local roles of regional councils, each of which is defined in Table 19.2. These regional council roles (regional and local) were identified in literature of the National Association of Regional Councils (1980, 1987, 1988), defining council roles and functions. Two sets of roles (regional and local) were classified by a panel of experts as either predominantly consultative/diplomatic (CD) or direct service/advocacy (DSA) roles (see Table 19.2). This classification represented a preliminary attempt to group regional council roles in a way that would be useful for

Table 19.2

Prominent Roles of Regional Councils Exercised on a Regional and Local Basis

Regional Roles/Classification[a]	Legal Roles/Classification[a]
1. Forum for identifying and solving regional problems—CD	1. Technical assistance and training for council member organizations and/or governments—CD
2. Working with the private sector on key issues of regional concern such as economic development, air and water quality, and hazardous waste disposal—CD	2. Working with the private sector on key issues of local concern, such as job development and training, encouraging small business entrepreneurship, development of small business incubators—DSA
3. Regional infrastructure planning and services delivery in such areas as transportation, solid waste disposal, and water and sewage treatment—DSA	3. Sponsorship of cooperative services between and/or among council members—CD
4. Growth management and regional planning—DSA	4. Local government advocacy and consistency building; lobbying for local interests at state or federal levels—DSA
5. Supportive services such as providing census information and regional data—CD	
6. Regional human services delivery such as services for the aging, the homeless, drug abusers, and the unemployed—DSA	

Source: Roles were identified from analyses of roles conducted by NARC (1980, 1987, 1988).
[a]Roles were classified by a panel of five experts (two practitioners and three academics). Panelists were asked to classify each role as predominantly consultative/diplomatic (CD) or direct service/advocacy (DSA). Agreement of three of five panelists was required for classification. Criteria used for classification: CD = Consultative/diplomatic—emphasis on negotiation, skillful mediation, and team building; and a capacity to compromise and to exercise "nonjurisdictional power" (Gardner 1990). DSM = Direct service/advocacy—emphasis on aggressive, systematic management of program elements and resources and/or resourceful and persistent lobbying as an advocate of local and regional interests

developing hypotheses about relationships of current council leadership styles to expected future roles.

Council executive directors were asked to report council priorities for these roles for three time periods: five years previous (1985), the present (1990), and five years hence (1995).[3] The last part of the analysis investigates relationships of leadership styles to council roles expected in the future. Data are reported which relate to the central question: Is there a mismatch between council leadership styles today and their expected roles for the future?

Hypotheses

Leadership Styles

It was predicted that regional councils, largely voluntary organizations, would most likely favor a participative leadership style in today's regional environment. Today's councils are engaged in regional issues as participants, but most still lack powers that would be needed to take a more directive leadership role. It also was expected that many councils prefer the supportive leadership role.

Hypothesis 1: The dominant style of leadership among regional councils will be the participative leadership style, and the supportive leadership style also will be a strong preference. The directive leadership style will be least preferred.

Leadership Styles and Future Regional Council Roles

There was emphasis at all levels of government on privatization in the 1980s, sometimes without regard for careful consideration of its merit (Donahue 1989). This emphasis was expected to lead to changes in regional council roles over the period 1985–95. In particular, priorities for future council involvement with the private sector were expected to increase relative to other regional council roles.

Given these changes, leadership styles were expected to relate to future expected council roles in predictable ways.

Hypothesis 2: Participative leadership will be associated with high priorities for consultative/diplomatic regional council roles in the future.

Several of the consultative roles are oriented toward broader strategic questions about regional problems and issues (see Table 19.2). These questions typically involve key public and private sector leadership. Consultative roles are particularly important for the regional council mission because they are likely to involve questions of policy and the use of political power and influence to attain regional objectives.

It is believed that regional councils are likely to use a participative leadership style in consultative roles for several reasons. For example, regional councils tend to be highly aware of their lack of formal governmental powers. They have been reluctant to assume a directive approach without such powers and fearful of alienating, either directly or indirectly, elements of their voluntary membership bases.

The directive leadership style was hypothesized to be related to a different cluster of roles.

Hypothesis 3: Directive leadership will be related to high priorities for direct service/advocacy roles in the future.

Direct service/advocacy roles are believed to be less problematic for regional councils than consultative/diplomatic roles. In the former, councils typically have program authority, either by statute or delegation. Role definition also is somewhat clearer and more specific for direct service/advocacy roles (see Table 19.2).

The supportive leadership style is rather passive. It is basically an information provision activity: generation and dissemination of information on regional issues, plans, and concerns. This role has been performed to some degree by almost all regional councils. It is not expected to be useful in differentiating among council roles for the future.

Hypothesis 4: There will be no relationship between supportive leadership and council priorities for consultative or direct services roles in the future.

Table 19.3

Executive Directors' Ratings of Use of Three Styles of Leadership in Their Regional Councils

Ratings[a]	Participative		Directive		Supportive	
	No.	Percent	No.	Percent	No.	Percent
Strong	140	46.2	59	19.5	95	31.4
Moderate	140	46.2	161	53.3	158	52.3
Weak	23	7.6	82	27.2	49	16.2
Total	303	100.0	302	100.0	302	100.0
Average rating		2.39		1.92		2.15

[a]Ratings were measured on a three-point continuum ranging from strong (3) to weak (1).

Incongruity Between Leadership Styles and Future Regional Council Roles

Regional councils have traditionally been more adept at regional planning and less adept at plan implementation. Their lack of governmental power has been a limitation in assuming a leadership role in implementing their plans and in solving regional problems. It is proposed that regional councils frequently, and inappropriately, choose the participative style of leadership in dealing with regional problems in consultative roles. They do this rather than adopt a more directive style of leadership, even though the directive style could be more effective. It is also proposed that those councils that do maintain a directive leadership approach will be more involved, by their own report, in making key regional decisions. It is reasonable to believe that their greater involvement over time in the processes of making key regional decisions will lead to greater effectiveness.

Hypothesis 5: Regional councils with directive leadership styles will be more likely to report that they are more fully involved in making key regional decisions than councils with participative leadership styles. Consequently, they have a better chance of being effective in regional decision making.

Results

Leadership Styles

Executive directors of regional councils indicated that their councils prefer the participative style of leadership. Table 19.3 shows that the participative leadership style received the highest average ratings of the three leadership styles (2.39 out of a possible 3.00). Almost half of the executive directors (46.2 percent) rated their councils as strong on the participative leadership style. The supportive role also received a relatively strong rating (2.15). In contrast, only 19.5 percent of executive directors gave their regional councils strong ratings on directive leadership.

Thus, as hypothesized, the participative leadership style emerged as the preferred leadership style among regional councils today. Hypothesis 1 was supported by these results.

Figure 19.1 **Regional Role Priorities over Time**

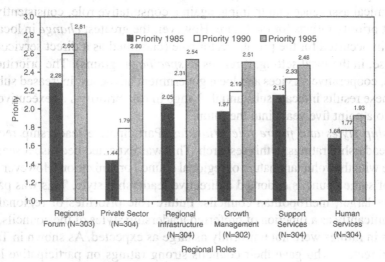

Figure 19.2 **Local Role Priorities over Time**

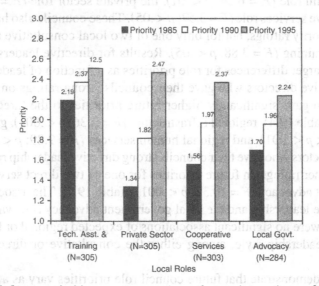

Note: For both figures, priorities were measured on a three-point continuum from 3 (high priority) to 1 (low priority).

Relationships of Leadership Styles to Regional Council Roles

Change and future priorities. Among the six regional roles, the regional forum role, a consultative role, was given the highest future priority ratings (Figure 19.1). However, the *change* in priority ratings given to the private sector role, also a consultative role, was the greatest for any of the six regional roles presented in Figure 19.1.

A similar pattern is apparent in Figure 19.2, which reports priorities for the four local roles. Technical assistance and training, again a consultative role, consistently received the highest priority ratings for the future. However, the greatest *change* in local role priorities again occurred for the private sector role (classified as a direct service/advocacy role because, in the local setting, it relates to *specific* programs). The priorities for two other roles, cooperative services and local government advocacy, increased substantially as well. These results indicate substantial change in role priorities as executive directors projected to a point five years into the future.

Leadership styles and future role priorities. Participative leadership received the strongest leadership ratings in this research. This was expected because it seemed more compatible with the voluntary nature of regional council organization. However, executive directors of some councils endorsed a directive leadership style. This was particularly true for the larger, metropolitan councils. Future role priorities of regional councils varied significantly as a function of preferred leadership styles of the councils, although differences in ratings were not uniformly as large as expected. As shown in Table 19.4, executive directors who gave their councils strong ratings on participative leadership styles also gave significantly higher future priorities to three consultative regional roles: the regional forum role *(F = 6.24; p < .01)*, the private sector role *(F = 5.41; p < .05)*, and the supportive services role *(F = 3.57; p < .05)*. These councils also had significantly higher future priority ratings, but for only one of two local consultative roles: technical assistance and training *(F = 3.88, p < .05)*. Results for directive leadership were more definitive, with larger differences for role priorities as a function of leadership style. As expected, executive directors who gave their councils strong ratings on directive leadership styles also gave significantly higher future priorities to the three direct service regional roles (Table 19.4): regional infrastructure *(F = 9.36; p < .001)*, growth management *(F = 10.74; p < .001)*, and regional human services *(F = 9.89; p < .001)*.

Executive directors who gave their councils strong directive leadership ratings also gave significantly higher ratings on future priorities for one of two direct service local roles: local government advocacy *(F = 10.32; p < .001)* (Table 19.4). The association between levels of directive leadership and the local government advocacy role was strong.

Finally, there were no significant associations of expected regional or local roles with the supportive leadership style, among either the consultative or direct service roles (Table 19.4).

These results demonstrate that future council role priorities vary as a function of regional council leadership styles. There was substantial support for Hypotheses 2 and 3, and reasonable support for Hypothesis 4.

Mismatch Between Leadership Styles and Future Regional Roles

Executive directors of regional councils were asked to indicate involvement of their councils in making key regional decisions in their respective regions. Less than 40 percent (112) indicated that most key regional decisions were made *by* their councils. However, 60 percent (174) indicated that most key regional decisions were made *outside* of their

Table 19.4

Expected Leadership Styles, Five Years Hence (1995), of Regional Councils and Regional and Local Roles

| | Mean scores for regional roles | | | | | | Mean scores for local roles | | | |
| | Consultative roles (CD) | | | Direct service roles (DSA) | | | Consultative roles (CD) | | Direct service roles (DSA) | |
Leadership style (number)	Regional forum	Work with private sector	Support services	Regional infrastructure management	Growth management	Regional human services	Technical assistance and training	Cooperative services delivery	Private sector small business development	Local government advocacy
Participative										
Strong (130)	2.87	2.70	2.60	2.60	2.52	1.98	2.59	2.49	2.48	2.31
Moderate (125)	2.80	2.53	2.38	2.48	2.44	1.90	2.46	2.31	2.44	2.23
Weak (20)	2.45	2.35	2.40	2.55	2.35	1.95	2.20	2.15	2.10	2.05
Total (275)	2.81	2.60	2.49	2.54	2.60	1.94	2.50	2.38	2.44	2.25
Range of averages	0.42	0.35	0.25	0.12	0.16	0.08	0.39	0.34	0.38	0.26
F Ratio	6.24**	5.41**	3.57*	0.85	0.76	0.29	3.88*	2.84	2.88	1.11
Directive										
Strong (49)	2.71	2.73	2.51	2.73	2.85	2.24	2.51	2.46	2.59	2.61
Moderate (152)	2.87	2.66	2.52	2.67	2.53	2.01	2.50	2.34	2.46	2.26
Weak (72)	2.71	2.38	2.39	2.17	2.16	1.61	2.49	2.45	2.29	2.00
Total (273)	2.81	2.60	2.48	2.55	2.49	1.95	2.51	2.39	2.44	2.26
Range of averages	0.16	0.35	0.12	0.56	0.69	0.63	0.02	0.12	0.30	0.61
F Ratio	2.28	5.12**	0.98	9.36***	10.74***	9.89***	0.03	1.49	2.16	10.32***
Supportive										
Strong (81)	2.79	2.65	2.47	2.58	2.51	1.81	2.57	2.37	2.37	2.19
Moderate (151)	2.81	2.59	2.52	2.51	2.46	1.98	2.44	2.38	2.48	2.24
Weak (40)	2.85	2.54	2.37	2.62	2.55	2.05	2.60	2.45	2.45	2.48
Total (272)	2.81	2.60	2.48	2.54	2.49	1.95	2.50	2.39	2.44	2.26
Range of averages	0.06	0.11	0.14	0.12	0.09	0.24	0.16	0.08	0.11	0.29
F Ratio	0.24	0.79	0.72	0.51	0.34	1.05	1.49	0.20	0.77	2.14

$*p < .05$; $**p < .01$; $***p < .001$.

Table 19.5

Involvement in Regional Decision Making and Leadership Style

| | Mean scores on leadership style | | | |
| | Directive | | Participative | |
Most key regional decisions are made:	Mean	Number	Mean	Number
By regional council	2.31	112	2.00	112
Outside of regional council	1.63	174	2.64	174
Total	1.90	266	2.39	286
Range of averages	0.68		0.64	
F Ratio	44.43***		42.43***	

***$p < .001$.

regional councils. Even if one allows for plausible tendency of executive directors to overstate the extent to which key regional decisions are made *by* councils, these results are somewhat sobering.

It was proposed that those councils that are more involved in making key regional decisions will probably be more effective in their regions than councils that are less involved in making key decisions. Results show (Table 19.5) that those directors who indicate that most key regional decisions are made by their councils do give the councils significantly higher ratings on directive leadership (2.31) than those who indicated that most key decisions were made outside their councils (1.63, $F = 44.43, p < .001$). Directors who indicate that most key regional decisions are made by their councils also indicate that their councils give less preference to the participatory leadership style (2.00) than do directors who indicate that most key regional decisions occur outside their councils (2.64, $F = 42.43, p < .001$).

Thus, it appears that regional councils that choose the participative style of leadership are actually less involved in making key regional decisions and therefore probably are less effective in regional policymaking. Unfortunately, council directors indicate that their councils make greater use of the participative style of leadership today (Table 19.3). They tend to match the participative leadership style with the broader, consultative roles, both regional and local in scope (Table 19.4). This appears to be a mismatch of leadership style with roles that is likely to result in less effective involvement in regional decision making. These results support Hypothesis 5.

Conclusions

The results of this research indicate that the dominant mode of leadership of regional councils today is participative leadership. The results also show that council leadership styles are related to the priorities executive directors expect to place on various regional and local roles in the future. Councils that take a participative leadership approach tend to give higher priorities to consultative roles for the future, whereas councils that take a more directive leadership approach tend to give higher priorities to direct service/advocacy roles for the future.

The question arises: Is the dominant pattern of leadership, participative leadership, preferable for regional councils in particular, and for substate regionalism more generally? Unfortunately, the answer most likely is no! Results of this research suggest that those councils that are most involved in key regional decisions prefer the directive style of leadership. Conversely, those councils that are *least* involved in key regional decisions give highest preference to the participative style of leadership. Yet councils indicate they prefer participative leadership to accomplish critical consultative tasks. Consultative roles tend to be broader and more strategic roles that are more important for solving key regional problems.

It certainly appears that regional councils do need to find ways to exert a more directive leadership style in broad consultative roles. It is in these roles that they currently and inappropriately use a participative leadership style. Data from this research show that many regional councils are familiar with directive leadership. They tend to employ a more directive leadership style in direct service and advocacy roles. To correct the mismatch, they need to increasingly apply this directive leadership style to their consultative roles. Executive directors, who indicated that their council preferred participative leadership, frequently confided that a somewhat more directive leadership style was needed, particularly in their council's role as a regional forum.

Gardner's analysis of leadership skill areas has promise for helping council leadership to use directive leadership. Gardner (1990, 118–20) suggests that five leadership skill areas are important for managing interconnectedness. Among these skill areas are: exercising nonjurisdictional power (other legitimate forms of power such as the power of the media and of public opinion, the power of ideas, and the power that accrues to those who understand how various systems work); and agreement building, with skills in conflict resolution, mediation, compromise, and coalition building.

Gardner indicates that these leadership skills can be learned. Council leaders can become more proficient in using nonjurisdictional forms of power and building agreement in the face of conflict. These skills can help regional councils move from the current participative style toward a more directive style of leadership. These skills certainly are compatible with the projected demands of working more closely with private sector leadership. They promote a nonconfrontational approach. By changing in this manner, regional councils should be more able to maintain the initiative in solving regional problems today and in the future.

Notes

1. The term *regional councils,* as it is used throughout this article, refers to different kinds of regional organizations including regional planning associations, regional commissions, regional resource planning and management committees, and regional councils of government. This usage follows the general National Association of Regional Councils [NARC] definition of the term: "a regional council is a public organization encompassing a multi-jurisdictional regional community and is founded, sustained and directly tied to local governments through local and/or state government laws" (1985, 3).

2. The survey was cosponsored by NARC, the Denver Regional Council of Governments (DRCOG) and the Graduate School of Public Affairs, University of Colorado at Denver (GSPA). The author is indebted to Richard C. Hartman, former NARC executive director, Robert D. Parley, DRCOG executive director, and Marshall Kaplan, GSPA dean, for their support.

3. Executive directors of regional councils tend to hold their positions longer than five years (Weaver and Wyman 1991). Consequently, it was possible to ask them to recall their councils' role priorities of five years ago.

References

Advisory Commission on Intergovernmental Relations (ACIR). 1966. *Metropolitan Councils of Government.* Washington, DC: Government Printing Office (GPO).

———. 1973. *Substate Regionalism and the Federal System.* Washington, DC: GPO.

———. 1982. *State and Local Roles in the Federal System.* Washington, DC: GPO.

Committee for Economic Development. 1982. *Public-private Partnership: An Opportunity for Urban Communities.* New York: Committee for Economic Development.

DeGrove, John M. 1991. "Evolving Regional Roles in State Planning and Growth Management Systems: What It Means to Planners and Developers." Paper presented at ALI-ABA Land Use Institute on Planning, Regulation, Litigation, Eminent Domain and Compensation, July 31, Coronado, California.

Dodge, William R. 1989. "The Emergence of Intercommunity Partnerships in the 1980s." *National Civic Review* 78 (January–February): 5–14.

———. 1990. "Regional Problem Solving in the 1990s: Experimentation with Local Governance for the 21st Century." *National Civic Review* 79 (July–August): 354–66.

Donahue, John D. 1989. *The Privatization Decision.* New York: Basic Books.

Fosler, Robert S., and Renee A. Berger. 1982. *Public-private Partnership in American Cities: Seven Case Studies.* New York: Lexington Books.

Gage, Robert W. 1988. "Regional Councils of Governments at the Crossroads: Implications for Intergovernmental Management and Networks." *International Journal of Public Administration* 11, no. 4: 467–501.

Gardner, John W. 1990. *On Leadership.* New York: Free Press.

Hersey, Paul. 1984. *The Situational Leader.* New York: Warner Books.

House, Robert J., and Terence R. Mitchell. 1974. "Path-goal Theory of Leadership." *Contemporary Business* 3 (Fall): 81–98.

Kingdon, John W. 1984. *Agendas, Alternatives, and Public Policies.* Boston: Little, Brown.

Kotter, John P. 1982. *The General Managers.* New York: Free Press.

McDowell, Bruce D. 1980. "Substate Regionalism Matures Gradually." *Intergovernmental Perspective* 6 (Fall): 20–26.

National Association of Regional Councils (NARC). 1980. *Regional Councils: Future Models (Special Report No. 55).* Washington, DC: NARC.

———. 1985. *Directory of Regional Councils: 1985–86.* Washington, DC: NARC.

———. 1987. *The Future of Regionalism in the United States with Special Attention to Regional Councils and Their Roles (Special Report No. 126).* Washington, DC: NARC.

———. 1988. *Future Regional Roles in Reality.* Washington, DC: NARC.

———. 1989. *Regional Council Programs and Activities: 1988 Survey.* Washington, DC: NARC.

Weaver, Robert, and Sherman Wyman. 1991. "Regional Councils and Their Managers: Profiles, Problems and Prospects." Paper presented at annual conference of Urban Affairs Association, April 18, Vancouver, BC.

Yukl, Gary A. 1989. *Leadership in Organizations,* 2d ed. Englewood Cliffs, NJ: Prentice Hall.

CHAPTER 20

RESEARCH AND INTERVENTIONS FOR STRESS REDUCTION IN A HOSPITAL SETTING

SUSAN R. RAYNIS AND MARGARET A. CLEEK

Current contingency models of leadership are based on the assumption that situational and subordinate characteristics play an important role in determining the most effective approach to leadership in a given setting. In particular, hospitals have environments and staff characteristics that suggest the appropriateness of certain approaches over others. Using House's (1971) Path-Goal theory of leadership, the following characteristics of hospitals and hospital employees are found to be critical in identifying an effective style of leadership.

Path-Goal theory defines four leadership styles: directive, supportive, participative, and achievement-oriented. Directive leadership is defined as task-oriented while supportive leadership is defined as person-oriented. Participative leaders spend their energy building employee involvement in the workplace. Finally, achievement-oriented leadership assumes that subordinates are willing and able to perform their tasks and therefore concentrates on motivating subordinates to reach high levels of performance. Given subordinate characteristics alone, the Path-Goal model would encourage hospital supervisors to engage in achievement-oriented leadership since hospital employees tend to be well-educated professionals with a great deal of dedication to their field.

However, situational factors also play an important role in determining which leadership styles will be the most effective, and one of the most salient features of hospitals as work environments is the high level of stress present (Marshall 1980). As a result of the uncertainty, unpredictability, role ambiguity, and role conflict that characterize hospital settings, Path-Goal theory suggests that leader behaviors should be directed at reducing those stressors in order to decrease the amount of stress experienced by hospital staff, thereby increasing job satisfaction and productivity.

According to the Path-Goal theory, the presence of a large number of stressors implies the need for a more participative style on the part of the supervisor, thus increasing subordinate control over the environment, and also the need to attend to subordinates' emotional needs. Therefore, although the highly professional nature of the staff might seem to indicate that an achievement-oriented leadership style would be the most effective, the situational characteristics point to a more participative, supportive leadership style with an emphasis on increasing clarity and predictability to the extent that these characteristics can be provided in a hospital setting. In support of this assumption, at least two studies have demonstrated that leadership consideration and sensitivity reduce the amount of stress experienced by hospital nurses (Sheridan and Vredenburgh 1978; Vredenburgh and Trinkaus 1980).

The present study involved a survey of hospital supervisors and their subordinates in which both groups were asked to rate the supervisors along a number of leadership dimensions. It was hypothesized that, if stress was the most salient feature of the hospital work situation, subordinates would express a desire for more structure and support whereas if the above-mentioned stressors were less salient, then the staff, given their high level of training and professionalism, would express a desire for more autonomy.

Method and Results

A group of 36 hospital supervisors rated themselves on twelve dimensions of leadership behavior, using Form XH of the Leader Behavior Description Questionnaire or LBDQ (Stogdill 1963). In addition, 180 subordinates used the LBDQ to rate the superiors on how they were currently performing as leaders ("is now") as well as how the subordinates would like them to behave as leaders ("would like"). Thus, it was possible to assess the amount of congruence between superior and subordinate perceptions of leadership via the "is now" responses, and also to examine any perceived deficits in leader behavior via the "would like" ratings.

Comparisons indicate that supervisors were accurate in assessing their performance of task-oriented leadership behaviors, but tended to overrate the degree to which they engaged in group-maintenance and person-oriented behaviors as represented by the dimensions of consideration and integration (Table 20.1). Stodgill (1963) defines the dimension of consideration as concern for the comfort and well-being of subordinates, while the dimension of integration involves maintaining a closely knit group and resolving intragroup conflicts. In addition, supervisors perceived that they were providing more predictability to the work situation than was perceived by their subordinates. All three of these dimensions are directly related to stress reduction.

An examination of supervisor self-ratings versus subordinate "would like" ratings demonstrated that subordinates desired higher levels of most leadership behaviors, including structuring, communication, and supportive activities, but did not desire additional performance pressure or ambiguity (Table 20.2). These responses suggest the presence of two sources of stress in the work environment: ambiguity and heavy task demands. The subordinates desired more supervisory behaviors that would counteract these stressors, expecially activities that would increase structure (demand reconciliation), support, and communication.

Discussion

It is interesting to note that the discrepancies in ratings of the supervisors' leadership behavior occurred primarily along the personal support dimension. Several explanations

Table 20.1

Supervisor Self-Ratings Versus Subordinate "Is Now" Ratings of the Supervisors' Leadership Behavior

LBDQ scale	Supervisors		Subordinates			
	M	(SD)a	M	(SD)b	t	(df)
Representation	20.10	(2.37)	19.47	(4.29)	0.77	(168)
Demand reconciliation	18.80	(2.54)	18.50	(3.92)	0.40	(175)
Tolerance of uncertainty	31.97	(4.66)	33.79	(7.18)	−1.33	(164)
Persuasiveness	37.41	(3.20)	36.38	(7.75)	0.70	(166)
Initiation of structure	40.93	(4.46)	39.96	(6.80)	0.74	(166)
Tolerance of freedom	37.48	(3.08)	36.47	(7.16)	0.74	(166)
Role assumption	39.21	(3.37)	37.95	(7.75)	0.86	(164)
Consideration	39.47	(3.80)	35.91	(8.24)	2.31	(170)*
Production emphasis	36.24	(4.67)	36.38	(5.74)	−0.12	(165)
Predictive accuracy	19.13	(1.94)	17.70	(3.52)	2.16	(175)*
Integration	21.41	(2.29)	18.94	(4.91)	2.65	(173)
Superior orientation	38.24	(3.47)	36.50	(5.62)	1.60	(165)

*p < .05
**p < .01
[a]n = 29 to 30, depending on missing data
[b]n = 136 to 147, depending on missing data

Table 20.2

Supervisor Self-Ratings Versus Subordinate "Would Like" Ratings of the Supervisors' Leadership Behavior

LBDQ scale	Supervisors		Subordinates			
	M	(SD)a	M	(SD)b	t	(df)
Representation	20.10	(2.37)	21.49	(2.88)	−2.49	(177)*
Demand reconciliation	18.80	(2.54)	22.76	(2.46)	−8.00	(175)**
Tolerance of uncertainty	31.97	(4.66)	37.52	(4.18)	−6.50	(173)
Persuasiveness	37.41	(3.20)	41.70	(4.48)	−4.90	(171)*
Initiation of structure	40.93	(4.46)	42.78	(4.01)	−2.22	(171)*
Tolerance of freedom	37.48	(3.08)	37.74	(4.75)	−0.28	(170)
Role assumption	39.21	(3.37)	44.22	(5.25)	−4.94	(171)ns,*
Consideration	39.47	(3.80)	42.89	(3.50)	−4.80	(171)*
Production emphasis	36.24	(4.67)	35.71	(5.21)	0.51	(172)
Predictive accuracy	19.13	(1.94)	20.67	(2.79)	−2.87	(175)ns,*
Integration	21.41	(2.29)	22.94	(2.20)	−3.40	(173)
Superior orientation	38.24	(3.47)	42.72	(4.28)	−5.30	(173)*

[ns]p > .50, nonsignificant
*p < .05
[a]n = 29 to 30, depending on missing data
[b]n = 136 to 147, depending on missing data

are possible as to why there was congruence on task-oriented dimensions but not on the two person-related dimensions of consideration and integration.

The most straightforward explanation is that the supervisors were simply not adequately attending to this area and were not giving consideration the attention which their subordinates believed it deserved. It is entirely possible that supervisors may have unknowingly de-emphasized "softer" person-oriented behaviors in the face of the daily time pressures of the tasks and the more results-oriented nature of many of the task-oriented dimensions.

It is also possible that the task-oriented behaviors of supervisors were more salient to the subordinates, whereas consideration and group maintenance behaviors were perhaps less likely to be directly observed by subordinates. For example, when a supervisor goes to bat for a subordinate with his or her own supervisor, the extent and scope of this may not be known to the subordinate. If a supervisor tries to make out a schedule which minimizes the number of weekends a subordinate must work, this activity may not be directly observed by the subordinate. Thus, the less salient nature of some of these behaviors might lead subordinates to perceive lower levels of the behaviors in comparison to the perception of their supervisors.

Still another explanation for the discrepancy is that the high stress nature of the environment makes it exceedingly difficult for most supervisors to provide the level of emotional support that the subordinates feel they need. Several researchers have documented the existence of staff stress in hospitals (cf. Marshall 1980; Pines 1982; Seuntjens 1982). Several factors make hospital staff especially vulnerable to continued stress on the job. The stress may be generated from the job itself (Seuntjens 1982). Hospital work is often physically demanding; it is sometimes unpleasant (Marshall 1980); and the often uncertain and unpredictable changes in the state of patients condition can, as many laboratory studies have shown (Miller 1980), serve as a stressor. Finally, the around-the-clock schedule of many hospital employees can result in atypical and shifting work hours which disrupt the private lives of staff. Especially noteworthy are the negative effects of role ambiguity and role conflict on staff satisfaction and performance (see, for example, research by Brief and Aldag 1976; Pines 1982; Posner and Randolph 1980). The results of the present study suggest that the factors cited above may also impact negatively upon subordinates' perceptions of supervisory ability in the areas of consideration and support.

The "would like" ratings indicated that subordinates did not want any more role ambiguity than was already present in the supervisory-subordinate relationship. Subordinates also did not desire greater pressure for productive output. However, they expressed a desire for an increase in all other types of behaviors, including structuring activities, communication, and person-oriented behaviors. These results, combined with the discrepancy in perceptions, point to a need for supervision that is more supportive rather than more achievement-oriented. In particular, providing personal and group support, increasing predictability in the work environment, and decreasing role ambiguity were the critical aspects of leadership identified by both the discrepancies in perception and the type of leader behaviors desired by subordinates. Thus, in applying Path-Goal theory, the most salient contingency factors in this setting was found to be stress, as reflected in the expressed desire for leader behavior that directly mitigate the effects of stress.

Implications for Applications

It is important to consider the application of these findings and to try to develop methods to encourage the kind of leader behavior and work environment which workers report that they need. Further, it is important to attempt to increase the levels of congruence in perceived behaviors on the part of supervisors and subordinates so that misunderstandings and blaming do not interfere with job effectiveness and impact negatively on job satisfaction.

These findings indicate that hospital employees have a real need and desire for the types of leader behaviors that can reduce the levels of stress which they experience on the job. In particular, subordinates in the present study expressed an inability to handle increased levels of role ambiguity and an inability to handle greater pressure for productivity. On the other hand, subordinates expressed a need for greater structuring of their activities and a greater need for communication and support-oriented behaviors.

One way to meet these needs is to change the leadership style either by selection or the training of managers. Leader behavior occurs in the context of the organizational environment and, relatedly, it may be very difficult if not impossible to accomplish these objectives unless we address the context in which leader behaviors are occurring. Contextual approaches to change, such as organizational development, operate to reduce the negative effects of stress in the workplace through changes in the setting in which the leader is operating. It is suggested, therefore, that interventions are needed which are more macro in scope and impact on the organization as a whole and not just the individual leader, while they also allow for the types of leader behaviors which reduce the sources of stress.

An array of organizational interventions exist which can be utilized to accomplish various organizational objectives. The present results indicate that any organizational intervention enjoyed in a health-care setting should be designed to reduce role ambiguity and role conflict, minimize pressure for output, provide structure, increase communication and support in the workplace, and allow for a more participative leadership style on the part of the manager.

The most straightforward way of reducing role ambiguity is simply to define jobs as closely as possible and to assure that workers have the resources to meet these expectations. A health care professional who understands role expectations and has the time, staff, and knowledge to meet these expectations can be expected to experience lowered levels of felt stress. Clarifying responsibility is one of the major activities of the manager and is a critical issue in the Path-Goal model, yet many managers fail to provide this clarification and instead parcel out activities in bits and pieces, making the subordinates unsure of their next move. In the worst case, the manager performs the role of fire chief, with staff being sent off to react to each new emergency. In such an environment, there is little follow-up because one is off to the next disaster and employees get little sense of closure on the tasks and duties which they perform. If employees have a sense of control over a well-defined area of responsibility, they are better able to set realistic expectations and goals for themselves and identify and act upon factors which impede work performance and goal accomplishment.

Among the established Organizational Development techniques are several which specifically address role clarity. In particular, value clarification, goal setting, and role negotiation exercises can serve this end. The process can also be institutionalized in a Management by Objectives program which would have the added bonus of clarifying organizational goals as well as work unit goals and responsibilities.

Since, for most workers, the really troublesome stressors arise from the structure of the job itself, one potential intervention is job redesign. Job redesign, which is usually directed toward job enrichment, has been proposed as a means of creating a better work environment in the health-care setting (Cleek and Karuza 1985). According to the job enrichment model, increasing employees' involvement in their work by enriching their jobs leads to improved staff morale, increased productivity, and reduced turnover. The characteristics of work identified by Hackman and Oldham (1975) which create job enrichment include:

- *Task variety*—the range of skills and abilities an individual utilizes in performing a certain job. Does the job require a single skill or no skill at all or are several abilities brought to the task?
- *Task identity*—the perceived fit of the job into the total context. Does the person know how his/her job contributes to the total service?
- *Task significance*—the importance of the job. Does the person feel that his/her job makes a contribution and is of value?

These first three characteristics comprise the experienced meaningfulness of work. When these characteristics are perceived as absent, work will be meaningless and low work motivation and low quality work will result.

Two other Hackman/Oldham characteristics need to be noted. In brief:

- *Autonomy*—the degree of control a person has over the methods and procedures of work. Is a person required to perform a task according to set procedures and at a controlled pace. This characteristic relates to responsibility for work outcomes. Without job autonomy, workers are unwilling to accept responsibility. No one wants to take responsibility something over which he has no control.
- *Feedback*—the degree to which a person has knowledge of results concerning the work in progress or upon completion. Feedback contributes to higher satisfaction with the work, continued involvement, and reduced turnover and absenteeism.

The current research suggests some caution with regard to job enrichment. Increasing the degree of task variety and autonomy may stress the staff. Results indicate that subordinates want more structure and clarity without additional performance pressure. Research by Hall and Schneider (1973) indicates that supervision which is characterized by a high level of support and which does not reduce the subordinate's level of autonomy is what is needed. Any job enrichment effort which seeks to increase the dimensions of autonomy and task variety needs to pay careful attention that these dimensions are increased only in a supportive environment or the intervention may increase rather than reduce perceived levels of stress.

Task identity and task significance are characteristics which contribute to experienced meaningfulness. People are often doing important jobs but no one ever acknowledges the importance of these jobs. Although it may seem to be obvious, simply communicating to someone how and why the work he/she does makes an important contribution can increase the perception of these dimensions. The current findings indicate that managers should indeed exert more energy to attend to this support function.

The results reported here strongly support the need for greater results communication (feedback). That is best accomplished with relevant and frequent performance review sessions. These reviews should be non-threatening, developmental in nature, constructive, not linked to pay, and, if possible, tied to role clarification. Further, supervisors should be trained to recognize symptoms of stress through the observation of performance required for these sessions and address them at this time.

The issue which deserves the greatest emphasis here is that the supervisor needs to create a supportive and nondefensive environment if he or she is to reduce stress for employees and maintain efficiency. Properly implemented and controlled, Team Building can go a long way toward the accomplishment of this objective. In the hospital environment, the interdisciplinary team can be formed within the work unit to meet the purposes of improved quality of care, improved communication, and, when skillfully handled, increased communication, feedback, and support. The interdisciplinary team within a work unit can also be a forum for increasing commitment. If the leader allows for participation in a supportive environment, the result can be increased commitment to goals, greater work involvement, and a more cooperative environment.

Finally, building and maintaining support systems in the workplace is clearly associated with a reduction in perceived stress (Beehr 1976). Support systems create a climate of openness and participation. The current research indicates that supervisors are not attending to this function to the degree that their subordinates desire. Supervisors need to realize that support, communication, feedback, and clarification of expectations are not just "the soft stuff" that needs to take a back seat to the "real" task related aspects of their job, but rather as a vital concern which in its absence prevents workers from delivering the quality of work that they would otherwise be capable.

Such concerns are particularly salient in the health care environment for, as levels of stress increase, the worker will "burnout," and burnout in the health care services is associated with, among other things, dehumanization of the patients and thus decreased liking for them (Cherniss 1980). In the health care environment, stress affects not only the worker's performance, but the quality of care experienced by the patient.

References

Beehr, T.A. 1976. "Perceived Situational Moderators of the Relationship Between Subjective Role Ambiguity and Role Strain." *Journal of Applied Psychology* 61: 35–40.

Brief, A. and R. Aldag. 1976. "Correlates of Role Indices." *Journal of Applied Psychology* 61: 468–72.

Cherniss, C. 1980. *Staff Burnout: Job Stress in the Human Services.* Beverly Hills: Sage.

Cleek, M.A. and J. Karuza, Jr. 1985. "Strategies for Increased Satisfaction and Retention of Nursing Home Personnel." Paper presented at the American Psychological Association Meeting in Los Angeles.

Golembiewski, R.T. 1982. "Organization Development (OD) Interventions: Changing Interaction, Structures, and Policies," in W.S. Paine (ed.). *Job Stress and Burnout: Research, Theory, and Intervention Perspectives.* Beverly Hills: Sage.

Hall, D.T. and B. Schneider. 1973. *Organizational Climates and Career: The Work Lives of Priests.* New York: Seminar Press.

House. R.A. 1974. "A Path-Goal Theory of Leadership." *Administrative Science Quarterly* 16: 321–38.

Marshall, J. 1980. "Stress Amongst Nurses," in C. Cooper and J. Marshall (eds.). *White Collar and Professional Stress.* London: John Wiley.

Pines. A. 1982. "Staff Burnout," in T.A. Wills (ed.). *Basic Processes in Helping Relationships.* New York: Academic Press.

Posner, B. and W.A. Randolf. 1980. "Moderators of Role Stress Among Hospital Personnel." *Journal of Psychology* 105: 215–24.

Seutjens, A. 1982. "Burnout in Nursing—What It Is and How to Prevent It." *Nursing Administration Quarterly* (Fall): 12–19.

Seybolt. J., C. Petett, and D. Walker. 1978. "Turnover among Nurses: It Can Be Managed." *Journal of Nursing Administration* 8: 4–9.

Sheridan. J.E. and D.J. Vrendenburgh. 1982. "Usefulness of Leadership Behavior and Social Power Variables in Predicting Job Tension, Performance, and Turnover of Nursing Employees." *Journal of Applied Psychology* 63(1): 89–95.

Stodtrill. R.M. 1983. *Manual for the Leader Behavior Description Questionnaire—Form XII: An Experimental Revision.* Columbus: Ohio State University, Bureau of Business Research.

Vrendenburgh, D.J. and R.J. Trinkaus. 1983. "The Analysis of Role Stress Among Hospital Nurses." *Journal of Vocational Behavior* 22(1): 82–96.

PART 6

WHAT ARE THE BEST TECHNIQUES FOR ADMINISTRATIVE LEADERS TO USE?

Although traits and skills provide the reservoir of talent, and styles provide the approach to the leadership task, it is through specific techniques or behaviors that leaders ultimately act in an attempt to fulfill their goals. There are numerous behavioral competencies in the simplest leadership position. When administrative leaders get comprehensive feedback through standard survey feedback instruments, it is generally the concrete behavioral competencies that are identified and evaluated. Leadership is made difficult by the large number of competencies that leaders must excel in, generally under great time constraints.

Although broad discussions of leader characteristics and style have their uses, concrete discussions of specific leader strengths and weaknesses require an analysis of what leaders actually do. Therefore, behavior competencies tend to be the basis of classification, training programs, personal development initiatives, and rigorous appraisal systems.

In this introduction, leader behaviors are divided into task, people, and organizational activities. Each of these domains is further sorted into assessment/evaluation, formulation and planning, implementation, and change functions. For example, the assessment activity for task behavior is monitoring the work; for people behavior it is consulting; and for organizational behavior it is scanning the environment. In all, twenty-one behaviors are defined in this taxonomy.

Task Behaviors

Monitoring, as with the assessment activities in each domain, is generally critical for the effective use of task behaviors such as planning, clarifying, and problem solving, as well as people behaviors such as motivating and developing. Monitoring gathers information about individuals, service or product quality, and the effectiveness of programs. It can be conducted by direct observation of work, reviewing productivity data, reading reports, attending progress or quality meetings, inspecting work samples, or conducting after-work reviews. All effective managers/leaders spend a good deal of time monitoring, although it may be done indirectly while outwardly performing other functions.

There are many types of planning, but our interest here is work process planning, also known as operations planning. It is the division and coordination of work; that is, how the work will be divided by processes and individuals, and how this division of labor will be combined consistently, efficiently and effectively. Operations planning is conducted through analysis of data (collected during the monitoring process); involves the coordination of multiple, often competing, interests; and produces schedules (who, what, and when) and performance goals (quantity and quality). Effective managers build operations planning into their routine schedule so that deadlines are met and there is ample time for plan refinement and change. To the degree that operations planning can be appropriately delegated without planning quality loss, it gives workers greater self-determination and allows managers more time for higher-level and longer-range planning activities.

Clarifying roles and objectives involves defining job responsibilities, establishing performance goals, and providing instruction on task accomplishment. It occurs verbally in individual and group meetings in both formal and informal settings. It is often followed with, and sometimes preceded by, written information. Effective managers do not assume that role clarity exists and that performance standards are known; they constantly check to make sure that follower knowledge and understandings are correct and consistent.

While the competency *clarifying* focuses on narrower role responsibilities, *informing* focuses on broader communication needs having to do with group performance and achievements, and notification of problems and changes. It is conducted through a wide array of mechanisms: messages, meetings, newsletters, email, bulletin boards, briefings, reports, and so on. Effective managers realize that they are a kind of nerve center that is not functioning well unless information flows out as well as in. It is especially critical when there is a major change or crisis.

Delegating, as used in this broad context, is when subordinates are allowed to have a degree of responsibility and discretion—from modest to full—in carrying out their work, handling problems, and making decisions. Delegating can be informally done at the manager's discretion on a case-by-case basis, or it can be made a formal part of employees' job descriptions. Effective managers seek to maximize participation of employees in decision making, knowing that many factors, such as worker knowledge, worker commitment, goal congruence, and time constraints, must constrain the latitude of delegation (Vroom and Jago 1988).

Problem solving is the act of identifying and analyzing operational problems, choosing from alternative solutions, and following up on the consequences (evaluation). One of the largest functions of leadership is making good choices, which is divided into three major behaviors in this discussion. Planning, already discussed, involves advance decision making about the division and coordination of work; decision making, to be discussed, involves broader choices having to do with organizational change and strategy; and problem solving involves responding to the implementation issues related to both operations planning and organizational decision making. Therefore, the time frame is inevitably shorter, the pattern is unpredictable, and it is a major contributor to the interruptions and stress that plague supervisors through executives. Effective managers select the problems to work on judiciously, handle them quickly, and do not let them crowd out the more contemplative forms of decision making (including contingency planning, which can be used to avert many problems in the first place).

Managing change is always a key leadership competency, but when organizations face greater competition for resources or when organizational structures are shifting, it is considered by some experts to be *the* key leadership competency. Because of its importance and its breadth of applications, change is subdivided here into three dimensions at the task, people, and organization levels. At the task or technical level, managing innovation and creativity is facilitating change that is either incremental or on a small scale, especially as a bottom-up process. As Kanter (1983) and others have pointed out, technical innovations do not primarily come from executives. More often than not, it is line workers or line supervisors who discover better ways of doing things, and it is mid-level managers who recognize and champion these insights. Thus leadership of innovation and creativity requires a mind-set that empowers people to recognize and make change within appropriate parameters, encourages systems thinking, creates an appreciation of flexibility and careful risk-taking, learns not only from successes but from failures and problems as well, and uncovers mental models that underlie peoples' actions so that habits and values can be understood (Argyris 1993; Senge 1990).

Interpersonal Behaviors

Consulting is the act of soliciting ideas and sentiments from others with an interpersonal, rather than operations, thrust (as in monitoring). In consulting, the enrichment of the individual being sought out is as important as the information gleaned by the leader. Because they are related, monitoring and consulting often occur simultaneously, but it is possible, and sometimes desirable, to do one without the other. For example, a supervisor focusing on consulting can discover how best to motivate a specific employee, identify beneficial types of employee development activities, and get suggestions that might never occur in a monitoring mode. Consulting can occur in many ways but is generally most powerful when done on a one-on-one basis in private.

Planning/organizing staff is determining the long-term objectives and strategies to use with regard to personnel and personnel functions. Just as operations planning focuses on deciding how best to allocate resources (including personnel) to accomplish work efficiently and effectively, planning and organizing personnel focuses on how best to allocate and adjust work to support personnel. Planning and organizing personnel occurs most visibly through hiring processes, work selection based on individual competencies, performance appraisal (when it is robust), social events related to work, team building, and recognition and rewards activities. In the short term it leads to more content and involved workers, and in the long run it assists with the management of the organizational culture.

Developing staff is providing a range of support, from knowledge- and skill-related training activities to broad "developmental" career advice (Van Wart, Cayer, and Cook 1993). It is conducted though formal training programs on and off the job site, through coaching in technical skills and special task requirements, and through mentoring. It also involves counseling on those issues that are likely to derail a person's career (e.g., "blind spots") and occasionally those personal (non-job) problems that interfere with work performance.

Motivating is the use of influence tactics that appeal to logic, action, or inspiration in order to generate enthusiasm and commitment for work. Much worker motivation is inherent to the worker's interest in the work itself; nonetheless, good leaders can have an enormous effect on the overall level and consistency of motivation. One common motivation tactic is the use of rational persuasion: providing evidence, reasons, benefits, comparisons, and explanations of problem avoidance. A second common motivation tactic is the use of involvement: asking for suggestions, assistance in decision making, and help in planning and implementation. A third motivation tactic is the use of inspiration: appeals to the personal dimensions such as professionalism, self-image, and ideals, as well as group and high-performance dimensions such as the use of an appealing future vision and setting high standards.

Building and managing teams not only requires an ability to facilitate cooperation and identification of people with various types of work units, but it also requires an understanding of the many types of team structures and the different needs that they have (Katzenbach and Smith 1993). "Team" structures can vary from the standard work team, which performs normal operational duties and which may be leader-led or self-managed, to project teams, whose members are generally assembled on a part-time basis for a specific purpose and that include cross-functional improvement teams, quality circles, task forces, and various types of management teams. For example, in setting up cross-functional teams leaders must pay attention to establishing a clear group mission or objective, selecting the appropriate number of people with a good balance of skills, making sure that the team has a grant of authority and is clear about its scope of power, providing the team with incentives to be successful, and ensuring that the team has, or will receive, training on team skills.

A special type of problem solving is managing conflict, which may stem from a variety of causes such as incompatible personalities, power struggles, competition for resources, work ambiguity, dysfunctional communication, or contradictory goals. Leaders must be able to deal with conflict among others as a third party and sometimes as a direct participant. There may be either "problem" or "relationship" elements to conflicts, and often both are involved, so an ability to use appropriate tactics in both areas is necessary. An example of a problem-oriented tactic is identifying specific reasons for the conflict, while an example of a relations-oriented tactic is remaining impartial and showing acceptance toward both parties.

Managing personnel change involves facilitating people to accept and participate in the change itself. It is a necessary component of both technical and organizational change. People have natural resistance to change so leaders must be able to minimize the restraining forces while encouraging the positive elements of change (Lewin 1951). Among the many tactics that leaders can use are creating a sense of urgency, helping people deal with the trauma of change, keeping people informed, demonstrating commitment to change, creating a new social identification for individuals, using high expectations and an achievement orientation to motivate, exciting people about the opportunity to make an important contribution, encouraging transcendence of personal needs to the needs of the common good, and simply demonstrating confidence.

Organizational Behaviors

Environmental scanning is the assessment function at the organizational level. It involves looking outside the specific unit or organization at other units and organizations for opportunities and threats. Some of the major sources of information for public organizations may be other agencies at the same or different level of government, organizations in the private sector, clients and customers, and legislative or other oversight bodies with influence. Environmental scanning is a quintessential executive skill (leaders who are "surprised" by external events may put the entire organization at risk), and becomes increasingly important in dynamic environments.

Planning and structuring organizational alignment involves both the determination of strategic goals and the identification of broad strategies. This behavior is commonly referred to as strategic planning. Strategic planning requires leaders to have done an adequate job in environmental scanning, know the current strengths (especially core competencies) and weaknesses, be able to determine a balanced set of intermediate and long-term goals and objectives with others, determine key areas for change, and identify promising implementation strategies.

Networking and partnering involve development of contacts outside the unit or agency through both formal and, especially, informal means. The more senior the position and the more lateral dependence a unit or agency has, the more important networking and partnering will be. These activities produce information used in scanning, opportunities for collaboration, solutions or assistance with concrete problems, and a source of political alliances. Although some networking and partnering occur at formal functions, most of these activities take place at or through conferences, lunches, social events, courtesy calls, informational meetings, and so on.

A variety of general management functions is required of all organizational leaders, although the types and extent of importance will diverge considerably. From supervisor to chief executive officer, the functions that most leaders have to perform, to one degree or another, include human resource management, budgeting, information management, and figurehead functions. Thus a first-line supervisor in a county public works department might need extensive human resource management skills while having virtually no budgetary or figurehead responsibilities, while the secretary of a federal agency might be called on to perform extensive figurehead and budget allocation functions but be almost totally removed from human resource functions outside her or his own office.

Articulating the mission and vision is communicating and positively affecting followers' sense of individual and organizational purpose and desire to strive for a better future state. Articulating mission and vision can be thought of as occurring at both transactional and transformational levels. At the transactional level, this behavior requires communication clarity that results in a clear focus on purpose and future operational strategies. Simple rational explanations of what the organization is about and where it is going may help to minimize follower disaffection and confusion. However, transformational leaders must go well beyond the more basic transformational requirements since this behavior is critical to major change. They must also provide intellectual stimulation and charisma (Bass 1985). The intellectual stimulation includes an inspiration for high standards and encouragement to think about old problems in new ways (entrepreneurialism). Charisma results from strong leader-follower bonding, and has two facets. Charisma is primarily achieved when followers believe in the leader because of competence, role modeling,

Table P6.1

The Functional Techniques of Organizational Leaders

	Leader actions: Behavior domains		
	Task	People	Organizational
Assessment/evaluation	1. Monitor and assess tasks	1. Consult	1. Scan the environment
Formulation and planning functions	2. Operations planning	2. Plan and organize personnel	2. Strategic planning
Implementation functions	3. Clarify roles and objectives	3. Develop staff	3. Network and partner
	4. Inform	4. Motivate	4. Perform general management functions
	5. Delegate	5. Build and manage teams	5. Articulate the mission and vision
"Change" functions	6. Problem solving	6. Manage conflict	6. Decision making
	7. Manage innovation and creativity	7. Manage personnel change	7. Manage organizational change

past successes, and a variety of appealing personal characteristics and is also enhanced by leaders' belief in followers themselves.

Although problem solving (discussed earlier) and decision making have similar intellectual structures, the scope is vastly different. Decision making, in this context, involves broader choices having to do with organizational change and strategy, and has a major effect on the organization or unit's well-being or operations. For example, problem solving in a land management agency might include fixing an unacceptable procurement lag, adding a new element to a training program, or working with a constituency to better service their needs under existing policy. Decision making might include a complete overhaul of the procurement policy, including a request for a change in legislation; changing the philosophy of training programs; or establishing a new relationship with constituency groups. The rational elements of decision making mirror those of problem solving: problem identification and clarification, alternatives generation, data collection regarding alternatives, choice, and evaluation (Van Wart 1998). However, the cognitive complexity in decision making becomes more pronounced (Hunt 1996).

Managing organizational change is facilitating and implementing major process and system changes, especially mission and vision changes that have occurred through the strategic planning process. When the environment of the organization is dynamic, or when organizational performance is lagging, many academic and popular theorists assert that this is the single most important leadership behavior. Managing organizational change largely picks up where strategic planning leaves off. It relies on both action planning and change management (Mintzberg 1994). Action planning essentially involves the scheduling of change: identifying the necessary steps and their sequence, setting deadlines, assigning responsibility, and developing coordinating and tracking systems. Good change management includes involving key stakeholders in the change process and forming coalitions to implement them, adapting strategic goals to ensure wide appeal and "buy-in," ensuring that one or more competent change masters is overseeing the process, identifying the relevant parts of the old ideology to keep and those to change, and bolstering cultural change and psychological attachment through the use of symbols and rituals.

In summary, it is easier to talk of leadership in broad generalities such as in discussions of style or leader characteristics. Such broad discussion can be useful for some purposes, but is not helpful when examining the specific strengths and weaknesses of individual leaders or classes of leaders. For more concrete uses, specific leader behavior taxonomies, which provide a detailed description of what leaders actually do, are necessary. As an introduction to the topic, twenty-one competencies were briefly reviewed. These behavior competencies are summarized in Table P6.1.

Review of the Selections in Part 6

Because of the vastness of the literature, leader techniques are not covered as comprehensively in the readings as some of the other topics. The first reading, "Gender Differences and Managerial Competencies" (1998) by Daley and Naff, however, serves as an excellent overview. Their analysis is derived from a framework by the Office of Personnel Management (OPM), and includes the identification of twelve leader behaviors, which they call management functions, and nine effectiveness characteristics (essentially the traits and skills discussed in part 4). A review of these competencies reveals three important trends. First, leadership taxonomies in the behavior and trait-skill areas vary extensively by nomenclature. For example, what Daley and Naff call external awareness is more commonly called environmental scanning in the academic literature; what they call interpretation is more often called informing. Because of a lack of consistent terminology, inevitably one must look at the operational definitions to compare different commentators' frameworks, rather than simply using a cursory perusal of the category names. Second, the conceptual breadth varies substantially. Consider the difference in conceptual breadth of a simple dichotomous framework (initiating structure and consideration), versus the twelve behavioral categories in the Management Excellence Inventory presented by Daley and Naff, and the twenty-one presented in Table P6.1. Third, one must consider the specific group and purpose for whom the framework is developed. Because the Daley and Naff framework is intended for supervisors, it is little wonder that some of the core supervisor responsibilities such as operations planning are so well covered (e.g., coordination, work unit planning, and material resources administration), while some of the organizational-level skills are relatively glossed over (e.g., organizational decision making and change). Of course their specific research focus is about gender differences and managerial competencies. Overall they find that the differences between male and female supervisors are extremely small, with the sole exception of budgeting where men performed significantly better. Men in the study also did slightly better in work unit planning; women did slightly better at work unit guidance, interpretation and supervision. To the authors, the results clearly indicate that women are as capable as men and that they could easily perform at the same level in budgeting with the requisite training and mentoring. That is, women are generally already functioning well within the traditional, which is to say male-oriented, model. The more provocative, but conjectural, aspect of the discussion is about what, if any, special "cultural" competence women might bring to management in an era when the fundamental competencies are shifting to greater teamwork and delegated achievement models.

The selection by Boss, Boss, and Johnson, "The Cost of Not Listening to Employees: The Case of a Union Movement at Bradford Hospital" (1990), is an excellent case study that focuses on the people-oriented behaviors of leadership. In the case, hospital administrators do not listen to nurses regarding their grievances, the nurses resort to union organizing, and the hospital successfully mobilizes its resources to defeat the union ratification but at great expense both financially and in terms of morale. Overall, the case fits an almost archetypal pattern, and supports the management adage that bad leadership breeds unions. Listening is an enormous component of consulting, as well as being related to other assessment/evaluation competencies such as monitoring and environmental scanning. If assessment functions are weak, other management functions tend to operate far less effectively because they are starved for good information. The case also highlights the importance of other human relations aspects of leadership such as motivating, team building, and managing conflict.

The selection "Loose Cannons and Rule Breakers, or Enterprising Leaders? Some Evidence about Innovative Public Managers" (2000), by Sandford Borins, focuses on the change functions of administrative leadership. In the private sector the management of change has long been acknowledged as either one of the most important competency clusters, or the single most important element (in the transformational school). In the public sector there is greater reserve about the role of administrative leaders' (those not specifically placed in policy-making roles) being active in change functions that have policy ramifications. But that immediately begs two questions. When is an administrative change really a policy issue? And can administrators really be isolated from policy making and be truly technically neutral? Borins presents a case that clearly comes down on the side of greater change management by administrators at all levels. As important as his factual analysis of administrative innovation, however, is his assertion that his evidence shows that innovative administrators use due process and go through appropriate democratic-process channels. Indeed, part of their success would seem to be their willingness and ability to work with others at different operational and functional levels, and be trusted to carry out the reform or change with integrity and competence. The tough question that critics of entrepreneurialism may ask, however, is to what degree is this list of award nominees a fair representation of the entrepreneurial universe, or is it biased toward an ideal subpopulation?

The next selection is a "classic" based on an earlier classic piece. Charles E. Lindblom (1959) and Amitai Etzioni (1967) both look at an aspect critical to leadership: decision making. Using the terminology supplied in Table P6.1, their discussions apply to problem solving, innovation and creativity, personnel change, decision making, and organizational change as well as environmental scanning, strategic planning, and mission-vision articulation. In "The Science of Muddling Through," Lindblom (not reprinted here) presents two ideals of decision making. In the "scientific" or rational-comprehensive version, administrators gather all relevant data and make a fundamentally fresh assessment based on that data. They dig all the way "to the root" of the issue and are prepared to make changes that affect the root as well. In the incremental or "branch" version, administrators only gather data that are useful in answering specific, narrower operational questions and seem worth the time and effort given the crush of concerns that they deal with. The approach assumes the course of prevailing policy and that the need is for only modest course corrections. He points out that the former approach is much advocated by theorists of the day, while the latter approach continues to be the general approach of most practitioners. As importantly, he asserts that there are sound reasons why administrators use an incremental approach. For example, in "the root method, the inevitable exclusion of factors is accidental, unsystematic, and not defensible by any argument developed, while in the branch method the exclusions are deliberate, systematic, and defensible." Also, more often than not the whole endeavor of policy making is a succession of approximations "to some desired objectives in which what is desired itself continues to change under reconsideration." Thus, incrementalism is not only commonly practiced, but, according to Lindblom, the "science of muddling through" is actually the sensible mode of operation much of the time.

Etzioni's article "Mixed-Scanning: A 'Third' Approach to Decision-Making" takes up where Lindblom leaves off. He rails against a simple dichotomous approach to decision making, and disagrees that incrementalism is either the most common or the best approach to take. His mixed scanning method employs "two cameras: a broad-angle camera that would cover all parts of the sky but not in great detail, and a second one which would zero in on those areas revealed by the first camera to require a more in-depth examination." He notes that "it is essential to differentiate fundamental decisions from incremental ones." This implies that fundamental decisions will tend to use more of a rationalistic approach with full information gathering and analysis, while narrower decisions would use the streamlined approach. The decision about the information needs and depth of decision analysis can only be known, he posits, if the decision maker has initially engaged in mixed scanning (especially environmental scanning). Although both Lindblom and Etzioni help us understand the subtleties of decision making better than if we simply adopted an unrealistic notion that the rationalist approach is always best, or even excessively rely on an ad hoc strategy when more radical change is needed, they also leave managers with a complex set of factors to weigh. Ultimately, in considering the decision-making model to adopt, it all depends on the situation at hand.

References

Argyris, Chris. 1993. *Knowledge for Action: A Guide to Overcoming Barriers to Organizational Change.* San Francisco: Jossey-Bass.

Bass, Bernard M. 1985. *Leadership and Performance Beyond Expectations.* New York: Free Press.

Hunt, James G. 1996. *Leadership: A New Synthesis.* Newbury Park, CA: Sage.

Kanter, Rosabeth M. 1983. *The Change Masters.* New York: Simon & Schuster.

Katzenbach, Jon R., and Douglas K. Smith. 1993. *The Wisdom of Teams: Creating the High-Performance Organization.* Boston: Harvard Business School Press.

Lewin, Kurt. 1951. *Field Theory in Social Science: Selected Theoretical Papers,* D. Cartwright (ed.). New York: Harper and Row.

Mintzberg, Henry. 1994. *The Rise and Fall of Strategic Planning.* New York: Free Press.

Senge, Peter. 1990. *The Fifth Discipline: The Art and Practice of the Learning Organization.* New York: Doubleday Currency.

Van Wart, Montgomery. 1998. *Changing Public Sector Values.* New York: Garland.

Van Wart, Montgomery, N. Joseph Cayer, and Steve Cook. 1993. *Handbook of Training and Development in the Public Sector.* San Francisco: Jossey-Bass.

Vroom, Victor H., and Arthur G. Jago. 1988. *The New Leadership: Managing Participating in Organizations.* Upper Saddle River, NJ: Prentice Hall.

CHAPTER 21

GENDER DIFFERENCES AND MANAGERIAL COMPETENCIES

DENNIS M. DALEY AND KATHERINE C. NAFF

The past two decades have witnessed a remarkable increase in the proportion of women holding supervisory and management positions. In the federal government, women's share of white-collar supervisory jobs grew from 18 percent in 1976 to 30 percent in 1996 (Central Personnel Data File). This growth has been accompanied by substantial debate about whether women perceive themselves, or are perceived by others, as having the abilities and traits required for management jobs (e.g., to act decisively, to make tough decisions, etc.) (Duerst-Lahti and Johnson 1992; Schein 1973; Ezell, Odewahn and Sherman 1980; Dubno 1985; Stewart 1990). Also at issue is whether women approach management in the same way as men, or whether they bring uniquely feminine characteristics and approaches to the job. This continuing controversy takes on particular significance at a time when some management theorists are suggesting that not only are new leadership qualities required in today's environment, but for organizations to remain viable, they must become flatter and more flexible, and structured to encourage information sharing and teamwork (Boyett and Conn 1991; Garvin 1995; Bartlett and Ghoshal 1995a, 1995b; Mohrman, Cohen and Mohrman 1995).

This study contributes to the discussion of the differences, if any, between men's and women's managerial style by analyzing responses from first-line federal supervisors to a questionnaire administered in 1991. That survey asked supervisors to rate the importance of and their own ability to do 118 management tasks. This paper assesses whether there is a difference between men's and women's perceptions of their own abilities to do these tasks, and whether men's and women's responses demonstrate a difference in the importance they attach to what they do as supervisors.

Prior Research

In 1943, the Office of the Secretary of War issued a pamphlet to War Department personnel entitled "You're Going to Employ Women" which included the following observation:

A woman worker is not a man; in many jobs she is a substitute—like plastics instead

From *Review of Public Personnel Administration,* vol.18, no. 2 (Spring 1998): 41–56. Copyright © 1998 by Sage Publications, Inc. Reprinted with permission.

of metal—she has special characteristics that lend themselves to new and sometimes much superior uses (Office of the Secretary of War 1943). To put the best face on the need for women to take the jobs vacated by men fighting overseas, supervisors had to be convinced that women were not only capable of doing the work, but in some ways were even better suited to certain kinds of work. Indeed, during the four decades following the end of World War II the labor force participation of 25–54-year-old women jumped from about 30 percent to 70 percent (Shank 1988). During that time, women's equal ability to perform work traditionally done by men became increasingly accepted.

By the 1970s concern shifted from women's right to equal opportunity and treatment in the workplace, in general, to the dearth of women in supervisory and management positions. Since then, considerable research has focused on whether women are given opportunities equal with men to climb the ladder into these positions (e.g., Morrison, White and van Velsor 1987; Department of Labor 1991; Merit Systems Protection Board 1992a; Lewis 1986; Guy 1992, 1994; Dugan et. al 1993; Naff 1994; Newman 1993).

Another stream of research has focused on whether women have the characteristics traditionally associated with effective management or whether women have different traits that make them equally qualified or even superior managers in today's environment (Amason 1996; Calas and Smircich 1993; Russell Reynolds and Associates 1990).

An early and notable example of the perception that women are not suited for management was a study conducted by Virginia Schein (1973). Schein asked male managers to characterize "women in general," "men in general," and "successful middle managers." The attributes associated with successful managers, including self-confidence, forcefulness, ambition, and leadership ability were also associated with "men in general" but not with "women in general." Subsequent research has documented the persistence of this perceived mismatch between managerial characteristics and female characteristics, a view held by many women and men alike (Ezell, Odewahn and Sherman 1980; Dubno 1985; Heilman, Block, Martell and Simon 1989; Brenner, Tomkiewicz and Schein 1989; Naff 1994).

A competing set of studies has sought to "prove" that women are just as capable of exhibiting leadership qualities as men (e.g., Russell Reynolds Associates, Inc. 1990). These studies focus on gender as a nonsignificant factor. While life experiences may presently interact on a temporary basis with gender, gender itself is seen as managerially irrelevant (see also Duerst-Lahti and Johnson 1992).

Researchers have also suggested that such stereotypes of women as lacking management potential are part of the "glass ceiling" that inhibits women's career advancement (Gallese 1991; Merit Systems Protection Board 1992a; Harriman 1996; Department of Labor 1991; Kanter 1977). The pervasiveness of this stereotype has probably also contributed to findings that some women have less confidence in their job performance in some situations than men (Jackson, Gardner and Sullivan 1992; Terborg 1977; Ezell, Odewahn and Sherman 1980). One question examined in this article is whether female first-line supervisors in the federal sector tend to rate their own abilities to perform managerial tasks less positively than their male colleagues. Ironically, while sex role stereotypes can have adverse effects on women's advancement into supervisory and managerial positions, another stream of literature not only recognizes a gender difference but claims that the "female" approach to management is perhaps better suited to the demands of today's environment than the "male" approach. Some of this thinking is rooted in studies conducted by Carol Gilligan (1982) from which she concluded that women are guided by a morality of care and responsibility whereas men are oriented toward justice and rights. Whether this basic, philosophic difference between men and women ultimately results in different styles of management has been the subject of considerable research and debate.

Several studies have found a "notable difference in male and female behavioral styles" (Kelly 1991, 123). That there should be a difference between men and women who have successfully achieved management status in some ways seems self evident since their backgrounds, and career paths, and experiences in the organization are distinct from those of men in many ways (Morrison, White and van Velsor 1987; Naff and Thomas 1994; Guy 1993; Cannings and Montmarquette 1991; Fine, Johnson and Ryan 1990).

Women are said to be more nurturing, accommodating, and interested in sharing power and information (Edlund 1993; Rosener 1990; Rosen and Jerdee 1995) and naturally create "webs of inclusions" rather than hierarchical structures (Hegelson 1990). A study by Russell Reynolds Associates showed that, contrary to popular belief, women were more likely than men to display "leadership" qualities defined as "visionary, initiatory, charismatic, innovative, and strategic" (Russell Reynolds and Associates 1990, 4). Analysis of the responses of federal middle-managers to a government wide survey found that women were significantly less satisfied with their supervisors' leadership and "people skills," although their responses to other questions regarding job satisfaction and treatment were very similar (Lewis 1992). A meta-analysis of laboratory, assessment, and organizational studies of differences in men's and women's leadership styles found that women tend to be more democratic than men even in organizational settings (Eagly and Johnson 1990).

Other research has found either little or no differences in men's and women's management style (Morrison, White and van Velsor 1987; Rizzo and Mendez 1988; Vertz 1985; Lynn and Vaden 1979; Powell 1988, 1990; Duerst-Lahti and Johnson 1992) or has concluded that differences are situational-based (Harriman 1996; Guy 1992) or diluted by socialization and training that tends to produce uniformity (Eagly and Johnson 1990; Guy 1993; Bayes 1991). An advantage of this study of first-line supervisors may be that first line supervisors are less likely to have had extensive managerial experience and effective training (Rusaw 1994), and therefore are less likely to have been socialized into a common management style. On the other hand, we have to recognize the limitations of looking for differences in a structure that has historically ignored gender differences (Stivers 1993).

It is important to note at this juncture that the qualities attributed to women are celebrated in some circles because they are more consistent with what management theorists argue is the kind of management and leadership needed in today's increasingly competitive and fluid environment. This literature calls on organizations to be flatter, team-based, and to emphasize sharing information with and empowering employees so that they can be creative and committed to achieving organizational goals (Garvin 1995; Bartlett and Ghoshal 1995a,

1995b). In fact, it has been suggested that in tomorrow's organization, first-line supervisors performing the traditional supervisory tasks will be unneeded and instead will be replaced by "leaders" oriented toward effectively communicating a vision, keeping employees informed, and holding work units accountable for results (Boyett and Conn 1991). The Clinton administration's governmentwide reform effort—the National Performance Review—also called for flattening organizations and increasing employee empowerment (National Performance Review 1993). Some public management scholars go even further, suggesting that traditional functional organizations are "living dinosaurs" that cannot compete with the self-managed work teams of the new horizontal organization (Hyde 1995). Management theorist Tom Peters, among others, suggests that women are better suited to this environment: "It's perfectly obvious that women should be better managers than men in today's topsy-turvy business environment. As we rush into the 1990s, there is little disagreement about what business must become: less hierarchical, more flexible and team-oriented, faster and more fluid. In my opinion, one group of people has an enormous advantage realizing this necessary new vision: women" (quoted in Calas and Smircich 1993, 71).

In summary, the influx of women into the labor force and, more recently, into management has resulted in sometimes conflicting controversies. Yet, women continue to be perceived as lacking what it takes to be effective managers, a stereotype that has hindered their own advancement and, at times, even their own self-confidence. On the other hand, considerable research has attempted to identify whether women indeed have a different approach to management, much of it arguing that their unique approach is even superior to men's, particularly in the turbulent environment of the present and future. This study updates and extends this literature by analyzing responses from first-line federal government supervisors to a questionnaire in which they were asked to rate the importance of, and their own ability to perform, 118 management tasks.

Data and Methods

This study analyzes data from a survey of first-line, federal supervisors administered in April 1991 by the Merit Systems Protection Board (MSPB) as part of its effort to assess the quality of those managing federal programs (MSPB 1992b). MSPB based its instrument on a Management Excellence Inventory (MEI) developed by the Office of Personnel Management (OPM) in the early 1980s (Flanders and Utterback 1985). OPM surveyed federal managers (GS/GM 13–15 and SES) about their job roles, conducted critical incident interviews and performed comprehensive, subject-matter expert (i.e., job incumbent) job analyses to develop the MEI. Developers of the MEI identified 118 tasks that they grouped into 21 indices (see Figure 21.1 for index descriptions). Twelve of the indices assess the functions (or "what") of management (e.g., external awareness, interpretation, coordination, work unit planning, budgeting) and nine indices represent effectiveness characteristics (or "how" of effective management; e.g., broad perspective, flexibility, communication). The MSPB dropped a tenth MEI effectiveness characteristic, technical competence, from their survey of first-line supervisors because they believed it was too job-specific in its focus.

Figure 21.1 **Management Excellence Inventory**

The "What" of Management: Functions

1. External Awareness
   Identifying and keeping up-to-date with key agency policies and priorities and/or external issues and trends (e.g., economic, political, social, technological) likely to affect the work unit.
2. Interpretation
   Keeping subordinates informed about key agency and work unit policies, priorities, issues, and trends and how these are to be incorporated in work unit activities and products.
3. Representation
   Presenting, explaining, selling, and defending the work unit's activities to the supervisor in the agency, and/or persons and groups outside the agency
4. Coordination
   Performing liaison functions and integrating work unit activities with the activities of other organizations.
5. Work Unit Planning
   Developing and deciding upon longer-term goals, objectives, and priorities; and developing and deciding among alternative courses of action
6. Work Unit Guidance
   Converting plans to actions by setting short-term objectives and priorities; scheduling/sequencing activities; and establishing effectiveness and efficiency standards/guidelines.
7. Budgeting
   Preparing, justifying and/or administering the work unit's budget.
8. Material Resources Administration
   Assuring the availability of adequate supplies, equipment, facilities; overseeing procurement/ contracting activities; and/or overseeing logistical operations.
9. Personnel Management
   Projecting the number and type of staff needed by the work unit, and using various personnel management system components (e.g., recruitment, selection, promotion, performance appraisal) in managing the work unit.
10. Supervision
    Providing day-to-day guidance and oversight of subordinates (e.g., work assignments, consultation, etc); and actively working to promote and recognize performance.
11. Work Unit Monitoring
    Keeping up-to-date on the overall status of activities in the work unit, identifying problem areas, and taking corrective actions (e.g., rescheduling, reallocating resources, etc.).
12. Program Evaluation
    Critically assessing the degree to which program/project goals are achieved and overall effectiveness/ efficiency of work unit operations, to identify means for improving work unit performance.

The "How" of Management: Effectiveness Characteristics

13. Broad Perspective
    Broad, long-term view; balancing short- and long-term considerations.
14. Strategic View
    Collecting/assessing/analyzing information; diagnoses; anticipation; judgment.
15. Environmental Sensitivity
    "Tuned into" agency and its environment; awareness of importance of non-technical factors.
16. Leadership
    Individual; group; willingness to lead and manage, and accept responsibility.
17. Flexibility
    Openness to new information; behavioral flexibility; tolerance for stress/ambiguity/change; innovativeness.
18. Action Orientation
    Independence, proactivity; calculated risk-taking; problem solving; decisiveness.
19. Results Focus
    Concern with goal achievement; follow through, tenacity.
20. Communication
    Speaking; writing; listening.
21. Interpersonal Sensitivity
    Self-knowledge and awareness of impact on others; sensitivity to needs/strengths/weaknesses of others; negotiation; conflict resolution; persuasion.

Source: From "The Management Excellence Inventory: A Tool for Management," by L.R. Flanders and D. Utterback, 1985, *Public Administration Review*, 45 (3), p. 405.

Because the MEI was constructed using information from job incumbents, it possesses face and content validity. Additional independent studies were used to cross-validate the instrument. Cronbach-alpha tests showed high reliability, ranging from .6 to .8 (Flanders and Utterback 1985). Since the purpose of the MEI was to address managerial effectiveness, validation did not substantially focus on male and female differences. Therefore, the MEI's structure reflects the predominantly male managerial world of the 1980s.

Nevertheless, the MSPB used the MEI to develop three questionnaires to assess the quality of first-line supervisors. First-line supervisors, their subordinates, and their supervisors were asked to rate the importance of the 118 tasks of management and how well the first-line supervisor him or herself performs them. The set of surveys was designed to give a 360-degree view of the tasks of management. In other words, the performance of the first-line supervisor was evaluated in a more complete manner than the traditional top-down view in that the performance of first-line supervisors was rated from three perspectives: their own self-appraisal, their employees' subordinate appraisals, and their second-line supervisors' "traditional" appraisal. For this study, which is interested in whether male and female first-line supervisors rate the importance and their performance of the tasks differently, only the responses from the first-line supervisors are used.

Because the study also addressed special managerial concerns regarding supply clerks/technicians (GS-2005) and accountants (GS-510), a stratified sampling frame was used to insure sufficient respondents in these categories. The Central Personnel Data file (CPDF) was employed to sample 500 non-supervisory employees and 1,500 first-line supervisors in each of the three job stratums (i.e., supply clerks/technicians, accountants, and all others). A total of 2533 out of 4500 first-line supervisor (56 percent) questionnaires were returned. Since we are not concerned with the supply clerk/technician and accountant aspects of the MSPB investigation, the first-line supervisor sample ($N = 2533$) is adjusted to reflect the appropriate general population proportions for the federal job series. Supply clerk/technician and accountant categories respectively make up roughly 1 and 2 percent of federal supervisors; the remaining category encompasses some 97 percent of all supervisors. Responses in each occupational category were weighted by these percentages. These adjustments, while retaining all cases, reduce the weighted sample to the equivalent of 950 first-line supervisors. This weighted sample divides (factoring in missing values) into 646 (70 percent) male and 276 (30 percent) female supervisors.

Each of the 21 indices representing management functions and effectiveness characteristics is made up of 3 to 18 individual items (for a total of 118 items). These items represent tasks which first-line supervisors were asked to rate along two dimensions. The first dimension was the extent to which the supervisor believes each task (management functions and effectiveness characteristics are not distinguished in the survey) is important for performing his or her job on a scale ranging from 1 (to no extent) to 5 (to a very great extent). Responses indicating that they do not perform the task, or that they "can't judge" its importance is coded as missing. The second dimension was the respondent's own rating of his or her ability to perform each task, using a scale ranging from 1 (cannot do this task at an acceptable level) to 5 (can do this task exceptionally well). Those marking a 6th choice (can't judge) is coded as missing.

The attitudes that constitute this analysis are unlikely to be transient. They tap central and important concepts that are the foundation of an individual's job (and, hence, personal) identity.

Whereas the MSPB (1992b) analysis focuses on the specific items, this study uses their broad-based, composite indexes. Each index was constructed in two steps. First, the individual items were summed (excluding missing values and "Can't Judge" responses). Second, this summary score was divided by a count of the total number of items without missing values (to adjust for the specific number of items to which an individual had responded). This two-step procedure prevents the exclusion of a respondent from the analysis if one of the index items were to register a missing value (as occurs when using an additive index). Virtually identical results are obtained from analysis conducted using a more restrictive additive index that discarded all cases with missing values.

In this analysis, index scores, rather than ratings on individual tasks, are used as dependent variables. The overall means from these indexes were used to construct a general ranking for the twenty-one indexes for perceived performance level and for importance. Indexes were ranked on the basis of the numeric value of their mean scores. Individuals were not directly asked to comparatively assess these twenty-one functions and effectiveness characteristics (or their constituent items).

Findings and Discussion

Men's and Women's Self-Assessments

Previous research has consistently provided evidence that both men and women have doubts about whether women can effectively perform the tasks of management (Schein 1973; Ezell, Odewahn and Sherman 1980; Dubno 1985; Heilman, Block, Martell and Simon 1989) and that, possibly as a result of these doubts, women sometimes lack confidence in their own job performance (Jackson, Gardner and Sullivan 1992; Terborg 1977; Ezell, Odewahn and Sherman 1980). Table 21.1 displays men's and women's mean ratings and rankings of their own performance for each of the 21 management functions and effectiveness characteristics.

Overall, men and women display equal (and a high degree of) confidence in their ability to perform the functions and effectiveness characteristics of management. Their rankings are, in general, similar with a Spearman rank-order correlation of .95. Both rated coordination, communication, and leadership as the top three kinds of tasks they are best at performing. In only two areas did women rate themselves significantly lower than men—work unit planning (estimating needed resources and their projected allocation) and budgeting (financial forecasting and cost accounting)—and even men's self-ratings on budgeting were, on average, the lowest of all 21 indices. These results indicate that despite the findings of previous researchers, women who are first-line supervisors in the federal government do not have less confidence in their own ability to perform the tasks of management than men.

Table 21.1

How Well Performed Are Management Functions and Effectiveness Characteristics? Index Mean (Ranking[1])

	General		Men		Women	
Functions						
External awareness	3.99	(18)	4.00	(18)	3.97	(17.5)
Interpretation	4.18	(5.5)	4.16	(6.5)	4.22	(6)
Representation	4.17	(7)	4.16	(6.5)	4.20	(8)
Coordination	4.30	(1)	4.29	(1)	4.34	(1)
Wu planning*	4.04	(15)	4.08	(13)	3.94	(19)
Wu guidance	4.18	(5.5)	4.16	(6.5)	4.23	(5)
Budgeting*	3.86	(21)	3.93	(21)	3.65	(21)
Material resources	3.95	(20)	3.96	(19.5)	3.91	(20)
Personnel	4.07	(14)	4.06	(15)	4.09	(13)
Supervision	4.15	(9.5)	4.13	(10)	4.21	(7)
Wu monitoring	4.09	(13)	4.07	(14)	4.13	(11)
Program evaluation	3.96	(19)	3.96	(19.5)	3.97	(17.5)
Effectiveness characteristics						
Broad perspective	4.01	(17)	4.01	(17)	4.02	(15)
Strategic view	4.10	(12)	4.11	(12)	4.06	(14)
Environmental sensitivity	4.03	(16)	4.04	(16)	4.01	(16)
Leadership	4.28	(2)	4.27	(2)	4.28	(3)
Flexibility	4.22	(4)	4.21	(4)	4.25	(4)
Action orientation	4.13	(11)	4.12	(11)	4.16	(10)
Results focus	4.16	(8)	4.15	(9)	4.18	(9)
Communication	4.26	(3)	4.25	(3)	4.29	(2)
Interpersonal	4.15	(9.5)	4.16	(6.5)	4.12	(12)

Note: Spearman's rank-order correlation $rs = .95$.

*F-test for male/female difference of means $p < .05$.

[1]In case of ties the median ranking is assigned. For example, two scales tied for second and third place would both be assigned a ranking of 2.5. In the case of three scales tied for ninth, tenth, and eleventh, a ranking of 10 would be assigned on all three.

Men's and Women's Views as to the Importance of Management Functions and Effectiveness Characteristics

Recent literature concerning women in management has suggested that women have a different approach to management than men that emphasizes the importance of non-hierarchical coach and coordinate work structures, teamwork and cooperation, and sharing power and information (Edlund 1993; Rosener 1990; Rosen and Jerdee 1995; Hegelson 1990). If this is the case, differences should be apparent in how men and women rate the importance of various tasks of, and approaches to, management. Table 21.2 displays the mean scores and rankings of the 21 indices measuring federal first-line supervisors' importance ratings.

Male and female respondents clearly believe that, overall, indices measuring management effectiveness are more important than those measuring the performance of specific functions. Male-female agreement on rankings records a Spearman rank-order correlation of .98. Six of the nine indices measuring effectiveness (communication, leadership,

Table 21.2

**How Important Are Management Functions and Effectiveness Characteristics?
Index Mean** (Ranking[1])

	General		Men		Women	
Functions						
External awareness*	4.01	(15)	3.98	(15.5)	4.08	(15)
Interpretation*	4.15	(9)	4.08	(9.5)	4.33	(7.5)
Representation*	3.95	(17)	3.92	(17.5)	4.02	(16.5)
Coordination*	4.34	(3)	4.31	(3)	4.41	(3.5)
Wu planning*	3.87	(19)	3.92	(18.5)	3.76	(19)
Wu guidance*	4.16	(8)	4.10	(8)	4.31	(9)
Budgeting*	3.62	(21)	3.71	(20)	3.35	(21)
Material resources	3.67	(20)	3.66	(21)	3.69	(20)
Personnel*	4.06	(13)	3.99	(13.5)	4.21	(12)
Supervision*	4.14	(10)	4.08	(9.5)	4.29	(10)
Wu monitoring*	4.06	(13)	3.99	(13.5)	4.22	(11)
Program evaluation*	3.93	(18)	3.89	(19)	4.02	(16.5)
Effectiveness characteristics						
Broad perspective*	4.06	(13)	4.02	(12)	4.15	(14)
Strategic view*	4.09	(11)	4.06	(11)	4.16	(13)
Environmental sensitivity	3.99	(16)	3.98	(15.5)	4.00	(18)
Leadership*	4.36	(2)	4.32	(2)	4.44	(1.5)
Flexibility*	4.30	(4)	4.25	(4)	4.41	(3.5)
Action orientation*	4.27	(5)	4.23	(5)	4.37	(5)
Results focus*	4.24	(6)	4.20	(6)	4.34	(6)
Communication	4.41	(1)	4.39	(1)	4.44	(1.5)
Interpersonal*	4.22	(7)	4.17	(7)	4.33	(7.5)

Note: Spearman's rank-order correlation $rs = .98$.

*F-test for male/female difference of means $p < .05$.

[1]In case of ties the median ranking is assigned. For example, two scales tied for second and third place would both be assigned a ranking of 2.5. In the case of three scales tied for ninth, tenth, and eleventh, a ranking of 10 would be assigned to all three.

flexibility, action orientation, results focus, and interpersonal sensitivity) are ranked among the most important or top tasks performed by managers. However, only one index representing managerial functions—coordination—is included among the top seven. This is consistent with MSPB's item-based finding that ten of the fourteen tasks that 85 percent or more of supervisors rated as being important to a considerable or great extent represented effectiveness rather than functions (MSPB 1992b, 10). Overall then, it seems that federal first-line supervisors find how they approach supervision to be of greater importance than the specific functions they are required to do as supervisors. Men's and women's agreement, in general, on what is important about their job is also reflected in the similarity in how the tasks were ranked in their minds.

Having said that, it should be clear that there were significant differences between men and women in the average importance rating given nearly every index represented in the survey (17 out of 21—see Table 21.2). In most cases, women simply rated these items as more important than men did, while their relative importance, as demonstrated in the rankings, remained about the same for men as women. That women rate most of the management tasks as more important than men may be a reflection of having less tenure as supervisors, overall, resulting in less experience by which to evaluate what is really important and what is not. It may also reflect the greater availability of mentoring social networks (or good old boy buddy systems) for male managers. Social networks and mentoring can serve to provide subjective assessments which substitute for or reduce the importance of objective management functions and effectiveness characteristics (Daley 1996). Exceptions to this pattern are work unit planning and budgeting, which, on average, women rated as less important than men did. Recall that these are also the tasks for which women's self-performance rating was also lower than men's were.

Finally, in order to assess whether male and female first-line supervisors best perform the tasks they see as most important (the basis for many performance appraisal ratings), an importance-performance measure was developed by multiplying the importance attached to a task by the supervisor's self-performance rating (not shown). Overall results indicated that the importance-performance rankings were positively correlated (Spearman rank-order correlation = .96) and demonstrated the same patterns for men and women reported in Table 21.2. Both men and women direct their effort at what they mutually deem to be the important tasks of management.

Conclusion

This study sought to shed light on two issues that have been the subject of much debate in recent years: (1) do women display less confidence than men in their ability to perform managerial tasks; and, (2) do women and men place the same importance on the various functions of, and approaches to, management? These questions are particularly important at a time when women are rapidly increasing their representation in supervisory jobs, and when management theorists are calling for new ways to manage (or "lead") the workforce.

Survey responses showed little differences between the way female and male first-line supervisors in the federal government rate their own performance on, and the importance of, the many supervisory tasks for which they are responsible. Overall, both sets of supervisors rated their performance of the tasks as represented by twelve functional indices and nine indices measuring management effectiveness as above average, and the importance of the same tasks as important at least to some extent. There were only two differences found between men and women in the specific ratings they provided: (1) women rated both the importance of, and their performance of, tasks related to work unit planning and budgeting lower than men; and (2) women gave higher ratings to their performance of instrumental goal interpretation and program implementation than men did. Women also tended to place greater importance on nearly all of the twenty-one management functions and characteristics than men did.

The similarity in performance ratings certainly suggests that women are as confident as men are in their ability to supervise their workforces. This is an encouraging finding, particularly in light of previous research which found that women often doubt their own abilities in managerial roles (Heilman, Block, Martell and Simon 1989; Naff 1994; Jackson, Gardner and Sullivan 1992; Terborg 1977; Ezell, Odewahn and Sherman 1980).

These findings, particularly those suggesting that men and women show little differ-ence in the way they rate the importance of the management tasks, could lend support to the theory that women and men in fact exhibit little or no difference in the way they approach management (Morrison, White and van Velsor 1987; Rizzo and Mendez 1988; Powell 1988, 1990; Lynn and Vaden 1977; Duerst-Lahti and Johnson 1992). It could also be the case that a difference would have been apparent if differences in the situations in which these supervisors find themselves could have been taken into account (Harriman 1996; Guy 1992). Such situational aspects (e.g., the nature of the work they are supervis-ing, the organization's culture, their work-related experiences) unfortunately could not be assessed given the nature and composition of the survey instrument.

It has also been suggested that differences between male and female managers are less likely where they have been subject to uniform selection and training methods (Eagly and Johnson 1990). Although first-line federal supervisors generally receive little effective training (Rusaw 1994), they do tend to be selected through fairly generic methods (MSPB 1989). Since the questionnaire did not ask supervisors about how they were selected or the training they had received, this hypothesis could not be tested.

Finally, it could be that the very structure of the bureaucracy has developed along masculine lines (Stivers 1993), leaving little room for a uniquely female approach to be considered by women in pursuit of managerial jobs. Moreover, the instrument itself may reflect a male profile that does not allow for a particular female perspective to emerge because the Management Excellence Inventory that formed the basis of this survey was developed through surveys and interviews with incumbent federal managers, the vast majority of whom were men. In other words, the analysis originally performed by the instrument developers found relationships among the various tasks that were then used to construct the indices that served as the dependent variables in our analysis. It is pos-sible that had indices been constructed based on women's conceptions of management (or women and men's combined conception of management), they would have formed different constructs, and differences between women and men would have been more apparent.

These findings, though necessarily tentative, do have implications for several human resource functions, including training, selection, and career development. While current management literature anticipates that traditional supervisory roles will be replaced by team leaders and "coaches" who facilitate, guide, and enable rather than direct work (Boyett and Conn 1991), many of the functions and effectiveness characteristics rated as important in this study are consistent with this concept. A willingness to lead, a capacity to communicate effectively, and the ability to effectively integrate work unit activities are among the proficiencies that will become even more important for team leaders and members to acquire as organizations become flatter and the workforce becomes more empowered and self-managed.

Although in no case were the self-performance ratings especially low, those responsible for developing training programs for new supervisors or team leaders should certainly take note of the areas where men and women tended to rate their own performance as relatively poorer. While these self-ratings do not confirm that their performance really is poorer with respect to these functions, they do suggest these as areas where current supervisors may lack complete self-confidence. For example, in terms of management functions, both men and women gave themselves comparatively low marks in budgeting and administering material resources. Given the enduring era of resource scarcity in which the government finds itself, it might be worth focusing more attention on providing those in leadership positions with training in these skills. It would seem that women might also benefit from training in work unit planning, including how to develop longer-term goals and priorities and strategies for deciding among alternative courses of action.

The findings with respect to importance ratings provide cues as to how selection decisions should be made. Male and female supervisors rated communication, leadership, and coordination to be the most important functions and characteristics of their jobs. It would seem worthwhile to ensure that applicants for higher level jobs be evaluated for their proficiency in these areas. Selecting officials should also be assured despite literature that suggests women are often thought to be less capable as managers (e.g., Schein 1973, 1989; Ezwell, Odewahn and Sherman 1980; Dubno 1985), and that they are better suited to management in today's environment (e.g., Russell Reynolds and Associates 1990; Rosener 1990). Women and men gave equivalent ratings to the importance of and their performance of these tasks. The importance-performance measure developed in this study has implications for the design of career development programs because it links the functions and characteristics that incumbent supervisors rate as important with their assessment of their own performance in these areas. The results of this analysis showed that not only do supervisors rate leadership, coordination and communication as among the most important aspects of their jobs, but they rate highly their own performance in these areas. It would be useful for those seeking to fashion career development programs to learn from these supervisors how they were able to develop these skills, and then to ensure the acquisition of these skills is central to the management development plan.

Further research is required to definitively support or dismiss the findings of this study. A next step would be to develop a survey instrument, validated for women as well as men, that also includes questions about the work environment, the means by which the respondents were recruited and trained for their supervisory jobs, and any other factors (besides gender) thought to influence managerial style. Because the emerging organizational environment demands a very different managerial approach than has been required in the past (Boyett and Conn 1991), it would be particularly timely to reexamine the tasks associated with the "what" and "how" of management.

References

Amason, A.C. 1996. "Distinguishing the Effects of Functional and Dysfunctional Conflict on Strategic Decision Making: Resolving a Paradox for Top Management Teams." *Academy of Management Journal,* 39 (1), 123–48.

Bartlett, C.A. and Ghoshal, S. 1995a. "Changing the Role of Top Management: Beyond Structure to Process." *Harvard Business Review,* 73 (1), 86–96.

Bartlett, C.A. and Ghoshal, S. 1995b. "Changing the Role of Top Management: Beyond Systems to People." *Harvard Business Review,* 73 (3), 132–42.

Bayes, J. 1991. "Women in Public Administration in the United States." *Women and Politics,* 11 (4), 85–109.

Boyett, J.H. and Conn, H.P. 1991. *Workplace 2000: The Revolution Reshaping American Business.* New York: Penguin Group.

Brenner, O., Tomkiewicz, J. and Schein, V.E. 1989. "The Relationship Between Sex Role Stereotypes and Requisite Management Characteristics Revisited." *Academy of Management Journal,* 32 (3), 662–69.

Calas, M.B. and Smircich, L. 1993. "Dangerous Liaisons: The 'Feminine-in-Management' Meets 'Globalization.'" *Business Horizons,* 36, 71–81.

Cannings, K. and Montmarquette, C. 1991. "Managerial Momentum: A Simultaneous Model of the Career Progress of Male and Female Managers." *Industrial and Labor Relations Review,* 44 (2), 212–28.

Daley, D.M. 1996. "Paths of Glory and the Glass Ceiling: Differing Patterns of Career Advancement Among Women and Minority Federal Employees." *Public Administration Quarterly,* 20 (2), 143–62.

Department of Labor. 1991. *A Report on the Glass Ceiling Initiative.* Washington, DC: U.S. Department of Labor.

Dubno, P. 1985. "Attitudes Toward Women Executives: A Longitudinal Approach." *Academy of Management Journal,* 28 (1), 235–39.

Duerst-Lahti, G. and Johnson, C.M. 1992. "Management Styles, Stereotypes, and Advantages." In M.E. Guy (ed.), *Women and Men of the States.* Armonk, NY: M.E. Sharpe.

Dugan, B. et al. 1993. *The Glass Ceiling: Potential Causes and Possible Solutions.* Alexandria, VA: Human Resources Research Organization.

Eagly, A.H. and Johnson, B.T. 1990. "Gender and Leadership Style: A Meta-Analysis." *Psychological Bulletin,* 108 (2), 233–56.

Edlund, C.J. 1993. "Learning from Women's Leadership Styles: Female Public Managers." Paper presented to the annual meeting of the American Society for Public Administration, San Francisco, July 17–21.

Ezell, H.E. Odewahn, C.A. and Sherman, J.D. 1980. "Perceived Competence of Women Managers in Public Human Service Organizations: A Comparative View." *Journal of Management,* 6 (2), 135–144.

Fine, M.G., Johnson, F.L. and Ryan, M.S. 1990. "Cultural Diversity in the Workplace." *Public Personnel Management,* 19 (3), 305–19.

Flanders, L.R. and Utterback, D. 1985. "The Management Excellence Inventory: A Tool for Management." *Public Administration Review,* 45 (3), 403–10.

Gallese, L. 1991, April. "Why Women Aren't Making It to the Top." *Across the Board,* 1822.

Garvin, D.A. 1995. "Leveraging Processes for Strategic Advantage." *Harvard Business Review,* 73 (5), 77–90.

Gilligan, C. 1982. *In a Different Voice.* Cambridge: Harvard University Press.

Guy, M.E. 1992. "The Feminization of Public Administration: Today's Reality and Tomorrow's Promise." In M.T. Bailey and R.T. Mayer (eds.), *Public Management in an Interconnected World.* New York: Greenwood Press.

Guy, M.E. 1993. "Two Steps Forward, Two Steps Backward: The Status of Women's Integration into Public Management." *Public Administration Review,* 53 (4), 285–92.

Guy, M.E. 1994. "Organizational Architecture, Gender, and Women's Careers." *Review of Public Personnel Administration,* 14 (2), 77–90.

Harriman, A. 1996. *Women/Men/Management.* Westport, CT: Praeger.

Heilman, M.E., Block, C., Martell, R.E., and Simon, M. 1989. "Has Anything Changed? Current Characterizations of Men, Women, and Managers." *Journal of Applied Psychology,* 74 (6), 935–42.

Hegelson, S. 1990. *The Female Advantage.* New York: Doubleday Currency.

Hyde, A.C. 1997. "Managing Change—Changing Management: Rethinking the Roles of Public Executives." *The Public Manager,* 26 (1), 7–12.

Jackson, L.A., Gardner, P.D. and Sullivan, L.A. 1992. "Explaining Gender Differences in Self-Pay Expectations: Social Comparison Standards and Perceptions of Self Pay." *Journal of Applied Psychology,* 77 (5), 651–63.

Kanter, R.M. 1977. *Men and Women of the Corporation.* New York: Basic Books.

Kelly, R.M. 1991. *The Gendered Economy.* Newbury Park, CA: Sage.

Lewis, G.B. 1992. "Men and Women Toward the Top: Backgrounds, Careers, and Potential of Federal Middle Managers." *Public Personnel Management,* 21 (4), 473–85.

Lewis, G.B. 1986. "Gender and Promotions: Promotion Chances of White Men and Women in Federal White-Collar Employment." *Journal of Human Resources,* 21 (3), 406–19.

Lynn, N.B. and Vaden, R.E. 1979, July/August. "Toward a Non-Sexist Personnel Opportunity Structure: The Federal Executive Bureaucracy." *Public Personnel Management,* 209–15.

Merit Systems Protection Board. 1992a. *A Question of Equity: Women and the Glass Ceiling in the Federal Government.* Washington, DC: U.S. Merit Systems Protection Board.

Merit Systems Protection Board. 1992b. *Federal First-Line Supervisors: How Good Are They?* Washington, DC: U.S. Merit Systems Protection Board.

Morrison, A.M., White, R.P. and van Velsor, E. 1987. *Breaking the Glass Ceiling: Can Women Reach the Top of America's Largest Corporations.* Reading, MA: Addison-Wesley.

Naff, K.C. 1994. "Through the Glass Ceiling: Prospects for the Advancement of Women in the Federal Civil Service." *Public Administration Review,* 54 (6), 507–14.

Naff, K.C. and Thomas, S. 1994. "The Glass Ceiling Revisited: Determinant of Federal Job Advancement." *Policy Studies Review,* 13, (34), 249–69.

National Performance Review. 1993, September 7. *From Red Tape to Results: Creating a Government That Works Better and Costs Less.* Washington, DC: Office of the Vice President.

Newman, M.A. 1993. "Career Advancement: Does Gender Make a Difference?" *American Review of Public Administration,* 23 (4), 361–84.

Office of the Secretary of War 1943. *You're Going to Employ Women.* Washington, DC: U.S. Government Printing Office.

Powell, G.N. 1988. *Women and Men in Management.* Newbury Park, CA: Sage.

Powell, G.N. 1990. "One More Time: Do Female and Male Managers Differ?" *Academy of Management Executive* 4 (3), 68–75.

Rizzo, A.M. and Mendez, C. 1988. "Making Things Happen in Organizations: Does Gender Make a Difference?" *Public Personnel Management,* 17 (1), 9–20.

Rosen, B. and Jerdee, T.H. 1995. *The Persistence of Age and Sex Stereotypes in the 1990s.* Public Policy Institute Issue Brief. Washington, DC: American Association of Retired Persons.

Rosener, J.B. 1990. "Ways Women Lead." *Harvard Business Review,* 63 (6), 119–25.

Rusaw, A.C. 1994, Summer. "Mobility for Federal Women Managers: Is Training Enough?" *Public Personnel Management,* 23 (2), 257–62.

Russell Reynolds and Associates, Inc. 1990. *Men, Women, and Leadership.* New York: Russell Reynolds Associates, Inc.

Schein, V.E. 1973. "The Relationship Between Sex Role Stereotypes and Requisite Management Characteristics." *Journal of Applied Psychology,* 60, 95–100.

Shank, S.E. 1988, March. "Women and the Labor Market: The Link Grows Stronger." *Monthly Labor Review,* 3–8.

Stewart, D.W. 1990. "Women in Public Administration." In N.B. Lynn and A. Wildavsky (eds.), *Public Administration: The State of the Discipline.* Chatham, NJ: Chatham House.

Stivers, C. 1993. *Gender Images in Public Administration.* Newbury Park: Sage.

Terborg, J.R. 1977. "Women in Management: A Research Review." *Journal of Applied Psychology,* 62 (6), 647–64.

Vertz, L.L. 1985. "Women, Occupational Advancement, and Mentoring: An Analysis of One Public Organization." *Public Administration Review,* 45 (3), 415–23.

CHAPTER 22

THE COST OF NOT LISTENING TO EMPLOYEES

The Case of a Union Movement at Bradford Hospital

R. WAYNE BOSS, LESLEE BOSS, AND JAMES A. JOHNSON

Accurate information is an essential component of effective management. In order to get the necessary information, managers need lots of help, particularly from their employees, and the best way to get that help is to listen to them. By listening we mean, at the very least, hearing information, analyzing it, recalling it at a later time, drawing conclusions from it, and then doing something about it. Listening is an important part of the communication process. When managers stop listening, employees often respond by not communicating, leading to great difficulty for the organization by shutting down internal communications. Furthermore, as stated by Boss (1989), "Leaders must be willing to listen to their people, both intellectually and emotionally, and to respond to what they hear. Some problems require nothing more than a listening ear. Others necessitate immediate action. Whatever the need, it is important that the leader give people what they need to grow and develop."

This case describes the problems faced by a hospital in which the managers and supervisors stopped listening to their employees. In the mid-1980s, the reorganization of services for patients and a falling patient census posed serious challenges to management. The hospital authorities responded with a series of decisions about staffing that eventually led the hospital's nurses to seek union representation. Though management "successfully" resisted the nurses' attempt to unionize, the cost was enormous in terms of time, energy, credibility in the medical community, and money. Those who spearheaded the union movement later maintained that they never would have requested union representation had their leaders listened to their concerns.

Background

Bradford Hospital, a 200-bed regional medical center with 1,100 employees, is located in the southeastern part of the United States. For years it had been plagued with commu-

From *Journal of Health and Human Resources Administration*, vol. 13, no. 1 (Summer 1990): 71–80. Copyright © 1990 by Southern Public Administration Education Foundation, Inc. Reprinted with permission.

nication problems and authoritarian leadership. In the fall of 1985, the hospital's Chief Operating Officer (COO) of six years was appointed Chief Executive Officer (CEO) and expectations for improvement significantly increased. In June 1986 he accepted the resignation of the Vice President for Patient Care Services, a nurse who had held that position for fifteen years and had a reputation as a tight-fisted autocrat who ruled by fear. Her position was filled six months later. Between the time of her resignation and the appointment of her successor eight months later, the nursing services responsibilities were shared by the Director of Maternal Child Care, the Director of Critical Care, and the Director of Surgery. These three reported directly to the new CEO and were told to run their areas with as little outside assistance as possible.

The implementation of diagnostic related groups (DRGs) caused such serious problems for the hospital that in late 1986 the administration laid off 200 people including a number of qualified RNs and LPNs. The result was a great deal of turmoil throughout the nursing services department. The layoff of the LPNs was particularly problematic since the RNs had to assume the duties of the LPNs.

Since work assignments had to be readjusted to cover the LPN duties and since there was also a surplus of RNs, the nursing administration required all RNs to reapply for their jobs. The final decision on staff assignments were based on seniority, and employees hired before 1986 had a choice of jobs throughout the hospital. To provide jobs for all the RNs, the nursing administration cut back the number of hours each RN worked and assigned some to undesirable shifts.

Shortly thereafter the patient census dropped and nurses were sent home for several weeks because of overstaffing. Since employees in other departments were not sent home, the nurses resented what they perceived as unfair treatment and were angry that they had been singled out to carry the burden of the low census. The administrators ignored these complaints and argued that only in the nursing division did they have the flexibility to adjust quickly.

Job Assignments and Nurse Reactions

Since job assignments were based primarily on seniority, some people were assigned to work undesirable shifts in areas for which they had no training. Take Sally, a part-time maternity nurse, who had been working two eight-hour night shifts per week. When she was bumped from her position by someone who had more seniority but no maternity experience and reassigned to work from 5:00–9:00 P.M. Monday through Thursday on the medical/surgical floor, she was irate. The new schedule made it impossible for her to fulfill her responsibilities as a single parent with three elementary school children and also forced her to work in an area in which she had received virtually no training. When Sally asked the reasons for the reassignment, she was told that the change was made to help another nurse continue working full-time. Furthermore, if Sally did not like the change, she could quit.

When Sally phoned the state nursing association and inquired about the legality of the hospital changing both her schedule and position, she learned that four other nurses had made similar calls. During the next week, these five met with an association representative.

Meanwhile, the nurses in the maternity area were concerned about patient care, staffing, and how the unit was managed. Each time they spoke privately with Cathy, the head nurse, she gave the same pat answers: "I'll look into it," "That's just the way things are," or "We can't do anything about it." When they talked to Lucy, the Director of Maternal-Child Care and Cathy's boss, they got the same answers. Simply put, the leaders refused to listen and made no response to the nurses' requests.

Organization of the "Maternity Task Force"

Since their one-to-one approach had failed, Sally and her four colleagues decided to confront Cathy in a group setting. In early February, they organized themselves into a maternity task force, called a meeting at the home of one of the nurses, and invited Cathy and the rest of the maternity nurses. Cathy refused to participate. On the other hand, all but two of the available RNs attended—a marked contrast to normal department meetings in which no more than five nurses participated.

Predictably, the staff nurses used this meeting as a forum to vent their frustrations and hostile feelings. They then decided that a positive approach would get them more mileage so they tried to be as constructive as possible. They listed their problems, set priorities, and suggested two or three alternative solutions, at least one of which cost no money. To build commitment and test out their solutions, the task force circulated the proposal to all their maternity RNs for approval. Their issues included the following items:

- The nurses were short staffed due to the higher census and shortage of nurses.
- The nurses were required to float to areas for which they had no technical training, and they were concerned about patient safety.
- The nurses were afraid that they might lose their license if a patient was harmed because they were forced to work in an area for which they had no training.
- The nurses felt neither valued nor appreciated, and the main reason for these feelings was that their leader refused to listen to their concerns.

In early March when the proposal was completed, the task force members invited Cathy to a meeting to discuss the problems. Lucy had not been invited, but came anyway. Her stated purpose was to support Cathy in this difficult process and to "get those nurses in line." Cathy and Lucy immediately took charge of the meeting and proposed that each nurse tell what she thought was the problem. When the nurses explained that they had already done that, Lucy said, "That's tough, because you are going to have to do it again."

As an alternative, the nurses suggested that one or two RNs review the process they had used to identify their concerns, describe the problems, and explain their alternative solutions. Lucy told them that she would not listen to one or two nurses because it was too much like a union. She said, "We will never have a union at this hospital."

To placate their leaders, the nurses agreed to take turns identifying problems and suggesting solutions. At the conclusion of each presentation, Cathy and Lucy said, "Fine" and then went on to the next person. They made no comments, took no notes, and made no commitments to action. The meeting was a disaster. Cathy and Lucy felt attacked by the united front the nurses presented and by the accusation that working conditions were undesirable. The nurses, on the other hand, felt ignored and devalued by the lack of attention paid to their concerns. They were particularly insulted when Lucy said, "We are the leaders and we will make the decisions. It is your job to carry them out, and you will do it if you want to continue to work here."

Two weeks later a second meeting was set up. Cathy came with a list of problems which included a few of the maternity task force items and asked for volunteers to work on each one. Reluctantly, the nurses signed up. Cathy herself refused to participate, stating that she was too busy with administrative duties to spend time on departmental problems. Besides, the resolution of the problems needed to be a group effort. In short she wanted the RNs to do all the work and she would then determine if their work was acceptable. The nurses felt ignored and insulted. One week later, Cathy resigned, stating that she could not stand the pressure.

In mid-April the labor/delivery and maternity units were combined. Judy, the clinical nurse manager for labor/delivery who became responsible for both units, had no experience working in maternity. Two days after the merger was announced, members of the maternity task force asked to meet with Judy. Judy agreed only to talk with each member alone which solidified the nurses' perception that she intended to ignore their concerns. During each meeting she took no notes and made no commitments to address their issues. The task force concluded that she had not listened to them and that no action would be taken.

Final Straws

Three additional incidents broke the camel's back and insured a request for union representation. The first took place in early May, two weeks after the merger of maternity and labor/delivery, the second and third followed shortly thereafter.

Susan, an outstanding nurse who had been with the hospital for three years, was left alone with a graduate nurse on the nurse's first day of work. The two were expected to care for sixteen patients, half of whom had just delivered babies. Then Judy asked Susan to send the new graduate to the labor and delivery area to help out. At that point, Susan confronted Judy about what she saw as irresponsible behavior. An argument ensued and Judy agreed to let the new nurse remain with Susan. The next day, however, Judy called Susan into her office and demanded that they discuss the matter. Susan, still angry, asked that they postpone the conversation until a later time when she felt more in control. One hour later Susan was called back into Judy's office for a disciplinary meeting with Judy and Lucy.

Lucy began the meeting by taking Susan to task for insubordinate behavior. Rather than asking Susan to explain her side of the story, Lucy gave her a three-day suspension, put her on probation for three months, scheduled her to get help with the employee assistance program to learn to deal with her anger, and ordered her to leave the hospital. In taking this action, Lucy contravened hospital policy which dictated that a person receive a verbal warning for the first offense, suspension for the third offense, and probation for the fourth offense.

Although Susan said nothing to anyone about the meeting, word of the suspension spread immediately throughout the hospital. Within minutes calls were coming in to the maternity unit; Susan received a dozen calls from people who thought she had been treated unfairly. A pediatrician and an obstetrician, who had observed the initial confrontation between Judy and Susan, wrote letters supporting Susan.

On the following Monday, Susan met with Pat, the new Vice President of Patient Care Services. Pat was supportive, but decided that, if she reversed Judy's decision, Judy would never have a chance to succeed in her position. So Pat let the decision stand. But she told Susan that the disciplinary record would be removed from her personnel file at the end of the three-month probation if there were no further incidents.

Susan saw this as a compromise and agreed to go along with the decision. The other maternity nurses, however, saw Pat's action as additional evidence of administrative unfairness and incompetence. Susan had an impeccable record; her evaluation at the end of her first six months of service was the highest that had been given in the history of the hospital and her subsequent performance evaluations were outstanding. Judy already had a reputation as a hard-nosed manager and the incident reinforced the perception that "You don't cross Judy or you will be sorry!" Furthermore, since the nurses had been told they would be fired if they approached Pat, they were powerless. In short, the nurses concluded that they could get no help from the nursing administrators and needed representation from someone outside the hospital.

Two additional incidents confirmed that conclusion. When a seasoned maternity nurse was ordered to "float" to the oncology floor, she refused because she had no technical competence in that area. Although this was her first offense, she was given written warning. The next day an outstanding labor and delivery nurse with more than twenty years' experience at the hospital was also asked to float to the oncology floor. When she refused because of her lack of experience and training in that area, Lucy ordered her to go anyway. The nurse resigned on the spot and started work the next morning at the competing hospital.

NLRB Petitioned

Two days later, the maternity nurses began collecting signatures to petition the National Labor Relations Board (NLRB) for permission to vote for union representation. Within one week they collected the number required, the NLRB intervened, and a vote was scheduled. When the petition arrived, the administration was taken completely off guard. They had no idea that anything was wrong in the nursing department and that the RNs were dissatisfied.

However, as soon as the petition was filed, the hospital administrators took immediate action. They immediately hired a consultant who had an excellent reputation as a union-buster and then retained the legal counsel of a firm with a national reputation in labor relations. They organized the department managers in all areas of the hospital and began a singularly focused campaign to keep the union out. Six months later, they successfully defeated the union by a three-to-one margin. The hospital administrator estimated the cost of the union effort to exceed $2.5 million actual costs ($500,000 in consulting and legal fees, $1.4 million in estimated labor costs, and-$600,000 in turnover among nurses).[1] There was also an additional $5 million in opportunity costs because of

- a 20–25 percent decrease in census during the twelve months after the official union movement began;
- a loss of credibility in the medical community, which two years later contributed to a nursing shortage at Bradford, while the competing hospital had a surplus of nurses;
- a loss of trust by the employees; and
- a loss of confidence in the community.

The irony of it all is that the entire problem could have been prevented if the line managers had paid more attention to their nurses and addressed their problems. As Sally later explained:

> We have never really wanted a union in the first place. We have the best financial and benefits package in the state. The physical conditions under which we work are excellent. We simply didn't like the way we were treated. It was an emotional issue, not an issue of fact.

Susan had similar observations:

> I knew at the outset that we didn't have the votes to win the election. In fact, we never had any intention of winning. But we wanted to make it absolutely clear to the administration that they could no longer refuse to listen to us and get away with it. When we go to them with problems, we expect them to listen to us and to treat us with respect. We are highly trained professionals, and most of us are at least as smart, if not smarter, than the administrators. We are not going to let them get away with treating us like children and refusing to pay attention to our concerns. Hopefully we will never have to go through something like this again. But if that is what it takes to get their attention, then it was worth the hassle. I hope they have learned their lesson.

Conclusion

Many factors contributed to the problems at Bradford, and it may never be possible to sort out the extent to which the layoff, the absence of leadership, the lowered census, and the governmental regulations played a role in the final outcome. However, one thing is certain. The nurses who initiated the union movement maintain that the major reason for soliciting outside help was that their leaders would not listen to them. Therefore, the only way they could get their attention was to solicit union representation.

Admittedly, the results cited in this case may be peculiar to Bradford Hospital and, therefore, the degree to which these findings may be generalized is questionable. However, one thing is clear: listening to employees is vital to successful organizations. When managers cease to listen to their people, regardless of the reason, the costs of this mistake can be enormous. Hospitals must begin to realize the value of their employees and acknowledge their importance to the organization. With the myriad changes occurring in health care and the subsequent demands placed on health service organizations there is an increasing need for attention to human resource planning, management, and development (Johnson 1988). As shown in this case, lack of attention to human resources will likely lead to difficulties and increased costs for the organization.

Note

1. Based on the replacement costs (recruitment, orientation, etc.) of one nurse at $20,000. See Droste, T. 1987. "High Price Tag on Nursing Recruitment." *Hospitals* (October 5): 150.

References

Boss, R.W. 1989. *Organization Development in Health Care.* Reading, MA: Addison-Wesley.

Johnson, J.A. 1988. "Human Resource Demands in a Changing Environment." *Journal of Health and Human Resources Administration* 10 (Spring): 331–35.

CHAPTER 23

LOOSE CANNONS AND RULE BREAKERS, OR ENTERPRISING LEADERS?

Some Evidence About Innovative Public Managers

SANDFORD BORINS

Introduction

One of the many controversial aspects of the New Public Management is its encouragement of public-sector entrepreneurship. In his review of Osborne and Gaebler's *Reinventing Government*, Goodsell (1993) points out that entrepreneurship could conflict with traditional values such as due process and accountability. In a seminal article defining the New Public Management, Hood (1991) notes that its emphasis on the values of economy and parsimony could come at the cost of the ethical values of honesty and fairness and the organizational values of robustness and resilience. Similarly, Jane Jacobs (1993) differentiates between commercial values and guardian, or traditional public-sector values, and argues that transposing one sector's values to another sector's institutions will lead to ethical lapses.

This theme has also been taken up in discussions of public-sector ethics. Gawthrop (1999) provides a number of cases that demonstrate an increasing preoccupation on the part of public servants with entrepreneurship, competition, efficiency, and performance management that could undercut values such as benevolence and justice. On the other hand, Cohen and Eimicke (1999) analyze a number of cases considered to be examples of failed public-sector entrepreneurship, and they conclude that the problems could have been avoided had the individuals involved followed simple ethical guidelines, such as "ensure thorough analysis" and "act with compassion and empathy." In their view, public-sector entrepreneurship should be encouraged, and the application of these ethical guidelines will mitigate any risk of increased corruption. Similarly, Kernaghan (2000) calls for the creation of governmentwide statements of key values that will incorporate both new values (service, innovation, quality) and traditional values (fairness, accountability, honesty) and will serve as the basis for ethical standards and training.

The pages of this journal have seen a particularly sharp debate over the merits of

From *Public Administration Review,* vol. 60, no. 6 (November/December 2000): 498–507. Copyright © 2000 by American Society for Public Administration. Reprinted with permission.

public-sector entrepreneurship. In the 1998 symposium on leadership, democracy, and the New Public Management, Terry (1998, 197) argued that public-sector entrepreneurs are obsessed with rule breaking, self-promotion, power politics, and risk taking, and concluded that their "penchant for rule-breaking and for manipulating public authority for private gain has been, and continues to be, a threat to democratic governance." On the other side, Behn (1998) felt that public servants should "exercise leadership about issues for which the elected chief [who is rightly concentrating on key priorities] either lacks the inclination or the time." The frequent failure of legislation to provide clear direction for public servants, coupled with other systemic failures, led him to urge public managers to display "leadership that takes astute initiatives designed to help the agency not only to achieve its purposes today but also to create new capacity to achieve its objectives tomorrow" (220). Recently, deLeon and Denhardt (2000, 92), following Terry, have claimed that public-sector entrepreneurs' "single-mindedness, tenacity, and willingness to bend the rules make them very difficult to control. They can become loose cannons."

One problem with this debate is that it has been conducted in the abstract or on the basis of a small number of examples given by either side of the laudatory or blameworthy behavior about which they generalize. DeLeon and Denhardt (2000, 92) do acknowledge Hyman Rickover, Herbert Hoover, and Robert Moses as "giants among public managers" who bent rather than broke the rules and pushed the limits of what was possible, but they suggest that this approach on the part of lesser mortals would lead to questionable results.

The objective of this article is to use a body of evidence about entrepreneurial public servants, some giants like Hoover and Moses, others far less exalted, to see whether they fit the deLeon-Denhardt-Terry image of loose cannons and rule breakers, or Behn's counterimage of enterprising leaders. The body of evidence comprises two large samples of the best applications to the Ford Foundation—Kennedy School of Government (Ford-KSG) Innovations in American Government Awards Program: 217 semifinalists from 1990 to 1994, encompassing state and local government, and 104 finalists between 1995 and 1998, including the federal government as well. Semifinalist applications detail the nature of the innovation and characteristics of the process of innovation—where in the organization it initiated, who supported the innovation, and how the innovators overcame obstacles.

It could be argued that this is an inappropriate sample for this purpose, because it includes only the applications deemed best by the judges of the Ford-KSG awards program. The judges determine merit on the basis of the application's novelty, results achieved, and replication or replicability. The innovative process itself is not taken into account in choosing the best programs, so winning programs could emerge from processes that deLeon, Denhardt, and Terry would find illegitimate. The Methodology section addresses this issue in detail, noting that only semifinalists were asked detailed questions about the innovative process, making it impossible to sample all applications.

This article will focus on five characteristics of the two samples: (1) the level in the organization where the innovations originated; (2) the nature of the innovations; (3) the factors leading to the innovations; (4) where the innovators received support; and (5) the obstacles the innovators faced and how they overcame them. Taken together, these characteristics should provide evidence to allow us to draw a portrait of actual public-management innovations and innovators and to compare it to the expectations of deLeon, Denhardt, and Terry on the one hand, and Behn on the other. Additionally, the two samples will enable us to see whether the results are consistent from the earlier sample to the later, and between state and local government and the federal government.

Methodology

The academic literature on innovation distinguishes between *invention*, the creation of a new idea, and *innovation*, the adoption of an existing idea for the first time by a given organization (Rogers 1995). Public-management innovation awards do not recognize new but unproven ideas; they choose the best applications on the basis of results (such as improvements in the well-being of program clients, service improvements, or reduced cost), as well as replication and originality. Ideally, the winning applications are relatively recent inventions that have been in operation long enough to show results and to be replicated. If the diffusion of an innovation is represented by a logistic (S-shaped) curve, with time on the horizontal axis and the percentage of the relevant community using the innovation on the vertical axis, then the judges of innovation competitions are attempting to give awards to programs on the lower end of the curve. As they are making the award relatively early in the life of the innovation, they are predicting that future adoption of the innovation will trace out a rising logistic curve.

Any policy area will have a number of innovations spreading more or less rapidly throughout its population of agencies at any given time. Since the Ford-KSG awards program does not limit applications by theme, its best applications encompass many policy areas. The common denominator is that they are all at relatively early points in the diffusion process. The program allocates substantial resources to eliciting as many initial applications as possible—for example, sending applications to all government departments and agencies, searching for newspaper articles about innovative programs and encouraging the managers to apply, and working through professional networks in many policy areas. Therefore, its initial applications constitute a representative sample of innovative activity in all policy areas.

The initial application asks about the characteristics of the program, in particular how it is innovative; the program's beneficiaries; the program's funding sources; verifiable evidence of the program's achievements; and the program's replicability. From approximately 1,500 initial applications received each year, juries of academics and practitioners with expert knowledge of the relevant policy areas choose 75 semifinalists, who represent each policy area in the same proportion as the 1,500 applications. Semifinalists complete a more detailed questionnaire, including many questions about the innovative process. The present study initially analyzed a large, coded sample of 217 of the 350 open-ended semifinalist questionnaires completed between 1990 and 1994, when the awards program was open only to state and local government. Two coders were used for each questionnaire, and levels of inter-coder reliability were a respectable 80 percent (Borins 1998,

Table 23.1

Initiators of Innovations (percent)

Initiator	1990–94 state, local	1995–98 total	1995–98 federal	1995–98 state	1995–98 local
Politician	18	27	14	30	36
Agency head	23	28	24	25	36
Other public servant	48	57	72	46	58
Middle managers	n.a.	43	62	30	45
Front-line staff	n.a.	27	24	27	29
Interest group, nonprofit	13	14	0	16	26
Individual citizen	6	10	0	16	10
Clients of program	2	5	10	2	3
Other	4	10	10	11	7
Total initiators	114	151	130	146	176
N	217	104	29	44	31

N = number of innovations.

Table entries are the percentage of a given group displaying a particular characteristic. For example, the "18" in the first cell of the first column means that in 18 percent of the 217 innovations in the 1990–94 sample, one of the initiators of the innovation was a politician.

Totals add to more than 100 percent because some innovations had more than one initiator.

Correlation coefficient (r) between 1990–94 distribution and total 1995–98 distribution = .99, t = 15.7, significant at .01 with 5 degrees of freedom.

Correlation coefficient (r) between 1995–98 federal and 1995–98 sate and local distributions = .66, t = 2.45, significant at .05 with 6 degrees of freedom.

12–18). This study did not attempt to define innovation a priori, but rather used the judges' choices to determine what constitutes innovation in each policy area.

A similar procedure was applied to the 1995–98 sample, which includes 104 finalists. Twenty-five finalists are chosen from the 75 semifinalists on the basis of expert evaluation of the detailed semifinalist questionnaire. The award was changed in 1995 to include the federal government. The 104 finalists in this sample include 29 federal, 44 state, and 31 local applications. The total sample includes 104 applications because 30, rather than 25 semifinalists were chosen in 1995, and because one program was a finalist twice, but was coded only once. The appendix lists the questions discussed in this paper.

Local Heroes

Table 23.1 identifies the initiators of the innovations, that is, the person(s) who conceived the idea. (Because more than one initiator could be cited for a given innovation, the percentages sum to more than 100.) A surprising result in the 1990–94 sample is that the most frequent initiators of innovations were not politicians (18 percent) or even agency heads like Rickover, Moses, or Hoover (23 percent), but career public servants below the agency-head level, that is, middle managers and front-line staff (48 percent). A strongly similar result was obtained for the later sample, and the correlation between the frequencies of the different initiators in 1990–94 and 1995–98 was .99, significant at .01.

This result might appear to be at odds with one of the basic tenets of American democracy: Voters elect politicians to develop new programs or to terminate existing ones. The most senior appointments to agencies are political, precisely to make the bureaucracy responsive to politicians and, in turn, to the public who elected them. The standard model of public bureaucracy emphasizes the existence of stringent central-agency constraints on public servants' entrepreneurship and innovativeness to minimize corruption and ensure due process (Barzelay 1992). The legislative branch often micromanages the executive. The media's interest in exposing public-sector failings (management in a fishbowl) is yet another impediment to innovation. For all these reasons, career public servants may not be rewarded for successful innovation and will likely be punished for unsuccessful innovation. A consequence of these asymmetric incentives is adverse selection, namely that innovative people do not choose careers in the public sector. Despite controls, asymmetric incentives, and adverse selection, career public servants—front-line staff and middle managers—do innovate.

The 1995–98 sample was used to probe this result in several ways. In the coding, a distinction was made between middle managers and front-line staff. Middle managers were the most frequent initiators (43 percent), but front-line staff (27 percent) were initiators as frequently as politicians (27 percent) and agency heads (28 percent). The data were analyzed to distinguish among cases with one initiator, two initiators, and three or more initiators. The most frequent sole originators were middle managers (19 cases), agency heads (10 cases), politicians (9), and front-line staff (8). By far, the most frequent pair of initiators was middle manager and front-line worker (9 cases), followed by politician and middle manager (3), public-interest group and middle manager (3), and agency head and middle manager (2). The data were also disaggregated by level of government: Both politicians (14 percent federal, 30 percent state, 36 percent local) and agency heads (24 percent federal, 25 percent state, 36 percent local) were more frequently initiators in smaller governments, while middle managers and front-line staff (72 percent federal, 46 percent state, 58 percent local) were more frequently initiators in larger governments (albeit an imperfect ranking, because large cities such as New York, Chicago, and Los Angeles have larger governments than many small states).

These data demonstrate that in addition to elected politicians, agency heads, middle managers, and front-line staff are frequent innovators. The question considered in the following sections is whether the data show that those public servants who innovate are loose cannons and rule breakers or that they are enterprising leaders.

Characteristics of Innovations

Table 23.2 presents the characteristics of the innovations as identified by the applicants. The table entries indicate the percentage of programs displaying a given characteristic. Where responses are closely related, the union of responses is provided. For example, an innovation was considered holistic if the applicant said that it takes a systems approach to analyzing a problem, coordinates the activities of several organizations, or provides multiple services to clients. If an application displayed one or more of

Table 23.2

Characteristics of Innovations (percent)

Characteristic	1990–94	1995–98
Takes a systems approach to problem	26	66
Coordinates organizations	29	57
Provides multiple services to clients	28	25
Total holistic	61	85
New technology	28	31
Simplified technology	2	2
Total technology	29	31
Faster process	31	35
Simpler process	7	8
Total process improvement	34	38
Empowerment of citizens or communities	34	17
Prevention of a problem	16	19
Uses incentives, not regulation	8	15
Use of private sector for public purposes	17	30
Use of volunteers	7	9
New management philosophy	15	13
Changes public attitudes	13	7
Lays groundwork for other programs	6	10
Spillover of benefits from program	8	12
Pilot program	1	18
Total (percent)	249	304
N	217	104

N = number of observations.

Correlation coefficient (r) between 1990–94 and 1995–98 distributions = .88, $t = 5.99$, significant at .01 with 11 degrees of freedom.

these characteristics, it was counted as holistic. That is why "total holistic" is always less than the sum of "systems approach," "coordinates organizations," and "multiple services."

Five characteristics stand out in both samples: holism (85 percent in the later sample and 61 percent in the earlier), the use of new technology, usually new information technology (approximately 30 percent in both samples), process improvement (approximately 35 percent in both samples), empowerment of communities or citizens (17 percent in the later sample and 34 percent in the earlier), and using the private sector to achieve public purposes (30 percent in the later sample and 17 percent in the earlier). The correlation coefficient between the frequencies of the characteristics of each sample is .88, significant at .01.

The theme of holism was developed in the original study (Borins 1998, 19–22, 26–9). Borins approached the data with his own classification scheme for the characteristics of the innovations, one component of which was partnerships. In coding the applicants' own testimony about what made their programs innovative, it became clear that, while some programs were formal partnerships, other applicants were often referring to a wider range of interorganizational arrangements. (This category would also include the case of two municipalities sharing two expensive pieces of road maintenance equipment that deLeon and Denhardt (2000, 92) cite as "sav[ing] the taxpayers money through their effective use of resources.") Applicants, particularly in social service programs, often described their innovations as dealing with the whole person, rather than any one problem a person faced. Finally, a third group of applicants emphasized their programs' focus on developing a systemic understanding of how the problem they were attempting to solve interacted with other problems and programs. Thus, the overarching category of holism was introduced to encapsulate the three concepts that applicants most often expressed. This finding is consistent with other contemporary research on public-sector innovation; for example, Bardach (1998) examined a sample of successful interagency collaborative programs to deduce smart practices in developing and maintaining such arrangements.

Information technology (IT) innovations appear in the first sample as ingenious applications devised by middle managers with a technical background who saw opportunities that politicians and agency heads were unaware of. In the 1995–98 sample, awareness of IT's potential was more widespread, evidenced by innovations with greater involvement by politicians and agency heads, entailing extensive transformation of the manner in which agencies conduct their business. For example, they often involved creating new information systems, such as using employment records to enforce child-support obligations of noncustodial parents (U.S. Department of Health and Human Services 1998) or using crime data from precincts to drive outcome-oriented policing (NYPD 1996). Web sites did not figure in the sample because the rapid spread of Internet technology in the public sector in the mid-1990s meant that they were quickly considered standard practice.

The third characteristic frequently observed—process improvement—refers to innovations designed to make governmental processes faster, friendlier, or more accessible. These initiatives often involved "one-stop shopping" for recipients of related government services; applications of the Pareto rule to separate a few complicated cases from many uncomplicated ones (U.S. Department of Labor 1995); separation of high-and low-value users through payment mechanisms such as electronic toll roads (California Department of Transportation 1997); voluntary compliance, especially in the regulation of business (U.S. Consumer Product Safety Commission 1998); and alternative dispute resolution (Vermont Department of Corrections 1998)—a process that deLeon and Denhardt (2000, 94) advocate. Voluntary compliance and alternative dispute resolution initiatives begin by recognizing that judicial processes are expensive, adversarial, and time consuming and looking for ways to streamline or circumvent them. Empowerment initiatives involve consultation with citizens' or community groups in policy making or inviting them to play a role in policy implementation (U.S. Department of Agriculture 1998).

Using the private sector to achieve public purposes sometimes involved initiatives opening up public-sector activities, such as municipal services or military supply, to private-sector competition (City of Indianapolis 1995), but also used voluntary or nongovernmental organizations for program delivery in job training and placement (City of San Antonio 1995).

Analyzing these most often cited characteristics discloses a set of approaches and behaviors that challenge the image of public-sector innovators as self-promoters, rule breakers, and individuals intent on manipulating public authority for private gain. Getting autonomous agencies to work together requires both a commitment to the effectiveness of the partnership and a renunciation of egotism and the desire for individual dominance. Similarly, process improvement and new technology initiatives seek to help the public sector do its work faster, more effectively, and more compassionately, with little scope for grandstanding or self-promotion. Finally, initiatives that empower citizens or communities, by definition, entail a willingness to share power and renounce some measure of control. While deLeon and Denhardt (2000, 95) fear that reinvention represents a narrowing of the political sphere and an expansion of the market sphere, that theme was not observed very frequently in these samples. The image that emerges from the description is that the innovators developed creative solutions to public-sector problems, using tools such as interorganizational cooperation, process reengineering, information technology, citizen empowerment, and assistance from the private or voluntary sectors.

Why Innovate?

In their narratives, innovators described the different conditions or challenges that led to their innovations. These conditions fell into five groups: (1) initiatives coming from the political system, due to an election mandate, legislation enabling an innovation, or pressure by politicians; (2) new leadership, whether from outside or inside the organization; (3) a crisis, defined as a current or anticipated publicly visible failure or problem; (4) a variety of internal problems (failing to respond to a changing environment, inability to reach a target population, inability to meet demand for a program, resource constraints, or an inability to coordinate policies); and (5) new opportunities, created by technology or other causes. The frequency of these causes is shown in Table 23.3. Political initiatives, internal problems, and opportunities were all comprised of two or more subcategories, and the table reports the union of the subcategories in the same way that Table 23.2 reported the union of the three subcategories of holism.

By far, the most frequent impetus for innovation was internal problems, appearing in 49 percent of the earlier sample and 64 percent of the later. Although the definition of "crisis" was broad, crises appeared in only 30 percent of the earlier sample and 25 percent of the later sample, calling into question the view that public-sector innovation occurs primarily in response to a major crisis (Levin and Sanger 1994; Wilson 1966). The argument underlying this view is that many agencies, because they are monopolies and because they lack performance measures, perform poorly for a long time without improvement until they encounter a publicly visible crisis. The relative infrequency of crisis-driven innovation, however, suggests that crises are not a necessary condition for public-sector innovation. Innovators are more likely to respond to internal problems before they reach crisis proportions or take advantage of opportunities, such as the availability of new information technology. It could be argued that a risk-seeking self-

Table 23.3

Conditions Leading to Innovations (percent)

Condition	1990–44 total	1995–98 total	1995–98 federal	1995–98 state	1995–98 local
Election	2	5	6	5	7
Legislation	11	18	17	27	7
Pressure, lobbying	6	22	17	34	10
All political	19	40	35	54	26
New leader (from outside)	6	14	21	7	19
New leader (from inside)	4	2	0	5	0
New leader	9	16	21	11	19
Crisis	30	25	31	21	26
Environment changes	8	23	28	18	26
Can not reach market	29	29	38	23	29
Can not meet demand	11	14	17	14	13
Resource constraint	10	15	17	18	10
No policy coordination	4	4	7	0	7
All internal	49	64	79	57	61
Technology opportunity	18	8	10	7	7
Other new opportunity	16	9	3	14	7
Total opportunity	33	15	10	21	13
Total conditions	154	162	179	143	146
N	217	104	29	44	31

N = number of observations.
  Correlation coefficient (r) between 1990–94 and total 1995–98 = .60, t = 2.49, significant at .05 with 11 degrees of freedom.
  Correlation coefficient (r) between 1995–98 federal and 1995–98 state and local = .85, t = 5.35.
  Significant at .01 with 11 degrees of freedom.

promoter would even seek to create a crisis because it would provide an opportunity for dramatic action.

The original study explored differences among innovations conceived by politicians, agency heads, and middle managers or front-line staff. Politicians were more likely to conceive of innovations that responded to crises, agency heads were more likely to innovate when they took over the reins, and public servants were more likely to innovate in response to internal problems or to take advantage of technological opportunities (Borins 1998, 48–49). Repeating these correlations for the 1995–98 sample produced similar results, which is consistent with Behn's picture of leadership at the political and bureaucratic levels. Politicians tend to focus on their chosen priorities or on crises. Public servants tend to innovate in areas that are not high on the political agenda, doing so by taking advantage of opportunities or proactively solving problems before they escalate to crises. This does not look like rule breaking or self-promotion on the part of public servants.

Finally, the correlation coefficient between the frequencies of the different conditions leading to innovation in the 1990–94 and 1995–98 samples was .6, significant at .05, while the correlation coefficient between the 1995–98 federal and total state and local frequencies was .85, significant at .01, again showing the similarity of the results over time and across levels of government.

Table 23.4

Supporters of Innovations, 1995–98 (percent)

Type of supporter	Total	Federal	State	Local
Supervisor	20	35	7	26
Agency head	27	28	27	26
Middle manager in agency	23	35	14	26
Other senior managers, board	24	35	16	26
Total within agency	62	79	46	68
Public-sector unions	15	17	11	19
Other agencies	44	48	36	52
Total other public sector	53	59	43	61
Political head of agency	23	24	21	26
President, governor, mayor	40	14	57	42
Other politicians	14	14	18	6
Legislative body	36	24	50	26
Total political	67	55	80	61
Public interest group	37	24	46	36
Clients of agency	36	45	39	23
Business lobby	39	35	46	32
Media	5	3	7	7
General public	23	17	27	23
Total public	91	90	96	97
N	104	29	44	31

N = number of observations.

Gathering Support

Applicants to the awards program were asked who their strongest supporters were. Table 23.4 shows the results for the 1995–98 sample. (It was not coded in the earlier sample.) The table shows supporters within the agency, elsewhere in the public sector, at the political level, and in the public. For each of these four groups, the table shows its union, that is the percentage of the total number of applications receiving support from one or more of the parties in the group.

It is noteworthy that the innovators received support for their ideas from many sources, both inside and outside the public sector. Still, there are significant patterns. Table 23.1 shows that the highest proportion of initiators at the federal level were public servants, and Table 23.4 shows that the highest percentage of innovations receiving support within the agency and from elsewhere in the public sector was in the federal government. Conversely, the highest proportion of political initiators was at the state level, and the highest percentage of innovations receiving support at the political level was in state government. Correlations were calculated between the initiators of the innovations and the nature of their supporters. Innovations initiated by public servants had a positive correlation with support from immediate supervisors and a negative correlation with support from the president or governor, the legislature, business lobbies, and the general public. Innovations initiated by agency heads had a positive correlation with support from the political head of the agency and business lobbies. Innovations initiated by politicians had a positive correlation with support from the president or governor, the legislature, business lobbies, the media, and the general public. These correlations indicate relatively independent paths to innovation. Public servants worked through bureaucratic channels, rather than going over the heads of their colleagues to appeal directly for political support, and politicians went through political channels and mobilized public support. Working through appropriate channels is the hallmark of a responsible public servant whose commitment to desired ends does not negate respect for due process.

Winning Hearts and Minds

Question 5 asked about obstacles to the innovative program or policy initiative, how the initiator attempted to overcome them, and whether, in fact, they were overcome. Table 23.5 outlines the obstacles identified and compares the relative frequency of occurrence for both samples. The obstacles were divided into three groups. The first, obstacles arising primarily within the bureaucracy, included attitudes in the bureaucracy, turf wars, difficulty coordinating organizations, logistical problems, difficulty maintaining the enthusiasm of program staff, difficulty implementing a new technology, opposition by unions, opposition by middle management, and opposition to entrepreneurial action within the public sector. The second group identified obstacles arising in the political environment, such as inadequate funding or other resources, legislative or regulatory constraints, and political opposition. One obstacle with both bureaucratic and political aspects was inadequate resources, which could result from funding decisions made at the bureaucratic or the political level. The third group addressed obstacles in the environment outside the public sector, such as public doubts about the effectiveness of the program, difficulty reaching the target group, opposition by affected private-sector interests, public opposition, and opposition from private-sector entities that, as a result of the innovation, would be forced to compete with the public sector.

The three groups of obstacles appear with similar frequencies in both samples. In addition, the correlation coefficient using the frequencies of all obstacles is .86, with a t-statistic of 6.9 with 16 degrees of freedom, significant at .01 in a two-tail test. The largest number of obstacles arose within the public sector, reflecting the tendency of these innovations to change occupational patterns, standard operating procedures, and power structures. Many instances of obstructive attitudes were cited, particularly on the part of occupational or professional groups. For example, police officers were sometimes opposed to community policing initiatives because it required them to do what they considered "social work." Health professionals opposed initiatives that employed community health workers or advocates in outreach programs. To generalize, programs often encounter opposition by professional groups when they require professions normally having little contact to work together; when they require professionals to do something not traditionally viewed as being within the scope of their work; and when they use volunteers, community workers, or paraprofessionals (Borins 1998, 67, 288). The internal obstacle encountered least frequently was opposition to acting entrepreneurially, which constituted only 1 percent of the occurrences in both samples. If innovators were in fact behaving in the irresponsible

Table 23.5

Obstacles to Innovation

	1995–98		1990–94	
Obstacles	Occurrences	Percent of total	Occurrences	Percent of total
Internal obstacles				
Bureaucratic attitudes	18	8.7	48	9.4
Turf fights	3	1.4	9	1.8
Other bureaucratic resistance	15	7.2	35	6.8
Total bureaucratic	36	17.4	92	18
Difficulty coordinating	14	6.8	52	10.2
Logistics	15	7.2	51	10
Maintaining enthusiasm, burnout	5	2.4	33	6.4
Implementing technology	9	4.3	30	5.9
Union opposition	6	2.9	7	1.4
Middle-management opposition	4	1.9	7	1.4
Opposition to entrepreneurs	2	1	4	0.8
Total internal	91	44	276	53.9
Political environment				
Inadequate resources	24	11.6	89	17.4
Legislative, regulatory constraints	14	6.8	34	6.6
Political opposition	13	6.3	8	1.6
Total political	51	24.6	131	25.6
External obstacles				
External doubts	22	10.6	48	9.4
Reaching target group	19	9.2	30	5.9
Affected private-sector interests	14	6.8	14	2.8
Public opposition	6	2.9	7	1.4
Private-sector competitors	6	2.9	6	1.2
Total external	65	32.1	105	20.5
Total	207	100	512	100

Correlation coefficient (r) between 1990–94 and 1995–98 = .86, t = 6.9, significant at .01 with 16 degrees of freedom.

and freewheeling manner of which they stand accused, we would expect to see a much higher incidence of opposition based on the perceived illegitimacy of their initiatives. Instead, most innovators experienced reactions to the anticipated effects of successfully planned programs.

Under political obstacles, lack of resources appeared most frequently. This can be explained by the fact that many innovations, particularly in the social services, were pilot programs looking for additional resources to increase their scale of operations. Legislative or regulatory constraints occurred when an innovator was hampered by existing legislation or by regulations that had previously been enacted, for other reasons. Opposition from elected politicians appeared least frequently. It occurred more frequently in the later sample (6.3 percent of the total number of obstacles) than in the earlier (1.6 percent of the total) because the later sample had a somewhat greater incidence of innovations initiated at the political level, particularly in state government. The infrequency of political obstacles may mean that bureaucratic innovators are working far enough from the political level that their work is not very noticeable to politicians or, if their work is noticeable, that they understand what is and is not politically feasible and gauge their actions accordingly. In those cases in the earlier sample where there was political or public opposition, however, it was overcome approximately 70 percent of the time (Borins 1998, 67).

The third set of obstacles—external obstacles—includes problems of program design, such as reaching the program's target population, public doubts about a program (approximately 10 percent of all obstacles in both samples), and more active public opposition (approximately 2 percent of all obstacles in both samples). The earlier study showed that external doubts were overcome 90 percent of the time and public opposition approximately 70 percent of the time (Borins 1998, 67). The infrequency of both political and public opposition and the substantial frequency with which obstacles were overcome suggests that the public recognizes that the performance of the public sector can be enhanced and that policy outcomes in many areas can be improved. They are not wedded to existing policies nor to existing procedures, and they are receptive to innovation and change.

Table 23.6 shows various tactics that were used to overcome the obstacles to innovation and the number of times each was cited for both samples. The correlation coefficient of the frequencies of the different obstacles between the two samples was .82, significant at .01, again showing stability over time. The tactics most commonly used in both samples could be described broadly as persuasion—showing the benefits of an innovation, establishing demonstration projects, and social marketing—and accommodation—consultation with affected parties, co-optation of affected parties by involving them in the governance of the innovation, providing training for those whose work would be affected by the innovation, compensating losers, and making a program culturally or linguistically sensitive. The innovators took objections seriously and attempted to change the minds of opponents or skeptics or modified the innovation so that opponents or skeptics would be more comfortable with it.

It is instructive that the tactic used least frequently in both samples was something that might be considered a "power politics" approach—changing the manager responsible for program implementation. The innovators usually attempted to persuade or accommodate their opponents, rather than appealing to superiors to use their authority to overcome them. They were using consensus-building rather than strong-arm tactics.

The earlier study matched up the individual obstacles presented in Table 23.5 with the tactics used to overcome them, presented in Table 23.6 (Borins 1998, 73). For example, there were ninety-two instances of bureaucratic opposition, and innovators most frequently responded by providing training (24 percent), demonstrating the benefits of the innovation (23 percent), consultation with affected parties (20 percent), and persistence (20 percent). When the obstacle was difficulty coordinating organizations, something often faced by holistic innovations, the most frequent responses were consultation with affected parties (31 percent), co-optation of affected parties (27 percent), focusing attention on the most important aspects of the innovation (19 percent), persistence (15 percent), and providing training (12 percent). These tactics are explicit examples of how an innovator who wants to make a holistic innovation succeed would renounce egotism and individual dominance.

The most frequent responses to legislative or regulatory constraints were attempting

Table 23.6

Tactics to Overcome Obstacles to Innovation, Total Frequency Used

	1990–94		1995–98	
Tactic	Number of cities	Percent of total	Number of cities	Percent of total
Demonstrate to opponents that program really advances their interests, provides benefits to them	56	11	17	8
Social marketing	29	5	23	10
Demonstration project	28	5	13	6
Total persuasion	113	21	53	24
Training affected parties	51	10	25	11
Consultation with affected parties	50	9	25	11
Cooptation/buy-in (opponents/skeptics become participants)	40	8	20	9
Program design made linguistically, culturally sensitive	14	3	2	1
Compensation for losers, design so that losers not worse off	5	1	6	3
Total accommodation	160	30	76	34
Finding additional resources of any kind	55	10	17	8
Persistence, effort	49	9	20	9
Logistical problems were resolved	41	8	11	5
Other	28	5	8	4
Gaining political support, building alliances	25	5	11	5
Focus on most important aspects of innovation, develop a clear vision	21	4	6	3
Technology was modified	20	4	6	3
Legislation or regulations were changed	10	2	10	4
Provide recognition for program participants or supporters	7	1	2	1
Changing managers responsible for program implementation	4	1	4	2
Total use of tactics	533	100	224	100

Correlation coefficient (r) between 1990–94 and total 1995–98 = .82, t = 5.7, significant at .01 with 16 degrees of freedom.

to change the legislation or regulations to permit the innovation (27 percent), building political support for the innovation (23 percent), persistence (20 percent), demonstrating the benefits of the innovation (9 percent), and consultation (6 percent). This is not breaking or bending rules, but rather accepting the need to conform to current rules while working to change them. Political opposition was most frequently overcome by building political support for the innovation (25 percent), demonstrating the innovation's benefits (25 percent), and persistence (25 percent). Finally, public doubts were most frequently overcome by demonstrating the benefits of the program to opponents or skeptics (31 percent), consultation with affected parties (23 percent), demonstration projects (21 percent), co-optation of affected parties (19 percent), and social marketing (17 percent).

Overall, the responses to the obstacles raised show that the innovators took objections seriously and attempted to meet objectors on their own terms, rather than appealing to authority or using strong-arm tactics. They did not necessarily view opposition to change as a bad thing, but rather as a challenge to communicate their message more clearly and a suggestion about how to improve the design of their programs.

Conclusion

Previous research based on the 1990–94 sample argued that innovators demonstrated integrity in innovation in numerous ways: by proactively solving problems before they became crises; by taking opposition seriously and attempting to deal with it forthrightly through persuasion or accommodation, rather than through power politics; by developing a clear vision of an innovation and staying focused on that vision; and by objectively evaluating an innovation to see if it is working (Borins 1998, 283–89). The results of the 1995–98 sample strongly replicate the earlier sample, as demonstrated by the statistically significant correlations. This evidence from the Ford-KSG awards paints a picture of public-management innovators that is far closer to Behn's vision of enterprising leaders taking astute initiatives than it is to deLeon, Denhardt, and Terry's loose cannons, rule breakers, self-promoters, power politicians, and manipulators of public authority for private gain.

Research advances by accumulating evidence. Those who hold the viewpoint expressed by deLeon, Denhardt, and Terry may be unconvinced by the evidence presented in this paper. If so, let them design their own empirical studies of public-management innovators to search for the reckless self-promoters, the irresponsible entrepreneurs, and the profiteers in reformers' clothing. Undoubtedly there will be such cases; one who most readily comes to mind is Robert Citron, the elected treasurer who bankrupted Orange County through risky investments in derivative securities (Cohen and Eimicke 1999). The question to be explored, however, is whether there are many such cases, or at most a handful. Has the reinvention movement turned loose upon American government a plague of rule breakers, profiteers, and self-promoters? An objective accumulation of evidence would determine whether such fears are justified or exaggerated.

The debate over public entrepreneurship is a debate about trade-offs. Proponents of reinvention call for a relaxation of central-agency controls and advocate experimentation, for example in the federal government's reinvention labs. While it is in the nature of experimentation that some individual experiments will not be successful, they argue that, on balance, these initiatives will enhance public-sector effectiveness and efficiency, with little degradation in other important values, such as probity, fairness, and justice (Jones and Thompson 1999). Critics believe the potential gains are smaller and the risks in terms of other values greater. This debate is not merely academic, but will influence the regulations governing public servants. The vast majority of the innovators discussed in this study did not work in reinvention labs or in other environments that were particularly supportive of innovation. If elected politicians take to heart the fears expressed by the critics, the public sector will likely become increasingly inhospitable to innovation. That would be most unfortunate, because the evidence presented here shows innovators who achieved beneficial results—such as enhanced client well-being, improved service, and lower cost—and did it with integrity.

Appendix. Questions Discussed in This Paper

1. What individuals or groups are considered the primary initiators of the program or policy initiative? Please specify their position or organizational affiliation at the time they initiated the program or policy initiative (see Table 23.1).
2. What makes your program or policy initiative innovative? Compare it with other programs currently operating in your region, state, or nationally that address the same problem. How does your approach differ (asked in 1990–94)? Describe your innovation; include the specific problem it addresses, and how it has changed previous practice (asked in 1995–98) (see Table 23.2).
3. When and how was the program or policy initiative originally conceived in your jurisdiction? Please describe any specific incidents or circumstances that led to the initiative (see Table 23.3).
4. What individuals or organizations are the strongest supporters of the program or policy initiative and why (see Table 23.4)?
5. Please describe the most significant obstacle(s) encountered thus far by your program or policy initiative. How did you deal with each of the obstacles? Which implementation obstacles or difficulties remain (see Tables 23.5 and 23.6)?

Acknowledgments

The research assistance of Marianna Marysheva, Marina Ninkovic, and Salim Rajwani, the comments of Bob Behn, Beth Herst, and three anonymous *PAR* reviewers, the financial support of the Innovations in American Government Awards Program, and the institutional support of the Goldman School of Public Policy at the University of California at Berkeley are all gratefully acknowledged. Earlier versions of this paper were presented at faculty seminars at the Goldman School of Public Policy and the Kennedy School of Government, and the insightful comments of colleagues at these seminars helped to shape this article.

References

Bardach, Eugene. 1998. *Managerial Craftsmanship: Getting Agencies to Work Together.* Washington, DC: The Brookings Institution.
Barzelay, Michael. 1992. *Breaking through Bureaucracy: A New Vision for Managing in Government.* Berkeley, CA: University of California Press.
Behn, Robert. 1998. "What Right Do Public Managers Have to Lead?" *Public Administration Review* 58(3): 209–24.
Borins, Sandford. 1998. *Innovating with Integrity: How Local Heroes Are Transforming American Government.* Washington, DC: Georgetown University Press.
California Department of Transportation. 1997. AB 680 Program. Application to the Innovations in American Government Awards Program.
City of Indianapolis. 1995. Competition and Costing. Application to the Innovations in American Government Awards Program.
City of San Antonio. 1995. Project Quest. Application to the Innovations in American Government Awards Program.

Cohen, Stephen, and William Eimicke. 1999. "Is Public Entrepreneurship Ethical?" *Public Integrity* 1(1): 54–74.

deLeon, Linda, and Robert B. Denhardt. 2000. "The Political Theory of Reinvention." *Public Administration Review* 60 (2): 89–97.

Gawthrop, Louis C. 1999. "Public Entrepreneurship in the Lands of Oz and Uz." *Public Integrity* 1(1): 75–86.

Goodsell, Charles T. 1993. "Reinvent Government or Rediscover It?" *Public Administration Review* 53(1): 85–87.

Hood, Christopher. 1991. "A Public Management for All Seasons?" *Public Administration* 69(1): 3–19.

Jacobs, Jane. 1993. *Systems of Survival.* New York: Random House.

Jones, Lawrence R., and Fred Thompson. 1999. *Public Management: Institutional Renewal for the Twenty-First Century.* Stamford, CT: JAI Press.

Kernaghan, Kenneth. 2000. "The Post-Bureaucratic Organization and Public Service Values." *International Review of Administrative Sciences* 66(1): 91–104.

Levin, Martin A., and Mary Bryna Sanger. 1994. *Making Government Work: How Entrepreneurial Executives Turn Bright Ideas into Real Results.* San Francisco, CA: Jossey-Bass.

New York Police Department. 1996. Compstat. Application to the Innovations in American Government Awards Program.

Rogers, Everett M. 1995. *Diffusion of Innovations.* 4th ed. New York: Free Press.

Terry, Larry D. 1998. "Administrative Leadership, Neo-Managerialism, and the Public Management Movement." *Public Administration Review* 58(3): 194–200.

U.S. Consumer Product Safety Commission. 1998. Fast Track Product Recall Program. Application to the Innovations in American Government Awards Program.

U.S. Department of Agriculture, Forest Service. 1998. Northern New Mexico Collaborative Stewardship. Application to the Innovations in American Government Awards Program.

U.S. Department of Health and Human Services, Office of Child Support Enforcement. 1998. National New Hire Reporting. Application to the Innovations in American Government Awards Program.

U.S. Department of Labor, Pension Benefit Guaranty Corporation. 1995. Early Warning Program. Application to the Innovations in American Government Awards Program.

Vermont Department of Corrections. 1998. Vermont Reparative Probation. Application to the Innovations in American Government Awards Program.

Wilson, James Q. 1966. "Innovation in Organization: Notes Toward a Theory." In *Approaches to Organization Design,* edited by James D. Thompson. Pittsburgh, PA: University of Pittsburgh Press.

CHAPTER 24

MIXED-SCANNING

A "Third" Approach to Decision Making

AMITAI ETZIONI

In the concept of social decision making, vague commitments of a normative and political nature are translated into specific commitments to one or more specific courses of action. Since decision making includes an element of choice, it is the most deliberate and voluntaristic aspect of social conduct. As such, it raises the question: To what extent can social actors decide what their course will be, and to what extent are they compelled to follow a course set by forces beyond their control? Three conceptions of decision making are considered here with assumptions that give varying weights to the conscious choice of the decision makers.

Rationalistic models tend to posit a high degree of control over the decision making situation on the part of the decision maker. The incrementalist approach presents an alternative model, referred to as the art of "muddling through," which assumes much less command over the environment. Finally, the article outlines a third approach to social decision making which, in combining elements of both earlier approaches, is neither as Utopian in its assumptions as the first model nor as conservative as the second. For reasons which will become evident, this third approach is referred to as mixed-scanning.

The Rationalistic Approach

Rationalistic models are widely held conceptions about how decisions are and ought to be made. An actor becomes aware of a problem, posits a goal, carefully weighs alternative means, and chooses among them according to his estimates of their respective merit, with reference to the state of affairs he prefers. Incrementalists' criticism of this approach focuses on the disparity between the requirements of the model and the capacities of decision makers.[1] Social decision-making centers, it is pointed out, frequently do not have a specific, agreed upon set of values that could provide the criteria for evaluating alternatives. Values, rather, are fluid and are affected by, as well as affect, the decisions made. Moreover, in actual practice, the rationalistic assumption that values and facts, means and ends, can be clearly distinguished seems inapplicable:

From *Public Administration Review*, vol. 27, no. 5 (December 1967): 385–92. Copyright © 1967 by American Society for Public Administration. Reprinted with permission.

. . . Public controversy . . . has surrounded the proposal to construct a branch of the Cook County Hospital on the South Side in or near the Negro area. Several questions of policy are involved in the matter, but the ones which have caused one of the few public debates of an issue in the Negro community concern whether, or to what extent, building such a branch would result in an all-Negro or "Jim Crow" hospital and whether such a hospital is desirable as a means of providing added medical facilities for Negro patients. Involved are both an issue of fact (whether the hospital would be segregated, intentionally or unintentionally, as a result of the character of the neighborhood in which it would be located) and an issue of value (whether even an all-Negro hospital would be preferable to no hospital at all in the area). In reality, however, the factions have aligned themselves in such a way and the debate has proceeded in such a manner that the fact issue and the value issue have been collapsed into the single question of whether to build or not to build. Those in favor of the proposal will argue that the facts do not bear out the charge of "Jim Crowism"—"the proposed site . . . is not considered to be placed in a segregated area for the exclusive use of one racial or minority group"; or "no responsible officials would try to develop a new hospital to further segregation"; or "establishing a branch hospital for the . . . more adequate care of the indigent patient load, from the facts thus presented, does not represent Jim Crowism." At the same time, these proponents argue that whatever the facts, the factual issue is secondary to the overriding consideration that "there is a here-and-now need for more hospital beds. . . . Integration may be the long-run goal, but in the short-run we need more facilities."[2]

In addition, information about consequences is, at best, fractional. Decision makers have neither the assets nor the time to collect the information required for rational choice. While knowledge technology, especially computers, does aid in the collection and processing of information, it cannot provide for the computation required by the rationalist model. (This holds even for chess playing, let alone "real-life" decisions.) Finally, rather than being confronted with a limited universe of relevant consequences, decision makers face an open system of variables, a world in which all consequences cannot be surveyed.[3] A decision maker, attempting to adhere to the tenets of a rationalistic model, will become frustrated, exhaust his resources without coming to a decision, and remain without an effective decision-making model to guide him. Rationalistic models are thus rejected as being at once unrealistic and undesirable.

The Incrementalist Approach

A less demanding model of decision making has been outlined in the strategy of "disjointed incrementalism" advanced by Charles E. Lindblom and others.[4] Disjointed incrementalism seeks to adapt decision-making strategies to the limited cognitive capacities of decision makers and to reduce the scope and cost of information collection and computation. Lindblom summarized the six primary requirements of the model in this way:[5]

1. Rather than attempting a comprehensive survey and evaluation of all alternatives, the decision maker focuses only on those policies which differ incrementally from existing policies.

2. Only a relatively small number of policy alternatives are considered.
3. For each policy alternative, only a restricted number of "important" consequences are evaluated.
4. The problem confronting the decision maker is continually redefined: Incrementalism allows for countless ends-means and means-ends adjustments which, in effect, make the problem more manageable.
5. Thus, there is no one decision or "right" solution but a "never-ending series of attacks" on the issues at hand through serial analyses and evaluation.
6. As such, incremental decision making is described as remedial, geared more to the alleviation of present, concrete social imperfections than to the promotion of future social goals.

Morphological Assumptions of the Incremental Approach

Beyond a model and a strategy of decision making, disjointed incrementalism also posits a structure model; it is presented as the typical decision-making process of pluralistic societies, as contrasted with the master planning of totalitarian societies. Influenced by the free competition model of economics, incrementalists reject the notion that policies can be guided in terms of central institutions of a society expressing the collective "good." Policies, rather, are the outcome of a give-and-take among numerous societal "partisans." The measure of a good decision is the decision-makers' agreement about it. Poor decisions are those which exclude actors capable of affecting the projected course of action; decisions of this type tend to be blocked or modified later.

Partisan "mutual-adjustment" is held to provide for a measure of coordination of decisions among a multiplicity of decision makers and, in effect, to compensate on the societal level for the inadequacies of the individual incremental decision maker and for the society's inability to make decisions effectively from one center. Incremental decision making is claimed to be both a realistic account of how the American polity and other modern democracies decide and the most effective approach to societal decision making, i.e., both a descriptive and a normative model.

A Critique of the Incremental Approach as a Normative Model

Decisions by consent among partisans without a societywide regulatory center and guiding institutions should not be viewed as the preferred approach to decision making. In the first place, decisions so reached would, of necessity, reflect the interests of the most powerful, since partisans invariably differ in their respective power positions; demands of the underprivileged and politically unorganized would be underrepresented.

Secondly, incrementalism would tend to neglect *basic* societal innovations, as it focuses on the short run and seeks no more than limited variations from past policies. While an accumulation of small steps could lead to a significant change, there is nothing in this approach to guide the accumulation; the steps may be circular—leading back to where they started, or dispersed—leading in many directions at once but leading nowhere. Boulding comments that, according to this approach, "we do stagger through history like a drunk putting one disjointed incremental foot after another."[6]

In addition, incrementalists seem to underestimate *their* impact on the decision makers. As Dror put it, "Although Lindblom's thesis includes a number of reservations, these are insufficient to alter its main impact as an ideological reinforcement of the pro-inertia and anti-innovation forces."[7]

A Conceptual and Empirical Critique of Incrementalism

Incrementalist strategy clearly recognizes one subset of situations to which it does not apply—namely, "large" or fundamental decisions,[8] such as a declaration of war. While incremental decisions greatly outnumber fundamental ones, the latter's significance for societal decision making is not commensurate with their number; it is thus a mistake to relegate nonincremental decisions to the category of exceptions. Moreover, it is often the fundamental decisions which set the context for the numerous incremental ones. Although fundamental decisions are frequently "prepared" by incremental ones in order that the final decision will initiate a less abrupt change, these decisions may still be considered relatively fundamental. The incremental steps which follow cannot be understood without them, and the preceding steps are useless unless they lead to fundamental decisions.

Thus, while the incrementalists hold that decision making involves a choice between the two kinds of decision-making models, it should be noted that (1) *most incremental decisions specify or anticipate fundamental decisions,* and (2) *the cumulative value of the incremental decisions is greatly affected by the related fundamental decisions.*

Thus, it is not enough to show, as Fenno did, that Congress makes primarily marginal changes in the federal budget (a comparison of one year's budget for a federal agency with that of the preceding year showed on many occasions only a 10 percent difference[9]), or that for long periods the defense budget does not change much in terms of its percentage of the federal budget, or that the federal budget changes little each year in terms of its percentage of the Gross National Product.[10] These incremental changes are often the unfolding of trends initiated at critical turning points at which fundamental decisions were made. The American defense budget jumped at the beginning of the Korean War in 1950 from 5 percent of the GNP to 10.3 percent in 1951. The fact that it stayed at about this level, ranging between 9 and 11.3 percent of the GNP after the war ended (1954–60), did reflect incremental decisions, but these were made within the context of the decision to engage in the Korean War.[11] Fenno's own figures show almost an equal number of changes above the 20 percent level as below it; seven changes represented an increase of 100 percent or more and 24 changes increased 50 percent or more.[12]

It is clear that, while Congress or other societal decision-making bodies do make some cumulative incremental decisions without facing the fundamental one implied, many other decisions which appear to be a series of incremental ones are, in effect, the implementation or elaboration of a fundamental decision.

For example, after Congress set up a national space agency in 1958 and consented to back President Kennedy's space goals, it made "incremental" additional commitments for several years. Initially, however, a fundamental decision had been made. Congress in 1958, drawing on past experiences and on an understanding of the dynamics of incremental processes, could not have been unaware that once a fundamental commitment is made it is difficult to reverse it. While the initial space budget was relatively small, the very act of setting up a space agency amounted to subscribing to additional budget increments in future years.[13]

Incrementalists argue that incremental decisions tend to be remedial; small steps are taken in the "right" direction, or, when it is evident the direction is "wrong," the course is altered. But if the decision maker evaluates his incremental decisions and small steps, which he must do if he is to decide whether or not the direction is right, his judgment will be greatly affected by the evaluative criteria he applies. Here, again, we have to go outside the incrementalist model to ascertain the ways in which these criteria are set.

Thus, while actors make both kinds of decisions, the number and role of fundamental decisions are significantly greater than incrementalists state, and when the fundamental ones are missing, incremental decision making amounts to drifting—action without direction. A more active approach to societal decision making requires two sets of mechanisms: (1) high-order, fundamental policy-making processes which set basic directions and (2) incremental processes which prepare for fundamental decisions and work them out after they have been reached. This is provided by mixed-scanning.

The Mixed-Scanning Approach

Mixed-scanning provides both a realistic description of the strategy used by actors in a large variety of fields and the strategy for effective actors to follow. Let us first illustrate this approach in a simple situation and then explore its societal dimensions. Assume we are about to set up a worldwide weather observation system using weather satellites. The rationalistic approach would seek an exhaustive survey of weather conditions by using cameras capable of detailed observations and by scheduling reviews of the entire sky as often as possible. This would yield an avalanche of details, costly to analyze and likely to overwhelm our action capacities (e.g., "seeding" cloud formations that could develop into hurricanes or bring rain to arid areas). Incrementalism would focus on those areas in which similar patterns developed in the recent past and, perhaps, on a few nearby regions; it would thus ignore all formations which might deserve attention if they arose in unexpected areas.

A mixed-scanning strategy would include elements of both approaches by employing two cameras: a broad-angle camera that would cover all parts of the sky but not in great detail, and a second one which would zero in on those areas revealed by the first camera to require a more in-depth examination. While mixed-scanning might miss areas in which only a detailed camera could reveal trouble, it is less likely than incrementalism to miss obvious trouble spots in unfamiliar areas.

From an abstract viewpoint mixed-scanning provides a particular procedure for the collection of information (e.g., the surveying or "scanning" of weather conditions), a strategy about the allocation of resources (e.g., "seeding"), and—we shall see—guidelines for the relations between the two. The strategy combines a detailed ("rationalistic") examination of some sectors—which, unlike the exhaustive examination of the entire area, is feasible—with a "truncated" review of other sectors. The relative investment in the two kinds of scanning—full detail and truncated—as well as in the very act of scanning, depends on how costly it would be to miss, for example, one hurricane; the cost of additional scanning; and the amount of time it would take.

Scanning may be divided into more than two levels; there can be several levels with varying degrees of detail and coverage, though it seems most effective to include an all-encompassing level (so that no major option will be left uncovered) and a highly detailed level (so that the option selected can be explored as fully as is feasible).

The decision on how the investment of assets and time it to be allocated among the levels of scanning is, in fact, part of the strategy. The actual amount of assets and time spent depends on the total amount available and on experimentation with various inter-level combinations. Also, the amount spent is best changed over time. Effective decision-making requires that sporadically, or at set intervals, investment in encompassing (high-coverage) scanning be increased to check for far removed but "obvious" dangers and to search for better lines of approach. Annual budget reviews and the State of the Union messages provide, in principle, such occasions.

An increase in investment of this type is also effective when the actor realizes that the environment radically changes or when he sees that the early chain of increments brings no improvement in the situation or brings even a "worsening." If, at this point, the actor decides to drop the course of action, the effectiveness of his decision making is reduced, since, through some high-coverage scanning, he may discover that a continuation of the "loss" is about to lead to a solution. (An obvious example is the selling of a declining stock if a further review reveals that the corporation is expected to improve its earning next year, after several years of decline.) Reality cannot be assumed to be structured in straight lines where each step towards a goal leads directly to another and where the accumulation of small steps in effect solves the problem. Often what from an incremental viewpoint is a step away from the goal ("worsening") may from a broader perspective be a step in the right direction, as when the temperature of a patient is allowed to rise because this will hasten his recovery. Thus mixed-scanning not only combines various levels of scanning but also provides a set of criteria for situations in which one level or another is to be emphasized.

In the exploration of mixed-scanning, it is essential to differentiate fundamental decisions from incremental ones. Fundamental decisions are made by exploring the main alternatives the actor sees in view of his conception of his goals, but—unlike what rationalism would indicate—details and specifications are omitted so that an overview is feasible. Incremental decisions are made but within the contexts set by fundamental decisions (and fundamental reviews). Thus, each of the two elements in mixed-scanning helps to reduce the effects of the particular shortcomings of the other; incrementalism reduces the unrealistic aspects of rationalism by limiting the details required in fundamental decisions, and contextuating rationalism helps to overcome the conservative slant of incrementalism by exploring longer-run alternatives. Together, empirical tests and comparative study of decision makers would show that these elements make for a third approach which is at once more realistic and more effective than its components.

Can Decisions Be Evaluated?

The preceding discussion assumes that both the observer and the actor have a capacity to evaluate decision-making strategies and to determine which is the more effective. Incrementalists, however, argue that since values cannot be scaled and summarized, "good" decisions cannot be defined and, hence, evaluation is not possible. In contrast, it is reasonable to expect that the decision makers, as well as the observers, can summarize their values and rank them, at least in an ordinal scale.

For example, many societal projects have one primary goal such as increasing birth control, economically desalting sea water, or reducing price inflation by one-half over a two-year period. Other goals which are also served are secondary, e.g., increasing the country's R & D sector by investing in desalting. The actor, hence, may deal with the degree to which the *primary* goal was realized and make this the central evaluative measure for a "good" policy, while noting its effects on secondary goals. When he compares projects in these terms, he, in effect, weighs the primary goal as several times as important as all the secondary goals combined. This procedure amounts to saying, "As I care very much about one goal and little about the others, if the project does not serve the first goal, it is no good and I do not have to worry about measuring and totaling up whatever other gains it may be providing for my secondary values."

When there are two or even three primary goals (e.g., teaching, therapy, and research in a university hospital), the actor can still compare projects in terms of the extent to which they realize each primary goal. He can establish that project X is good for research but not for teaching while project Y is very good for teaching but not as good for research, etc., without having to raise the additional difficulties of combining the effectiveness measures into one numerical index. In effect, he proceeds as if they had identical weights.

Finally, an informal scaling of values is not as difficult as the incrementalists imagine. Most actors are able to rank their goals to some extent (e.g., faculty is more concerned about the quality of research than the quality of teaching).

> One of the most imaginative attempts to evaluate the effectiveness of programs with hard-to-assess objectives is a method devised by David Osborn, Deputy Assistant Secretary of State for Educational and Cultural Affairs. . . . Osborn recommends a scheme of cross-multiplying the costs of the activities with a number representing the rank of its objectives on a scale. For instance, the exchange of Fulbright professors may contribute to "cultural prestige and mutual respect," "educational development," and gaining "entree," which might be given scale numbers such as 8, 6, and 5, respectively. These numbers are then multiplied with the costs of the program, and the resulting figure is in turn multiplied with an ingenious figure called a "country number." The latter is an attempt to get a rough measure of the importance to the U.S. of the countries with which we have cultural relations. It is arrived at by putting together in complicated ways certain key data, weighed to reflect cultural and educational matters, such as the country's population, Gross National Product, number of

college students, rate of illiteracy, and so forth. The resulting numbers are then revised in the light of working experience, as when, because of its high per capita income, a certain tiny middle-eastern country turns out to be more important to the U.S. than a large eastern European one. At this point, country numbers are revised on the basis of judgment and experience, as are other numbers at other points. But those who make such revisions have a basic framework to start with, a set of numbers arranged on the basis of many factors, rather than single arbitrary guesses."[14]

Thus, in evaluation as in decision making itself, while full detailed rationalism may well be impossible, truncated reviews are feasible, and this approach may be expected to be more effective in terms of the actors' goals than "muddling through."

Morphological Factors

The structures within which interactions among actors take place become more significant the more we recognize that the bases of decisions neither are nor can be a fully ordered set of values and an exhaustive examination of reality. In part, the strategy followed is determined neither by values nor by information but by the positions of and power relations among the decision makers. For example, the extent to which one element of mixed-scanning is stressed as against the other is affected by the relationship between higher and lower organizational ranks. In some situations, the higher in rank, concerned only with the overall picture, are impatient with details, while lower ranks—especially experts—are more likely to focus on details. In other situations, the higher ranks, to avoid facing the overall picture, seek to bury themselves, their administration, and the public in details.

Next, the environment should be taken into account. For instance, a highly incremental approach would perhaps be adequate if the situation were more stable and the decisions made were effective from the start. This approach is expected to be less appropriate when conditions are rapidly changing and when the initial course was wrong. Thus, there seems to be no one effective decision-making strategy in the abstract, apart from the societal environment into which it is introduced. Mixed-scanning is flexible; changes in the relative investment in scanning in general as well as among the various levels of scanning permit it to adapt to the specific situation. For example, more encompassing scanning is called for when the environment is more malleable.

Another major consideration here is the capacities of the actor. This is illustrated with regard to interagency relations by the following statement: ". . . the State Department was hopelessly behind. Its cryptographic equipment was obsolescent, which slowed communications, and it had no central situation room at all."[15] The author goes on to show how as a consequence the State Department was less able to act than was the Defense Department.

An actor with a low capacity to mobilize power to implement his decisions may do better to rely less on encompassing scanning; even if remote outcomes are anticipated, he will be able to do little about them. More generally, the greater a unit's control capacities the more encompassing scanning it can undertake, and the more such scanning, the more effective its decision making. This points to an interesting paradox: The developing nations, with much lower control capacities than the modern ones, tend to favor much more planning, although they may have to make do with a relatively high degree of incrementalism. Yet modern pluralistic societies—which are much more able to scan and, at least in some dimensions, are much more able to control—tend to plan less.

Two different factors are involved which highlight the difference in this regard among modern societies. While all have a higher capacity to scan and some control advantages as compared to nonmodern societies, they differ sharply in their capacity to build consensus. Democracies must accept a relatively high degree of incrementalism (though not as high as developing nations) because of their greater need to gain support for new decisions from many and conflicting subsocieties, a need which reduces their capacity to follow a long-run plan. It is easier to reach consensus under noncrisis situations, on increments similar to existing policies, than to gain support for a new policy. However, the role of crises is significant; in relatively less passive democracies, crises serve to build consensus for major changes of direction which are overdue (e.g., desegregation).

Totalitarian societies, more centralist and relying on powers which are less dependent on consensus, can plan more but they tend to overshoot the mark. Unlike democracies which first seek to build up a consensus and then proceed, often doing less than necessary later than necessary, totalitarian societies, lacking the capacity for consensus-building or even for assessing the various resistances, usually try for too much too early. They are then forced to adjust their plans after initiation, with the revised policies often scaled down and involving more "consensus" than the original one. While totalitarian gross misplanning constitutes a large waste of resources, some initial overplanning and later down-scaling is as much a decision-making strategy as is disjointed incrementalism, and is the one for which totalitarian societies may be best suited. A society more able to effectively handle its problems (one referred to elsewhere as an active society)[16] would require:

1. A higher capacity to build consensus than even democracies command.
2. More effective though not necessarily more numerous means of control than totalitarian societies employ (which new knowledge technology and better analysis through the social sciences may make feasible).
3. A mixed-scanning strategy which is not as rationalistic as that which the totalitarian societies attempt to pursue and not as incremental as the strategy democracies advocate.

Notes

1. See David Braybrooke and Charles E. Lindblom, *A Strategy of Decision* (New York: Free Press, 1968), pp. 48–50 and pp. 111–43; Charles E. Lindblom, *The Intelligence of Democracy* (New York: Free Press, 1965), pp. 137–39. See also Jerome S. Bruner, Jacqueline J. Goodnow, and George A. Austin, *A Study of Thinking* (New York: John Wiley, 1956) chapters 4–5.

2. James Q. Wilson, *Negro Politics* (New York: Free Press, 1960), p. 189.

3. See review of *A Strategy of Decision* by Kenneth J. Arrow in *Political Science Quarterly*, vol. 79 (1964), p. 585. See also Herbert A. Simon, *Models of Man* (New York: Wiley, 1957), p. 198, and Aaron

Wildavsky, *The Politics of the Budgetary Process* (Boston: Little, Brown, 1964), pp. 147–52.

4. Charles E. Lindblom, "The Science of 'Muddling Through,'" *Public Administration Review*, vol. 19 (1959), pp. 79–99; Robert A. Dahl and Charles E. Lindblom, *Politics, Economics and Welfare* (New York: Harper, 1953); *Strategy of Decision*, op. cit.; and *The Intelligence of Democracy*, op. cit.

5. Lindblom, *The Intelligence of Democracy*, op. cit., pp. 144–48.

6. Kenneth E. Boulding in a review of *A Strategy of Decision* in the *American Sociological Review*, vol. 29 (1964), p. 931.

7. Yehezkel Dror, "Muddling Through—'Science' or Inertia?" *Public Administration Review*, vol. 24 (1964), p. 155.

8. Braybrooke and Lindblom, *A Strategy of Decision*, op. cit., pp. 66–69.

9. Richard Fenno, Jr., *The Power of the Purse* (Boston: Little, Brown, 1966), pp. 266ff. See also Otto A. Davis, M.A.H. Dempster, and Aaron Wildavsky, "A Theory of the Budgetary Process," *American Political Science Review*, vol. 60 (1966), esp. pp. 530–31.

10. Samuel P. Huntington, quoted by Nelson E. Polsby, *Congress and the Presidency* (Englewood Cliffs, NJ: Prentice Hall, 1964), p. 86.

11. Ibid.

12. Fenno, *The Power of the Purse*, loc. cit.

13. For an example involving the Supreme Court's decision on desegregation, see Martin Shapiro, "Stability and Change in Judicial Decision-Making: Incrementalism or Stare Decisis," *Law in Transition Quarterly*, vol. 2 (1965), pp. 134–57. See also a commentary by Bruce L.R. Smith, *American Political Science Review*, vol. 61 (1967), esp. p. 151.

14. Virginia Held, "PPBS Comes to Washington," *The Public Interest*, No. 4 (Summer 1966), pp. 102–15, quotation from pp. 112–13.

15. Roger Hilsman, *To Move a Nation: The Politics of Foreign Policy in the Administration of John F. Kennedy* (Garden City, NY: Doubleday & Co., 1967), p. 27.

16. Amitai Etzioni, *The Active Society: A Theory of Societal and Political Processes* (New York: Free Press, 1968).

PART 7

HOW DO YOU EVALUATE LEADERSHIP IN THE PUBLIC SECTOR?

Leader Evaluation of Organization and Self

Leader evaluation is the end of one cycle, but it is the basis for much of the next cycle's assessment as well. It should occur at regular intervals, but ultimately it is an ongoing activity too. First and foremost, leaders should examine the appropriate balance among the organization's technical performance, follower development, and organizational alignment. Which areas need the primary focus of the leader in the upcoming period?

In terms of change focus, leaders should examine the success of past strategic initiatives and the concrete change management that accompanied them. Is the overall strategy sound? Is the change implementation at an operational level working? Leaders also look at the operational aspects of business systems to see whether quality improvements are necessary and they must look at the evolutionary stages of organizational need and how this fits with the environment, strategy, and operations.

Finally, leaders must look at themselves and their roles. Do they need to redeploy their own energies based on their evaluation? Do they need to change their style in particular situations or perhaps in general to meet evolving conditions? And are they continuing to develop themselves and to accommodate the changing needs of the organization?

Challenges in Evaluating Leader Performance

Ideally, one could evaluate leader performance strictly by looking at organizational performance. This is particularly appealing in the private sector, with its neat profit-and-loss statements and generally narrower missions. Indeed, in the last decade there has been increased interest in emphasizing results-oriented leadership that produces tangible results. However, there are at least two enormous problems in relying solely on organizational performance to evaluate leader performance.

The first problem in using organizational performance as an exact one-to-one corollary for leader performance is that leader effectiveness is only one of many factors that contribute to organizational performance. The environment, client characteristics, treatments, and structures also affect organizational effectiveness. A recession in the environment makes an executive's job much more challenging because demand for services may go up while funding is reduced. Schoolchildren (clients) in an old, run-down suburban neighborhood may increasingly come to school with decreased educational readiness and increased personal distractions. Policies about the nature of treatment can be changed dramatically without an administrative leader's input. Consider the major changes that have occurred in welfare (Hollar 2003), NASA space programs (Romzek and Dubnick 1987), Big Science projects (Lambright 1998), and contracting out (Boyne 1998). All of these policy changes introduced major implementation challenges. Although many policy changes are improvements, some are not, and result in Herculean challenges. Consider the savings and loan regulatory leaders in the 1980s as they pleaded, and even fought with, both Congress and the White House over disastrous policies (Riccucci 1995). Structure influences organizational effectiveness by making the division and coordination of work easier or more difficult; consider the effort to enhance national security by consolidating many disparate agencies into a single Department of Homeland Security with a cabinet-level secretary (Donley and Pollard 2002; Newmann 2002; Wise and Nader 2002). In many circumstances it might be argued that leadership is the single most important factor for organizational effectiveness, but it can also be demonstrated that high-quality leadership may only minimize the deterioration of organizational performance under harsh conditions (such as in the savings and loan case).

There is another problem with excessive reliance on organizational performance as a sole criterion for leader effectiveness related to time frame. Short-term strategies are often not effective in the long term. Political leaders who "borrow" money from pension trust funds to fix today's economic pinch know that the fiscal liability will not seriously affect the political economy for a decade or more (when they are likely to be long gone). The private-sector chief executive officer who spends all of his/her time cutting corporate costs, including large downsizing initiatives, to balance expenditures and revenues in the short term may fail to rebuild corporate loyalty or champion new product lines down the road. At its worst, an excessive reliance on short-term results can become a vicious cycle in which leaders spend all their time "fixing" today's problems but never take time to work on the future. Great leaders are those whose initiatives today—in personnel, culture changes, new programs, and so on—may not yield full results for five to ten years. For example, when in the 1980s Paul Volcker introduced strict monetary discipline to the Federal Reserve System, he experienced years of unpopularity. Yet he contributed enormously to the longest economic boom in U.S. history in the 1990s, which was fueled by low interest rates and monetary discipline.

Alternatives to Organizational Performance as a Sole Criterion of Leader Effectiveness

Organizational effectiveness is only one among a number of factors that are generally considered when evaluating leaders. What are other possible factors? One is the old standby—leader characteristics. What are the characteristics of leaders that make a difference over time: high-quality communication, decisiveness, influence skills, drive, energy, and so on? This generally reduces to a holistic analysis that is impressionistic and subjective, but still should relate to demonstrable leader actions.

A related approach is to look at specific leader behaviors in context. These behaviors may be captured largely by critical incidents: those events that define exceptional performance at either end of the spectrum. A critical incident might be acting decisively in curtailing spending before a fiscal crisis evolves, or failing to handle a difficult employee who disrupts operations for an entire unit. Or, the evaluator may want a fuller assessment of the performance in context, especially as it results in specific goal achievement. The advantage of using behavioral factors is that they are more concrete and specific criteria. The disadvantage is the number and complexity of the factors to record and consider. Leaders act in so many different areas, and so many different projects occur simultaneously, that evaluation of all of them is difficult.

A final major factor to consider is the difficulty of the leadership context. This really gets back to the idea that organizational performance is affected by many factors in addition to leadership itself, and sometimes these factors make leadership easier or more difficult. The leader who assumes responsibility of a well-organized unit where revenues are plentiful hardly has the same challenge as a leader who assumes responsibility of a chaotic unit that is understaffed and that is nonetheless receiving funding cuts.

Review of the Selections in Part 7

The first selection is by Steven A. Cohen, "Defining and Measuring Effectiveness in Public Management" (1993). He rehearses the type of arguments made above; organizational effectiveness and leader effectiveness are related to be sure, but only loosely, "because of the hundreds of contextual variables." He recommends that leader evaluation review the specific context of leader needs (which strongly echo those already outlined in this book), such as signs that indicate that a leader is:

- learning about what the organization is doing (assessment);
- determining what the organization needs to do (goal setting and prioritization);
- establishing systems and procedures to ensure that the organization's work gets done and encourage innovative ways (technical implementation strategies);
- deploying incentives to convince organizational members to conduct the activities of the organization (personnel strategies);
- representing the aspirations and fulfilling the social and psychological needs of the organization's members to the extent necessary to maintain the organization (organizational strategies);
- ensuring that the organization accomplishes what it needs to accomplish (evaluation).

Cohen recommends that *simultaneously* seven attribute clusters be examined, such as the "ability to listen, to learn, and to distinguish critical from peripheral facts, values, and concepts." His article, then, provides a very good, if very complex, global overview of leader evaluation.

In "Executive Evaluation: Assessing the Probability for Success in the Job" (1983), Lawrence Buck squarely takes on the issue of job difficulty. When two leaders have jobs of entirely different levels of difficulty, how do you evaluate them fairly? This challenge is often glossed over in organizations, resulting in difficult jobs' being avoided by savvy managers. Indeed, often the weakest managers are given the most difficult jobs because they are the lowest in the pecking order. In order to avoid this problem and to promote fairness, Buck describes a weighted rating system that takes into account job difficulty as a primary feature. Although this self-conscious approach to job difficulty has not been widely adopted, the concept is critical to keep in mind when reviewing leader accomplishments.

In conclusion, leader evaluation is generally far more difficult than it might seem on the surface. Organizational performance is weakly correlated because of powerful externalities. Job challenges may be equalized by difficulty coefficients in such cases. Even looking at leader performance in narrower contexts has its challenges. It is hard not to come back to some form of combined trait-behavior assessment, but these are prone to bias if not carefully linked to organizational needs (Cohen). However such evaluations are done, it should be clear that they take time to develop, take time to implement, and, if they are to be rigorous, will probably need multiple assessors and evaluation clusters.

References

Boyne, George A. 1998. "Bureaucratic Theory Meets Reality: Public Choice and Service Contracting in U.S. Local Government." *Public Administration Review* 58 (6): 474–84.

Donley, Michael B., and Neal A. Pollard. 2002. "Homeland Security: The Difference Between a Vision and a Wish." *Public Administration Review* 62 (special edition): 138–44.

Hollar, Danielle. 2003. "A Holistic Theoretical Model for Examining Welfare Reform: Quality of Life." *Public Administration Review* 63 (1): 90–104.

Lambright, W. Henry. 1998. "Downsizing Big Science: Strategic Choices." *Public Administration Review* 58 (3): 259–68.

Newmann, William W. 2002. "Reorganizing for National Security and Homeland Security." *Public Administration Review* 62 (special edition): 126–37.

Riccucci, Norma M. 1995. *Unsung Heroes: Federal Execucrats Making a Difference*. Washington, DC: Georgetown University Press.

Romzek, Barbara S., and Melvin J. Dubnick. 1987. "Accountability in the Public Sector: Lessons from the Challenger Tragedy." *Public Administration Review* 47 (3): 227–38.

Wise, Charles R., and Rania Nader. 2002. "Organizing the Federal System for Homeland Security: Problems, Issues, and Dilemmas." *Public Administration Review* 62 (special edition): 44–57.

CHAPTER 25

DEFINING AND MEASURING EFFECTIVENESS IN PUBLIC MANAGEMENT

STEVEN A. COHEN

> Public management research should focus on improving
> the performance of public managers.

This article begins with a discussion of the concepts of management and leadership. I seek to integrate these two concepts by specifying dimensions of leadership and management in which a public manager strives to be effective. Next, I will discuss the concept of effectiveness as it applies to public management. For each dimension of management I will propose indicators for assessing effectiveness. Finally, I will discuss how these indicators might be used in empirical studies of management effectiveness.

I want to know what is meant by the terms *effectiveness* and *management*. The unit of analysis is the manager. I am attempting to assess effective management performance, not effective organizational performance. This emphasis is best represented in the management literature by Henry Mintzberg (1973) and his focus on the work of managers, Robert Behn's recent work (1991, 1992), and by Herbert Kaufman's (1981) similar work on the behavior of federal bureau chiefs. It is difficult to discuss effective management without understanding what managers do. However, management cannot be understood simply by studying and describing the behaviors of managers. The sociology literature in organization theory and the business literature in management present us with a number of different slants on the definition of management and leadership (Stogdill 1974). Review of this literature makes it clear that we are looking at a complex, multidimensional concept. Each particular scholarly emphasis provides useful insight on some dimension of management. I do not believe it is necessary to choose between these schools of thought: by drawing on all of them we can develop a comprehensive definition of management (Cohen 1991).

For some time now scholars of private sector management have pursued a behavioral approach to the study of management. To date, however, they have failed to relate managerial effectiveness to organizational effectiveness. The additional complexity of public management environments makes it even more difficult to study and understand

From *Public Productivity & Management Review*, vol. 17, no. 1 (Fall 1993): 45–57. Copyright © 1993 by Jossey-Bass. Reprinted with permission of M.E. Sharpe, Inc.

the behavior of public managers. Nevertheless, if we do not observe the work of public managers, we cannot hope to understand and improve their performance.

Leadership and Management

In the management literature a distinction is often made between leadership and management. According to this literature, management is the task of setting up control structures and standard operating procedures (SOPs), while leadership involves stimulating organizational change by articulating a vision and inspiring a sense of mission. John Kotter (1990) has done an excellent job of defining these two concepts. Kotter (1990, 103) observes that "leadership and management are two distinct and complementary systems of action. Each has its own function and characteristic activities." Kotter (1990, 107) concludes by noting:

> According to the logic of management, control mechanisms compare system behavior with the plan and take action when a deviation is detected. In a well-managed factory, for example, this means the planning process establishes sensible quality targets, the organizing process builds an organization that can achieve those targets, and a control process makes sure that quality lapses are spotted immediately. . . .
>
> For some of the same reasons that control is so central to management, highly motivated or inspired behavior is almost irrelevant. Managerial processes must be as close as possible to fail-safe and risk free. That means they cannot be dependent on the unusual or hard to obtain. The whole purpose of systems and structures is to help normal people who behave in normal ways to complete routine jobs successfully, day after day. It's not exciting or glamorous. But that's management.
>
> Leadership is different. . . . Motivation and inspiration energizes people, not by pushing them in the right direction as control mechanisms do but by satisfying basic human needs for achievement, a sense of belonging, recognition, self esteem, a feeling of control over one's life and the ability to live up to one's ideals.

Here Kotter is describing two functions that are basic to management: (1) establishing and maintaining production systems, and (2) inspiring people to contribute the effort needed to implement and change work processes. The analytic advantage to separating these two functions is that it ensures that each receives separate focused attention. However, my own view is that control systems and motivational factors must be connected in both analysis and practice. People frequently have greater or lesser comfort with either the "system" side of the shop or with the "human interaction" part of the operation. However, control structures and SOPs only perform at peak efficiency when the people within the organization are motivated to implement and change them. Otherwise they quickly become outmoded. Indeed, Kotter agrees that both "leadership" and "management" are needed for a successful organization.

My fear is that by not subsuming them under a single concept, we run the risk of emphasizing one over the other in both analysis and practice. I have seen people who hide behind their elegant control structures complaining about the "damn fools" in the organization who simply will not play their designated role in the system. I have also seen managers who focus on vision exclusively, leaving the less glamorous implementation tasks to "lesser" staff who inevitably allow the vision to be compromised in the day-to-day world of real work. Finally, I have also observed "touchy-feely" human relations experts so caught up in perfecting group processes that they ignore the importance of production systems and organizational outputs. In terms of analysis, formal structures and control systems are more amenable to quantitative study and development than are soft topics such as motivation and vision. Academics tend to focus research on phenomena that enable them to use sophisticated methodologies. After all, they have invested considerable effort learning these techniques, and frequently enjoy using them.

But it is possible to integrate "soft" management with "hard" management. Total quality management (TQM) is an effort to integrate the "soft management techniques of organizational development and human resource management with the "hard" quantitative techniques of statistical process control (Cohen and Brand 1990, 100–2). While TQM aims to improve an organization's systems and SOPs, it utilizes staff energy and enthusiasm to do so. Systems development and human relations are not divorced because SOPs are developed by staff for their own use.

In this article I am seeking to develop a multidimensional definition of management, and then attempting to develop a method for measuring management effectiveness. I am not seeking to distinguish management from other concepts, but instead to build a more comprehensive definition.

Defining Management

To define management I suggest we focus on two distinct units of analysis. The first is the functions of management; the second is the attributes of managers. Managers must perform the following functions:

1. Learn what the organization is doing.
2. Determine what the organization needs to do.
3. Encourage innovative ways of doing what the organization needs to do.
4. Deploy incentives to convince the organization's members to conduct the activities that the organization needs to do.
5. Represent the aspirations and fulfill the social and psychological needs of the organization's members to the extent necessary to maintain the organization.
6. Ensure that the organization accomplishes what it needs to accomplish.

To perform these functions, managers require the following skills or attributes:

1. The ability to listen, to learn, and to distinguish critical from peripheral facts, values, and concepts.
2. A personality that matches the needs of the particular organization's social structure and internal composition, environment, and goals.

3. Skill and sensitivity in distributing resources, deploying incentives, and exercising power. This requires an ability to read people, interpret behavior, act intuitively, and correctly mix the use of emotional appeals, reason, incentives, and one's own power to influence organizational behaviors.

4. The ability to identify and achieve appropriate goals. In the public sector, goal setting is often a complex act requiring the manager to juggle conflicting claims and ambiguous policy directions. As incremental theory indicates, sometimes public managers are not trying to accomplish anything new, but simply trying to keep a bad situation from getting worse.

5. The ability to clearly communicate roles, tasks, goals, and missions.

6. Creativity.

7. The ability to inspire.

Defining Effectiveness

According to Lynn (1987, 18), "Success in public management is a product of the interaction of personality and circumstances: the skillful use of many approaches—structural, political, symbolic—to produce movement toward personal goals in specific situations. Executives' beliefs and temperaments define and impart direction to ambiguous reality." As Lynn indicates, the critical point to understand in defining effectiveness is that it is always situational. The definition of effectiveness will vary with different organizational environments, different organizational types, and different organizational goals. Each of the functions and the attributes needed to perform those functions I just listed will vary in different organizational settings. One can easily imagine a manager in a crisis situation who has excellent listening skills, but who listens too much and does not act when he or she should. Or perhaps we might imagine another manager running a directionless organization: this particular manager has terrific communication skills but has poor skills as a strategist—the wrong situation for this person's talents.

However, I have observed some general traits shared by effective public managers. In the *Effective Public Manager* (Cohen 1988) I discussed the general behaviors exhibited by these managers. In this section I will summarize some of the points I made in my book to provide an overview of the concept of effectiveness.

Effectiveness, as Lynn indicates, requires craftsmanship and an ability to give shape to vague and ambiguous policy environments. An effective public manager seeks to shape events rather than be shaped by them. The most effective public managers learn to adjust programs rapidly to reflect changed priorities. They anticipate changes in policy direction and build organizations capable of rapid redirection. Developing management systems and understanding budget formulation and financial management are only part of the job. To achieve effective management, a manager must be able to influence human beings to act in a desired manner. An effective manager must have both the most up-to-date information and an excellent staff to respond to and act quickly in a changing environment.

The most effective public managers are careful people who understand that actions that are poorly thought through can result in unanticipated bad consequences. However, they do not allow wise caution to degenerate into inertia. They must learn to judge when caution is the prudent course and when risk is necessary. This kind of judgment takes intuition, guesswork, wisdom, and experience. Since very little is ever achieved in conflict-free environments, a good manager must not only accept conflict as an inevitable part of accomplishing goals, but she or he must learn to feel comfortable working with it. The effective public manager must have flexibility, resilience, and persistence.

Effective public management requires managers who are not afraid to take aggressive and even risky actions to overcome constraints and obstacles. The entrepreneurial public manager assumes risk for the sake of organization gain. However, the risks are made in a calculated fashion and as part of a realistic (possibly unwritten) organizational strategy. Good managers must take risks to assure performance. Effective public managers try to make things happen; they pursue programmatic goals and objectives by thinking and acting strategically. They attempt to understand why things are happening and how things can be changed. This requires constant contact with an informal network of informants who provide feedback on ideas and initiatives, and who themselves are constantly learning, teaching, experimenting, and changing.

Effective management requires defining and redefining the mission and activities of the organization. The manager must keep in close contact with the needs and views of both staff and customers while designing and executing programs. It is the responsibility of the manager to ensure that the organization's performance results in accomplishments and products that serve public needs. This responsibility requires entrepreneurial risks. The effective public manager works continually to interpret the public's changing needs and design creative responses to fulfill those needs. Put simply, the effective public manager has a can-do attitude and believes that all problems have a solution; the secret is to persist until the solution is found.

Indicators of Effectiveness

These general sentiments are useful in providing a feel for the nuances of effectiveness, but they lack the type of specificity required for research. To provide the type of specificity I am looking for I will take each dimension of management—its functions and the attributes of managers—and propose indicators of effectiveness or at least an approach for determining effectiveness for that particular dimension. I should mention that these indicators do not imply any assumptions about their relative weight in assessing effectiveness. One of the first tasks I would recommend in utilizing these indicators is to assess the situation (the nature of the organization, its goals, and its environment) and decide what indicators are most important. Let me also note that I look at these management dimensions and indicators as a first step in operationally defining effective management. They will need to be modified in the light of empirical research on actual public managers.

Indicators of Effective Performance of Management Functions

1. Signs that indicate a manager is learning about what the organization is doing include:

Presence of a management information and/or financial control system, as well as evidence of actual use of the system in decision making.

Presence of processes for describing and reporting work, such as regular staff meetings.

Evidence of informal communication patterns—management by apparent wandering around, social events, travel, phone contacts, and the like.

Evidence of changed management behavior in response to information about what the organization is actually doing.

2. Signs that indicate that a manager is determining what the organization needs to do include:

Presence of a process for formulating organizational strategy. This need not (and probably should not) be a formal process resulting in a written document.

Evidence of frequent contact with external parties—for example, other units within the organization, legislators, other executive branch organizations, the media, academics, industry, and interest groups.

Documentation or evidence of an evolving strategy in response to changed external conditions.

3. Signs that indicate that a manager has established systems and procedures to ensure that the organization's work gets done and encourages innovative ways of doing what the organization needs to do include:

Presence and use of SOPs or rules governing work processes.

A record of efforts to change SOPs.

Evidence of efforts to change SOPs.

Evidence of pilot projects to test innovations and documentation of adoption of new policies, processes, and technologies.

4. Signs that indicate that a manager is deploying incentives to convince organizational members to conduct the activities that the organization needs to do include:

Documentation of methods for describing and assessing staff performance; again, we are not looking for a formal written performance assessment system.

Evidence that the manager understands the specific incentives most effective at motivating particular staff.

Documentation of deployment of resources for incentives to encourage, discourage, or reward specific behaviors; such incentives might include awards, new equipment, higher pay, promotions, exhortation, praise, admonitions, warnings, and assignments.

Evidence of changed behavior as a result of the deployment of incentives.

5. Signs that indicate that a manager is representing the aspirations and fulfilling the social and psychological needs of the organization's members to the extent necessary to maintain the organization include:

  Evidence of high morale among those directly supervised, for example, in terms of staff attitudes toward the organization, or staff willingness to interact with other staff and managers after normal work hours for both work and socializing.

  Data on staff turnover among those directly supervised. There are no quantitative rules here, but a 0 percent turnover rate and a 100 percent turnover rate are equally negative indicators of effectiveness.

6. Signs that indicate that a manager is ensuring that the organization accomplishes what it needs to accomplish include:

  Data on organizational outputs. Do standard performance measures indicate a relationship between the organization's strategy and its accomplishments? How much of what the organization sets out to accomplish is completed?

  Evidence that the organization has anticipated problems, or otherwise prevented damage to the organization's functions or mission. For example, in regard to the organization's media coverage, Are negatives effectively countered? Are the organization's problems exaggerated, ignored, or accurately reported?

If we are to build a body of research on the effectiveness of public managers, we must first study the impact that managers have had on their organizations. The indicators I have just discussed provide a framework for that type of research. I assume that the actions of managers are the independent variable and the behavior of their organizations are the dependent variables. However we must move beyond assumptions and directly study the behavior of managers. To directly study managerial behavior, we must identify other independent variables and seek to explain variation in managerial behavior. The unit of analysis for this inquiry is the effectiveness of managers, not the effectiveness of organizations. Organizational behavior is a surrogate measure for management effectiveness; it is not the focus of this article.

Indicators That Managers Possess the Skills Needed to Be Effective

1. Signs that a manager has the ability to listen, learn, and distinguish critical from peripheral facts, values, and concepts include:

  Evidence that a manager regularly changes his or her views in response to communications from staff.
  Evidence of efforts to integrate disparate facts into central themes or findings.
  Examples of incidence in which the manager communicates to staff the organiza-

tion's core values and mission, and evidence of efforts to apply these values to organizational tasks and to use them in discarding tasks and information seen as peripheral.

Direct observation of efforts to elicit the views of staff. Does the manager dominate all meetings, or are other voices heard? Does the staff feel that their input is considered when the manager makes decisions?

2. Signs that a manager has a personality that matches the needs of the particular organization's social structure and internal composition, environment, and goals include:

Measures of the manager's professional reputation among peers and staff—especially as related to the current job; evidence of support and opposition among the staff.

Analysis of manager personality—perhaps via Meyers/Briggs or similar classification scheme matched to an analysis of the organization's needs. (For example, at this phase in the organization's life, does it need an inspirational visionary, or someone good at minding the organization's basic "nuts-and-bolts" routines? Are there external threats requiring someone who performs well in front of TV cameras, or would strengths as a legislative insider be more helpful?)

3. Signs that a manager has skill and sensitivity in distributing resources, deploying incentives, and exercising power include:

Measures of the manager's reputation for overall competence among peers and staff.

Evidence that the manager is perceived as a skillful practitioner. Is the manager perceived as judicious, prudent, timid, aggressive, or a "hothead"? Does the manager inspire staff and peers' respect and admiration, fear and loathing, or scorn and pity?

Evidence of the manager's ability to correctly predict events and the behavior of people. Does the manager attempt to anticipate reaction to his or her actions, for example, and how often are the manager's guestimates correct?

Evidence of the manager's ability to correctly predict the effect of the deployment of resources on the behavior of key staff.

4. Signs that a manager has the ability to identify and accomplish appropriate goals include:

Evidence that the manager is directly involved in setting goals and directing activities that contribute to their accomplishment. This evidence might include analysis of calendars and formal memos to identify activities related to goal setting and tracking, or detailed case analysis following the articulation of a goal and identification of specific management activities that led to staff behaviors that contributed to accomplishing that goal.

Evidence that demonstrates that the manager takes into account the organization's environment and internal resources when setting goals and monitoring accomplishments.

Evidence of external support for the organization directly attributed to the direction the manager has set for the organization.

Evidence that the manager was able to change the organization's direction and outputs in response to specific external stimuli.

5. Signs that a manager has the ability to facilitate development of systems of work processes and to clearly communicate roles, tasks, goals, and missions include:

Analysis of the manager's ability to organize and structure work. Does the manager have good skills at planning and organizing projects (measured by means of self-perceptions, staff perception, and documented project plans)? If the manager lacks these skills, does he or she have the self-awareness to delegate these functions to someone else?

Analysis of overlap of manager and staff understanding of roles, tasks, goals, and missions.

Analysis of internal formal memoranda articulating and implementing roles, tasks, goals, and missions to assess the quality of the communicating process. Does staff understand what the manager is trying to say and do? What types of questions are raised in formal communications? Do they indicate resistance, poor communication, or simply a need for more detail?

The amount of training and experience the manager has had in spoken and written communication.

Staff and peer perceptions of the quality of the manager's communication skills.

Expert analysis of the manager's communication skills. Does the manager have the technical skills in speaking and writing needed to communicate clearly? Is the manager able to compensate for any lack of formal technical communication skills, for example, through more frequent communication efforts, through an engaging informal style, or by using subordinates as surrogate communicators?

6. Signs that a manager has creativity include:

The frequency that the manager's advice is sought when developing new programs, policies, and procedures. Does staff seek the manager's involvement to prevent a veto or to tap into his or her ability to frame creative proposals?

Evidence that the manager encourages experimentation to modify established practices.

Examples of new ideas that can be directly attributed to the manager.

Staff and peer perceptions of the quality of the manager's creative powers.

7. Signs that a manager has the ability to inspire include:

Evidence that the manager makes an effort to communicate his or her vision of the organization and its role in the world.

Evidence that the manager's vision is expressed without prompting by members of the organizations, and that it is accepted as an important and credible guide to action.

Staff and peer perceptions of the manager's ability to inspire.

Evidence of changed organizational behavior that can be directly attributed to the manager's ability to inspire, for example, staff statements such as "I wasn't too sure this would work, but X says it will and I really believe in what she says and stands for. So I did it her way."

Studying Management Effectiveness

Obviously the concept of management effectiveness and indicators of effectiveness open up a thicket of definitional and measurement issues. My purpose here is not to attempt to conclude a discussion of management effectiveness but to contribute to a dialogue. I believe that if we are to improve management performance, we must study that performance empirically. However, we should not build a body of research that simply describes and categorizes management behavior. Such scholarship may have its place in less applied disciplines, but in the field of public management we need to study effectiveness for a purpose: that purpose is to improve the performance of public managers. As workers in the field, we should be very interested in studies that attempt to define what we are looking for in a manager—what I am calling effectiveness—and then assess management performance in the light of explicit criteria.

In some sense this is a retreat from efforts to assess organizational effectiveness. Some evaluation experts, such as Joseph S. Wholey (1983), have developed practical tools for evaluating organizational effectiveness and for obtaining what Wholey terms "results-oriented management." It is clear that studies of organizational effectiveness and operational indicators of organizational effectiveness have an important place in professional practice and scholarship. In particular, those responsible for running organizations need tools for measuring the performance of the entity they are responsible for. However, in his recent work, *Understanding and Managing Public Organizations,* Hal Rainey (1991, 208) reviewed the literature on organizational effectiveness and noted that organizational experts "emphasize the difficulty of defining and determining organizational effectiveness. . . . [T]hose who set out to study effectiveness soon realized that assessing whether an organization does its job well involved numerous technical, economic, ethical and ideological issues."

Studying the effectiveness of an entire organization presents many daunting practical measurement problems, although a number of evaluation experts believe that this task is feasible. An accurate empirical organizational study must describe a large number of people and their behaviors. Researchers must develop practical summary measures of organizational outputs. We must also seek methods of summarizing the behaviors that lead to particular outputs. I believe that these measurement tasks can and will be done and assume that the organization will remain an important unit of analysis in public management research.

However, while indicators of organizational output can be useful in understanding current levels of organizational performance, I am not certain that there is any benefit in measuring the overall effectiveness of an organization. How can this information be used? If you know that one organization meets its targets more often than another, what do you know about the organization? You may know that its leadership is good at setting low targets. Or you may know that it is good at meeting the numbers it wishes to be measured against. But you have no way of knowing which output indicator is most important, unless you have conducted a qualitative assessment of the organization's operations.

Even if you were able to figure out that one organization performed better than another, an emphasis on output and impact indicators would not tell you what led to those different performance levels. If you then decide to study organizational processes in order to understand the causes of various performance levels, you end up observing the behavior of managers in instituting and changing SOPs. In the end you still find yourself describing and analyzing the behavior of managers. By emphasizing the manager as the unit of analysis we may be able to understand the ingredients of a manager's relative effectiveness (or ineffectiveness) and therefore teach managers how to perform better.

While studying the behavior of managers within organizations presents some of the same problems as studying organizations, one can at least focus observations on a finite discrete case. Identifying causal links between an individual and an organization is a difficult, but feasible research task. One can observe different managers running the same organization at different points in time. The same manager might be studied in a variety of settings. I am arguing that public management scholars should increase their efforts to borrow methodologies developed for individual and clinical psychological studies and in-depth anthropological fieldwork rather than utilize the macro level methodologies more characteristic of sociology and political science large-scale survey research. A manager's performance must be assessed in light of information about a large number of subtle and complex environmental factors. What is the organization's history? What type of issue areas is it working in? What kind of political and media visibility does the issue area generate? What is the constellation of political support for the organization? What type of programs does the organization implement? Is the organization's work technically and socially ambitious (for example, space travel or homeless families) or simple and straightforward (for example, highway construction or processing Social Security checks)? What type of personnel and organizational capacity did the manager inherit? There are hundreds of similar contextual variables that must be understood to measure management effectiveness. This requires a methodology that allows the researcher to live and breathe the organization he or she is studying. The methodologies appropriate to this study are those that enable a scholar to become immersed in the organization and its work. Robert Behn has termed this approach "case analysis research." In his view, theory on management effectiveness must be built on empirical research. According to Behn (1991, 11):

> Case analysis research is based on the assumption that if you want to develop a theory about effective practice you have to understand a lot of observations of effective practice. What makes an individual an effective manager in particular situations is not at all obvious—or logical. If you really want to know the best way to lead an organization to the top of sand dunes, you have to observe a lot of organizational efforts to climb sand dunes. And then you have to cull out the commonalities of success—at least of particular kinds of success in particular conditions—and attempt to develop a theoretical framework to explain such limited and conditional successes.

Public management research to date has focused on organizational performance and developing indicators of organizational success. While I believe that these indicators are useful as one method (hopefully among many) for measuring current levels of organizational performance, such indicators have been overinterpreted and misinterpreted. The effort to develop output and impact measures that serve as a surrogate bottom line for public sector organizations can lead to artificial bean counting. Given the incremental nature of public sector problem solving, the results we sometimes manage for are difficult to measure using the type of management indicators I have seen used in government. I worry about goal-setting efforts that result in meaningless or misleading organizational output and process indicators. This is not to say that management information systems (MIS) do not have a role in public organizations. Tracking the current level of an organization's performance is an essential element of any effort to improve performance. However, the use of this data to set and manage against numerical goals seems to distort organizational performance by driving out less quantifiable priorities and creating the type of last-minute rush typically seen in Russian factories.

Finally, as an educator of future public managers, I am attracted to the manager as a unit of analysis because I teach future managers. I do not teach organizations. Research on the effectiveness of managers may provide me with insights I can use in teaching future public managers. I believe that this type of research focus has greater potential for helping to create a research tradition more closely linked to professional practice.

In a strict behavioral sense, organizations do not "behave" but managers and staff do. Improving organizational performance is not simply a matter of manipulating organizational and control structures, legal authority, and financial resources. Each of those factors can be seen as independent variables that influence the behavior of management and staff. If we are attempting to improve management effectiveness, we are attempting to stimulate management behaviors, and those behaviors should be the ultimate dependent variable in our analysis.

References

Behn, R.D. "Management by Groping Along." *Journal of Policy Analysis and Management* 7 (4), 643–63.

Behn, R.D. 1991. "Case-Analysis Research and Management Effectiveness: Learning How to Lead Organizations Up Sand Dunes." Paper presented at the National Public Management Research Conference, Maxwell School, Syracuse University, Syracuse, NY, September 19–21, 1991.

Behn, R.D. 1992. "Management and the Neutrino: The Search for Meaningful Metaphors." *Public Administration Review,* 52, 409–19.

Cohen, S. 1988. *The Effective Public Manager: Achieving Success in Government.* San Francisco: Jossey Bass, 1988.

Cohen, S. 1991. "Measuring Effectiveness in Public Management." Paper presented at the 1991 annual research meeting of the Association of Public Policy Analysis and Management, Bethesda, Maryland, October 24–26, 1991.

Cohen, S., and Brand, R. 1990. "Total Quality Management in the U.S. Environmental Protection Agency." *Public Productivity and Management Review,* 14(1), 99–113.

Kaufman, H. 1981. *The Administrative Behavior of Federal Bureau Chiefs.* Washington, DC: Brookings Institution.

Kotter, J.P. 1990. "What Leaders Really Do." *Harvard Business Review,* 68, 103–11.

Kotter, J.P. 1992. *Corporate Culture and Performance.* New York: Free Press.

Lynn, L. 1987. *Managing Public Policy.* Boston: Little, Brown.

Mintzberg, H. 1973. *The Nature of Managerial Work.* New York: HarperCollins.

Rainey, H.G. 1991. *Understanding and Managing Public Organizations.* San Francisco: Jossey-Bass.

Stogdill, R.M. 1974. *Handbook of Leadership.* New York: Free Press.

Wholey, J.S. 1983. *Evaluation and Effective Public Management.* Boston: Little, Brown.

CHAPTER 26

EXECUTIVE EVALUATION

Assessing the Probability for Success in the Job

LAWRENCE S. BUCK

Introduction

The accurate and objective evaluation of executives' job performance has long been a matter of concern in the public and private sectors. While large amounts of money are spent recruiting and training executives, systems for assessing their on-the-job performance have tended to be subjective and trait-based in nature. More objective and job-related evaluation systems are needed to evaluate executives' performance accurately. Such systems, in addition to protecting the employer's interest, also protect the employee's interests, particularly when personnel actions or financial rewards are based on performance evaluations.

In the federal government, the passage of the Civil Service Reform Act of 1978 (CSRA) cast the performance appraisal issue in a new light. The CSRA created a new Senior Executive Service (SES) and required that an objective, job-related, measurable performance evaluation system that would provide for summary performance ratings at different levels be developed for senior executives. The CSRA also required that executives' evaluations serve as a basis for a variety of personnel actions, including performance awards (cash bonuses) to be paid in a lump sum.

While an organization has a commitment to its executive to ensure that their performance is objectively and fairly evaluated, the organization is also committed to the accomplishment of its objectives. In this respect, a performance evaluation system must meet both the needs of the organization and its executives. Ralph (1980, 145–47) dichotomizes the purposes that performance evaluation systems can serve into "administrative" and "behavioral." ". . . the administrative purposes are those the *organization* will *do to* the individual. The behavioral purposes . . . are those which the *individual* must bring about himself."

To meets its "behaviorial" purposes, the Department of Agriculture implemented a performance appraisal system for its senior executives. This system is based, at least

---

in theory, on objective, job-related performance elements and standards. This article describes an additional evaluation system developed in the department to serve its "administrative" purposes relative to the award provisions of the CSRA. This evaluation system embodies a concept called the position coefficient and results in a rating that is combined with the performance appraisal rating to determine the performance award recipients.

Background

The CSRA stipulates that performance bonuses be limited in number to no more than 50 percent of the senior executives in an agency. Further limitations on the number of executives who could receive specific bonus amounts were imposed by the Office of Personnel Management (OPM). These limitations created problems for the bonus process since bonuses were to be based primarily on performance and yet performance ratings were not to be subjected to forced distribution. Historically in the department, executives' ratings have clustered at the upper levels of the scale with little variance. Given the likelihood that such rating patterns would continue, how would the finer discriminations necessary for selection of bonus recipients be effected? The position coefficient concept was the department's answer to these problems.

Prior to implementation of the department's SES performance appraisal system, a panel of departmental executives convened to develop a means of facilitating the performance bonus process that would be objective, fair, and consistent. Philosophically the panel was in agreement that some jobs are easier than others, some more controllable, some demand more conservative execution, and that these aspects of an executive's position can be measured (rated). The position coefficient is a rating of these differences between positions in terms of the probability for success in a position based on the risk/difficulty level of the position where success equates to performance. This rating is combined with the performance rating to determine award eligibility. Contrary to performance ratings, the distribution of position coefficient ratings is forced, providing more differentiation among executives.

Stimson (1980, 42) points out a problem common to award systems in that ". . . rewards are sometimes allocated to units on a fair share basis, resulting in the inequitable process of giving rewards to managers in low performance units who are not as deserving as managers not receiving awards in higher performance units." Brumback (1981, 270) discusses another potential problem with reward systems in that:

> Because individuals have different performance objectives, instances sometimes occur in which two or more individuals reach the same levels of achievement, but the values of the achievements to the organization are not the same. When such instances do occur and are not somehow resolved . . . performance-based decisions can produce serious inequities.

The position coefficient concept offers a resolution to both of these problems in that awards are granted on an individual basis and, by taking the demands placed on one's position into consideration, those who succeed under the most trying conditions are rewarded. In this respect, executives receiving high ratings due in part to the lack of demands on their positions will not necessarily be advantaged over executives receiving lower ratings due in large part to excessive demands on their positions.

Performance Review Boards

The CSRA (1978) requires that "each agency shall establish . . . one or more performance review boards . . . to make recommendations to the appropriate appointing authority of the agency relating to the performance of senior executives in the agency." The performance review boards (PRBs) are also required to make recommendations relative to performance bonus recipients. The department established nine PRBs to review supervisors' performance ratings and to make recommendations to the Secretary of Agriculture as appropriate. Each PRB is responsible for the position coefficient ratings for those executives under its jurisdiction. The PRBs also recommend to the Secretary of Agriculture those senior executives to be awarded performance bonuses.

Each PRB consists of a minimum of eight voting members designated by the Secretary of Agriculture. The PRBs are generally chaired by a Deputy Assistant Secretary and include the administrators of the agencies under their jurisdiction. Senior executives from other departmental agencies and/or program areas make up the remaining members of each PRB. The PRBs are established along organization lines to ensure that programs with related functions and responsibilities are grouped together. This manner of composing the PRBs is important, since the position coefficient concept is most effective when the positions being rated do not involve significantly different executive functions. Care is taken to assure that no executive is a member of a PRB that would act on his or her performance or position coefficient rating.

The Rating Process

The PRBs assign position coefficient ratings on a scale of one to five, where one represents a low risk/difficulty position, three a typical position, and five a high risk/difficulty position. Expressed in a different manner, a rating of one reflects a position with a high probability for success on the job (low risk/difficulty), while a rating of five reflects a position with a low probability for success (high risk/difficulty). These ratings are assigned to each career executive based on the PRBs collective perception of the risk/difficulty level of the executive's position relative to the positions occupied by the other career executives under the PRBs jurisdiction. That is, within a particular PRB, executives' positions are compared with each other and not with those of executives under other PRBs. In this respect, an executive's position might be considered the most risky and difficult relative to the other executives under his or her PRB and yet, if considered department-wide, the position might rank far down the line.

The position coefficient ratings are based on an evaluation of the career positions for four of the following five factors:

Figure 26.1   **Award Matrix** (position coefficient)

Performance Rating	1	2	3	4	5
1	X	X	X	X	X
2	X	X	X	X	X
3	15	14	12	9	6
4	13	11	8	5	3
5	10	7	4	2	1

- integration of internal and external program/policy issues;
- organizational representation and liaison;
- direction and guidance of program, projects, or policy development;
- resource acquisition and administration;
- scientific research and personal accomplishments.

The PRBs are aided in the rating process by narratives provided for each of the four selected factors by the supervisor, the executive, and where appropriate, the second-level supervisor. A forced distribution of ratings is ensured by providing to each PRB points equal to three times the number of executives under its jurisdiction that are eligible for performance bonuses. For example, if a PRB had 13 eligible executives, it would be assigned 39 points to distribute, resulting in an average rating of three.

The Award Matrix

To provide a means of combining the position coefficient and performance ratings, an award matrix was designed (Figure 26.1). The matrix is divided into cells and an executive's cell placement is determined by his or her combined performance and position coefficient ratings. The cutoff for bonus eligibility was established at the cell corresponding to a performance rating of three and a position coefficient rating of one (cell 15) since the CSRA requires acceptable performance for eligibility for performance bonuses (under the department's five-level performance evaluation system, a rating of three corresponds to acceptable performance).

The cell corresponding to a performance rating of five and a position coefficient of five is the highest possible cell (cell 1). The numbers in the cells reflect the rank order of the cells. As Figure 26.1 illustrates, the performance rating is weighted more than the position coefficient rating. For example, a performance rating of five with a coefficient of four (cell 2) is ranked higher than a performance rating of four with a coefficient of five (cell 3). Within a cell, executives are rank-ordered according to their composite performance ratings expressed to the nearest tenth. If three executives were in cell 3 with performance ratings of 4.1, 4.3, and 4.6 and the PRB could award bonuses to only two of them, the executives with the 4.6 and 4.3 ratings would receive the bonuses.

As the plan was originally conceived, all eligible executives in the department would have been placed in one matrix and each matrix cell weighted to determine the bonus amount attached to each cell, contingent on the number of bonuses payable. However, because of severe limitations placed by Congress and OPM on the number of bonuses payable, the award matrix was not used in this manner. Congress stipulated that an agency could award bonuses equal in number to no more than 25 percent of the agency's executive positions; OPM further reduced this to 20 percent of the career executives in an agency. In round figures, these actions reduced from 200 to 60 the number of potential bonus recipients in the department for the first performance award cycle.

Due to limitations on the number of payable bonuses, the department established allocations for each PRB and the award matrix was used within each PRB rather than across all PRBs. Each PRB assigned performance ratings and position coefficient ratings for each eligible executive and placed them in the matrix. In accordance with its specific allocation, each PRB would then recommend those in the highest cells for bonuses. The Secretary's PRB (which has oversight responsibilities for the program PRBs) reviewed the results of each PRB's actions and, unless there were special circumstances, honored the recommendations of the PRBs. In this respect, rating differences between PRB did not affect the chances of a PRB's recommendees. The Secretary's PRB then recommended the specific bonus amounts to be awarded to each bonus recipient and forwarded its recommendations to the Secretary of Agriculture for final approval.

Executives' Reactions

The position coefficient was utilized in the department for each of the first two annual performance award cycles and will continue to be used for the third cycle. The concept has, however, met with mixed reactions from the department's executives. Executives' attitudes toward the concept were assessed in part through an attitude survey administered to 243 executives. The survey was part of an ongoing evaluation of the department's SES. Twelve of the forty-eight survey questions addressed issues related to the position coefficient concept. The return rate was 62 percent.

It was obvious from the survey results as well as other feedback gathered less systematically that there is a considerable amount of negativism toward the concept. For example, 61 percent of the survey respondents felt that the position coefficient unfairly discriminates against senior executives in terms of their potential for performance bonuses, 18 percent did not consider the coefficient discriminatory, and the remainder were undecided. With respect to the continued use of the position coefficient, 53 percent of the respondents were opposed, 26 percent favored its continuation, and 21 percent were undecided. As to determining bonus recipients strictly on the basis of their performance ratings, 65 percent were in favor, and 31 percent favored the use of performance ratings and a modified position coefficient concept for the bonus process. On the question of whether the risk/difficulty aspects of their positions could be observed and rated, 49 percent of the respondents were in agreement, while 43 percent did not agree with the concept; the remainder were undecided.

A number of other concerns with the position coefficient concept were raised through written comments received with the survey returns, as well as other feedback from de-

Table 26.1

Comparisons Between 1980 and 1981 Position Coefficient Ratings
(N = 177)

Increase			Decrease			Stay the same		
Rating	N	% Total N	Rating	N	% Total N	Rating	N	% Total N
1–2	1	.6	5–4	3	2	2	30	17
1–3	1	.6	5–3	1	.6	3	48	27
2–3	22	12	5–2	1	.6	4	17	10
2–4	4	2	4–3	20	11			
2–5	1	.6	4–2	3	2			
3–4	7	4	3–2	13	7			
3–5	2	1	2–1	1	.6			
4–5	2	1						

partmental executives. Many executives were concerned that once a position coefficient rating was assigned, the rating would remain with the position for the next rating cycle. If this were the case, an executive with a low position coefficient would have little chance of receiving a bonus the next year regardless of his or her performance and, therefore, less incentive to perform well. This was neither the intent of the position coefficient, nor the manner in which it operated. Rather, factors such as shifts in priorities and direction, reorganizations, or self-induced changes may impact on the relative degree of risk/difficulty in a position. The Mt. St. Helens eruption and the Mediterranean fruit-fly crisis serve as two examples of situational factors that radically altered the demands placed on various executives and thus resulted in a position coefficient different from that assigned the previous year.

Table 26.1 illustrates the fact that position coefficient ratings are not static from one year to the next. There were 177 executives who were rated under the department's appraisal system in both 1980 and 1981. Of these ratings, nearly half changed from 1980 to 1981. The greatest percentage of increased ratings was from a rating of two to a coefficient of three while the greatest percentage of decreased ratings was from a rating of four to a rating of three.

Of these 177 executives for whom 1980 and 1981 ratings were available, 35 received bonuses in 1981. Of these, fifteen had coefficient ratings which had increased from 1980 to 1981; three had decreased ratings, and seventeen had the same ratings. This further illustrates that not only will ratings change from year to year, but also that the change may be beneficial to the executive.

Many executives consider the paperwork and time requirements associated with the use of the position coefficient to be excessive and counterproductive. Others believe that the position coefficient rating is weighted more heavily than the performance rating and that the opposite should hold. In addition, a number of executives consider the position coefficient biased in favor of higher level management positions, thereby reducing the chances for executives in lower level positions to receive performance awards. Depending on their frame of reference, others consider the coefficient to be biased against scientific

Table 26.2

Departmental Senior Executives and Bonus Recipients by Location

Location	SES population 1980	SES population 1981	Percent 1980	Percent 1981	Bonuses paid 1980	Bonuses paid 1981	Percent of bonus recipients 1980	Percent of bonus recipients 1981
Headquarters	177	189	66	76	49	41	75	79
Field	91	61	34	24	16	11	25	21

positions, field positions (as opposed to headquarters), and/or administrative positions.

Table 26.2 shows the breakdown for 1980 and 1981 of headquarters versus field executives and of bonus recipients. While the data would probably not put to rest the notion of a bias in favor of headquarter executives, the discrepancies are not as great as many executives considered them to be.

On the other side of the picture, the PRB members have generally, although reluctantly, agreed that the position coefficient concept works, that it facilitates the bonus decision process, and that they have been satisfied with the resulting decisions. Based on administrative interactions with the PRBs, it appears evident that the position coefficient formalizes a seemingly inevitable part of the PRB rating process. That is, in determining bonus recipients (and often performance ratings as well) the risk or difficulty aspects of executives' positions are considered. This contention has also been supported by discussions with representatives of other federal agencies who have been involved in the bonus and performance appraisal processes. Formalization of this apparently inevitable aspect of the rating process should increase the overall objectivity of the bonus process.

The PRBs are so constituted that all members will not be equally familiar with the executives or positions being rated. Allowing the supervisor, the executive, and the second-level supervisor to provide relevant input can only increase the fairness of the rating process and of any subsequent decisions. Without the position coefficient, the potential is great for manipulation of performance ratings to ensure the desired rank order of those appraised. Such a practice would bring into serious question the credibility of the performance rating process as well as being contrary to the requirements of the CSRA. With the use of the position coefficient, the credibility of the performance rating process can be maintained. This is not to imply that the position coefficient is used strictly to effect a desired rank order. Rather, it allows the organization to reward those most deserving, those who perform and perform well in the most demanding positions, in a fair and objective manner.

Other Potential Uses

Although the position coefficient concept has been used solely for the performance award process, it would appear to have some potential for other situations. By tracking executives' performance ratings over a period of time as well as the coefficient ratings for positions served in, organizations could develop performance profiles for their executives. These profiles would provide indices of executives' abilities to function under adverse conditions as well as their experiences or lack of same in risky/difficult positions. Where possible, the primary reason for changes in position coefficient ratings should also be noted. The profiles would then provide additional information of value to the organization. In this respect, where changes in coefficient ratings were a result of situational or environmental factors, a measure of the executive's ability to function under changing and adverse conditions could be derived. Where changes were primarily self-induced, the ability of the executive to introduce risk into a position rather than perpetuating the status quo could be evaluated.

The organization could then use the executives' profiles for assigning them to positions where the ability to function under risky/difficult conditions is a factor to be considered. Executives with a proven track record of success in such conditions would be assigned to difficult positions. Executives with a record of successfully introducing change into positions could be assigned where change is needed. In situations where executives are routinely rotated into different positions, the use of the position coefficient concept could help ensure that the right people are placed in the right situations.

Summary and Conclusion

The SES has be depicted as "on the one hand, a personnel and career system which impacts on present and prospective members and, on the other, a means of pursuing organization objectives through the management of an agency's senior administrators" (Institute for Social Research 1981). In developing the position coefficient the goals of the department were to facilitate the accomplishment of departmental objectives relative to the performance award program while at the same time providing its executives with a fair and objective process for awarding bonuses. That the concept has been less than favorably received is not surprising given the inherently discriminatory nature of the bonus program, which has been exacerbated by severe limitations placed by Congress and OPM on the number of bonuses awardable. In fact, a number of executives have suggested the cancellation of the bonus program because of its negative impact.

In spite of the criticisms, the bottom line is that the PRBs and the department's management have not been dissatisfied with the position coefficient or the quality and caliber of the bonus recipients. The concept provides a means of rewarding those who succeed, in spite of the odds against them and whose performance ratings may be somewhat low because of the difficult positions they serve in. At the same time, executives with high performance ratings due in part to the lack of risk and difficulty in their positions retain their high ratings but not at the expense of supplanting more deserving executives as award recipients. The fact is that equal performance ratings do not equate to equal performance or equal worth to the organization. In one sense then, the concept preserves the integrity of the performance appraisal system. In addition, the standardization and formalization of this process increases the overall objectivity of the award determination process since a consideration of the risk/difficulty level of executives' positions seems to be an inevitable part of the evaluation process.

Note

The author was employed by the Department of Agriculture from November 1979 to June 1982. Endorsement of the author's views by the U.S. Department of Agriculture is not implied and should not be inferred.

References

Brumback, G.B. 1981. "Revisiting an Approach to Managing Behaviors and Results." *Public Personnel Management* 10, 1: 270–77.
Institute for Social Research. 1981. *Organizational Assessments of the Effects of Civil Service Reform.* Ann Arbor: University of Michigan.
Ralph, P.M. 1980. "Performance Evaluation: One More Try." *Public Personnel Management* 9, 3: 145–53.
Stimson, R.A. 1980. "Performance Pay: Will It Work?" *The Bureaucrat* 9 (Summer): 39–47.

PART 8

HOW DO YOU DEVELOP LEADERS?

Several erroneous assumptions are often made about leadership development. First, an understanding of leadership does not necessarily mean that one knows how to develop it. Another assumption is that leadership development is achieved primarily through education and training (probably because that is the name given to a class of training programs). A final erroneous assumption is that leadership development is a fairly straightforward affair, once there is a commitment to promoting it. As it turns out, understanding leadership helps promote development practices but cannot guarantee them. Formal instruction is only one aspect of leadership development, albeit a critical part in order to enhance consistently high-caliber candidates and incumbents. Finally, building leadership development programs and evaluating them are extremely difficult undertakings that are fraught with difficulties even when resources and support are forthcoming.

What Are the Different Means of Developing Leaders?

The single most common method of developing leadership is through experience and trial and error. Experience inculcates knowledge about technical data, people, and organizational systems, demonstrates what works, and clarifies what mistakes not to repeat. Since people spend years at their jobs, it is the method that dwarfs all others in terms of time spent. It is certainly very powerful when it works well. The astute learner has time to absorb lessons, which are integrated into personal experience in a natural developmental flow. Some of the methods of enhancing experience as a leadership development tool are: job rotation, challenging assignments, and opportunities to process and critique work products or incidents. For example, some organizations purposely place management interns in a wide variety of staff and line assignments for rotational breadth. "Up-and-comers" are given a series of increasingly difficult assignments to handle in order to provide experiential variety and confidence, and to test the mettle of those aspiring for higher positions. Good managers and leaders provide individual and group analysis sessions, such as public safety commanders who debrief a major fire, drug bust, or crime sweep to emphasize best practices, discourage improper or rogue behavior, and uncover developing trends.

Another important method of developing leadership is through networking. Networking is the process of learning through talking to others. Commonly this means talking to others in the organization or in similar jobs (such as at professional meetings). Networking allows people to find their own "teachers" and to compare their problems with others of a similar, but not identical, nature. It provides a good opportunity to learn from others' mistakes. Networking also assists people in socializing into various organizational and disciplinary cultures. Networking is enhanced by encouraging people in the organization with unstructured opportunities to get together and socialize at events such as receptions and mixers, as well as through structured opportunities to meet and discuss such as retreats, problem-solving meetings, user groups, and open-ended operational meetings. External networking is enhanced by encouraging people to participate in professional groups and in the local community (and providing the time and resources to do so).

Mentoring is a self-conscious activity that provides coaching and counseling to individuals who are in the beginning developmental phases. Coaching (in leadership development) is the act of providing feedback on specific performance issues in a job setting. Good leadership mentors analyze what the mentee is doing and provide useful, timely feedback. Counseling provides the mentee with opportunities to discuss career development paths and alternatives, organizational culture, and personal issues. Unlike networking, which tends to be ad hoc and learner directed, good mentoring is a conscious effort to ensure that the mentee knows what they do *not* know. Because mentoring is time consuming and largely unnoticed by anyone other than the mentee, it is often best encouraged by formalizing mentoring programs so that the contribution is recognized and responsibility is more formally assigned.

Education is the final, major category of leadership development. It can be informal and largely self-directed, such as personal reading about management and leadership, or a self-analysis of personal strengths and weaknesses. The most visible means is formal education in structured settings such as classrooms. The variety of types is enormous. Formal education programs vary by level of participant, purpose, and the resources devoted, to mention only a few of many variables. Formal education is very dense and efficient, despite its reputation to the contrary, when you consider the time involved in other leadership development alternatives. This is especially true for basic competencies and skills of a technical and professional nature. Other strengths are its ability to bring in experts and to target the issues needed by the organization, the learner, or both. It can best be enhanced at the organizational level by self-consciously planning a series of development programs, both inside and outside the organization, of which those seeking to advance can clearly understand and avail themselves. The organization must also commit the resources to producing and evaluating the quality of such programs (further discussed below). At the individual level, leadership development programs are more powerful when participants have a positive attitude and use them to resolve and improve current issues with which they are dealing.

The question is often posed: What is the best means of leadership development? A far more productive version of the inquiry is: What is the best *combination* of approaches? Because leadership is an extraordinarily complex and difficult undertaking, no single approach is likely to adequately fulfill all development needs. Leaders who are not experienced, connected, "groomed," and trained generally have difficulty advancing and are more prone to major weaknesses or to being professionally "derailed." Overreliance on any single method brings us to the next topic, the difficulties of the various methods.

Weaknesses in Various Leadership Development Approaches

Powerful though it may be as teacher, experience has many glaring weaknesses from a learning perspective. Experience is a slow teacher at best, is haphazard in the leadership lessons it provides, and it is highly inefficient if good timing is important. Dramatic though some experiences may be, subtle leadership lessons may be unclear to the perceiver or improperly learned. For example, a supervisor may have a bad experience in working with an employee, and deduce that he needs to be more forceful in the future, when in actuality he may need to work on interpersonal skills such as listening, respect, and patience. Sole reliance on experience allows the individual to make costly and career-damaging mistakes. Finally, excessive reliance on experience can allow individuals to become proficient in substandard or nonideal management and leadership practices, of which in all likelihood they are quite unaware. Unlearning these practices may be difficult, if and when they are later discerned.

Networking, too, is a haphazard way to learn and it is inefficient and time consuming. Feedback is generally limited to the originator's request, not necessarily his or her real need. Sometimes one's network does not include the expertise that is needed. At other times the nature of the problem is more substantial than can be addressed in the typical network situation. That is to say, networking is rarely detailed enough for many developmental purposes. It is a useful auxiliary, but rarely a mainstay of leadership development.

Like networking, mentoring is a very good auxiliary approach to leadership development but rarely a foundation. Mentoring is more difficult than it seems and finding good mentors is not always easy. Because good leaders are always in short supply, the pool of potentially good mentors is in short supply too. Often people who are good leaders agree to be mentors but later find that because they are good they have many other similar competing demands. Poor leaders may be willing to be mentors but may actually confuse the development of those trying to advance.

The problems with education and training are well known. Basic education may be watered down or out-of-date. Advanced education and training is exceedingly difficult to do because of participants' high expectations, competing demands, and resource constraints. Education and training are expensive and generally take people away from their jobs. Poor training fails to motivate and enthuse them, teaches things of little value, or does not relate effectively back to the participant's home environment.

The Developmental Skill Hierarchy for Leaders

A near universally held proposition is that leaders need different skill sets at different times (see, for example, Katz 1955; Hunt 1996; Jacques 1989). Frontline supervisors, mid-level managers, and chief executive officers all need a somewhat different mix of skills in order to be successful. Thus, training and development needs should also vary.

The general notion is that frontline supervisors use technical skills most. They often fill in for others, must troubleshoot problems, and provide the technical training for new employees. Indeed, true administrative functions may be a small part of their position.

Middle managers spend much more time managing programs, with the people issues and problems that such programs entail. Who is the right person for a job, who should be on a committee, and how can operations be adjusted to improve productivity? Thus, interpersonal relations and analytic and conceptual skills become more important to the mid-level manager as she or he seeks to integrate her/his programs into the organizational system.

Senior managers and executives focus almost exclusively on the organizational system or major elements of it, and thus they must have very strong conceptual skills. They are incapable of keeping abreast of all the technical information in all the areas that report to them personally, but generally know about such changes. Senior managers and executives continue to need good interpersonal skills, but the emphasis of such skills becomes more large-scale and public relations–oriented. They are increasingly responsible for official relations outside the agency or department. As major organizational changes are implemented, senior managers must understand the ramifications for all parts of the system.

From a training perspective, then, the frontline manager may still be interested in a good deal of technical skill building in their own substantive area, in basic management techniques such as human resource management, information systems, and financial management. Mid-level managers increasingly need to hone supervision skills, such as appraisal techniques, negotiation, motivation, meeting management, project management, and so on. Finally, senior managers need advanced planning (especially strategic) skills, change management, policy analysis, greater cultural awareness, and public speaking.

How Do You Evaluate Training and Education?

The classic evaluation scheme for evaluating training programs was put forth by Donald Kirkpatrick (1959). It points out that there are four levels of evaluation possible.

The first level is reaction. How do participants react to the program? This type of evaluation is captured by participant evaluations. Typically these evaluations are heavily influenced by emotional elements: the "entertainment" value and how they felt treated.

The second level is learning. How much did the participants learn in the program? Evaluating this level requires some proof of performance, such as a test or skill demonstration. From a strict evaluation perspective, it is important to know what the baseline skill was prior to the program. It can also be important to measure how much understanding is retained after a substantial period of time, such as six months.

The third level is behavior. How different are the participant's actions in the work setting? If the training program is about improving motivation and listening skills, how much more and better is the participant observed to be in listening and encouraging others? Often such assessments are gathered from subordinates and superiors, rather than from the participant.

The most global level is results. What result does the training have on the productivity of the unit or organization? If an extensive program on supervision skills and human resource management techniques is provided, is there a documentable decrease in grievances, litigation, or absences? If there is a management program in reengineering techniques, is there an absolute reduction in organizational expenses along with an improvement in cycle time?

The first two types of evaluation—reaction and learning—are typical of all good training programs of significant duration. Learning outcomes actually keep participants as accountable as those who are providing the training. However, the latter two types of evaluation—behavior and results—are far more difficult to do. First, these levels of evaluation generally require access to organizational systems and evaluators must have the buy-in of both the participants and executives in the organization. Second, documenting an effect in the work setting is generally challenging given the many variables that operate there and the subtlety of what is generally being measured. Unlike the measurement of workers' productivity, which is relatively easy to document through cases processed, error rates, absence rates, and so on, managers' work is reflected in a longer time frame and affects the motivation and perceptions of others.

A final issue in evaluation is the degree of effect that a training program should have. How much effect should a forty-hour training program be expected to have in a 2,000-hour work year, two years (or 4,000 hours) later? This also brings up such issues as critical mass (the amount of time and the number of participants in the organization included in the training program), executive buy-in, and "booster" programs (elements of the program that occur after the initial basic training to encourage use and resolve problems).

Review of the Selections in Part 8

James Conant's article "The Manager's View of Management Education and Training" (1996) provides valuable data regarding the development approaches discussed above. Although derived from a single case study (state-level managers in one state), his data give us a clear sense of managers' perceptions. For example, managers at all levels believe that the most powerful source of development is experience (learning from the results of one's own actions), followed by networking (learning from interaction with other managers), and finally with formal training, mentors, and departmental meetings playing a smaller but significant role. Another interesting finding is that although less than half of the managers were involved in a substantial training in any given year, 61 percent would support a mandate to require a minimum floor of training every year. However, the managers were strongly against a mandated program from any single source. When it came to generalized sources they preferred departmental training, technical training, and mentoring. Similarly, when trying to improve their department as a whole, they recommended departmentally sponsored management training and mentoring, and clearer objectives, which might infer better communications, role clarity, and strategic planning. Interestingly, university-based training for managers in their jobs did not score well in this case study.

Dahlia Bradshaw Lynn's article "Succession Management Strategies in Public Sector Organizations" (2001) focuses on succession planning, which deals with the selection and grooming of managers, as well as their initial support. She says, "[t]here is justifiable concern over the present capacity of the public sector to recognize, teach, groom, and reward employees." She further notes: "Whether public or private, the ability of an institution to survive turbulent times is based on the organization's capacity to produce sustained and high quality leadership over time." Succession planning requires organizational assessment, identifying a pool of high-potential candidates, providing them with robust development processes, and making the actual selection of candidates for specific positions. She notes that two fundamental philosophies are possible. First, it is possible to view succession management as a simple replacement strategy in which all employees are offered equal opportunities for all training. This "egalitarian" model means that the quality of training will be moderate because resources will be so broadly dispersed. A second model used for management and executive training is to create an elite cadre who are specifically groomed for management through rotation, training, and mentoring. This restricted model requires making advanced judgments about the candidates and their potential, but allows much more focused and extensive training. For example, a number of government agencies at both the city and federal level use management intern programs as fast-track options in which superior graduate students are groomed for higher-level positions. Lynn notes that the challenges to succession planning are severe. These include a lack of resources and attention to problems associated with management development, confusion over which model to use, and a gap between the ideal in succession planning (such as starting with organizational needs and connecting them with job descriptions) and actual practice.

In "Reflections on 'Educating Executives'" (1959), Raymond A. Katzell looks at six executive development programs by reviewing their overarching purposes: administrative knowledge and skills, broadening executive perspective, and broadening cultural perspective. He also considers short- versus long-term goals. The training parameters he examines include content and basic objectives, training methods, training provider, and participant level. He notes that the programs tended to sort the technical versus conceptual focus out by level of participant, very much as Corson and others recommend. His suggestion that such programs use more methods to simulate experience (such as case studies) and more rigorous reduction of psychological barriers to change is very much in line with the later work of Argyris (1970, 1985, 1990) and others. While very much a proponent of executive development, Katzell warns against poorly designed programs that can actually be harmful by wasting resources and discouraging individuals from meaningful development. While his particular diagnosis is less interesting because of its specificity to the circumstance he is investigating, the types of questions that he raises and the method he uses to come to his conclusions are classic. Finally, he notes that the best ways to ensure that executive programs are appropriate is by (1) a thorough analysis of executives' developmental needs in the agency context, and (2) better evaluation of the programs themselves.

References

Argyris, Chris. 1970. *Intervention Theory and Method*. Reading, MA: Addison.
Argyris, Chris. 1985. *Strategy, Change and Defensive Routines*. New York: Harper Business.
Argyris, Chris. 1990. *Knowledge for Action*. San Francisco: Jossey-Bass.
Blake, Robert, and Jane S. Mouton. 1964. *The Managerial Grid*. Houston, TX: Gulf.
Hunt, James G. 1996. *Leadership: A New Synthesis*. Newbury Park, CA: Sage.
Jacques, Elliott. 1989. *Requisite Organization*. Arlington, VA: Carson Hall.
Katz, Robert L. 1955. "The Skills of an Effective Administrator." *Harvard Business Review* 33, (1): 33–42.
Kirkpatrick, Donald C. 1959. "Techniques for Evaluating Training Programs." *Journal of ASTD* 13 (11): 3–9.

CHAPTER 27

THE MANAGER'S VIEW OF MANAGEMENT EDUCATION AND TRAINING

JAMES K. CONANT

It is an old adage that "experience is the best teacher." To the extent this is true, the day-to-day practice of management is the best means for public managers to gain the knowledge and skills they need to function effectively. Yet, public affairs and administration programs seem to be built upon a different assumption. The university perspective generally assumes that formal classroom education is the best way for public managers to gain the knowledge and skills they require. Although most public administration programs have come into being since 1960, the primary presumption on which they operate can be traced back to 1887. In his article, "The Study of Administration," Woodrow Wilson argued that public managers (and prospective candidates for the public service) needed training in a "science of administration." This training, Wilson contended, was necessary to save administration from the "costliness of empirical experiment."

Since Wilson's time, a long list of academicians, blue ribbon government commissions, and even elected officials have proposed management education and training as a means for improving the performance of government organizations. Yet, despite the large volume of material that has been published in public affairs and administration journals over the past 100 years, empirically based studies of public sector management education and training efforts remain in remarkably short supply. Furthermore, attempts to present the executive branch manager's view of the relative value of experience and classroom education and training appear to be virtually nonexistent. Even at the state level where, during the past decade or so, a number of publications have provided useful findings about the financial, administrative, programmatic, and even political dimensions of the states' management education and training activities, no data on the managers' view of the states' activities have been published (Hays 1996; Conant 1995; 1993; 1992; 1990; Conant and Housel 1995; Vanagunas and Webb 1994; Sherwood 1992; Van Wart 1992; Sims, et al. 1987; Finkle 1985; and Henning and Wilson 1979).

Perhaps the presumption about the value of classroom education is so deeply ingrained

From *Review of Public Personnel Administration,* vol. 16, no. 3 (Summer 1996): 23–37. Copyright © 1996 by Sage Publications, Inc. Reprinted with permission.

in the public affairs profession that the manager's view of management education and training has not been deemed worthy of empirical examination. Or, perhaps there are other explanations. Whatever the reason, the gap in the literature should be filled. Data on the manager's view could be useful to people who make decisions about the delivery of management education and training activities—such as elected officials, department secretaries, managers and staff in human resources departments, and faculty in schools of public affairs and administration. The data might also be useful to executive branch managers themselves as they contemplate the options they have for developing their knowledge and skills.

The research findings presented in this article are focused on six key questions:

1. Do public managers think that experience or classroom education and training has been more important in the development of their knowledge and skills?
2. How often are managers likely to participate in education and training classes?
3. What sources are managers most likely to select for their classes?
4. Which source of classroom instruction do managers think is the best source for enhancing their own knowledge and skill?
5. What do public managers think is the best means to improve the performance of the entire management team in their division or department?
6. Do public managers think that management education and training should be voluntary or mandatory?

Data, Methodology, and Definitions

The data presented and analyzed in this article are drawn from the state of Wisconsin. In some respects, Wisconsin seems like an ideal state for studying the relative value that executive branch managers place on experience and classroom education. With its Progressive tradition dating back to the 1890s, the state has a longstanding reputation for clean politics, institutional innovation, policy leadership, and a highly professionalized public service. The University of Wisconsin–Madison campus is only one mile from the State Capitol, and many of the state's policy innovations have emerged through cooperative partnerships between the university and the state government.

The data contained in this article were collected through a comprehensive study of the state's management education and training activities. The study was conducted in 1990 and 1991; data were collected through both a field study and a survey of executive branch managers. The basic design for the study was provided by the author of this article, but a team of state government managers and staff made important contributions to both the content of the survey questionnaire and to the task of the collection of data in the field study.[1] Most of the data presented in this article are derived from the survey, but findings from the field study are employed as a tool for interpreting, analyzing, and supplementing the survey data.

When this study was conducted, there were approximately 60,000 employees in Wisconsin state government. Approximately one-half of those employees worked in the executive branch departments and agencies, 45 percent of the state's employees worked in the University of Wisconsin system, and the remaining 5 percent worked in the office of the governor, the legislature, and the state supreme court. Of the 30,000 executive branch employees, more than five thousand had supervisory or managerial rank.

Time and resource constraints required the selection of a subset of executive branch departments and agencies for the study.[2] An effort was made to choose departments that varied on the basis of size and function. An additional objective was to ensure that a substantial proportion (15 to 25 percent) of the executive branch population was included in the study. The departments selected included Administration (general services administration and state budget office), Natural Resources (natural resource management and pollution control), Revenue (tax collection), and Transportation (road building and maintenance, licensing, etc.).[3] Approximately 26 percent of all executive branch employees worked in these four departments; approximately 28 percent of the state's managers and supervisors work in them. By Wisconsin standards, two departments were medium sized (Administration and Revenue) and two were large (Natural Resources and Transportation). The survey questionnaire was mailed to 600 supervisors and managers selected randomly from the full management cadre in Administration, Natural Resources, Revenue, and Transportation. Almost 90 percent of the managers surveyed responded to the questionnaire. The questionnaire was pretested with small groups of managers from each of the four departments.

In this article, the managers' views about management education and training are presented in two ways: (1) as a single group or body, and (2) by level of management. In the latter case, the groupings include political appointees, senior managers, middle managers, and first-line managers or supervisors. Most department and agency secretaries, deputy secretaries, and division administrators in Wisconsin are political appointees.[4] There are approximately 120 such positions in Wisconsin state government.

Senior managers are next in the organizational hierarchy. Senior managers generally hold the title of bureau director. Most senior managers are promoted to their positions through the civil service system. There are approximately 400 senior managers in Wisconsin's executive branch departments and agencies. Middle managers are the third-level of managers in the executive branch departments. Middle managers have direct supervisory responsibility of first-line managers. Most middle managers are civil servants. There are approximately 1,375 middle managers in Wisconsin's executive branch departments and agencies.

First-line managers are at the bottom of the management hierarchy. These managers generally have the rank of supervisor or section chief, and most of the managers who hold these titles are civil servants. There are approximately 3,300 first-line managers. Thus, first-line managers constitute the largest group within the state's management corps.

Experience and the Classroom: Contributions to Knowledge and Skill Development

As part of the survey, executive branch managers in Wisconsin were asked to rate several different ways of learning about management. Specifically, managers were asked to state

Table 27.1

Importance of Experience, Classroom Education, and Training, etc., in Management Knowledge and Skill Development (percentile giving rating of "very important")

	All managers	Political appointees	Senior managers	Middle managers	First-line managers
Learning from results of own actions	70.9	82.1	84.8	78.9	78.8
Learning from interaction with other managers	55.6	60.7	64.1	58.1	53.3
Management education and training courses	34.6	28.6	32.6	38.0	33.8
Training provided by mentor(s)	29.1	32.1	32.2	29.8	28.3
Formal meetings required by department	27.3	28.6	25.0	29.1	26.9

whether the form of learning identified was "very important, somewhat important," or "not very important" in the development of their knowledge and skills. In this section, we first look at the ratings given by the entire group of managers in the survey, then we consider the ratings given by each level of management.

The survey results underscore the strength of the old adage about experience. Almost 80 percent of the managers rated "on the job learning from the results of actions they had taken" as "very important" in the development of their knowledge and skills. Experience was also considered important in another way, too. Almost 56 percent of the managers considered "informal on the job learning through interaction with other managers" in activities like planning, analysis, and problem solving to be "very important."

Classroom education and training was considered "very important" by just over one-third of the managers. "On-the-job training through a mentor or mentors" was rated "very important" by 29.1 percent, and "formal on the job training that occurred through required departmental activities such as planning sessions, decision-making sessions and monthly meetings" was considered "very important" by 27.3 percent. The data are presented in Table 27.1.

The survey data show some variation by management level in the responses to classroom experience. Indeed, the data show that the valuation of classroom instruction varied inversely with the position a manager held in the hierarchy For example, political appointees and senior managers were less likely to give classroom education a "very important" rating than were middle managers and first-line managers.

Of particular interest for some, here, might be the middle managers' views. They were more likely than managers at the three other levels to give classroom education a "very important" rating. Additionally, middle managers were least likely to rate classroom education training as "not very important," while political appointees were most likely to do so. Twenty-five percent of political appointees gave classroom education and training a "not very important" rating, while only 11.6 percent of middle managers, 13.3 percent of supervisors, and 18.5 percent of senior managers did so.

Variation in response by management level can also be seen for the other four categories of learning, but the pattern of the variation differs somewhat from category to category. For example, "very important" ratings given for "informal on the job learning through interaction with other managers" grew stronger as one moved up the hierarchy. Fifty-three percent of supervisors rated learning through interaction with other managers "very important"; the same rating was given by 58.1 percent of middle managers, 64.1 percent of senior managers, and 60.7 percent of political appointees.[5] Perhaps this pattern can be explained by the fact that both the latitude for and frequency of interaction with others is likely to go up substantially as one moves up the hierarchy.

Variation in response also corresponded to vertical movement up the hierarchy in two other categories, but the range of variation was not as great as it was in the two categories discussed previously. For example, 78.8 percent of the first-line supervisors rated "learning from one's own actions" as very important, 78.9 percent of the middle managers did the same, while 84.8 percent of senior managers and 82.1 percent of political appointees thought that this form of experience was very important. Likewise, senior managers and political appointees were more likely to select a mentor or mentors as "very important" than were middle managers or supervisors. In the final category, however, responses did not reflect positions in the hierarchy. Middle managers and political appointees gave "formal on-the-job learning through required departmental meetings," stronger ratings than did the senior managers and first-line supervisors.

Participation Rates in Classroom Sessions and Programs

In some respects, the finding that most managers rate experience as a more important contributor to their management knowledge and skills than classroom education is not surprising. After all, the practice of management is a continuous activity, and managers can learn from it hour-by-hour, day-by-day, month-by-month, and year-by-year. In contrast, data presented in this article show that classroom education and training for most executive branch managers is likely to be sporadic and of very limited duration. It is likely to consist of only a single "course" each year, and that course is likely to run for only a day or two. Only a small percentage of the managers studied (about 2 percent) participate in MPA or MBA programs in a given year. A somewhat larger percentage participate in nondegree certificate programs, such as the Certified Public Manager Program. The managers who participate in programs requiring regular class attendance over an extended period are the clear exception rather than the rule.[6]

Findings on participation rates in classroom education are presented in Table 27.2. Results regarding the type of classroom sessions the managers are likely to choose in any given year are presented in the next section. The survey questionnaire asked managers whether they had participated in a management education and training course (outside of the state-mandated supervisory course) during the fiscal years 1986–90. The data show that participation rates ranged from a low of 44 percent in 1986 to a high of 61.7 percent in 1989. The findings for the five-year period show a clear upward trend in participation rates from 1986 through 1989; in 1990, however, there was a rather sharp drop-off. No single factor would seem to explain the decline, but a problem of resource

Table 27.2

Participation in Management Education and Training Activities, FY 1986–90
(percent taking at least "one course")

Year	All managers	Political appointees	Senior managers	Middle managers	First-line managers
1986	53.1	44.0	67.9	54.9	50.7
1987	55.8	57.7	66.2	60.6	52.2
1988	59.2	55.6	63.3	63.2	56.9
1989	61.7	52.0	75.0	61.0	60.5
1990	48.0	53.6	65.5	47.7	45.7

constraints was among the factors mentioned most frequently during the interviews and focus group sessions.

Averaging the yearly participation rates, we find that approximately one out of every two managers is likely to participate in formal classroom sessions in any given year. One is moved to ask why is the rate so low? A host of factors seem to come into play here, including time constraints, resource limitations, and the inconvenient timing and location of course offerings. During interviews and focus group sessions, these factors were regularly identified by managers who expressed a desire to participate in classroom sessions on a regular basis but indicated they were unable to do so. Another factor mentioned with surprising frequency by managers was an organizational culture in which formal training was not perceived to be highly valued. Finally, one other factor mentioned during interviews and focus groups by some managers was lack of interest in classroom education and training.

Source of Education and Training Classes/Programs Selected

Executive branch managers in Wisconsin, as with many states, could select education and training classes from a number of providers. Of those who participated in management education and training activities in FY 1990, more than 80 percent took a course from their own department. These half-day, one-day or sometimes two-day "courses" were offered through the Human Resources Office of the division or department in which the manager worked. The courses were given by departmental staff, private sector providers, departmental managers, staff from other departments, and occasionally by university faculty.

As the data in Table 27.3 show, private sector providers were the source selected with the second highest degree of frequency, followed by the Department of Employee Relations. Professional conferences were the fourth most commonly used source, followed by the University of Wisconsin–Extension, other providers (unspecified sources), business schools in the University of Wisconsin System, vocational-technical schools, and public administration programs in the state university system.

The findings displayed in Table 27.3 reveal several interesting patterns. First, all forms of university-based classroom sessions are located in the bottom half of the list. Second, the University of Wisconsin–Extension was more likely to be used as a source

Table 27.3

Source of Management Education and Training Classes Taken, FY1990
(percent taking at least "one course" of each type listed)

Source	All managers	Political appointees	Senior managers	Middle managers	First-line managers
Manager's department	80.4	60.8	80.0	83.3	80.2
Private sector provider	30.9	13.3	21.7	27.2	34.9
Employee relations department	26.7	40.0	16.7	21.9	29.9
Professional conferences	21.1	6.7	23.3	27.5	18.7
University extension	11.1		6.7	6.4	3.5
Other	5.2	13.3	5.0	7.9	3.8
University business school	4.5		6.7	6.4	3.5
Vocational technical school	2.7		1.7	4.1	2.4
University public administration program	1.4		3.3		1.8

for classes than were the university's business schools or public affairs programs. Third, public administration programs were the least likely of all sources to be selected by managers.

The interviews and focus group sessions conducted as part of the field study provided a basis for at least a partial explanation of the managers' choices for classroom instruction. It is important to remember that managers operate within a set of rigid constraints. Time is limited, resources are scarce, and classes may not be offered at times or in places that mesh with a manager's workday requirements. For example, most managers can fit a half-day, one-day, or even a two-day classroom session into their schedules. Semester-long, year-long, or multiple-year degree programs such as the MPA or MBA, however, are much more difficult to accommodate. Thus, to the extent that university programs limit their offerings to semester-long courses, they will not be a viable option for most managers. In contrast, the managers' departments, private sector providers, professional conferences, and the Department of Employee Relations offer courses that fit "market" circumstances.

This is a key part of the explanation for the position of the University of Wisconsin–Extension at the top of the university-based programs. The Extension's Public Affairs Department had seminars that fit these market requirements well. The Extension also had a Certified Public Manager Program that did not require the time, energy, and resources needed to complete an MPA or MBA program. Furthermore, the business school's ranking ahead of public affairs programs can be explained in part because, at least at the University of Wisconsin–Madison, the business school had an outreach division that offered one-day or two-day courses on a variety of management topics and issues. The offerings of the public administration program, in contrast, were limited almost exclusively to semester-long courses.

Best Classroom Sources for Development of Own Knowledge and Skills

The data in previous sections highlight the types of classroom settings managers selected in the year immediately preceding the study. The survey questionnaire also asked managers to identify the classroom source or program type they thought would be the "best source" for the future development of the knowledge and skills they needed to function effectively in their jobs. The managers were asked to choose from ten options. These options differed in an important way from the options given on the question asking about courses taken in the previous year. For this question, most of the options were framed as program-based options—that is to say, there was an assumption of a class schedule that proceeded over a period of time.

In the order they were presented on the questionnaire, the ten options were: (1) technical training courses in your university discipline or your professional specialization that are offered by a university, your department, or private sector providers; (2) a state-mandated supervisory program offered by the Department of Employment Relations; (3) a supervisory training program designed for managers in your department; (4) a state-mandated management training program offered by the Department of Employment Relations; (5) a management training program designed for managers in your department; (6) a university MPA or MBA graduate degree program; (7) having a mentor or mentors in your department; (8) a certified Public Manager Program offered by the University of Wisconsin–Extension; (9) professional conferences; and, (10) other (please specify). The managers' responses to the options posed by this question are displayed in Table 27.4. As in previous tables, the results show that the managers have a strong preference for options that are department-based.

By a substantial margin the top choice was a department-based management education and training program that was designed for the department's managers. It was the first choice in the ratings for the management cadre as a whole, and its was the first choice for each level of management. Indeed, for senior managers, this option was the overwhelming favorite; for first-line managers, this option came just ahead of a department-based supervisory program.

The second highest ratings were given to a department-based supervisory training program. Support for this option, not surprisingly, was stronger at the bottom end of the hierarchy than it was at the top. Technical training courses received the third highest concentration of responses. Perhaps the most surprising element of this ranking is that a higher percentage of political appointees chose this option than did first-line managers.

The fourth choice was a mentor in the department. The highest concentration of managers selecting this option was at the top and the bottom of the hierarchy. The fifth choice was "Other." Private sector providers were mentioned with considerable frequency here. The sixth choice was a Certified Public Manager Program run by the University of Wisconsin–Extension. Given the fact that the CPM program in Wisconsin was quite new in 1991, this is a very interesting finding. The professional conference option was selected with greater frequency than was the MPA/MBA option, but the MPA/MBA came ahead

Table 27.4

Best Classroom/Program Source for Development of Own Knowledge and Skills
(listed in order of percentile rankings by all managers)

Source	All managers	Political appointees	Senior managers	Middle managers	First-line managers
Department-based management training program	30.2	32.1	52.7	32.8	26.2
Department-based supervisory training program	19.7	10.7	7.7	13.8	23.9
Technical training courses	10.5	17.9	7.7	12.2	10.6
Mentor in department	9.9	14.3	8.8	8.0	10.5
Other	6.7	3.6	5.5	8.3	5.9
Certified Public Manager program	6.0	7.1	4.4	7.6	5.6
Professional conference	5.9	10.7	4.4	8.0	5.2
University MPA or MBA	4.3	3.6	4.4	3.1	4.6
Mandated management program given by Employee Relations Department	4.0		4.4	3.1	4.3
Mandated supervisory program given by Employee Relations Department	2.8			3.1	3.1

of either a state-mandated management or supervisory program run by the Department of Employee Relations.

Best Means to Improve the Performance of the Whole Management Team

In addition to asking managers to give their views about the best source for improving their own knowledge and skills, the survey questionnaire also asked them to give their views on "the best vehicle for improving the performance of the whole management team in your division or department." There were eight options from which to choose. Two of the options were management education and training options; five options were related to the structure and operation of their department. The eighth option was open-ended; it allowed them to select "other," and then specify what they meant by this choice.

In the order in which they were presented on the questionnaire, the options were: (1) a management education and training program designed for all supervisors and managers in your division or department; (2) new computer hardware or software; (3) a requirement that all managers complete an MPA or MBA; (4) improved information and control systems (budget, accounting, etc.); (5) a new departmental or divisional organization structure; (6) an active mentoring process; (7) more clearly defined objectives for managers and the rest of the staff; and, (8) other.

The manager's responses seem to provide good news for those who think that classroom training can make a significant contribution to the performance of a management team

Table 27.5

Best Vehicle for Improving Performance of Whole Management Team
(listed in order of percentile rankings by all managers)

Best vehicle	All managers	Political appointees	Senior managers	Middle managers	First-line managers
Management training program for department managers	49.2	51.9	65.6	45.6	48.5
More clearly defined objectives	18.6	22.2	13.3	17.5	19.6
Active mentoring process	9.7	11.1	5.6	7.7	11.0
Other	7.8	11.1	8.9	11.6	6.0
New organization structure	7.6	3.7	3.3	9.1	7.7
Improved information/control system	4.5		1.1	5.5	4.8
Require MPA/MBA for all managers	1.7		2.2	1.7	1.8
New computer hardware and software	.8			.3	.5

and a department. As the findings reported in Table 27.5 show, most managers selected "a management education and training program designed for all supervisors and manager in your division or department."

The management training program was not only the first choice of the entire cadre of managers, but it was also the first choice of all four levels. Senior managers gave this choice the strongest rating, followed by political appointees. While the percentage of middle and first-line managers favoring this option was somewhat smaller than their superiors in the hierarchy, nearly half of the middle and first-line managers selected this option as their first choice.

The option chosen with the second highest rate of frequency by the managers was "more clearly defined objectives for managers and the rest of the staff." Among the options specified under "other" were new departmental leadership, new political leadership, more resources, and the installation of a department-wide quality improvement program. A new organizational structure was fifth among the choices, followed by improved information and control systems, a requirement that all managers take an MPA or MBA program, and finally, new computer hardware or software.

Why was "a management education and training program designed for the managers of your department" selected as the best means for improving the performance of the whole management team? One part of the explanation undoubtedly has to do with the strong preference managers have for department-based classroom activities. However, there are some other factors that come into play here, too. Perhaps the most important of these factors were the (large) size of the organizations in which these managers worked and something that might be called the "social" dimension of management.

During the interview and focus group sessions, some of the first-line and middle levels reported having limited (or even very limited) interaction with managers up the hierarchy and across the organization. Some said that they had never met or talked to the senior managers or political appointees in their division or department. Equally important, some reported that their contact with other managers up the hierarchy was limited to brief encounters, such as addressing a crisis. Thus, there was little time to get to know other managers. Could a department-based management education and training program designed for the managers in a particular department serve to provide some of the social glue that several of these executive branch managers seemed to want? It could, especially if that program was similar in design to the one given in the Department of Natural Resources (DNR). The DNR program was designed and delivered by the political appointees and the senior managers of that department. The program was delivered twice each year to thirty managers during a week-long session. Applicants for the program were selected on a competitive basis. In order to be considered, managers had to meet a set of prerequisites, which included completion of basic supervisory and management courses. Applicants also had to write an essay explaining why they wanted to be in the program. The week-long training session was carefully choreographed to include presentations, question and answer sessions, role playing, and small group and large group sessions. The agenda also included social events during the evenings. The author of this article was given the chance to sit through one of these week-long sessions. During informal interviews held with managers attending the session, the author heard a common refrain—namely, this training session was much coveted because it provided middle and first-line managers an opportunity to meet and interact with the department's senior managers and political appointees. Through this interaction, managers had the opportunity to learn firsthand about the values, preferences and priorities of the senior managers and political appointees in their department.

The fact that the DNR's first-line and middle managers placed such a high premium on learning about the values, preferences and priorities of the political appointees and senior managers is not difficult to understand. Particularly in a large public organization, where the direct interaction middle and first-line managers have with managers at the top of the hierarchy is very limited, there may be considerable confusion about the organization's priorities. The political appointees and senior managers may get their cues about what the organization's priorities should be from elected officials and interest groups. Yet, the cues may not be shared with or understood by those lower in the hierarchy. Furthermore, since the priorities of elected officials can shift rapidly, political appointees and senior managers may be changing the organization's priorities on an ongoing basis. This, too, can create confusion for the middle level and first-line managers.

Given these circumstances, it is not surprising to find that the option the managers selected as the second best option for improving the performance of their management team was "more clearly defined objectives for managers and staff of the department." As noted above, discussions about objectives and priorities can be incorporated into a department-based management education and training program. Likewise, a department-based management education and training program can incorporate what the managers identified as the third best vehicle for improving the performance of their management team: active mentoring. Mentoring activities can be built into the design of a department-based program, and they can be continued after the classroom sessions are completed.

Table 27.6

Require Management Education and Training Class(es) Each Year?
(responses in percentile)

	All managers	Political appointees	Senior managers	Middle managers	First-line managers
Yes	61.2	69.2	63.7	58.5	61.6
No	38.8	30.8	36.3	41.5	38.4

Mandates for Classroom Education and Training

The sixth and final question addressed in this manuscript is whether executive branch managers think that classroom training should be required each year for all managers. The survey questionnaire employed in the Wisconsin study asked respondents to take a yes or no position on this issue. Given the fact that less than a third of the managers considered classroom education and training a "very important" part of their knowledge and skill development, one might predict a strong negative response. Surprisingly, a majority of the managers favored such a mandate. The managers' responses are presented in Table 27.6.

The results set forth in Table 27.6 show that 61.2 percent of the executive branch managers favored a requirement that all managers take at least one classroom session a year. This seems somewhat remarkable in and of itself, but it seems even more remarkable when one considers that the strongest support of the mandate came from the political appointees. After all, political appointees were the least likely of the four levels to rate classroom sessions as "very important" in their own knowledge and skill development. Furthermore, they were most likely to rate classroom education and training as "not very important." To add to the irony here, middle managers were the least supportive of the classroom requirement, even though they were the most positive about the contribution classroom education and training made to their knowledge and skill development (see Table 27.1).

Summary and Conclusion

The manager's view of management education and training has been presented in this article. Because the empirical data for the study are drawn from a single state, and because there are no published data from other states to which this study can be compared, the findings reported herein must be considered suggestive and preliminary only. Among the key questions addressed in this article was whether managers view experience or classroom education and training as more important in the development of their knowledge and skill. The findings suggest that almost 80 percent of the managers viewed experience as a "very important" contributor to their knowledge and skills, while fewer than 30 percent of the managers gave classroom education this rating. Thus, if experience and classroom education were exclusive choices, experience wins hands down. Fortunately, however, they need not be considered exclusive choices; classroom education can precede and supplement experience.

As a supplement to experience, the intensive form of classroom education and training envisioned by Woodrow Wilson and offered by MPA programs is preferred by only a very small proportion of executive branch managers. In any given year, most managers engage in classroom education and training activities that are limited to only a day or two. Furthermore, to the extent that department managers are willing to extend their classroom work, they want to do so in a department-based program.

Executive branch managers think that department-based programs are the best way to develop their own skills; they also think these programs are the best way to improve the performance of the whole departmental management team. A number of factors that underlie this view have been discussed in this article, including time, energy, and resource constraints, the need for social "glue" in an organization, the need for greater clarity of departmental objectives and priorities, and the desire to have a mentoring process. The managers' preferences on these topics could be viewed by university faculty with quiet disapproval, since these preferences do not line up neatly with the regular MPA curriculum offerings. However, an understanding of the manager's view on these matters, as well as some of the constraints that condition that view, may contribute to a more favorable response by MPA faculty. Such a response may, in turn, facilitate faculty efforts to work with top-level department managers and staff in the design, delivery, and evaluation of department-based management education and training programs.

Acknowledgements

Financial support for this study was provided by the Robert M. LaFollette Institute of Public Affairs, University of Wisconsin–Madison and the Wisconsin Department of Administration. The author would like to thank Robert Havemen, Sheila Earl, Peter Eisinger, the Executive Committee at La Follette Institute and George Lightbourn, at the Department of Administration, for their early and ongoing support of this study. Other state government officials who made important contributions to or lent their support to this study include: Don Bach, Buzz Besadny, Tom Bierrenkott, Bruce Braun, Diane Brown, Mark Bugher, Ron Fiedler, Don Jorgenson, James Klauser, John Litscher, Toya Nelson and Ron Semann.

Notes

1. The team consisted of managers and staff from each of the four departments included in this study. All of the participants were volunteers.

2. Although considerable care was taken in the selection of the subset, for a variety of reasons it is not possible to select a "representative sample" of agencies. A key factor in the make-up of the subset used here was the department secretaries' willingness to have the department included in the study. Fortunately, all four department secretaries of the agencies the author selected as first choice for the subset agreed to participate in the study.

3. The Department of Administration had 855 full-time and 40 part-time employees; Revenue had 1,137 full-time and 663 part-time employees; Natural Resources had 2,880 fulltime and 1,350 part-time employees; Transportation had 3,958 full-time and 568 part-time employees.

4. Most departmental secretaries are nominated by the governor, confirmed (or rejected) by the State Senate, and serve at the pleasure of the governor. However, some departmental secretaries are nominated by departmental boards or commissions. Most agency secretaries, deputy secretaries, and division administrators are nominated or appointed by the agency's board or commission. Most nominees need Senate confirmation.

5. It is also worth noting that only a very small percentage of the managers at the bottom (3.6 percent) and top (3.1 percent) of the hierarchy thought this form of education was "not very important." At the middle level, 8.7 percent thought learning by interaction was "not very important" in their knowledge and skill development, while 6.7 percent of senior managers took this position.

6. For a discussion of the time and resource costs associated with participation in MPA and CPM programs, see Conant and Housel 1995, and Conant 1990.

References

Conant, J.K. 1995. "The Certified Public Manager Program (CPM): A Cross State Study." *State and Local Government Review* 27: 144–58.

———. 1993. "Management Education and Training in the States: The Fiscal, Administrative, and Political Dimensions of Policy Options." *State and Local Government Review* 25: 173–84.

———. 1992. "Management Education and Training in Wisconsin: A Description, an Appraisal, and Recommendation for Improvement." Madison, WI: Wisconsin Department of Administration.

———. 1990. "Management Education and Training in New Jersey: A Description, an Appraisal and Recommendations for Improvement." East Orange: The Fund for New Jersey.

Conant, J.K. and S. Housel. 1995. "MPA and CPM Programs: Competitors or Complements in Public Service Management Education?" *Review of Public Personnel Administration* 15: 5–21.

Finkle, A. 1985. "CPM—Professionalizing Professionalism." *Public Administration Quarterly* 9: 47–54.

Hays, S.W. (Forthcoming). "Professional Certification in Public Management: A Status Report and a Proposal." *Public Administration Review.*

Henning, K.K. and L.D. Wilson. 1979. "The Georgia Certified Public Manager (CPM) Program." *Southern Review of Public Administration* 6: 428–30.

Sherwood, F. 1992. "Institutionalizing Executive Development and Attendant Problems." *Public Productivity and Management Review* 15: 449–61.

Sims, R.R., J.G. Veres, T.S. Locklear and R.B. Wells. 1987. "Training for Public Managers: The Alabama Certified Public Manager Program." *Journal of European Industrial Training* 11: 11–13.

Vanagunas, S. and J. Webb. 1994. "Administrative Innovation and the Training of Public Managers." *Public Personnel Management* 23: 437–46.

Van Wart, M. 1992. "Connecting Management and Executive Development in the States." *Public Productivity and Management Review* 15: 477–86.

Wilson, W. 1887. "The Study of Administration." *Political Science Quarterly* 2 (June).

CHAPTER 28

SUCCESSION MANAGEMENT STRATEGIES IN PUBLIC SECTOR ORGANIZATIONS

DAHLIA BRADSHAW LYNN

Introduction

An essential employee in a public sector agency unexpectedly resigns leaving the organization with a substantial gap in institutional memory, knowledge, and leadership. Institutional personnel, community leaders, and stakeholders are asking critical questions. How long will it take to have a replacement? Are there internal candidates? Where can the right person be found? Why is someone not ready for this job? Why did not the organization plan for this occurrence?

According to Blunt (2000), growing the next generation of public sector leaders may be "the single most critical responsibility of senior public service leaders today" (4). The natural ebb and flow of human events—retirement, career mobility, ill health, termination, or even death—require institutional responses to the leadership gaps all organizations inevitably face (Friedman and Singh 1989; Hesselbien, Goldsmith, and Beckhard 1996; Vancil 1987). The importance of the identification and development of leadership potential and the process chosen by an organization cannot be underestimated (Zald 1970), for "outcomes of leadership succession choices may . . . have a large impact on organizational directions and policies" (245).

Current systems for developing future public managers have been characterized as "largely serendipitous" (Huddleston 1999). Efforts to address the question of leadership capacity confirm what many leaders and practitioners already know—there is a growing gap of leadership talent in the public service (Eastman 1995; The Leadership Development and Education Institute 1999).

There are varieties of alternative strategies in the selection of new leaders. Public and private sector response have involved different approaches to the identification and development of institutional leadership capacity. Public sector leadership is primarily predicated on open competition, merit, and competitive testing mechanisms or seniority (incorporating collective bargaining as a subset of a civil service personnel system). Conversely, the private sector response to executive replacement not only includes

From *Review of Public Personnel Administration*, vol. 21, no. 2 (Summer 2001): 114–32. Copyright © 2001 by Sage Publications, Inc. Reprinted with permission.

open competition and competitive test mechanisms but may also encompass a number of different strategies involving the early recognition of high-potential candidates, providing opportunities for professional development and ultimately advancement with the organization.

Although the indicators of organizational change may vary, public and private organizations increasingly share a common experience. Whether public or private, the ability of an institution to survive turbulent times is based on the organization's capacity to produce sustained and high quality leadership over time. "Sustained innovation," the ability to keep change alive, extends beyond sector characteristics and encompasses the leadership capacity of all organizations (Schall 1997). Thus, effective and sustained leadership contributes toward an organization's weathering storms of change, whether caused by downsizing, technology, or public expectations (National Academy of Public Administration [NAPA] 1997).

How organizations address leadership capacity building is an important indicator of an organization's ability to develop the intellectual capacity necessary for it to thrive. This is no less the case for public sector agencies facing formidable challenges in identifying and nurturing the next generation of public service leaders. Increasingly, leadership capacity building is receiving renewed attention as governmental and other public sector agencies face mounting pressures to ensure organizational sustainability, flexibility, and responsiveness in the face of increasing uncertainty and limitations.

The inability of the public sector to meet leadership needs is similar to that of the private sector. What stands in marked contrast is the way each sector has responded to the challenge of building leadership capacity. Leadership strength within public organizations has traditionally rested on the ability of public managers to provide reliable and predictable direction in an environment characterized by incremental change and improvement (NAPA 1997). Increasing turbulence in the public sector environment, characterized by organizational restructuring, funding uncertainties, and increasing program complexities, has substantial effects on the ways public sector organizations respond to leadership replacement (Caudron 1966).

This study is concerned with the nature of succession management strategies and the potential usefulness of strategic human resource management (HRM) tools in identifying and developing leadership capacity in public sector organizations. One of its purposes is to be descriptive, expanding the base of information about the succession management process. It also reports on the results of three focus groups conducted with public sector managers and human resource professionals. Group participants assessed their individual organization's readiness to resolve leadership gaps through the establishment of formalized leadership succession programs, their own involvement in such activities, and the extent to which such efforts were seen as valuable.

Protecting the Institutional Knowledge Base

The continued vitality of an organization is linked to its ability to survive a leadership void. In the private sector, where financial stability is a function of an organization's

Figure 28.1 **The Succession Management Process**

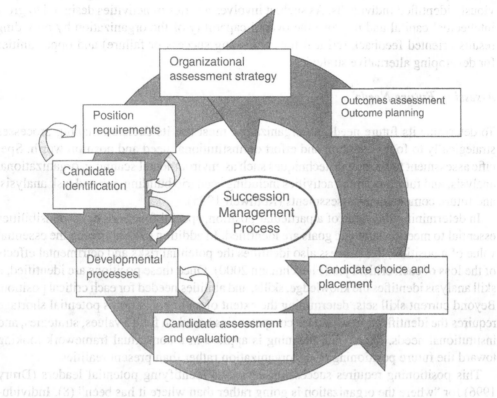

Organizational
assessment strategy

Outcomes assessment
Outcome planning

Position
requirements

Candidate
identification

Succession
Management
Process

Developmental
processes

Candidate choice and
placement

Candidate assessment
and evaluation

perceived strength plus its ability to survive takeover attempts, succession plans mark the ability of an organization to withstand financial predators. Consequently, what a private sector organization can survive (Kesner and Sebora 1994) is "significantly influenced by how and to whom power and authority are passed" (38). This makes the succession of leaders a defining event for virtually every organization (Chaganti, Mahajan, and Sharina 1985; Jauch, Martin, and Osborn 1980; Zald 1970). The significance of a chief executive officer's (CEO) impact on the firm and the symbolism attendant to succession are seen as signals regarding an institution's continued viability (Beatty and Zajac 1987).

Three important dimensions bound succession management as a leadership development process: The future requirements of the organization, the identification and development of leadership talent, and the ability to identify results. As conceptualized in Figure 28.1, there is a two-directional relationship between elements of the succession management process (SMP). This cyclical process is designed to ensure organizational continuity through timely, adaptive, and ongoing change in the development and deployment of leadership talent.

SMP occurs in sequential steps including the (1) deliberate and systematic identification of organizational needs; (2) discovery of a pool of high-potential candidates; (3) intentional learning experiences designed to increase the knowledge, skills, and abilities

of these potential leaders; and (4) actual selection of leaders from among the pool of previously identified individuals. As such, it involves a series of activities designed to grow
intellectual capital and improve the overall capability of the organization by providing
results-oriented feedback (critical for confirming success or failure) and opportunities
for developing alternative strategies.

Assessing Future Needs

To determine its future needs, an organization must use its decision-making processes
strategically to focus attention and effort on institutional need and position worth. Specific assessment tools include techniques such as environmental scanning, organizational
analysis, and future-oriented activities including scenario building, job and task analysis,
and future competencies assessments (Rothwell 1995).

In determining the value of a particular position, special functions or responsibilities
essential to meeting strategic goals are identified. In addition to establishing the essential
value of a position, this process also identifies the potential risks and detrimental effects
of the loss of each critical job (Fleischmann 2000). Once these positions are identified, a
skill analysis identifies the knowledge, skills, and abilities needed for each critical position.
Beyond current skill sets, determining the extent of an organization's potential shortage
requires the identification of needed competencies based on future values, strategies, and
institutional needs. Succession planning is applied in a contextual framework looking
toward the future positioning of the organization rather than present realities.

This positioning requires succession decisions identifying potential leaders (Drury
1996) for "where the organization is going rather than where it has been" (8). Individuals and the organizations they manage engage in vision-oriented thinking encapsulating
core competencies and skill sets required to achieve the envisioned organization. Vision-
oriented reflection requires the organization to ask several important future-oriented
questions about the emergence of key positions, the nature of work requirements (knowledge, skills and abilities, and other characteristics), and the best method to identify and
develop the potential of individuals to fit these future needs (Brady and Helmich 1982).
The premise of such efforts rests on an ongoing analysis of an organization's external
environment, identifying its strengths, weaknesses, opportunities, and threats. The final
element of the organizational needs assessment process involves a comparison of the
critical skill sets for essential positions with the experience of employees in those positions. These planning discussions require organizations to examine present and future
core competencies, staffing patterns (often driven by attrition and internal movement),
and the efficacy of development plans (including education, project or job assignments,
and other learning experiences).

The assessment process is strategic, requiring an understanding of organizational
goals, present workforce competencies, and future needs and skill sets. In addition, it
requires decision makers to undertake HRM strategies maximizing the flow of people
into the organization, ensuring the most competent people fill the most critical positions
(Berwick 1993; Fleischmann 2000). As an aid to formulating both short- and long-term

strategies, organizational needs assessment is subject to continually changing assumptions and limitations concerning time and information.

Identifying Potential Leaders

The value-added nature of succession management as an HRM strategy does not exist in isolation. It is based not only on the individual chosen for succession but also on matching individual competencies to current and anticipated organizational needs. Attaining that optimal match is realized through various succession management strategies, including simple replacement, full replacement, and talent pool development (Rothwell 1995). Within each alternative, there are several levels of employee leadership readiness. Although some individuals are prepared for immediate succession, others are within a few years of advancement, and some have identified potential for long-term development (Dutton 1996).

Simple replacement strategy relies primarily on an organizational chart to identify the next generation of leadership talent. Replacement is based on identification of gaps in leadership coupled with preselected internal replacements. Often this means the slotting of a number of names for possible replacement, usually among the key employees reporting to the CEO or director. This creates a system built on a position-person-matching model or replacement charting. Full replacement strategy emphasizes identification of possible replacements, extending the candidate identification process deeper into the organization by considering middle or lower management employees as well. Both simple and full replacement strategies assume relatively stable environments, high career predictability, and the assumption of linear and long-term career growth investment by organizations (Metz 1998). Often the resulting replacement "queues" are ranked in order of candidate readiness; those employees able to assume positions immediately (usually on an emergency basis) and those employees considered "planned successors" (Peterson 1985; Rothwell 1995).

However, uncertainty within the organizational environment can make targeting future promotional opportunities problematic. Organizational transitions, such as restructuring, require organizations to maximize their abilities when responding to either opportunity or decline. Rather than invest heavily in one or two potential successors for specific positions, a talent pool strategy provides "depth at the bench" for any number of vacancies (whether unforeseen, planned, or newly created) by creating a cadre of employees with needed competencies and skill sets. In addition, given the competition for leadership talent, high-potential employees with strong leadership competencies are also highly marketable. Talent pool strategy provides a way to give strongly skilled employees an indicator of possible advancement opportunities in their organization. These options stress recruitment and development of organizational talent below essential positions to build the talent pool needed to sustain the organization over long periods. Ultimately, as argued by Rainey and Wechsler (1998), "Whether one adapts a broad or more specific approach to organizational performance and productivity, effective transition management is essential to achieving positive results" (156).

Identifying Results

Open communications policies regarding the identification of high potential employees generates immediate benefits. Increasing the visibility and exposure of such programs increases respect for the institutionalized leadership development process, ultimately ensuring a level of rigor that can withstand scrutiny (Cope 1998). The ability to pinpoint and communicate what characterizes success enables organizations to develop learner opportunities for individuals to develop those skills. This requires organizations to commit to practices supporting and enhancing the quality of the leadership talent pool. Formal organizational assessment contributes to the process, providing significant information to the candidate choice process.

Evaluative information shared with individual employees enables potential candidates to express an interest in leadership opportunities. These assessment strategies provide additional avenues for employees to self-identify while also supporting individual responsibility for career development and growth. This encourages an environment that is comment intensive, incorporating continual review systems. This also encourages performance-planning initiatives that incorporate individual manager ratings and a multidimensional feedback process. Finally, it is essential the SMP include identifying and tracking organizational performance in achieving leadership depth.

Literature Review

Kesner and Sebora (1994) found the literature of succession management research in the private sector to be robust, with more than 150 articles over the past 40 years. Their integration of those writings provides a general model of the succession process identifying four key elements of the succession event: (1) succession contingencies (industry issues, organizational characteristics, and selector variables including incumbent and board power); (2) succession antecedents (initiating forces for CEO departure, CEO roles, and candidate issues); (3) the succession event (process, candidate, and choice issues); and (4) succession consequences (organizational effectiveness, stakeholder issues, and evaluation outcomes) (Fredrickson, Hambrick, and Bauman 1988; Friedman and Singh 1989; Goulder 1950; Odiorne 1984; Rhodes and Walker 1984).

The extent of research on succession management in the public sector has been less comprehensive. There is uniform recognition that the subject of succession management in the public sector has received scant attention (Austin and Gilmore 1993; Greenblatt 1983; Rainey and Wechsler 1998; Schall 1997). Less than thirty articles characterize work in the area over the past forty years. Using Kesner and Sebora's (1994) framework, it appears most public sector literature focuses on either succession antecedents (particularly executive level transition) or succession contingencies (organizational characteristics and selector issues) (Greenblatt 1983; Kesner and Sebora 1994; Rainey and Wechsler 1998).

Other research has focused on the nature of succession planning within federal agencies. Acknowledging the somewhat disjointed, often transitory nature of service at the executive levels of federal service, survey results from fifty-four public sector organizations lend support to the contention that succession management has been largely absent from strategic human resource planning at the federal level (NAPA 1997). According to the survey, only 28 percent of government respondents had implemented or planned to implement a succession management program. Yet at the same time, over half of all respondents believed their organizations did not have sufficient leaders to meet emerging changes (NAPA 1997). Even where an agency emphasized the leadership development model, only 11 percent of the NAPA respondents linked succession efforts to strategic plans; only 15 percent prioritized succession management efforts as part of ongoing fiscal commitments. Scant public sector research centers on efforts using succession management as an ongoing human resource process or as a strategic management strategy (Grusky 1969; NAPA 1992; Riedman 1990; Schall 1997).

Having considered the extant literature and noting the lack of public sector research, this article now shifts its focus to redressing one area of that paucity. The research presented below examines how public sector leaders view succession management strategies and the potential usefulness of such a process in identifying, developing, and enabling leadership growth in their organizations.

The Succession Planning Process

Several key elements characterize a successful management succession process. First among them is an organizational assessment linking succession management to an organization strategic plan (Leibman, Bruer, and Maki 1996; National Association of Corporate Directors 1998). Based on this strategy, a leadership template of competencies is established identifying position requirements. This guides the development of a cadre of leadership candidates. Figure 28.2 delineates the process.

Once established, these competencies become part of the candidate identification process and touchstones for the development of individuals who have gaps in important leadership competencies. Development plans for potential leaders represent the institutional commitment to address skill or knowledge areas identified as underdeveloped. Once identified, key personnel and management executives choose among performance strategies designed to strengthen knowledge, skills, and abilities. These include job training, practical leadership experiences, mentoring, and task force/project assignments (Executive Knowledgeworks 1998; Gilmore and Ronchi 1995).

The ability to identify and communicate success enables organizations to develop opportunities for individuals to learn and develop those skills. Developmental assignments are linked to performance plans and work opportunities tailored to employee and organizational needs (Walker 1998). Candidate development, based on job assignments supplemented by training, requires a more intensive and focused approach to strategic competencies. The basis for the system is ultimately a combination of candidate assessment and evaluation wherein traditional analysis is expanded to establish an "action profile" or results-oriented job description of performance outcomes (Burnett and Waters 1984; Klinger and Nalbandian 1997). Employing 360-degree evaluations and emphasizing organizational vision and values further strengthens the evaluative process (Leibman et al. 1996).

Figure 28.2 **Organizational Assessment Strategies**

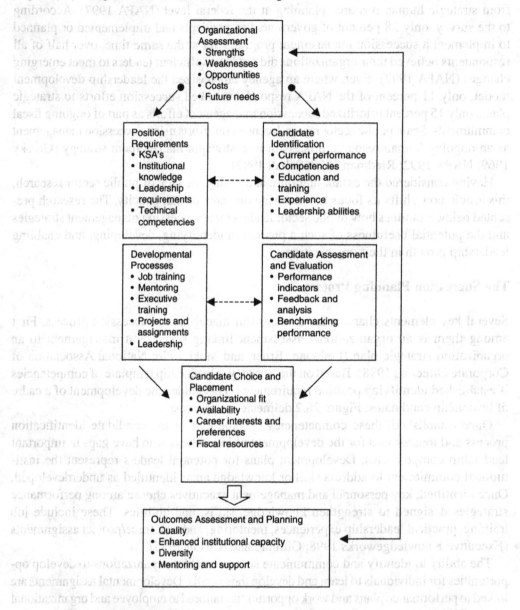

This effort is supported by institutionalizing succession planning as part of the organization's strategic planning efforts. Strategic-level questioning of the type of leadership competencies needed, the processes and resources required, and the organizational performance outcomes anticipated is encouraged by this process (Laurstein 1980; NAPA 1997). Thus, the integration of succession and strategic plans enables the development of sufficient support and experience to link these efforts to the ongoing work of the organization. The creation of a leadership template enables organizations to close the gap between strategic intent and current performance by identifying needed additional core competencies. Once identified, the organization can develop expertise among leadership candidates to meet emerging competency needs. The last element of the process involves the use of outcome assessments and planning to track organizational performance in achieving leadership depth.

Succession Management: Current Initiatives

Several succession management efforts in the public sector are noteworthy as examples of emerging leadership strategies and workforce planning efforts. The U.S. Internal Revenue Service (IRS) has implemented a restructuring initiative that creates operating divisions serving specific customer segments and enhancing customer focus. As a critical component of this effort, the IRS is designing a leadership life-cycle process based on competencies and behaviors linked to executive and managerial responsibilities. These competencies will ultimately drive selection, development, evaluation, compensation, recognition, and succession planning. Also included are a uniform coaching model for successful leadership behavior and sequenced educational opportunities for all leadership levels (Sanders 2000).

A broader effort involving workforce planning and succession management is underway as part of the U.S. Department of Health and Human Services' "Building Successful Organizations" initiative of the Workforce Planning Project. Under the auspices of the division of Human Resources Services (HRS), the project is designed to assist the development of current and future competency models, the allocation of resources for future competency training, the identification and prioritization of gaps in competencies between current workforce skills and future organizational needs, and the periodic and systematic review of succession management plans to meet changes in agency mission and objectives (Office of Human Resources 1999).

Also noteworthy are the efforts by the Quebec government in conjunction with the Ecole Nationale d'Administration Publique [National School of Public Administration] (ENAP) to study the provinces' public sector management succession needs. At the government's invitation (Boudreau 1995), "the ENAP Board of Governors established the *Commission concerant les besoins de la relève des gestionnaires pour la fonction publique quebeçoise* (Commission respecting management succession needs for Quebec's public service) to conduct a prospective needs assessment regarding replacement levels and supervisory function and skills profile" (3). As part of the findings, the Commission report included a desired skill profile for future public managers, including the capabilities of strategic management, client service orientation, and least-cost management and the ability to motivate, mobilize, and manage people.

At the state level, two efforts underway in Oklahoma and Minnesota hold the potential for significant results. Begun in 1990, the leadership of the Minnesota Department of Transportation (MnDOT) initiated an internal leadership development process designed to address competencies essential to the future of the transportation department An organizational assessment process initiated by senior leadership incorporated potential individual needs, organizational changes, diversity status, and the core competencies of leadership, strategic and systems thinking, and people skills. Designed as a voluntary process, employees self-identify for an intensive "cascade review" process, resulting in their selection to a leadership pool. Those employees then create individual development plans with their immediate supervisors and are provided targeted developmental opportunities to fill individual knowledge/skill gaps. As part of the MnDOT leadership pool, they are considered corporate assets for both future development and selection for senior management positions (Blunt and Clark 1997).

In another example, the State of Oklahoma's Department of Corrections has begun a succession management effort focusing on job transitions as significant points for organizational and individual learning. The Oklahoma model is predicated on executive development opportunities for middle- to high-level management and incorporates four elements: placement for development opportunities, formal executive training, a commitment to internal promotion and advancement, and broad-based job assignments to increase individual capacity. A key feature of the Oklahoma process is the incorporation of "learning journeys" to build networking ties and to gain insights and expertise on the inner workings and history of the agency. As their sole task, newly assigned managers take part in a series of interviews over a two- or three-week period with key staff and management throughout the department to identify sources of support and to develop a contextual framework of their new position (Riedman 1990).

Survey Assessment

Given the growing recognition of the importance associated with developing internal leadership capacity, it appeared useful to assess the extent to which public sector managers are preparing to respond to leadership gaps through formalized succession programs. What follows are the results of three focus-group discussions held with forty-eight public sectors leaders to discuss their involvement in management succession programs, the success of these strategies, and plans for expanding such programs.

Method

The use of focus groups provides a source of detailed information and is an effective way to produce data and insights often less accessible without group interaction (Morgan 1998: Sauliner 2000). As a research tool, this method enables the collection of information from a specific population, in this case, participants involved in the development of leadership talent in their respective organizations. The focus group approach enabled participants to provide insights into the complexity of the succession management process, as well as to discuss the readiness of their organizations to identify and nurture the next generation of leaders.

Findings

The mix of participants in the three focus groups included government and nonprofit managers and public-sector human resource professionals. The majority (60.5 percent) were either agency directors or human resource managers working for municipal government agencies with more than fifty employees. Of the participants, 12 (25 percent) were associated with not-for-profit organizations as executive directors; 7 (14.5 percent) were employed in state agencies. Although almost half indicated their organizations were prepared to replace an essential position under unforeseen circumstances, none of the forty-eight indicated their respective organizations had a formalized management succession program.

Even where civil service systems operated, replacement strategies undertaken by a majority of group members (82 percent) were characterized as reactive and ad hoc. Leadership gap remediation strategy was often determined on a case-by-case basis, tending to focus on identifying an interim or acting replacement until a formal plan was initiated. Among the twelve nonprofit agency participants, ten indicated their small professional staffs precluded formal replacement strategies and frequently involved dividing duties associated with a vacant position until a replacement strategy was developed.

The lack of an ongoing programmatic response to future leadership needs was evident by the overwhelming percentage of group members (87.5 percent) who revealed their organizations did not rely on a process for the systematic development of individuals for future leadership positions. Only seven out of forty-eight (14.5 percent) indicated their organization used some sort of employee development process. All seven participants from municipal and state agencies characterized such efforts as situation-based or linked to developing specific skills needed within a particular job category. Yet, 65 percent of those responding indicated there was a link between leadership development and the organization's strategic planning efforts. This outcome suggests that although the individuals surveyed have a conceptual commitment to employee development, opportunities directly tied to professional growth have not been established within their agencies.

Another important aspect of succession planning involves the development of evaluative strategies designed to identify employees with the requisite knowledge, skills, and abilities, or readiness, for promotion. Asked to describe the extent to which ongoing formalized review systems contribute to the identification of potential leaders, only nine participants remarked on the use of standardized performance appraisals or other review systems as part of that process. Yet, almost 50 percent indicated evaluation efforts are part of an objective assessment of employee competencies. Arguably then, these review systems are utilized retrospectively, providing managers the opportunity to examine prior efforts and performance outcomes rather than prospectively identifying future needs and skill sets of employees.

The success of succession management as a leadership development strategy is attributable to many factors, not the least of which is the overall acceptance of the strategy by senior-level decision makers. The involvement of top executives reflects the institutional commitment to the development of internal leadership capacity. A significant portion of the groups (66 percent) indicated a high degree of expectation of involvement in these decisions. However, only eight (16 percent) noted they played a major role in the process and only two had developed their organization's policy; twelve (25 percent) indicated they played no part in the development of leadership strategies. Senior level administrators, such as executive directors, senior executives, and board members, were routinely identified as potentially important decision makers regarding succession planning. This was as expected and is indicative of the NAPA (1997) findings that indicated the importance of high-level organizational involvement in the development of internal leadership capacity. Although immediate supervisors and managers were ranked as second most important in the process, human resource professionals were seen as critical actors in the succession planning process. However, only eight participants indicated HR and management worked in concert to ensure the viability of their organization's succession efforts. Although seeing succession management as an important human resource activity, participants said most organizations do not automatically involve HR managers in strategic planning, needs assessment, or forecasting. Last, participants were asked the extent to which they had explored the issue of succession management in any conference or training seminar opportunities. Underscoring the public sector's weakness in succession planning, none of the forty-eight focus-group members indicated that had occurred.

Conclusion

In an environment of early retirements, reorganizations, and lean hierarchies, often with depleted pools of middle management, there are many challenges facing the public sector in regard to developing and selecting leaders (Byham 1999). Within federal agencies and in at least twelve states, the recruitment and utilization of highly qualified individuals has involved the establishment of a senior executive personnel system. However, Sherwood and Beyer's (1987) study of state executive systems concluded such systems had done "little to alleviate critical problems of attracting people to leadership roles in the states; to utilize available resources effectively; and to develop leadership personnel of the future" (410). There are internal barriers to leadership development in the public sector: organizational culture, low priority, insufficient resources, inadequate rewards for initiative/risk, limited mobility, and lack of role models (Centers for Creative Leadership 1996; NAPA 1997; Schall 1997). As Schall (1997) also pointed out, there are impediments to taking public sector succession efforts seriously, including issues of scope, confusion over replacement versus positioning, and a lack of planning techniques in the face of political and other constraints. In addition, the window of opportunity is often short-lived for managerial political appointees, affecting the development of succession strategies.

The traditional view of the public personnel management system is centered on the concept of a merit-based civil service supporting the values of equity and fairness. Merit-based civil service systems, an important departure from patronage and political favor, explains in part the hesitancy of public HRM managers and the leadership of their organizations to support programs that identify preselected replacements for positions. Career service and political appointees are reluctant to embrace a process that potentially flies in the face of longstanding commitments to merit. Despite growing government complexity and the need for leadership continuity, the traditional commitment to egalitarianism can outweigh the desirability of a system perceived as elitist (Musolf 1971; Sherwood and Beyer 1987).

In addition, there are often gaps between the promises of succession planning and the reality of its outcomes. Plans, even if well conceived, often go awry. The fragile nature of site-specific work locations, flexible working relationships, and new technologies, coupled with changing societal expectations of work and family plus an increasingly diverse workplace, create new organizational landscapes (Leibman et al. 1996; Mills 1985). The potential for highly political outcomes and the possible appointment of external candidates not in the talent pool, create frustration and undermine the overall success of such plans. Effective plan implementation requires better and earlier identification of candidates and strategies for dealing with lack of senior management support and resources. Increasingly, public organizations are simultaneously confronting new and often ill-defined environments, expectations, and internal demands.

The pace of succession management is often considered too slow and too likely to fail in the long-term to produce candidates with the capabilities to lead. This can also lead to the loss of top candidates who move elsewhere or to the escalation of frustration among internal candidates passed over in favor of external hires. New competencies, organizational reengineering, transformational efforts, and general uncertainties in the economy can transform succession decisions into make or buy choices (develop internally or recruit externally) (Walker 1998). Finally, the lack of explicit, ongoing executive support for succession management sends an important message throughout the organization; programs that become staff-driven have limited credibility.

These conclusions are preliminary, based on only three focus groups in two settings. However, the results do point to important aspects for further study. Based on the reactions of the focus group participants, public sector managers and HRM professionals are concerned with the directions of their organizations and identifying who in the organization is capable of leading. Investment beyond the traditional methods, not only ensuring the training and education of potential leaders but also tracking the progress of their systematic enhancement of competencies and continuously identifying further critical areas for development, is crucial to creating a viable leadership succession process. Human resource professionals are fundamental to implementing this type of strategy. Their role includes providing managers and executives with tools for developing new competencies in the workforce, training to improve core competencies, performing workforce and gap analysis, and developing succession planning models.

With the often abbreviated tenure of many government and public sector leaders, career service executives and human resource personnel must be able to move their organizations toward a succession management process as a strategic endeavor—one designed to ensure both the sustainability and depth of leadership capital necessary for the success of public agencies in carrying out their missions. There is justifiable concern over the present capacity of the public sector to recognize, teach, groom, and reward employees (Conan 1990). The success of the succession management process, as with other employee development efforts, ultimately rests with commitment from top management.

References

Austin, M.J., and Gilmore, T.N. 1993. "Executive Exit: Multiple Perspectives on Managing Leadership Transition." *Administration in Social Work,* 77(1): 47–80.

Beany, R.P., and Zajac, E.J. 1987. "CEO Change and Firm Performance in Corporations: Succession Effects and Manager Shifts." *Strategic Management Journal,* 8: 305–17.

Berwick, C. 1993. "Eight Ways to Assess Succession Plans." *Human Resource Magazine,* 38(5): 109–13.

Blunt, R. 2000. "Leaders Growing Leaders: Preparing the Next Generation of Public Service Executives." Washington, DC: Council for Excellence in Government.

Blunt, R., and Clark, H. 1997. "Growing Public Service Leaders." *Public Manager,* 26(2): 87–92.

Boudreau, T.J. 1995 (Summer). "Management Succession Needs for Quebec's Public Service: Report of the Commission." *Journal of Public Sector Management,* 3–9.

Brady, G., and Helmich, D. 1982. "The Hospital Administrator and Organizational Change: Do We Recruit from the Outside?" *Hospital and Health Services Administration,* 27: 53–62.

Burnett, R.S., and Waters, J.S. 1984. (May/June). "The Action Profile: A Practical Aid to Career Development and Succession Planning." *Business Horizons,* 15–21.

Byham, W.C. 1999. "Grooming Next-Millennium Leaders." *Personnel Management,* 44(2): 46–51.

Caudron, S. 1966. "The Looming Succession Crisis." *Workforce,* 75(9): 72–76.

Chaganti, R., Mahajan, V. and Sharina, S. 1985. "Corporate Board Size, Composition, and Corporate Failures." *Journal of Management Studies,* 22: 400–16.

Conan, J.K. 1990. *Management Education and Training in New Jersey: A Description, an Appraisal, and Recommendations for Improvement.* East Orange, NJ: Fund for New Jersey.

Cope, F. 1998. "Current Issues in Selecting High Potentials." *Human Resource Planning,* 21: 120–34.

Drury, D.H. 1996. "Administrative Innovation Applied to Systems Adaption." *International Journal of Management,* 12(1): 5–19.

Dutton, G. 1996. "Executive Succession." *Management Review,* 55(8).

Eastman, L. 1995. *Succession Planning: An Annotated Bibliography and Summary of Commonly Reported Organizational Practices.* Greensboro, NC: Center for Creative Leadership.

Executive Knowledgeworks. 1988. *Succession Planning in America's Corporations.* Palatine, IL: Anthony J. Fresina.

Fleischmann, S.T. 2000 (Summer). "Succession Management for the Entire Organization." *Employment Relations Today,* 53–62.

Fredrickson, J.W., Hambrick, D.C, and Bauman, S. 1988. "A Model of CEO Dismissal." *Academy of Management Review,* 13(2), 255–70.

Friedman, S.D., and Singh, H. 1989. "Succession and Stockholder Reaction." *Academy of Management Journal,* 32(4), 718–44.

Gilmore, T.N., and Ronchi, D. 1995. "Managing Predecessors' Shadows in Executive Transitions." *Human Resource Management,* 34(1), 11–26.

Goulder, A.W. 1950. "The Problem of Succession and Bureaucracy." In A.W. Goulder (ed.), *Studies in Leadership* (pp. 644–62). New York: Harper.

Greenblatt, M. 1983. *Management Succession: Some Major Parameters.* San Francisco: Human Science Press.

Grusky, O. 1969. "Succession with an Ally." *Administrative Science Quarterly,* 14, 155–70.

Hesselbien, F., Goldsmith, M., and Beckhard, R. 1996. *The Leader of the Future: New Visions, Strategies and Practices for the Next Era.* San Francisco: Jossey-Bass.

Huddleston, M.W. 1999. *Profiles in Excellence: Conversations with the Best of America's Career Executive Service.* Washington, DC: The PriceWaterhouseCoopers Endowment for the Business of Government.

Jauch, L, Martin, T., and Osborn, R. 1980. "Top Management under Fire." *Journal of Business Strategy,* 1, 33–41.

Kesner, L.E., and Sebora, T.C. 1994. "Executive Succession: Past, Present and Future." *Journal of Management,* 20(2), 327–72.

Klingner, D., and Nalbandian, J. 1997. *Public Personnel: Context and Strategies* (4th ed.) Englewood Cliffs, NJ: Prentice Hall.

Laurstein, M. 1980 (June). "Boards of Directors: The Need for a Strategic Concept." *Journal of Business Strategy,* 66–68.

The Leadership Development and Education Institute. 1999. *The National Survey on Public Leadership: Abridged Results.* Boulder, CO: Author.

Leibman, M., Bruer, R.A., and B.R. Maid. 1996. "Succession Management: The Next Generation of Succession Planning." *Human Resource Planning,* 19(5), 16.

Metz,. E.J. 1998. "Designing Succession Systems for New Competitive Realities." *Journal of Human Resource Planning,* 21, 356.

Mills, D.Q. 1985 (July/August). "Planning with People in Mind." *Harvard Business Review,* 97–105.

Morgan, D.L. 1998. *The Focus Group Guidebook.* Thousand Oaks, CA: Sage.

Musolf, L. 1971. "Separate Career Executive Systems: Egalitarianism and Neutrality." *Public Administration Review,* 31, 678–89.

National Academy of Public Administration. 1992. *Paths to Leadership: Executive Succession Planning in the Federal Government.* Washington, DC: Author.

National Academy of Public Administration. 1997. *Managing Succession and Developing Leadership: Growing the Next Generation of Public Service Leaders.* Washington, DC: Author.

National Association of Directors. 1998 (July). *Chief Executive Officers: Selection and Appointment and CEO Succession.* Report of the National Association of Corporate Directors, Washington, DC.

Odiorne, G.S. 1984 (November). "Match Organizational Requirements to Corporate Human Potential." *Management Review,* 157–73.

Office of Human Resources, Department of Health and Human Services. 1999. *Building Successful Organizations: Workforce Planning in HHS.* Washington, DC: Author [Online]. Available: www.hhs.gov/progorg/ohr/wrpguide.html.

Peterson, A.H. 2000. "Succession Management." *Credit Union Magazine,* 66(1).

Peterson, M. 1985. "Attitudinal Differences Among Leaders: What Do They Reflect?" *Academy of Management Journal,* 28(3).

Rainey, H.G., and Wechsler, B. 1998. *Executive-level Transition: Executive Succession Planning in the Federal Government.* Washington, DC: National Academy of Public Administration.

Rhodes, D.W., and Walker, J.W. 1984. "Management Succession and Development Planning." *Journal of Human Resource Planning,* 14, 157–73.

Riedman, S. 1990. "Succession Systems in the Public Sector: Lessons from the Oklahoma Department of Corrections." *Public Personnel Management,* 19(3), 291–303.

Rothwell, W.J. 1995. "Beyond Training and Development." *Management Review,* 84(9).

Sanders, R. 1999. *The Executive Decision Making Process: Identifying Problems and Assessing Outcomes.* Westport, CT: Quorum.

Sauliner, C. 2000. "Groups as Data Collection Method and Data Analysis Technique." *Small Group Research,* 31(5), 607–28.

Schall, E. 1997. "Public Sector Succession: A Strategic Approach to Sustaining Innovation." *Public Administration Review,* 57(1), 1129–45.

Sherwood, E. and Beyer, L. 1987. "Executive Personnel Systems in the States." *Public Administration Review,* 47(5), 410–16.

Sullivan, J. 1999. *Workforce Planning Helps Growth* [Online]. Available: www.workforceonline.com/members/research/workforce_planning/31065.html.

Vancil, R.F. 1987. *Passing the Baton: Managing the Process of CEO Succession.* Boston: Harvard Business School Press.

Walker, J.W. 1998. "Do We Need Succession Planning?" *Journal of Human Resource Planning,* 21, 239–56.

Zald, M.N. 1970. "Political Economy: A Framework for Comparative Analysis," In M.N. Zald (Ed.), *Power in Organizations* (pp. 221–61). Nashville, TN: Vanderbilt University Press.

CHAPTER 29

REFLECTIONS ON "EDUCATING EXECUTIVES"

RAYMOND A. KATZELL

The symposium, "Educating Executives," in the Autumn, 1958, *Review* provides a panorama of educational programs to develop executives in industry and public agencies. All were instituted within the past few years and therefore present a contemporary overview.

What can we learn from these reports? We can observe what the programs tried to accomplish, how they were conducted, and something of their outcomes. Some of us may spot characteristics that we may wish to adapt to our own purposes, practices that we may decide to avoid, or needs that we may regard as still unfulfilled.

It may therefore be helpful to approach this array of programs by analyzing first their apparent similarities and differences. Aggregate trends may then be compared with what is known of other programs and some comparative judgments made.

Major dimensions in terms of which these similarities and differences may be analyzed are: Objectives, Content, Method, Educational Agency, and Job Level of Trainees. Let us examine more closely these facets of the programs reported.

A Combined Analysis of the Programs

A. *Basic objectives.* All executive development programs, including those cited here, have the comprehensive goal of modifying executive thinking and behavior through learning. However, there may be important differences among programs in the particular levels and patterns of behavior which they attempt to change. Four such target areas may be identified, some more explicitly than others, in the reports under review:

1. improving the executive "as a man" by enhancing the scope of his cultural background;
2. broadening his outlook on executive responsibilities, presumably leading to some redirection of executive attention and action;
3. increasing his specific administrative knowledge and skills;
4. modifying his patterns of adjustment and relationships to his world, involving some change in personality processes.

From *Public Administration Review,* vol. 19, no. 1 (1959): 1–6. Copyright © 1959 by American Society for Public Administration. Reprinted with permission.

The first objective is most clearly represented in the liberal arts programs described by Nelson. The second, or "broadening" objective, is paramount in most of the other programs described. The main difference between these two objectives, irrespective of content or method, is the greater emphasis in the second objective on change in *job* behavior. As Nelson puts it, ". . . the liberal arts do not stand or fall according to whether they make better business managers or better public administrators." However, one may infer that programs to educate the whole man would have few employer sponsors without the assumption that attaining this objective also helps create better executives. This inference is supported by the attention Nelson devotes to the ways in which it may be "possible for the liberal arts to transform the practices of an administrator" and by the objectives cited for the liberal arts program undertaken by Bell Telephone. Thus, in the last analysis, objectives one and two may not differ markedly.

The third objective, that relating to skills training, is the major target of none of the programs reviewed here, although several devote considerable attention to it in the course of pursuing the second (Mailick, Grundstein, Reynolds, Mowitz). This circumstance should not blind us to the possibility that programs which focus primarily on improving specific administrative skills may play an important and legitimate role in executive development. Such programs are widely represented in the seminars and workshops conducted by various universities, by professional and management associations, and intramurally by many companies and agencies, on such topics as work simplification, public speaking, cost control, budget management, etc.

The fourth target area for development exists on the level of changing the individual's perceptions and feelings of himself, his colleagues, and his environment. The improvements sought in this connection are dependent not so much on factual knowledge as on the removal of the psychological barriers to effective understanding and action and on the development of personal insights that cannot be readily communicated by the spoken and written word.

Of the programs described here, the only one that explicitly embraces this fourth objective is that reported by Grundstein. Here, there was a dual focus on the organization and the executive's self. Referring to the changes stimulated by the executive's experiences, Grundstein points out: "Some of the changes are in the conceptual (thinking) area, with no challenge to one's image of self, but some changes are directed to altering one's image of self. I attempted to get into this area of perception of self and others through a sensitivity sequence that was directed to raising the level of consciousness regarding one's behavior."

Thus, these several programs range from considerable concern with improving job performance of the executive to relatively little attention to such short-range payoffs; from attention to specific administrative skills through intellectual broadening to personality change. Yet, there is a recurrent theme: the aim of raising the executive's sights, of sensitizing him to a wider diversity of factors affecting his responsibilities, of stimulating his growth toward statesmanlike leadership.

B. *Content.* The subject-matter of a development program may be regarded as an operating definition of its objective. We may therefore analyze content under the same rubrics as we did objectives.

The programs dedicated to the intellectual development of the whole man have stressed the liberal arts, particularly philosophy, economics, aesthetics, natural sciences, social sciences, literature, and contemporary civilization.

Programs addressed to the broadening of the executive as an executive have differed widely in specifics, but there are common general themes. Chief among them are: the setting of public administration in its political, economic, and social context; organizational and administrative theory; planning and policy making, including their ethical and moral facets; administrative behavior and human relations. The process of decision making appears to have served as a convenient core on which more than one program undertook to integrate various topics.

Several programs included training in specific administrative techniques. Prominent among these were budgeting and accounting, personnel administration, oral and written communication, decision-making skills, techniques of motivating people, and principles and techniques of scientific management. As previously mentioned, practically none of the programs was devoted mainly to such skill-subjects; usually they were articulated with broader, more theoretical treatments of the type listed in the preceding paragraph.

It is more difficult to classify the subject-matter related to the psychological development of the individual. We have already seen that Grundstein devoted attention to this subject, but the article furnishes only a few details on content. Also, most of the other programs devoted some attention to interpersonal relations and the implications of behavioral sciences; presumably, at least part of the intention may have been to modify the executive's self-understanding and adaptive behavior. The liberal arts, too, have traditionally been held to improve one's self-knowledge and approach to life. But as to these latter efforts, we must not fail to make a distinction between cognitive learning *about* human nature, and the more intimate, self-directed, and emotional process of learning new behavior patterns and modes of adjustment. Grundstein's program aside, we must therefore question whether any of the programs contained subject matter effectively directed to personality change.

C. *Method.* The basic educational method most widely employed in these programs appears to have been the seminar or discussion-group led by an expert in the subject at hand. The lecture and lecture-discussion also were widely used, either as the major method of instruction or interspersed among seminars.

Readings were employed universally as an ancillary educational method but never as the exclusive one. Other ancillary methods, each used by one or two programs, included workshops, consultations with high-level administrators, the case method, and the syndicate method.

It is apparent that these programs were, for the most part, cast in the mold of traditional academic practices. The program which in its essence deviated most from that tradition was that of the Brookings Institution, which emphasized the conference method and encouraged continued development through the formation of alumni groups. Continued innovation along these lines is essential if we are to implement our view that development is a continuing rather than a one-shot affair.

The auxiliary use of discussions with outside administrators (Reynolds) and of workshops (Mailick) represent interesting efforts to move from the plane of abstraction and generality to that of specificity and particularization—another field in which more innovation is needed if development is to bring behavioral change.

D. *Development agency.* Another aspect of method is the locus of the training activity, i.e., which agency or institution plays the major role in carrying out the development program. All of the programs were executed by an agent outside the government—usually a university. However, in most instances, the government unit or group whose personnel were enrolled in the program played an active part in its planning and design.

In this respect, then, our sample of programs is restricted for it does not include representatives of intramurally conducted programs, a type which is common in private industry and not unknown in government. One might guess that intramural programs would have stronger representation of skill-subjects and relatively little of the liberal arts as such. Intramural programs may also be expected, more typically, to examine problems and implications germane to the company or agency itself, which may be a mixed blessing.

E. *Levels of executives.* The programs reported here collectively attempted to cover the needs of a wide range of job levels, ranging upward from approximately the equivalent of GS-5. However, each program typically defined a limited executive stratum to which it was addressed. For example, the Brookings program was aimed at career executives at the level of GS-16 and above, while that at the University of Chicago was directed at GS-12 and above. Apparently the feeling was widespread that great heterogeneity of job levels would not make for effective programs. Another evidence of this was the establishment of separate programs for different job levels where the range was wide (e.g., Reynolds, Mowitz).

Not unexpectedly there seems to be some interaction between the job levels comprehended by a program and its objectives, content, and educational methods. Our limited data indicate that the programs addressed to higher-level executives tended toward greater emphasis on broadening and liberalizing objectives and subject-matter, whereas those designed for the lower levels were more concerned with skills and techniques. In educational method, the former programs were more likely to be characterized by more active roles for participants (conferences, seminars), whereas the programs addressed to lower levels exhibited greater structure and spoon-feeding. One might hazard a guess that such differences in method depend more on expediency than on educational philosophy. Or at least one hopes so.

Evaluating the Composite Program

One way of summarizing the nature of executive development programs furnished in the six reports is to draw a composite picture made up of their modal characteristics: (1) a program offered by a university (2) mainly for intermediate-level executives (3) with the aim of assisting in the intellectual development (4) of a broad-gauge executive—a man who is aware of the scope of his responsibilities, cognizant of the social, economic, and moral boundaries within which policies must be formulated, and at least somewhat understanding of the nature of complex organizations and the people who compose them.

The content of the program accordingly comprises organizational theory, the economic, social, and political environment of public agencies, the process of planning and policy setting, principles and theories of management, human relations, and some attention to advanced administrative skills such as decision making, budgeting, or motivating people. This subject-matter is considered in lectures and discussion groups, supported by readings from selected bibliographies.

Of course individual programs deviate from the mode, but the composite portrait may give us a general feel for what has been going on and serve as a point of departure for general comment.

On the positive side, it is apparent that our composite program is up-to-date in the sense that it reflects contemporary thinking regarding executive functions and the administrative process. Moreover, it tries commendably to challenge the executive by involving him in the consideration and discussion of new ideas and syntheses. The composite also properly recognizes that the effective executive is neither merely a repository of advanced information in his technical specialty nor an administrative specialist furnished with a battery of techniques for organizing and supervising subordinates; clearly, the note struck here is one of responsible leadership of complex organizations in a multi-faceted environment.

From some standpoints, however, our composite program is rather old fashioned. For one thing, it is centered around the hallowed tradition of developing people by getting them together in a course, in which they listen, read, and discuss. Should not more attention be given (as some of the programs did) to "newer" educational practices that attempt to simulate something of life, such as the case method, the laboratory method, or the syndicate method?

And why is there no attention to individualized programs of development, such as job rotation, counseling, coaching, subsidized adult and graduate education, correspondence courses, or participation in development, programs of various professional and managerial associations? In this connection, it should be noted that executives usually report that the most profound influence on their own development has been confrontation with new and challenging responsibilities, pointing to the importance of planned on-the-job experience in the development of the individual. Is it that individualized programs of development are harder to conceive or to administer—have they been tried and failed?—or is it just that we comfortably fall back on our familiar educational heritage? Some of these agencies may have individual development programs in addition to outside educational courses, though they were mentioned only by Mailick. If so, there is need to integrate them with the courses. Failure to mention them would suggest the absence of an over-all developmental plan.

The composite program is conventional in another way as well—in its emphasis on the intellectual growth of the executive, i.e., on learning or cognitive understanding. However, we now know that behavior is only in part a function of cognition. Accurate perception of relationships, skill in responding appropriately to situations, and the elimination of emotional and affective barriers to realistic perception and action also are potent factors in effectiveness. While laudable efforts have been noted among the programs to accommodate some of these considerations, such efforts form a relatively small part of the total picture. Of course it may be appropriate for the composite program to focus on growth in knowledge if this is really the area in which most executives are especially lacking, but one rather doubts that ignorance plays a more prominent part in executive ineffectiveness than does inability to put extant knowledge to use in specific situations.

There is another emphasis in the composite program which may create an imbalance if it is true of the whole field of executive development. The past few decades have seen increasing crystallization of the concept of management as a general profession, irrespective of the particular business, agency, or executive's special field. Certainly many essential executive skills are general in nature and transcend the specific setting or job, but it does not follow that all an executive needs to function effectively is this kit of general attitudes and skills. There are substantive aspects of the work of a particular agency, or subdivision, which are special to the work of that organization. It is almost a truism that the executive needs such substantive or technical competence over and beyond his general administrative and leadership skill.[1] It therefore follows that the development of executives involves enhancement not only of their general administrative abilities, but also, up to a point, of their technical competence in the field in which their organization operates, be this manufacturing, agriculture, finance, diplomacy, or what have you. This need probably is particularly strong at the lower and middle managerial levels.

It would seem to be too much to ask that our programs reviewed here also incorporate such technical subject-matter, since they were obviously addressed to the development of the general executive abilities. However, let this discussion serve as a *caveat* to the field at large not to think of executive development solely in these terms. Otherwise we may repeat the mistake of extremists in teacher education who concentrated on the *how* of teaching to the detriment of the *what*.

"Bad" Executive Development

There is a final *caveat: an organized executive development program is not necessarily "good"—it may sometimes be "bad."*

An executive development program is good when it will help the executive better to realize his potentialities through more effective and self-satisfying performance of his job. It is bad to the extent that it hampers or detracts from this process.

Under what circumstances might programs be bad? The major ones are these:

A. The problem identified for solution may be wrong, i.e., developmental objectives may not correspond to the executives' needs. The case comes to mind of the company president who, finding that his managers often failed to note things that were buried in the memoranda and reports which deluged them, decided they should improve their reading skills.

B. The program may be inadequate for the objectives. A common example is the "quickie" course in human relations, a field which is far too complex and emotionally charged for "how-to-do-its." Poorly designed programs are bad because they waste the executives' time, misdirect their attention, and sometimes even misinform them.

C. The program may be out of step with the organizational climate. The effectiveness of an executive's behavior depends in part on its articulation with the behaviors, needs, and expectations of others in his organization. A program which undertakes to develop managerial attitudes and behaviors that are out of phase with such established relationships is unlikely to do either the manager or his organization any good, no matter how desirable these behaviors may be under other circumstances.[2] It is in this context that one of Nelson's points becomes especially significant: the importance of having in positions of policy leadership persons who are sensitive to and sympathetic with the values, approaches, and methods that may be developed through a program for career executives. The same may be said about higher-level career executives in relation to the development of their subordinate executives within an agency.

D. The program may be directed toward problems which lie outside of the control of the executives who participate in it. A common reaction of those in high echelons to symptoms of organizational ineffectiveness or malfunctioning is to feel that the answer lies in improving the caliber of their subordinate executives. While this diagnosis may be correct, it may also be that executive performance is about as good as can be expected under current policies, traditions, and conditions. If the latter is the case (as may too often be true), then the organization of executive development programs to remedy the situation will be bad. In addition to wasting time, effort, and money, they may increase the frustration of the subordinate executives, and divert effort from attacking the roots of the problems. We must be particularly wary of this origin of bad programs, since it is so much easier to inaugurate training programs than to change organizational aims, policies, and traditions.

Assuring Effective Programs

If development programs can be bad as well as good, how can we ensure the latter? One indispensable requirement is a thorough study of the development needs of the executives in an organization. Basically, such a study entails the establishment of empirical standards of effective executive behavior, and a survey of the extent to which, and respects in which, executive performance falls below these standards. Given this information, it should be possible to judge whether executive ability needs development or whether the major target should be policy and procedure revision, and, if the former, in what directions development is most needed.

Another requirement is better evaluation of the consequences of various types of programs and methods. To their everlasting credit, practically all contributors to the symposium were sensitive to this need. To the extent that they reported evaluative data, they will help us all in the design of future programs. But I am sure they would join me in entering a plea for greater future support of controlled and systematic research on the relations between the characteristics of development programs and their outcomes.

It is, after all, a basic law of psychology that we improve in direct proportion to our knowledge of the results of our efforts.

Notes

1. Empirical studies support this belief by indicating that technical ability is an important factor in managerial effectiveness. See, for example: Baumgartel, H. "Leadership, Motivation, and Attitudes in Research Laboratories" in *Journal of Social Issues* Number 2, pp. 24–31 (1956); and Comrey, A.L. et al. *Factors Influencing Organizational Effectiveness* (University of Southern California, 1954).

2. Research evidence on this point may be found in: Fleishman, E.A. et al. *Leadership and Supervision in Industry: An Evaluation of a Supervisory Training Program* (Bureau of Business Research, Ohio State University, 1955); and Hariton, T. "Conditions Influencing the Effects of Training Foremen in New Human Relations Principles." Doctoral Dissertation, University of Michigan, 1951.

PART 9

EXAMPLES AND EXEMPLARS OF PUBLIC-SECTOR LEADERSHIP

Having talked so long about administrative leadership, it is now time to highlight some examples and exemplars. But this brings us to one of the great conundrums of the field. Where are the good examples in the journal literature? Unfortunately, most journal articles tend to feature either elected political figures or political appointees in their administrative roles. It is also unfortunate that the examples are often negative (such as a Robert Citron who in his administrative capacity risked and lost billions of dollars in his failed investment scheme) or extreme (such as the public leaders who stood up to President Nixon and were fired by him in the "Saturday night massacre"). The reader should not conclude, however, that excellent leaders are not to be found.

The problem associated with providing good examples of administrative leadership is technical—how do you document and discuss the dozens of variables that highlight good leadership in a *short* treatment, especially since the contextual environment itself is so complex? What theoretical framework do you use if it is a scholarly journal? Given the detail that must be provided, how do you ensure that the treatment is interesting, and not a compendium of details or a syrupy story? Writing a good scholarly case study of administrative leadership is a difficult task and generally not encouraged. (A major exception is the "exemplar profile" solicited by *Public Integrity*.) Nonetheless, a few good examples of such scholarship can be found.

What Is *Great* Administrative Leadership?

This book has spent the bulk of its space talking about *good* administrative leadership. Is *great* administrative leadership simply more of the same? That is, good administrative leadership is deft and efficient technical production, firm and compassionate utilization of human resources, a clear sensibility of what the organization needs to be doing and how it needs to adapt, and a sense of integrity that overlays it all. Certainly that is a great deal. However, is doing all of these things very well great administrative leadership? Or is more required of greatness? Does such leadership require a profound element such as a great vision that is dedicated to the public good? What if that vision is not achieved? Does such leadership require a weighty success? Stated differently, does great administrative leadership require a legacy? Or perhaps such administrative leadership is attained not so much by the achievement as by the challenge experienced and the sacrifice made. In other words, does great administrative leadership require a heroic element such as an act of moral courage? Of course there are no definitive answers; this section of readings, however, does indeed raise these questions.

One final question raised by this section is the problem of moral lapses. At what point do moral lapses diminish or entirely deny legitimate claims to greatness in administrative leadership? Although only briefly mentioned in this section, some of the most famous "administrative" leaders of the twentieth century were highly flawed. Indeed, it almost seems that in order to achieve the great things that they did in an environment that demanded incredible slowness, mediocrity, compromise, and conventionality that they had to be bold, decisive, demanding, uncompromising, and unconventional. This opens the door rather widely for egotism, self-promotion, and bullying. It also raises the age-old question: Should leaders with clearly great capacities and extraordinary accomplishments be held to the same standards, or should they be given some allowance for their peccadilloes?

Review of the Selections in Part 9

The first article, "The Patriotism of Exit and Voice: The Case of Gloria Flora" (2001) by H. George Frederickson and Meredith Newman, is about moral courage. Federal employees in the West who were in charge of land management were increasingly being subjected to various types of harassment and threats as various parts of the community advocated for increased rights over federal lands. In response to what she viewed as outrageous behavior from not only the local community but elected officials as well, Flora resigned as a form of protest. Readers will want to ask: When and how is this type of sacrifice and courage appropriate for a leader? No matter whether one thinks that the sacrifice was justified in this particular case, Flora clearly demonstrates many of the traits, skills, and behaviors that promote leader effectiveness, such as vision, hard work, integrity, public service motivation, intelligence, political savvy, and a variety of interpersonal skills.

The next reading is another portion of the book review used in part 1, "Leaders and Leadership" (1980) by John Corson. Reviewing Eugene Lewis's book on public entrepreneurship, Corson discusses Hyman Rickover, J. Edgar Hoover, and Robert Moses. Rickover was the admiral who led the U.S. Navy into the nuclear age. He was successful at the modernization effort that made the U.S. Navy the envy of the world, but his bigger-than-life personality seemed to rival Patton in World War II and MacArthur in the Korean War. Hoover took a small division in the Justice Department and fashioned it into a world-class national police force with independent status. He also blackmailed presidents, ruthlessly controlled his employees, and built an administrative empire from which it was almost impossible to depose him. Likewise, Moses's control of the parks, throughways, bridges, tunnels, and ports in the New York area was extraordinary. While he single-handedly redesigned New York, which was an eighteenth-century city in the beginning of his tenure, into the modern city it is today, he also administratively blackmailed politicians and used elitist preferences in his building designs. (For example, when he designed Jones Beach he forbade access by public transportation to discourage the poor from using it.) How do we evaluate figures with such mixed contributions?

Ironically, the final selection, written by Robert Behn, "Branch Rickey as a Public Manager: Fulfilling the Eight Responsibilities of Public Management" (1997), is about a "public manager" who actually is in the private sector. Branch Rickey is the famous general manager of the New York Yankees who successfully integrated baseball in 1947 with the inclusion of Jackie Robinson. Behn identifies eight characteristics of leadership, with the first being a hallmark distinctive of public leadership: seek to achieve an important public purpose. Behn carefully argues that Rickey's public purpose was enormous: the integration of America's favorite pastime. His technical success in doing so ensures his hall-of-fame status. This exceptionally well-crafted case study demonstrates that not only can a theoretical framework be successfully applied to particular individuals, but it can be done in a fascinating and illuminating way.

CHAPTER 30

THE PATRIOTISM OF EXIT AND VOICE

The Case of Gloria Flora

H. GEORGE FREDERICKSON AND MEREDITH NEWMAN

In 1998 Gloria Flora was appointed supervisor of the Humboldt-Toiyabe National Forest in Nevada, the largest national forest in the lower forty-eight states. In less than two years, Flora resigned in a highly public protest. This resignation was accompanied by Flora's use of Albert Hirschman's (1970) exit option to shine a spotlight both on the plight of Forest Service employees charged with administering the nation's land management policies and on the vulnerability and deterioration of the land itself. And, pace Hirschman, she gave voice to these same issues in public forums across the country. This is the story of her decision and her moral episode (Hart 1992) and why Gloria Flora is an exemplar.

The Intergovernmental Context

Sagebrush Rebellion

It is claimed that the Sagebrush Rebellion originated in Nevada's 1979 legislative session as a result of pressure from old westerners to assert state claims to some 50 million acres of federal lands. Approximately 85 percent of all Nevada land is owned by the federal government (Morin and Herzik 2000). Rural Nevada ranchers and others claim that the federal government (which some refer to as the "occupying government") does not have a legitimate right to decide matters of cattle grazing, road building, mining, or mineral and oil exploration in the West. The outcome was the passage by the Nevada state legislature of the Sagebrush Bill, authored in large part by Wayne Hage. He would become part of Flora's story some twenty years hence.

This bill was a reaction to the passage of the Federal Land Policy and Management Act (FLPMA) of 1976, which declared that the classification of any lands in dispute would remain public. This was essentially a reversal of federal land policy of previous decades that sought to dispose of public lands. The act gave the Bureau of Land Management (BLM)

From *Public Integrity*, vol. 3, no. 4 (Fall 2001): 347–62. Copyright © 2001 by American Society for Public Administration. Reprinted by permission of M.E. Sharpe, Inc.

authority over these lands and resulted in controversial grazing fees and the requirement that mining claims be recorded with the BLM rather than at the county courthouse. The FLPMA followed on the heels of the environmental legislation of the 1960s and early 1970s (e.g., the Multiple Use/Sustained Yield Act of 1960, the Wilderness Act of 1964, the Water Quality Act of 1965, the National Environmental Policy Act of 1969, the Clean Air Act of 1970, and the Endangered Species Act of 1973). Many Nevadans (and other westerners) were increasingly feeling the pinch of what they believed to be restrictive legislative policies. Confrontation was virtually inevitable (Cawley 1993, 81). The movement quickly gained momentum and scope—from ranchers initially protesting over public land to timber and energy groups, and subsequently to off-road vehicle users. Together they found a common cause against the federal government and its representatives, and the Sagebrush Rebellion was in full cry.

Wise Use and County Supremacy Movements

In the late 1980s advocates of wise use joined the cause of the Sagebrush rebels. The wise use movement organized to prevent government regulation on public lands, in contrast to the earlier Sagebrush focus on protecting property rights. The philosophical leader of this movement was Ron Arnold, executive vice president of the Center for the Defense of Free Enterprise, a group that claimed to be "representatives of a new balance, of a middle way between extreme environmentalism and extreme industrialism" (Cawley 1993, 166).[1] The refrain of the wise users is notable for its strongly antigovernment rhetoric, as exemplified in these words: "It is time to take the government off the public lands, get it out of the business of regulating private land use, and free the people to pursue their happiness unhindered by the dead hand of Washington's extreme environmentalists" (Echeverria and Eby 1995, 45). The wise use agenda of 1988 included opening all public lands to mining, oil drilling, logging, and commercial development (including wilderness areas and national parks), clear-cutting all remaining old-growth forests, opening all public lands to unrestricted off-road vehicle access, and privatizing public rangelands. Compared with the Sagebrush Rebellion, this movement includes a broader coalition of ideological and economic interests that stand to profit from deregulation of industry and the weakening of environmental regulations than its precursor (Echeverria and Eby 1995, 82).

The story of Gloria Flora would not be complete without reference to the county supremacy movement. Counties are at the forefront of growing local-versus-federal conflict. This movement, with its employment of wise use, or county supremacy, ordinances, aims to make federal decisions regarding land use subject to county approval. Although county supremacy ordinances take several forms, they share an assertion of the county's legitimate claims to sovereignty over all land in the county, even land that is federally owned, as well as a general distrust of federal land management practices. An important feature of the movement—and central to our story—is the involvement of elected county officials with their focus on the county as the unit of government that protects local interests (Witt and Aim 1997).

The Transition from the Old West to the New West

The cliche "change is inevitable" may be lost on many western rural communities that cling to the traditional way of life of the old West and are fearful of an unknown future. Gloria Flora captures the essence of the issue: "My grandfather made a living selling ice from a horse-drawn wagon. If I were in the family business today, I'd be selling stainless steel-clad Frigidaires with ice-makers on-line. Same business, updated product and delivery. Survival requires change" (Flora 2000a). Externally imposed changes threaten the comfortable regularity of traditional life. According to Flora, "some embrace change and adapt; others head to the bunkers, blindly fighting for an unsustainable status quo" (Flora 2000b).

Control of federally owned public lands represents the flash point of the inevitability of change. For most of us, the old rural West conjures up images of rugged individualism, the frontier, wide-open spaces, ranches, cowboys, and multiple use of resources through logging, mining, and grazing. The old West ideology holds that nature exists to be used by and for man, that productive lands and water should be privately owned, and that concerns about depletion of energy and other mineral resources are greatly exaggerated (Maughan and Nilson 1993). The new, mostly urban West is characterized by the collective mentality of "green," Sierra Club, environmentalism, sustainability, spirituality, and the common good. The Forest Service and the BLM tend to identify with the new West and the modern environmental legal and statutory base that undergird this newer view. The Forest Service Roadless Initiative is the most recent manifestation of the new West view.

The issue of control of roads and road building activities on public lands features prominently in Gloria Flora's story. The roadless initiative, a directive from President Clinton, bans new road construction on 43 million acres of federal land with the aim of designating 40–60 million acres of federally owned land as roadless. The essence of the new West is captured in a speech by President Clinton: "The national forests are more than a source of timber, they are places of renewal of the human spirit and our natural environment. . . . environmental protection and economic growth can, and must, go hand in hand" (Clinton 1999). When all of these movements are taken together, they set the stage for an escalation of the clash of cultures between old West traditionalists and new West values.

The Montana Controversy

The Socialization of Gloria Flora

"There's always room for a good one on top." These words, spoken to Gloria Flora by her mother when she was quite young, became an inspirational mantra during her formative years. Born on September 24, 1955, in Bellevue, Pennsylvania, Gloria Flora had a traditional upbringing as the youngest of three children. Her mother and father both graduated from high school. Her father was a self-employed laborer, her mother a homemaker. She recounts how her parents, especially her mother, were very supportive of their children, urging them to always do the best they could.

Flora earned a B.S. in landscape architecture in 1977 from Pennsylvania State University, and she continued her higher education at Montana State University in 1983 (forest habitat types) and Clemson University in 1984 (advanced outdoor recreation management). Flora's formal academic credentials have been supplemented over the years with training in leadership, negotiations, communications, watershed management, wildlife and fisheries, fire dynamics, lands adjustments, and partnerships.

Her professional experience with the U.S. Forest Service began immediately after graduation in 1977, when, at the age of twenty-one, she started as a landscape architect trainee (GS-5) on the Shasta-Trinity National Forest in northern California. She went on to become the forest landscape architect (GS-11) in the Kootenai National Forest in Idaho. From her biographical sketch it is clear that Flora's career in the Forest Service has been on a fast track. At the age of thirty, she was promoted to Selway district ranger (GS-12) in 1986 on the Nez Perce National Forest in Idaho—one of only thirty-five female district rangers on the nation's 617 forest districts and younger than most of her employees. Four years later, in 1990, she was appointed ecology resources group leader of Bridger-Teton National Forest in Jackson, Wyoming (GM-13). She was detailed for four months with the BLM as acting district manager of the Salt Lake District (GM-14) in 1994. The following year, in 1995, she was promoted to Lewis and Clark National Forest supervisor (GS-14) in Great Falls, Montana. Three years later, in July 1998, she was appointed as Humboldt-Toiyabe Forest supervisor in Reno, Nevada (GS-15). With each promotion the scope and level of her responsibility and authority increased. For example, during her three-year tenure as supervisor of the Lewis and Clark National Forest, she oversaw a 1.9–million acre forest. Her promotion to supervisor of the Humboldt-Toiyabe Forest in 1998 entrusted her with the largest national forest in the continental United States—6.3 million acres, over three hundred employees, $21 million budget—the jewel in the crown of the Forest Service. Some people were asserting that Flora had the potential to become the first female chief of the Forest Service. By all accounts, she was a rising star with a stellar record.

Consistent with the Hart schema (1992), Flora's story embodies conscious moral work and a number of confrontations or moral episodes in which she risked career and livelihood in order to do the right thing as she saw it (Stivers 1992, 168). One such confrontation that gained national recognition, which included both a moral episode and the exercise of her voice, occurred during her tenure as the Lewis and Clark National Forest supervisor in Montana. Her decision to ban gas leasing on the Rocky Mountain Front was both controversial and courageous. It similarly defined her leadership style and environmental ethic, and it strengthened the conviction of her values of stewardship.

The Rocky Mountain Front

Some of the largest tracts of unprotected wilderness in the continental United States lie in northwestern Montana, along the rugged windswept eastern slope of the Rocky Mountains. This area, known as the Rocky Mountain Front, was at the center of an intensifying dispute over drilling for oil and gas. Petroleum companies were (and still are) eager to use drilling leases they had purchased from the federal government during the Reagan administration. However, the Clinton administration and environmental activists believed that the front represents a fragile ecosystem that deserves permanent wilderness designation. As a stopgap, Secretary of the Interior Bruce Babbitt placed a temporary moratorium on all oil and gas activity in the Badger-Two Medicine, a 116,000–acre section of the national forest on the front and part of a federally designated grizzly bear recovery zone. The Blackfeet Nation joined the fray to protect their sacred lands of the Badger-Two Medicine. This moratorium was subsequently superseded by a suspension of existing drilling leases.

On June 30, 1997, Flora testified before the Congressional Subcommittee on Energy and Mineral Resources as part of an oversight hearing on Bureau of Land Management and U.S. Forest Service oil and gas regulations regarding access and permitting issues. Flora had been supervisor of the Lewis and Clark National Forest for some two years, and she was no stranger to making—and justifying—difficult decisions. In her testimony she stated that the history of oil and gas leasing on the front is complex and heated. Her agency had received almost 1,500 comments from the public, 80 percent of which favored less development than called for in the preferred alternative. In the face of significant industry and political pressure, Flora announced her imposition of a ban on oil and gas leasing on September 23, 1997, three months following her congressional testimony. Her decision placed the front off limits to future oil and gas leasing for the next twenty years and settled a bitter, two-decades–long fight between energy interests and environmentalists (Kenworthy 1997). Flora would later draw from her upbringing, her academic and professional experiences, and the Rocky Mountain Front episode in order to prepare for her next assignment—and showdown—in Jarbidge.

The Jarbidge Revolt

This episode, referred to colloquially as the Son of Sage, is illuminated by the words on the back of Flora's business card: "There are two things that interest me, the relationship of people to their landscape and of people to each other" (Aldo Leopold). Flora states that "how we treat each other is often reflected in how we treat the land" (Flora 2000a). At Jarbidge, Flora had to wrestle with what she believed to be the mistreatment and abuse of both people and land.

The Issues

The ostensible issue was the wild and native Dolly Varden (or bull trout), found only in Idaho, Oregon, and Nevada. In the watersheds in these states the beautiful Dolly Varden is either officially listed as threatened or regarded as requiring "monitoring." Squeezed into a narrow and steep canyon of the Jarbidge River near the town of Jarbidge, Nevada (population 14), is an old (1911) gravel road leading only to a wilderness trailhead. Elko County claims to own this road, although it is located with the Humboldt-Toiyabe National Forest. The last mile and a half of the road washed out. After considerable deliberation, the Forest Service made a preliminary decision to protect the gravel riverbed adjacent to the washed-out road for Dolly Varden spawning and not rebuild the road. The agency asked the county to collaborate in locating the trailhead at the site of the washout.

This request brings us to the real issue. The Elko County commissioners used the road washout issue as a platform for their claims of county supremacy and states rights. In the tradition of the Sagebrush Rebellion, they sent a bulldozer up the canyon to rebuild the road. In this abortive effort, only fifty feet of rough road was built, but the riparian vegetation was removed and the river was channelized, creating 900 feet of slow-moving warm water, which was harmful to the Dolly Varden. The state of Nevada ordered the county to stop. Months later, when a Nevada state assemblyman, John Carpenter, organized a volunteer group to rebuild the road, a federal judge issued a temporary restraining order for fear of a violent confrontation between officials of the Forest Service and the volunteers.

Having served in the West throughout her career, Flora represented a seasoned veteran of the Sagebrush Rebellion. Skirmishes such as the Jarbidge Road washout were nothing new to her. But what happened next was another matter.

The Precursors to Resignation

Representatives Helen Chenoweth-Hage (R-Idaho) and Jim Gibbons (R-Nev.) announced congressional hearings on the Jarbidge matter, to be held in Elko in late November 1999. As chair of the House Resources Subcommittee on Forest and Forest Health, Chenoweth-Hage intended to use her subpoena authority to force Forest Service officials to answer questions (Sonner 1999a). For his part, Representative Gibbons made it known that he was prepared to use the appropriations process to withhold funding from the Forest Service (Dorsey 1999). Chenoweth-Hage, as well as senators Frank Murkowski (R-Alaska) and Larry Craig (R-Idaho), joined the threat to severely cut the agency's budget (Knickerbocker 1998). The list of those who were to testify included employees of the Forest Service and the BLM and "ex-pens," almost all of whom were critics of federal government ownership and control of western land.

That was not unusual; such hearings are often a kind of public grandstanding for political purposes. Flora understood that congressional hearings of this kind are intended to demean federal employees rather than lead to a substantive outcome. This list of witnesses, however, included the personal attorney of Wayne Hage, Representative Chenoweth-Hage's husband, who has a ten-year history of defying the federal government on his extensive land holdings in Nevada. (Hage is the philosophical leader of the Sagebrush Rebellion and author of *Storm over Rangelands: Private Rights in Federal Lands*, 1994). He is currently suing the Humboldt-Toiyabe National Forest for $26 million over grazing and water rights on Forest Service lands. When asked about this, Representative Gibbons dismissed any charges of conflict of interest on the part of Representative Chenoweth-Hage and said: "That's nonsense, [Chenoweth-Hage is] coming to Nevada at my request to gather facts. There's absolutely no conflict of interest in that at all. That statement I find almost to be laughable. There's no logic behind it" (Sonner 1999a). In addition, the hearings were to be followed by a fund-raiser for Chenoweth-Hage and Gibbons.

It seemed to Flora that federal government employees were to serve as the public service punching bags for Representatives Chenoweth-Hage and Gibbons prior to their political fund-raiser. In the words of a *Missoulian* (the primary newspaper in Missoula, Montana) editorial, the purpose of the hearing was "to skewer federal employees" ("Once Again Gloria" 1999). Flora decided that she would have none of it. In a letter to her employees dated November 8, 1999, and in advance of the congressional "hearing," she resigned as the forest supervisor for the Humboldt-Toiyabe National Forest:

> When a member of the United States Congress joins force with them, using the power of the office to stage a public inquisition of federal employees followed by a political fund-raiser, I must protest. . . . Enough is enough. . . . I refuse to continue to participate in this charade of normalcy. (Flora 1999)

On December 27, 1999, Jack Blackwell, intermountain regional forester, appointed Robert Vaught to replace Gloria Flora as forest supervisor of the Humboldt-Toiyabe National Forest. Anyone who reads between the lines of the following excerpt from Blackwell's introductory speech will discern a lack of support for Flora and her decision:

> Vaught's selection comes at a time when Forest Service relationships within the state of Nevada are strained. . . . We heard loud and clear about the importance of selecting a new forest supervisor who understands the people, issues and culture of Nevada. I think Bob Vaught truly fits the bill. . . . He also has a great reputation of successfully working with people. We're very pleased with the selection.

Blackwell's words can be seen as minimizing or trivializing Flora's twenty-two years of professional experience with the Forest Service throughout the intermountain West and undermining her credibility. Blackwell squandered a highly visible opportunity to voice his public support for Flora and acknowledge the full significance of her resignation, choosing instead to placate and appease local interests. Such an approach only serves to embolden her adversaries, who are likely to become Vaught's nemesis in turn (Flora 2000a). In summary, the Jarbidge revolt represented a moral episode for Flora that had profound consequences for her personal and professional life.

Discussion

Nevada is ground zero for the Sagebrush Rebellion. It is not always clear whether the Sagebrush rebels' goal is the privatization of federal lands or the overthrow of the federal government itself. As the Jarbidge episode demonstrates, there is an angry and hateful tone to their rhetoric. Some of this goes with the territory in the rural West. Running a national forest is not for the faint of heart. Employees for the Forest Service, BLM, and other federal agencies endure suspicion, antagonistic attitudes, intimidation, harassment, threats, and even acts of violence. In the case of Jarbidge, however, the violence and emotional rage reached a particularly high level. A chairman of a county public land use advisory committee in Nevada wrote at length, comparing the Forest Service with the Vichy government in Nazi-occupied France. Along with accusations against specific employees, he included thinly veiled threats against collaborators. Flora states: "To evoke the image of fascism and compare it to contemporary public land management in America is at best delusional and at worst a disgrace to the memories of those who suffered unimaginable terror at the hands of the Nazi regime. . . . Exaggeration and incendiary language do nothing to elucidate issues" (Flora 2000a).

Jarbidge also exposes the growing tendency among some politicians to openly condone and exploit distrust, even threatening armed insurrection. Flora reminds us that all elected officials, as well as Forest Service employees, sign an oath of office to uphold the Constitution and the laws of the United States. She does not take her oath of office lightly. "Those who wish to selectively support the laws, that is, only the ones that please them personally, should recognize that they are violating their oath of office and doing a disservice to the public" (Flora 2000a). In a letter written on December 30, 1998, Gary Woodbury, the district attorney in Elko County, urged an economic boycott against Forest Service employees. He stated, "Don't sell goods or services to them until they come to their senses" (Associated Press 2000). As a further example, Tony Lesperance, an Elko County commissioner, said: "Ultimately the issue is who owns the county, the federal government or the people. We will rebuild the road, come hell or high water. . . . We are not afraid to defy . . . the Forest Service or anybody else" (Vogel 1999). In September 1999, Assemblyman John Carpenter (R-Elko) spearheaded the citizen movement against the closure of the South Canyon Road and encouraged their rebellion. Thousands of shovels were sent to Elko and to the "rebels" in their "war" against the federal government. In January 2000, a twenty-eight–foot shovel was erected in front of the Elko County Courthouse, a symbol of the Shovel Brigade rebels. For his part, the governor of Nevada, Kenny Guinn, publicly supported the protests against the Forest Service: "Sometimes the only way to get their attention is to stand up for our rights" (Sonner 2000). These and other elected officials tended to characterize the federal government as engaging in a war on the West. Flora advocated a different approach—civil discourse. "One of the least effective ways of seeking resolution is to vilify the federal employees who are stewards of this land we all share. What sense does it make to shoot the federal employees who are messengers?" (Flora 2000a).

For a small minority in Elko, Nevada, "fed bashing" is a favorite pastime. The public is largely silent, as if watching a spectator sport. Flora described an "open season" on federal employees in Nevada and fed bashing as a "state-sanctioned sport." In Elko this is politically correct behavior. To Flora, fed bashing is the dark side of the lack of civility and is synonymous with racism. "You pick a class of people, you decide they are the source of your problems and you proceed to systematically make them unwelcome in your community. . . . In response to my expressed concerns about the treatment of my employees and their families in Nevada, a member of Congress casually quipped, 'You're federal employees, what do you expect?'" (Flora 2000a).

In a telephone interview, Flora recounted the story of a woman who publicly voiced her objection to the shovel monument.[2] This woman is married to a prominent local doctor but does not share his last name. In response to her criticism, Assemblyman

John Carpenter telephoned the woman's home at seven o'clock the following morning and said, "We know who your husband is." He then broadcast the name of her husband on the radio—the purpose being to publicly castigate a member of the community as a "collaborator." Such hostile tactics served to mute further dissension, and public voices were intimidated and silenced.

In her open letter explaining her resignation, Flora refers to a lack of voice in the Forest Service. "All people have a right to speak. . . . However, I learned that in Nevada, as a federal employee, you have no right to speak, no right to do your job and certainly no right to be treated with respect." As supervisor, Flora was the frequent target of verbal abuse. "When I speak against the diatribes and half-truths of the Sagebrush Rebellion, I am labeled a liar and personally vilified in an attempt to silence me." The attacks on Flora were sometimes personal. Her husband, Marc, responded to an editorial in the *Elko Daily Free Press* that was the latest in a series of personal attacks against Flora. Fully aware that the *Free Press* was owned by an ultraconservative group, Marc wrote a heartfelt letter to the editor, asking that the editor stop the personal attacks against Gloria—because they were false and they were fomenting violence. The editor replied that he was not at the point of advocating violence yet but predicted that it would happen. He had no intention of stopping the personal attacks and called Flora a duplicitous liar. In a series of exchanges between Marc Flora and the editor, the editor concluded, "Well obviously your wife couldn't take it and you are both dirt bags." The fact that Flora was a woman provided further fuel for the personal criticisms. For example, responding to her resignation, the chairman of the Elko County Republican Party is quoted as saying that she "had some kind of a breakdown and decided she'd rather quit than testify" (Foster 2000).

After Jarbidge

The Investigation

Flora had resigned, but her allegations of harassment and discrimination against her staff prompted Forest Service chief Mike Dombeck and regional forester Jack Blackwell to investigate the situation. A team of five investigators was sent to the area to interview employees, citizens, public officials, and a tribal representative about their perceptions of the "working environment for employees and the quality of external relationships" (U.S. Forest Service 2000). In their twenty-two–page report, the team concluded, in part, that there were "no incidents worthy of attention from the Justice Department" (Morrison 2000). This finding, however, may have missed the point, since much of the harassment was of a nonprosecutorial character—such is the nature of harassment, intimidation, and ostracism. However, the internal investigation was not the only inquiry.

Public Employees for Environmental Responsibility (PEER), a nonprofit group that advocates for federal employees facing harassment, completed its own investigation and made its findings public. PEER was openly critical of Nevada's U.S. attorney, Kathryn Landreth, for her unwillingness to prosecute criminal complaints brought forth by the Forest Service, including criminal acts other than the harassment of individuals. Landreth's office has declined to prosecute dozens of cases referred to it by the Forest Service since 1990—at least twenty-one felonies and fifty-two misdemeanors involving more than a hundred people (Sonner 1999b). PEER's statistics show that from 1992 to 1998, only eight prosecutions were brought of eighteen cases that were referred for prosecution. The record of Landreth's office ranks in the bottom quarter (36th out of 47th) among U.S. attorneys with measurable referrals in terms of willingness to act on complaints lodged by the Forest Service.

According to PEER's national field director, "the record of the U.S. attorney in Nevada suggests that environmental crimes committed on the Humboldt-Toiyabe will go unpunished" (Public Employees for Environmental Responsibility 2000). Moreover, the director of law enforcement and investigations for the U.S. Forest Service estimates that his agency's employees and property are attacked 350 times a year. "Forest Service offices have been the targets of several recent bombings and arsons. None of them have been solved by authorities" (Public Employees for Environmental Responsibility 1997). One notable example is the bombing of the van and home of the Carson District Forest Service ranger that took place in Carson City, Nevada, on August 4, 1995, and remains unsolved as a felony investigation by local authorities (Barnum 1995). This act of terrorism (Costello 1995) followed an earlier bomb attack outside this same ranger's office on March 30, 1995. Taken together, Flora's charges, rather than being the "hysterical exaggerations" that Representative Chenoweth-Hage suggests, appear to understate the problem.

In a telephone interview, Flora called the Forest Service investigative report "sad." She said that the investigative team was a fine group of people who did the best they could. But it was a neutral, bureaucratic report. She characterized the report as "Dickensonian."[3] Moreover, people lied to the investigators. At a public hearing on the roadless initiative, Elko County officials addressed the crowd in true Sagebrush Rebellion language, a far cry from the collaboration and cooperation they professed to support to the investigators just that same morning. Flora recounted a four-month collaborative effort to resolve the Jarbidge situation. During the final meeting, two Elko County commissioners and the city manager of Elko had taken a conciliatory tone with the group, reaching consensus on the scientific evidence that to rebuild the South Canyon Road would harm bull trout. Less than twenty-four hours later when speaking to the press, the commissioners backtracked, stating that they had in fact rejected the evidence. Those who witnessed this reversal, including Senator Harry Reid's chief of staff, were silent. The internal investigative report effectively muted Flora's message, and the collective allegations were whitewashed.

Where Things Stand

The South Canyon Road has not been rebuilt, and the issue of ownership over the road remains unresolved. Elko County claims ownership under Nevada Revised Statute 2477, which refers to the 1866 Mining Act holding that a right of way for roads across public lands not previously reserved is hereby granted. The Forest Service disputes this claim. In March 2000, in an effort to settle the dispute, a federal district court judge ordered all parties into mediation. At the conclusion of the mediation in June, a proposed settlement was placed before the county commissioners, who have since refused to accede. The deputy district attorney has advised the commissioners that there is no practical difference between the mediation right of way and the RS 2477 right of way. The county has sought outside legal opinion, and the issue remains in limbo. In July, Nevada U.S. Attorney Kathryn Landreth notified the court that the Forest Service and the Fish and Wildlife Service did not intend to permit the county to sit indefinitely on this proposed settlement. Accordingly, in early September, a motion to lift the court order stay was filed. At the end of September, the district judge issued an order saying he was not going to allow this issue to remain in limbo. He gave the parties until November 22, 2000, to either agree to a settlement or proceed with litigation.

Flora's insights into this standoff are revealing. She is convinced that the county is not seeking mediation but victory, success in throwing the federal government out of Elko County. She refers to the minutes of the commissioner's meetings, which illuminate their goal: "[we have] got to win, have to win the revolution. . . . we must overthrow the tyranny of the national government." Given such intransigence, a peaceful and lasting resolution seems unlikely, despite the efforts of Flora and her predecessor.

The New Man in Charge

We interviewed a longtime manager in the Forest Service (who prefers to remain anonymous) stationed on the Humboldt-Toiyabe. "Because politics tends to be a transitory function, it's not something that gives the Forest Service a rooting in what we feel is important. Forest Service employees are all motivated by a belief that we are making the hard choices for the right reasons, namely, good stewardship of the land. Gloria Flora exemplified this, as did her predecessor. Gloria was able to make the hard decisions. We were willing to take the knocks because of the belief that we were doing the good job. This has now been undermined" (Anonymous 2000).

The Flora Legacy

We asked our contact about Flora's legacy. The following remarks are some of the comments that were made: "One of the things that I think Gloria left us in Nevada was feeling good about ourselves. It's been a rough haul for the Forest Service in Nevada. Gloria came in at a time when the previous forest supervisor had retired under a cloud. Gloria came in and helped us feel good about ourselves. She recognized people for what they could contribute to the Forest Service. She recognized how each individual was a part of the whole and, regardless of rank and position, was equally valuable. This leadership style is part of her legacy here." The commentary continued:

> That "feel good" sentiment changed when Gloria left. Some people were hurt. Some women took it personally—they felt abandoned to some extent, and concerned that her resignation was a sign of weakness. They don't feel that way now. The initial hurt was just a reaction to the decision. Now they see it as an act of courage—to give up a promising career, to possibly become the first female chief of the agency. She was a role model for a number of

women who were just enamored and wowed by her leadership style—that it's okay to be a strong woman, that it's not an oxymoron. Gloria brought intelligence and courage to her position. She is well read and is able to process and utilize information. The bottom line is that she spoke truthfully and wouldn't sugarcoat things, but she did so in a manner that is respectful of people.

As an aside, the interview ended as follows: "Jarbidge is like a soap opera. When we need to smile, we refer to Jarbidge, the musical!"

A Retrospective

How has Flora fared? What wounds did Jarbidge inflict, and have they healed? Does she feel differently now about her moral stance than she did immediately upon resigning? We asked her these and other questions, and here are some of the things she said. We also refer to her September 2000 speech, "Letting Spirit Inspire Action" (Flora 2000b).

First, this was a high-profile resignation to underscore the significance of issues associated with the open and sanctioned mistreatment of federal civil servants. She could no longer stand by and not speak out for all of the employees under her supervision. By leaving, she gave voice to these important issues.

Second, there are only a few things that draw public attention to such issues—bombings, killings (one thinks of Oklahoma City), or high-profile resignations. Since she could not both openly criticize elected officials and supervise the forest, she chose the former strategy.

Third, the price was high. Her decision may have effectively terminated her career in the Forest Service. She was two and a half years away from being vested in Civil Service retirement. She is at peace with her decision and consequently is healing well. She views all traumas as growth opportunities. She does not consider herself a victim, nor does she have any regrets.

Fourth, honesty, integrity, and ethical behavior are the qualities necessary to ensure right action: compromise in determining specific action but do not compromise values. Protect resource integrity and "kick butt," but do it compassionately. She embraces the philosophy captured by the following benediction: Let us make peace with the life force, befriend our fellow creatures, and speak for the voiceless wilderness. In the spiral of time, when the eyes of the future gaze into ours, pray we see no tears because we failed to act.

Conclusion

From the time she was hired by the Forest Service twenty-three years ago, Gloria Flora has been at the forefront of changes in the West. She represented the rise of a new generation of conservation-minded Forest Service managers. She saw her influence grow as the Forest Service adopted "ecosystem management" as its mantra (Foster 2000). Flora is an exemplary public administrator, displaying character and leadership in the service of the government—a form of moral patriotism. Her courage earned Flora the Wilderness

Society's Public Land Manager of the Year Award in recognition of taking "significant risks"—to her safety and that of her employees, to political integrity, to professional survival—to promote environmental conservation.

These risks culminated in her decision to resign. Reflecting on Hirschman's (1970) thesis, Flora's voice was not being heard, and when the safety of her subordinates was compromised, exit was her only option. This is not to deny that Flora had other choices (e.g., to stay and fight or to build political support for her position). Flora, however, refused to continue this charade of normalcy and the inherent risks to the safety of her employees. For Flora, there was no other moral choice but to resign in protest—with voice (see also Weisband and Franck 1975). Her resignation can be viewed as a reflection of virtue and courage. In order to clarify Flora's reasoning, we asked her about her motivation and values, and about issues of character and moral work, as well as the lessons from her story.

She was motivated to act as she did out of a sense of responsibility. Although her decision to exit with voice had negative effects on herself and her family, she believes her actions were for the greatest positive benefit for the greatest number of people. She was able to make this and earlier hard decisions by drawing on her values—integrity and honesty from her parents, and ethical behavior and personal responsibility from her experience. She also learned from people who behave poorly—they are great teachers of how not to act. She is very concerned with growing evidence of unsustainable consumption and the destruction of natural resources. Her values include a profound respect for the land. She feels strongly that if you live by your values, every choice you make and every life you touch should be a demonstration of those values. She describes her moral work as respect for the earth and respect for other people—a high moral charge. Flora believes that people should follow their highest sense of ethical behavior and choice and live congruently with those values. Social and environmental conditions are uplifted when people share their gifts and talents for the common good.

For the practice and study of public administration, the story of Gloria Flora is a moral example of why it is sometimes necessary to exercise the options to exit and speak out. It is a lesson that career survival is sometimes a failure to do what is right. It is a lesson that personal integrity will always trump career, money, or power.

It could be argued that public administration leaders such as Flora should always be neutral and objective. The evidence indicates that great public management leaders are seldom neutral. Would we want a school superintendent who is neutral about education? No. Would we want the chair of the Joint Chiefs of Staff to be neutral about national defense? No. We expect our leaders to be passionately engaged in the work of their agency and dedicated to its purposes. That is, we expect practitioners to be passionate, not about some private ax they wish to grind, but about the specific mission of the agency with which they are entrusted. In these terms, Flora represents a deep dedication to environmental issues and is not neutral about them.

What is Flora doing now? Currently on leave without pay from the Forest Service, she continues to be very active in her professional pursuits. Living with her husband in Helena, Montana, she speaks frequently about the sustainability of natural resources on public lands and researches techniques for incorporating sustainability criteria into land management. Flora is far from unemployable. She has left the door open with the Forest Service and may be considering other possibilities as well. She is reconciled with what happened, has no regrets, and is ready for the next assignment. Her long-term moral work on behalf of the Forest Service and the lessons of those experiences should serve her well, whatever that assignment may be.

Notes

This chapter was prepared with the research assistance of Kelly Benson, Andrea Breyton, Sharon Brown, William Ezell, and Alyson Galloway.

1. The Center for the Defense of Free Enterprise, founded in 1976 and located in Bellevue, Washington, is a nonprofit, nonpartisan, tax-exempt foundation. Its board of directors includes Alan Gottlieb, president, and Samuel Slom, vice president.

2. This story came to light on a National Public Radio *Morning Edition* piece on Flora's resignation and Elko County by Howard Berkes, aired on March 28, 2000.

3. Flora is referring to Dicken's *A Tale of Two Cities*, which begins with the line: "It was the best of times, it was the worst of times."

References

Anonymous. 2000. Telephone interview by Meredith A. Newman, October 14.

Associated Press. 2000. "Elko Official Urged Boycott of Forest Service." *Las Vegas Review-Journal*, March 9.

Barnum, Alex. 1995. "Crossfire: Battle over U.S. Land Gets Nasty, Personal." *San Francisco Chronicle*, August 14.

Cawley, R. McGreggor. 1993. *Federal Land, Western Anger: The Sagebrush Rebellion and Environmental Politics*. Lawrence: University of Kansas Press.

Clinton, William Jefferson. 1999. Speech on the Roadless Initiative, October 13.

Costello, Michael. 1995. "Of Course, Chenoweth Opposes Terrorism." *Lewiston Morning Tribune*, August 19.

Dorsey, Christine. 1999. "State Lawmakers Lobby for Bill to Sell Public Lands." *Las Vegas Review-Journal*, September 22.

Echeverria, J., and R. Booth Eby. 1995. *Let the People Judge: Wise Use and Private Property Rights Movement*. Washington, DC: Island.

Flora, Gloria. 2000a. "Towards Civil Discourse: The Need for Civility in Public Land Management." Speech delivered in Helena, Montana, January.

———. 2000b. "Letting Spirit Inspire Action." Keynote speech to the Wilderness Society National Conference, September.

———. 1999. Open Letter to the Employees of the Humboldt-Toiyabe National Forest, November 8.

Foster, David. 2000. "Wild Ride: A Feisty Forester Blazes Her Way Across the New West" *Associated Press State and Local Wire*, June 1.

Hage, Wayne. 1994. *Storm over Rangelands: Private Rights in Federal Lands*. 3rd ed. Bellevue, WA: Free Enterprise Press.

Hart, David K. 1992. "The Moral Exemplar in an Organizational Society." In Terry L. Cooper and N. Dale Wright, eds., *Exemplary Public Administrators: Character and Leadership in Government*, 9–29. San Francisco: Jossey-Bass.

Hirschman, Albert O. 1970. *Exit, Voice, and Loyalty: Responses to Decline in Firms, Organizations, and States*. Cambridge: Harvard University Press.

Kenworthy, T. 1997. "U.S. Forbids Oil, Gas Leases in Montana Rockies Gateway." *Washington Post,* September 24, Al.

Knickerbocker, Brad. 1998. "New Twists in Debate over Public Land. 'Sagebrush Rebellion' Is Stoked by a Senator's Proposal to Sell More Federal Land Each Year." *Christian Science Monitor,* April 23.

Maughan, Ralph, and Douglas Nilson. 1993. *What's Old and What's New About the Wise Use Movement,* www.nwcitizen.com.

Morin, Robert P., and Eric B. Herzik. 2000. "Nevada." In Dale Krane, Platon N. Rigos, and Melvin Hill, eds., *Home Rule in America: A Fifty-State Handbook,* 269–76. Washington, DC: Congressional Quarterly Press.

Morrison, Robyn. 2000. "Fed-bashing Investigated." *High Country News,* February 28, 324.

"Once Again Gloria Stands Tall." 1999. *Missoulian,* November 11.

Public Employees for Environmental Responsibility. 2000. "Forest Service Complaints Ignored by Justice in Nevada." February 10. www.peer.org/action.

———. 1997. "Epidemic of Violence Hitting Land Management Agencies: Agencies in Denial." April 21. www.peer.org/action.

Sonner, Scott. 1999a. "Chenoweth Likely to Subpoena Forest Service in Fish Dispute." *Associated Press State and Local Wire,* October 29.

———. 1999b. "Forest Workers in Nevada Fear for Safety, Memo Says." *Seattle Times,* November 19.

———. 2000. "10,000 Shovels Arrive in Nevada; Gov. Guinn Backs Protest." *Las Vegas Sun,* January 29.

Stivers, Camilla. 1992. "Beverlee A. Myers: Power, Virtue, and Womanhood in Public Administration." In Terry L. Cooper and N. Dale Wright, eds., *Exemplary Public Administrators: Character and Leadership in Government,* 166–92. San Francisco: Jossey-Bass.

U.S. Forest Service. 2000. Fact Finding Report, February 4.

Vogel, Ed. 1999. "Elko County Official Vows to Build Road." *Las Vegas Review-Journal,* November 14.

Weisband, Edward, and Thomas M. Franck. 1975. *Resignation in Protest: Political and Ethical Choices Between Loyalty to Team and Loyalty to Conscience in American Public Life.* New York: Grossman.

Wilkinson, Todd. 1998. *Science Under Siege: The Politicians' War on Nature and Truth.* Boulder: NetLibrary.

Witt, Stephanie, and Leslie R. Aim. 1997. "County Government and the Public Lands: A Review of the County Supremacy Movement in Four Western States." In Brent S. Steel, ed., *Public Lands Management in the West: Citizens, Interest Groups, and Values,* 95–110. Westport, CT: Praeger.

CHAPTER 31

LEADERS AND LEADERSHIP

JOHN J. CORSON

[Eugene Lewis's book *Public Entrepreneurship: Toward a Theory of Bureaucratic Political Power* is examined in the following excerpt from John J. Corson's book review,
"Leaders and Leadership." Corson's review highlights the inherent difficulties in evaluating administrative leadership when individuals demonstrate paradoxical (both "good"
and "bad") administrative behaviors, or when at least some of their actions conflict with
moral norms or political expectations.—Eds.]

[I]n his *Public Entrepreneurship: Toward a Theory of Bureaucratic Political Power*
Lewis defines a public entrepreneur "as a person who creates or profoundly elaborates
a public organization so as to alter greatly the existing pattern of allocation of scarce
public resources." Surely, Hyman G. Rickover, J. Edgar Hoover, and Robert Moses are
widely known for their accomplishments in appointive, public service posts and for the
organizations they developed. But were they leaders?

Rickover forced the U.S. Navy to become stronger through the use of nuclear power.
He was aided by fear generated by the Cold War and the technological promise of nuclear
energy. He was enough of an engineer to direct the adaptation of nuclear power, first to
the submarine and then to the whole fleet, enough of an organizer to build an almost
autonomous and an effective structure with Navy, enough of a politician to gain not
only the resources needed to advance the nuclear submarine and the nuclear fleet but to
advance his personal status, enough of a publicist to gain renown for his, as well as his
organization's, technological accomplishments and contributions to national security.
Was he a leader?

J. Edgar Hoover started in 1924, at the age of twenty-nine, as "acting director" of a
bureau of ill repute within the Justice Department. He benefited from the sponsorship of
Harlan Fiske Stone, then attorney general and later chief justice of the Supreme Court.
He fired a number of "crooks and hacks" and instituted non-political personnel practices
and accepted managerial practices. He reinforced these innovations by establishing in
1935 what became the FBI National Academy. He expanded the FBI's scope substantially, professionalized the police investigative function, persistently publicized its and

---

Excerpted from *Public Administration Review,* vol. 40, no. 6 (November/December 1980): 632.

his accomplishments, aggressively built an unprecedented autonomy for the FBI, and for himself unparalleled stature. Was he a leader?

Robert Moses, like Rickover and Hoover, was a career public servant. Son of well-to-do parents, he was well educated (Yale, B.A. and Phi Beta Kappa; Oxford, M.A.; Columbia, Ph.D.) and through his parents, well connected. By dint of hard work he became in turn an authority on the civil service, an expert on governmental organization, knowledgeable with respect to architecture and civil engineering, and an acknowledged authority on planning and funding public works. Between 1933 and 1968, Moses effectively controlled the physical development—the planning and construction of bridges, tunnels, highways, parks, public housing and other public works—of the New York metropolitan area while serving as an advisor to other cities, states and countries. He fashioned governmental organizations (particularly highway and parkway authorities) that enabled them to exercise uncontrolled power. He mobilized—and mercilessly drove—efficient staffs. He brooked no interference from, and did not hesitate to challenge, mayors (LaGuardia and Lindsay), governors (Dewey and Rockefeller) and federal authorities (Ickes). Was he a leader?

I suggest the answers to these rhetorical questions must be, No. Each was able to mobilize the persons and resources needed to achieve, within highly competitive and conflicting contexts, goals that each established, in large part unilaterally. Each disregarded on occasion the prevailing public policy as defined by legislative or executive authorities. Each made sanctimonious claims of serving the public—as they defined its interests—while aggressively expanding their agencies and their individual statures. Each was a master of the crafts of the manager and the politician. But were they leaders?

Did not each lack a moral quality that may be expected of a public servant in a democracy? May they be more accurately described as successful administrative despots, rather than leaders in the public service?

The best of Lewis' book, the concluding chapter, poses a key question. In a society marked by a trend toward public enterprise and increasingly large organizations, are such "public enterpreneurs" needed? Are their crafty, guileful, self-aggrandizing ways, their drives to accomplish the goals that they define "by any means at all," needed to overcome the constraints of large bureaucracies? Are their tough hides and astute dominating, political skills essential for the survival of administrative leaders in modern public administration?

CHAPTER 32

BRANCH RICKEY AS A PUBLIC MANAGER

Fulfilling the Eight Responsibilities of Public Management

ROBERT D. BEHN

Branch Rickey was a public manager. Admittedly, he never was appointed to head a public agency. Nor was he ever elected to public office (though he was offered the Republican nominations for both governor and senator of Missouri). On paper, Branch Rickey was a business manager—a very successful business manager. He invented baseball's farm system and a number of innovative instructional techniques. He helped create the position of general manager and developed a cadre of managerial protégés (Frick 1973, 169–71). His teams won pennants in St. Louis, Brooklyn, and Pittsburgh.

But Branch Rickey is most remembered as the president and general manager of the Brooklyn Dodgers who broke the color line in baseball. And to do that, Branch Rickey had to be not only a manager but a public manager—an excellent public manager.

It was Jackie Robinson, of course, not Branch Rickey, who actually broke the color barrier. It was Robinson, not Rickey, who had to learn to hit the major-league curveball, who had to learn to go to his right on a ground ball, who had to cope with the beanballs and the spikings, who suffered the humiliations and received the death threats. It took Robinson, not Rickey, to implement Rickey's scheme for integrating major-league baseball.

Robinson was essential, but so was Rickey. If Robinson had not been such a superior—and intelligent—athlete, if he had not been capable of dealing with psychological pressures and personal burdens that few of us can even imagine, it might have been many years before baseball was integrated on the field. But if Rickey had not conceived and implemented his plan so intelligently and carefully the same would have been true.

Before moving to Brooklyn, Branch Rickey served as vice president of the St. Louis Cardinals for over two decades. In 1942, Rickey's Cardinals won 106 games to capture the National League pennant and then defeated the New York Yankees in the World Series. Branch Rickey never got a hit for that team, never pitched a ball, never played. Yet Rickey and his system created that winning team. The Cardinals won the pennant again in 1943 and in 1944 won both the pennant and the World Series; by then, however, Rickey

Excerpted from *Journal of Public Administration Research and Theory*, vol. 7, no. 1 (January 1997): 1–33. Copyright © 1997 by Public Management Research Association. Reprinted with permission.

had left St. Louis for Brooklyn. And yet, the Cardinals' success in 1943 and 1944 can be directly attributed to Rickey. The Brooklyn Dodgers won pennants—and even a World Series—after Rickey left Brooklyn, and the Pittsburgh Pirates won the World Series in 1960, after Rickey had built that team and again left town. Rickey was essential to the success achieved by those teams in St. Louis, Brooklyn, and Pittsburgh.

Similarly, Branch Rickey was essential to the integration of baseball. How long after 1947 would it have taken if Rickey had not assumed the initiative—and done it well? That question, of course, is impossible to answer definitively. Historian Carl Prince concludes, however, that Rickey "was singlehandedly responsible for moving African Americans into organized white ball a full decade earlier than it might otherwise have occurred had he not forced the issue with both wisdom and political acuity" (1996, 34). "The credit for banishing Jim Crow from baseball belongs solely to Branch Rickey and the strategy that he pursued must be judged overwhelmingly effective," concludes historian Jules Tygiel. Nevertheless, Tygiel thinks the integration of baseball could have happened—and soon—without Rickey: "With public pressure mounting, particularly in the New York area, it seems likely that political events would have forced the issue within the next few years" (1983, 207). Yet, even if outside politics had indeed forced baseball's hierarchy to attend to the issue, would the fractious process of integrating the sport (or of integrating anything) have been as successful without the thoughtful guidance of someone like Rickey?

Branch Rickey was a mediocre baseball player. In four seasons with the St. Louis Browns and New York Highlanders (who became the Yankees), he batted .239 in just 119 games (Wolf 1990, 1378); as a catcher, he established a major-league record by allowing thirteen stolen bases in one game (Ward and Burns 1994, 129). As a field manager, he was not much better, winning less than half of his games over ten years with the St. Louis Browns and Cardinals (Wolf 1990, 602).

But as a front-office manager (what today is called the general manager) Rickey excelled. He was a master at strategy and teaching. He was a master at identifying talent and creating winning teams. He was a master at making money—both for himself and for his teams' owners. And he was a master at orchestrating social change. Branch Rickey was a master manager—a master public manager.

The Eight Responsibilities of Public Management

What did Branch Rickey do that made him a public manager? What did he do—actually do—that means he was more than a very successful baseball executive, more than just another successful business manager?

To be effective—to accomplish significant public purposes—public managers have to fulfill eight different responsibilities. Excellent public managers must

- seek to achieve an important public purpose;
- possess a clear definition of success, including benchmarks along the way;
- have an overall strategy for achieving their purpose;

- be analytical about everything;
- pay attention to the details of implementation;
- influence people by building coalitions, motivating individuals and teams, and creating a favorable climate of public opinion;
- recognize and exploit their luck and, when they are not lucky, keep focused on their public purpose and grope their way toward it; and
- leave the organization better than they found it.

Excellent business managers do many of these things. It might even be argued that they do all of these things—at least all of these things except seek to achieve an important public purpose. But that first responsibility does more than simply define what the manager is attempting to accomplish; it does more than establish why the manager undertakes these other tasks. The important public purpose also shapes how the public manager approaches each responsibility. . . .

Public Purpose

Public management is different from private management—for the purposes to be achieved by public managers are quite different from those of their counterparts. Kenneth Andrews, a former editor of the *Harvard Business Review*, argues that a business (and thus its managers) should seek to make an "economic and noneconomic contribution . . . to its shareholders, employees, customers, and communities" (1980, 18). And many do so. Nevertheless, the essential test of effective private-sector management is whether the firm makes money for its stockholders; if a firm fails to make a significant economic contribution to its shareholders, all its other contributions are irrelevant. . . .

Branch Rickey had a clear public purpose: to integrate major-league baseball. Moreover, this was a significant public purpose. After World War II, baseball was indeed the national pastime. It was a uniquely American game—except that it was all white. Rickey set out to change that. It was a public purpose on a scale that few public managers—before, then, or after—have tackled. Many a president of the United States has found numerous reasons to avoid the issue of racial integration. Yet Rickey seized it completely. He did not attempt to move baseball a little. He set out to change baseball—and American society—radically.

Why did Rickey do it? What were his motivations? . . .

The first possible explanation is that Rickey wanted to make a contribution beyond baseball. At twenty-one, before his first game ever as a coach—of the Ohio Wesleyan University baseball team—Rickey insisted that Kentucky would play his team with Charles Thomas, a black, at first base or it would not play at all. When he took his team to play Notre Dame, the Oliver Hotel refused to admit Thomas. Rickey's conniving got Thomas to stay with him in his room, but Thomas just sat there saying "Black skin, black skin. If I could only make 'em white." Rickey was later to say, "For forty years, I've had recurrent visions of him wiping off his skin" (Polner 1982, 32–35).

Of himself, Rickey once observed: "I wonder why a man trained for the law devotes his life to something so cosmically unimportant as a game" (Monteleone 1995, 98). Integrating baseball gave Rickey something cosmically important to do.

The alternative explanation is that Rickey simply wanted to make money for himself and the owners of the Dodgers. Rickey understood that black players would attract black fans (both at Ebbets Field in Brooklyn and in the ballparks around the league) and that talented black players would improve the Dodgers on the field—giving his team a significant advantage. Given Rickey's well-established reputation as a baseball genius,[7] he figured out before anyone else the benefits from being the first team to field black stars.

Which explanation reflects Rickey's true motives? Even Rickey's own words do not settle the question:

- "I'm out to win a pennant. If this fellow [Robinson] can help me more to win the pennant as a team fact, I'm going to employ him. And I did" (Monteleone 1995, 84).
- "I couldn't face my God much longer knowing that His black creatures are held separate and distinct from His white creatures in the game that has given me all I own" (Ribowsky 1995, 267).
- "I don't mean to be a crusader. My only purpose is to be fair to all people and my selfish objective is to win baseball games" (Goldstein 1991, 255).
- "I want ballplayers. I don't care if they're purple or green or have hair all over them and arms that reach down to their ankles, just so they can win the World Series" (Lipman 1966, 9).

Despite his various protests, however, Rickey seems clearly to have been motivated by what he called the cause (Honig 1981, 112).

If Rickey had really been motivated only by making money he would have devoted his energies to making a success of the Brown Dodgers, the team he created in 1945 to play in the new black United States League. After all, the New York Yankees and other teams made a lot of money while their own clubs were on the road by renting their stadiums to black teams, which drew very large crowds (Ribowsky 1995, 268; Oakley 1994, 20). Thus not only would the integration of the major leagues kill the Negro Leagues, it also would eliminate this source of extra income for many major-league teams. Although the Brooklyn club did not benefit as much from this practice as other teams, it certainly was possible for it to make more money with a second, organized black team that would fill Ebbets Field while the white Dodgers played seventy-seven away games each year.

There is one more piece of evidence to suggest that Rickey was motivated more by social justice than by winning pennants or making money. In 1948, Roy Campanella had spent a year in the minors and was ready to be Brooklyn's full-time catcher. Indeed, the Dodger manager, Leo Durocher, urgently wanted Campanella. But during the first month of the season, Rickey would only let Durocher use Campanella in the outfield. Then, when all major-league teams had to reduce their rosters to twenty-five players by May 15, Rickey sent Campanella to the Dodger farm team in St. Paul to "do something bigger"—to integrate the American Association (Campanella 1995, 135–36). A month and a half later, after hitting .325, homering thirteen times, and driving in thirty-three runs, Campanella was back in Brooklyn as the regular catcher. Yet "by using Campanella as a pawn in the integration campaign," concludes Tygiel, Rickey "probably cost the Dodgers the 1948 pennant" (1983, 241).

What was Rickey's motivation: more money or social justice? It hardly makes much difference. Regardless of his motivation, if he was to integrate baseball, Rickey had to do it right. He could not just bring in one black to play for a few years; such a strategy made little sense either financially or socially. Doing that took as much energy and created as much strife as integrating baseball completely. After all, almost everywhere that Robinson and the Dodgers went, they integrated something—whether that was a southern baseball diamond (Mann 1957, 267) or a northern hotel.

And doing it right was a complex task. This was not simply the management challenge involved in bringing out a new product—such as Post-it notes—that people had never dreamed of using. This was more than bringing out a new product—such as a personal computer—that would change the work habits and life styles of millions of people. If integrated baseball was a new product, it was one that would challenge the thinking and values of almost everyone in the country.

"All the men in baseball understood the code" that prevented blacks from playing, noted Red Barber, the Dodger's popular radio broadcaster from 1939 until 1954. Moreover, "a code is harder to break than an actual law." . . . Rickey, the public manager, was not trying to change a law or get a public agency to implement a law. He was out to change one of society's most basic codes: Jim Crow behavior in baseball and in America.

Regardless of Rickey's personal motives, he had undertaken to achieve a public purpose. Thus he could not merely approach this task as a traditional business manager. Moreover, he knew that. Even if Rickey was only attempting to maximize his own income, to do so by integrating baseball, he had to behave as a public manager.

Clear Definition of Success

Because public managers lack the obvious measure of success that drives their business counterparts—the economic contribution to stockholders—they need to create explicit measures to see if they are, in fact, achieving their public purpose—to see if they are making a contribution to society. In fact, the lack of an obvious measure to drive behavior may be the deficiency that most frustrates effective public management across agencies and jurisdictions.

Rickey, of course, had two very immediate measures of success: first, in 1946, Robinson had to make it in the minors as a regular on the Dodgers' AAA farm team, the Montreal Royals. Then, in 1947, Robinson had to make it as a regular, every-day, major-league player. Robinson had to be sufficiently effective, offensively and defensively, to be in the Brooklyn line-up every day. Otherwise, he would not make money for the Dodgers; a someday player would not attract new fans. Otherwise, the Robinson strategy would not integrate baseball; other teams would certainly not bother to sign blacks to be utility players. . . .

To achieve his private and public purposes, Rickey had to achieve a number of very clear benchmarks of success: Robinson had to make the Dodger team on his merits. He had to make it as a regular. He had to make it as a star. Robinson had to make it in a way that permitted Rickey to sign other black players—regulars and stars—to the Dodgers.

Finally, Robinson and his black teammates had to make it in such a way that other major-league teams—all other major-league teams—fielded teams with black players. Other teams also had to start signing and playing blacks or Rickey's experiment would be little more than a stunt—remembered alongside Bill Veeck's sending the midget Eddie Gaedel up to bat to get a walk for the Cleveland Indians. To really be successful, to really integrate organized baseball, all the teams in the American and National Leagues had to sign and play blacks. That was Rickey's final benchmark—the ultimate measure of success. . . .

Rickey once observed, "If a man wants to do something and you want to help him, give him an objective. This is true in cultivating skills in any profession" (Monteleone 1995, 52). Rickey applied this principle when dealing with his players, coaches, and managers. He also applied it to himself when it came to integrating baseball, for this specific, measurable public purpose required him to cultivate some new skills and to use some existing skills in different ways. To accomplish his new public purpose, Rickey had to think differently, analyze new problems, create a new strategy, and develop new tactics to get to his benchmarks. . . .

Overall Strategy

Good intentions are not enough; good purposes are not enough. Public managers have to understand how to realize their public purposes. Rickey, the teetotaler, understood this well when, in 1944, he told the Brooklyn Rotary Club: "The cause of prohibition, a most worthy one, was thrown back a hundred years by the Volstead Act. Very possibly the introduction of a Negro into baseball, even without force, might similarly throw back their cause of racial equality a quarter century or more" (Mann 1957, 217).

To integrate major-league baseball required both someone who possessed this lofty public purpose and someone with a practical way of achieving it. And Rickey combined these characteristics. "Two strains come through from the life of Branch Rickey," wrote Larry Merchant in the *Philadelphia Daily News*. "One was his idealism; the other was his pragmatism" (Monteleone 1995, 131). Rickey's idealism gave him purpose; Rickey's pragmatism gave him strategy.

Much of the discussion of Rickey's strategy has focused on his selection of Jackie Robinson to be the pioneer. Some thought Robinson was a poor choice. He was certainly not the best player in the Negro Leagues; when Rickey signed Robinson in the fall of 1945, he had played with the Kansas City Monarchs for only one season; he had a lot to learn about baseball. But Rickey—and others—recognized that the pioneer needed more than baseball skills. The pioneer would have to be intelligent. The pioneer would have to be able to take the inevitable abuse. At the same time, Rickey recognized that the pioneer would have to be a fighter.

But Rickey's strategy consisted of more than finding the right pioneer. Later, Rickey recalled that he had "worked out" a plan with "six essential points":

- "The man we finally chose had to be right off the field. *Off* the field."
- "He had to be right on the field. If he turned out to be a lemon, our efforts would fail for that reason alone."
- "The reaction of his own race had to be right."
- "The reaction of the press and public had to be right."
- "We had to have a place to put him [in the Dodger system]."
- "The reaction of his fellow players had to be right" (Holland 1955, 62–63).

Arthur Mann, who worked for Rickey in Brooklyn, also reported later that Rickey developed a "six-part plan to integrate baseball," but Mann's list does not include having a place to put the pioneer. Instead, Mann's number one item focused on "the backing and sympathy of the Dodgers' directors and stockholders, whose investment and civic standing had to be considered and protected" (1957, 214). In reality, Rickey's plan included much more than these six or seven steps.

Clearly, Rickey's strategy consisted of more—much more—than selecting the right player. Nevertheless, the core of his six-part plan was really a "lone-pioneer strategy"; it depended upon using a single, individual black player to integrate one club and thus, by implication, all of organized baseball. . . .

In the 1940s, there were a variety of alternative strategies for integrating major-league baseball. Yet, as Tygiel writes, "So total was Robinson's triumph, so dominant his personality, that few people have questioned the strategies and values that underpinned Branch Rickey's 'noble experiment'" (1983, 206).

Was Rickey's strategy *the* correct one? Certainly, it was *a* correct one. But there is no reason (other than our subconscious faith in scientific management) to believe there was only one correct strategy. With the right attention to details and tactics, with the right efforts at influencing the right people, with appropriate attention to all the responsibilities of public management, many . . . other strategies might have worked as well.

But Rickey had something on one else—including those advocating integration—had: He had a *strategy*. And a *strategy* beats *no strategy* every time (Boswell 1982).

Analysis

Branch Rickey was analytical about everything he did. "Rickey could think," recalled Red Barber. "He never got in a situation he didn't think his way out of. He also had the courage and the patience to execute his thinking." In 1926 with the Cardinals, Barber noted, Rickey "won a World Series with his brain and not with money" (1982, 7, 6). Ford Frick, president of the National League and commissioner of baseball, observed, "Anyone who knew Mr. Rickey knew he never acted on impulse. Every move he made was well planned. . . ." (1973, 95).

Branch Rickey was certainly analytical about baseball—about everything from teaching hitting to building pennant winners. He was the first person in baseball to hire a team statistician. He was analytical about strategy and analytical about tactics; he was analytical about the relationships between the big purposes he was trying to achieve and the details of what it took to achieve those purposes. Even if Rickey had never taken on the challenge of integrating the major leagues he would have been famous within baseball circles for the analytical way he invented and perfected the farm system.

In the 1920s, as manager and general manager of the St. Louis Cardinals, Rickey realized that his poor team—poor both in finances and in player talent—could never compete with the rich teams from New York and Chicago when it came to buying the contracts of promising minor-league players. The Cardinals would always be outbid. So Rickey convinced the team's owner, Sam Breadon, that it made sense to invest in minor-league teams and develop their own players. And thus Rickey created the Cardinal's system of teams—from Class D through Class AAA—that won National League pennants in 1928, 1930, 1931, 1934, 1942, 1943, and 1944 and that was copied by every other major-league club. Rickey believed that "the development of a major-league club on any permanent basis should involve planning not only for one succeeding season but for the permanency of a proud position in all succeeding seasons" (Monteleone 1995, 64).

Rickey did more than just create a hierarchy of minor-league teams. He created a system of development, instruction, and evaluation. He wanted his farm teams to develop minor-league players so that they could play in the majors. He believed that to make the major leagues a ballplayer needed a number of unteachable physical characteristics—especially speed—combined with desire. He believed that there were some basic principles for identifying good prospects. He also believed in certain fundamentals—that there was a best way to hit a ball, bunt a ball, execute a run-down play, take a lead off a base. At a time when scientific management was much in vogue, Rickey was applying it to baseball. . . .

When Rickey decided to integrate major-league baseball, he applied the same approach. He would not do it whimsically. He would do it right. He would do it analytically. That did not just mean getting the macro strategy right; it also meant thinking through the entire process of implementation. . . .

The Details of Implementation

To achieve their purposes, public managers need more than a grand strategy. They also need to pay attention to the critical details and tactics of implementing that strategy. . . .

To implement the lone-pioneer strategy, the most important detail was to find the right man to be the lone pioneer. And from what his scouts told him, Robinson was the right man—at least the right man on the field. But what about off the field? Again, the information that the scouts provided about Robinson suggested that he would be. Robinson had been to college and had played on integrated teams. Moreover, he possessed a number of personal characteristics that Rickey valued: Robinson did not drink, did not smoke, attended church, and was engaged to an educated woman (Oakley 1994, 26). But could he stand the pressure? Rickey "wanted a man of exceptional intelligence, a man who was able to grasp and control the responsibilities of himself to his race and could carry that load. That was the greatest danger point of all" (Monteleone 1995, 80–81).

To resolve this question, Rickey first flew to California to check out Robinson the person. Then, he talked with Robinson personally. Explaining to a surprised Robinson his true purpose, Rickey proceeded to enact, extremely explicitly, the kind of abuse that Robinson could expect to get, both on and off the field. "His acting was so convincing," Robinson recalled later, "that I found myself chain-gripping my fingers behind my back" (Tygiel 1983, 66). At one point, as Rickey berated him, Robinson asked, "Mr. Rickey do you want a ballplayer who's afraid to fight back?" to which Rickey responded, "I want a ballplayer with guts enough not to fight back" (Rowan 1960, 117).

At the end of their three-hour meeting . . . Rickey and Robinson agreed that he would sign with the Dodgers—linking them forever together in the history of sports and race relations.

Having selected Robinson, Rickey had to prepare him for his ordeal. Indeed, the lone-pioneer strategy was predicated on the assumption that there would inevitably be a personal ordeal. This required Rickey to analyze the nature of this upcoming ordeal and to develop ways to buffer Robinson and prepare him as well. After all, from his earliest coaching days at Ohio Wesleyan, Rickey had seen the ordeal that Charles Thomas faced and, reports Cohen, "began to appreciate what it took to survive as a minority of one: the competitive determination, the moral conviction, the emotional restraint. And he remembered" (1990, 78).

Rickey worried about Robinson's isolation, so he signed first John Wright and then Roy Partlow, two black pitchers, to be with Robinson during his first year of white ball with the Montreal Royals. Rickey worried about who Robinson would room with on the road, so when Robinson was promoted to Brooklyn, he hired Wendell Smith, a black sportswriter for the *Pittsburgh Courier*, to travel with Robinson. Rickey worried about how Robinson would be treated in Florida during spring training, so for 1946, he made special arrangements in Florida and then, for 1947, he moved the Dodgers training camp to Cuba.

At the end of 1947, Rickey understood that the battle was still not completely won—not in baseball, not even on the Dodger team. So, to use Prince's word, he northernized the team—trading away those, like Dixie Walker (a fan favorite in Brooklyn, "The Peepul's Cherce"), who opposed Robinson (1996, 4).

Did Branch Rickey worry too much about the details of implementation? Was all this attention to so many particulars really necessary? Tygiel thinks not: "Rickey's preparations, in retrospect, also appear overelaborate and unnecessary" (1983, 207). And yet, previous efforts had failed. In 1944, William Benswanger, president of the Pittsburgh Pirates, noting that "Colored men are American citizens with American rights," was considering two of the top stars from the Negro Leagues, Josh Gibson, and Buck Leonard. But when the criticisms rolled in, he backed off (Polner 1982, 152). And baseball's hierarchy, despite its public statements, was hardly supportive. Given the history of subsequent efforts to integrate other American institutions, the analytical care with which Rickey executed his strategy hardly seems overelaborate or unnecessary.

Influencing People

No manager does it all. In fact, by definition, a manager is someone who gets people to work together to achieve a common purpose in a way that is more effective and efficient than if they each worked alone. This means influencing the behavior of others. This means motivating people and building coalitions. This means affecting public opinion. And, at least for managers who are pursuing a public purpose, this means relying on some people at some critical junctures to—independently—do the right thing.

To achieve his very public purpose, to integrate baseball, Rickey could not do it all. As a manager, he needed to get a number of other people to work toward that common purpose. Some of these would be people who worked within the Dodger organization, and Rickey might have an easier (though not necessarily easy) time influencing their behavior. Others whose decisions and actions would be critical did not, however, work for the Dodgers; influencing these people would be more difficult. Like every public manager, to accomplish his most significant purposes Rickey needed to influence the behavior of others who did not work within his organization.

Moreover, like other public managers, Rickey had to influence public opinion. He was not merely making a small, internal change in the Dodger organization. He was about to do something that would be news. Robinson—and everything about him—would be the subject of debate—of public debate in the news media and of private debate at the dinner table. Moreover, although the public could not appeal to their elected officials to fire Rickey, the public did have a vote—a big vote.

Rickey [also] had to influence the Dodger players to accept Robinson as a teammate. He had to create an informal coalition within organized baseball that would at least tolerate his experiment. And he had to create a favorable climate of public opinion so that Robinson would attract rather than drive away fans.

Given the lone-pioneer strategy, Rickey's ability to influence others depended in large part upon selecting the right pioneer—the right person on the field and off the field. As a public manager, Rickey was not going to influence most of the critical people directly. Rather, he could influence them only indirectly—through the selection, instruction, and cultivation of his pioneer. That is why he extracted from Robinson the famous promise that he refrain from retaliating against physical and verbal abuse for a full three years.

Rickey understood that he could not order even his own players to accept his pioneer. But he could select a pioneer who would win the acceptance and respect of some of his teammates, of some of his on-field opponents, and of some of the public.

Moreover, Rickey did not need to influence the behavior of everyone. He needed a winning coalition—not in the legislative sense, but in the implementation sense. He knew there would be opposition; he needed others to neutralize that opposition. For his implementation coalition, Rickey did not need the cooperation or support of everyone. But he needed enough Dodgers, enough major-league players, enough owners, enough journalists and opinion leaders, and enough fans. There would be important confrontations, and he needed enough people to do the right thing during enough of these disputes to ensure that his crusade was not defeated. He needed enough people who wanted to support Robinson the principle and enough people who learned to appreciate Robinson the person. . . .

Fortunately, in seeking to influence those both inside and outside the Dodger organization, Rickey had one big advantage. The big public purpose he was attempting to achieve was the right thing to do. Moreover, it was socially, culturally, and ethically important—not just a trivial action, such as improving market share of one brand of jeans against another. Consequently, to influence the behavior of others, Rickey could draw on more than their narrow self-interest. Rickey could count on their desire to do the right thing—or at least to appear publicly to do the right thing. . . .

Rickey's lone-pioneer strategy called for secrecy in its early, preannouncement stages; thus he did not seek to build a public coalition. Nevertheless, he began to engage people in his strategy. As soon as he arrived in Brooklyn, Rickey began building his coalition, and within a few months he had the support of the Dodgers' owners. Moreover, they never wavered in their support of Rickey's plan. When given the opportunity, the Dodger owners did the right thing.

So did Red Barber. Born in Mississippi and raised in Florida, Barber did the Dodger radio broadcasts in his slow, soft, southern voice. Culturally, he could not imagine whites and blacks playing baseball on the same field. But early on, Rickey divulged his secret plan to Barber. "There is a Negro player coming to the Dodgers," Rickey told Barber before the 1945 season. "I don't know who he is and I don't know where he is, and I don't know when he is coming. But he is coming. And he is coming soon" (Barber 1968, 265).

Barber's immediate reaction was to seek employment with another team. But his wife talked him out of a hasty decision, and eventually Barber concluded that his job was simply to tell his listeners what was happening on the field—to "broadcast the ball"—and ignore whether the player was black or white (Tygiel 1983, 55; Barber 1982, 63–65). Within the Dodger organization, Rickey needed to choose and prepare his people carefully. He had to get them accustomed to the idea of integration. Rickey gave Barber enough time to think it over, and, when given the chance, Red Barber did the right thing.

So did Leo Durocher. Late one night in March 1947, while the Brooklyn and Montreal squads were playing spring-training exhibition games in Panama, Durocher, the Dodgers' manager, learned that Dixie Walker and some southern teammates were circulating a petition saying that they would not play if Robinson was promoted from Montreal to Brooklyn. Durocher immediately called a midnight meeting. Standing in the team's kitchen wearing pajamas and a yellow bathrobe, Durocher put down the rebellion:

> [. . .] I don't care if a guy is yellow or black, or it he has stripes like a fuckin' zebra. I'm the manager of this team, and I say he plays. What's more, I say he can make all of us rich . . . An' if any of you can't use the money, I'll see that you're traded. (Parrott 1976, 208–9)

For Durocher, observes Roger Kahn, this "was probably the finest hour of his life" (1993, 35). When given the chance, Leo Durocher did the right thing. . . .

Indeed, when faced with the choice, most of the Dodgers did the right thing. Reese explained how he and his teammates reacted to Robinson that first year:

You saw how he stood there at the plate and dared them to hit him with the ball, and you began to put yourself in his shoes. You'd think of yourself trying to break into the black leagues, maybe, and what it would be like—and I know that I couldn't have done it. In a word, he was winning respect. (Monteleone 1995, 87)

Robinson, concurred Duke Snider, "put up with far more than the rest of us could have" (1988, 27).

Rickey had anticipated that most of Robinson's teammates would react this way. Toward the end of spring training in 1947, Rickey observed, "First they'll endure Robinson, then pity him, then embrace him" (Monteleone 1995, 87). He understood that Robinson would take abuse; he also understood that, if Robinson reacted properly, his teammates would too. And, thus, even the infamous attack by Chapman and his Phillies went according to Rickey's script:

Chapman did more than anybody to make Dixie Walker, Eddie Stanky and other Dodgers speak up on Robinson's behalf. When he poured out that string of unconscionable abuse, he solidified and unified thirty men, not one of whom was willing to sit by and see someone kick around a man who had his hands tied behind his back. Chapman created in Robinson's behalf a thing called sympathy, the most unifying word in the world. That word has a Greek origin; it means to suffer. Thus, to say I sympathize with you is meaningful only because it means 'I suffer with you.' That is what Chapman did. He caused men like Stanky to suffer with Robinson and he made this Negro a real member of the Dodgers. (Rowan 1960, 183–84)

. . . As every public manager laments, business managers have an advantage. They function with many fewer constraints, many fewer rules concerning financing, personnel, and procurement. They are not subjected to microscopic media scrutiny of their smallest actions. They have access to more resources. They can use money as a motivator.

But public managers have an advantage, too (Behn 1994b). After all, money is not the only motivator (Herzberg 1968; Maslow 1943)—particularly for people who choose to work in the public sector. Most of them choose public employment because they want to accomplish something. They want to do something important. They want to do the right thing. . . .

At the start of the 1947 season, it was not necessarily obvious to the Dodger players that Robinson—despite his outstanding play in Montreal and during spring training in Panama—would become a Hall of Fame player. Robinson's colleagues supported him not only because he would help the team but also because it was the right thing to do.

Luck

All public managers are lucky. But being lucky is not enough. For the luck to count, for the luck to contribute to success, the manager has to recognize and exploit it.

In many ways, Branch Rickey was lucky. But this luck was helpful only because Rickey discerned it and because he was able to capitalize on it.

Rickey was lucky. By the end of World War II, pressure was building to integrate the major leagues (Oakley 1994, 22–23). He could capitalize on the existence and efforts of this diverse, unorganized coalition without having to formally join it. He was further lucky that a number of influential black journalists—particularly Wendell Smith of the *Pittsburgh Courier*, Sam Lacy of the *Baltimore Afro-American*, and Joe Bostic who wrote for the communist *Daily Worker* and the black *People's Voice*—had been pressing for the integration of baseball (Tygiel 1983, 35–36). They all wanted Robinson to succeed, and Rickey easily accepted both their journalistic work and their willingness to personally support Robinson during the early years.

Rickey was lucky in 1944; Commissioner Landis died. Hired as baseball's first commissioner to restore the game's integrity after the Black Sox scandal of 1919, Landis had the complete authority to act however he believed to be in the "best interests" of baseball. And he deployed this power arbitrarily and without restraint. The owners tolerated Landis's dictatorial ways because he had saved their business. But whoever they chose to replace Landis would never be given such absolute authority—and would be less rigid, at least, in opposing integration.

Rickey was lucky in 1942; he was in an irresolvable conflict with Sam Breadon, owner of the Cardinals, and felt compelled to resign (Polner 1982, 115–16; Mann 1957, 208–10). "During the 1940s," writes Roger Kahn, "the St. Louis Cardinals were the closest thing in the major leagues to a team representing the Old South," and the city "was militantly southern" (1993, 54). Rickey could never have brought Robinson to St. Louis.

But was Rickey really lucky that Commissioner Chandler suspended Leo Durocher, the Dodgers' field manager, on April 9, 1947, the day before Rickey announced the promotion of Robinson from Montreal to Brooklyn? The conventional wisdom is that the loss of Durocher meant a loss of support for Robinson. Durocher played to win—"It doesn't matter how you win, just so you win" (Oakley 1994, 51)—and he already had shown in his defense of Robinson in Panama that he thought Robinson would be a significant asset in his effort to win.

Nevertheless, the suspension of Durocher distracted attention from Robinson. Rickey's promotion of Robinson "had to share space in the sports pages" with the story about Durocher's suspension which, at that moment, was bigger news (Oakley 1994, 50). And others, such as Reese, stepped in to replace Durocher as Robinson's champion; they were much more subtle and, in the long run, more effective. . . .

Rickey was lucky that the Dodger's AAA farm team was in Montreal, Canada—a city with a small black population and thus without much experience with racial animosity or conflict. Consequently, Rickey had a relatively unhostile environment to which he could send Robinson for his first year in organized white baseball.

And, of course, Rickey was lucky that after he was dismissed in St. Louis he was hired by the Dodgers of Brooklyn. The Dodgers were not the New York Dodgers. They were the *Brooklyn* Dodgers. They belonged to the Borough of Brooklyn, which was still quite sure—a half-century later—that it never should have merged with the rest of New York. It was, Prince reports (1996), a city of cultural, social, and ethnic cleavages. (See Golenbock, p. 183.) But those were internal. Brooklyn also had an us-against-the-world attitude, which was reflected in their support for their team, for *their* "Bums."

. . . Thus Brooklyn's fans responded to Robinson just as his teammates had. Regardless of their general views on integration, when Robinson put on the Dodger uniform he represented Brooklyn, and the fans supported him aggressively. . . .

Sure, Rickey was lucky in many (though often small) ways. But he was also analytical enough to recognize and then take advantage of even the seemingly most trivial cases of luck. Yet Rickey himself emphasized planning:

> Things worthwhile generally don't just happen. Luck is a fact, but should not be a factor. Good luck is what is left over after intelligence and effort have combined at their best. Negligence or indifference or inattention are usually reviewed from an unlucky seat. The law of cause and effect and causality both work the same with inexorable exactitudes.

Branch Rickey would often emphasize: "Luck is the residue of design" (Monteleone 1995, 11).

When public managers are lucky, they need to recognize it. When they are not lucky, they need to keep focused on their public purpose and grope their way toward their next benchmark.

A Better Organization for the Future

Public managers not only have a responsibility to accomplish something—some public purpose—while they hold their jobs, they also have a responsibility to leave their organizations in better shape then they found them—to create the human and institutional capabilities to accomplish other public purposes in the future.

In St. Louis, Brooklyn, and Pittsburgh, Branch Rickey left behind talented teams—teams that he staffed and developed. Within a few years after he left, the Cardinals, the Dodgers, and the Pirates each won a World Series.

But Branch Rickey left more than just his teams better off. He also left baseball better off—much better off.

In the 1950s, 1960s, and later, Americans integrated a number of their institutions: public transportation, lunch counters, school systems, juries, public and private universities, businesses, unions, state legislatures. And the struggle that resulted usually involved much conflict and often violence. The integration of major-league baseball, too, was not without its conflict. Yet throughout the saga, not a single regular-season game—either in the minor or major leagues—failed to be played because of Robinson's presence. Throughout the 1950s, those black baseball players who were making their way up through the minor leagues in the South—Hank Aaron, Curt Flood, Bob Gibson, Frank Robinson, Bill White—continued to face the same kind of harassment and discrimination that Robinson had faced (Tygiel 1983, 279–84). Professional baseball is still not free of discrimination. Yet on a comparative scale, Rickey and Robinson accomplished what others could not do without chaos, disorder, riots, and violence. How many other American industries integrated their employment practices without losing a day of work to racial conflict?

The leaders of many American institutions—public and private—could have served themselves and their organizations well had they adapted Rickey's strategy and tactics to their own situations. Public managers, then and now, would benefit from observing how Rickey fulfilled the eight responsibilities of public management.

To many, Branch Rickey was a hero. "He was not only a top flight executive, but the greatest revolutionary the game has ever known," wrote Lou Smith of the *Cincinnati Enquirer.* "Branch Rickey was probably the most glamorous name in all baseball history" (Monteleone 1995, 132). "To say that Branch Rickey was the finest man ever brought to the game of baseball is to damn with the faintest praise—like describing [Isaac] Stern as a lively fiddler," wrote the famous sports columnist, Red Smith (Monteleone 1995, xvii). To Smith, Robinson's "arrival in Brooklyn was a turning point in the history and the character of the game; it may not be stretching things to say it was a turning point in the history of this country" (Berkow 1986, 113).

. . . Rickey's accomplishments as a traditional business manager and as a public manager are monumental. Those who aspire to be effective public managers would be wise to examine how Rickey sought to fulfill the eight responsibilities of public management. Every public manager would be proud to have Branch Rickey's record for accomplishing important public purposes. He left baseball—and the country—much better than he found it.

References

Alien, Maury. 1987. *Jackie Robinson: A Life Remembered.* New York: Franklin Watts.
Andrews, Kenneth R. 1971. *The Concept of Corporate Strategy.* Homewood, IL: Dow Jones-Irwin. Revised edition, 1980.
Barber, Red. 1968. *Rhubarb in the Catbird Seat.* Garden City, NY: Doubleday.
Behn. Robert D. 1988. "Management by Groping Along." *Journal of Policy Analysis and Management* 7:4: 643–63.
———. 1991. *Leadership Counts: Lessons for Public Managers.* Cambridge, MA: Harvard University Press.
———. 1994a. "Bottom-Line Government." Durham, NC: The Governors Center at Duke University.
———. 1994b. "The Importance of Importance." *Governing:* (September): 78.
Berkow, Ira. 1986. *Red: A Biography of Red Smith.* New York: Times Books.
Boswell, Thomas. 1982. "In Baseball, the Courage of Convictions Is Rewarded." *Washington Post.* July 7.
Campanella, Roy. 1995. *It's Good to Be Alive.* Lincoln: University of Nebraska Press.
Cohen, Stanley. 1990. *Dodgers! The First 100 Years.* New York: Carol Publishing.
Dickson, Paul. 1991. *Baseball's Greatest Quotations.* New York: HarperCollins.
Durocher, Leo. 1975. *Nice Guys Finish Last.* New York: Pocket Books.
Falkner, David. 1995. *Great Time Coming: The Life of Jackie Robinson from Baseball to Birmingham.* New York: Simon & Schuster.
Frick, Ford C. 1973. *Games, Asterisks, and People: Memoirs of a Lucky Fan.* New York: Crown.
Goldstein, Richard. 1991. *Superstars and Screwballs: 100 Years of Brooklyn Baseball.* New York: Dutton.
Golenbock, Peter. 1984. *Bums: An Oral History of the Brooklyn Dodgers.* New York: Putnam's.
Gough, David. 1994. *Burt Shotton, Dodgers Manager: A Baseball Biography.* Jefferson, NC: McFarland.
Herzberg, Frederick. 1968. "One More Time: How Do You Motivate Employees?" *Harvard Business Review* 46:1: 53–62.

Holland, Gerald. 1955. "Mr. Rickey and the Game." *Sports Illustrated* (March):38: 59–65.

Honig, Donald. 1981. *The Brooklyn Dodgers: An Illustrated Tribute.* New York: St. Martin's.

Kahn, Roger. 1993. *The Era. 1947–1957: When the Yankees, the Giants, and the Dodgers Ruled the World.* New York: Ticknor & Fields.

Koppett, Leonard. 1993. *The Man in the Dugout: Baseball's Top Managers and How They Got That Way.* New York: Crown.

Lipman, David. 1966. *Mr. Baseball: The Story of Branch Rickey.* New York: Putnam.

Mann, Arthur. 1957. *Branch Rickey: American in Action.* Boston: Houghton Mifflin.

Maslow, Abraham. 1943. "A Theory of Human Motivation." *Psychological Review* 50:(July): 370–96.

Monteleone, John J., ed. 1995. *Branch Rickey's Little Blue Book: Wit and Strategy from Baseball's Last Wise Man.* New York: Macmillan.

Oakley, J. Ronald. 1994. *Baseball's Last Golden Age, 1946–1960: The National Pastime in a Time of Glory and Change.* Jefferson, NC: McFarland.

Parrott, Harold. 1976. *The Lords of Baseball.* New York: Praeger.

Polner, Murray. 1982. *Branch Rickey: A Biography.* New York: Antheneum.

Prince, Carl E. 1996. *Brooklyn's Dodgers: The Bums, the Borough, and the Best of Baseball 1947–1957.* New York: Oxford University Press.

Ribowsky, Mark. 1995. *A Complete History of the Negro Leagues: 1884 to 1955.* New York: Carol Publishing.

Rickey, Branch. 1965. *The American Diamond: A Documentary of the Game of Baseball.* New York: Simon & Schuster.

Robinson, Jackie. 1995. *I Never Had It Made.* Hopewell, NJ: Ecco.

Rowan, Carl T. 1960. *Wait Till Next Year.* New York: Random House.

Snider, Duke. 1988. *The Duke of Flatbush.* New York: Zebra.

Taylor, Frederick W. 1912. "Scientific Management." Testimony before the U.S. House of Representatives, January 25. Reprinted in Jay M. Shafritz and Albert C. Hyde, 1992. *Classics of Public Administration,* 3rd ed. Pacific Grove, CA: Brooks/Cole, 29–32.

Tygiel, Jules. 1983. *Baseball's Great Experiment: Jackie Robinson and His Legacy.* New York: Vintage.

Ward, Geoffrey C., and Burns, Ken. 1994. *Baseball: An Illustrated History.* New York: Knopf.

Wolf, Rick, ed. 1990. *The Baseball Encyclopedia: The Compete and Official Record of Major League Baseball,* 8th ed. New York: Macmillan.

INDEX

Italic page references indicate tables, charts, and graphs.

ABOUT THE EDITORS

Montgomery (Monty) Van Wart is Professor and Chair at California State University–San Bernardino. He received his Ph.D. from Arizona State University. As a scholar, Dr. Van Wart has over forty publications, including five books and a substantial number of articles in the leading journals. His research areas are administrative leadership, human resource management, training and development, administrative values and ethics, organizational behavior, and general management. He also serves on numerous editorial boards. He has taught leadership classes to public-sector managers for all levels of government. His book on leadership, *The Dynamics of Leadership: Theory and Practice* (M.E. Sharpe 2005), was highly recommended in *Choice*, which stated that it is a "very impressive and successful effort." His article recently published in *Public Administration Review* is one of the most electronically accessed articles, according to the journal.

Lisa A. Dicke (Ph.D.–Utah) is Associate Professor and MPA coordinator in the Department of Public Administration at the University of North Texas. Her teaching and research interests are in government accountability, nonprofit management, and intersectoral relations. Dr. Dicke's work has appeared in the *American Review of Public Administration, Public Organization Review, Public Integrity, Public Productivity and Management Review, International Journal of Organization Theory & Behavior*, and the *Journal of Public Affairs Education,* and in several edited books.